IFRS™ / US GAAP Comparison

A comparison between International Financial Reporting Standards and US GAAP by the Financial Reporting Group of Ernst & Young

Principal Authors and Editors from Ernst & Young's
Financial Reporting Group

David Cook

Larissa Connor

Richard Crisp

Pieter Dekker

Margaret Pankhurst

Allister Wilson

D0843926

**International
Accounting Standards Committee
Foundation®**

ERNST & YOUNG

This publication has been carefully prepared, but it necessarily contains information in summary form and is therefore intended for general guidance only, and is not intended to be a substitute for detailed research or the exercise of professional judgement. Ernst & Young LLP and the International Accounting Standards Committee Foundation can accept no responsibility for loss occasioned to any person acting or refraining from action as a result of any material in this publication. On any specific matter, reference should be made to the appropriate adviser.

Ernst & Young LLP is authorised by the Institute of Chartered Accountants in England and Wales to carry on investment business. The United Kingdom firm of Ernst & Young is a member of Ernst & Young Global.

Apart from any fair dealing for the purposes of research or private study, or criticism or review, as permitted under the Copyright, Designs and Patents Act, 1988, this publication may only be reproduced, stored or transmitted, in any form or by any means, with the prior permission in writing of the publishers, or in the case of reprographic reproduction in accordance with the terms of licences issued by the Copyright Licensing Agency, 90 Tottenham Court Road, London, W19 9HE, United Kingdom. Enquiries concerning reproduction outside those terms should be sent to the authors at the following address:

Foreword

Sir David Tweedie

Chairman International Accounting Standards Board

The International Accounting Standards Board is committed to developing, in the public interest, a single set of high quality, global accounting standards that require transparent and comparable information in general purpose financial statements. IFRSs are being used in more than 90 countries.

In pursuit of its objective, the IASB cooperates with national accounting standard-setters to achieve convergence in accounting standards around the world. Now that the rush to 2005 is over, convergence is the IASB's principal strategic goal.

Since October 2002 the IASB and the Financial Accounting Standards Board have been working together. Their program of work melds convergence of standards and improvement of financial reporting in the following way:

- Short-term convergence projects deal with narrow issues. Where the standard of one of the Boards appears to have a superior approach on a narrow issue, the other Board adopts it without alteration.
- Medium-term convergence projects deal with topics where the standards of the two Boards are broadly similar, but have elements that could be improved.
- In some cases the standards of both Boards need significant change to improve financial reporting. These will be long-term joint projects with the aim of producing a new common standard.

One measure of the achievement of convergence is the number of items appearing in reconciliation statements prepared by companies filing with the US Securities and Exchange Commission.

Another measure of convergence is a comparative study of IFRSs and US GAAP such as this one. This book reveals the extent of the task ahead of us, and provides valuable information for companies and regulators. But we will take up the challenge. Dare I suggest that we are striving to eliminate future demand for such comparative studies.

London
May 2005

Sir David Tweedie
International Accounting Standards Board

Authors' preface

The long-awaited 2005 deadline has now been reached. A comprehensive 'stable platform' of generally high quality International Financial Reporting Standards (IFRSs) has now been promulgated by the International Accounting Standards Board (IASB), and many countries around the world are committed to adopt IFRSs directly, or to align their national standards with IFRSs, from 2005 or later.

At the same time, one of the most talked about issues surrounding IFRSs is their convergence with US GAAP. For some, it cannot happen quickly enough, whilst others are more cautious, concerned that convergence may lead to the introduction of US GAAP-style rules in place of the IASB's principles-based standards.

Nevertheless, few can take issue with the desirability of developing a single set of global standards that is recognised by all the international capital markets. However, this is the end destination of a very long journey that will take many years to complete and which has many stops along the way. One of those stops – which, in our view, has already been reached – is equivalence. Importantly, equivalence should not be confused with convergence. Convergence is the long-term goal of a single set of globally accepted standards; equivalence is the short-term imperative that implies broad comparability – not uniformity – and the acceptance by national regulators of different systems without the need for reconciliation.

The Committee of European Securities' Regulators (CESR) believes that two systems of GAAP can be declared equivalent when financial statements prepared under either system enable investors to take a similar decision in terms of whether to invest or divest. We strongly support this approach. Any insistence on a uniform treatment of the same transaction would put enormous strain on the IASB to develop rules-based standards for the many areas where US GAAP has specific rules. A principles-based approach would not be sufficient, because US GAAP tends to deal with transactions on a case-by-case basis.

The extent of this book bears testimony to the fact that there are very many differences of detail between IFRSs and US GAAP. This is the case even in areas such as employee benefits, deferred tax and business combinations, where the respective standards are broadly similar. Consequently, it will often be the case that uniform treatment is achieved more by luck than by design. Not only does this exemplify the sheer scale of the convergence task, but it also illustrates why convergence should not be viewed as a pre-condition for mutual recognition on the basis of equivalence.

The continued insistence of the US SEC to require Foreign Private Issuers to reconcile their net income and equity to US GAAP is increasingly being questioned by many constituencies, including the European Commission. Companies are questioning not only the value to investors of these reconciliations, but also their appropriateness in the light of the new and improved standards issued by the IASB over the past two years. We are encouraged that the FASB is now proposing a new US GAAP hierarchy that includes IFRSs. We hope that this might act as further encouragement to the SEC to remove the reconciliation requirement in the immediate future.

In the meantime, we offer this book to preparers, users, auditors and regulators of accounts – as well as to the accounting standard-setters – as a practical tool to be used to identify and understand the many differences in detail between IFRSs and US GAAP.

Finally, we are deeply indebted to many of our colleagues within the global organisation of Ernst & Young for their selfless assistance in the publication of this book. Our thanks go particularly to those who reviewed drafts, most notably Buddy Aiken, Elisa Alfieri, Mike Bonham, Thomas Bures, Olof Cederberg, Matthew Curtis, Mike Davies, Tim Denton, Melinda Evans, Charles Feeney, Sven Hayn, Liz Hickey, Martin Hoogendoorn, Eskild Jakobsen, Richard Jenkins, Richard Jones, David Kane, Patricia LaValle, Richard Lynch, Francine Mellors, Richard Moore, Alejandro Moran, Eric Ohlund, Victor Oliveira, Craig Parks, Lars Pettersen, Ruth Picker, Carlo Pippolo, Nigel Reid, Hedy Richards, Robert Royall, George Schleier, Jeffrey Scott, Nagaraj Sivaram, Jeffrey Slate, Gary Smith, Michael Tamulis, Eric Tarleton, Leo van der Tas and Gregory Wilkinson-Riddle.

As authors, however, we take responsibility for all the opinions expressed in this book, and the blame for all its faults.

London
May 2005

David Cook
Larissa Connor
Richard Crisp
Pieter Dekker
Margaret Pankhurst
Allister Wilson

List of chapters

Detailed contents

CHAPTER 3   DETAILED COMPARISON BETWEEN IFRSs AND US GAAP

Abbreviations

The following abbreviations are used in this book:

Professional and regulatory bodies

AICPA	American Institute of Certified Public Accountants
APB	Accounting Principles Board (of the AICPA, predecessor of the FASB)
ARC	Accounting Regulatory Committee of representatives of EU Member States
CESR	Committee of European Securities Regulators
EC	European Commission
EFRAG	European Financial Reporting Advisory Group
EITF	Emerging Issues Task Force in the US
EU	European Union
FASB	United States Financial Accounting Standards Board
G4+1	The (now disbanded) group of four plus 1, actually with six members, that comprised an informal 'think tank' of standard setters from Australia, Canada, New Zealand, UK, and USA, plus the IASC
IASB	International Accounting Standards Board
IASC	International Accounting Standards Committee
IFAC	International Federation of Accountants
IFRIC	International Financial Reporting Interpretations Committee
IOSCO	International Organisation of Securities Commissions
SAC	Standards Advisory Council
SEC	United States Securities and Exchange Commission
SIC	Standing Interpretations Committee of the IASC (replaced by IFRIC)

References to authoritative literature under IFRSs

ED	Exposure Draft
Framework	IASB's Framework for the preparation and presentation of financial statements
IAS	International Accounting Standard(s) (issued by the IASC and IASB)
IFRIC	Interpretation by the IFRIC
IFRS	International Financial Reporting Standard (issued by the IASB)

IFRSs   Standards and Interpretations adopted by the IASB. They comprise:

         (a) International Financial Reporting Standards;

         (b) International Accounting Standards; and

         (c) Interpretations originated by the IFRIC or the former SIC.

SIC   Interpretation by the SIC

Paragraph references to IFRSs, IASs, Interpretations and supporting documentation

AG   Application Guidance

AV   Alternative View

BC   Basis for Conclusions

DO   Dissenting Opinion

IE   Illustrative Examples

IG   Implementation Guidance

IN   Introduction

References to authoritative literature in the US

AIN-APB   Accounting Interpretation of an Accounting Principles Board (issued by the AICPA)

APB   Opinion of the APB

ARB   Accounting Research Bulletin of the AICPA

ASR   Accounting Series Release (issued by SEC; later codified into FRR 1)

CON   Statement of Financial Accounting Concepts (issued by the FASB)

EITF   Consensus of the Emerging Issues Task Force of the FASB

FAS   Statement of Financial Accounting Standards (issued by the FASB)

FAQ   Special report issued by SEC Staff addressing questions on implementing a particular SAB

FIN   Interpretation of Financial Accounting Standards (issued by the FASB)

FRR   Financial Reporting Release (issued by the SEC)

FTB   Technical Bulletins (issued by the staff of the FASB)

SAB   Staff Accounting Bulletin (interpretations/practices of the SEC staff)

SAS   Statement on Auditing Standards (issued by the Auditing Standards Board of the AICPA)

SOP   Statement of Position (issued by the Accounting Standards Division of the AICPA)

S-K   Regulation S-K (SEC regulations on non-financial statement disclosures)

S-X   Regulation S-X (SEC regulations governing the form, content and periods to be covered in financial statements included in registration statements and periodic reports)

Q&A   A special report issued by FASB staff addressing questions on implementing a particular standard

20-F   Form for the registration of securities and annual and transition reports of foreign private issuers under the Securities and Exchange Act of 1934

Authoritative literature

IFRSs

This book takes into account authoritative literature published up to the end of April 2005 and includes:

- IFRS 6
- IAS 41
- IFRIC 5
- SIC-33

US GAAP

This book takes into account authoritative literature published up to the end of April 2005 and includes:

- FAS 153 and CON No. 7
- FIN 47 and TB 01-1
- SAB 107 and FRR 71
- SOP 04-2

Chapter 1   Regulatory background to IFRS and US financial reporting

1   THE INTERNATIONAL ACCOUNTING STANDARDS BOARD

1.1   The formal structure of the IASC Foundation

The governance of the IASC Organisation is ultimately in the hands of the Trustees of the IASC Foundation.   The Trustees were appointed during the second half of 2000 by a Nominating Committee that was set up for that sole purpose under the Chairmanship of the then US SEC Chairman, Mr. Arthur Levitt.   There are nineteen Trustees from diverse career backgrounds, under the Chairmanship of Mr. Paul A. Volcker, a Former Chairman of the US Federal Reserve Board.   To ensure a broad international representation, there are six Trustees from North America, six from Europe, four from the Asia/Pacific region and three from any area, subject to establishing an overall geographical balance. The appointment of all subsequent Trustees to fill vacancies caused by routine retirement or other reasons is the responsibility of the existing Trustees.   The appointment of the Trustees is normally for a term of three years, renewable once. However, to provide continuity, some of the initial Trustees will serve staggered terms so as to retire after four or five years.

The first act of the Board of Trustees was to appoint Sir David Tweedie (who had just completed a highly distinguished period of ten years as the Chairman of the UK's Accounting Standards Board) as the first Chairman of the new International Accounting Standards Board (IASB).   Subsequently, in January 2001, the Trustees appointed the thirteen other members of the IASB.   The Trustees are responsible also for appointing the members of the International Financial Reporting Interpretations Committee (IFRIC) and Standards Advisory Council (SAC).   In addition, their duties include the following:

- fundraising;
- reviewing annually the strategy of the IASC Foundation and the IASB and their effectiveness;
- approving annually the budget of the IASC Foundation and determining the basis for funding;
- reviewing broad strategic issues affecting accounting standards, promoting the IASC Foundation and its work and promoting the objective of rigorous application of International Accounting Standards and International Financial Reporting Standards (the Trustees are, however, excluded from involvement in technical matters relating to accounting standards);

- establishing and amending operating procedures for the IASB, IFRIC and the SAC;
- approving amendments to the Constitution after following a due process, including consultation with the SAC and publication of an Exposure Draft for public comment;
- exercising all powers of the IASC Foundation except for those expressly reserved to the IASB, IFRIC and the SAC; and
- publishing an annual report on the IASC's activities, including audited financial statements and priorities for the coming year.

With effect from 1 April 2001, the IASB assumed international accounting standard setting responsibilities from its predecessor body, the International Accounting Standards Committee (IASC).

The IASB structure has the following main features: the IASC Foundation is an independent organisation having two main bodies, the Trustees and the IASB, as well as a Standards Advisory Council and the International Financial Reporting Interpretations Committee. The IASC Foundation Trustees appoint the IASB Members, exercise oversight and raise the funds needed, whereas the IASB has sole responsibility for setting accounting standards.

Set out below is a graphical representation of the IASC Foundation structure:

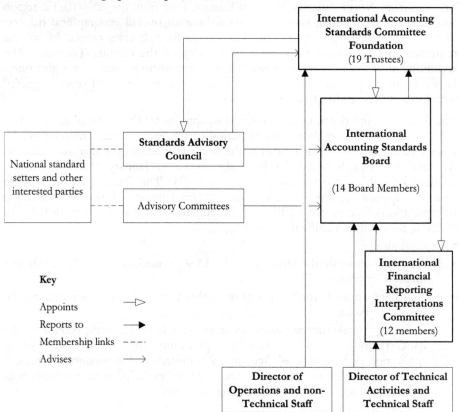

1.1.1   The IASC Foundation Constitution

The IASC Foundation Constitution was approved in its original form by the Board of the former International Accounting Standards Committee in March 2000 and by the members of IASC at a meeting in Edinburgh on 24 May 2000. The Foundation was formed as a not-for-profit corporation incorporated in the State of Delaware, USA, and is the parent entity of the IASB, which is based in London.

The Constitution sets out the basic structural and procedural framework for the various bodies of the IASC Organisation. Article 2 of the Constitution sets the objectives of the IASC Foundation as follows:

- to develop, in the public interest, a single set of high quality, understandable and enforceable global accounting standards that require high quality, transparent and comparable information in financial statements and other financial reporting to help participants in the world's capital markets and other users make economic decisions;
- to promote the use and rigorous application of those standards; and
- to bring about convergence of national accounting standards and International Accounting Standards and International Financial Reporting Standards to high quality solutions.

1.1.2   The International Accounting Standards Board (IASB)

In accordance with Article 19 of the Constitution, the IASC Foundation Trustees appointed twelve of the IASB Members to full-time positions, including the Chairman and the Vice-Chairman, and two to part-time positions. To encourage cooperation among the new Board and national standard-setters, the Trustees appointed seven of the IASB Members as official liaisons to national bodies. These liaison IASB Members must maintain close contact with their respective national standard-setters and are responsible for coordinating agendas and ensuring that the IASB and national bodies are working toward the goal of convergence on a single set of high quality standards around the world. Countries with formal liaisons are Australia and New Zealand together, Canada, France, Germany, Japan, the United States, and the United Kingdom. In addition, IASB Members have frequent contacts with organisations such as the European Commission and the SEC, financial regulators and central banks, private industry, analysts, and academics throughout the world.

Following the appointment of the members of the IASB, Sir David Tweedie stated the following: 'The mission of the newly-created IASB is simple. In partnership with national standard setters, we will aim to increase the transparency of financial reporting by achieving a single, global method of accounting for transactions – whether in Stuttgart, Sydney, Seattle or Singapore. The potential benefit to the world economy by removing barriers to investment through applying uniform, high-quality standards is enormous.'

The members of the IASB are not selected based on geographical representation. However, the Constitution stipulates that the Trustees shall ensure that the IASB is not dominated by any particular constituency or geographical interest. The foremost qualification for membership of the IASB is technical expertise. The IASB should comprise a group of people representing, within that group, the best available combination of technical skills and background experience of relevant international business and market conditions to contribute to the development of high quality, global accounting standards. No individual can be Trustee and IASB Member at the same time.

To achieve a balance of perspectives and experience, a minimum of five members of the IASB must have a background as practising auditors, a minimum of three a background as users of financial statements, a minimum of three a background in the preparation of financial statements, and at least one an academic background.

The responsibilities of the IASB are listed in Article 32 of the Constitution. The primary role of the IASB is to have complete responsibility for all technical matters including the preparation and publication of International Financial Reporting Standards and Exposure Drafts, both of which shall include any dissenting opinions, and final approval of Interpretations by IFRIC. Decisions by the IASB require only a simple majority (i.e. eight out of fourteen votes) to be adopted. The IASB has full discretion over its technical agenda and over project assignments on technical matters. It must, however, consult the SAC on major projects, agenda decisions and work priorities.

The IASB (whose meetings are open to the public) met in technical session for the first time in April 2001. During this meeting, it approved a resolution to adopt the existing body of International Accounting Standards and Interpretations issued by the former IASC Board and the Standing Interpretations Committee (SIC). The IASB announced also that the IASC Foundation Trustees had agreed that the accounting standards issued by the IASB would be designated 'International Financial Reporting Standards (IFRS)'. The existing pronouncements will, however, continue to be designated 'International Accounting Standards (IAS)'.

1.1.3 The Standards Advisory Council (SAC)

The SAC provides a forum for participation by organisations and individuals with an interest in international financial reporting, who have diverse geographic and functional backgrounds, with the objective of (a) giving advice to the IASB on agenda decisions and priorities in the Board's work, (b) informing the IASB of the views of the SAC members on major standard setting projects and (c) giving other advice to the IASB or the Trustees.

The SAC must be consulted by the IASB in advance of Board decisions on major projects and by the Trustees in advance of any proposed changes to the Constitution.

In June 2001, the Trustees of the IASC Foundation announced the appointment of 49 SAC members. The members include chief financial and accounting officers from some of the world's largest corporations and international organisations, leading financial analysts and academics, regulators, accounting standard setters, and partners from leading accounting firms. The members of the SAC are drawn from six continents, 29 countries, and five international organisations. In addition, the European Commission, the US Securities and Exchange Commission, and the Financial Services Agency of Japan attend as observers.

The SAC (whose meetings are open to the public) normally meets three times a year under the chairmanship of the IASB Chairman. The SAC met for the first time with the IASB in July 2001.

1.1.4   The International Financial Reporting Interpretations Committee (IFRIC)

In 2001, the Board amended the mandate and operating procedures of the SIC, which was formed in 1997 under the former IASC structure, and renamed the committee IFRIC. In accordance with paragraphs 34 to 37 of the Constitution, the role of IFRIC is to:

- interpret the application of IAS and IFRSs and provide timely guidance on financial reporting issues not specifically addressed in IAS and IFRSs, in the context of the IASB Framework, and undertake other tasks at the request of the IASB. In carrying out this work, IFRIC should have regard to the IASB's objective of working actively with national standard-setters to bring about convergence of national accounting standards and IAS and IFRSs to high quality solutions;

- publish after clearance by the IASB Draft Interpretations for public comment and consider comments made within a reasonable period before finalising an Interpretation; and

- report to the IASB and obtain its approval for final Interpretations.

The Trustees appoint the twelve voting members of IFRIC for renewable terms of three years. They also appoint a non-voting chair, who should be an IASB member, a senior member of the IASB technical staff or an individual from outside the IASB. The Trustees can appoint non-voting observer representatives of regulatory organisations, who shall have the right to attend and speak at meetings. Currently the European Commission and the International Organisation of Securities Commissions (IOSCO) have observer status on IFRIC. Approval of Draft or final Interpretations requires that not more than three voting members vote against the Draft or final Interpretation.

IFRIC meets about every two months. All technical decisions are taken at sessions that are open to public observation. The Committee addresses issues of reasonably widespread importance, and not issues of concern to only a small set of entities. The interpretations cover both:

- newly identified financial reporting issues not specifically addressed in IFRSs; or

- issues where unsatisfactory or conflicting interpretations have developed, or seem likely to develop in the absence of authoritative guidance, with a view to reaching a consensus on the appropriate treatment.

The due process for each IFRIC project normally, but not necessarily, involves the following steps (the steps that are required under the terms of the IASC Foundation Constitution are indicated by an asterisk *):

- the staff are asked to identify and review all the issues associated with the topic and to consider the application of the Framework to the issues;

- study of national accounting requirements and practice and an exchange of views about the issues with national standard-setters, including national committees that have responsibility for interpretations of national standards;

- publication of a draft interpretation for public comment if no more than three IFRIC members have voted against the proposal;*
- consideration of all comments received within the comment period on a draft interpretation;*
- approval by the IFRIC of an interpretation if no more than three IFRIC members have voted against the interpretation after considering public comments on the draft interpretation;* and
- approval of the interpretation by at least eight votes of the IASB.*

Initially the output from IFRIC had been somewhat limited, with the Committee taking more than two years to issue its first Interpretation. In reality, IFRIC has acted much more in the capacity of a Steering Committee of the IASB, as opposed to a conventional interpretations committee. Currently, however, IFRIC has approximately ten items under consideration, including some important issues such as service concession arrangements.

1.1.5 The IASC Foundation's Constitution review

As part of the governance structure of the IASC Foundation, the Constitution requires that the Trustees of the IASC Foundation undertake a review of the entire structure of the IASC Foundation and its effectiveness. The Constitution specifies that this review should commence three years after the coming into force of the Constitution, with the objective of implementing any agreed changes five years after the coming into force of the Constitution (i.e. 6 February 2006).

At a meeting on 4 November 2003, the Trustees discussed the need to consult interested parties on the full range of issues raised by the Constitution, and agreed on various aspects of the review, including the procedures for conducting the review, the extent of consultation, staffing, and the issues to be discussed. On 12 November 2003, the Trustees announced that they had initiated a review of the Foundation's constitutional arrangements that govern the operating procedures of the Foundation and the IASB. In launching this, the Trustees emphasised that they were willing to examine any aspect of the Constitution and would be consulting a wide range of organisations. To coordinate the process, the Trustees established an internal committee (the 'Constitution Committee'), chaired by Paul Volcker.

As the first step of the review, comments were invited on a consultation paper that discussed the issues to be considered by the Trustees and posed some preliminary questions to those interested in participating in the review. On the basis of the comment letters received, the Constitution Committee determined the key issues to be taken forward and, on 22 March 2004, the Committee posted a paper – *Next Steps for the Constitution Review following initial consultation* – on the IASC Foundation Website. The paper noted that the Constitution Committee:
- had identified ten main issues for consideration, but had not yet reached conclusions on them;
- would be establishing a subcommittee of the Standards Advisory Council (SAC) to provide guidance on the Constitution Review; and
- would hold a series of public hearings to provide an additional opportunity for public comment.

The ten main issues for consideration were listed as follows:

- Whether the objectives of the IASC Foundation should expressly refer to the challenges facing small- and medium-sized entities (SMEs);
- The number of Trustees and their geographical and professional distribution;
- The oversight role of the Trustees;
- Funding of the IASC Foundation;
- The composition of the IASB;
- The appropriateness of the IASB's existing formal liaison relationships;
- Consultative arrangements of the IASB;
- Voting procedures of the IASB;
- Resources and effectiveness of IFRIC; and
- The composition, role, and effectiveness of the SAC.

On 7 May 2004, the Constitution Committee published a paper – *An Update on the Constitution Review and Information regarding Public Hearings* – outlining possible approaches to the ten issues identified by the Committee in the Constitution Review. These approaches were not formal recommendations but were meant to stimulate discussion at the public hearings.

The Constitution Committee finalised the recommendations to be presented to the full Trustees on 25 October 2004 in the form of a detailed report. The report also included a description of the philosophy that underpinned the Committee's analysis and the rationale for decisions taken. Once the Trustees have reached a common position on recommendations, they will publish a report with proposed constitutional changes for public comment. The Trustees are only required to implement any constitutional changes by February 2006.

In the meantime, on 24 March 2004, the IASB announced that it had initiated an internal review of its own deliberative procedures alongside the Trustees' Constitution Review. In so doing, the IASB published a consultation paper – *Strengthening the IASB's deliberative processes* – which set out its preliminary findings and inviting public comment on improvements to its procedures that were already in progress. Particular attention was given to the following matters:

- the accessibility and transparency of the IASB's deliberative process;
- the IASB's responsiveness to constituents' comments; and
- the extent of consultation before releasing proposals and Standards.

The deadline for comments was 25 June 2004. The IASC Foundation Trustees have stated that their Constitution Committee will review the IASB's conclusions on the deliberative process as part of its broader consideration of possible changes to the Constitution.

The Board received 50 comment letters on the consultation paper, and these were discussed at its September 2004 meeting. With the exception of five comments on the publication of near-final drafts, there was strong support for the steps proposed.

After considering further actions recommended by some respondents, the Board tentatively decided:

- to continue to make observer notes available on its website, with paragraph numbers corresponding to those in the Board's papers;
- to make all public meetings available, if possible, by internet or audio;
- to publish near-final drafts of final documents only;
- to enhance the due process procedures as proposed and to explain its reasons when it decides not to undertake a non-mandatory step of its due process;
- to conduct field tests when appropriate;
- to distinguish clearly field tests, field visits and other means of obtaining input from constituents while an IFRS is being developed;
- to vary the length of comment periods, taking account of the complexity of the project and with sensitivity to the problems of translation; and
- to clarify the procedure for adding items to its agenda.

1.2 The IASB's current technical agenda

The IASB has several projects in progress at the moment. These cover a wide range of topics, some of which could potentially have a fundamental impact on financial reporting under IFRSs. In addition, it has identified other topics that it may place on its agenda as resources permit.

The IASB's current agenda includes the following:

- various issues relating to accounting for financial instruments, such as disclosures and shares puttable at fair value;
- business combinations phase II – application of the purchase method and related issues such as minority interests and intangible assets;
- reporting comprehensive income;
- revenue and related liabilities;
- conceptual framework;
- various convergence projects, including:
  - income taxes;
  - provisions, contingent liabilities and contingent assets;
  - disclosures about segments; and
  - government grants;
- standards for non-publicly accountable entities;
- consolidation (including special purpose entities);
- insurance contracts phase II; and
- liabilities and equity.

In addition, the IASB has embarked on active research, in collaboration with others, on the following topics:

- extractive activities;
- financial instruments, improvements to existing standards;
- hyperinflationary economies;
- financial instruments: interest margin hedging;

- intangible assets;
- investment entities;
- joint ventures;
- leases;
- management commentary; and
- measurement objectives.

The intention is that, when the preparatory work on these research projects is concluded, they will be moved to the IASB's main agenda.

Furthermore, in response to the criticism that the IASB has received regarding its consultative procedures, the Board has announced the formation of three new advisory groups. The IASB has stated that it is establishing these groups to bring together expertise from a broad range of perspectives on three critical projects – insurance contracts, financial instruments and performance reporting. In selecting the advisory groups' membership, the IASB has sought a balance of geographical and professional backgrounds in these three complex and controversial areas.

Building on the advice of these groups, the IASB expects to produce discussion papers on the insurance and performance reporting projects and any potential overhaul of IAS 39. In this way, the Board hopes to encourage people and organisations with a wide range of perspectives around the world to join the debate on the IASB's projects. In due course Exposure Drafts will follow, but that may well be several years into the future.

1.2.1   Changed format of new IFRSs

When the new IASB took office on 1 April 2001, it announced that the IASC Foundation Trustees had agreed that the accounting standards issued by the IASB would be designated 'International Financial Reporting Standards (IFRS)', whilst the existing standards would continue to be designated 'International Accounting Standards (IAS)'.

In addition, the new IFRSs issued by the IASB have adopted an entirely new format. In future, all IFRSs will incorporate some or all of the following components:

- An introduction to the IFRS
- The text of the IFRS itself
- Appendices that form part of the standards:
  - Defined terms
  - Application Guidance
  - Amendments to other IFRS
- Statement of Approval of the IFRS by the Board
- Basis for Conclusions, that does not form part of the IFRS
- Dissenting Opinions of Board Members
- Illustrative Examples, that do not form part of the IFRS
- Implementation Guidance, that does not form part of the IFRS

This new format represents a substantial improvement over the old style IAS. However, there are those that express the concern that principles-based standards will be turned into rules-based standards through the imposition of extensive mandatory application guidance.

It should be noted also that the EU's process of adopting an IFRS applies only to the IFRS itself and those appendices that the IASB designates as forming part of the standard. This means that all appendices that do not form part of the standard, including the basis for conclusions, illustrative examples and implementation guidance do not form part of 'adopted' IFRSs in the EU.

1.2.2   First-time application of IFRSs

The adoption by the European Union of IFRSs as the financial reporting basis for all listed EU companies from 2005 (see section 2 below) made it a priority for the IASB to develop IFRS 1 *First-time Adoption of International Financial Reporting Standards*. The requirements of that standard are discussed separately in Chapter 2.

1.3   Financial reporting in compliance with International Financial Reporting Standards

1.3.1   Statement of compliance with IFRSs

Although IFRSs, in themselves, do not have the force of law, they have become internationally accepted and are applied by a growing number of companies. More importantly, though, 2005 is a watershed year for IFRSs with a significant number of countries adopting IFRSs as their principal financial reporting regime – either directly (for example, by the 25 Member States in the European Union), or by aligning their national standards with IFRSs (for example, Australia and South Africa).

The main document setting out the basis on which financial statements should be presented under IFRSs, and the required contents of those financial statements, is IAS 1 – *Presentation of Financial Statements*. An entity whose financial statements comply with IFRSs should make an explicit and unreserved statement of such compliance in the notes. IFRS compliance involves compliance with all the recognition, measurement and disclosure provisions of the standards and interpretations. For this reason, IAS 1 states that financial statements shall not be described as complying with IFRSs unless they comply with all the requirements of IFRSs. The IASB has therefore established unambiguously the principle that full application of its standards and related interpretations is a necessary prerequisite for a company to assert that its financial statements comply with International Financial Reporting Standards.

1.3.2   Fair presentation and compliance with IFRSs

Paragraph 13 of IAS 1 requires that financial statements should present fairly the financial position, financial performance and cash flows of an entity. It goes on to state that fair presentation requires the faithful representation of the effects of transactions, other events and conditions in accordance with the definitions and recognition criteria for assets, liabilities, income and expenses set out in the *Framework*. The application of IFRSs, with additional disclosure when necessary, is presumed to result in financial statements that achieve a fair presentation.

IAS 1 states that in virtually all circumstances, a fair presentation is achieved by compliance with applicable IFRSs. A fair presentation under IFRSs also requires an entity:

- to select and apply accounting policies in accordance with IAS 8 – *Accounting Policies, Changes in Accounting Estimates and Errors*. IAS 8 sets out a hierarchy of authoritative guidance that management considers in the absence of a Standard or an Interpretation that specifically applies to an item;

- to present information, including accounting policies, in a manner that provides relevant, reliable, comparable and understandable information; and

- to provide additional disclosures when compliance with the specific requirements in IFRSs is insufficient to enable users to understand the impact of particular transactions, other events and conditions on the entity's financial position and financial performance.

1.3.3   The fair presentation override

The IASB strategy relies upon accounting standards that are couched in terms of broad principles, with a minimum of detailed accounting rules – indeed some practitioners criticise the IASB for the lack of detailed guidance it provides with some of its more complex standards. IAS 1 makes it clear that inappropriate accounting policies are not rectified either by disclosure of the accounting policies used or by notes or explanatory material. For this reason, the standard was required to cater for those situations where compliance with a standard or interpretation would distort fair presentation. Consequently, the standard provides that in the extremely rare circumstances in which management concludes that compliance with a requirement in a Standard or an Interpretation would be so misleading that it would conflict with the objective of financial statements set out in the *Framework*, the entity shall depart from that requirement if the relevant regulatory framework requires, or otherwise does not prohibit, such a departure.

When an entity applies the override in these circumstances, it must disclose the following:

- that management has concluded that the financial statements present fairly the entity's financial position, financial performance and cash flows;

- that it has complied with applicable Standards and Interpretations, except that it has departed from a particular requirement to achieve a fair presentation;

- the title of the Standard or Interpretation from which the entity has departed, the nature of the departure, including the treatment that the Standard or Interpretation would require, the reason why that treatment would be so misleading in the circumstances that it would conflict with the objective of financial statements set out in the *Framework*, and the treatment adopted; and

- for each period presented, the financial impact of the departure on each item in the financial statements that would have been reported in complying with the requirement.

When an entity has departed from a requirement of a Standard or an Interpretation in a prior period, and that departure affects the amounts recognised in the financial statements for the current period, the standard requires it to make the disclosures set out in the third and fourth bullet above.

It is worth noting that the fair presentation override is a requirement (not an option) of IAS 1 to be applied in the extremely rare circumstances in which management concludes that compliance with a requirement in a Standard or an Interpretation would be so misleading that it would conflict with the objective of financial statements set out in the *Framework*.

However, at the same time, the IASB has introduced a somewhat contradictory twist to the application of the override. As stated above, the override can be applied only if the relevant regulatory framework requires, or otherwise does not prohibit its use. This means that the Board has built into IAS 1 the possibility of regulatory intervention in its application. Paragraph 21 of IAS 1 provides for the situation where 'the relevant regulatory framework' prohibits departure from a requirement in a particular standard or interpretation. In such cases, the standard requires an entity, to the maximum extent possible, to reduce the perceived misleading aspects of compliance by disclosing:

- the title of the Standard or Interpretation in question, the nature of the requirement, and the reason why management has concluded that complying with that requirement is so misleading in the circumstances that it conflicts with the objective of financial statements set out in the *Framework*; and

- for each period presented, the adjustments to each item in the financial statements that management has concluded would be necessary to achieve a fair presentation.

This seems to contradict the clear statement in paragraph 16 of IAS 1 that inappropriate accounting policies are not rectified either by disclosure of the accounting policies used or by notes or explanatory material. It seems also to create the unwelcome precedent of a standard formally giving regulators the ability to determine how standards should be applied.

2   THE MOVE TO IFRSs IN THE EUROPEAN UNION

2.1   Historical differences in European accounting

European accounting is the product of disparate social, economic and political factors, which have resulted in a number of deep-rooted differences in financial reporting practice throughout the region. The factors that have caused these differences include a variety of legal and tax systems, the perceived objectives of financial reporting and the significance of different sources of finance.

In contrast to IFRSs and US GAAP, there is no broad-based statement of generally accepted theoretical principles that underpins financial reporting in the European Union (EU). Clearly, though, it is not the lack of such a conceptual framework that has caused the European differences in financial reporting practices. European accounting has evolved over many centuries, and the differences that exist throughout Europe have been shaped by the conditions in each European country.

Until recently, the principal mechanism employed by the European Union to reduce these differences has been through the adoption of Directives under its company law harmonisation programme. These Directives are not laws that apply directly to companies, but instructions to Member States to alter, if necessary, their own national legislation to ensure compliance with the provisions of the Directive. In most cases, the Directives lay down minimum requirements only, so that there is nothing to prevent a Member State having supplementary requirements of a more stringent nature, provided that these are not incompatible with the Directives.

The most significant Directives in the area of financial reporting are the Fourth and Seventh, which were adopted into national legislation by most EU countries during the 1980s. The principal objective of the Fourth Directive was to achieve harmonisation in respect of formats, valuation rules and note disclosure, whilst the Seventh established a requirement for EU companies to prepare consolidated accounts on a common basis.

However, in negotiating the Fourth and Seventh Directives with the EU Member States, the European Commission found that the deep-rooted differences in European accounting could be reconciled only through compromise.

2.2   Harmonisation achieved by the Fourth and Seventh Directives

Historically, the objectives of financial reporting have varied in different countries, and this fact is reflected in the relative importance given to the various parties who have an interest in accounting information. For example, financial reporting in certain countries has developed on the basis of considering shareholders as being the most important party entitled to receive financial information. This approach arose from the situation where businesses had obtained a substantial proportion of their funds from the public generally and where responsibility for the conduct of the operations of the business was divorced from ownership. Investors required regular reports to assess the performance achieved by management and future prospects, and annual accounts ensured that the stewardship function was being exercised properly.

On the other hand, in other countries financial reporting has evolved from the premise that accounts were provided largely for the tax authorities and other government bodies interested in national economic planning. The assessment of liabilities to tax had to be based on standard rules regarding the recognition of income, deduction of expenses and valuation of assets; in this way, all businesses would be subject to tax on the same basis.

These contrasting attitudes to the purpose of financial reporting have adversely affected harmonisation of accounting law and practice in the EU. This being the case, it is probable that the harmonisation programme under the Directives has been only partially successful. This is clearly evidenced by the fact that harmonisation has not been achieved in the areas of recognition and measurement – both of which are fundamental to achieving comparability in financial reporting. Nevertheless, it is clear also that the Fourth and Seventh Directives have provided a base level for harmonisation of financial reporting in the EU, and have undoubtedly led to improvements in the quality and comparability of company accounts throughout the Union over the last twenty years. They have contributed also to improving the conditions for cross-border business and have allowed the mutual recognition of accounts for the purposes of quotation on securities exchanges throughout the EU. Moreover, a further important contribution of the Directives is in the area of creditor protection through the public availability of financial information. In contrast to the US, where only SEC registrant companies are required to publish financial statements, all limited liability companies in the EU are required to produce and publish financial information.

2.3 The European Commission's 1995 Communication on international harmonisation

In 1995, the European Commission issued a Communication (i.e. policy statement) stating that, while EU legislation has considerably improved the quality of financial reporting in the Union, the Directives do not provide answers to all the problems facing preparers and users of accounts and accounting standard setters. In the Commission's view, the most urgent problem to be addressed concerns European companies with an 'international vocation' (the so-called 'global players') and the need to facilitate the access of such European global players to the international capital markets. The accounts prepared by those companies in accordance with their national legislation (based on the Accounting Directives) are not acceptable for international capital market purposes. These companies are therefore obliged to prepare two sets of accounts, one set which is in conformity with the Accounting Directives and another set required by the international capital markets.

The Commission examined several possible approaches to dealing with the issue of 'upgrading' EU accounting legislation. After careful consideration, the Commission suggested that a closer cooperation between the EU and the IASC, with the objective of ultimately adopting International Accounting Standards at the EU level, was the preferred solution. Referring to the 1995 agreement between IOSCO and the IASC to produce a core set of international accounting standards which would be endorsed by IOSCO, the Commission concluded that 'rather than amend the existing Directives, the proposal is to improve the present situation by associating the EU with the efforts undertaken by IASC and IOSCO towards a broader international harmonisation of accounting standards'.

This policy statement of the Commission paved the way to the acceptance of IFRSs by the EU. Unfortunately, the Commission could not anticipate in 1995 that the ultimate endorsement of IFRSs by IOSCO in May 2000 would only be a qualified acceptance of the standards. As it turned out, one of the main objectives of the Commission in moving towards IFRSs (access of European companies to international capital markets without having to provide reconciliations to any National GAAP) was only partly achieved.

2.4 The European Commission's Financial Services Action Plan

As part of its strategy to embrace IFRSs, and in response to its growing use by EU multinational companies, the Commission carried out an ongoing examination of the conformity between the Accounting Directives and IAS and SIC Interpretations. Generally, these comparisons concluded that (with the exception of IAS 39 – see below) there are few conflicts between the Accounting Directives and IFRSs. Those minor conflicts that did exist would be addressed by the Commission in the context of the modernisation of the Accounting Directives that took place during the next two years or so. The Commission's programme of modernising the Accounting Directives not only removed existing conflicts between IFRSs and the Directives, but also ensured that all the options then available under IFRSs would be available to EU companies.

In May 1999, the Commission issued its Financial Services Action Plan. The plan confirmed the Commission's position that comparable, transparent and reliable financial information is fundamental to an efficient and integrated EU capital market, and that International Accounting Standards seemed the most appropriate benchmark for a single set of financial reporting requirements which would be the catalyst for the development of a single EU capital market.

This initiative was given further impetus by the summit of the European Heads of Government held in Lisbon in March 2000, where it was agreed that a single European capital market should be developed as a matter of priority. It was acknowledged further that the adoption of a single financial reporting framework for the European Union was a vital element in that process. The summit conclusions stressed the need to accelerate completion of the internal market for financial services and set a deadline of 2005 to implement the Commission's Financial Services Action Plan.

Following this lead by the European Heads of Government, the Commission announced in June 2000 that it would present proposals to:

- introduce the requirement that all listed EU companies report in accordance with IFRSs by 2005; and
- modernise the EU Accounting Directives to reduce potential conflicts with IFRSs and bring the Directives into line with modern accounting developments.

Meanwhile, EU companies reporting at the time under IFRSs faced an immediate problem with respect to IAS 39 – *Financial instruments: recognition and measurement.* IAS 39 requires that certain financial instruments are valued at fair value and that, in some cases, the changes in fair value are recorded in the profit and loss account. These requirements meant that there was a significant conflict between IFRSs and the Accounting Directives, with the result that EU companies would not be able to continue to apply IFRSs unless significant amendments were made to the Directives. Consequently, because IAS 39 became operative for financial statements covering financial years beginning on or after 1 January 2001, there arose an urgent need to amend the Directives in order to allow the application of IAS 39 by EU companies.

Accordingly, the Commission put forward a proposal to amend the Fourth and Seventh Directives in order to enable EU companies to comply with IAS 39, and therefore prepare their financial statements in conformity with IFRSs. This was eventually approved by the Council and by the European Parliament in May 2001 in the form of a Directive (the 'Fair Value' Directive) that amended the Fourth, Seventh and Bank Accounts Directives.

Although the Commission wanted to provide more flexibility in the Fair Value Directive in order to anticipate future developments in accounting for financial instruments, the EU Member States insisted on including certain restrictions in the Directive in order to make it as close as possible to the then current version of IAS 39 as possible. Unfortunately, as a result, these restrictions mean that the IASB's extension of the fair value provisions in IAS 39 (the 'full fair value option') has created new conflicts with the Fourth Directive, which will in all probability have to be addressed through further amendments to the Directive.

2.5   The European Commission's Regulation on the application of IFRSs in the European Union

On 13 February 2001, the European Commission published a draft EU Regulation that would require publicly traded EU incorporated companies to prepare, by 2005 at the latest, their consolidated accounts under IFRSs 'adopted' (see below) for application within the EU. This was adopted unanimously by the Council, and on 12 March 2002, by a vote of 492 for, five against, and 29 abstentions, the European Parliament endorsed this proposal. This was adopted as Regulation No. 1606/2002 of the European Parliament and of the Council on 19 July 2002.

An EU Regulation has direct effect on companies, without the need for national legislation. However, the Regulation also provides an option for Member States to permit or require the application of adopted IFRSs in the preparation of annual (unconsolidated) accounts and to permit or require the application of adopted IFRSs by unlisted companies. This means that Member States can require the uniform application of adopted IFRSs to important sectors such as banking or insurance, regardless of whether or not companies are listed.

The Regulation established also the basic rules for the creation of an endorsement mechanism for the adoption of IFRSs, the timetable for implementation and a review clause to permit an assessment of the overall approach proposed. The endorsement mechanism is discussed below.

The Regulation provides the facility for individual Member States, at their option, to defer the application of the Regulation until 2007 for those companies publicly traded both in the EU and on a regulated third-country market which are already applying 'another set of internationally accepted standards' (essentially, US GAAP) as the primary basis for their consolidated accounts as well as for companies which have only publicly traded debt securities. However, the Regulation states that it is nonetheless crucial that by 2007 at the latest IFRSs are applied by all EU companies publicly traded on a EU regulated market.

To date, Denmark, Finland, Germany, Poland and Sweden have announced that they will allow this transitional provision to be applied by companies whose debt securities only are traded on a regulated market, with Austria, Belgium, France and Luxembourg likely to do so as well. However, only Germany has announced formally that it will provide the transitional relief to companies currently reporting under US GAAP, although Austria and Belgium are likely to do so as well.

There are currently approximately 7,000 companies listed on EU regulated markets that will be subject to the proposed Regulation. Only about 275 of these companies applied IFRSs prior to 2005.

2.6   The EU endorsement mechanism

The Regulation defines the EU endorsement mechanism, which was already foreseen in the Commission's June 2000 Communication. The Commission took the view that an endorsement mechanism is needed to provide the necessary public oversight. The Commission considered also that it was not appropriate, politically or legally, to delegate accounting standard setting unconditionally and irrevocably to a private organisation over which the EU has no influence. In addition, the endorsement mechanism has the responsibility of examining whether the standards adopted by the IASB conform with EU public policy concerns.

The role of the endorsement mechanism is not to reformulate or replace IFRSs, but to oversee the adoption of new standards and interpretations, intervening only when these contain material deficiencies or have failed to cater for features specific to the EU economic or legal environments. The central task of this mechanism is to confirm that IFRSs provide a suitable basis for financial reporting by listed EU companies. The mechanism is based on a two-tier structure, combining a regulatory level with an expert level, to assist the Commission in its endorsement role.

The recitals to the Regulation state that the endorsement mechanism should act expeditiously on proposed international accounting standards and also be a means to deliberate, reflect and exchange information on international accounting standards among the main parties concerned, in particular national accounting standard setters, supervisors in the fields of securities, banking and insurance, central banks including the European Central Bank (ECB), the accounting profession and users and preparers of accounts. The mechanism should be a means to foster common understanding of adopted international accounting standards in the Community.

There are three criteria set out in the Regulation on the application of IFRSs in the EU with which any individual IFRS must comply if it is to be adopted:

- the standard should not be contrary to the principle of true and fair in conformity with the Accounting Directives;
- the standard should be conducive to the European public good; and
- the standard should meet basic criteria as to the quality of information required for financial statements to be useful to users.

These criteria, although wide, are fundamentally reasonable and cannot be considered overly difficult or burdensome in view of the substantial power the EU is effectively vesting in the IASB, a body not accountable to the EU electorate in any manner. It is important to note that whilst a standard or interpretation can only be adopted if all three criteria are met, this does not mean that if all three criteria are met that a standard or interpretation must necessarily be adopted. However, if a standard or interpretation is not adopted, EU companies are free to apply it, except in those cases where such application would be in conflict with binding EU law.

2.6.1   *Regulatory level of the endorsement mechanism*

An Accounting Regulatory Committee (ARC) has been formed, composed of representatives of the Member States and chaired by a representative of the Commission. The ARC operates on the basis of appropriate institutional arrangements and under existing comitology rules that will ensure full transparency and accountability towards the Council and the European Parliament.

Under these rules, the Commission presents to the ARC a report that is required to identify the standard and examine both its conformity with the conditions set out in the Regulation and its suitability as a basis for financial reporting in the EU. The ARC must decide, on the basis of qualified majority voting, whether to recommend to the European Commission that it should adopt or reject a standard for application in the EU. The same procedure applies to the adoption of amendments to previously adopted Standards and Interpretations.

2.6.2   *The European Financial Reporting Advisory Group (EFRAG)*

The European Financial Reporting Advisory Group (EFRAG) was established as a private-sector initiative by ten key constituents interested in financial reporting in Europe, including the European Federation of Accountants (FEE), the Union des Confédérations de l'Industrie et des Employeurs d'Europe (UNICE), the European Banking Federation (EBF), and the Comité Européen des Assurances (CEA).

EFRAG is a two-tier organisation, comprising:

- a group of eleven highly qualified experts (the EFRAG Technical Expert Group), to carry out the technical work; and
- a Supervisory Board of European Organisations (the EFRAG Supervisory Board), to guarantee representation of the full European interest and to enhance the legitimacy and credibility of EFRAG.

The manner in which EFRAG fits into the EC comitology framework of endorsement of IFRSs is shown diagrammatically below:

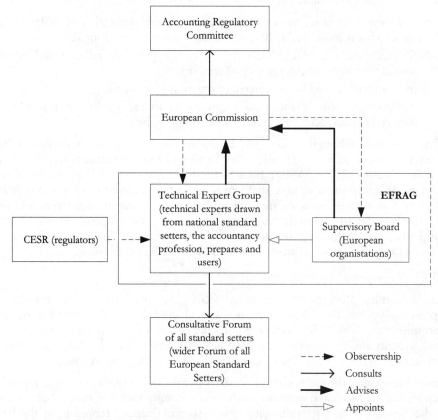

The principal aim of EFRAG is to provide proactive input into the work of the IASB. EFRAG will advise the Commission on the technical assessment of IFRSs and Interpretations, for application in the EU. The technical work of EFRAG will be carried out by the Technical Expert Group on the basis of a wide consultation process. National standard setters of Europe have access to EFRAG through a number of routes. In common with other consultative organisations, they receive regular updates of EFRAG agenda items and decisions. Additionally, they comprise EFRAG's Consultative Forum, meeting at least twice a year to engage in technical debate on matters arising from the EFRAG agenda.

The Technical Expert Group was set up by EFRAG on 26 June 2001. Its role is to provide the private sector support and expertise needed to assess the standards and interpretations developed by the IASB on a timely basis. It also has the responsibility to provide input into the IASB standard setting process at all stages of a particular project, and particularly in the early phases. The Technical Expert Group will ensure that EU users and preparers are involved in the preparatory discussions of the standards at the international level, and in the technical assessment of the standards, before their adoption by the EU. The meetings of the Technical Expert Group are open to public observation.

The Technical Expert Group provides advice to the Commission on the adoption of existing IFRSs for their use in the EU, and it advises the Commission also on whether or not an amendment to the Directives is recommended in the light of international accounting developments. However, the Technical Expert Group has a somewhat uneasy voting arrangement: EFRAG cannot recommend non-endorsement of a standard unless there is a two thirds majority vote against the standard. As the Group comprises eleven members, including the Chairman, this means that at least eight must vote against a particular IFRSs or Interpretation in order to be able to recommend non-endorsement. The situation can therefore arise, and has arisen, where a majority of the technical expert group vote against recommending a standard; but EFRAG is still not empowered to recommend its non-endorsement.

In addition, a special sub-committee of EFRAG has been established in close co-operation with the European Insurers' Association (CEA) to deal with insurance matters. Insurance has priority in Europe, given the fact that there is no comprehensive IFRS on accounting for insurance contracts yet, even though listed insurance undertakings will have to apply adopted IFRSs from the financial year 2005 onwards, in line with other listed companies.

2.7   Enforcement and regulation in an integrated European capital market

The European Commission has set an ambitious agenda for the European Union to become the world's most competitive economy by 2010. However, progress with European capital market integration – a vital ingredient of this agenda – so far has been slow. Nevertheless, the economic gains to be derived from an integrated pan-European financial and capital market are considerable. European companies will have greater access to a deep and liquid market at lower costs of capital; and European consumers will enjoy wider investment choice and increasing net returns on their investments. The macroeconomic benefits could be substantial also, as increased investment implies stronger job creation and GDP growth.

However, the basic structures needed for an integrated market are not yet in place. In Europe, trans-national companies have to report to regulators in twenty-five member states. They face a wide variety of different rules and regulations and investors have to negotiate fragmented markets that frustrate cross-border trading.

By contrast, the US capital markets provide clear evidence that efficiencies are forced upon businesses once their performances are easily comparable; without these pressures, inefficiency can go unnoticed. Globalisation of competition will punish less efficient businesses that cannot be price-competitive, and their revenues will reduce. Businesses enjoying semi-protected markets for their services, under less than transparent financing arrangements, will not be able to enjoy that shelter indefinitely.

Consequently, the greatest challenge facing Europe in delivering an efficient single capital market is the task of efficient regulation and enforcement. The absence of an effective and coordinated enforcement mechanism severely limits the credibility of any financial reporting regime. Clearly, the adoption of IFRSs in Europe will improve the functioning of the securities markets only when it is properly and rigorously enforced. This means that the supervisors of the European capital markets have a crucial role to play in ensuring that companies comply with financial reporting requirements. This can be achieved only through the establishment of an efficient and lean Europe-wide regulatory system. This implies the co-operative development and implementation of a common EU approach to regulation that would establish a level playing field for EU financial reporting, maintained by rigorous enforcement that will prevent regulatory arbitrage.

In introducing the IAS Regulation, the European Commission stated that one of its key actions would be the development of an enforcement infrastructure that will ensure the rigorous application of IFRSs by listed companies in the EU. The focus of this initiative will be on disseminating implementation guidance, encouraging high quality auditing, and reinforcing coordinated regulatory oversight. A coordinating body has been set up, as described below.

2.7.1 The Committee of European Securities Regulators (CESR)

The Committee of European Securities Regulators (CESR) was established by the European Commission Decision of June 2001. CESR is an independent Committee whose members comprise senior representatives from national public authorities competent in the field of securities. CESR has set out its own operational arrangements in its Charter.

The CESR Chair and Vice-Chair are elected from among the Members for a period of two years. The Committee meets at least four times a year. CESR works with the support of a secretariat headed by a Secretary General. A representative of the European Commission is entitled to participate actively in all discussions held by CESR.

CESR submits an Annual Report to the European Commission, which is also sent to the European Parliament and the Council. The Chair of CESR reports regularly to the European Parliament and maintains strong links with the European Securities Committee.

The main roles of CESR are to:

- improve coordination among European Securities Regulators;

- act as an advisory group to assist the European Commission, in particular in its preparation of draft implementing measures to support the legislative framework for the regulation of Europe's securities markets; and

- work to ensure more consistent and timely day-to-day implementation of the European legislative framework in the Member States.

In doing so, CESR advises the European Commission on securities policy issues relating to Europe's securities markets and responds to mandates given by the European Commission. To foster common and uniform implementation of EU securities law, CESR may issue guidelines, recommendations and standards.

2.7.2   CESR Standard No. 1

During the seventh meeting of CESR held in Paris in March 2003, the first CESR standard on *Financial Information: Enforcement of standards on financial information in Europe*, was approved. The standard represents a significant part of CESR's contribution to the task of developing and implementing a common approach to the enforcement of IFRSs in Europe.

The standard sets down 21 principles on which, in CESR's view, harmonisation of the institutional oversight systems in Europe may be achieved. In particular, a definition of enforcement of standards on financial information, its scope, the selection techniques applicable by the enforcers and the responsibility of the different parties involved are outlined.

The standard states that for financial information other than prospectuses, ex-post enforcement is the normal procedure, whilst for prospectuses ex-ante approval is the normal procedure. Enforcement of all financial information should normally be achieved by selecting a number of issuers and documents to be examined. The preferred models for selecting financial information for enforcement purposes are mixed models whereby a risk-based approach is combined with a rotation and/or a sampling approach.

Where a material misstatement in the financial information is detected, enforcers are required to take appropriate actions to achieve an appropriate disclosure and where relevant, public correction of misstatement. Enforcers should periodically report to the public on their activities providing, as a minimum, information on the enforcement policies adopted and decisions taken in individual cases including accounting and disclosure matters.

2.7.3   CESR Recommendation on communication of the impact of IFRSs

In December 2003, CESR published a recommendation for regulators on how listed EU companies can effectively manage the communication of the financial impact of transitioning to IFRSs in 2005. CESR considers it essential that the transition must be monitored carefully by regulators to ensure that every company continues to meet its reporting requirements and that investors are able to understand the effect of the new reporting standards on the financial position of listed companies.

2.7.4 CESR Standard No. 2

In April 2004, CESR issued a standard on the organisation of greater co-ordination of enforcement activities by supervisors of financial information in Europe. The standard's aim is further to contribute to the creation within Europe of robust and consistent enforcement of IFRSs. The key principles introduced by Standard No. 2 include:

- discussion of enforcement decisions and experiences within a formalised structure;
- the principle that all supervisors should take into account existing decisions taken by EU National Enforcers; and
- the development of a database as a practical reference tool that sets out decisions taken by EU National Enforcers to provide a record of previous decisions reached in particular cases.

2.7.5 CESR equivalency project

In June 2005, after receipt of a mandate from the European Commission, CESR started work on considering the equivalence between certain third countries' GAAP and IFRSs. Both the EU Prospectus Regulation and the EU Transparency Directive state that non-EU issuers who have their securities admitted to trading on an EU regulated market, or who wish to make a public offer of their securities in Europe, will be required to prepare and present the financial statements that they publish on the basis of EU endorsed IFRSs or on the basis of the third country's national accounting standards if they have been endorsed as equivalent to IFRSs.

As a first step in developing its final advice to the European Commission, CESR issued in October 2004 a concepts paper on how it intends to measure equivalence between third country GAAP and IFRSs. In February 2005, CESR issued its final concepts paper in which it articulated the following key principles:

- that equivalence should not be interpreted as requiring the third country GAAP to be identical; CESR believes that a third country GAAP can be declared as equivalent to IFRSs when financial statements prepared under such third country GAAP enable investors to take a similar decision in terms of whether to invest or divest;
- that CESR's approach to assessing equivalence will be to limit its analysis to the difference commonly found in practice or known to be significant as such by the financial and audit community in Europe and in third countries;
- the assessment process is likely to result in three potential outcomes:
  - a third country GAAP may be found equivalent and no adjustment is needed;
  - there may be a finding of non-equivalence of a third country GAAP in which case restatement is the only solution; and
  - there is a range of instances where third country GAAP could be considered as equivalent subject to 'remedies'. CESR's view is that the objective of the 'remedies' should be to enable investors to make similar investment decisions;

- the concept paper describes the potential 'remedies' which might be appropriate, depending on the nature of the difference between the accounting models;

- in describing the third countries enforcement mechanisms as requested by the European Commission, CESR's confirms in the concept paper that it is not its task under the EC mandate to make an assessment of the effectiveness and efficiency of such mechanisms, nor to evaluate the quality of enforcements systems in third countries. In order to prepare the description of enforcement systems in place, CESR will use as a benchmark the principles identified in CESR Standard No 1 on *Financial Information-Enforcement of Standards on Financial Information.*

CESR aims to complete its public consultation in the second quarter of 2005 with the aim to issue its final advice to the European Commission by 30 June 2005.

3   THE ADOPTION OF IFRSs IN OTHER COUNTRIES

A comprehensive 'stable platform' of generally high quality International Financial Reporting Standards has now been promulgated, and nearly 100 countries are committed to adopt IFRSs directly, or to align their national standards with IFRSs, from 2005 or later. Although the European Union, comprising twenty-five Member States, will almost certainly be the IASB's most significant constituency, there are also a number of other economically developed countries that will be adopting IFRSs as their primary system of GAAP. Set out below is a brief summary of the basis on which some of these countries have adopted IFRSs.

3.1   Australia

The Australian Financial Reporting Council (FRC) is a statutory body established under the *Australian Securities and Investments Commission Act 2001, as amended by the Corporate Law Economic Reform Program (Audit Reform and Corporate Disclosure) Act 2004.* The FRC is responsible for providing broad oversight of the process for setting accounting and auditing standards as well as monitoring the effectiveness of auditor independence requirements in Australia and providing the Australian Government with reports and advice on these matters. It comprises key stakeholders from the business community, the professional accounting bodies, governments and regulatory agencies.

In July 2002, the Chairman of the FRC announced that the FRC had formalised its support for the adoption by Australia of international accounting standards by 1 January 2005. In accordance with this strategic directive, the Australian Accounting Standards Board (AASB) issued Australian equivalents to IFRSs on 15 July 2004. The issuing of the Australian equivalents to international standards achieves the FRC's strategic directive of ensuring that for-profit entities applying AASB standards for reporting periods beginning on or after 1 January 2005 will also be complying with IASB standards.

In adopting the IASB's standards, the AASB's overall approach is to adopt the content and wording of the standards. Words are only being changed where there is a need to accommodate the Australian legislative environment. In addition, subject to due process, the AASB sometimes permits only one of a number of optional treatments available in IASB standards and sometimes requires additional disclosures, particularly where these are already required under existing AASB standards.

In some cases, existing AASB standards contain helpful commentary that is not included in the equivalent IASB standards. The AASB has retained this commentary as guidance that is not part of the standards where it is considered to be of benefit to users of AASB standards, and provided it does not contradict the content of Australian equivalents to IASB standards. Such guidance may, for example, deal with situations that are commonly encountered in the Australian environment but which are not catered for in the IASB standards.

The AASB plans to continue to work to maintain consistency with the IASB's standards in order that the FRC's strategic directive continues to be met.

3.2   China and Hong Kong

3.2.1   China

The developments in IFRSs have been playing an important role in the development of accounting standards and practices in China. The Ministry of Finance (the "MOF") is responsible for the promulgation of accounting standards. In 1993, the MOF started a work programme to develop a set of *Accounting Standards for Business Enterprises*. To date, sixteen accounting standards have been published, as well as several exposure drafts covering a number of topics.

The overall approach is to converge, as far as is practicable, with international practices and, in particular, with IFRSs. Many of the accounting standards published to date are similar to the corresponding IFRSs. For instance, the requirements set out in the local accounting standards on revenue, construction contracts, post balance sheet date events, cash flow statements are very similar to those in IAS 18, IAS 11, IAS 10 and IAS 7, respectively. However, there are accounting standards that do not have an IFRS equivalent, and the requirements contained therein may not be in line entirely with international practices. Notable examples are the accounting standards on non-monetary transactions and on debt restructuring, the accounting treatments of which are based on carrying value instead of fair value.

The MOF also promulgated the *Accounting System for Business Enterprises*, which codifies the accounting practices introduced by the accounting standards into a single volume of accounting rules.

The publication of the accounting standards and the *Accounting System for Business Enterprises* are important milestones in the convergence process. Prior to their publication, the local accounting regulations and practices were primarily tax-driven, with virtually no provisions, for example, for impairment testing. Thus, whilst there are still some historic differences between local and international practices, the convergence process is closing the gap, particularly during the last few years where significant progress has been made.

3.2.2   Hong Kong

The Hong Kong Institute of Certified Public Accountants ("HKICPA"), formerly the Hong Kong Society of Accountants, a statutory body established under the Professional Accountants Ordinance, is the principal source of accounting principles in Hong Kong. These include a series of Hong Kong Financial Reporting Standards ("HKFRS"), accounting standards referred to as Statements of Standard Accounting Practice ("SSAPs") and Interpretations issued by the HKICPA. The term "Hong Kong Financial Reporting Standards" is deemed to include all of the foregoing. While HKFRS have no direct legal force, they derive their authority from the HKICPA, which may take disciplinary action against any of its members responsible, as preparer or as auditor, for financial statements that do not follow the requirements of the pronouncements.

In 2001, the HKICPA Council mandated a strategy of achieving convergence of its accounting standards with IFRSs issued by the IASB. Today the overwhelming majority of extant HKFRS are based on their equivalent IFRS, IAS and Interpretations promulgated by the IASB. The HKICPA Council supports the integration of its standard setting process with that of the IASB.

As of October 2004, IFRSs 1 to 5 had been adopted as HKFRS 1 to 5 and, with effect from 1 January 2005, all the existing SSAPs and Interpretations for which there are equivalent IAS and SIC Interpretations will be replaced by Hong Kong Accounting Standards and Hong Kong Accounting Standards Interpretations with numbers corresponding to the equivalent IAS and SIC Interpretations, respectively. There will be 31 such standards and 11 such Interpretations.

Although the HKICPA Council has a policy to achieve convergence of HKFRSs with IFRSs, the HKICPA Council may consider it appropriate to include additional disclosure requirements in a HKFRS or, in some exceptional cases, to deviate from an IFRS. Each HKFRS issued by Council contains information about the extent of compliance with the equivalent IFRS. Where the requirements of a HKFRS and an IFRS differ, the HKFRS should be followed by entities reporting within the area of application of the HKFRSs. However, such situations are relatively few.

HKFRS are considered to be strongly persuasive in interpreting the legal requirement that financial statements should give a true and fair view. HKFRSs set out recognition, measurement, presentation and disclosure requirements dealing with transactions and events that are important in general purpose financial statements. They may also set out such requirements for transactions and events that arise mainly in specific industries. HKFRSs are based on a Framework, adopted from IFRSs, which addresses the concepts underlying the information presented in general purpose financial statements. The objective of the Framework is to facilitate the consistent and logical formulation of HKFRSs. The Framework also provides a basis for the use of judgement in resolving accounting issues.

HKFRSs are designed to apply to the general purpose financial statements and other financial reporting of all profit-oriented entities. Profit-oriented entities include those engaged in commercial, industrial, financial and similar activities, whether organised in corporate or in other forms. They include organisations such as mutual insurance companies and other mutual cooperative entities that provide dividends or other economic benefits directly and proportionately to their owners, members or participants. Although HKFRSs are not designed to apply to not-for-profit activities in the private sector, public sector or government, entities with such activities may find them appropriate.

3.3   Norway

Norway is not a member of the EU. However, as a member of the European Economic Agreement (EEA), Norway is obligated to adopt the EU Regulation requiring all entities in the EU listed on a regulated market to their prepare consolidated accounts in accordance with IFRSs by 2005 ('the mandatory scope'). Clearly, this puts a constraint on the development of Norwegian financial reporting in the future.

Financial reporting in Norway is regulated by legislation. The Norwegian Accounting Act of 1998 does not contain detailed rules and may best be characterised as a legal framework. This legal framework, as opposed to a set of detailed rules, leaves room for the exercise of professional judgment. The concept of 'good accounting practice' (GAP) plays a fundamental role in the framework. A basic principle set out in the legislation is that financial reports should be prepared in accordance with GAP. Underlying the GAP concept are accounting principles and concepts developed in a transaction based historical cost model.

The legal framework approach assumes an active standard setting body. Norsk RegnskapsStiftelse (NRS, 'The Norwegian Accounting Standards Board' (NASB)) is the standard setting body in Norway. Today, in addition to the NASB accounting standards, pronouncements made by the Oslo Stock Exchange are considered authoritative GAP literature. Similarly, pronouncements made by the Norwegian Institute of Public Accountants (DnR) are generally considered to have impact on Norwegian GAP.

Norwegian GAP has traditionally drawn on the accounting standards issued by the FASB in the US, the ASB in the UK, and the IASB in its standard setting process. The leading role of US GAAP in international accounting practice has greatly influenced Norwegian GAP. However, the increased importance of the IFRSs in the international accounting harmonisation process led to a shift in the Norwegian approach in the mid-nineties. In the preamble of the Accounting Act 1998, the Parliament assumes that harmonisation towards IFRSs should be regarded an objective in accounting standard setting. The international harmonisation process led the NASB to adopt a strategy in 2001 where harmonization with IFRSs was the primary objective.

In any event, though, as a result of the EU Regulation and the EEA, listed Norwegian companies will be required to adopt full IFRS in their consolidated accounts by 2005, and the enforcement mechanism assumed under the Regulation applies to Norway as well. However, it has not yet been determined whether IFRS reporting will be allowed or required for other than listed companies and whether IFRS reporting will be allowed or required in the separate accounts. In the report of the Accounting Act Committee of 2002, which was commissioned to assess the demand for changes in the current accounting legislation to meet the requirements of the EU Regulation, it was proposed that other than listed companies should be allowed, but not required, to apply IFRSs in their consolidated accounts by 2005.

However, the report recommended also that neither listed nor unlisted companies should be allowed to apply IFRSs in the separate accounts. Nevertheless, in spite of this recommendation, a government bill on the subject was released in June 2004, suggesting that the application of IFRSs in the separate accounts of companies should be permitted.

The report of the Accounting Act Committee also proposed changes in the Accounting Act that would allow accounting policies that are permissible under IFRSs to be adopted under Norwegian GAP as well (with the exception of the revaluation alternative under IAS 16). Thus, even though a two-tier system of both IFRSs and Norwegian GAP most likely will apply in Norway from 2005, Norwegian GAP is intended to allow companies applying it to adopt IFRS accounting policies even though these companies are not applying IFRSs *per se.*

The harmonisation of Norwegian GAP with IFRSs outside the mandatory scope of the EU Regulation creates difficult challenges, both conceptually and in practice. The Norwegian legal framework and Norwegian GAP are focused on revenue and expense recognition and the main objective is to provide a framework for meaningful income measurement, as opposed to the emphasis on asset and liability recognition under IFRSs.

The NASB will in the future not only develop accounting standards dealing with Norwegian GAP, but will also issue recommendations or guidelines on the interpretation of IFRSs on issues specific to Norwegian companies. For instance, there may be issues relating to the oil and gas, hydroelectric power generating and shipping industries that may specific to Norwegian companies. The NASB has so far issued one document dealing with the interpretation of IFRSs: in an exposure draft dealing the public and private pension arrangements in Norway in the context of IFRSs, the NASB discusses guidelines for the application of IAS 19.

3.4   South Africa

In 1994 the South African standard setting body, the Accounting Practices Board, made the decision to base future accounting standards on international standards issued by the IASC. As a result, the South African standards that were issued were generally the same as the equivalent IASs, but with a few minor differences. These differences mainly related to certain additional disclosures that were included in the South African standards, and in addition, the South African standards did not incorporate the allowed alternative method for a change in accounting policy. Some of the international standards were issued in South Africa after they were issued internationally, meaning that some standards had different effective dates. For example, on the one hand IAS 41 – *Agriculture* – was issued in South Africa with an unchanged effective date, while on the other hand South Africa did not have an accounting standard dealing with business combinations until years beginning on or after 1 January 2000, although IAS 22 – *Business Combinations* – had been initially issued in 1993.

In 2003, the Accounting Standards Board decided to remove the remaining differences, as far as possible, between IFRSs and South African standards. As a result, in the first half of 2004 all international standards in issue at that time were adopted in South Africa. Consequently, the standards have a dual number, namely an international and South African number (for example IFRS 1/AC 138) to reflect the fact that the Accounting Practices Board has approved them for use in South Africa.

Whilst this harmonisation process has left some historic differences in effective dates, which are included by way of footnote in the accounting standards, for IFRSs issued since the end of 2003 there are none. In addition, South Africa has issued its own interpretation on one issue, dealing with an additional tax payable when dividends are declared, as a result of the IASB deciding not to issue an opinion on an issue that was considered to be specific to South Africa.

The South African securities exchange, the JSE Securities Exchange, revised its listing requirements in 2003, and with effect from periods beginning on or after 1 January 2005 listed companies will be required to prepare financial statements under IFRSs.

The Companies Act, together with its related Fourth Schedule that governs the disclosure requirements for South African companies, and the securities exchange's listing requirements have certain disclosure requirements that are additional to those contained in IFRSs.

3.5   Switzerland

In Switzerland, Swiss GAAP Financial Reporting Standards (FER) came into life in the mid 1980s to address the need for a Swiss set of financial accounting standards that presented a true and fair view of the state of affairs of companies (as opposed to the generally conservative tax- or creditor-oriented financial statements prepared under statutory rules applicable to all companies). Swiss GAAP FER had (and has) as one of its goals to 'embrace the concepts of IAS' and to not conflict with IAS, but rather, to allow further alternatives than those included under IAS. In the early years, Swiss GAAP FER allowed many alternative treatments and implementation was very diverse. As time passed, many alternative treatments were abandoned and Swiss GAAP FER today can be viewed as a fairly complete set of standards with more flexibility and less required disclosure than IAS. It is now targeted at small and medium-sized enterprises.

However, international accounting standards have played a very significant role since the beginning of the 1990s, when consolidated accounts became required for the first time. Because the local Swiss accounting standards and practices in those days were primarily tax-driven and creditor-oriented, global companies were forced to look to a set of accounting standards more accepted on the world stage. As a result, many of the large Swiss multinational companies implemented IAS for their consolidated accounts. Over time, the importance of IAS (and US GAAP) grew, and by the mid-nineties, virtually all large listed companies were applying either IAS or US GAAP. The majority of these currently apply IFRSs. The Swiss Exchange (SWX) requires the adoption of either IFRSs or US GAAP for all registrants on the main exchange with effect from 2005, whilst for those companies not listed on the main exchange, Swiss GAAP FER provides a minimum standard (although IFRSs or US GAAP are also allowed).

4   WHAT CONSTITUTES INTERNATIONAL GAAP?

4.1   Generally accepted practice

It is clear that 2005 is a watershed year for IFRSs with a significant number of countries adopting it as their principal financial reporting regime. However, to date, no substantial body of custom, practice or generally accepted ways of employing IFRSs has had an opportunity to develop. Indeed, one of the challenges is to put in place a regime under which an 'International GAAP' that is understood and commonly applied throughout the world, can develop. Paradoxically, it may be that this situation best illustrates the real meaning of GAAP in an IFRS context. A comprehensive set of IFRSs exists, but no GAAP as yet.

So what else has to happen before 'International GAAP' can be said to have emerged? The extra element, which only time, practical application, and the inevitable disputes and compromises can supply, is generally accepted practice. It will only be after a number of years of full implementation by a representative cross-section of businesses in a number of countries, that a consensus will emerge over the way that in practice, and in the context of real commercial transactions, IFRSs is actually to be applied.

The term 'generally accepted' does not necessarily imply that there must exist a large number of actual applications of a particular accounting practice. For example, new areas of accounting that have not yet been generally applied may be accepted as part of GAAP. Similarly, alternative accounting treatments for similar items may both be generally accepted.

In the developing context of IFRSs, 'generally accepted' will refer to accounting practices that are regarded as permissible by the accounting profession and regulators internationally – which means a broad consensus will come to exist between users, preparers, auditors, regulators and the markets, across what are currently regarded as national boundaries.

In general, any accounting practice which is legitimate in the circumstances under which it has been applied has come to be regarded as GAAP. The decision as to whether or not a particular practice is permissible or legitimate is normally governed by one or more of the following factors, which may therefore be expected to apply to the emergence of 'International GAAP':

- Is the practice addressed in accounting standards or other official pronouncements?
- Is the practice addressed in accounting standards that deal with similar and related issues?
- If the practice is not addressed in accounting standards, is it dealt with in the standards of another country that could reasonably be considered to offer authoritative guidance?
- Is the practice consistent with the needs of users and the objectives of financial reporting?
- Does the practice have authoritative support in the accounting literature?
- Is the practice consistent with the underlying conceptual framework document?

- Does the practice meet basic criteria as to the quality of information required for financial statements to be useful to users?
- Does the practice fairly reflect the economic substance of the transaction involved?
- Is the practice consistent with the fundamental concept of 'fair presentation'?
- Are other companies in similar situations generally applying the practice?

In an IFRSs context, these factors build on the requirements set out in paragraphs 10 to 12 of IAS 8, which state that, in the absence of a Standard or an Interpretation that specifically applies to a transaction, other event or condition, management is required to use its judgement in developing and applying an accounting policy that results in information that is:

(a) relevant to the economic decision-making needs of users; and

(b) reliable, in that the financial statements:

   (i) represent faithfully the financial position, financial performance and cash flows of the entity;

   (ii) reflect the economic substance of transactions, other events and conditions, and not merely the legal form;

   (iii) are neutral, i.e. free from bias;

   (iv) are prudent; and

   (v) are complete in all material respects.

In support of this primary requirement, the standard gives guidance on how management should apply this judgement. This guidance comes in two 'strengths' – certain things which management is required to consider, and others which it 'may' consider, as follows.

In making this judgement, management *shall* refer to, and consider the applicability of, the following sources in descending order:

(a) the requirements and guidance in standards and interpretations dealing with similar and related issues; and

(b) the definitions, recognition criteria and measurement concepts for assets, liabilities, income and expenses in the Framework; and

in making this judgement, management *may also* consider the most recent pronouncements of other standard-setting bodies that use a similar conceptual framework to develop accounting standards, other accounting literature and accepted industry practices, to the extent that these do not conflict with the sources in (a) and (b) above.

4.2 Practical interpretations of IFRSs

Relatively speaking, IFRS financial reporting is still in its infancy. However, in 2005 IFRSs becomes the global standard for financial reporting outside North America virtually overnight, therefore significant questions of interpretation will inevitably arise. Many of these will be issues of precedent and will have cross-border implications. The biggest challenge facing regulators is to ensure that national variations in the interpretation and application of IFRSs do not emerge. Although IFRIC does exist as the IASB's interpretations arm, IFRIC is neither able to, nor can it be expected to, deal with issues of interpretation that will arise on a day-to-day basis. IFRIC took more than two years to issue its first interpretation, and it is fruitless for companies to expect either IFRIC or the IASB to provide immediate answers to every practical issue as it arises.

In reality, the day-to-day issues of interpretation will be decided, initially, by company management and their auditors. Thereafter, regulators may become influential to a greater or lesser extent. However, the role of IFRIC and the IASB will principally be to monitor the practical application of standards and, if deemed necessary, issue an interpretation or amend a standard in response to what they consider to be the development of divergent or unacceptable treatments or inappropriate practices.

4.3   Who 'owns' International GAAP?

The adoption of IFRSs in the European Union as the single financial reporting framework for listed companies will mean that it has become a major force in world accounting. Its adoption by thousands of EU companies, including some of the largest companies in the world, will inevitably ensure its prominence. Combine this with other countries such as Australia, China and Switzerland, and it will not be long before the question of the 'ownership' of International GAAP arises, and who, therefore, is the ultimate authority when the inevitable differences of opinion and judgements occur.

This issue has a number of practical implications for companies applying IFRSs, for example:

- What happens in cases where different (and potentially conflicting) interpretations of the same standard are given by different regulators?
- There is uncertainty surrounding the legal issue of who has jurisdiction in cases of conflict between two parties on the question of the conformity of a specific set of financial statements with IFRSs. For example, what are the roles of the national courts, the European Court of Justice, National Regulators, the IASB, IFRIC etc.?

However there is a possibility of an even greater level of uncertainty being created as the custom and practice that are an essential part of any GAAP, begin to accrue. Hitherto, all standard setting bodies have been given their legitimacy by, and have operated within, national legislative frameworks; by contrast, the IASB is a private sector body, with no political accountability. In theory at least, all it does is set the standards; issues of compliance and enforcement are outside its frame of reference. As International GAAP develops there will no longer be a supreme legislative body that can decide, for all concerned with applying International GAAP, what does and does not constitute conformity with it. Moreover, pronouncements, rulings, and interpretations issued by others outside the IASB setup, will inevitably become part of International GAAP.

Therefore, it seems that it is only a matter of time before the ultimate ownership and authority of International GAAP is tested. Paradoxically it may be that the more successful International GAAP becomes as a global financial reporting system, the more its interpretation, integrity and meaning will be disputed.

5   FINANCIAL REPORTING IN THE UNITED STATES

To understand the regulation of financial reporting in the US it is necessary to understand the workings of the Securities and Exchange Commission (SEC) and its relationship with the FASB.   Before the 1930s, there were no authoritative or enforceable US standards governing corporate financial reports.   This lack of any statutory underpinning meant that the accounting profession had no authority to establish ground rules for corporations to use as a basis for their financial statements.

However, the abuses in stock exchange practices, in the financing of securities, and the defects in corporate reporting, which were revealed after the 1929 stock market crash, led the US Congress to enact the Securities Act of 1933, the Securities Exchange Act of 1934, and several other securities laws.   Under this legislation, companies offering new issues of securities for inter-state sale (other than for certain exempted issuers and certain exempted securities) and all companies whose securities are traded publicly, must register and file periodic reports with the SEC. These laws, taken together, emphasise full disclosure by issuers of securities and others acting in the US securities markets.   They are intended to provide investors with information about the issuer of a security as well as the terms of the security being offered, so that informed decisions on the investment merits of securities can be made, and to ensure that fair trading practices prevail in the primary and secondary markets.   The SEC, though given wide power to require that full disclosures be made, was not empowered to pass judgement on the quality or merit of an investment.   These aspects of financial reporting in the US are discussed in more detail in the following sections.

5.1   The role of the SEC

The SEC was created under the 1934 Act to enforce and administer the federal securities laws subject to the oversight of Congress.   Securities involved solely in intrastate transactions are subject to the separate securities laws of the state concerned, but not ordinarily to the federal securities laws.   The SEC is composed of five commissioners who are nominated by the President for five-year terms (the persons nominated must be confirmed by Congress in open proceedings) one of whom serves as the chairman.   It has a staff of lawyers, accountants, engineers, and financial analysts.   Despite its relatively small size (by US federal standards), the SEC has earned a reputation as one of the most ably administered federal regulatory agencies.   Its small size has been achieved, in part, through transferring the burden of monitoring compliance with its regulations onto securities issuers and their professional advisers.   This has been achieved through severe legal penalties for non-compliance, backed up by vigorous enforcement activities, and through various discretionary powers granted by Congress.   Though many other federal regulatory agencies are involved in various aspects of financial reporting, particularly in the financial services sector of the US economy, none has the pervasive influence of the SEC.

The SEC was given statutory power to set US generally accepted accounting principles (US GAAP) for companies subject to the federal securities laws; however, with limited exceptions, it has allowed the private sector (for example, at present, the FASB) to establish financial accounting standards and has viewed generally accepted accounting principles as those which have 'substantial authoritative support'. This term was first introduced in the SEC's Accounting Series Release (ASR) No. 4, which was issued in 1938 and stated that 'in cases where financial statements filed with the Commission ... are prepared in accordance with accounting principles for which there is no substantial authoritative support, such financial statements will be presumed to be misleading or inaccurate despite disclosures contained in the certificate of the accountant or in footnotes to the statements provided the matters involved are material'.

The separate accounting rules and regulations of the SEC have for the most part dealt with disclosure and classification standards rather than with the establishment of basic measurement principles and, in many areas, have required accounting disclosure by registrants beyond that specified for general purpose US GAAP financial statements. The SEC has stated that disclosures required by US GAAP set a minimum standard of disclosure to which should be added such further material information as is necessary to make financial statements filed with the SEC, in the light of the circumstances under which they are prepared, not misleading. The SEC has nevertheless exerted significant influence on the development of measurement principles whenever it has believed that accounting principles were not being addressed by the private sector in a timely or appropriate manner. Apart from audited issuer financial statements, the SEC rules can also necessitate the presentation of other financial statements in defined circumstances. Such other financial statements, which must also be audited, are most frequently encountered when the security offered is guaranteed by another party, when the issuer has acquired other businesses, and when investees of the issuer accounted for under the equity method are significant to its consolidated financial statements.

The content of US financial statements is designed for the general use of investors, creditors and regulators. Accordingly, they do not include financial information not considered necessary for a fair presentation of financial position and results of operations. The SEC has always considered consolidated financial statements to be the most meaningful and parent-company financial statements to be relatively unimportant – unless there are contractual or other restrictions on a parent's ability to receive funds by dividend, loan, or otherwise from its subsidiaries. In general, US GAAP is applicable to all legal forms of an entity and the SEC follows this approach also. Financial statements are widely used, distributed and understood in the US and the litigious US environment has resulted in numerous court cases and legal opinions regarding their content and purpose. Releases following an SEC enforcement investigation and activities of the SEC practice section of the American Institute of Certified Public Accountants (AICPA) (e.g. Peer Reviews and other quality control procedures) additionally support the objectives of fair and consistent financial reporting in the US. It is essential that any inconsistency in applying accounting principles or other lack of comparability between accounting periods be clearly disclosed.

The scope of the company laws of each of the US states is generally limited to non-financial reporting matters. In short, state company law is not a factor in US financial reporting. Other than for some federally chartered banks, there is no such thing as a US federal company law. Moreover, virtually none of the federal, state and local taxing authorities in the US use general purpose US GAAP financial statements for tax assessment or reporting purposes, nor do the tax laws usually directly influence the manner in which such financial statements are prepared. Instead, each taxing jurisdiction requires tax returns to be prepared and filed using tax accounting principles. The main exception to this general approach relates to the permitted use of the LIFO method for determining the cost of inventory.

Until the early 1980s, the SEC's focus was principally domestic. However, since 1982 a body of rules generally running in tandem with, but in certain respects less onerous than, the domestic regime has been developed for so-called 'foreign private issuers.' The term 'foreign private issuer' means any foreign issuer (other than a foreign governmental issuer), unless (1) more than 50 percent of the outstanding voting securities of such issuer are held of record either directly or through voting trust certificates or depositary receipts by residents of the US and (2) (i) the majority of the executive officers or directors of the issuer are US citizens or residents or (ii) more than 50 percent of the assets of the issuer are located in the US or (iii) the business of the issuer is administered principally in the US.

Failure to meet the foreign private issuer definition results in an entity, though incorporated or located outside the US, still being subject to the SEC's domestic rules. Special rules apply to an entity, which is wholly-owned by a foreign government, or agency thereof and these are not dealt with in this book because of their narrow application. Non-US and non-government owned companies meeting the foreign private issuer definition who offer debt or equity securities in a US public distribution, or wish to list on a US stock exchange, are required to register with the SEC beforehand and subsequently to file periodic disclosure reports.

At present, such registrations and annual disclosure reports must include audited consolidated financial statements for the latest three fiscal years. The auditor for this purpose is usually the company's incumbent auditor, though the SEC's auditor independence standards must be met and the audit must be performed under US auditing standards. The consolidated financial statements can be in accordance with the registrant's home-country accounting practices provided that, if equity securities are offered, all the disclosures required by US GAAP are added and provided that a reconciliation of reported net income and shareholders' equity to their approximate amounts, had US GAAP been applied, is presented. When non-convertible debt is offered, certain reliefs from the full gamut of US GAAP disclosure are permitted – though no relief from the reconciliation to US GAAP is available.

5.2   The SEC report filing system

Before a security (which is extremely broadly defined in the US) can be sold or offered for sale in a public interstate transaction by a non-exempted issuer, it must be registered with the SEC pursuant to the Securities Act of 1933, as amended. Rule 144A under the 1933 Act allows offers of unlisted securities to qualified institutional investors without SEC registration. The Securities Exchange Act of 1934 separately requires registration with the SEC of securities before they can be listed for trading on a US stock exchange or quoted on NASDAQ. Rules made by the SEC under the 1934 Act specify the subsequent annual and interim reporting obligations of a registrant and govern proxy solicitations in respect of shareholder meetings as well as tender and other offers to purchase.

Since the early 1980s, the 1933 and 1934 Acts have been administered under an integrated approach. Essentially this means that the disclosures required under each Act have, wherever practicable, been conformed, with the result that a registrant under the 1934 Act can use its reports under that Act to fulfil its disclosures under the 1933 Act if a transaction subject to registration under the 1933 Act is contemplated. For larger companies which have filed, in all respects, in compliance with the 1934 Act, which have been registrants for some time and which are not in default under the terms of any outstanding debt or preferred stock, an abbreviated 1933 Act registration statement can be used. Such 'short-form' registration statements, often in the form of 'shelf-registrations', incorporate by reference all reports filed under the 1934 Act and as a result can be extremely brief.

While the integrated disclosure system has simplified and streamlined the registration process, the specific disclosure requirements, for both registration statements and periodic disclosure reports, are nevertheless significantly more extensive and detailed than the requirements in most other countries. The principal rules and regulations governing disclosure in such filings are: Regulation S-X, which deals with the periods to be covered, form and content of financial statements; and Regulation S-K, which deals with the non-financial statement disclosures. In addition, the SEC Staff have detailed requirements and practice concerning financial statements included in SEC filings, and these are to be found in Staff speeches and the Division of Corporation Finance's Staff Training Manual. Where SEC rules require audited financial statements to be filed, the audit must be conducted in accordance with US generally accepted auditing standards. In practice, the SEC will not accept a filing containing an audit qualification due to a departure from GAAP or to management imposing scope limitations.

The main reporting obligation under the 1934 Act for US companies is an annual report (on Form 10-K) due within 90 days of the year end which must, amongst many other matters, include or incorporate by reference audited financial statements and applicable supplementary analytical financial statement schedules for the three most recent financial years. The other main reports by the 1934 Act for US companies are the quarterly report (on Form 10-Q) due in respect of the first three quarters of each financial year within 45 days of the quarter end, and the current events report (on Form 8-K) due in respect of any material events to which the registrant is a party, e.g. the material acquisition or disposition of assets or businesses, usually within four business days of the event reported.

The filing of annual and quarterly reports by reporting companies that are 'accelerated filers' has been accelerated, although the final phase-in period for acceleration was postponed for one year.

Under the amended rules, the deadline for an accelerated filer to file its annual report for its fiscal year ending on or after December 15, 2004 will remain at 75 days after fiscal year end. Similarly, the quarterly report deadlines for the three subsequently filed quarterly reports will remain at 40 days after quarter end. The phase-in schedule will then resume such that an accelerated filer will have to file its annual report within 60 days after its fiscal year ending on or after 15 December 2005. The company will then have to file its next three quarterly reports within 35 days after quarter end. The 60-day and 35-day deadlines then remain in place for accelerated filers for all subsequent periods.

An 'accelerated filer' is an issuer that meets the following conditions as of the end of its fiscal year:

- the issuer has a public float of US$ 75 million or more as computed on the last business day of the issuer's most recently completed second fiscal quarter;
- the issuer has been subject to Exchange Act reporting requirements for at least 12 calendar months;
- the issuer has filed at least one annual report; and
- the issuer is not a small business issuer as defined in Rule 405.

Eligible non-US companies (meeting the definition of a 'foreign private issuer') similarly must register with the SEC if they wish to enter the US public equity or debt capital markets. Such foreign private issuers are required to provide a broadly similar level of information to that provided by US companies in their SEC registration statements and periodic reports. The annual reports for foreign private issuers are filed on Form 20-F, which is due 180 days after the year-end. Form 20-F is also used by foreign private issuers for registration under the 1934 Act where, for example, a foreign private issuer seeks a secondary listing on a US stock exchange or NASDAQ. Certain reliefs from the domestic SEC regime are available to foreign private issuers.

Financial statements may be provided as specified in Item 17 of Form 20-F if the financial statements are presented pursuant to a registration under the 1934 Act, or to an offering of investment grade debt securities under the 1933 Act. The registration of equity and non-investment grade debt requires financial statements to be provided pursuant to Item 18.

The SEC Staff encourage, but do not require, foreign private issuers to provide the financial statements and related information specified under Item 18 in lieu of Item 17. In practice, financial statements under Item 18 are almost always required in any 1933 Act offering.

5.3 The financial accounting standard-setting system in the US

Since 1973 the Financial Accounting Standards Board (FASB) has been the officially recognised body charged with the task of establishing financial reporting standards in the US. It is financed by contributions from such private sources as accounting firms, investors and industry groups. It has seven full time members who must not be connected to any other business or profession while they serve on the FASB.

The FASB are responsible for, and issue, Statements and Interpretations, Technical Bulletins and EITF consensuses. Statements and Interpretations generally address accounting and reporting issues with substantial and pervasive implications and may significantly change practice in an area. Prior to being issued, Financial Accounting Standards (FASs) are subject to extensive due process. This includes: the debate of the proposed provisions in a FAS in open forum; exposure drafts which are issued for comment; and public hearings where oral arguments can be presented to the FASB on issues in the proposed statement.

Technical Bulletins provide guidance on applying FASs and for resolving issues not directly addressed by them. Bulletins are generally issued when the guidance they contain is not expected to cause a major change in current practice, does not conflict with accepted fundamental principles, and where the cost of implementing the guidance is not expected to be significant.

The Emerging Issues Task Force (EITF) was established by the FASB in 1984 to assist in the early identification of issues and problems affecting financial reporting. It is composed of individuals who are knowledgeable and aware of accounting matters. The EITF issues consensuses that address quite narrow issues and these may only be issued if no more than one third of the twelve voting members object. The SEC will challenge any accounting that differs from an EITF consensus because it considers a consensus represents the best thinking on areas where there are no specific standards.

The standard form audit report in the US refers to fair presentation in accordance with 'generally accepted accounting principles', which is broadly equivalent to the words 'present fairly in all material respects in accordance with International Financial Reporting Standards' that would normally be found in an audit report on IFRS financial statements. However, the FASB have taken a rather different strategic approach to accounting standard setting from that adopted by the IASB. The IASB strategy relies upon accounting standards that are couched in terms of broad principles, with a minimum of detailed accounting rules – indeed some practitioners criticise the IASB for the lack of detailed guidance it provides with some of its more complex standards. As a result, financial reporting under IFRSs requires a considerable measure of judgement to be exercised in the application of many of the applicable standards.

By contrast the characteristic of the FASB's system is one of highly detailed rules, which arguably may have obscured the concept of fair presentation in some instances.

5.4   Adoption by the US Financial Reporting System of a Principles-Based Accounting System

The recent spate of major corporate accounting scandals in the US (such as Waste Management and Enron) suggested to many that the US system of corporate governance and financial reporting was in need of improvement. To many it appeared that, at least in some cases, the checks-and-balances within the US financial reporting system-ranging from management to auditors, audit committees, boards of directors, analysts, rating agencies, corporate counsel, standard setters, regulators, banks and the investors themselves-failed to prevent or detect large-scale fraud in major corporations that were carried out over extended periods of time.

The US Congress responded by passing the Sarbanes-Oxley Act of 2002 ('the Act'), the most significant piece of US securities legislation since the 1930s. Much of the Act may be viewed as a legislative attempt to align better the incentives of management, auditors and other professionals with those of investors. For example, with respect to corporate management, the Act increased penalties for violations of securities laws and required certification of financial results by key corporate officers.

In summary, the Act called for improvement in the checks and balances that govern the production of financial information provided to investors. However, the question arose as to whether these actions addressed fully the causes of the recent corporate scandals. Many questioned whether the accounting standards themselves might have played some role in facilitating or even encouraging the behaviour of some of the individuals involved. More generally, many asked whether technical compliance with US accounting standards necessarily results in financial reporting that fairly reflects the underlying economic reality of reporting entities.

Amongst these concerns, there was a growing sense that the standard setting process in the US may have become overly rule-based. Three of the more significant and commonly-accepted shortcomings of rule-based standards are that they:

- contain numerous 'bright-line' tests, which ultimately can be misused by financial engineers as a roadmap to comply with the letter, but not the spirit, of standards;

- contain numerous exceptions to the principles purportedly underlying the standards, resulting in inconsistencies in accounting treatment of transactions and events with similar economic substance; and

- further a need and demand for voluminously detailed implementation guidance on the application of the standard, creating complexity in, and uncertainty about, the application of the standard.

Accordingly, Section 108(d) of the Act called upon the staff of the US Securities and Exchange Commission to conduct a study on the adoption by the US financial reporting system of a principles-based accounting system and for the SEC to submit a report thereon to the US Congress by 30 July 2003. The Act mandated that the study should include: (i) the extent to which principles-based accounting and financial reporting exists in the US; (ii) the length of time required for change from a rules-based to a principles-based financial reporting system; (iii) the feasibility of and proposed methods by which a principles-based system may be implemented; and (iv) a thorough economic analysis of the implementation of a principles-based system. The SEC staff submitted its study to the US Congress during July 2003.

The study asserts that imperfections exist when standards are established on either a rules-based or a principles-only basis. Principles-only standards may present enforcement difficulties because they provide little guidance or structure for exercising professional judgment by preparers and auditors. Rules-based standards often provide a vehicle for circumventing the intention of the standard. As a result, the SEC staff recommended that those involved in the standard-setting process should develop standards more consistently on a principles-based or 'objectives-oriented' basis. According to the study, such standards should have the following characteristics:

- be based on an improved and consistently applied conceptual framework;

- clearly state the accounting objective of the standard;

- provide sufficient detail and structure so that the standard can be 'operationalised' and applied on a consistent basis;

- minimise exceptions from the standard; and

- avoid use of percentage tests ('bright-lines') that allow financial engineers to achieve technical compliance with the standard while evading the intent of the standard.

According to the SEC staff, neither US GAAP nor IFRSs, as currently drafted, are representative of the optimal type of principles-based standards. In their view, an optimal standard involves a concise statement of substantive accounting principle where the accounting objective has been included at an appropriate level of specificity as an integral part of the standard and where few, if any, exceptions or conceptual inconsistencies are included in the standard. Further, such a standard should provide an appropriate amount of implementation guidance given the nature of the class of transactions or events and should be devoid of 'bright-line' tests. Finally, such a standard should be consistent with, and derive from, a coherent conceptual framework of financial reporting.

The SEC staff refers to this system as 'objectives-oriented' standard setting, and distinguishes it from a principles-only approach, which they believe typically provides insufficient guidance to make the standards reliably operational. The assertion is that objectives-oriented standards explicitly charge management with the responsibility for capturing within the company's financial reports the economic substance of transactions and events – not abstractly, but as defined specifically and framed by the substantive objectives built into each pertinent standard. In turn, auditors would be held responsible for reporting whether management has fulfilled that responsibility. Accordingly, it is considered that objectives-oriented standards place greater emphasis on the responsibility of both management and auditors to ensure that the financial reporting captures the objectives of the standard than is the case with either rules-based standards or principles-only standards. Further, if properly constructed, the SEC staff believes that objectives-oriented standards may require less use of judgment than either rules-based or principles-only standards, and thus, may serve better to facilitate consistency and compliance with the intention of the standards.

However, as noted in the study, a move towards more objectives-oriented standards will require a change in behaviour of standard setters, preparers, auditors and investors, including the ways in which standards are interpreted and applied and professional judgment is exercised. It could well take several years for the necessary changes in behaviour, attitude and expertise to take root – particularly given the legal and regulatory frameworks in the US. In any event, the first step must be for the FASB and IASB to develop jointly an agreed conceptual framework to be used as the foundation for the preparation of truly globally accepted objectives-oriented standards. It is for this reason that we believe that IFRSs and US GAAP convergence should involve the development of new standards based on a sound conceptual framework, rather than the elimination of detailed differences between existing IFRSs and US GAAP. The establishment in 2004 by the IASB and the FASB of a joint project to develop a common conceptual framework may be the first step in achieving this goal.

5.5   Recent standard-setting developments in the US

The FASB and the IASB have agreed to undertake a project aimed at removing differences between US GAAP and IFRSs. The convergence project is being conducted in two parts, a short-term convergence project and a longer-term research project. The short-term, limited scope project is being undertaken jointly to resolve differences between US and International Standards that are narrow in scope and which can be resolved in a relatively short timeframe usually be selecting between existing IFRSs and US GAAP. The Boards plan to complete the short-term convergence through a series of specific projects. The first project, Phase 1, has addressed a number of areas of difference identified by the Boards in October 2002. The FASB issued FAS 151 on inventory costs, FAS 153 on non-monetary exchanges at the end of 2004 and is re-deliberating exposure drafts on accounting changes/error corrections and earnings per share. Phase 1 is expected to be completed by the first quarter of 2005. A second joint project with the IASB is addressing accounting for income taxes and in a third project the FASB may revisit accounting for research and development. The FASB aims to issue an exposure draft of a proposed amendment to FAS 109 *Accounting for Income Taxes* early in 2005. Differences related to issues requiring comprehensive reconsideration by either Board have been deferred to a longer-term research project. The FASB and IASB are also working together on projects involving purchase-method procedures, financial performance, and revenue recognition.

As part of the FASB's joint efforts with the SEC to study the feasibility of a principles-based approach to standard setting, the FASB has issued for public comment a proposal incorporating general principles that would be established for the fundamental recognition, measurement and reporting requirements. In that document, the Board stated that creating two levels of literature (authoritative and non-authoritative) and elevating the conceptual framework within the generally accepted accounting principles (GAAP) hierarchy are key elements of the Board's goal of improving the quality of the GAAP hierarchy and, therefore, the quality and transparency of standards and the standard-setting process. The first step is a project to move the generally accepted accounting principles hierarchy from the AICPA's Statement of Auditing Standards No. 69, *The Meaning of Present Fairly in Conformity with Generally Accepted Accounting Principles in the Independent Auditor's Report*, to FASB standards and to define the meaning of authoritative literature. The FASB expects to issue an exposure draft on the GAAP hierarchy early in 2005.

5.5.1   The Sarbanes-Oxley Act

In response to recent corporate scandals, on 30 July 2002, President Bush signed into US law the Public Company Accounting Reform and Investor Protection Act of 2002 (now universally known by its short-form title the Sarbanes-Oxley Act of 2002). The Sarbanes-Oxley Act was designed to better protect investors by improving the accuracy and reliability of public company disclosures and is applicable to all public companies (domestic and foreign) that report to the SEC. The Act mandated a number of reforms to enhance corporate responsibility, enhance financial disclosures and combat corporate and accounting fraud. It also created the Public Company Accounting Oversight Board, to oversee the activities of the auditing profession.

5.5.2   The Public Company Accounting Oversight Board

Accounting firms are required to register with, and be subject to oversight by, the Public Company Accounting Oversight Board (PCAOB) in order to conduct audits of public companies. The mandate of the PCAOB is to enforce compliance with auditing, quality control, ethics, independence and other standards relating to the preparation of audit reports. The SEC is charged with the organisation and oversight of the PCAOB. The PCAOB's rulemaking process results in the adoption of rules that are then submitted to the SEC for approval. PCAOB rules do not take effect unless approved by the SEC. PCAOB rules include auditing and related Professional Practice Standards, Forms, and the Board's Bylaws and Ethics Code.

Since July 2002, the SEC has issued many final rules on aspects of financial reporting specified under the Sarbanes-Oxley Act, including rules related to:

- certification of disclosures in quarterly and annual reports;
- disclosure of audit committee financial expert and implementation of code of ethics for senior financial officers;
- use of non GAAP financial measures;
- disclosure of off-balance sheet arrangements and aggregate contractual obligations;
- mandated electronic filing; and
- management's report on internal control over financial reporting; and, additional Form 8-K disclosure requirements and accelerated filing dates.

5.6   The FASB's Technical Agenda

The following summarises the FASB's plan for major projects, application and implementation projects and other technical activities at January 2005.

Short-Term International Convergence – Phase 1

The objective of the joint FASB and IASB short-term convergence project is to achieve compatibility by identifying common, high-quality solutions. Under phase 1 of the project, the FASB issued FAS 151, *Inventory Costs,* in November 2004, and FAS 153, *Exchanges of Nonmonetary Assets,* in December 2004. A final Statement covering accounting changes is expected to be issued in the first quarter of 2005 and a final Statement covering earnings per share is expected to be issued in the second quarter of 2005. Income taxes and research and development are being addressed in a second phase of the project.

Short-Term International Convergence – Phase 2

Income Taxes

Both FAS 109 *Accounting for Income Taxes* and IAS 12 *Income Taxes* are based on similar principles but there are differences in application which the FASB and IASB are deliberating. The FASB hopes to issue an exposure draft of a proposed Standard in the second quarter of 2005.

Research and development

The objective of this phase of the project is to identify existing differences between US GAAP and IFRSs that might be eliminated through a future specific convergence project.

Businesss Combinations: Purchase Method Procedures

This project is the second phase of the FASB's overall project on business combinations and is a joint project with the IASB as part of the wider international convergence project. The objectives of the project are to revise the existing guidance for the application of the purchase method of accounting to improve (1) transparency of information provided to users of financial statements and (2) the consistency of that guidance with the conceptual framework. The Boards expect to issue common exposure drafts in the second quarter of 2005. The proposed Statement would replace FAS 141 *Business Combinations.*

Business Combinations: Noncontrolling Interests

This is another phase of the Board's project on business combinations and is also a joint project with the IASB. Both this project and the FASB's project on financial instruments, liabilities and equity include issues relating to the accounting for and reporting of noncontrolling (minority) interests. The Board plans to issue an exposure draft of a proposed Standard that would replace ARB 51 *Consolidated Financial Statements* in the second quarter of 2005.

Business Combinations: Combinations of Not-for-Profit Organizations

The object of this project, which is yet another phase of the overall business combinations project, is to provide guidance for combinations of not-for-profit organisations which is consistent with that for combinations of business entities. The Board expects that the requirements in FAS 141 *Business Combinations* (as amended by the Business Combinations: Purchase Method Procedures project) will be relevant for combinations of not-for-profit organisations unless circumstances require different accounting, when specific accounting guidance will be provided. The Board plans to issue an exposure draft in the third quarter of 2005.

Conceptual Framework

In October 2004, the FASB and IASB added a joint conceptual framework project to their agendas to update, complete, and converge their existing conceptual frameworks. An upcoming *Understanding the Issues* will explain this project in greater detail by (a) discussing the role of the FASB Concepts Statements and the IASB Framework, (b) indicating the areas needing improvement, and (c) explaining the Boards' planned approach to the project. FASB expects to distribute *Understanding the Issues* in the second quarter of 2005.

Fair Value Measurement

The overall objective of this project is to provide a single reference source for guidance on how to measure fair value when other accounting pronouncements require a fair value measurement. The short-term objective is to provide a single definition of fair value and a measurement framework. The longer term objective is to improve related conceptual guidance, especially around measurement reliability. An exposure draft was issued in June 2004. The Board plans to issue a final Statement in the third quarter of 2005.

Financial Instruments: Liabilities and Equity

This project is part of a broader initiative to improve accounting for financial instruments. In May 2003 the Board issued FAS 150 *Accounting for Certain Financial Instruments with Characteristics of both Liabilities and Equity.* FAS 150 requires that financial instruments within its limited scope be classified as liabilities, but FSP FAS 150-3 indefinitely defers the effective date of FAS 150 for certain mandatorily redeemable noncontrolling interests. The objective of this project is to discuss proposed changes to Concept Statement 6 and to issue a Statement dealing with the effect of those changes on the classification of certain financial instruments.

Financial Performance Reporting by Business Enterprises

The objective of this joint project with the IASB is to establish standards for the presentation of financial information in financial statements that would improve the usefulness of that information in assessing the financial performance of a business entity. Those standards will address the classification, aggregation and display of information on the face of the basic financial statements.

Liability Extinguishment

This project will support the revenue recognition project by (1) analysing how the liability extinguishment criteria in FAS 140 *Accounting for Transfers and Servicing of Financial Assets and Extinguishment of Liabilities* would be applied to performance obligations arising from revenue arrangements (2) addressing the application of extinguishment guidance in FAS 140 to certain financial instrument transactions, and (3) considering whether the liability derecognition guidance in FAS 140 should apply to liabilities excluded from its scope.

Revenue Recognition

The objective of the revenue recognition project is to develop conceptual guidance for revenue recognition and a comprehensive Statement based on those concepts. The FASB intends that a comprehensive Statement will eliminate inconsistencies in existing literature, fill voids that have emerged in revenue recognition guidance, and provide direction for addressing issues that arise in the future. This is a convergence project conducted jointly with the IASB.

Application and Implementation Projects

FAS 140: Qualifying Special-Purpose Entities and Isolation of Transferred Assets

The Board issued an exposure draft *Qualifying Special-Purpose Entities and Isolation of Transferred Assets* in June 2003. In response to comment letters received, the Board decided to draft a revised exposure draft which it expects to issue in the third quarter of 2005. A final Statement is expected in the first quarter of 2006.

FAS 140: Beneficial Interests in Securitized Financial Assets

This project was added to the FASB agenda to resolve the issues that led to the interim guidance in FAS 133 *Accounting for Derivative Instruments and Hedging Activities* Implementation Issue No. D1. This interim guidance stated that beneficial interests in securitised financial assets are not subject to FAS 133. The resolution of these issues could require amendment to or interpretive guidance for FAS 133 and certain provisions of FAS 140 and could require more beneficial interests to be accounted for as derivatives. Clarification of the types of derivative instruments to which a qualifying special purpose entity may be a party could also be required. The FASB expects to issue an exposure draft in the third quarter of 2005 and a final Statement in the first quarter of 2006.

FAS 140: Beneficial Interests in Securitized Financial Assets

This project will reconsider the accounting for mortgage servicing rights following comments on the June 2003 exposure draft *Qualifying Special-Purpose Entities and Isolation of Transferred Assets* which emphasised the need for fair value accounting. The Board recognises that this project may result in amendment to FAS 140 *Accounting for Transfers and Servicing of Financial Assets and Extinguishment of Liabilities* and FAS 65 *Accounting for Certain Mortgage Banking Activities.* During its deliberations, the Board expanded the scope of the project to reconsider the accounting for all servicing rights. The FASB aims to issue an exposure draft in the third quarter of 2005 and a final Statement in the first quarter of 2006.

Fair Value Option

The objective of this project is to determine whether to permit entities a one-time election to report certain financial instruments (or similar non-financial instruments) at fair value with the changes in fair value included in earnings. In the near future the FASB will consider scope issues, such as whether to extend the election to other recognised non-financial assets and liabilities and whether (and if so what) criteria should be imposed to qualify for the election.

Interpretation of FAS 87/Amendment of FAS 35

This project will provide guidance for 'cash balance' pension funds which are not specifically addressed in FAS 87 *Employers' Accounting for Pensions.*

Interpretation of the Liability Recognition Provisions of FAS 143

The objective of this project is to clarify the application of FAS 143 *Accounting for Asset Retirement Obligations* to legal obligations to perform asset retirement activities that are conditional on a future event.

In addition to the projects discussed above, the FASB has identified a number of research projects that will study technical issues for the purpose of developing the nature and scope of future major projects. The following research projects are on the FASB's current agenda:

- Conceptual Framework;
- International Convergence;
- Financial Instruments; and
- Consolidations: Policy and Procedure.

6   CONVERGENCE BETWEEN IFRSs AND US GAAP

6.1   The Norwalk Agreement

In the past, co-operation between the IASC/IASB and national standard setters occurred at a mostly informal level through a variety of bodies such as the G4+1 group of standard-setters (an informal grouping of staff members of the accounting standard-setting bodies of Australia, Canada, New Zealand, the UK, the US and the IASC) and the Joint Working Group on financial instruments (comprising representatives from the IASC, the FASB and eight other international bodies). However, in 2002 the co-operation specifically between the IASB and US Financial Accounting Standards Board (FASB) was placed on a more formal footing.

On 29 October 2002, the IASB and FASB issued a memorandum of understanding that marked a significant step towards the two Boards formalising their commitment to the convergence of IFRSs and US GAAP. This agreement was reached at a joint meeting held at the FASB's offices in Norwalk, Connecticut, USA on 18 September 2002, where the two Boards each acknowledged their commitment to the development of high-quality, compatible accounting standards that could be used for both domestic and cross-border financial reporting. At that meeting, both Boards pledged to use their best efforts to (a) make their existing financial reporting standards fully compatible as soon as is practicable and (b) to coordinate their future work programs to ensure that once achieved, compatibility is maintained.

To achieve compatibility, the two Boards agreed, as a matter of high priority, to:

- undertake a short-term project aimed at removing a variety of individual differences between US GAAP and IFRSs;
- remove other differences between IFRSs and US GAAP that remain at 1 January 2005, through coordination of their future work programs; that is, through the mutual undertaking of discrete, substantial projects that both Boards would address concurrently;
- continue progress on the joint projects that they are currently undertaking; and,
- encourage their respective interpretative bodies to coordinate their activities.

The Boards agreed to commit the necessary resources to complete such a major undertaking and to start deliberating differences identified for resolution in the short-term project with the objective of achieving compatibility by identifying common, high-quality solutions. Both Boards agreed also to use their best efforts to issue an exposure draft of proposed changes to US GAAP or IFRSs that reflected common solutions to some, and perhaps all, of the differences identified for inclusion in the short-term project during 2003.

6.2   What does convergence mean in practice?

Significant progress has already been made towards global convergence with the commitment of a significant number of countries around the globe to adopt IFRSs directly or to align their national standards with IFRSs from 2005 or later. However, the world's largest capital market – the US – has not yet committed to adopt IFRSs. Consequently, from 2005 onwards convergence will largely be an IFRSs/US GAAP issue, and it is therefore encouraging that the IASB and FASB have committed to joint working arrangements on all major projects with the aim of achieving convergence of IFRSs and US GAAP in the long term.

The first real evidence of 'convergence' can be found in IFRS 5 – *Non-current Assets Held for Sale and Discontinued Operations* – which was published in April 2004. IFRS 5 is virtually identical to the equivalent US standard, SFAS 144 – *Accounting for the Impairment or Disposal of Long-Lived Assets*. However, this has attracted certain criticism, since SFAS 144 is not generally regarded as a 'high quality' standard, and IFRS 5 cannot be seen as being a superior solution to the standard that it superseded, IAS 35 – *Discontinuing Operations*.

Some difficulties may arise from the fact that the FASB has its own governance arrangements that are based on the US GAAP preparer and user communities and regulatory and legal environments. In the light of the joint working arrangements that have now been agreed by the IASB and the FASB, it is particularly important that an appropriate balance is maintained between the respective interests of users of IFRSs and users of US GAAP as convergence between IFRSs and US GAAP is sought.

There is a real concern amongst the IASB's constituency that IFRSs/US GAAP convergence means the adoption of US GAAP into IFRSs through the back door – as evidenced by the IFRS 5 example. These concerns have not been allayed by the IASB's recently announced intention to adopt the US standards dealing with segment reporting (SFAS 131), and restructuring provisions and employee termination benefits (SFAS 146). The underlying problem is that IFRSs and US GAAP are two fundamentally different systems of financial reporting. US GAAP is a highly detailed rules-based system that places emphasis on the legal form of transactions and arrangements over their economic substance. In contrast, IFRSs have traditionally been principles-based and substantially less detailed, with much greater emphasis placed on economic reality and the exercise of judgment. However, it is a concern that, although based on principles, recently issued IFRSs increasingly include detailed rules. Although members of the IASB frequently emphasise the need for professional judgment to be used in the application of IFRSs, the standards often are drafted in a manner that appears to de-emphasise the use of judgment and, in some cases, may appear driven by a desire to achieve short-term convergence with US GAAP.

6.3 US GAAP convergence and the SEC reconciliation requirement for foreign private issuers

A significant proportion of the world's largest companies outside the US are listed on the New York Stock Exchange and NASDAQ and are therefore subject to SEC regulation. For those that file a Form 20-F, there is a requirement to provide reconciliations from National GAAP to US GAAP for both income and equity.

Consequently, the Norwalk Agreement was warmly welcomed around the world – particularly by those SEC-registered foreign private issuer companies that are currently required to provide US GAAP reconciliations, who saw this as a means of removing the reconciliation requirement. In addition, a European Commission statement welcomed the IASB/FASB commitment to achieving real convergence between their respective accounting standards by 2005, when listed EU companies would be required to apply IFRSs. The EU statement made the point that the announcement heralded a major step towards a global system of accounting standards and hoped that it would, in particular, help the SEC to accept financial statements prepared by EU companies in accordance with IFRSs, without reconciliation to US GAAP, for the purposes of listing on the US markets.

There was therefore the widespread hope that the IASB/FASB short-term convergence project would obviate the necessity for foreign private issuer companies reporting under IFRSs to prepare US GAAP reconciliations beyond 2005. However, the present disposition of the SEC is that this will still take some time to achieve. Global convergence around new accounting solutions is a long-term objective; whether or not the reconciliation is removed in the short-term is therefore not a matter of convergence – it is an issue of mutual recognition on the basis of equivalence. However, it seems that the unconditional acceptance of IFRSs by the SEC will still involve a long process of political negotiation.

Chapter 2 First-time adoption of IFRSs

1   INTRODUCTION

In 1997 the former IASC Board asked its Standing Interpretations Committee to address the issue of how first-time adopters should account for the transition to IFRSs.   This resulted, in July 1998, in the adoption of SIC-8 *First-Time Application of IASs as the Primary Basis of Accounting*. SIC-8 required that in the period when IASs are applied in full for the first time as the primary accounting basis, the financial statements of an enterprise should be prepared and presented as if the financial statements had always been prepared in accordance with the Standards and Interpretations effective for the period of first-time application.   It became clear shortly after SIC-8 was issued that, although theoretically sound, the approach taken by the interpretation could give rise to substantial practical difficulties for entities adopting IFRSs for the first time.

The spotlight was placed firmly on first-time adoption of IFRSs when the European Commission proposed to require all publicly traded EU incorporated companies to prepare their consolidated accounts under IFRSs, by 2005 at the latest.   After the IASB had been made aware of the considerable practical difficulties surrounding first-time application under SIC-8, it announced that it would undertake a separate project on this subject. Consequently, in July 2002, the IASB published ED 1 *First-time Application of International Financial Reporting Standards*.   The Board made significant changes to the exposure draft before finalising it in June 2003 as IFRS 1 *First-time Adoption of International Financial Reporting Standards*.

IFRS 1 offers many significant improvements over SIC-8, but it also has a number of weaknesses. Firstly, given the IASB's worldwide constituency, IFRS 1 had to be written in a way that completely ignores a first-time adopter's previous GAAP. One of the IASB's aims in developing IFRS 1 was 'to find solutions that will be appropriate for any entity, in any part of the world, regardless of whether adoption occurs in 2005 or at a different time'.[1]   Consequently, first-time adoption exemptions are made available to all first-time adopters, even those first-time adopters whose previous GAAP was very close to IFRSs. A first-time adopter will be able to make considerable adjustments to its opening IFRS balance sheet, using the available exemptions in IFRS 1, even if the difference between its previous GAAP and IFRSs was only minor.   It may even be that such adjustments are required to be made by IFRS 1.

Secondly, in its basis for conclusions, the IASB notes that ideally a regime for the first-time adoption of IFRSs would achieve comparability between the financial statements of an entity over time, between different first-time adopters, and between first-time adopters and entities already applying IFRSs.[2] SIC-8 gave priority to ensuring comparability between a first-time adopter and entities already adopting IFRSs.   Inevitably there are tensions between these objectives, and IFRS 1 gives priority to achieving 'comparability over time within a first-time adopter's first IFRS financial statements and between different entities adopting

IFRSs for the first time at a given date; achieving comparability between first-time adopters and entities that already apply IFRSs is a secondary objective'.[3]

2   SCOPE AND DEFINITIONS

The underlying principle in IFRS 1 is that a first-time adopter should prepare financial statements as if it had always applied IFRSs, but there are a number of exemptions and exceptions that allow or require a first-time adopter to deviate from this general rule. The objective of IFRS 1 is to ensure that an entity's first IFRS financial statements and its first IFRS interim financial statements contain high quality financial information that:[4]

- is transparent for users and comparable over all periods presented;
- provides a suitable starting point for accounting under IFRSs; and
- can be generated at a cost that does not exceed the benefits to users.

2.1   What counts as first-time adoption?

Clearly, given the differing regimes between first-time adopters and entities already using IFRSs, what counts as first-time adoption is a question of some importance. IFRS 1 defines an entity's first IFRS financial statements as being the first annual financial statements in which an entity adopts IFRSs by an 'explicit and unreserved statement' of compliance with IFRSs in those financial statements.[5] The decisive factor is whether or not the entity made that explicit and unreserved statement. Even if an entity departed from certain IFRSs (whether recognition, measurement or disclosure) in its previous financial statements, if it made an explicit and unreserved statement of compliance, that entity is *not* considered to be a first-time adopter. Accordingly, such an entity is not allowed to apply IFRS 1 in accounting for changes in its accounting policies.

IFRS 1 states that an entity's first IFRS financial statements will be subject to IFRS 1 even if it presented its most recent previous financial statements in conformity with IFRSs in all respects except that they did not contain an explicit and unreserved statement.[6] An entity's financial statements are considered its first IFRS financial statements, and thus fall within the scope of IFRS 1, when it:[7]

- presented its most recent previous financial statements:
    - (i)   under national requirements that are not consistent with IFRSs in all respects;
    - (ii)   in conformity with IFRSs in all respects, except that the financial statements did not contain an explicit and unreserved statement that they complied with IFRSs;
    - (iii)   containing an explicit statement of compliance with some, but not all, IFRSs;
    - (iv)   under national requirements inconsistent with IFRSs, using some individual IFRSs to account for items for which national requirements did not exist; or
    - (v)   under national requirements, with a reconciliation of some amounts to the amounts determined under IFRSs;

- prepared financial statements under IFRSs for internal use only, without making them available to the entity's owners or any other external users;
- prepared a reporting package under IFRSs for consolidation purposes without preparing a complete set of financial statements as defined in IAS 1 *Presentation of Financial Statements*; or
- did not present financial statements for previous periods.

Therefore, an entity whose most recent previous financial statements contained an explicit and unreserved statement of compliance with IFRSs can never be considered a first-time adopter. This is the case even in the following circumstances:[8]

- the entity issued financial statements claiming to comply both with national GAAP and IFRSs, and subsequently drops the national GAAP compliance claim; or
- the auditors issued a qualified audit report on the IFRS financial statements; or
- the entity stops presenting a separate set of financial statements under national requirements.

The IASB could have introduced special rules that would have required an entity that significantly departed from IFRSs to apply IFRS 1. However, the IASB considered that such rules would lead to 'complexity and uncertainty'.[9] In addition, this would have given entities applying 'IFRS-lite' (i.e. entities not applying IFRSs rigorously in all respects) an option to side-step the requirements of IAS 8.[10]

An entity that is not a first-time adopter cannot apply IFRS 1 to changes in its accounting policies. Instead, such an entity should apply:[11]

- the requirements of IAS 8; and
- specific transitional requirements in other IFRSs.

2.2   When should IFRS 1 be applied?

An entity that presents its first IFRS financial statements is a first-time adopter[12] and should apply IFRS 1 in preparing those financial statements.[13] It should also apply the standard in each interim financial report that it presents in compliance with IAS 34 *Interim Financial Reporting* for a part of the period covered by its first IFRS financial statements.[14] However, a first-time adopter that only issues a 'trading statement' at its interim reporting dates, which is not described as complying with IAS 34 or IFRSs, is not required to apply IAS 34.[15] Therefore, IFRS 1 does not apply to such interim reports.

2.3   First-time adoption timeline

IFRS 1 defines the following terms in connection with the transition to IFRSs:[16]

Date of transition to IFRSs: The beginning of the earliest period for which an entity presents full comparative information under IFRSs in its first IFRS financial statements.

Reporting date: The end of the latest period covered by financial statements or by an interim financial report.

First IFRS financial statements: The first annual financial statements in which an entity adopts International Financial Reporting Standards, by an explicit and unreserved statement of compliance with IFRSs.

First IFRS reporting period: The reporting period ending on the reporting date of an entity's first IFRS financial statements.

Opening IFRS balance sheet: An entity's balance sheet (published or unpublished) at the date of transition to IFRSs.

International Financial Reporting Standards: Standards and Interpretations adopted by the International Accounting Standards Board (IASB). They comprise:

- International Financial Reporting Standards;
- International Accounting Standards; and
- Interpretations originated by the International Financial Reporting Interpretations Committee (IFRIC) or the former Standing Interpretations Committee (SIC).

Previous GAAP: The basis of accounting that a first-time adopter used immediately before adopting IFRSs.

An entity's first IFRS financial statements must include at least one comparative period, but an entity may elect or be required to provide more than one comparative period.[17] The beginning of the earliest comparative period for which the entity presents full comparative information under IFRSs will be treated as its date of transition to IFRSs. The diagram below shows how for an entity with a December year-end the above terms are related:

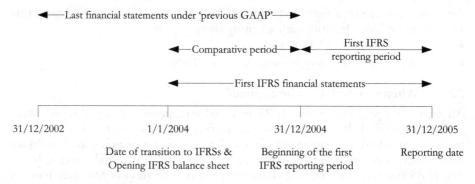

The diagram above also illustrates that there is a period of overlap, for the financial year 2004, which is reported first under the entity's previous GAAP and then as a comparative period under IFRSs.

2.3.1 First-time adoption timeline for SEC registrants

The US Securities and Exchange Commission (SEC) have published a final amendment to Form 20-F that changes the filing requirements for foreign private issuers that are first-time adopters of IFRSs.[18] The amendment 'permits eligible foreign private issuers for their first year of reporting under IFRSs to file two years rather than three years of statements of income, changes in shareholders' equity and cash flows prepared in accordance with IFRSs, with appropriate related disclosure. The accommodation retains current requirements regarding the reconciliation of financial statement items to generally accepted accounting principles (GAAP) as used in the United States (US GAAP).'[19] The amendment applies to a foreign private issuer:

- that is a 'first-time adopter' of IFRSs, as defined in IFRS 1; and
- that adopts IFRSs as their basis of accounting prior to or for the first financial year starting on or after 1 January 2007.

The accommodation is only available to a foreign private issuer that is able to state unreservedly and explicitly that its financial statements comply with IFRSs, and are not subject to any qualification relating to the application of IFRSs as issued by the IASB. However, the accommodation is available to a foreign private issuer that prepares its financial statements in accordance with IFRSs as adopted by the EU if it also provides an audited reconciliation to IFRSs as published by the IASB.

Foreign private issuers relying on the accommodation will continue to be required to provide an audited reconciliation to US GAAP for the two financial years presented under IFRSs. An issuer that applies IFRSs as adopted by the EU may use the required reconciliation to IFRSs as published by the IASB as the basis for their reconciliation to US GAAP.

First-time adopters that rely on the accommodation will be allowed, but not required, to include, incorporate by reference or refer to any financial statements or other financial information based on their previous GAAP. If first-time adopters do include or incorporate by reference such information, they should (1) include or incorporate narrative disclosure of their operating and financial review and prospects for the periods covered by that information, and (2) include cautionary language to disclose that the filing contains financial information based on their previous GAAP, which is not comparable to financial information based on IFRSs. There is no prescribed specific placement of any financial information based on an issuer's previous GAAP, but presentation in a side-by-side columnar format with IFRSs information is prohibited.

In addition, the proposed accommodation will only require entities to provide selected historical financial data based on IFRSs for the two most recent financial years. Selected historical financial data based on US GAAP will continue to be required for the five most recent financial years. The amendments neither require nor prohibit entities from including or incorporating by reference selected financial data based on previous GAAP, but as with the audited financial statements, information prepared under IFRSs and information prepared under previous GAAP should not be presented in a side-by-side columnar format.

Where a narrative discussion of its financial condition is provided, the accommodation requires management to focus on the financial statements prepared under IFRSs and the reconciliation to US GAAP for the past two financial years. In addition, management should explain any differences between IFRSs and US GAAP that are not otherwise discussed in the reconciliation necessary for an understanding of the financial statements as a whole. An entity should not include any discussion relating to the financial statements prepared under its previous GAAP unless it has elected to include such financial information.

IFRS 1 requires a first-time adopter to present a reconciliation from its previous GAAP to IFRSs in the notes to its financial statements and allows certain exceptions from full retrospective application of IFRSs in deriving the relevant data. Under the SEC's amendment to Form 20-F, any issuer relying on any of the elective or mandatory exceptions from IFRSs that are contained within IFRS 1 will have to disclose the following additional information:

- the items or class of items to which an exception was applied;
- a description of what accounting principles were used and how they were applied;
- when relying on an elective exception, where material, qualitative disclosure of the impact on the financial condition, changes in the financial condition, and results of operations; and
- when relying on a mandatory exception, a description of the exception and a statement that it complied.

The amendments to Form 20-F permit first-time adopters of IFRSs to file two years rather than three years of statements of income, changes in shareholders' equity and cash flows. However, in exchange for that accommodation a first-time adopter would need to provide a certain amount of additional disclosure. Consequently, first-time adopters that are SEC registrants need to consider carefully the costs and benefits before deciding whether or not to use the accommodation.

2.4   Fair value and deemed cost

Some exemptions in IFRS 1 refer to 'fair value' and 'deemed cost', and the standard defines these terms. These definitions are important to the practical application of IFRS 1 and an understanding of the exemptions it contains:[20]

Deemed cost: An amount used as a surrogate for cost or depreciated cost at a given date. Subsequent depreciation or amortisation assumes that the entity had initially recognised the asset or liability at the given date and that its cost was equal to the deemed cost.

Fair value: The amount for which an asset could be exchanged, or a liability settled, between knowledgeable, willing parties in an arm's length transaction.

In determining the fair value of items, a first-time adopter should use the guidance in IFRS 3 *Business Combinations* unless 'another IFRS contains more specific guidance on the determination of fair values for the asset or liability in question'. The fair values determined by a first-time adopter should reflect the conditions that existed at the date for which they were determined,[21] i.e. the first-time adopter should not apply hindsight in measuring the fair value at an earlier date.

3   RECOGNITION AND MEASUREMENT PRINCIPLES

3.1   Opening IFRS balance sheet and accounting policies

At the date of transition to IFRSs (i.e. 1 January 2004 for an entity presenting one year of comparative figures and reporting at 31 December 2005) an entity should prepare an opening IFRS balance sheet that is the starting point for its accounting under IFRSs. This opening balance sheet does not have to be published in the first IFRS financial statements.[22] However, it is required for, and integral to an equity reconciliation that has to be presented in an entity's first IFRS financial statements (see section 10.2 below).

The requirement to prepare an opening IFRS balance sheet and 'reset the clock' at that date poses a number of challenges for first-time adopters. Even a first-time adopter that already applies a standard that is directly based on an IFRS may need to restate items in its opening IFRS balance sheet. This happens, for example, in the case of an entity applying a pensions standard that is based on IAS 19 *Employee Benefits* before an entity's date of transition to IFRSs that elects to recognise all cumulative actuarial gains and losses at the date of transition to IFRSs, even though it continues to use the corridor approach for subsequent actuarial gains and losses (see section 7.1 below).

With the exception of financial instruments and insurance contracts (see section 6.1 below), in principle IFRS 1 requires a first-time adopter to use the same accounting policies in its opening IFRS balance sheet and all periods presented in its first IFRS financial statements. However, the principle is modified because IFRS 1 allows, and in some cases requires, the entity to take into account a number of exemptions from some IFRSs, and exceptions to retrospective application of others (see section 3.3 below).[23] In other words, the fundamental principle of IFRS 1 is to require full retrospective application of the standards in force at an entity's reporting date, but with limited exceptions.[24] The diagram below shows how the process of selecting IFRS accounting policies for a first-time adopter operates.

The requirement to apply the same accounting policies to all periods prohibits a first-time adopter from applying previous versions of standards that were effective at earlier dates.[25] The IASB believes that this:

- enhances comparability because the first IFRS financial statements are prepared on a consistent basis over time;
- gives users comparative information that is based on IFRSs that are superior to superseded versions of those standards; and
- avoids unnecessary costs.[26]

For similar reasons, IFRS 1 also permits an entity to apply a new IFRS that is not yet mandatory if that standard allows early application.[27] Users of financial statements should be aware that, depending on an entity's reporting date, it may or may not have the option to choose which version of a particular standard it may apply, as can be seen in the following diagram.

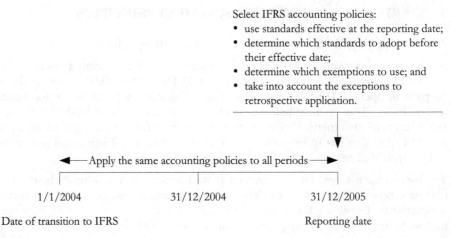

Date of transition to IFRS

Reporting date

Opening IFRS balance sheet

Apart from when the exceptions in section 3.3 below apply, an entity should in preparing its opening IFRS balance sheet:[28]

- recognise all assets and liabilities whose recognition is required by IFRSs;
- not recognise items as assets or liabilities if IFRSs do not permit such recognition;
- reclassify any items recognised under previous GAAP as one type of asset, liability or component of equity, that under IFRSs should be classified as a different type of asset, liability or component of equity; and
- apply IFRSs in measuring all recognised assets and liabilities.

Any change in accounting policies on adoption of IFRSs may cause changes in the amounts previously recorded as a result of events and transactions that occurred before the date of transition. These adjustments should be recognised at the date of transition to IFRSs in either retained earnings or another category of equity, if this is appropriate.[29] For example, an entity that applies the IAS 16 *Property, Plant and Equipment* revaluation model in its first IFRS financial statements would recognise the difference between cost and the revalued amount of property, plant and equipment as a revaluation surplus in equity. Conversely, an entity that had applied a revaluation model under its previous GAAP, but decided to apply the cost model under IAS 16 would reallocate the revaluation surplus to retained earnings.

3.2 Transitional provisions in other standards

The transitional provisions in other IFRSs only apply to entities that already report under IFRSs. For a first-time adopter, the requirements in IFRS 1 override the transitional provisions in other IFRSs.[30] There are limited exceptions to this general rule relating to (1) insurance contracts and (2) assets classified as held for sale and discontinued operations. In these cases IFRS 1 specifically requires application of the transition rules in the relevant IFRSs (see sections 7.4 and 8.2 below). It is important to note that the transition rules for first-time adopters and entities that already report under IFRSs may differ significantly.

When it issues a new IFRS, the IASB will consider whether a first-time adopter should apply that IFRS retrospectively or prospectively. In the limited number of cases that the IASB considers prospective application more appropriate it will amend IFRS 1.[31] Furthermore, the IASB also amended IFRS 1 to introduce a special first-time adoption regime for IAS 32 *Financial Instruments: Disclosure and Presentation*, IAS 39 *Financial Instruments: Recognition and Measurement* and IFRS 4 *Insurance Contracts* (see section 6.1 below).

The IASB's desire to ensure that IFRS 1 comprises all first-time adoption rules has meant that IFRS 1 has been amended by all the standards that the Board has subsequently issued as well as by several IFRIC interpretations.

3.3   Departures from full retrospective application of IFRSs

The IASB's *Framework* recognises that the necessity of striking a balance between the cost and benefit of providing information is a constraint that may limit the provision of relevant and reliable information in financial reporting.[32] In developing IFRS 1 the IASB specifically considered this cost-benefit constraint, which resulted in a number of exceptions from the general principle of retrospective application. It is worthwhile noting that the IASB 'expects that most first-time adopters will begin planning on a timely basis for the transition to IFRSs. Accordingly, in balancing benefits and costs, the Board took as its benchmark an entity that plans the transition well in advance and can collect most information needed for its opening IFRS balance sheet at, or very soon after, the date of transition to IFRSs.'[33]

IFRS 1 establishes two types of departure from the principle of full retrospective application of standards in force at the date of transition to IFRSs:[34]

- it allows a number of optional exemptions from some of the requirements of other IFRSs;[35] and

- it requires a number of mandatory exceptions from the requirement for the retrospective application of other IFRSs.[36]

3.3.1   *Optional exemptions from the requirements of other IFRSs*

IFRS 1 grants limited *exemptions* from the general requirement of full retrospective application of the standards in force at an entity's reporting date when 'the cost of complying with them would be likely to exceed the benefits to users of financial statements'.[37] The standard establishes exemptions in relation to:[38]

- business combinations (see section 4 below);

- the use of fair value or revaluation as deemed cost of property, plant and equipment, investment properties and certain intangible assets (see section 5 below);

- financial instruments:
  - restatement of comparative information (see section 6.1 below);
  - designation of previously recognised financial instruments (see section 6.2 below);
  - compound financial instruments (see section 6.3 below);

- employee benefits (see section 7.1 below);

- cumulative translation differences (see section 7.2 below);

- share-based payment transactions (see section 7.3 below);
- insurance contracts (see section 7.4 below); and
- assets and liabilities of subsidiaries, associates and joint ventures (see section 7.5 below). Some commentators have argued that this is not really an exemption, because it is not optional and actually requires a parent to use the IFRS measurements already used in a subsidiary's separate IFRS financial statements.

It is specifically prohibited under IFRS 1 to apply these exemptions by analogy to other items.[39]

Application of these exemptions is entirely optional, i.e. a first-time adopter can pick and choose the exemptions that it wants to apply. Importantly, the IASB did not establish a hierarchy of exemptions. Therefore, when an item is covered by more than one exemption, a first-time adopter has a free choice in determining the order in which it applies the exemptions.

3.3.2 *Exceptions to retrospective application of other IFRSs*

In addition to the optional *exemptions* discussed above, IFRS 1 also defines a number of mandatory *exceptions* that prohibit 'retrospective application of IFRSs in some areas, particularly where retrospective application would require judgements by management about past conditions after the outcome of a particular transaction is already known'.[40] The mandatory *exceptions* in IFRS 1 cover the following situations:[41]

- financial instruments:
  - derecognition of financial assets and financial liabilities (see section 6.4 below);
  - hedge accounting (see section 6.5 below);
- estimates (see section 8.1 below); and
- assets classified as held for sale and discontinued operations (see section 8.2 below).

The reasoning behind these exceptions is that retrospective application of IFRSs in these situations could easily result in an unacceptable use of hindsight and lead to arbitrary or biased restatements, which would be neither relevant nor reliable.

4   BUSINESS COMBINATIONS EXEMPTION

The business combinations exemption in IFRS 1 is probably the single most important exemption in the standard, as it permits a first-time adopter not to restate business combinations prior to its date of transition to IFRSs. The detailed guidance on the application of the business combinations exemption is contained in a separate appendix to IFRS 1 and is described below.[42]

4.1   Option to restate business combinations retrospectively

A first-time adopter must account for business combinations after its date of transition to IFRSs under IFRS 3. However, it may elect not to apply IFRS 3 to any business combination before that date. However, if a first-time adopter restates any business combination prior to its date of transition to comply with IFRS 3 it must also restate all subsequent business combinations under IFRS 3 and apply both IAS 36 (revised 2004) *Impairment of Assets* and IAS 38 (revised 2004) *Intangible Assets* from that date onwards.[43] In other words, as shown on the diagram below, a first-time adopter is allowed to choose any date in the past and account for business combinations going forward under IFRS 3 without having to restate business combinations prior to the earliest IFRS 3 restatement.

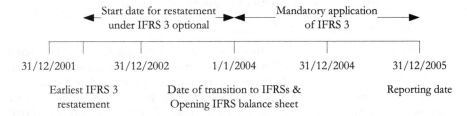

This exemption for past business combinations applies also to past acquisitions of associates and interests in joint ventures. However, it is important to note that the date selected for the first restatement of business combinations should also be applied to the restatement of acquisitions of associates and interests in joint ventures.[44]

4.2   Classification of business combinations

IFRSs mandate that business combinations should be accounted for as acquisitions or reverse acquisitions. An entity's previous GAAP may be based on a different definition of, for example, a business combination, an acquisition, a merger and a reverse acquisition. An important benefit of the business combinations exemption is that a first-time adopter will not have to determine the classification of past business combinations in accordance with IFRS 3.[45] For example, a transaction that was accounted for as a merger or uniting of interests using the pooling-of-interests method under an entity's previous GAAP will not have to be reclassified and accounted for under the IFRS 3 purchase method. However, an entity may still elect to do so if it so wishes – subject, of course, to the conditions set out in section 4.1 above.

The business combinations exemption applies only to 'business combinations that the entity recognised before the date of transition to IFRSs'.[46] The business combinations exemption does not apply to a transaction that IFRSs consider to be an acquisition of an asset, rather than a combination. First-time adopters will therefore have to consider whether past transactions qualify as business combinations under IFRSs, which are defined as 'the bringing together of separate entities or businesses into one reporting entity'.[47] A business is defined as an integrated set of activities and assets conducted and managed for the purpose of providing:[48]

(a)   a return to investors; or

(b)   lower costs or other economic benefits directly and proportionately to policyholders or participants. A business generally consists of inputs, processes applied to those inputs, and resulting outputs that are, or will be, used to generate revenues. If goodwill is present in a transferred set of activities and assets, the transferred set shall be presumed to be a business.

Furthermore, IFRS 3 states that 'if an entity obtains control of one or more other entities that are not businesses, the bringing together of those entities is not a business combination.'[49] Therefore, it is possible that under some national GAAPs, transactions that are not business combinations according to IFRSs (e.g. asset purchases) may have been accounted for as if they were business combinations.

4.3 Recognition and measurement of assets and liabilities

4.3.1 *Derecognition of assets and liabilities*

A first-time adopter should exclude from its opening IFRS balance sheet any items it recognised under its previous GAAP that do not qualify for recognition as an asset or liability under IFRSs. If the first-time adopter previously recognised an intangible asset, as part of a business combination, that does not qualify for recognition as an asset under IAS 38, it should reclassify that item and the related deferred tax and minority interests as part of goodwill (unless it previously deducted goodwill directly from equity under its previous GAAP) (see section 4.4 below). All other changes resulting from derecognition of such assets and liabilities should be accounted for as adjustments of retained earnings.[50]

4.3.2 *Recognition of assets and liabilities*

In its opening IFRS balance sheet, a first-time adopter should recognise all assets and liabilities that were acquired or assumed in a past business combination, with the exception of:[51]

- certain financial assets and liabilities that were derecognised and that fall under the derecognition exception (see section 6.4 below); and

- assets (including goodwill) and liabilities that were not recognised in the acquirer's consolidated balance sheet under its previous GAAP that would not qualify for recognition under IFRSs in the separate balance sheet of the acquiree.

The change resulting from the recognition of such assets and liabilities should be accounted for as an adjustment of retained earnings or another category of equity, if appropriate. However, if the change results from the recognition of an intangible asset that was previously subsumed in goodwill, it should be accounted for as an adjustment of that goodwill (see section 4.4.1 below).[52]

4.3.3 *Subsequent measurement under IFRSs not based on cost*

IFRSs require subsequent measurement of some assets and liabilities on a basis other than original cost, such as fair value. When a first-time adopter does not apply IFRS 3 retrospectively to a business combination, such assets and liabilities must be measured on that other basis in its opening IFRS balance sheet. Any change in the carrying amount of those assets and liabilities should be accounted for as an adjustment of retained earnings, or other appropriate category of equity, rather than as an adjustment of goodwill.[53]

4.3.4 *Subsequent measurement on a cost basis under IFRSs*

For assets and liabilities that are accounted for on a cost basis under IFRSs, the standard stipulates that, 'immediately after the business combination, the carrying amount under previous GAAP of assets acquired and liabilities assumed in that business combination shall be their deemed cost under IFRSs at that date. If IFRSs require a cost-based measurement of those assets and liabilities at a later date, that deemed cost shall be the basis for cost-based depreciation or amortisation from the date of the business combination.'[54]

4.3.5 Measurement of items not recognised under previous GAAP

An asset acquired or a liability assumed in a past business combination may not have been recognised under the entity's previous GAAP. However, this does not mean that such items have a deemed cost of zero in the opening IFRS balance sheet. Instead, the acquirer recognises and measures those items in its opening IFRS balance sheet on the basis that IFRSs would require in the balance sheet of the acquiree.[55] The change resulting from the recognition of such assets and liabilities should be accounted for as an adjustment of retained earnings or another category of equity, if appropriate. This requirement avoids 'an unjustifiable departure from the principle that the opening IFRS balance sheet should include all assets and liabilities'.[56]

4.4 Restatement of goodwill

4.4.1 Mandatory adjustments of goodwill

Under the business combinations exemption, a first-time adopter takes the carrying amount of goodwill under its previous GAAP at the date of transition to IFRSs as a starting point and only adjusts it as follows:[57]

- A first-time adopter increases goodwill at the date of transition by an amount equal to the carrying amount of an item that it recognised as an intangible asset acquired in a business combination under its previous GAAP (less any related deferred tax and minority interests), but which does not meet the recognition criteria under IFRSs. That is, the first-time adopter accounts for the change in classification prospectively and does not, for example, reverse the cumulative amortisation on the item that it recognised as an intangible asset under its previous GAAP;

- If a first-time adopter is required to recognise an intangible asset under IFRSs that was subsumed in goodwill under its previous GAAP, it decreases goodwill accordingly and adjusts deferred tax and minority interests;

- 'A contingency affecting the amount of the purchase consideration for a past business combination may have been resolved before the date of transition to IFRSs. If a reliable estimate of the contingent adjustment can be made and its payment is probable, the first-time adopter shall adjust the goodwill by that amount. Similarly, the first-time adopter shall adjust the carrying amount of goodwill if a previously recognised contingent adjustment can no longer be measured reliably or its payment is no longer probable';[58] and

- 'Regardless of whether there is any indication that the goodwill may be impaired, the first-time adopter shall apply IAS 36 *Impairment of Assets* in testing the goodwill for impairment at the date of transition to IFRSs and in recognising any resulting impairment loss in retained earnings (or, if so required by IAS 36, in revaluation surplus). The impairment test shall be based on conditions at the date of transition to IFRSs.'[59]

> The estimates used to determine whether a first-time adopter recognises an impairment loss or provision at the date of transition to IFRSs should be consistent with estimates made for the same date under previous GAAP (after adjustments to reflect any difference in accounting policies), unless there is objective evidence that those estimates were in error.[60] If a first-time adopter needs to make estimates for that date that were not necessary under its previous GAAP, such estimates and assumptions should not reflect conditions that arose after the date of transition to IFRSs.[61]
>
> If a first-time adopter's opening IFRS balance sheet reflects impairment losses, it recognises any later reversal of those impairment losses in the income statement unless IAS 36 requires that reversal to be treated as a revaluation. This applies to both impairment losses recognised under previous GAAP and additional impairment losses recognised on transition to IFRSs.[62]

Under IFRS 1, assets acquired and liabilities assumed in a business combination prior to the date of transition to IFRSs are not necessarily valued on a basis that is consistent with IFRS 3. Nevertheless, the IASB accepted that IFRS 1 'does not prevent the implicit recognition of internally generated goodwill that arose after the date of the business combination. However, the Board concluded that an attempt to exclude such internally generated goodwill would be costly and lead to arbitrary results.'[63]

4.4.2   Prohibition of other adjustments of goodwill

The IASB concluded that to 'avoid costs that would exceed the likely benefits to users', IFRS 1 should prohibit 'restatement of goodwill for most other adjustments reflected in the opening IFRS balance sheet, unless a first-time adopter elects to apply IFRS 3 retrospectively'.[64] Therefore, a first-time adopter electing not to apply IFRS 3 retrospectively is not permitted to make any adjustments to goodwill other than those described in section 4.4.1 above. For example, such a first-time adopter should not restate the carrying amount of goodwill:[65]

- to exclude in-process research and development acquired in that business combination (unless the related intangible asset would qualify for recognition under IAS 38 in the balance sheet of the acquiree);
- to adjust previous amortisation of goodwill;
- to reverse adjustments to goodwill that IFRS 3 would not permit, but were made under previous GAAP.

4.4.3   Derecognition of negative goodwill

IFRS 3 specifically requires derecognition of negative goodwill (which IFRS 3 calls excess of acquirer's interest in the net fair value of acquiree's identifiable assets, liabilities and contingent liabilities over cost) with a corresponding adjustment to the opening balance of retained earnings on adoption of the standard.[66] Although IFRS 1 does not specifically address accounting for negative goodwill recognised under a previous GAAP, negative goodwill should be derecognised by a first-time adopter because it is not permitted 'to recognise items or liabilities if IFRSs do not permit such recognition'.[67] Negative goodwill clearly does not meet the definition of a liability under the IASB's *Framework* and its recognition is not permitted under IFRS 3.

4.4.4   *Goodwill previously deducted from equity*

If a first-time adopter deducted goodwill from equity under its previous GAAP then 'it shall not recognise that goodwill in its opening IFRS balance sheet. Furthermore, it shall not transfer that goodwill to the income statement if it disposes of the subsidiary or if the investment in the subsidiary becomes impaired.'[68] Effectively, under IFRSs such goodwill ceases to exist.

If a first-time adopter deducted goodwill from equity under its previous GAAP then 'adjustments resulting from the subsequent resolution of a contingency affecting the purchase consideration shall be recognised in retained earnings'.[69] Effectively, the adjustment is being accounted for in the same way as the original goodwill that arose on the acquisition, rather than having to be adjusted against capitalised goodwill under IFRS 3. This requirement could affect, for example, the way a first-time adopter accounts for earn-out clauses relating to business combinations prior to its date of transition to IFRSs.

4.5   Currency adjustments to goodwill

IAS 21 *The Effects of Changes in Foreign Exchange Rates* requires that 'any goodwill arising on the acquisition of a foreign operation and any fair value adjustments to the carrying amounts of assets and liabilities arising on the acquisition of that foreign operation shall be treated as assets and liabilities of the foreign operation'.[70] For a first-time adopter it may be impracticable, especially after a corporate restructuring, to determine retrospectively the currency in which goodwill and fair value adjustments should be expressed. Consequently, under IFRS 1, a first-time adopter need not apply this requirement of IAS 21 'retrospectively to fair value adjustments and goodwill arising in business combinations that occurred before the date of transition to IFRSs'.[71] If IAS 21 is not applied retrospectively a first-time adopter should treat such fair value adjustments and goodwill 'as assets and liabilities of the entity rather than as assets and liabilities of the acquiree. Therefore, those goodwill and fair value adjustments either are already expressed in the entity's functional currency or are non-monetary foreign currency items, which are reported using the exchange rate applied under previous GAAP.'[72]

If a first-time adopter chooses not to take the exemption, it must apply IAS 21 retrospectively to fair value adjustments and goodwill arising in either:[73]

- all business combinations that occurred before the date of transition to IFRSs; or

- all business combinations that the entity elects to restate to comply with IFRS 3.

The decision to treat goodwill and fair value adjustments as either items denominated in the parent's or the acquiree's functional currency will also affect the extent to which the net investment in those foreign subsidiaries can be hedged.

It should also be noted that the above exemption is different from the 'cumulative translation differences' exemption, which is discussed in section 7.2 below.

4.6   Previously unconsolidated subsidiaries

Under its previous GAAP a first-time adopter may not have consolidated a subsidiary acquired in a past business combination, which it will have to consolidate under IFRSs. In that case a first-time adopter applying the business combinations exemption should adjust the carrying amounts of the subsidiary's assets and liabilities to the amounts that IFRSs would require in the subsidiary's balance sheet. The deemed cost of goodwill equals the difference at the date of transition to IFRSs between:[74]

- the parent's interest in those adjusted carrying amounts; and
- the cost in the parent's separate financial statements of its investment in the subsidiary.

The cost of a subsidiary in the parent's separate financial statements should be determined under the cost method of accounting under IAS 27. Thus, a first-time adopter does not have to calculate what the goodwill would have been at the date of the original acquisition. The deemed cost of goodwill will, however, be capitalised as an asset in the opening IFRS balance sheet.

If the original acquisition cost is lower than the net asset value at the date of transition to IFRSs, the difference is taken to retained earnings.

Slightly different rules apply to all other subsidiaries (i.e. those not acquired in a business combination) that an entity did not consolidate under its previous GAAP, the main difference being that goodwill should not be recognised in relation to those subsidiaries (see section 9.3 below).

It should be noted that in calculating the deemed cost of the goodwill, the first-time adopter is required to compare the historical cost of the investment to its share of the carrying amount of the net assets determined on a different date.

4.7   Previously consolidated entities that are not subsidiaries

A first-time adopter may have consolidated an investment under its previous GAAP that does not meet the definition of a subsidiary under IFRSs. In this case the entity should first determine the appropriate classification of the investment under IFRSs and then apply the first-time adoption rules in IFRS 1. Generally such previously consolidated investments should be accounted for as either:

- *an associate:* First-time adopters applying the business combinations exemption should also apply that exemption to past acquisitions of investments in associates. If the business combinations exemption is not applicable or the entity did not acquire the investment in the associate, IAS 28 *Investments in Associates* should be applied retrospectively;
- *a joint venture:* First-time adopters applying the business combinations exemption should also apply that exemption to past acquisitions of investments in joint ventures. If the business combinations exemption is not applicable or the entity did not acquire the investment in the joint venture, IAS 31 *Interests in Joint Ventures* should be applied retrospectively;
- *an investment under IAS 39* (see section 6.2 below); or
- *an executory contract* or *service concession arrangement:* There are no first-time adoption exemptions that apply; therefore, IFRSs should be applied retrospectively.

4.8   Measurement of deferred taxation and minority interests

Deferred taxation is calculated based on the difference between the carrying amount of assets and liabilities and their respective tax base. Therefore, deferred taxation should be calculated after all assets acquired and liabilities assumed have been adjusted under IFRS 1.[75]

Minority interest is defined in IAS 27 *Consolidated and Separate Financial Statements* as 'that portion of the profit or loss and net assets of a subsidiary attributable to equity interests that are not owned, directly or indirectly through subsidiaries, by the parent'.[76] Minority interests related to subsidiaries acquired in a business combination should be calculated after all assets acquired, liabilities assumed and deferred taxation have been adjusted under IFRS 1.[77]

Any resulting change in the carrying amount of deferred taxation and minority interests should be recognised by adjusting retained earnings (or, if appropriate, another category of equity), unless they relate to adjustments to intangible assets that are adjusted against goodwill.

5   FAIR VALUE OR REVALUATION AS DEEMED COST EXEMPTION

5.1   Background

IFRS 1 requires full retrospective application of standards extant at a first-time adopter's first IFRS reporting date. Therefore, in the absence of the deemed cost exemption, the requirements of IAS 16, IAS 38 and IAS 40 would have to be applied as if the first-time adopter had always applied these standards. This could be quite onerous because:

- these items are long-lived which means that accounting records for the period of acquisition may not be available anymore. In the case of formerly state-owned businesses, the required accounting records possibly never even existed;

- the entity may have revalued the items in the past as a matter of accounting policy or because this was required under national law; or

- even if the items were carried at depreciated cost, the accounting policy for recognition and depreciation may not have been IFRS compliant.

Given the significance of property, plant and equipment in particular in the balance sheet of most first-time adopters (and the sheer number of transactions affecting property, plant and equipment), restatement is not only extremely difficult but would often also involve undue cost and effort. Nevertheless, a first-time adopter needs a cost basis for the assets in its opening IFRS balance sheet. Therefore, the IASB decided to introduce the notion of a 'deemed cost' that is not the 'true' IFRS compliant cost basis of an asset, but a surrogate that is deemed to be a suitable starting point.

In its deliberations on IFRS 1, the IASB noted that reconstructed cost data might be less relevant to users, and less reliable, than current fair value data. Therefore, IFRS 1 permits an entity to use fair value as deemed cost in some cases without any need to demonstrate undue cost or effort.[78]

5.2 Scope of 'fair value or revaluation as deemed cost' exemption

To deal with the problem of restatement of long-lived assets upon first-time adoption of IFRSs, the standard permits a first-time adopter – for the categories of assets listed below – to measure an item in its opening IFRS balance sheet using an amount that is based on its deemed cost:[79]

- property, plant and equipment;[80]

- investment property, if an entity elects to use the cost model in IAS 40 *Investment Property*. The fact that the exemption can only be applied to investment property accounted for under the cost model will not pose any problems in practice as the fair value model under IAS 40 requires an entity to measure its investment property at fair value at its date of transition to IFRSs;[81] and

- intangible assets that meet:[82]
   - the recognition criteria in IAS 38 (including reliable measurement of original cost); and
   - the criteria in IAS 38 for revaluation (including the existence of an active market).

A first-time adopter cannot use a deemed cost approach for any other assets or liabilities.[83]

The use of fair value or revaluation as deemed cost for intangible assets will be very limited in practice because of the very restrictive definition of an active market in IAS 38.[84] It is therefore unlikely that a first-time adopter will be able to apply this exemption to any intangible assets.

The IASB argued that it is not necessary to restrict application of the exemption to classes of assets to prevent selective revaluations, because 'IAS 36 *Impairment of Assets* requires an impairment test if there is any indication that an asset is impaired. Thus, if an entity uses fair value as deemed cost for assets whose fair value is above cost, it cannot ignore indications that the recoverable amount of other assets may have fallen below their carrying amount. Therefore, the IFRS does not restrict the use of fair value as deemed cost to entire classes of asset.'[85]

5.3 Determining deemed cost

The deemed cost that a first-time adopter uses is either:

(1) the fair value of the item at the date of transition to IFRSs (see section 2.4 above);[86] or

(2) a revaluation under its previous GAAP at or before the date of transition to IFRSs, if the revaluation was, at the date of the revaluation, broadly comparable to:[87]
   - fair value; or
   - cost or depreciated cost under IFRSs, adjusted to reflect, for example, changes in a general or specific price index; or

(3) the deemed cost under its previous GAAP that was established by measuring items at their fair value at one particular date because of an event such as a privatisation or initial public offering.[88]

The revaluations referred to in (2) above need only be 'broadly comparable to fair value or reflect an index applied to a cost that is broadly comparable to cost determined under IFRSs'.[89] The flexibility in this area permits a cost-effective solution for the unique problem of transition to IFRSs. It allows a first-time adopter to establish a deemed cost using a measurement that is already available and is a reasonable starting point for a cost-based measurement.[90]

If the deemed cost of an asset was determined before the date of transition to IFRSs then an IFRS accounting policy needs to be applied to that deemed cost in the intervening period to determine what the carrying amount of the asset is in the opening IFRS balance sheet.

6   FINANCIAL INSTRUMENTS

6.1   Exemption from the requirement to restate comparative information

The IASB issued the revised IAS 32 and the revised IAS 39 in December 2003; and the amendment to IAS 39 *Fair Value Hedge Accounting for a Portfolio Hedge of Interest Rate Risk* in March 2004. To allow entities adopting IFRSs for the first time before 1 January 2006 sufficient time to comply with the requirements of those standards, the IASB decided not to require them to prepare comparative information under IAS 32, IAS 39 and IFRS 4 (see section 7.4).[91]

A first-time adopter that chooses to present comparative information that does not comply with IAS 32, IAS 39 and IFRS 4 in its first year of transition should:

- apply its previous GAAP in the comparative period to financial instruments that are within the scope of IAS 32 or IAS 39 and to insurance contracts with the scope of IFRS 4. In other words, this exemption also affects the application of certain aspects of other standards. For example, it overrides the requirements of IAS 1 on the balance sheet presentation of financial instruments and insurance contracts and IAS 18 *Revenue* on the application of the effective interest method; and
- make certain additional disclosures (see section 10.1.1).[92]

A first-time adopter that does not present comparative information under IAS 32, IAS 39 and IFRS 4 should use *the beginning of the first IFRS reporting period* (e.g. 1 January 2005 for an entity reporting at 31 December 2005) as the relevant date for the application of the first-time adoption rules in IFRS 1, and not the *date of transition to IFRSs*, for the purpose of these standards only.[93]

In applying this exemption a first-time adopter should be aware of the following:

- the wording of the standard does not explicitly require the exemption to be applied to IAS 32, IAS 39 and IFRS 4 as a package. Even though the transitional provisions in both IAS 32 and IAS 39 that require the standards to be adopted simultaneously do not apply to first-time adopters, the IASB clearly intended both standards to be adopted simultaneously. In any case, the many cross-references between the two standards make it virtually impossible to adopt one of the standards without the other. Therefore, the exemption applies to IAS 32 and IAS 39 as a package;

- a first-time adopter that presents two comparative periods under IFRSs will not be permitted to restate the most recent comparative financial period because the exemption must be applied as of the beginning of the first IFRS reporting period (e.g. an entity reporting at 31 December 2005 with two comparative periods would not be allowed to restate 2004 unless it also restated 2003);

- the exemption only covers items that are within the scope of IAS 32, IAS 39 and IFRS 4. The comparative information relating to all other items must be restated under IFRSs; and

- a first-time adopter not applying IAS 39 would need to apply its previous GAAP in accounting for hedges.

6.2 Designation of previously recognised financial instruments

IAS 39 permits a financial instrument to be designated on initial recognition as:

- a *financial asset or financial liability at fair value through profit or loss*, which is a financial instrument that is either classified as *held for trading* or is designated as such on initial recognition;[94] or

- an *available-for-sale financial asset*, which is a financial asset designated as 'available for sale', or which is not specifically classified as 'loans and receivables', 'held-to-maturity investments' or 'at fair value through profit or loss'.[95]

A first-time adopter is allowed to designate a financial instrument at the date of transition to IFRSs (or the beginning of the first IFRS reporting period, if comparatives are not restated) as a 'financial asset or financial liability at fair value through profit or loss' or as available-for-sale.[96] This exemption allowing retrospective designation by first-time adopters is based on the transitional rule applied by entities that already report under IFRSs.[97] Therefore, if upon initial application of IAS 39 the investment is classified as:[98]

- *at fair value through profit or loss*, the pre-IAS 39 revaluation gain that had been recognised in equity is reclassified into retained earnings on initial application of IAS 39;

- *available-for-sale*, then the pre-IAS 39 revaluation gain is recognised in a separate component of equity. Subsequently, the entity recognises gains and losses on the available-for-sale financial asset in that separate component of equity until the investment is impaired, sold, collected or otherwise disposed of. On subsequent derecognition or impairment of the available-for-sale financial asset, the first-time adopter transfers to profit or loss the cumulative gain or loss remaining in equity.

A first-time adopter that applies this exemption needs to make certain additional disclosures (see section 10.2.2 below).[99]

Retrospective designation of financial instruments as available-for-sale financial assets 'requires a first-time adopter to recognise the cumulative fair value changes in a separate component of equity in the opening IFRS balance sheet (or the balance sheet at the beginning of its first IFRS reporting period, if comparatives are not restated), and transfer those fair value changes to the income statement on subsequent disposal or impairment of the asset'.[100] The IASB recognised that this could give rise to a selective approach, whereby first-time adopters would only designate financial instruments with cumulative gains as available-for-sale, but it noted that a first-time adopter could achieve similar results by selectively disposing of some financial assets before the date of transition to IFRSs.[101] Therefore, IFRS 1 does not impose any additional restrictions on first-time adopters regarding the designation of financial instruments as available-for-sale financial assets.

6.3 Compound financial instruments

IAS 32 requires compound financial instruments (such as a convertible bond) to be split at inception into separate equity and liability components. If the liability component is no longer outstanding, a full retrospective application of IAS 32 would involve identifying two components, one representing the original equity component and the other representing the cumulative interest on the liability component, both of which are accounted for in equity. A first-time adopter does not need to make this allocation if the liability component is no longer outstanding at the date of transition to IFRSs (or the beginning of the first IFRS reporting period, if comparatives are not restated).[102] For example, in the case of a convertible bond that has been converted into equity, it is not necessary to make this split.

A first-time adopter applying this exemption can therefore avoid the possibly complex allocation process that would be involved. However, where the compound instrument is still outstanding at the date of transition to IFRSs (or the beginning of the first IFRS reporting period, if comparatives are not restated), then a split will need to be made.[103] In practice this exemption is of limited value because the number of different compound financial instruments outstanding at the date of transition to IFRSs (or the beginning of the first IFRS reporting period, if comparatives are not restated) is bound to be small.

6.4 Derecognition of financial assets and financial liabilities

A first-time adopter should apply the derecognition requirements in IAS 39 prospectively to transactions occurring on or after 1 January 2004. Therefore, if a first-time adopter derecognised non-derivative financial assets or non-derivative financial liabilities under its previous GAAP as a result of a transaction that occurred before 1 January 2004, it should not recognise those assets and liabilities under IFRSs (unless they qualify for recognition as a result of a later transaction or event).[104] Though this seems similar to the transitional rules that apply to existing IFRS reporting entities, first-time adopters do not have to apply IAS 39 (revised 2000) to transactions before 1 January 2004. A first-time adopter that wants to apply the derecognition requirements in IAS 39 retrospectively from a date of the entity's choosing can only do so 'provided that the information needed to apply IAS 39 to financial assets and financial liabilities derecognised as a result of past transactions was obtained at the time of initially accounting for those transactions'.[105] This will effectively ban most first-time adopters from restating transactions before 1 January 2004.

A first-time adopter that derecognised non-derivative financial assets and liabilities under its previous GAAP before 1 January 2004 will not have to recognise these items under IFRSs even if they meet the IAS 39 recognition criteria. However, a first-time adopter is not exempt from:

- SIC-12 *Consolidation – Special Purpose Entities* which requires consolidation of all SPEs; and
- the requirement under IAS 39 to measure all derivatives at fair value.

Therefore, not all previously derecognised items will remain off-balance sheet upon adoption of IFRSs.

6.5 Hedge accounting

6.5.1 Prohibition on retrospective application

IFRS 1 explains that entities are prohibited from applying retrospectively some of the hedge accounting provisions of IAS 39, because it is unlikely that many entities would have adopted IAS 39's criteria for (a) documenting hedges at their inception and (b) testing the hedges for effectiveness, even if they intended to continue the same hedging strategies after adopting IAS 39.[106]   Furthermore, retrospective designation of hedges (or retrospective reversal of their designation) could lead to selective designation of some hedges to report a particular result.

IAS 39 should be applied 'prospectively' in accordance with the requirements of IFRS 1, which are explained in section 6.5.2 below.

6.5.2 Hedge accounting: opening IFRS balance sheet

A Measurement of derivatives and elimination of deferred gains and losses

Under its previous GAAP an entity's accounting policies might have included a number of accounting treatments for derivatives that formed part of a hedge relationship. For example, accounting policies might have included those where the derivative was:

- not explicitly recognised as an asset or liability (e.g. in the case of a forward contract used to hedge an expected but uncontracted future transaction);
- recognised as an asset or liability but at an amount different from its fair value (e.g. a purchased option recognised at its original cost, perhaps less amortisation; or an interest rate swap accounted for by accruing the periodic interest payments and receipts); or
- subsumed within the accounting for another asset or liability (e.g. a foreign currency denominated monetary item and a matching forward contract or swap accounted for as a 'synthetic' functional currency denominated monetary item).

Whatever the previous accounting treatment, a first-time adopter should isolate and separately account for all derivatives in its opening IFRS balance sheet as assets or liabilities measured at fair value.[107]

The implementation guidance explains that all derivatives, other than those that are designated and effective hedging instruments, are classified as held for trading. Accordingly, the difference between the previous carrying amount of a derivative (which may have been zero) and its fair value should be recognised as an adjustment of the balance of retained earnings at the beginning of the financial year in which IFRS 1 is initially applied (other than for a derivative that is a designated and effective hedging instrument).[108]

Hedge accounting policies under an entity's previous GAAP might also have included one or both of the following accounting treatments:

- derivatives were measured at fair value but, to the extent they were regarded as hedging future transactions, the gain (or loss) arising was reported as a liability (or asset) such as deferred (or accrued) income;

- realised gains or losses arising on the termination of a previously unrecognised derivative used in a hedge relationship (such as an interest rate swap hedging a borrowing) were included in the balance sheet as deferred or accrued income and amortised over the remaining term of the hedged exposure.

In all cases an entity is required to eliminate deferred gains and losses arising on derivatives 'that were reported under previous GAAP as if they were assets or liabilities'.[109] Essentially this is because deferred gains and losses do not meet the definition of assets or liabilities under the IASB's *Framework*. In contrast to adjustments made to restate derivatives at fair value, the implementation guidance does not specify in general terms how to deal with adjustments to eliminate deferred gains or losses.

The requirement to eliminate deferred gains and losses does not appear to extend to those that have been included in the carrying amount of other assets or liabilities that will continue to be recognised under IFRSs. For example, under an entity's previous GAAP, the carrying amount of non-financial assets such as inventories or property, plant and equipment might have included the equivalent of a basis adjustment (i.e. hedging gains or losses were considered an integral part of the asset's cost). In fact, carrying forward this treatment into an entity's first set of IFRS financial statements would be consistent with the transitional provisions of the revised IAS 39. Of course entities should also consider any other provisions of IFRS 1 that apply to those hedged items.

The way in which an entity accounts for these adjustments will, to a large extent, dictate how its existing hedge relationships will be reflected in its ongoing IFRS financial statements. Particularly, an entity's future results will be different depending on whether the adjustments are taken to retained earnings or to a separate component of equity – in the latter case they would be recycled to profit or loss at a later date but would not in the former. Similarly, its future results would be affected if the carrying amount of related assets or liabilities are changed to reflect these adjustments (as opposed to the adjustments being made to retained earnings).

For short-term hedges (e.g. of sales and inventory purchases) these effects are likely to work their way out of the IFRS financial statements relatively quickly. However for other hedges (e.g. of long term borrowings) an entity's results may be affected for many years. The question of which hedge relationships should be reflected in an entity's opening IFRS balance sheet is dealt with in sections B to D below.

B   Hedge relationships reflected in the opening IFRS balance sheet

The standard states that a first-time adopter *should not* reflect a hedging relationship in its opening IFRS balance sheet (or the balance sheet at the beginning of its first IFRS reporting period, if comparatives are not restated) if that hedging relationship is of a type that *does not* qualify for hedge accounting under IAS 39. As examples of this it cites many hedging relationships where the hedging instrument is a cash instrument or written option; where the hedged item is a net position; or where the hedge covers interest risk in a held-to-maturity investment.[110]

However, if an entity had designated a net position as a hedged item under its previous GAAP then an individual item within that net position *may* be designated as a hedged item under IFRSs, provided that it does so no later than the date of transition to IFRSs (or the beginning of the first IFRS reporting period, if comparatives are not restated).[111] In other words, such designation could allow the hedge relationship to be reflected in the opening IFRS balance sheet (or the balance sheet at the beginning of its first IFRS reporting period, if comparatives are not restated).

Further, a first-time adopter is not permitted to designate hedges retrospectively in relation to transactions entered into before the date of transition to IFRSs (or the beginning of the first IFRS reporting period, if comparatives are not restated).[112] This would appear to prevent an entity from reflecting hedge relationships that it did not identify as such under its previous GAAP in its opening balance sheet of the first period in which it applies IAS 39.

It might seem to follow that a hedge relationship designated under an entity's previous GAAP *should* be reflected in its opening IFRS balance sheet (or the balance sheet at the beginning of its first IFRS reporting period, if comparatives are not restated) if that hedging relationship *is* of a type that *does* qualify for hedge accounting under IAS 39. In fact, if an entity was allowed not to reflect such a hedge in its opening IFRS balance sheet (or the balance sheet at the beginning of its first IFRS reporting period, if comparatives are not restated) this would effectively allow the retrospective reversal of the hedge designation. As noted in section A above, this is something the IASB has sought to avoid.[113] However, while such a 'principle' seems to be implied by the implementation guidance (see sections C and D below), the IASB has not specifically stated that this is the case.

There are, perhaps, a number of reasons for the IASB's reticence. For example, under an entity's previous GAAP, it might not have been clear whether a derivative instrument was actually designated as a hedge. Further, even if it were clear that a derivative had previously been designated as a hedge, the hedged item might not have been identified with sufficiently specifically to allow the effects of the hedge to be reflected in the opening IFRS balance sheet and/or, thereafter, to be 'unwound' at the appropriate time.

C   *Reflecting cash flow hedges in the opening IFRS balance sheet*

The implementation guidance to IFRS 1 explains that a first-time adopter may, under its previous GAAP, have deferred gains and losses on a cash flow hedge of a forecast transaction. If, at the date of transition to IFRSs (or the beginning of the first IFRS reporting period, if comparatives are not restated) the hedged forecast transaction is not highly probable, but is expected to occur, the entire deferred gain or loss should be recognised in equity.[114] To be consistent, this would be included in the same component of equity an entity would use to record future gains and losses on cash flow hedges.

This raises the question of how to deal with such a hedge if, at the date of transition to IFRSs (or the beginning of the first IFRS reporting period, if comparatives are not restated), the forecast transaction *was* highly probable. It would make no sense if the former was required to be reflected in the opening IFRS balance sheet, but the latter (which is clearly a 'better' hedge) was not. Therefore, it must follow that a cash flow hedge should be reflected in the opening IFRS balance sheet in the way set out above if the hedged item is a forecast transaction that is highly probable. Similarly, it follows that a cash flow hedge of the variability in cash flows attributable to a particular risk associated with a recognised asset or liability (such as all or some future interest payments on variable rate debt) should also be reflected in the opening balance sheet.

If, at the date of transition to IFRSs (or the beginning of the first IFRS reporting period, if comparatives are not restated), the forecast transaction was *not* expected to occur, this would be a relationship of a type that does not qualify for hedge accounting under IAS 39. Therefore the hedging relationship should not be reflected in the opening IFRS balance sheet.

It is possible to read parts of the implementation guidance as preventing hedge treatment if the hedge has not been designated in an effective hedge under IAS 39 by the date of transition (or the beginning of the first IFRS reporting period, if comparatives are not restated). Such an interpretation would allow an entity to choose not to designate (in accordance with IAS 39) certain cash flow hedges, say those that are in a loss position, until one day after its date of transition, thereby allowing associated hedging losses to bypass profit or loss completely. Some commentators have suggested that this literal interpretation is acceptable. However, this would effectively result in the retrospective de-designation of hedges to achieve a desired result, thereby breaching this general principle of IFRS 1. In our view it is clear that this general principle of the standard should take precedence over the implementation guidance.

D   Reflecting fair value hedges in the opening IFRS balance sheet

The implementation guidance to IFRS 1 explains that a first-time adopter may, under its previous GAAP, have deferred or not recognised gains and losses on a fair value hedge of a hedged item that is not measured at fair value. For such a fair value hedge, the entity should adjust the carrying amount of the hedged item at the date of transition to IFRSs (or the beginning of the first IFRS reporting period, if comparatives are not restated). The adjustment, which is essentially the effective part of the hedge that was not recognised in the carrying amount of the hedged item under the previous GAAP, should be calculated as the lower of:[115]

- that portion of the cumulative change in the fair value of the hedged item that reflects the designated hedged risk and was not recognised under previous GAAP; and

- that portion of the cumulative change in the fair value of the hedging instrument that reflects the designated hedged risk and, under previous GAAP, was either (i) not recognised or (ii) deferred in the balance sheet as an asset or liability.

Available-for-sale assets are measured at fair value so the guidance above would not appear to apply to fair value hedges of such instruments. However, it would be logical to apply an equivalent adjustment to the cost or amortised cost of such assets.

6.5.3   Hedge accounting: subsequent treatment

The implementation guidance explains that hedge accounting can be applied prospectively only from the date the hedge relationship is fully designated and documented. Therefore, if the hedging instrument is still held at the date of transition to IFRSs (or the beginning of the first IFRS reporting period, if comparatives are not restated) the designation and documentation of a hedge relationship must be completed on or before that date if the hedge relationship is to qualify for hedge accounting afterwards.[116]

An entity may, before the date of transition to IFRSs (or the beginning of the first IFRS reporting period, if comparatives are not restated), have designated a transaction as a hedge that does not meet the conditions for hedge accounting in IAS 39. In these cases it should follow the general requirements in IAS 39 for discontinuing hedge accounting.[117]

For cash flow hedges, any net cumulative gain or loss that was reclassified to equity on initial application of IAS 39 (see section 6.5.2 C above) should remain in equity until:[118]

- the forecast transaction subsequently results in the recognition of a non-financial asset or non-financial liability;

- the forecast transaction affects profit or loss; or

- subsequently circumstances change and the forecast transaction is no longer expected to occur, in which case any related net cumulative gain or loss that had been recognised directly in equity is recognised in profit or loss.

6.6   Derivatives, embedded derivatives and transaction costs

At the date of transition to IFRSs (or the beginning of the first IFRS reporting period, if comparatives are not restated), IAS 39 requires a first-time adopter to measure all derivatives at fair value and to eliminate deferred gains and losses arising 'on derivatives that were reported under previous GAAP as if they were assets or liabilities'.[119]

6.6.1   Derivatives

All derivatives, except for those that are designated and effective hedging instruments, are classified as held for trading under IAS 39. Therefore, the difference between a derivative's fair value and its previous carrying amount should be recognised as an adjustment to retained earnings at the beginning of the financial year in which IAS 39 is initially applied.[120]

6.6.2   Embedded derivatives

IAS 39 requires an entity to account separately for some embedded derivatives at fair value. Common examples of host contracts that can contain embedded derivatives include non-derivative financial instruments (especially debt instruments), leases, insurance contracts as well as contracts for the supply of goods or services. Embedded derivatives introduce foreign currency, credit, price or interest rate risks that are not closely related to (i.e. are not commonly found in) such host contracts. A first-time adopter will have to consider all contracts existing at its date of transition to IFRSs (or the beginning of the first IFRS reporting period, if comparatives are not restated) and decide whether or not they contain embedded derivatives. Any embedded derivatives that are identified and have to be accounted for separately should be recognised as assets or liabilities, and be measured at their fair value.

6.6.3   *Transaction costs*

To determine the amortised cost of a financial asset or liability using the effective interest rate method, a first-time adopter needs to establish the transaction costs incurred when the instrument was originated. Despite arguments by some commentators that this might involve undue cost or effort, the IASB concluded that the 'unamortised portion of transaction costs at the date of transition to IFRSs (or the beginning of the first IFRS reporting period, if comparatives are not restated) is unlikely to be material for most financial assets and financial liabilities' and therefore presumably does not require restatement.[121] The IASB presumes that 'even when the unamortised portion is material, reasonable estimates should be possible'.[122]

7   OTHER EXEMPTIONS

As discussed in section 3.3.1 above, IFRS 1 establishes exemptions from the requirements of other IFRSs. Those exemptions not already dealt with above are discussed in sections 7.1 to 7.5 below.

7.1   Employee benefits

Under IAS 19 an entity is allowed to use a 'corridor' approach that leaves some actuarial gains and losses on defined benefit plans unrecognised.[123] To calculate the net cumulative unrecognised gains or losses at the date of transition to IFRSs, a first-time adopter would need to determine actuarial gains or losses for each year since inception of each defined benefit plan. It is obvious that a full retrospective application of IAS 19 would be costly (if not impossible to achieve) and would not benefit users of the financial statements.[124] Therefore, the IASB introduced an exemption that allows a first-time adopter 'to recognise all cumulative actuarial gains and losses at the date of transition to IFRSs, even if it uses the corridor approach for later actuarial gains and losses'.[125] If a first-time adopter uses this exemption it will have to apply the exemption to all its defined benefit plans.

7.1.1   *Full actuarial valuations*

An entity's first IFRS financial statements may reflect its defined benefit liabilities at three different dates, that is, the reporting date, the end of the comparative period and the date of transition to IFRSs. An entity that presents two comparative periods would have to calculate its defined benefits liabilities at four different dates. Clearly, it is quite costly to require a first-time adopter to perform three, or possibly even four, actuarial valuations. However, the IASB decided against permitting 'an entity to use a single actuarial valuation, based, for example, on assumptions valid at the reporting date, with service costs and interest costs based on those assumptions for each of the periods presented'.[126] The IASB's main objection to such an exemption was that it 'would conflict with the objective of providing understandable, relevant, reliable and comparable information for users'.[127]   Nevertheless, the IASB agreed to the compromise position that if an entity obtains a full actuarial valuation at one or two dates, it is allowed to roll forward (or roll back) to another date but only as long as the roll forward (or roll back) reflects material transactions and other material events between those dates (including changes in market prices and interest rates).[128]

7.1.2   Actuarial assumptions

A first-time adopter's actuarial assumptions at its date of transition to IFRSs should be consistent with the ones it used for the same date under its previous GAAP, unless there is objective evidence that those assumptions were in error (see section 8.1 below). The impact of any later revisions to those assumptions is an actuarial gain or loss of the period in which the entity makes the revisions.[129] If a first-time adopter needs 'to make actuarial assumptions at the date of transition to IFRSs that were not necessary under its previous GAAP these actuarial assumptions should not reflect conditions that arose after the date of transition to IFRSs. In particular, discount rates and the fair value of plan assets at the date of transition to IFRSs must reflect market conditions at that date. Similarly, the entity's actuarial assumptions at the date of transition to IFRSs about future employee turnover rates should not reflect a significant increase in estimated employee turnover rates as a result of a curtailment of the pension plan that occurred after the date of transition to IFRSs.'[130]

7.1.3   Unrecognised past service costs

It is worth mentioning that the employee benefits exemption only applies to unrecognised actuarial gains or losses, it does not apply to unrecognised past service costs that relate to unvested benefits. The IASB decided that an exemption for past service cost was not justified because a full retrospective application of IAS 19 to unrecognised past service costs 'is less onerous than the retrospective application of the corridor for actuarial gains and losses, as it does not require retrospective calculation of data since the inception of the plan'.[131] A first-time adopter therefore needs to look at periods before its date of transition to IFRSs to determine the amount of unrecognised past service costs that relate to unvested benefits in accordance with IAS 19.

7.2   Cumulative translation differences

Exchange differences arising on a monetary item that forms part of a reporting entity's net investment in a foreign operation are recognised in a separate component of equity under IAS 21.[132] IAS 21 and IAS 39 require that, on disposal of a foreign operation, the cumulative amount of the exchange differences deferred in the separate component of equity relating to that foreign operation (which includes, for example, the cumulative translation difference for that foreign operation, the exchange differences arising on certain translations to a different presentation currency and any gains and losses on related hedges) should be recognised in profit or loss when the gain or loss on disposal is recognised.[133]

Full retrospective application of IAS 21 would require a first-time adopter to restate all financial statements of its foreign operations to IFRSs from their date of inception or later acquisition onwards, and then determine the cumulative translation differences arising in relation to each of these foreign operations. The costs of this restatement are likely to exceed the benefits to users of financial statements. For this reason a first-time adopter need not comply with these requirements for cumulative translation differences that existed at the date of transition to IFRSs. If a first-time adopter uses this exemption:

- the cumulative translation differences for all foreign operations are deemed to be zero at the date of transition to IFRSs; and

- the gain or loss on a subsequent disposal of any foreign operation shall exclude translation differences that arose before the date of transition to IFRSs and shall include later translation differences.[134]

IFRS 1 is unfortunately not entirely clear whether the exemption extends to similar gains and losses arising on related hedges. Therefore, entities will need to apply judgement in determining how and when the cumulative gains and losses on net investment hedges are reset to zero.

7.3   Share-based payment transactions

IFRS 2 *Share-based Payment* applies to accounting for the acquisition of goods or services in equity-settled share-based payment transactions, cash-settled share-based payment transactions and transactions in which the entity or counterparty has the option to choose between settlement in cash or equity. The transitional rules for first-time adopters are based on the transitional rules for existing IFRS reporting entities. However, the IASB added the following exemptions for first-time adopters:[135]

- a first-time adopter is not required to apply IFRS 2 to equity instruments that were granted after 7 November 2002 but that vested before the date of transition to IFRSs; and

- a first-time adopter is not required to apply IFRS 2 to liabilities arising from cash-settled share-based payment transactions if those liabilities were settled before 1 January 2005 or before the date of transition to IFRSs.

The IFRS 1 exemption for share-based payment transactions contains the following options and requirements:

- only if a first-time adopter 'has disclosed publicly the fair value of those equity instruments, determined at the measurement date, as defined in IFRS 2' is it encouraged but not required to apply IFRS 2 to:[136]

    (i)   equity instruments that were granted on or before 7 November 2002;

    (ii)   equity instruments that were granted after 7 November 2002 but vested before the later of (1) the date of transition to IFRSs and (2) 1 January 2005.

    Many first-time adopters will not have published the fair value of equity instruments granted and are, therefore, not allowed to apply IFRS 2 retrospectively to those share-based transactions;

- for all grants of equity instruments to which IFRS 2 has not been applied, a first-time adopter shall nevertheless disclose the information required by paragraphs 44 and 45 of IFRS 2;[137] and

- if a first-time adopter modifies the terms or conditions of a grant of equity instruments to which IFRS 2 has not been applied, the entity is not required to apply paragraphs 26-29 of IFRS 2 if the modification occurred before the later of (1) the date of transition to IFRSs and (2) 1 January 2005.[138]

Furthermore, if share-based payments give rise to liabilities, a first-time adopter is:[139]

- encouraged, but not required, to apply IFRS 2 to liabilities arising from share-based payment transactions that were settled before the date of transition to IFRSs;

- also encouraged, but not required, to apply IFRS 2 to liabilities that were settled before 1 January 2005 and

- not required to restate comparative information, for liabilities to which IFRS 2 is applied, to the extent that the information relates to a period or date that is earlier than 7 November 2002.

IFRS 1 allows a first-time adopter to pick and choose from these options as it sees fit, i.e. it does not encourage or require a first-time adopter to make consistent use of the options. However, the qualitative characteristics of financial statements as set out in the *Framework* would seem to dictate that a first-time adopter should not apply the above exemptions in a random fashion.[140]

7.4 Insurance contracts

A first-time adopter may apply the transitional provisions in IFRS 4. That standard limits an insurer to changing 'its accounting policies for insurance contracts if, and only if, the change makes the financial statements more relevant to the economic decision-making needs of users and no less reliable, or more reliable and no less relevant to those needs. An insurer shall judge relevance and reliability by the criteria in IAS 8.'[141] As discussed in section 6.1 above, an entity adopting IFRSs for the first time before 1 January 2006 is not required to prepare comparative information under IAS 32, IAS 39 and IFRS 4.[142] Instead, a first-time adopter that chooses to present comparative information that does not comply with IAS 32, IAS 39 and IFRS 4 in its first year of transition should:

- apply its previous GAAP in the comparative period to financial instruments that are within the scope of IAS 32, IAS 39 and IFRS 4; and

- make certain additional disclosures (see section 10.1.1 below).[143]

7.5 Assets and liabilities of subsidiaries, associates and joint ventures

7.5.1 *Subsidiary becomes a first-time adopter later than its parent*

Within groups, some subsidiaries, associates and joint ventures may have a different date of transition to IFRSs than the parent/investor (for example, national legislation required IFRSs after, or prohibited IFRSs at, the date of transition to IFRSs of the parent/investor). This could result in permanent differences between the IFRS figures in a subsidiary's own financial statements and those it reports to its parent. In turn this could force a subsidiary to keep two parallel sets of accounting records based on different dates of transition to IFRSs.[144] To mitigate this difficulty, the IASB introduced a special exemption regarding the assets and liabilities of subsidiaries, associates and joint ventures.

If a subsidiary becomes a first-time adopter later that its parent, it should in its financial statements measure its assets and liabilities at either:

'(a)   the carrying amounts that would be included in the parent's consolidated financial statements, based on the parent's date of transition to IFRSs, if no adjustments were made for consolidation procedures and for the effects of the business combination in which the parent acquired the subsidiary; or

(b)   the carrying amounts required by the rest of IFRS 1, based on the subsidiary's date of transition to IFRSs. These carrying amounts could differ from those described in (a):

(i)   when the exemptions in this IFRS result in measurements that depend on the date of transition to IFRSs.

(ii)   when the accounting policies used in the subsidiary's financial statements differ from those in the consolidated financial statements. For example, the subsidiary may use as its accounting policy the cost model in IAS 16 *Property, Plant and Equipment*, whereas the group may use the revaluation model.'[145]

A similar election is available to an associate or joint venture that becomes a first-time adopter later than an entity that has significant influence or joint control over it.[146]

Under option (b) a subsidiary would prepare its own IFRS financial statements, completely ignoring the IFRS reports that its parent uses in preparing its consolidated financial statements. Under option (a) the numbers in a subsidiary's IFRS financial statements will be as close to those used by its parent as possible. However, differences other than those arising from consolidation procedures and business combinations will still exist in many cases, for example:

- a subsidiary may have hedged an exposure by entering into a transaction with a fellow subsidiary, such transaction could qualify for hedge accounting in the subsidiary's own financial statements but not in the parent's consolidated financial statements; or

- a pension plan may have to be classified as a defined contribution plan from the subsidiary's point of view, but is accounted for as a defined benefit plan in the parent's consolidated financial statements.

Application of option (a) would be more difficult when a parent and its subsidiary (joint venture or associate) have different financial years. In that case, IFRS 1 would seem to require the IFRS information for the subsidiary (joint venture or associate) to be based on the parent's date of transition to IFRSs, which may not even coincide with an interim reporting date of the subsidiary (joint venture or associate).

A subsidiary may become a first-time adopter later than its parent, because it previously prepared a reporting package under IFRSs for consolidation purposes but did not present a full set of financial statements under IFRSs. The above election may be 'relevant not only when a subsidiary's reporting package complies fully with the recognition and measurement requirements of IFRSs, but also when it is adjusted centrally for matters such as post-balance sheet events review and central allocation of pension costs'.[147]   Adjustments made centrally to an unpublished reporting package are not considered to be corrections of errors for the purposes of the disclosure requirements in IFRS 1. However, a subsidiary is not permitted to ignore misstatements that are immaterial to the consolidated financial statements of its parent but material to its own financial statements.

The exemption is also available to associates and joint ventures. This means that in many cases an associate or joint venture that wants to apply option (a) will need to choose which shareholder it considers its 'parent' for IFRS 1 purposes and determine its IFRS carrying amount of its assets and liabilities by reference to that parent's date of transition to IFRSs.

7.5.2 Parent becomes a first-time adopter later than its subsidiary

If an entity becomes a first-time adopter later that its subsidiary, associate or joint venture the entity should 'in its consolidated financial statements, measure the assets and liabilities of the subsidiary (or associate or joint venture) at the same carrying amounts as in the financial statements of the subsidiary (or associate or joint venture), after adjusting for consolidation and equity accounting adjustments and for the effects of the business combination in which the entity acquired the subsidiary'.[148]

Whereas a subsidiary can choose to prepare its first IFRS financial statements by reference to its own date of transition to IFRSs or that of its parent, the parent itself must use the IFRS measurements already used in the subsidiary's separate financial statements, except to adjust for consolidation procedures and for the effects of the business combination in which the parent acquired the subsidiary.[149]

7.5.3 Implementation guidance on accounting for assets and liabilities of subsidiaries, associates and joint ventures

When an entity applies the rules discussed in sections 7.5.1 and 7.5.2 above, these do not override the requirements:[150]

- to apply Appendix B of IFRS 1 to assets acquired, and liabilities assumed, in a business combination that occurred before the acquirer's date of transition to IFRSs. However, the acquirer applies paragraph 25 to new assets acquired, and liabilities assumed, by the acquiree after that business combination and still held at the acquirer's date of transition to IFRSs.

- to apply the rest of the IFRS in measuring all assets and liabilities for which paragraphs 24 and 25 are not relevant.

- to give all disclosures required by the IFRS as of the first-time adopter's own date of transition to IFRSs.

7.5.4 Adoption of IFRSs on different dates in separate and consolidated financial statements

If a parent adopts IFRSs in its 'separate financial statements earlier or later than for its consolidated financial statements, it shall measure its assets and liabilities at the same amounts in both financial statements, except for consolidation adjustments'.[151] An entity that prepares both separate and consolidated IFRS financial statements is required to prepare them using the same date of transition to IFRSs for both, which greatly improves comparability. Although it might seem natural to use the earliest date of transition, the standard does not specifically require this.

8   OTHER EXCEPTIONS TO RETROSPECTIVE APPLICATION OF OTHER IFRSs

As discussed in section 3.3.2 above, IFRS 1 specifically prohibits retrospective application of IFRSs in a number of situations. The exceptions that have not been covered in sections 6.4 and 6.5 above are discussed below.

8.1   Estimates

IFRS 1 requires an entity to use estimates under IFRSs that are consistent with the estimates made for the same date under its previous GAAP – after adjusting for any difference in accounting policy – unless there is objective evidence that those estimates were in error.[152] IAS 8 defines prior period errors as:

> 'omissions from, and misstatements in, the entity's financial statements for one or more prior periods arising from a failure to use, or misuse of, reliable information that:
>
> (a)   was available when financial statements for those periods were authorised for issue; and
>
> (b)   could reasonably be expected to have been obtained and taken into account in the preparation and presentation of those financial statements.
>
> Such errors include the effects of mathematical mistakes, mistakes in applying accounting policies, oversights or misinterpretations of facts, and fraud.'[153]

Under IFRS 1 an entity cannot apply hindsight and make 'better' estimates when it prepares its first IFRS financial statements. It also means that an entity is not allowed to take account of any subsequent events that provide evidence of conditions that existed at that date, but that came to light after the date of its previous GAAP financial statements were finalised. The IASB considers that although 'some of those events might qualify as adjusting events under IAS 10 *Events After the Balance Sheet Date*, if the entity made those estimates on a basis consistent with IFRSs then it would be more helpful to users to recognise the revision of those estimates as income or expense in the period when the entity made the revision, rather than in preparing the opening IFRS balance sheet'.[154] Effectively, this prevents entities from using hindsight to 'clean up' their balance sheets by direct write-offs to equity as part of the opening IFRS balance sheet exercise.

The requirement that an entity should use estimates consistent with those made under its previous GAAP applies both to estimates made in respect of the date of transition to IFRSs and to those in respect of the end of any comparative period.[155] IFRS 1 provides the following guidance on how an entity should put this requirement into practice:

- When an entity receives information after the relevant date about estimates that it had made under previous GAAP, it treats this information in the same way as a non-adjusting event after the balance sheet date under IAS 10.[156] An entity can be in one of the following two positions:[157]

  - its previous GAAP accounting policy was consistent with IFRSs, in which case the adjustment is reflected in the period in which the revision is made; or

- its previous GAAP accounting policy was not consistent with IFRSs, in which case it will need to adjust the estimate for the difference in accounting policies.

  In both situations, if an entity later adjusts those estimates, it accounts for those estimates as events of the period in which it makes the revisions;[158]

- When an entity needs to make estimates under IFRSs at the relevant date that were not required under its previous GAAP, those estimates should be consistent with IAS 10 and reflect conditions that existed at the relevant date. This means, for example, that estimates of market prices, interest rates or foreign exchange rates should reflect market conditions at that date;[159] and

- IFRS 1 does not override the requirements in other IFRSs that require classifications or measurements to be based on circumstances existing at a particular date, such as for example:

  - the distinction between finance leases and operating leases;

  - the restrictions in IAS 38 that prohibit capitalisation of expenditure on an internally generated intangible asset if the asset did not qualify for recognition when the expenditure was incurred; and

  - the distinction between financial liabilities and equity instruments (see IAS 32).[160]

8.2 Assets classified as held for sale and discontinued operations

The transitional rules for existing IFRSs reporting entities in IFRS 5 *Non-current Assets Held for Sale and Discontinued Operations* require prospective application for financial periods starting on or after 1 January 2005. However, early adoption of IFRS 5 – at any date before its effective date – is permitted, provided the valuations and other information needed to apply the IFRSs were obtained at the time those criteria were originally met. These transitional rules have been extended to apply to first-time adopters whose date of transition to IFRSs is before 1 January 2005.[161]

The transitional rules for first-time adopters whose date of transition to IFRSs is on or after 1 January 2005 are different. They will need to apply IFRS 5 retrospectively.[162]

9 ADDITIONAL IFRS 1 IMPLEMENTATION GUIDANCE

Accounting areas that have not been covered above, but for which IFRS 1 provides specific implementation guidance, are discussed in sections 9.1 to 9.7 below.

9.1 Property, plant and equipment

9.1.1 *Depreciation method and rate*

If a first-time adopter's depreciation methods and rates under its previous GAAP are acceptable under IFRSs then it accounts for any change in estimated useful life or depreciation pattern prospectively from when it makes that change in estimate (see section 8.1 above). However, if the depreciation methods and rates are not acceptable under IFRSs and the difference has a material impact on the financial statements, a first-time adopter should adjust the accumulated depreciation in its opening IFRS balance sheet retrospectively.[163] If a restatement would be too onerous, a first-time adopter could opt instead to use fair value as the deemed cost.

9.1.2 Use of fair value or revaluation as deemed cost

As discussed in section 5 above, a first-time adopter may elect to use fair value or a revaluation as the deemed cost of an item of property, plant and equipment. When a first-time adopter uses a fair value or a revaluation as the deemed cost of an item of property, plant and equipment it will need to start depreciating the item 'from the date for which the entity established the fair value measurement or revaluation' and not from its date of transition to IFRSs.[164]

9.1.3 Revaluation model

A first-time adopter that chooses to account for some or all classes of property, plant and equipment under the revaluation model needs to present the cumulative revaluation surplus as a separate component of equity. However, IFRS 1 requires that the 'revaluation surplus at the date of transition to IFRSs is based on a comparison of the carrying amount of the asset at that date with its cost or deemed cost'.[165] If revaluations under previous GAAP did not satisfy the criteria in IFRS 1, a first-time adopter measures the revalued assets in its opening balance sheet on one of the following bases:[166]

- cost (or deemed cost) less any accumulated depreciation and any accumulated impairment losses under the cost model in IAS 16;
- deemed cost, being the fair value at the date of transition to IFRSs; or
- revalued amount, if the entity adopts the revaluation model in IAS 16 as its accounting policy under IFRSs for all items of property, plant and equipment in the same class.

A first-time adopter that uses fair value as the deemed cost for those classes of property, plant and equipment would be required to reset the cumulative revaluation surplus to zero.

9.1.4 Decommissioning provisions

Under IAS 16 the cost of an item of property, plant and equipment includes 'the initial estimate of the costs of dismantling and removing the item and restoring the site on which it is located, the obligation for which an entity incurs either when the item is acquired or as a consequence of having used the item during a particular period for purposes other than to produce inventories during that period'.[167] Therefore, a first-time adopter needs to ensure that cost includes an item representing the decommissioning provision as determined under IAS 37 *Provisions, Contingent Liabilities and Contingent Assets*.[168]

The entity applies IAS 16 in determining the resulting amount included in the cost of the asset, before depreciation and impairment losses. Items such as depreciation and impairment losses cause differences between the carrying amount of the liability and the amount included in the carrying amount of the asset. An entity accounts for changes in decommissioning provisions in accordance with IFRIC 1 *Changes in Existing Decommissioning, Restoration and Similar Liabilities*, but IFRS 1 provides an exemption for changes that occurred before the date of transition to IFRSs and prescribes an alternative treatment under which a first-time adopter should:[169]

- measure the liability as at the date of transition to IFRSs under IAS 37;

- to the extent that the liability is within the scope of IFRIC 1, estimate the amount that would have been included in the cost of the related asset when the liability first arose, by discounting the liability to that date using its best estimate of the historical risk-adjusted discount rate that would have applied for that liability over the intervening period; and

- calculate the accumulated depreciation on that amount, as at the date of transition to IFRSs, on the basis of the current estimate of the useful life of the asset, using the depreciation policy adopted by the entity under IFRSs.

9.2   Leases

IFRS 1 requires a first-time adopter to classify leases as operating or finance leases based on the circumstances existing at the inception of the lease and not those existing at the date of transition to IFRSs.[170] However, if 'at any time the lessee and the lessor agree to change the provisions of the lease, other than by renewing the lease, in a manner that would have resulted in a different classification of the lease if the changed terms had been in effect at the inception of the lease, the revised agreement is regarded as a new agreement over its term'.[171]

A first-time adopter should apply SIC-15 *Operating Leases – Incentives (amended 2003)* retrospectively to all leases.[172]

9.3   Subsidiaries and Special Purpose Entities

A first-time adopter should consolidate all subsidiaries and Special Purpose Entities, except when IAS 27 requires otherwise.[173] If a first-time adopter did not consolidate a subsidiary under its previous GAAP, it should in its opening IFRS balance sheet measure the subsidiary's assets and liabilities at either:[174]

- the same carrying amounts as in the separate IFRS financial statements of the subsidiary, after adjusting for consolidation procedures and for the effects of the business combination in which it acquired the subsidiary;[175] or

- if the subsidiary has not adopted IFRSs, the carrying amounts that IFRSs would require in the subsidiary's separate balance sheet.

If the parent acquired the subsidiary in a business combination it should recognise goodwill as explained in section 4.6 above. If the parent created the subsidiary it should not recognise goodwill.[176] The adjustment of the carrying amounts of assets and liabilities of a first-time adopter's subsidiaries may affect minority interests and deferred tax.[177]

9.4   Hyperinflation

The IASB decided not to exempt first-time adopters from retrospective application of IAS 29 *Financial Reporting in Hyperinflationary Economies*. Although the cost of restating financial statements for the effects of hyperinflation in periods before the date of transition to IFRSs might exceed the benefits, particularly if the currency is no longer hyperinflationary, the IASB concluded that a full retrospective 'restatement should be required, because hyperinflation can make unadjusted financial statements meaningless or misleading'.[178]

In preparing its opening IFRS balance sheet a first-time adopter should apply 'IAS 29 to any periods during which the economy of the functional currency or presentation currency was hyperinflationary'.[179] To make the restatement process less onerous, a first-time adopter may want to consider using fair value as deemed cost for long-lived assets such as property, plant and equipment, investment properties and certain intangible assets (see section 5 above).[180] If a first-time adopter applies the exemption to use fair value or a revaluation as deemed cost, 'it applies IAS 29 to periods after the date for which the revalued amount or fair value was determined'.[181]

9.5   Intangible assets

In its opening IFRS balance sheet a first-time adopter:[182]

- excludes all intangible assets and other intangible items that do not meet the criteria for recognition under IAS 38 at the date of transition to IFRSs; and

- includes all intangible assets that meet the recognition criteria in IAS 38 at that date, except for intangible assets acquired in a business combination that were not recognised in the acquirer's consolidated balance sheet under previous GAAP and also would not qualify for recognition under IAS 38 in the separate balance sheet of the acquiree (e.g. internally generated brands and customer lists).

An intangible asset is only capable of capitalisation under IAS 38 if it is probable that the future economic benefits attributable to the asset will flow to the entity and the cost of the asset can be measured reliably.[183] The standard imposes a number of additional criteria that further restrict capitalisation of internally generated intangible assets. An important restriction is the prohibition from using hindsight to conclude retrospectively that recognition criteria are met.[184] Therefore, a first-time adopter is only permitted to capitalise the costs of internally generated intangible assets when it:[185]

- concludes, based on an assessment made and documented at the date of that conclusion, that it is probable that future economic benefits from the asset will flow to the entity; and

- has a reliable system for accumulating the costs of internally generated intangible assets when, or shortly after, they are incurred.

In other words, it is not permitted under IFRS 1 to reconstruct retrospectively the costs of intangible assets. If an internally generated intangible asset qualifies for recognition at the date of transition to IFRSs, a first-time adopter recognises the asset in its opening IFRS balance sheet even if it had recognised the related expenditure as an expense under its previous GAAP.[186] However, first-time adopters that did not capitalise internally generated intangible assets are unlikely to have the type of documentation and systems required by IFRS 1 and will therefore not be able to capitalise these items in their opening IFRS balance sheet. Furthermore, if the asset does not qualify 'for recognition under IAS 38 until a later date, its cost is the sum of the expenditure incurred from that later date'.[187] Nonetheless, going forward, first-time adopters will need to implement the internal systems and procedures that enable them to determine whether or not any future internally generated intangible assets should be capitalised (for example, in the case of development costs). Capitalisation of separately acquired intangible assets will generally be easier because contemporaneous documentation that was prepared to support the investment decisions often exists.[188]

If a first-time adopter's 'amortisation methods and rates under previous GAAP would be acceptable under IFRSs, the entity does not restate the accumulated amortisation in its opening IFRS balance sheet. Instead, the entity accounts for any change in estimated useful life or amortisation pattern prospectively from the period when it makes that change in estimate ... However, in some cases, an entity's amortisation methods and rates under previous GAAP may differ from those that would be acceptable under IFRSs ... If those differences have a material effect on the financial statements, the entity adjusts the accumulated amortisation in its opening IFRS balance sheet retrospectively so that it complies with IFRSs.'[189]

9.6 Revenue recognition

If a first-time adopter 'has received amounts that do not yet qualify for recognition as revenue under IAS 18 (for example, the proceeds of a sale that does not qualify for revenue recognition), it recognises the amounts received as a liability in its opening IFRS balance sheet and measures that liability at the amount received'.[190] It is therefore possible that revenue that was already recognised under a first-time adopter's previous GAAP, will need to be deferred in its opening IFRS balance sheet and recognised again (this time under IFRSs) as revenue at a later date.

9.7 Borrowing costs

If on first-time adoption of IFRSs an entity 'adopts a policy of capitalising borrowing costs or not capitalising them then the entity should apply that policy consistently in its opening IFRS balance sheet and in all periods presented in its first IFRS financial statements'.[191] It is therefore not possible solely to capitalise borrowing costs prospectively from the date of transition. Instead, a first-time adopter that applies IAS 23's allowed alternative treatment to capitalise borrowing costs, should apply that treatment retrospectively, even for periods before the effective date of the standard.[192] However, if the entity established a deemed cost for an asset, it does not capitalise borrowing costs incurred before the date of the measurement that established the deemed cost.

10 PRESENTATION AND DISCLOSURE

As a general principle, IFRS 1 does not exempt a first-time adopter from any of the presentation and disclosure requirements in other IFRSs, with one noteworthy exception relating to comparative information under IAS 32, IAS 39 and IFRS 4 (see section 10.1.1 below).[193]

If an entity adopts IFRS 1 early, i.e. in its first IFRS financial statements for a period beginning before 1 January 2004, it should disclose the fact that it applies IFRS 1 and not SIC-8.[194]

10.1   Comparative information

IAS 1 requires (except where a standard or interpretation permits or requires otherwise) comparative information 'in respect of the previous period for all amounts reported in the financial statements' and 'for narrative and descriptive information when it is relevant to an understanding of the current period's financial statements'.[195] Accordingly, an entity's first IFRS financial statements should include at least one year of comparative information under IFRSs.[196] It is however not required to present its opening IFRS balance sheet in its first IFRS financial statements, although it is integral to the equity reconciliation at the date of transition that has to be presented in the entity's first IFRS financial statements (see section 10.2 below).[197] The IASB does not require a first-time adopter to present more than one comparative period under IFRS because 'such a requirement would impose costs out of proportion to the benefits to users, and increase the risk that preparers might need to make arbitrary assumptions in applying hindsight'.[198]

10.1.1   *Exemption from the requirement to restate comparative information for IAS 32, IAS 39 and IFRS 4*

As discussed in section 6.1 above, an entity adopting IFRSs for the first time before 1 January 2006 may elect to present comparative information that does not comply with IAS 32, IAS 39 and IFRS 4, in which case it needs to:[199]

- disclose that the comparative information does not comply with IAS 32, IAS 39 and IFRS 4, but that it has been prepared on the basis of its previous GAAP;

- disclose the nature, but not the amount, of the main adjustments that would make the information comply with IAS 32, IAS 39 and IFRS 4; and

- treat any adjustment between the balance sheet at the comparative period's reporting date and the start of the first IFRS reporting period as arising from a change in accounting policy. This difference is accounted for as an adjustment to the opening balance of each affected component of equity at the start of the first IFRS reporting period. The entity is required to make the disclosures prescribed by paragraphs 28(a)-(e) and (f)(i) of IAS 8.[200]

Originally IFRS 1 also required first-time adopters to prepare comparative information that complied with IAS 32 and IAS 39 because this improved comparability within the first IFRS financial statements and because the IASB believed that this should not be a problem for entities that planned the adoption of IFRSs in a timely manner.[201] Unfortunately, the less-than-timely publication of the revised IAS 32 and IAS 39 obliged the IASB to exempt entities adopting IFRSs before 1 January 2006 from applying these standards in preparing comparative information.

10.1.2   *Historical summaries*

Normally IFRSs require comparative information that is prepared on the same basis as information relating to the current reporting period. However, when an entity presents 'historical summaries of selected data for periods before the first period for which they present full comparative information under IFRSs', the standard does not 'require such summaries to comply with the recognition and measurement requirements of IFRSs'.[202]

As an entity is only allowed to apply IFRS 1 in its first IFRS financial statements, a literal reading of IFRS 1 would seem to suggest that the above exemption is not available to an entity that prepares its second IFRS financial statements. In practice this is not likely to cause a significant problem because this type of information is generally presented outside the financial statements where it is not covered by the requirements of IFRSs.

If an entity presents comparative information under its previous GAAP in addition to the comparative information required by IFRSs it should:[203]

- label the previous GAAP information prominently as not being prepared under IFRSs; and

- disclose the nature of the main adjustments that would make it comply with IFRSs. An entity need not quantify those adjustments.

10.2 Explanation of transition to IFRSs

A first-time adopter is required to explain how the transition from its previous GAAP to IFRSs affected its reported financial position, financial performance and cash flows.[204] The IASB decided 'that such disclosures are essential because they help users understand the effect and implications of the transition to IFRSs and how they need to change their analytical models to make the best use of information presented using IFRSs'.[205]

As indicated in section 3.3.1 above, IFRS 1 offers a wide range of exemptions that a first-time adopter may elect to apply. However, somewhat curiously, the standard does not explicitly require an entity to disclose which exemptions it has applied and how it applied them. In the case of, for example, the exemptions relating to employee benefits and cumulative translation differences it will be rather obvious whether or not an entity has chosen to apply the exemption. In other cases, users will have to rely on a first-time adopter disclosing those transitional accounting policies that are 'relevant to an understanding of the financial statements'.[206]

If a first-time adopter did not present financial statements for previous periods this fact should be disclosed.[207] In that case an explanation of how the transition to IFRSs affected the entity's reported financial position, financial performance and cash flows cannot be presented, because a relevant comparison under the entity's previous GAAP does not exist.

10.2.1 Reconciliations

A first-time adopter is required to present:

- reconciliations of its equity reported under previous GAAP to its equity under IFRSs at:[208]
  - the date of transition to IFRSs; and
  - the end of the latest period presented in the entity's most recent annual financial statements under previous GAAP;

- a reconciliation of the profit or loss reported under previous GAAP for the latest period in the entity's most recent annual financial statements to its profit or loss under IFRSs for the same period;[209] and
- an explanation of the material adjustments to the cash flow statement, if it presented one under its previous GAAP.[210]

First-time adopters should not apply the requirements of IAS 8 relating to the disclosure of changes in accounting policies because that standard does not deal with changes in accounting policies that occur when an entity first adopts IFRSs.

These requirements apply as follows to an entity whose first reporting date is 31 December 2005 and date of transition to IFRSs is 1 January 2004:

	1 January 2004	31 December 2004	31 December 2005
Balance sheet		●	●
Reconciliation of equity	●	●	
For the period ending			
Income statement		●	●
Cash flow statement		●	●
Statement of changes in equity		●	●
Reconciliation of profit or loss		●	
Explanation of material adjustments to cash flow statement		●	

These reconciliations should be sufficiently detailed 'to enable users to understand the material adjustments to the balance sheet and income statement'[211] and the entity should 'distinguish correction of ... errors from changes in accounting policies'.[212] While the standard does not prescribe a layout for these reconciliations, the Implementation Guidance contains an example of a reconciliation of equity and profit or loss that contains a line-by-line reconciliation of both balance sheet and income statement.[213] Such a presentation may be particularly appropriate when a first-time adopter needs to make transitional adjustments that affect a significant number of line items in the primary financial statements. If the adjustments are less pervasive a straightforward reconciliation of the equity and profit or loss figures may be able to provide an equally effective explanation of how the adoption of IFRSs affects the reported financial position, financial performance and cash flows.

If a first-time adopter recognised or reversed any impairment losses it should disclose the information that IAS 36 would have required 'if the entity had recognised those impairment losses or reversals in the period beginning with the date of transition to IFRSs'.[214] The purpose of this disclosure requirement is that while 'there is inevitably subjectivity about impairment losses the disclosure provides transparency about impairment losses recognised on transition to IFRSs. These losses might otherwise receive less attention than impairment losses recognised in earlier or later periods'.[215]

10.2.2   Designation of financial assets and financial liabilities

IAS 39 permits a financial instrument to be designated on initial recognition as a:

- *financial asset or financial liability at fair value through profit or loss*, which is a financial instrument that is either classified as *held for trading* or is designated as such on initial recognition; or

- *available-for-sale financial asset*, which is a financial asset designated as 'available for sale' or that is not specifically classified as 'loans and receivables', 'held-to-maturity investments' or 'at fair value through profit or loss'.

If a first-time adopter designates a previously recognised financial asset or financial liability as a 'financial asset or financial liability at fair value through profit or loss' or as available-for-sale (see section 6.2 above), it should disclose for each category:[216]

- the fair value of any financial assets or financial liabilities designated into it; and

- the classification and carrying amount in the previous financial statements.

10.2.3   Use of fair value as deemed cost

If a first-time adopter uses 'fair value in its opening IFRS balance sheet as deemed cost for an item of property, plant and equipment, an investment property or an intangible asset' (see section 5 above), it should disclose for each line item in the opening IFRS balance sheet:[217]

- the aggregate of those fair values; and

- the aggregate adjustment to the carrying amounts reported under previous GAAP.

10.3   Interim financial reports

If a first-time adopter presents an interim financial report under IAS 34 for part of the period covered by its first IFRS financial statements, that report should:[218]

- include reconciliations of:
  - its equity under previous GAAP at the end of that comparable interim period to its equity under IFRSs at that date; and
  - its profit or loss under previous GAAP for that comparable interim period, both on a current and year-to-date basis, to its profit or loss under IFRSs for that period; and

- include the reconciliations described in section 10.2.1 above or a cross-reference to another published document that includes these reconciliations.

For an entity presenting annual financial statements under IFRSs it is not compulsory to prepare interim financial reports under IAS 34. Therefore, the above requirements only apply to first-time adopters that prepare interim reports under IAS 34 on a voluntary basis or that are required to do so by a regulator or other party.[219] However, even if an entity does not present interim financial reports prepared in accordance with IAS 34, the accounting policies applied in preparing its interim financial statements should still be IFRS compliant.

Interim financial reports under IAS 34 contain considerably less detail than annual financial statements because they 'are based on the assumption that users of the interim financial report also have access to the most recent annual financial statements'.[220]   Therefore, a first-time adopter will have to ensure that its first interim financial report contains sufficient information about events or transactions that are material to an understanding of the current interim period. Hence it may be necessary for a first-time adopter to include in its first IFRS interim report significantly more information that it would normally include in an interim report; alternatively it could include a cross-reference to another published document that includes such information.

11   EFFECTIVE DATE

IFRS 1 is mandatory for an entity's first IFRS financial statements for a period beginning on or after 1 January 2004, although early application is encouraged. If an entity applies IFRS 1 early, it should disclose this fact (see section 10 above).[221]

References

1 IFRS 1, para. BC3.
2 IFRS 1, para. BC9.
3 IFRS 1, para. BC10.
4 IFRS 1, para. 1.
5 IFRS 1, para. 3 and Appendix A.
6 IFRS 1, para. 3.
7 IFRS 1, para. 3.
8 IFRS 1, para. 4.
9 IFRS 1, para. BC5.
10 IFRS 1, para. BC6.
11 IFRS 1, para. 5.
12 IFRS 1, Appendix A.
13 IFRS 1, para. 2.
14 IFRS 1, para. 2.
15 IFRS 1, para. 3.
16 IFRS 1, Appendix A.
17 IFRS 1, para. 36.
18 Release   No. 33-8567,   *First-Time Application of International Financial Reporting Standards*, Securities and Exchange Commission (SEC), 12 April 2005.
19 Release No. 33-8567.
20 IFRS 1, Appendix A.
21 IFRS 1, para. 14.
22 IFRS 1, para. 6.
23 IFRS 1, para. 7.
24 IFRS 1, paras. BC17-BC18.
25 IFRS 1, para. 8.
26 IFRS 1, para. BC11.
27 IFRS 1, para. 8.
28 IFRS 1, para. 10.
29 IFRS 1, para. 11.
30 IFRS 1, para. 9.
31 IFRS 1, para. BC14.

32 Framework, para. 44.
33 IFRS 1, para. BC27.
34 IFRS 1, para. 12.
35 IFRS 1, para. 13.
36 IFRS 1, para. 26.
37 IFRS 1, para. IN4.
38 IFRS 1, para. 36A.
39 IFRS 1, para. 13.
40 IFRS 1, para. IN4.
41 IFRS 1, para. 26.
42 IFRS 1, para. 15 and Appendix B.
43 IFRS 1, para. B1.
44 IFRS 1, para. B3.
45 IFRS 1, para. B2(a).
46 IFRS 1, para. 15.
47 IFRS 3, Appendix A.
48 IFRS 3, Appendix A.
49 IFRS 3, para. 4.
50 IFRS 1, para. B2(c).
51 IFRS 1, para. B2(b).
52 IFRS 1, para. B2(b).
53 IFRS 1, para. B2(d).
54 IFRS 1, para. B2(e).
55 IFRS 1, para. B2(f).
56 IFRS 1, para. BC35.
57 IFRS 1, para. B2(g).
58 IFRS 1, para. B2(g).
59 IFRS 1, para. B2(g).
60 IFRS 1, para. IG40.
61 IFRS 1, para. IG41.
62 IFRS 1, para. IG43.
63 IFRS 1, para. BC39.
64 IFRS 1, para. BC38.
65 IFRS 1, para. B2(h).
66 IFRS 3, para. 81.

67 IFRS 1, para. 10.
68 IFRS 1, para. B2(i).
69 IFRS 1, para. B2(i).
70 IAS 1, para. 47.
71 IFRS 1, paras. B1A and IG21A.
72 IFRS 1, para. B1A.
73 IFRS 1, para. B1B.
74 IFRS 1, para. B2(j).
75 IFRS 1, para. B2(k).
76 IAS 27, para. 4.
77 IFRS 1, para. B2(k).
78 IFRS 1, para. BC42.
79 IFRS 1, para. 16-17.
80 IFRS 1, para. 16.
81 IFRS 1, para. 18.
82 IFRS 1, para. 18.
83 IFRS 1, para. 18.
84 IFRS 1, para. IG50.
85 IFRS 1, para. BC45.
86 IFRS 1, para. 16.
87 IFRS 1, para. 17.
88 IFRS 1, para. 19.
89 IFRS 1, para. BC47.
90 IFRS 1, para. BC47.
91 IFRS 1, para. BC89A.
92 IFRS 1, para. 36A.
93 IFRS 1, para. 36A.
94 IAS 39, para. 9.
95 IAS 39, para. 9.
96 IFRS 1, para. 25A.
97 IFRS 1, para. BC63A.
98 IFRS 1, para. IG59.
99 IFRS 1, para. 43A.
100 IFRS 1, para. BC81.
101 IFRS 1, paras. BC81-BC82.
102 IFRS 1, para. 23.
103 IFRS 1, paras. IG35-IG36.
104 IFRS 1, para. 27.
105 IFRS 1, para. 27A.
106 IFRS 1, paras. 26(c) and BC75-BC76.
107 IFRS 1, para. 28.
108 IFRS 1, para. IG58A.
109 IFRS 1, para. 28.
110 IFRS 1, para. 29.
111 IFRS 1, para. 29.
112 IFRS 1, para. 30.
113 IFRS 1, para. BC75.
114 IFRS 1, para. IG60B.
115 IFRS 1, para. IG60A.
116 IFRS 1, paras. IG60 and IG60B.
117 IFRS 1, para. 30.
118 IFRS 1, para. IG60B.
119 IFRS 1, para. 28.
120 IFRS 1, para. IG58A.
121 IFRS 1, para. BC73.
122 IFRS 1, para. BC73.
123 IFRS 1, para. 20.
124 IFRS 1, para. BC48.
125 IFRS 1, paras. 20 and IG18.

126 IFRS 1, paras. BC50-BC51.
127 IFRS 1, para. BC51.
128 IFRS 1, paras. BC51 and IG21.
129 IFRS 1, para. IG19.
130 IFRS 1, para. IG20.
131 IFRS 1, para. BC52.
132 IFRS 1, para. 21 and IAS 21, paras. 32 and 39.
133 IFRS 1, para. 21 and IAS 21, para. 48.
134 IFRS 1, para. 22.
135 IFRS 1, para. BC63B.
136 IFRS 1, para. 25B.
137 IFRS 1, para. 25B.
138 IFRS 1, para. 25B.
139 IFRS 1, para. 25C.
140 Framework, paras. 25-28.
141 IFRS 1, para. 25D and IFRS 4, para. 22.
142 IFRS 1, para. BC89A.
143 IFRS 1, para. 36A.
144 IFRS 1, para. BC59.
145 IFRS 1, para. 24.
146 IFRS 1, para. 24.
147 IFRS 1, para. IG31.
148 IFRS 1, para. 25.
149 IFRS 1, para. BC63.
150 IFRS 1, para. IG30.
151 IFRS 1, para. 25.
152 IFRS 1, para. 31.
153 IAS 8, para. 5.
154 IFRS 1, para. BC84.
155 IFRS 1, para. 34.
156 IFRS 1, paras. 32 and IG2.
157 IFRS 1, para. IG3.
158 IFRS 1, para. IG3.
159 IFRS 1, paras. 33 and IG3.
160 IFRS 1, para. IG4.
161 IFRS 1, para. 34A.
162 IFRS 1, para. 34B.
163 IFRS 1, para. IG7.
164 IFRS 1, paras. IG8-IG9.
165 IFRS 1, para. IG10.
166 IFRS 1, para. IG11.
167 IAS 16, para. 16.
168 IFRS 1, para. IG13.
169 IFRS 1, paras. 25E and IG201-IG203.
170 IFRS 1, para. IG14.
171 IAS 17, para. 13.
172 IFRS 1, para. IG16.
173 IFRS 1, para. IG26.
174 IFRS 1, para. IG27.
175 IFRS 1, para. 25.
176 IFRS 1, para. IG27.
177 IFRS 1, para. IG28.
178 IFRS 1, para. BC67.
179 IFRS 1, para. IG32.
180 IFRS 1, para. IG33.
181 IFRS 1, para. IG34.
182 IFRS 1, para. IG44.
183 IAS 38, para. 21.

184 IAS 38, para. 71.
185 IFRS 1, para. IG46.
186 IFRS 1, para. IG47.
187 IFRS 1, para. IG47.
188 IFRS 1, para. IG48.
189 IFRS 1, para. IG51.
190 IFRS 1, para. IG17.
191 IFRS 1, para. IG23.
192 IFRS 1, para. IG25.
193 IFRS 1, para. 35.
194 IFRS 1, para. 47.
195 IAS 1, para. 36.
196 IFRS 1, para. 36.
197 IFRS 1, para. 6.
198 IFRS 1, para. BC86.
199 IFRS 1, para. 36A.
200 IAS 8, paras. 24 and 28.
201 IFRS 1, para. BC89.
202 IFRS 1, para. 37.
203 IFRS 1, para. 37.
204 IFRS 1, para. 38.
205 IFRS 1, para. BC91.
206 IAS 1, para. 108.
207 IFRS 1, para. 43.
208 IFRS 1, para. 39.
209 IFRS 1, para. 39.
210 IFRS 1, para. 40.
211 IFRS 1, para. 40.
212 IFRS 1, para. 41.
213 IFRS 1, para. IG63.
214 IFRS 1, para. 39.
215 IFRS 1, para. BC94.
216 IFRS 1, para. 43A.
217 IFRS 1, para. 44.
218 IFRS 1, para. 45.
219 IFRS 1, para. IG37.
220 IFRS 1, para. 46.
221 IFRS 1, para. 47.

Chapter 3

Detailed comparison between IFRSs and US GAAP

This chapter presents accounting measurement and disclosure requirements under IFRSs and US GAAP for a range of specific accounting topics in a manner that facilitates comparison. The requirements under IFRSs are based on the Standards and Interpretations adopted by the IASB, which comprise International Financial Reporting Standards, International Accounting Standards and Interpretations originated by the IFRIC or the former SIC. The corresponding requirements in the US are derived from the accounting principles that have substantial authoritative support (comprising primarily accounting standards and practices promulgated by the FASB and its predecessor bodies). Where appropriate, reference has also been made to the accounting rules and regulations of the SEC.

The chapter is divided into 30 sections, each of which allows a side-by-side comparison of a specific accounting topic. The accounting and disclosure requirements under IFRSs are summarised on the left-hand pages and the corresponding requirements in the US on the right-hand pages. Where appropriate, we have avoided repetition of areas of common practice and concentrated on areas where there are differences in accounting practice or disclosure requirements. As a result, the text is not exhaustive, and reference should therefore be made to the original accounting literature for detailed guidance on any specific area. The relevant authoritative literature is indicated at the beginning of each section and references to specific guidance are given in the margins.

The special accounting practices that apply in certain industries (for example, banking, insurance, oil and gas) are outside the scope of this book. Consequently, certain accounting standards issued by the FASB and the Accounting and Auditing Industry guides issued by the AICPA that deal with specialised industries are not covered. Reference should be made either to these pronouncements, where the issue relates to a specialised industry that is the subject of an accounting standard, or to other relevant guidance issued by the AICPA or other relevant body. The SEC also has special provisions in Industry Guides governing statistical data and other financial data for registrants with significant banking, insurance or oil and gas operations. Reference should be made to Regulation S-X for these.

Section 1   Presentation of financial statements

1.1   AUTHORITATIVE PRONOUNCEMENTS

- IAS 1
- IAS 8
- IAS 10
- IAS 12
- IAS 32
- IFRS 5

1.2   COMPONENTS OF FINANCIAL STATEMENTS

IAS 1.2-3   IAS 1 *Presentation of Financial Statements* applies to all general purpose financial statements prepared and presented in accordance with IFRS, i.e. those intended to meet the needs of users who are not in a position to demand tailored reports.

IAS 1.8,103-104   A complete set of financial statements comprises:
- a balance sheet;
- an income statement;
- a statement of changes in equity showing either all changes in equity or changes in equity other than those arising from transactions with equity holders acting in their capacity as such (see section 12.5.3);
- a cash flow statement (see section 27 for the requirements of IAS 7 *Cash Flow Statements*); and
- notes, comprising a summary of significant accounting policies and other explanatory notes.   IAS 1 explains that notes contain information in addition to that presented in the balance sheet, income statement, statement of changes in equity and cash flow statement, and provide narrative descriptions or

Section 1   Presentation of financial statements

1.1   AUTHORITATIVE PRONOUNCEMENTS

- ARB 43
- APB 9
- APB 10
- APB 17
- APB 20
- APB 22

- FAS 16
- FAS 130
- FAS 144
- FIN 20
- FIN 39

COMMENT

In December 2003, the FASB issued an exposure draft for a proposed Statement of Financial Accounting Standards *Accounting Changes and Error Corrections a replacement of APB Opinion No. 20 and FASB Statement No. 3.* The proposed Statement would require retrospective application for discretionary changes in accounting principle as well as changes in accounting principle required by the issuance of new accounting pronouncements, in the absence of specific transitional guidance, and would require that a change in depreciation method be accounted for as a change in estimate. The proposed Statement would carry forward the guidance in APB 20 for the justification for a change in accounting principle and reporting (1) the correction of an error, (2) a change in accounting estimate, and (3) a change in the reporting entity. The proposed standard is expected to be issued in the second quarter of 2005.

1.2   COMPONENTS OF FINANCIAL STATEMENTS

SEC registered entities must file the following consolidated financial information:

- balance sheet;   *S-X 3-01(a)*
- income statement;   *S-X 3-02(a)*
- comprehensive income statement;   *FAS 130*
- cash flow statement;   *S-X 3-04*
- an analysis of the changes in each caption of other stockholders' equity presented in the balance sheets; and
- related notes required by the comprehensive body of accounting standards pursuant to which the financial statements are prepared and any required schedules.

The same requirements apply to foreign private issuers. The financial statements of foreign private issuers may be prepared according to US GAAP or according to a comprehensive body of accounting principles other than US GAAP (e.g. IFRS) if reconciliations to US GAAP are prepared for net income, comprehensive income, cash flows and shareholders' equity, with explanations of the differences.   *20-F Item 8A, Items 17-18*

disaggregations of items disclosed in those statements and information about items that do not qualify for separate recognition in those statements. Notes should normally be presented in a systematic manner with cross-references from other statements.

IAS 1.9-10,44-46 Reports, such as a financial review by management, an environmental report or value added statements, may be presented outside the financial statements but within the same document. Such reports and statements are outside the scope of IFRS. The financial statements should be clearly identified and distinguished from other information and reports contained within the same document.

1.3   FAIR PRESENTATION

IAS 1.13-14 Entities whose financial statements comply with all the requirements of IFRSs should make an explicit and unreserved statement of such compliance in the notes. The application of IFRS, with additional disclosure when necessary, is presumed in virtually all circumstances to result in financial statements that achieve a fair presentation of an entity's financial position, financial performance and cash flows. Fair presentation requires the faithful representation of the effects of transactions, other events and conditions in accordance with the definitions and recognition criteria set out in the *Framework for the Preparation and Presentation of Financial Statements*.

IAS 1.15 Fair presentation also requires an entity to:

- select and apply accounting policies in accordance with IAS 8 *Accounting Policies, Changes in Accounting Estimates and Errors* (see section 1.4 below);

- present information in a manner that provides relevant, reliable, comparable and understandable information; and

- provide additional disclosures when compliance with the specific requirements of IFRSs is insufficient to enable users to understand the impact of particular transactions or events on the entity's financial position and financial performance.

IAS 1.16 Inappropriate accounting policies are not rectified either by disclosure of the accounting policies used or by notes or other explanatory material.

IAS 1.17-18,22 In extremely rare circumstances, an entity may conclude that compliance with an IFRS requirement would be so misleading as to conflict with the *Framework's* objective. In such cases, compliance would not represent faithfully the transactions, other events and conditions that an item of information either purports to represent or could reasonably be expected to represent and would therefore be likely to influence users' economic decisions. In such a situation, an entity should depart from the requirement in order to achieve a fair presentation provided the relevant regulatory framework requires, or otherwise does not prohibit, such a departure. Where an entity departs from a requirement in this way, it should disclose:

(a)   that management has concluded that the financial statements present fairly the entity's financial position, financial performance and cash flows;

(b)   that it has complied with applicable Standards and Interpretations except that it has departed from a particular requirement in order to achieve a fair presentation;

Reconciliations between the accounting principles used in preparing the primary financial statements and US GAAP, which describe and quantify each material variation are required:

- for each balance sheet presented; and

- for each year and any interim periods for which an income statement is presented. However, reconciliation of net income of the earliest of the three years may be omitted if that information has not previously been included in a filing made under the Securities Act or Exchange Act.

1.3   FAIR PRESENTATION

The notion of a true and fair override does exist under US GAAP but is not used in practice. Non-application of applicable accounting standards is not permissible unless, due to unusual circumstances, adhering to the pronouncements would make the financial statements misleading.

(c)   the title of the Standard or Interpretation from which it has departed, the nature of the departure, including the required treatment, the reason why that treatment would be so misleading that it would conflict with the *Framework's* objective and the treatment adopted; and

(d)   for each period presented, the financial impact of the departure on each item that would have been reported in complying with the requirement.

IAS 1.19   Where a departure in a prior period affects the amounts recognised in the current period, the disclosures outlined in c) and d) above should also be made.

IAS 1.21   In the extremely rare circumstances that compliance with a requirement would be misleading (as outlined above) but the relevant regulatory framework prohibits departure from the requirement, the entity should seek to minimise the perceived misleading aspects of compliance by disclosing:

- the title of the Standard or Interpretation in question, the nature of the requirement, the reason for the conclusion that compliance with the requirement is so misleading as to conflict with the *Framework's* objective for financial statements; and

- for each period presented, the adjustments to each item in the financial statements that management has concluded would be necessary for a fair presentation.

IAS 1.22   In making its assessment as to whether compliance with a requirement would be misleading management should consider why the objective of financial statements is not achieved in the particular circumstances and how the entity's circumstances differ from those of other entities that comply with the requirement. There is a rebuttable presumption that the entity's compliance would not be so misleading as to conflict with the objective if other entities in similar circumstances are in compliance.

1.4   ACCOUNTING POLICIES

IAS 1.108,112   A summary of significant accounting policies should be disclosed which includes:

- the measurement basis (or bases) used in preparing the financial statements; and

- the other accounting policies used that are relevant to an understanding of the financial statements.

An accounting policy may be significant because of the nature of the entity's operations even if amounts for the current and prior periods are not material (see section 1.5.1).

IAS 8.7-8   Where a Standard or Interpretation specifically applies to a transaction, other event or condition, application of that Standard or Interpretation, together with consideration of any relevant Implementation Guidance, should determine the accounting policy adopted. The policies within IFRSs need not be applied to immaterial balances and transactions, however it is inappropriate to make, or leave uncorrected, immaterial departures from IFRSs in order to achieve a particular presentation.

1.4   ACCOUNTING POLICIES

APB 22 requires reporting entities to disclose the accounting principles followed   *APB 22.12*
and the methods of applying those principles that materially affect the
determination of financial position, cash flows or results of operations.   The
disclosures should include important judgements as to the appropriateness of
principles relating to:

- recognition of revenue;
- allocation of asset costs to current and future periods; and
- those accounting principles and methods that involve any of the following:
  - a selection from existing acceptable alternatives;
  - principles and methods peculiar to the industry in which the reporting
    entity operates, even if such principles and methods are predominantly
    followed in that industry;
  - unusual or innovative applications of generally accepted accounting
    principles and of principles and methods peculiar to the industry in
    which the reporting entity operates.

IAS 8.10-12   Where there is no specific requirement under IFRS, an entity's management should use its judgement to develop accounting policies that result in information that is:

- relevant to the decision-making needs of users; and
- reliable, in that the financial statements:
    - represent faithfully the financial position, financial performance and cash flows of the entity;
    - reflect the economic substance of transactions, other events and conditions and not merely the legal form;
    - are neutral, i.e. free from bias;
    - are prudent; and
    - are complete in all material respects.

In making this judgement, management should refer to, and consider, the applicability of the following sources in descending order:

- the requirements and guidance in Standards and Interpretations dealing with similar and related issues; and
- the definitions, recognition criteria and measurement concepts for assets, liabilities, income and expenses set out in the *Framework*.

Management may also consider the most recent pronouncements of other standard-setting bodies that use a similar conceptual framework, other accounting literature and accepted industry practices to the extent that these do not conflict with the above sources.

IAS 8.13   Accounting policies should be selected and applied consistently for similar transactions, other events and conditions, unless a Standard or Interpretation specifically requires or permits categorisation of items for which different policies may be appropriate. Where categories are used, appropriate accounting policies should be selected and applied consistently to each category.

IAS 1.113   Within the summary of significant accounting policies or other notes, an entity should disclose the judgements (apart from those involving the key sources of estimation uncertainty – see below) made by management in applying the accounting policies that have the most significant effect on the amounts recognised in the financial statements.

IAS 1.116,120   Information should be disclosed in the notes about the key assumptions concerning the future, and other key sources of estimation uncertainty at the balance sheet date, that have a significant risk of causing a material adjustment to the carrying amount of assets and liabilities within the next financial year. The notes should include details of the nature of the assets and liabilities concerned and their carrying amount at the balance sheet date.

IAS 1.122   Where it is impracticable (i.e. an entity cannot apply the requirement after making every reasonable effort to do so) to disclose full information relating to the possible effects of a key assumption or another key source of estimation uncertainty at the balance sheet date, disclosure should be made of the fact that, based on existing knowledge, outcomes could differ and thus require a material adjustment to the balances affected.

Where an SEC registered entity has not adopted, due to a delayed effective date, a *SAB 74* recently issued accounting standard that is expected to have a material effect on *(Topic 11M)* future results of operations or financial position, the following information should be disclosed:

- A brief description of the new standard, the date that adoption is required, and the date that the entity plans to adopt, if earlier.

- A discussion of the methods of adoption allowed by the standard, and the method expected to be applied by the entity.

- A discussion of the impact that adoption of the standard is expected to have on the financial statements, unless not known or reasonably estimable, in which case a statement to that effect should be made.

- Disclosure of the potential impact of other significant matters that might result from adoption of the standard is encouraged (e.g. technical violations of debt covenant agreements).

1.5   BASIS OF PREPARATION

IAS 1.23-24 In preparing financial statements, management should make an assessment of the
IAS 10.14   entity's ability to continue as a going concern by considering all available
information about the future, which is at least, but not limited to, twelve months
from the balance sheet date.   Material uncertainties that may cast significant doubt
upon the entity's ability to continue as a going concern should be disclosed.

Financial statements should be prepared on a going concern basis unless
management either intends to liquidate the entity or to cease trading, or has no
realistic alternative but to do so.   If the financial statements are not prepared on a
going concern basis, that fact should be disclosed, together with the actual basis of
preparation and the reason why the entity is not considered to be a going concern.

IAS 1.25-26 Apart from cash flow information, financial statements should be prepared on an
accrual basis with items recognised in accordance with the definitions and
recognition criteria of the *Framework*.

IAS 1.27 The presentation and classification of items in the financial statements should be
applied consistently from one period to the next unless:

- it is apparent, following a significant change in the nature of the entity's
operations or a review of its financial statements that another presentation or
classification would be more appropriate having regard to IAS 8; or

- a Standard or Interpretation requires a change in presentation.

IAS 1.28 A revised presentation must provide information which is reliable and more relevant
to the users of the financial statements and must be expected to continue so that
comparability is not impaired.   A revised presentation requires restatement of
comparatives (see section 1.5.2 below).

1.5.1   Materiality

IAS 1.11   IAS 1 and IAS 8 define 'material' as follows: 'omissions or misstatements of items
IAS 8.5   are material if they could, individually or collectively, influence the economic
decisions of users taken on the basis of the financial statements.   Materiality
depends on the size and nature of the omission or misstatement judged in the
surrounding circumstances.   The size or nature of the item, or a combination of
both, could be the determining factor'.

IAS 1.29-31 The financial statements should present separately:

- each material class of similar items; and

- material items which are dissimilar in nature or function.

The final stage in the process of aggregation and classification of transactions or
other events is the presentation of condensed and classified data which form line
items in the financial statements.   If a line item is not individually material, it
should be aggregated with other items either on the face of the financial statements
or in the notes.   An item that is not sufficiently material to warrant separate
presentation on the face of the balance sheet, income statement, statement of
changes in equity or cash flow statement may nevertheless be sufficiently material
for separate presentation in the notes.

1.5   BASIS OF PRESENTATION

The assumption that an entity will be able to continue as a going concern is implicit in financial statements prepared in conformity with US GAAP in the absence of significant information to the contrary.   If it is clear that an entity will not be able to continue as a going concern, use of the liquidation basis of accounting may be appropriate.   Generally, use of the liquidation basis of accounting is required if the company is currently in the process of being liquidated or the owners have decided to dissolve or liquidate the company, or legal proceedings, including bankruptcy, have reached a point where liquidation of the company is imminent. *SAS 59* *FRR 607.02*

However, in many instances, conditions will exist or events will have occurred that raise a question about an entity's ability to continue as a going concern, but ultimate liquidation of the company cannot be assessed as imminent.   In these cases, use of the liquidation basis of accounting is not appropriate, and the financial statements should be prepared on a going concern basis.

Financial statements should be prepared, except for cash flow information, under the accrual basis of accounting (i.e. transactions and events are recognised when they occur, and not as cash or its equivalent is received or paid; and they are recorded in the accounting records and reported in the financial statements of the periods to which they relate). *CON 6.134-152*

Comparative financial information should be comparable with that disclosed for the most recent financial period presented; any exceptions to comparability should be clearly identified.   APB 20 specifies the manner of reporting each type of accounting change (e.g. an accounting principle, accounting estimate, or reporting entity). *ARB 43 Ch 2.5* *APB 20*

1.5.1   Materiality

Items are considered material if the magnitude of an omission or misstatement of accounting information makes it probable that the judgement of a reasonable person relying on the information would have been changed or influenced by the omission or misstatement.   In order to determine whether an item is material, the magnitude and nature of the item and the circumstances in which the judgement has to be made need to be taken into account. *CON 2.123-132*

SEC registrants are required to consider both quantitative and qualitative factors when assessing materiality.   In addition, intentional immaterial misstatements are not permissible and, in certain circumstances, are unlawful. *SAB 99*

A specific disclosure requirement or accounting policy in a Standard or Interpretation need not be applied to immaterial information (subject to IAS 8.8 – see section 1.4 above).

1.5.2   Periods presented and comparative information

IAS 1.49   Financial statements should be presented at least annually.   If an entity changes its balance sheet date so that the financial statements are presented for a period which is longer or shorter than one year, it should disclose the period covered by the financial statements, the reason for the longer or shorter period and the fact that the comparative information is not entirely comparable.

IAS 1.36   Comparative information should be disclosed for all amounts reported in the financial statements, unless a Standard or an Interpretation permits or requires otherwise.   It should be included for narrative and descriptive information when relevant to an understanding of the current period.

IAS 1.38-39   When the presentation or classification of items in the financial statements is amended, comparative amounts should be reclassified, unless reclassification is impracticable (i.e. an entity cannot apply the requirement after making every reasonable effort to do so). The nature, amount of, and reason for, any reclassification should be disclosed.   When it is impracticable to reclassify comparative amounts, an entity should disclose the reason for not reclassifying and the nature of the adjustments that would have been made if the amounts had been reclassified.

1.6   LAYOUT OF PRIMARY FINANCIAL STATEMENTS

1.6.1   Layout of balance sheet

IAS 1.68-68A   IFRSs do not prescribe standard layouts for the balance sheet, but does require that, as a minimum, the face of the balance sheet includes line items that present the following:
- property, plant and equipment;
- investment property;
- intangible assets;
- financial assets (excluding amounts shown under the headings marked*);
- investments accounted for using the equity method*;
- biological assets;
- inventories;
- trade and other receivables*;
- cash and cash equivalents*;
- trade and other payables;
- provisions;
- financial liabilities (excluding amounts shown under trade and other payables and provisions);
- liabilities and assets for current tax, as defined in IAS 12 *Income Taxes;*

1.5.2　Periods presented and comparative information

SEC registered entities must file audited balance sheets as of the end of each of the two most recent fiscal years and audited statements of income and cash flows for each of the three fiscal years preceding the date of the most recent balance sheet being filed, or such shorter period as the registrant has been in existence. Comprehensive income should be reported for each period for which an income statement is presented. *S-X 3-01(a)*　*S-X 3-02(a)*

A foreign private issuer would be required to provide a balance sheet for the earliest of the three fiscal years presented if that balance sheet is required by the relevant jurisdiction outside the United States. *20-F Item 8A*

1.6　LAYOUT OF PRIMARY FINANCIAL STATEMENTS

1.6.1　Layout of balance sheet

There is no general requirement under US GAAP for entities to prepare a balance sheet in accordance with a specific layout. However, SEC registrants are required to prepare their balance sheets in conformity with Regulation S-X, which requires the following line items (where applicable) to be shown on the face of the balance sheet or notes thereto: *S-X 5-02*

- current assets:
    - cash and cash items;
    - marketable securities;
    - accounts and notes receivable, stating separately amounts receivable from (1) customers (trade), (2) related parties, (3) underwriters, promoters, and employees (other than related parties) which arose in other than the ordinary course of business; and (4) others.

      If the aggregate amount of notes receivable exceeds 10% of the aggregate amount of receivables, the above information should be disclosed separately for accounts receivable and notes receivable.

      Certain additional disclosures are required if amounts due under long-term contracts are included in receivables;
    - allowances for doubtful accounts and notes receivable;
    - unearned income;

IAS 1.70 • deferred tax liabilities and deferred tax assets, as defined in IAS 12 (note that where an entity presents both current and non-current assets and liabilities, it should not classify any deferred tax balances as current);

• minority interest, presented within equity;

• issued capital and reserves attributable to equity holders of the parent;

• the total of assets classified as held for sale and assets included in disposal groups classified as held for sale in accordance with IFRS 5 *Non-current Assets Held for Sale and Discontinued Operations*; and

• liabilities included in disposal groups classified as held for sale in accordance with IFRS 5.

IAS 1.76-77 Various details for each class of share capital and a description of the nature and purpose of each reserve within equity are required either on the face of the balance sheet or in the notes.

IAS 1.69,72,74 Additional line items, headings and sub-totals should be presented on the face of the balance sheet when relevant to an understanding of the entity's financial position. Further sub-classifications of the line items presented, classified in a manner appropriate to the entity's operations, should be disclosed either on the face of the balance sheet or in the notes. An entity should consider the nature, liquidity and function of assets and the amount, nature and timing of liabilities in assessing whether additional line items or further sub-classification are required.

- inventories, stating separately in the balance sheet or in a note thereto, if practicable, the amounts of (1) finished goods, (2) inventoried costs relating to long-term contracts, (3) work in process, (4) raw materials, and (5) supplies. If inventories are valued at LIFO or include long-term contracts or programmes, certain additional disclosures are required;
- prepaid expenses;
- other current assets; and
- total current assets;
- non-current assets:
  - securities of related parties;
  - indebtedness of related parties – non current;
  - other investments;
  - property, plant and equipment;
  - accumulated depreciation, depletion, and amortisation of property, plant and equipment;
  - intangible assets;
  - accumulated depreciation and amortisation of intangible assets; and
  - other assets;
- total assets;
- current liabilities:
  - accounts and notes payable, stating separately amounts payable to (1) banks for borrowings, (2) factors or other financial institutions for borrowings, (3) holders of commercial paper, (4) trade creditors, (5) related parties, (6) underwriters, promoters, and employees (other than related parties), and (7) others;
  - the amount and terms of unused lines of credit for short-term financing must be disclosed, if significant, in the notes to the financial statements;
  - other current liabilities, stating separately, in the balance sheet or in a note thereto, any item in excess of 5 percent of total current liabilities; and
  - total current liabilities;
- long-term liabilities:
  - bonds, mortgages and other long-term debt, including capitalised leases, disclosing separately each issue or type of obligation and certain other information;
  - non-current indebtedness to related parties;
  - other liabilities;
  - commitments and contingent liabilities; and
  - deferred credits, stating separately amounts for deferred income taxes, deferred tax credits and material items of deferred income;
- minority interests in consolidated subsidiaries;
- preferred stocks subject to mandatory redemption requirements or whose redemption is outside the control of the issuer;

1.6.2 Distinction between current and non-current

IAS 1.51,55 IAS 1 requires presentation of current and non-current assets and current and non-current liabilities as separate classifications on the face of the balance sheet except when a presentation in order of liquidity provides reliable information which is more relevant. A mixed basis of presentation, showing some assets and liabilities using a current/non-current classification and others in order of liquidity, is also permitted when this provides information that is reliable and more relevant.

IAS 1.52 Whichever method of presentation is adopted, an entity should disclose the amount expected to be recovered or settled after more than twelve months for each asset and liability line item that combines amounts expected to be recovered or settled both within and after more than twelve months from the balance sheet date.

IAS 1.57 An asset should be classified as current when it satisfies any of the following criteria:
- it is expected to be realised in, or is intended for sale or consumption in, the entity's normal operating cycle;
- it is held primarily for the purpose of being traded;
- it is expected to be realised within twelve months after the balance sheet date; or
- it is cash or a cash equivalent (as defined in IAS 7 *Cash Flow Statements*) unless it is restricted from being exchanged or used to settle a liability for at least twelve months after the balance sheet date.

All other assets should be classified as non-current assets until they meet the criteria to be classified as held for sale in accordance with IFRS 5 *Non-current Assets Held for Sale and Discontinued Operations* (see section 1.9 below).

IAS 1.60-61 A liability should be classified as current when it satisfies any of the following criteria:
- it is expected to be settled in the entity's normal operating cycle;
- it is held primarily for the purpose of being traded;
- it is due to be settled within twelve months after the balance sheet date (even if the original term exceeded twelve months); or
- the entity does not have an unconditional right as at the balance sheet date to defer settlement of the liability for at least twelve months after the balance sheet date.

All other liabilities are classified as non-current liabilities.

IAS 1.63 An entity classifies its financial liabilities as current when they are due to be settled within twelve months after the balance sheet date, even if (i) the original term was for a period longer than twelve months and (ii) an agreement to refinance, or to

- preferred stocks which are not redeemable or are redeemable solely at the option of the issuer;

- each class of common stocks;

- other stockholders' equity, stating separately (1) additional paid-in capital, (2) other additional capital, (3) appropriated retained earnings and (4) unappropriated retained earnings;

- total liabilities and stockholders' equity.

1.6.2   Distinction between current and non-current

With the exception of certain industries, for which the current/non-current distinction is considered to have little relevance, most entities present classified balance sheets, i.e. current assets and current liabilities are shown separately, which permit ready determination of working capital.   *FAS 6.7*

Current liabilities are obligations, the liquidation of which is reasonably expected to require the use of existing resources classified as current assets or the creation of other current liabilities.   In practice, this classification is intended to include obligations that, by their terms, are due on demand or will be due on demand within one year, or operating cycle, if longer, after the balance sheet date, even though liquidation may not be expected within that period.   It also includes long-term debt that the company intends to repay within 12 months.   *ARB 43 Ch 3A.7-9*

A long-term obligation that is or will be callable by the lender, either because of a breach of the debt agreement at the balance sheet date or a breach that is not cured within a specified period of grace, should be classified as a current liability unless, before the balance sheet is issued, one of the following conditions is met: *FAS 78.5*

- the lender has waived or subsequently lost the right to demand repayment for more than one year (or operating cycle, if longer) from the balance sheet date; or

- for long-term obligations containing a grace period within which the breach may be remedied, it is probable that the violation will be cured within that period.

If a violation exists but the breach is waived for a stated period of time beyond the balance sheet date, the amount of the obligation and period of the waiver should be disclosed.   *S-X 4-08(c)*

Where a long-term debt agreement contains a subjective acceleration clause, the borrower should assess the likelihood that the lender will accelerate the debt's maturity under that clause.   In some situations, the circumstances, e.g. recurring losses or liquidity problems, would indicate that such debt should be classified as current.   Other situations would indicate only disclosure of the existence of such clauses.   Neither reclassification nor disclosure would be required if the likelihood of the acceleration of the due date were remote.   *FTB 79-3*

Short-term obligations, other than those arising from transactions in the normal course of business that are to be paid in customary terms, should be excluded from current liabilities only if the entity: *FAS 6.8-11*

- intends to refinance the obligation on a long-term basis, and

reschedule payments, on a long-term basis is completed after the balance sheet date and before the financial statements are authorised for issue.

IAS 1.59,61 Certain assets and liabilities that form part of the entity's working capital used in its normal operating cycle are classified as current assets and liabilities even when they will be realised or settled after more than twelve months. The same normal operating cycle applies to the classification of an entity's assets and liabilities and, when its duration is not clearly identifiable, is assumed to last twelve months.

IAS 1.67 Certain events which occur between the balance sheet date and the date the financial statements are authorised for issue, such as a refinancing, will qualify for disclosure as non-adjusting in accordance with IAS 10 *Events after the Balance Sheet Date* but will not result in the reclassification of a liability from current to non-current in the financial statements.

IAS 1.64 If an entity expects, and has the discretion, to refinance or roll over an obligation for at least twelve months after the balance sheet date under an existing loan facility, it classifies the obligation as non-current, even if it would otherwise be due within a shorter period. However, when refinancing or rolling over the obligation is not at the discretion of the entity (for example, there is no agreement to refinance), the potential to refinance is not considered and the obligation is classified as current.

IAS 1.65-66 When an entity breaches an undertaking under a long-term loan agreement on or before the balance sheet date with the effect that the liability becomes payable on demand, the liability is classified as current, even if the lender has agreed, after the balance sheet date and before the authorisation of the financial statements for issue, not to demand payment as a consequence of the breach. The liability is classified as current because, at the balance sheet date, the entity does not have an unconditional right to defer its settlement for at least twelve months after that date. However, the liability is classified as non-current if the lender agreed by the balance sheet date to provide a period of grace ending at least twelve months after the balance sheet date, within which the entity can rectify the breach and during which the lender cannot demand immediate repayment.

The classification and presentation requirements of IFRS 5 *Non-current Assets Held for Sale and Discontinued Operations*, which apply to disposal groups and all non-current assets recognised under IFRS, are addressed in section 1.9.3B.

1.6.3   Offsetting

IAS 1.32-35 Assets and liabilities and income and expenses should not be offset except where required or permitted by a Standard or Interpretation. Measuring assets net of valuation allowances, such as allowances for obsolescence or doubtful debts, is not offsetting.

Some transactions undertaken by an entity will be incidental to its main operating activities, for example disposal of non-current assets or reimbursement of expenditure relating to a provision. Presentation of the net income or expense is permitted in such cases where this reflects the substance of the transaction.

In addition, gains and losses arising from a group of similar transactions are reported on a net basis unless they are material in which case they should be reported separately.

- its ability to consummate the refinancing is demonstrated prior to the issuance of the financial statements in either of the following ways:

    (a)   an issue of a long-term obligation or equity securities occurring after the balance sheet date for the purpose of refinancing the short-term obligation on a long-term basis; or

    (b)   entering into a financing agreement, before the balance sheet is issued, which clearly permits the refinancing of the short-term obligation on a long-term basis on terms that are readily determinable, and all of the following conditions are met:

        (i)   the agreement does not expire within one year (or operating cycle) of the balance sheet date and during that period cannot be cancelled by the lender except for violation of a provision with which compliance is objectively determinable or measurable. A provision that can be evaluated differently by the parties to the agreement (such as 'a material adverse change' or 'failure to maintain satisfactory operations') is not objectively determinable;

        (ii)   there is no violation of any provision in the financing agreement at the balance sheet date nor in the period after that date but prior to the issuance of the balance sheet, or, if one exists at the balance sheet date or has occurred thereafter, a waiver has been obtained; and

        (iii) the lender is expected to be financially capable of honouring the agreement.

Although FAS 6 *Classification of Short-Term Obligations Expected to Be*   *FAS 6.13*
Refinanced requires the borrower to intend to refinance the short-term obligation on a long-term basis, this does not restrict the entity to refinance only using the committed facility available at the year end. An alternative source of financing could be used to refinance the short-term obligation when it becomes due; however, the entity must intend to exercise its rights under the existing facility if that other source does not materialise.

FAS 6 does not require that the lender and the provider of the facility be the same person or group of persons. A borrower should show short-term debt as long-term if it intends to refinance the debt on a long-term basis and, after the balance sheet date but before that balance sheet is issued, a long-term obligation or equity securities have been issued to refinance the short-term debt on a long-term basis.

1.6.3   Offsetting

It is a general principle of US GAAP that assets and liabilities should not be offset   *APB 10.7*
except where a right of set-off exists.

A right of set-off is a debtor's legal right (by contract or otherwise) to discharge all   *FIN 39.5-6*
or a portion of the debt owed to another party by applying against the debt an amount that the other party owes to the debtor. A right of set-off exists when all of the following conditions are met:

- each of two parties owes the other determinable amounts; the amounts do not have to be denominated in the same currency or bear the same interest rate nor do they need to have the same maturities. However, if the maturities are different, only the party with the nearer maturity can offset.

IAS 32.42   A financial asset and a financial liability should be offset and the net amount reported in the balance sheet when, and only when, an entity:

- currently has a legally enforceable right to set off the recognised amounts; and
- intends either to settle on a net basis, or to realise the asset and settle the liability simultaneously.

In accounting for a transfer of a financial asset that does not qualify for derecognition, the entity should not offset the transferred asset and the associated liability.

IAS 12.71   Deferred tax assets and deferred tax liabilities may be offset when certain strict criteria have been met.   These criteria are discussed in detail in section 17.4.1.

IAS 19.116   For pension plans, an entity may only offset an asset relating to one plan against a liability relating to another plan when it has a legally enforceable right to use a surplus in one plan to settle obligations under the other plan and it intends to settle the obligations on a net basis or simultaneously.

1.6.4   Layout of income statement

IAS 1.78,81   All items of income and expense recognised in a period should be included in the income statement unless another Standard or Interpretation requires otherwise. IAS 1 does not prescribe standard layouts for the income statement, but does require that the following information for the period be presented, as a minimum, on the face of the income statement:

- revenue;
- finance costs;
- share of the profit or loss of associates and joint ventures accounted for using the equity method;
- tax expense;
- a single amount comprising the total of (i) the post-tax profit or loss of discontinued operations and (ii) the post-tax gain or loss recognised on the measurement to fair value less costs to sell or on the disposal of the assets or disposal group(s) constituting the discontinued operation (see section 1.9.3A); and
- profit or loss.

IAS 1.82   The face of the income statement should also disclose the following items as allocations of the profit or loss for the period:

- profit or loss attributable to minority interest; and
- profit or loss attributable to equity holders of the parent.

IAS 1.86   If an item of income or expense is material, its nature and amount should be disclosed separately, either on the face of the income statement or in the notes.

IAS 1.95,125   The amount of dividends recognised as distributions to equity holders during the period and the related amount per share should be disclosed either on the face of the income statement or the statement of changes in equity (see section 1.6.6 below) or in the notes.   The notes should include details of dividends proposed or

- the reporting party has the right to set-off the amount owed with the amount owed by the other party;

- the reporting party intends to set-off; this criterion is met where there is acknowledgement of the intent by the reporting party and, if applicable, demonstration of the execution of the set-off in similar situations; and

- the right of set-off is enforceable at law. Legal constraints should be considered to determine whether the right will be enforceable.   *EITF D-43*

FIN 39 *Offsetting of Amounts Related to Certain Contracts* does not modify the requirements of other authoritative pronouncements which specify accounting treatments in circumstances that result in offsetting, e.g. FAS 87 *Employers' Accounting for Pensions* (accounting for pension plan assets and liabilities), FAS 109 *Accounting for Income Taxes* (net tax asset or liability amounts reported), AICPA Audit and Accounting Guides *Audits of Brokers and Dealers in Securities* (trade date accounting for trading portfolio positions).   *FIN 39.7*

The SEC staff's opinion is that even when items can be directly associated, it is not appropriate to offset assets and liabilities without the benefit of an existing legal right.   *SAB (Topic 11-D)*

1.6.4   Layout of income statement

There is no general requirement under US GAAP for entities to prepare an income statement in accordance with a specific layout. However, SEC registrants are required to prepare their income statements in conformity with Regulation S-X, which requires the following line items (where applicable) to be shown on the face of the income statement: *S-X 5-03*

- net sales and gross revenues:
  - net sales of tangible products;
  - operating revenues of public utilities or others;
  - income from rentals;
  - revenues from services; and
  - other revenues;

  each class which is not more than 10 % of the sum of the net sales and gross revenue items may be combined with another class, but if items are combined, related costs or expenses should be combined in a similar manner;

- costs and expenses applicable to sales and revenues:
  - cost of tangible goods sold;
  - operating expenses of public utilities or others;
  - expenses applicable to rental income;
  - cost of services; and
  - expenses applicable to other revenues;

- other operating costs and expenses;

- selling, general and administrative expenses;

- provision for doubtful accounts and notes;

- other general expenses;

- non-operating income (the following items may also be disclosed in the notes to the income statement):

declared before the issue of the financial statements but which were not recognised as a distribution in the period together with the amount of any cumulative preference dividends not recognised.

IAS 1.83-84 Additional line items, headings and sub-totals should be presented on the face of the income statement when such presentation is relevant to an understanding of the entity's financial performance.   Factors to be considered include materiality and the nature and function of the components of income and expenses.

IAS 1.85 Following the revision of IAS 1 in 2003, no item of income and expense may be presented as an extraordinary item, either on the face of the income statement or in the notes.

1.6.5   Classification of expenses

IAS 1.88-94 An entity should present an analysis of expenses using a classification based on either the nature of expenses or their function within the entity, whichever provides information that is reliable and more relevant.   Presentation of this analysis on the face of the income statement is encouraged.   Entities classifying expenses by function should disclose additional information on the nature of expenses, including depreciation, amortisation and employee benefits expenses.

1.6.6   Statement of changes in equity and comprehensive income

IAS 1.96-97 IFRSs do not prescribe a standard layout for the statement of changes in equity, but does require that the following information be presented on the face of the statement:

- profit or loss for the period;
- each item of income and expense for the period that, as required by other Standards or Interpretations, is recognised directly in equity, and the total of these items;
- total income and expense for the period (calculated as the sum of the above two items), showing separately the totals attributable to equity holders of the parent and to minority interest; and
- for each component of equity, the effects of changes in accounting policies and, separately, the correction of errors recognised in accordance with IAS 8.

- – dividends;
- – interest on securities;
- – profits on securities (net of losses); and
- – miscellaneous other income;

- interest and amortisation of debt discount and expense;
- non-operating expenses (the following items may also be disclosed in the notes to the income statement):
  - – losses on securities (net of profits); and
  - – miscellaneous income deductions;
- income or loss before income tax expense and appropriate items below;
- income tax expense (only taxes based on income);
- minority interest in income of consolidated subsidiaries;
- equity in earnings of unconsolidated subsidiaries and 50 percent or less owned persons;
- income or loss from continuing operations;
- discontinued operations;
- income or loss before extraordinary items and cumulative effects of changes in accounting principles;
- extraordinary items, less applicable tax;
- cumulative effects of changes in accounting principles;
- net income or loss; and
- earnings per share data.

1.6.5   Classification of expenses

There is no general requirement under US GAAP for entities to prepare an income statement in accordance with a specific layout.

1.6.6   Statement of changes in equity and comprehensive income

Comprehensive income is defined as the change in equity (net assets) of an entity during a period from transactions and other events and circumstances from non-owner sources. Under FAS 130 *Reporting Comprehensive Income*, comprehensive income is used to describe the total of all components of comprehensive income, i.e. net income plus other comprehensive income.

CON 6

FAS 130.10

All components of comprehensive income should be separately reported in the period in which they are recognised. A total amount for comprehensive income should be disclosed in the financial statements where the components of other comprehensive income are reported.

FAS 130.14

Comprehensive income and its components should be displayed in a financial statement with equal prominence to other financial statements that constitute a full

FAS 130.22-23

117

A statement of changes in equity that comprises only the items above should be titled a statement of recognised income and expense.

In addition, an entity should present, either on the face of the statement or in the notes:

- the amounts of transactions with equity holders in their capacity as such, showing distributions separately;
- the balance of retained earnings (i.e. accumulated profit or loss) at the beginning of the period and at the balance sheet date, and the changes during the period; and
- a reconciliation between the carrying amount of each class of contributed equity and each reserve at the beginning and the end of the period, separately disclosing each change.

IAS 1.100 Retrospective adjustments and restatements required by IAS 8 are made to the balance of retained earnings unless a Standard or Interpretation specifies that another component of equity should be adjusted. These adjustments are disclosed for each prior period and the beginning of the period.

Comprehensive income is not defined in IFRSs and there is currently no Standard which deals with the subject.

COMMENT

The IASB and the FASB have an ongoing project on the subject of Performance Reporting (Reporting Comprehensive Income). The project is intended to establish standards for the presentation of information in the financial statements in order to enhance the usefulness of that information in assessing the financial performance and financial position of an entity. The project includes consideration of whether there should be a requirement to produce a single statement of comprehensive income.

At the time of writing, the Boards expect to issue a public document in 2006.

1.7   UNUSUAL OR INFREQUENT ITEMS

1.7.1   Definition

IAS 1.11 Items are material if their omission or misstatement 'could, individually or collectively, influence the economic decisions of users taken on the basis of the financial statements. Materiality depends on the size and nature of the omission or misstatement judged in the surrounding circumstances. The size or nature of the item, or a combination of both, could be the determining factor'.

set of financial statements.   The following three alternative disclosure formats are permitted:

- a statement of income and comprehensive income with other comprehensive income items added to the income statement after net income;
- a separate statement of comprehensive income to include net income and other comprehensive income items; or
- in the statement of changes in shareholders' equity.

Items included in other comprehensive income should be classified based on their nature, e.g. foreign currency items, minimum pension liability adjustments, or unrealised gains and losses on certain investments in debt and equity securities.   *FAS 130.17*

Reclassification adjustments should be made to avoid including amounts in net income that had also been included in comprehensive income for the same, or a previous, period.   Reclassification adjustments should be displayed either gross on the face of the financial statement or net, with the gross change displayed in the notes to the financial statements, except minimum pension liability which should be displayed net.   *FAS 130.18-21*

The timing of recognition and measurement of items that make up comprehensive income are governed by other FASB statements.   *FAS 130.7*

FAS 130 requires the amount of income tax expense or benefit allocated to each component of other comprehensive income to be displayed either on the face of the financial statements or in a note.   *FAS 130.24-25*

The accumulated total of other comprehensive income is required to be disclosed separately from retained earnings and additional paid-in-capital in the equity section of the balance sheet.   The accumulated balances for each classification of other comprehensive income should be disclosed in the separate component of equity on the face of a statement of financial position, in a statement of changes in equity, or in notes to the financial statements.   The classifications should correspond to those used elsewhere in the financial statements.   *FAS 130.26*

COMMENT

The FASB and IASB have a joint project to establish standards for the presentation of information in financial statements that would improve the usefulness of that information.   The project will focus on form and content, classification and aggregation, and display of specified items and summarised amounts on the face of the basic financial statements (for both interim and annual periods).

The Boards anticipate that an initial public discussion document will be issued in late 2005.

1.7   UNUSUAL OR INFREQUENT ITEMS

1.7.1   Definition

A material event or transaction that is unusual in nature or occurs infrequently, but not both, should be reported as a separate component of income from continuing operations.   *APB 30.26*

1.7.2   Disclosure

IAS 1.29,86 Separate disclosure of the nature and amount of any material items of income or expense is required. For items which are not individually material, each material class of similar items should be presented separately in the financial statements. Items of a dissimilar nature or function should be presented separately unless they are immaterial (see also section 1.5.1 above).

1.8   EXTRAORDINARY ITEMS

1.8.1   Definition

IAS 1.85 Following the revision of IAS 1 in 2003 (effective for accounting periods beginning on or after 1 January 2005, although earlier application is encouraged), entities are not permitted to present any items of income or expense as extraordinary items, either on the face of the income statement or in the notes.

1.8.2   Disclosure

Separate disclosure of extraordinary items is not permitted under the revised version of IAS 1.

1.7.2   Disclosure

The nature and financial effects of each unusual or infrequent event or transaction should be disclosed on the face of the income statement or alternatively in the notes.   Such items should not be reported on the face of the income statement net of income taxes or in a manner that may imply that they are extraordinary items. The earnings per share effects of such items should not be disclosed on the face of the income statement. *APB 30.26*

For public companies, restructuring charges must be presented as a component of income from continuing operations and separately disclosed if material.   If presented separately, a restructuring charge should not be preceded by a sub-total showing 'income from continuing operations before restructuring charge'. *SAB 67 (Topic 5-P) EITF 87-4*

Charges that relate to activities for which the revenues and expenses have historically been included in operating income should generally be classified as an operating expense, separately disclosed if material.   Charges that relate to activities previously included under 'other income and expenses' should be similarly classified, also separately disclosed if material.

Disclosures required for restructuring charges are discussed in section 18.9.1.

1.8   EXTRAORDINARY ITEMS

1.8.1   Definition

Extraordinary items are events and transactions that are distinguished by their unusual nature and by the infrequency of their occurrence.   They should possess both of the following criteria: *APB 30.20*

- a high degree of abnormality, being of a type clearly unrelated to, or only incidentally related to, the ordinary and typical activities of the enterprise; and

- being of a type that would not reasonably be expected to recur in the foreseeable future, taking into account the environment in which the entity operates.

A   *Exceptions to the definition*

Negative goodwill (see section 3.4.5B) should be allocated to reduce proportionately the values assigned to the acquired assets, including research and development assets acquired and charged to expense, except (a) financial assets other than equity accounted investments, (b) assets to be disposed of by sale, (c) deferred tax assets, (d) prepaid assets relating to pension or other post-retirement benefit plans, and (e) any other current assets.   Any remainder should be recognised as an extraordinary gain. *FAS 141.44-46*

1.8.2   Disclosure

Extraordinary items should be disclosed after the results from operations. Descriptive captions and the amounts for individual extraordinary events or transactions should be disclosed, preferably on the face of the income statement. *APB 30.11*

The nature of an extraordinary event or transaction and the principal items entering in the determination of an extraordinary gain or loss should be described.

1.9   NON-CURRENT ASSETS HELD FOR SALE AND DISCONTINUED OPERATIONS

COMMENT

IFRS 5.43-44   IFRS 5 applies to accounting periods beginning on or after 1 January 2005 although earlier application is encouraged.   It should be applied prospectively to non-current assets (or disposal groups) that meet the criteria for classification as held for sale and operations that meet the criteria to be discontinued after the effective date of the Standard.   An entity may apply the Standard from any date before the effective date of 1 January 2005 provided the valuations and other information needed to apply IFRS 5 were obtained at the time the criteria were originally met.

1.9.1   Definitions

A   *Discontinued operations*

IFRS 5.31-32,   A discontinued operation is a component of an entity that either has been disposed
Appx A   of, or is classified as held for sale (see section 1.9.1B below), and:

- represents a separate major line of business or geographical area of operations;
- is part of a single co-ordinated plan to dispose of a separate major line of business or geographical area of operations; or
- is a subsidiary acquired exclusively with a view to resale.

A component of an entity comprises operations and cash flows that can be clearly distinguished from the rest of the entity, both operationally and for financial reporting purposes (i.e. it will have been a cash-generating unit or a group of such units while being held for use).

B   *Classification as held for sale*

IFRS 5.6-9   A non-current asset (or disposal group – see definition below) should be classified
IFRS 5.Appx B   as held for sale if its carrying amount will be recovered principally through sale rather than continuing use.   In order for this to be the case, the asset (or disposal group) must be available for immediate sale in its present condition subject only to terms that are usual and customary for the sale of such assets and the sale must be 'highly probable', which means that:

- the appropriate level of management must be committed to it;
- an active programme to find a buyer and complete the plan must have been initiated;
- the asset (or disposal group) must be actively marketed at a price which is reasonable in relation to its current fair value;
- there should be an expectation that the sale will be completed within twelve months of classification as held for sale (unless there is a delay due to events or circumstances beyond the entity's control and the entity remains committed to the plan); and

Taxes applicable to extraordinary items should be disclosed on the face of the income statement if practicable, and otherwise in the notes.

Earnings per share data for extraordinary items should be presented either on the face of the income statement or in the notes.

APB 30.12
FAS 128.37

1.9 NON-CURRENT ASSETS HELD FOR SALE AND DISCONTINUED OPERATIONS

1.9.1 Definitions

A   Discontinued operations

The term discontinued operations refers to the operations of a component of an entity that either:

FAS 144.42

- has been sold, abandoned, spun off, or otherwise disposed of; or
- is classified as 'held for sale' (see definition of measurement date in section 1.9.2A).

'Component of an entity' describes operations and cash flows that can be clearly distinguished from the remainder of the entity, both operationally and for financial reporting purposes.   A component of an entity may be an operating segment (as defined in FAS 131 – see section 21.3.1), a reporting unit (as defined in FAS 142 – see section 9.5), a subsidiary, or an asset group (a group of assets representing the lowest level for which identifiable cash flows are largely independent of the cash flows of other groups of assets and liabilities).

FAS 144.41

FAS 144.4

The results of operations of a component of an entity that either has been disposed of or is classified as held for sale should be disclosed as discontinued operations if both:

FAS 144.42

- the operations and cash flows of the component have been (or will be) eliminated from the ongoing operations of the entity following the disposal; and
- the entity will not have any significant continuing involvement in the operations of the component after the disposal.

The EITF has considered how the above criteria should be applied and reached the following consensus:

EITF 03-13

- An assessment period may extend beyond one year after the component is actually disposed of in situations in which events or circumstances beyond an entity's control extend the period required to eliminate the direct cash flows of the disposed component or eliminate the significant continuing involvement in the ongoing operations of the disposed component provided that the entity

- the actions required to complete the plan should indicate that significant changes to, or withdrawal from, the plan are unlikely.

IFRS 5.10   For the purposes of IFRS 5, sale transactions include exchanges of non-current assets when the exchange has commercial substance (see sections 6.2.3A, 7.2.1 and 8.2).

IFRS 5.Appx A   A disposal group is 'a group of assets to be disposed of, by sale or otherwise, together as a group in a single transaction, and liabilities directly associated with those assets that will be transferred in the transaction'.   A disposal group:

- may be a group of cash-generating units, a single cash-generating unit or part of a cash-generating unit.   Once classified as a disposal group, however, the relevant assets and liabilities will be treated separately from other cash-generating units;
- includes goodwill, where the disposal group is a cash-generating unit to which goodwill has been allocated or is an operation within such a unit; and
- may include any assets and liabilities of the entity, including current assets, current liabilities and assets which are excluded from the measurement requirements of IFRS 5 (see section 1.9.2A).

IFRS 5.11   Assets acquired specifically with the intention of sale should be classified as held for sale only if the one-year rule (referred to above) is met at the acquisition date and if it is highly probable that any of the criteria above which are not met at the acquisition date will be met shortly after the acquisition (usually within three months).

IFRS 5.13-14   A non-current asset (or disposal group) that is to be abandoned should not be classified as held for sale.   This includes assets which are to be held to the end of their economic life or closed rather than sold.   However, if the disposal group to be abandoned meets the criteria for being a discontinued operation, it should be treated as such in the income statement and notes from the date on which it ceases to be used (see sections 1.9.1A and 1.9.3).

A non-current asset that has temporarily been taken out of use should not be accounted for as if it had been abandoned and hence will not be disclosed as a discontinued operation.   Accounting for non-current assets and their presentation in the financial statements are also addressed in sections 6 to 8).

IFRS 5.12   If the held for sale criteria are not met until after the balance sheet date, the non-current asset (or disposal group) may not be classified as held for sale at the balance sheet date but disclosure should be made in accordance with IFRS 5 when the criteria are met before the financial statements are issued.

1.9.2   Measurement

A   *Measurement of a non-current asset (or disposal group) held for sale*

IFRS 5.15-16   A non-current asset (or disposal group) held for sale should be measured at the lower of its carrying amount and fair value less costs to sell.   If a newly acquired asset meets the held for sale criteria, it should initially be measured at the lower of its carrying amount had it not been classified as held for sale (for example, cost) and fair value less costs to sell.   Assets acquired in a business combination will therefore be measured at fair value less costs to sell.

IFRS 5.4-5,18-19   Immediately before initial classification as held for sale, the carrying amounts of the assets (or all the assets and liabilities in the disposal group) are measured in

(1) takes the actions necessary to respond to those situations and (2) expects to eliminate the direct cash flows and the significant continuing involvement.

- The evaluation of whether the criteria have been met for a component that is either disposed of or classified as held for sale at the balance sheet date should include significant events or circumstances that occur after the balance sheet date but before the issuance of the financial statements. This guidance is limited to whether the operations of a component should be presented as discontinued operations.

B   *Classification as 'held for sale'*

A component of an entity to be sold should be classified as held for sale in the period in which all of the following criteria are met: *FAS 144.30-32*

- management having the authority to approve the action commits to a plan to sell of the component of the entity;
- the component of the entity is available for immediate sale;
- an active programme of actions to complete the sale has been initiated;
- the sale is probable and is expected to be completed within one year (subject to events or circumstances beyond an entity's control);
- the component of the entity is being actively marketed at a reasonable price in relation to its current fair value; and
- it is unlikely that there will be significant changes to the plan or that the plan will be withdrawn.

A newly acquired long-lived asset or asset group that will be sold rather than held and used should be classified as held for sale at the acquisition date only if the sale is probable and is expected to be completed within one year (subject to events or circumstances beyond an entity's control) and the other criteria above are probable of being met within a short period (within three months) after the acquisition.

If at any time the above criteria are no longer met, the component of the entity   *FAS 144.38*
should be reclassified as held and used (i.e. a component of continuing operations).

1.9.2   Measurement

A component of an entity classified as held for sale should be measured at the lower   *FAS 144.34-35*
of its carrying amount and fair value less the incremental direct costs to complete the sale. Assets should not be depreciated while classified as held for sale.

Future expected operating losses are excluded from direct cost to sell and also should not be indirectly recognised by reducing the carrying amount of the component to less than its fair value less cost to sell.

Any recognised gains or losses arising on initial measurement or subsequent   *FAS 144.37*
adjustments to fair value less cost to sell should be included in the results of operations of the component in discontinued operations. Recognition of a gain is

accordance with applicable Standards. However, IFRS 5 does not apply to the measurement of liabilities within a disposal group nor to the following assets, even if part of a disposal group, which are covered by the specified standards:

- deferred tax assets (IAS 12 *Income Taxes* – see section 17);

- assets arising from employee benefits (IAS 19 *Employee Benefits* – see sections 23-25);

- financial assets within the scope of IAS 39 *Financial Instruments: Recognition and Measurement* – see section 11;

- investment property measured in accordance with the fair value model (IAS 40 – see section 8);

- biological assets or agricultural produce at the point of harvest assets (IAS 41); and

- contractual rights under insurance contracts (IFRS 4 *Insurance Contracts*).

On subsequent remeasurement, the carrying amounts of liabilities and assets outside the scope of measurement of IFRS 5 are remeasured in accordance with the applicable Standards, before the fair value less costs to sell of the disposal group is remeasured.

IFRS 5.17 When the sale is expected to occur after more than one year, the costs to sell should be measured at their present value with any increase over time recognised as a financing cost in profit or loss.

IFRS 5.25 An asset (or disposal group) classified as held for sale should not be depreciated (or amortised). However, interest and other expenses attributable to liabilities included in a disposal group held for sale should continue to be recognised.

B   Recognition of impairment losses and reversals

IFRS 5.20 An entity shall recognise an impairment loss for any initial or subsequent write-down of the asset (or disposal group) to fair value less costs to sell, to the extent not already recognised (as a result of measurement of assets and liabilities outside the scope of the measurement requirements of IFRS 5).

IFRS 5.21-22 A gain shall be recognised for an increase in fair value less costs to sell of an asset (or a disposal group, to the extent not already recognised), but not in excess of the cumulative impairment loss recognised either in accordance with IFRS 5, or previously in accordance with IAS 36 (see section 9).

IFRS 5.23 The impairment loss (or subsequent gain) for a disposal group reduces or increases the carrying amount of the non-current assets in the order of allocation set out in IAS 36 (see section 9.6).

IFRS 5.37 Gains or losses on remeasurement of a non-current asset (or disposal group) classified as held for sale are included within profits or losses from continuing operations, unless the definition of a discontinued operation is met.

C   Gain or loss on disposal

IFRS 5.24
IAS 36.104,122 Any gain or loss that has not been recognised by the date of the sale of a non-current asset (or disposal group) should be recognised at the date the asset (or disposal group) is derecognised. Requirements relating to derecognition are set out in IAS 16 for property, plant and equipment (see section 7.2.1) and IAS 38 for intangible assets (see section 6.4).

restricted to the cumulative loss previously recognised for a write-down to fair value less cost to sell.   Any previously unrecognised gain or loss arising from the sale of a component of an entity is recognised at the date of sale.

Adjustments to estimates of contingent liabilities or assets remaining after disposal of a component of an entity or that arose pursuant to the terms of the disposal transaction generally should be classified in discontinued operations.   *FAS 144.44*

A   Measurement date

A component of an entity is first recognised as a discontinued operation in the period in which it is either sold or otherwise disposed of, or is classified as held for sale.   A component of an entity is classified as held for sale only when all of the criteria set out in section 1.9.1A are met.   *FAS 144.42*

If the criteria in section 1.9.1A are met after the balance sheet date but before the financial statements are issued the component should be classified within continuing operations in those financial statements.   *FAS 144.33*

B   Gain or loss on disposal

The gain or loss on disposal should include such adjustments, costs, and expenses that are directly related to the disposal of the component.   *FAS 144.35*

Gains or losses from pension settlements and curtailments (see section 23.4.5) that are directly related to a disposal of a component of an entity also should be taken into account.   *FAS 106.96*

A gain or loss on the disposal of a component should be disclosed either on the face of the income statement or in the notes to the financial statements.   *FAS 144.47*

1.9.3　Presentation

A　Income statement

IFRS 5.33　An entity should disclose:

- a single amount on the face of the income statement comprising the total of:
  - the post-tax profit or loss of discontinued operations; and
  - the post-tax gain or loss recognised on the measurement to fair value less costs to sell or on the disposal of the assets or disposal group(s) constituting the discontinued operation.
- an analysis of the single amount above into:
  - the revenue, expenses and pre-tax profit or loss of discontinued operations;
  - the related income tax expense (see section 17.4.2);
  - the gain or loss recognised on the measurement to fair value less costs to sell or on the disposal of the assets or disposal group(s) constituting the discontinued operation; and
  - the related income tax expense (see section 17.4.2).

  The analysis may be presented either on the face of the income statement or in the notes. If presented on the face of the income statement, it should be presented separately from continuing operations in a section identified as relating to discontinued operations. The analysis is not required for newly acquired subsidiaries that, on acquisition, meet the criteria in paragraph 11 of IFRS 5 as held for sale.
- either in the notes or on the face of the financial statements, the net cash flows attributable to the operating, investing and financing activities of discontinued operations. This cash flow information is not required for newly acquired subsidiaries that, on acquisition, meet the criteria in paragraph 11 of IFRS 5 to be classified as held for sale.

IFRS 5.34　Comparative figures in the income statement should be restated in order to provide the above disclosures for all periods presented in respect of all operations which are discontinued as at the latest balance sheet date.

IFRS 5.35　Any adjustments made in the current period to amounts previously presented in discontinued operations that are directly related to the disposal of a discontinued operation in a prior period should be classified separately in discontinued operations. The nature and amount of such adjustments should be disclosed.

IFRS 5.36　If an entity ceases to classify a component of an entity as held for sale, any results of that component which were previously presented as part of discontinued operations should be reclassified to income from continuing operations for all periods presented. Comparative figures should be described as having been re-presented.

B　Balance sheet

IFRS 5.2　The classification and presentation requirements of IFRS 5 *Non-current Assets Held for Sale and Discontinued Operations* apply to all non-current assets recognised under IFRSs (including, in a liquidity presentation, those that include an amount expected to be recovered more than twelve months after the balance sheet date) and disposal groups.

1.9.3   Presentation

A   Income statement

The income statements for each period presented should be completely reclassified   *FAS 144.42-43*
so that the results of continuing operations are reported separately from
discontinued operations.

Income statements for current and prior periods that include the results of
discontinued operations should report those results, less applicable income taxes, as
a separate component of income before extraordinary items and the cumulative
effect of accounting changes (if applicable).

The results of discontinued operations should be reported in the period(s) in which
they occur and should include only income and costs directly related to the
discontinued operations.

General corporate overhead may not be allocated to discontinued operations.
Reorganisation or restructuring of continuing operations resulting from a sale or
termination should be included under continuing operations.

Interest on debt that is to be assumed by the buyer and interest on debt that is   *EITF 87-24*
required to be repaid as a result of the disposal transaction should be allocated to
discontinued operations.   The allocation to discontinued operations of other
consolidated interest that is not directly attributable to or related to other operations
of the enterprise is permitted but not required.

Any recognised gains or losses arising on adjustments to the carrying amounts of   *FAS 144.44*
discontinued operations, and any previously unrecognised gain or loss arising from
its sale, should be reported in discontinued operations.

IFRS 5.3,6   Assets classified as non-current, together with any assets which would normally be classified as non-current but which have been acquired exclusively for resale, should only be reclassified as current assets when they meet the criteria to be classified as held for sale in accordance with IFRS 5.   Assets (or disposal groups) which are held for sale are those assets whose carrying amount will be recovered principally through sale rather than continuing use.

IFRS 5.30,38-39   The aim of IFRS 5 is that entities should present and disclose information that enables users of the financial statements to evaluate the financial effects of disposals of non-current assets (or disposal groups).   It requires:

- non-current assets classified as held for sale (see section 1.9.1B) and the assets of a disposal group classified as held for sale to be presented separately from other assets in the balance sheet; and

- the liabilities of a disposal group classified as held for sale to be presented separately from other liabilities in the balance sheet.

The assets and liabilities may not be offset and presented as a single amount.

In addition to the above:

- the major classes of assets and liabilities classified as held for sale should normally be shown separately either on the face of the balance sheet or in the notes (although this is not required if the disposal group is a newly acquired subsidiary which, on acquisition, meets the criteria to be classified as held for sale); and

- any cumulative income or expense recognised directly in equity relating to a non-current asset (or disposal group) classified as held for sale should be presented separately.

IFRS 5.40   Amounts which were presented in the balance sheets for prior periods as non-current assets or as assets and liabilities of disposal groups should not be reclassified or re-presented to reflect the classification in the balance sheet for the latest period presented.

For joint ventures and associates however, prior periods are restated (see section 4.4.5).

1.9.4   Other disclosures

IFRS 5.41   The notes should include the following information in the period in which a non-current asset (or disposal group) has been either classified as held for sale or sold:

- a description of the non-current asset (or disposal group);

- a description of the facts and circumstances of the sale, or leading to the expected disposal, and the expected manner and timing of that disposal;

- the gain or loss recognised in accordance with IFRS 5 and, if not separately presented on the face of the income statement, the caption in that statement that includes the gain or loss; and

- if applicable, the segment in which the non-current asset (or disposal group) is presented in accordance with IAS 14 *Segment Reporting*.

IFRS 5.42   These disclosures are also required (with the exception of the gain or loss on remeasurement) where a non-current asset (or disposal group) has been classified as

1.9.4   Other disclosures

The notes to the financial statements should disclose, for a component of the entity   *FAS 144.47*
that is either disposed of or is held for sale:

- a description of the facts and circumstances surrounding the disposal, the expected manner and timing of the disposal, and, if not separately presented on the face of the statement, the carrying amount(s) of the major classes of assets and liabilities of component to be disposed of;

- the gain or loss and if not separately presented on the face of the income statement, the caption in the income statement that includes the gain or loss;

- if applicable, amounts of revenue and pre-tax profit or loss reported in discontinued operations; and

- if applicable, the segment in which the component is reported under FAS 131 (see section 21).

held for sale after the balance sheet date, but before issuance of the financial statements.

1.9.5   Other issues

A   Discontinued operations subsequently retained

IFRS 5.26,29,42   If a non-current asset (or disposal group) no longer meets the held for sale criteria or if an asset or liability is removed from a disposal group, an entity should cease to classify the asset (or disposal group) as held for sale and should disclose, in the period of the decision to change the plan, a description of the facts and circumstances leading to that decision and the effect of the decision on the results of operations for the period and any prior periods presented.

IFRS 5.27-28   An asset which ceases to be held for sale (or which ceases to be in a disposal group which is held for sale) should be measured at the lower of:

- its carrying amount before it was held for sale (as adjusted for any depreciation, amortisation or revaluations which would have taken place had it not been classified as held for sale); and

- its recoverable amount at the date of the decision not to sell.

Apart from any revaluation increases or decreases which should be treated in accordance with the requirements of IAS 16 or IAS 38 (see sections 6.2.5 and 7.2.2), any adjustments to the carrying amount as a result of the above remeasurement should be taken to income from continuing operations in the period in which the asset no longer qualifies as held for sale.   These adjustments should be presented in the same income statement caption used to present the prior gains or losses on remeasurement, if any.

IFRS 5.29   If an asset or liability is removed from a disposal group classified as held for sale, the remaining assets and liabilities should be measured as a disposal group only if they continue to meet the criteria.   Otherwise, non-current assets that continue to meet the criteria should be individually valued as at the date of the removal at the lower of their carrying amount and fair value less costs to sell.   Any other non-current assets should cease to be classified as held for sale.

IFRS 5.36   Where applicable, the income statement should be restated (see section 1.9.3A above).

B   Disposals and terminations that do not qualify as discontinued operations

Any disposal or termination which fails to meet the definition of a discontinued operation should be accounted for within continuing operations.

1.10   CHANGE IN ACCOUNTING POLICY

IAS 8.15   Users of financial statements need to be able to compare the financial statements of an entity over time to identify trends in its financial position, financial performance

If an entity decides to keep a component that it previously classified as held for sale, the notes to the financial statements should include a description of the facts and circumstances leading to the change in the disposal plan and disclose its effect on the results of operations for the period and any prior periods presented. *FAS 128.37*

Earnings per share data for a discontinued operation should be presented either on the face of the income statement or in the notes.

1.9.5   Other issues

A   Discontinued operations subsequently retained

If an entity decides to keep a component that it previously classified as held for sale, that component should be reclassified as held and used and the results of its operations previously reported in discontinued operations should be reclassified and included in income from continuing operations for all periods presented. The reclassified component should be measured at the lower of (1) carrying amount before classification as held for sale, adjusted for any depreciation/amortisation that would have been recognised had the component not been classified as held for sale, and (2) fair value at the date of the subsequent decision not to sell. *FAS 144.38-39*

B   Disposals and terminations that do not qualify as discontinued operations

The gain or loss on a sale of a portion of a line of business that is not a component of an entity (as defined in section 1.9.1) should be calculated in the same manner as if it were a component of an entity. However, the operating results should be included within continuing operations, possibly reported as a separate component of income from continuing operations (as an unusual or infrequent item – see section 1.7), it should not be reported on the face of the income statement in a manner that would suggest that it is a disposal of a component of an entity or a discontinued operation. Similarly, revenues and related costs and expenses of the operations for prior periods should not be segregated on the face of the income statement. The notes to the financial statements should contain the disclosures noted in section 1.9.4 if the information is known.

A component of an entity to be disposed of other than by sale (e.g. closure or abandonment) should continue to be classified and accounted for as a continuing operation until the disposal is completed. *FAS 144.27*

1.10   CHANGE IN ACCOUNTING POLICY

Accounting changes made in conformity with authoritative pronouncements should be implemented in accordance with guidance provided in those pronouncements. *APB 20.4*
FIN 20.5

and cash flows.   Consistent application of accounting policies therefore underpins the preparation of financial statements.

1.10.1   When can a change in accounting policy occur?

IAS 8.14   Accounting policies should be applied consistently unless a change:

- is required by a Standard or Interpretation; or
- results in the financial statements providing reliable and more relevant information.

IAS 8.16   IAS 8 clarifies that the following are not changes in accounting policy:

- the application of an accounting policy for transactions, other events or conditions that differ in substance from those previously occurring; and
- the application of a new accounting policy for transactions, other events or conditions that did not occur previously or were immaterial.

IAS 8.17   The initial application of a policy of asset revaluation in accordance with IAS 16 *Property, Plant and Equipment* or IAS 38 *Intangible Assets* is a change in an accounting policy but should be dealt with as a revaluation in accordance with those Standards rather than in accordance with IAS 8.

1.10.2   Reporting a change in accounting policy

IAS 8.19-20   A change in accounting policy in order to apply a Standard or an Interpretation for the first time must be accounted for in accordance with any specific transitional provisions of that Standard or Interpretation.   Where there are no such provisions, or where the change in policy is voluntary (this excludes early application of a Standard or Interpretation), the change should be applied retrospectively, i.e. as if it had always been applied.

IAS 8.5,22-24   Where retrospective application is impracticable (i.e. it cannot be done after making every reasonable effort to do so) because the period-specific effects for one or more comparative periods cannot be determined, the new policy should be applied to the carrying amounts of assets and liabilities from the beginning of the earliest period for which retrospective application is practicable, with a corresponding adjustment to the opening balance of each affected component of equity for that period.

IAS 8.25   When it is impracticable to determine the cumulative effect at the beginning of the current period of a change in accounting policy, the comparative information should be adjusted to apply the new accounting policy prospectively from the earliest date practicable.   The entity therefore disregards the portion of the cumulative adjustment arising before that date.

IAS 8.27,50-53   IAS 8 outlines the considerations an entity should make in assessing whether retrospective application and restatement are impracticable.   A distinction is drawn between information that provides evidence of circumstances that existed at the relevant date and would have been available when the financial statements for that period were authorised for issue and other information.   It is recognised that significant estimates are often required but hindsight should not be used when applying a new accounting policy to, or correcting amounts for, a prior period.

Accordingly, guidance contained here only applies in those circumstances where the pronouncement does not specify the manner in which a change in accounting principle upon adoption should be reported.

1.10.1   When can a change in accounting policy occur?

An enterprise must justify the use of an alternative accounting principle as being preferable and the nature and justification of the change must be disclosed.   *APB 20.16-17*

Domestic SEC registrants must obtain a preferability letter from the auditor for any accounting change. Item 601 of Regulation S-K states that a preferability letter is not required when an accounting change is made in response to standards adopted by the FASB. Also, the SEC staff's administrative practice is not to require a preferability letter for changes made on the initial adoption of a method of accounting prescribed by a SAB, an EITF Consensus, a FASB Technical Bulletin, an AICPA Statement of Position or an AICPA Accounting and Auditing Guide.

The issuance of a new accounting standard that expresses a preference for an accounting principle or rejects a specific accounting principle is sufficient support for a change in accounting principle.

1.10.2   Reporting a change in accounting policy

A   Cumulative catch up adjustments

With the exception of a few specific situations (discussed below), a change of accounting principle should be recognised by a cumulative 'catch-up' adjustment, which is included in income in the year of the change and disclosed between the captions 'extraordinary items' and 'net income'. Although prior period amounts are not restated, the income before extraordinary items and net income computed on a pro forma retroactive basis should be shown on the face of the income statement for all periods presented.   *APB 20.19-21*

Pro forma earnings per share amounts for income before extraordinary items and net income should be disclosed on the face of the income statement. Earnings per share amounts for the cumulative effect of an accounting change should also be shown either on the face of the income statement or in the related notes.   *APB 20.21*

A change in method of depreciation should be accounted for as an accounting change and the retroactive effect should be included in net income of the year of the change as a cumulative 'catch-up' adjustment if the new method is to be applied to previously recorded assets. A company is permitted to adopt a different method of depreciation for newly acquired assets only, but a description of the nature of the change in method and its effects on income before extraordinary items and net income of the period of the change, together with the related per share amounts, should be disclosed.   *APB 20.23-24*

Disclosure

IAS 8.28   When initial application of a Standard or Interpretation has an effect on the current or any prior period, would have such an effect except that it is impracticable to determine the adjustment or might have an effect on future periods, an entity should disclose:

(a)   the title of the Standard or Interpretation;

(b)   when applicable, that the change in accounting policy is made in accordance with its transitional provisions;

(c)   the nature of the change in the accounting policy;

(d)   when applicable, a description of the transitional provisions;

(e)   when applicable, the transitional provisions that might have an effect on future periods;

(f)   for the current period and each prior period presented, to the extent practicable, the amount of the adjustment for each financial statement line items affected and, where IAS 33 *Earnings Per Share* applies, the adjustment to basic and diluted earnings per share;

(g)   to the extent practicable, the amount of the adjustment relating to periods before those presented; and

(h)   if retrospective application is required but is impracticable for a particular prior period or for periods before those presented, the reason for this should be given together with a description of how, and from when, the change in accounting policy has been applied.

The financial statements of subsequent periods need not repeat these disclosures.

IAS 8.29   When a voluntary change in accounting policy has an effect on the current or any prior period, would have such an effect except that it is impracticable to determine the adjustment or might have an effect on future periods, an entity should make the disclosures set out in points (c) and (f)-(h) above and should also disclose the reasons why the new policy provides reliable and more relevant information.   Again, the financial statements of subsequent periods need not repeat these disclosures.

IAS 8.30-31   When an entity has not applied a new Standard or Interpretation that has been issued but is not yet effective, it should disclose this fact together with known or reasonably estimable information relevant to assessing the impact of the Standard or Interpretation on the entity's financial statements when it is first applied.

1.11   CHANGE IN ACCOUNTING ESTIMATE

IAS 8.33-34   The use of reasonable estimates is an essential part of the preparation of financial statements and does not undermine their reliability.   An estimate may need revision if changes occur in the circumstances on which the estimate was based or as a result of new information or more experience.   The revision of an estimate does not relate to prior periods and is not the correction of an error.

IAS 8.35   A change in the measurement basis is a change in accounting policy not the change of an estimate.   When it is difficult to distinguish between a change in accounting policy and a change in accounting estimate, the change is treated as a change in accounting estimate.

B Retroactive restatement

As mentioned earlier, certain changes in accounting principles should be reported by restatement of financial statements of all prior periods.   The following changes should be accounted for by retroactive restatement:

APB 20.27

- a change from the last-in, first-out method of inventory valuation to another method;

- a change in accounting for long-term construction type contracts;

- a change to or from the 'full cost' method in the extractive industries; and

- a change from retirement-replacement-betterment accounting to depreciation accounting.

The nature of, and justification for, a change in accounting principle should be disclosed in the period the change was adopted.

APB 20.28

The effect of the change on income before extraordinary items, net income and the related per share amounts should be disclosed for all periods presented, either on the face of the income statement or in the notes.   The effect on opening retained earnings must also be given.

APB 20.28
APB 20.App B

A retroactive restatement may be made for a change in principle by a company whose securities are not currently widely held and where financial statements are first issued for the purpose of obtaining equity capital, registering securities or effecting a business combination.

APB 20.29

> **COMMENT**
>
> The FASB's proposed Statement of Financial Accounting Standards *Accounting Changes and Error Corrections a Replacement of APB Opinion No. 20 and FASB Statement No.* 3 would require retrospective application for discretionary changes in accounting principle as well as changes in accounting principle required by the issuance of new accounting pronouncements, in the absence of specific transitional guidance.   The proposed Statement would carry forward the guidance in APB 20 for the justification for a change in accounting principle.   The proposed standard is expected to be issued in the second quarter of 2005.

1.11 CHANGE IN ACCOUNTING ESTIMATE

Prior periods should not be restated nor should pro forma amounts be disclosed. The effect should be included in current and, where applicable, future years' income and the effect on income should be disclosed if material.

APB 20.31-33

The effect on income before extraordinary items and net income of the current period should be disclosed for a change in estimate that affects several future periods, e.g. estimates of economic lives of fixed assets or actuarial assumptions affecting pension costs.

APB 20.33

IAS 8.36-37   To the extent that a change in accounting estimate gives rise to changes in assets and liabilities, or relates to an item of equity, it should be recognised by adjusting the relevant carrying amount in the period of change.   The effect of any other change in accounting estimates should be recognised prospectively by inclusion in the profit or loss of the period of change if only one period is affected or in the profit or loss of the period of the change and future periods if both are affected.

Disclosure

IAS 8.39-40   An entity should disclose the nature and amount of a change in accounting estimate that affects the current period or is expected to affect future periods.   The disclosure of the effect on future periods need not be made if it is impracticable to estimate the effect, but that fact should be disclosed.

1.12   CORRECTION OF AN ERROR IN PREVIOUSLY ISSUED FINANCIAL STATEMENTS

IAS 8.41   Errors can arise in the recognition, measurement, presentation or disclosure of elements of financial statements.   Financial statements are not in compliance with IFRSs if they contain either material errors or immaterial errors made intentionally to achieve a particular presentation.   Where material errors relating to an accounting period are not discovered until a subsequent period, they should be corrected in the comparative information presented in that subsequent period.

IAS 8.42-43   Except where retrospective restatement is impracticable, material prior period errors should be corrected in the first set of financial statements authorised for issue after their discovery by:

- restating the comparative amounts for the prior period(s) presented in which the error occurred; or

- if the error occurred before the earliest period presented, restating the opening balances for the earliest prior period presented.

IAS 8.44-45,47   Where it is impracticable to determine the period-specific effects of an error, the opening balances should be restated for the earliest period for which retrospective restatement is practicable (which may be the current period).

Where it is impracticable to determine the cumulative effect, at the beginning of the current period, of an error on all prior periods, the comparative information should be restated to correct the error prospectively from the earliest date practicable. The entity therefore disregards the portion of the cumulative adjustment arising before that date.

IAS 8.50-53   IAS 8 outlines the considerations an entity should make in assessing whether retrospective application and restatement are impracticable (see section 1.10.2 above).

Disclosure

IAS 8.49   The following disclosures should be made in relation to the correction of a prior period error:

- the nature of the prior period error;

- for each prior period presented, to the extent practicable, the amount of the

COMMENT

The FASB's proposed Statement of Financial Accounting Standards *Accounting Changes and Error Corrections a Replacement of APB Opinion No. 20 and FASB Statement No. 3* would require retrospective application for discretionary changes in accounting principle as well as changes in accounting principle required by the issuance of new accounting pronouncements, in the absence of specific transitional guidance. A change in accounting estimate that is effected by a change in accounting principle, for example, a change in depreciation method, would be recognised as a change in estimate to be accounted for prospectively. The proposed standard is expected to be issued in the second quarter of 2005.

1.12　CORRECTION OF AN ERROR IN PREVIOUSLY ISSUED FINANCIAL STATEMENTS

Errors in financial statements which result from mathematical mistakes, mistakes in the application of accounting principles, or oversight or misuse of facts that existed at the time the financial statements were prepared should be accounted for as prior period adjustments.
APB 20.13,36
FAS 16.11

Disclosures should be given of the nature of the error and the effect of its correction on income before extraordinary items and net income and the related per share effects in the period in which the error was discovered and corrected.
APB 20.37
APB 9.18,26

Where financial statements for more than one period are given, the effect on the net income of prior periods should also be disclosed. Such disclosure should include the amounts of tax applicable to the prior period adjustments.

correction for each financial statement line items and, where IAS 33 *Earnings Per Share* applies, for basic and diluted earnings per share;

- the amount of the correction at the beginning of the earliest prior period presented; and
- if retrospective restatement is impracticable for a particular period, the reason for this should be given together with a description of how and from when the error has been corrected.

The financial statements of subsequent periods need not repeat these disclosures.

1.13   DEVELOPMENT STAGE COMPANIES

There is no specific guidance under IFRSs on financial reporting for development stage companies.

1.13　DEVELOPMENT STAGE COMPANIES

A development stage company is an entity devoting substantially all of its efforts to establishing a new business and either its planned principal operations have not commenced or its planned principal operations have commenced but have not yet generated significant revenues.

FAS 7.8-9

The financial statements should be identified as those of a development stage company and should include a description of the nature of the development stage activities.　The financial statements also should disclose:

FAS 7.10-12
S-X 10-01(a)(7)

- a balance sheet including any cumulative net losses reported, under a descriptive caption such as 'deficit accumulated during the development stage' in the stockholders' equity section;

- an income statement showing amounts of revenues and expenses for each period covered by the income statement, as well as cumulative amounts from the company's inception;

- a statement of cash flows showing the cash inflows and cash outflows for each period for which an income statement is presented as well as cumulative amounts from the company's inception;

- a statement of comprehensive income; and

FAS 130.6

- a statement of stock holders' equity showing each issuance of stock and all other equity movements since inception, including the date and number of securities issued, the amount of consideration received, and the nature of any non-cash consideration and the basis for assigned amounts.

The disclosures of cumulative amounts in the income statement and cash flow statement should be presented in 'cumulative to-date' columns.

Generally accepted accounting principles that apply to established operating entities should be applied to determine revenue recognition for development stage companies and whether costs should be deferred or charged to expense as incurred.

The financial statements for the first fiscal year in which the company is no longer considered to be in the development stage should disclose that in prior years it had been in the development stage.

FAS 7.13

141

Section 2   Consolidated financial statements

2.1   AUTHORITATIVE PRONOUNCEMENTS

- IFRS 3
- IAS 27
- IAS 31

- IAS 32
- SIC-12

COMMENT

The IASB is engaged in two projects – Business Combinations (Phase II) and Consolidation – that will impact the accounting treatment of subsidiaries. Phase II of the Business Combinations project on application of the purchase method is conducted jointly with the FASB. An Exposure Draft is expected in 2005 (with an IFRS to follow later in that year, likely to be effective for periods beginning on or after 1 January 2007). Application is expected to be prospective, with the inclusion of special transitional arrangements. The Business Combinations Project Phase II proposes, inter alia, that:

- consolidated goodwill would include the minority's share of goodwill;
- the minority would bear their proportionate share of losses, even if these reduced the minority interest (to be known as non-controlling interest) below zero; and
- transactions between majority and minority shareholders, not resulting in a loss of control over the subsidiary, would be treated as equity transactions not giving rise to a profit or loss.

The Consolidation Project will lead to a new IFRS to replace IAS 27 *Consolidated and Separate Financial Statements* and SIC-12 *Consolidation – Special Purpose Entities.* It is likely to contain significant changes to the criteria giving rise to a presumption of control. This is discussed further in sections 2.3 and 2.6.

2.2   CONSOLIDATION POLICY

IAS 27.1,9,12   A parent company shall prepare consolidated financial statements in which all subsidiaries are consolidated.

IAS 27.10   A parent company need not prepare consolidated financial statements if and only if:

- it is a wholly owned subsidiary itself (or is a partially-owned subsidiary, and its other owners, including those not entitled to vote, have been informed about, and do not object to, the parent company not presenting consolidated financial statements);
- the parent's debt or equity instruments are not traded in a public market;
- the parent did not file, nor is in the process of filing, its financial statements with a securities commission or other regulatory organisation for the purpose of issuing any class of instruments in a public market; and

Section 2   Consolidated financial statements

2.1   AUTHORITATIVE PRONOUNCEMENTS

- FAS 94
- FAS 140
- FAS 144
- ARB 43, Chapter 12

- ARB 51
- APB 18
- FIN 46(R)

COMMENT

Consolidations have been on the FASB's agenda for almost 20 years and a final Statement was planned but in January 2001, the FASB determined that there was not sufficient Board member support to proceed.

The Board issued FIN 46 *Consolidation of Variable Interest Entities an interpretation of ARB 51* in January 2003 (revised December 2003). FIN 46(R) introduces a new consolidation model—the variable interests model which provides guidance on how to apply the controlling financial interest criteria in ARB 51 to variable interest entities. See section 2.7.

Currently, the FASB is partnering with the IASB on a joint project that represents the second phase of the Board's overall project on business combinations – reconsidering aspects of the purchase method of accounting that were not deliberated in FAS 141 and FAS 142. Phase II will revise FAS 141 to require all acquisitions of businesses to be measured at the fair value of the business acquired and provide specific guidance for applying the purchase method. The FASB issued a summary of tentative decisions on phase II of the business combinations project as of July 2004. The FASB and IASB are developing common exposure drafts of proposed standards which are expected to be issued in the first half of 2005.

2.2   CONSOLIDATION POLICY

If an enterprise has one or more subsidiaries, consolidated statements rather than parent company financial statements are the appropriate general-purpose financial statements.   *FAS 94.61*

There is a presumption that consolidated statements are more meaningful than separate statements and that they are usually necessary for fair presentation when one company has an indirect or direct controlling financial interest in one or more other companies.   *ARB 51.1*

Equity accounting is not a valid substitute for consolidation.   *FAS 94.15(c)*

- the ultimate or any intermediate parent of the parent produces consolidated financial statements available for public use that comply with International Financial Reporting Standards.

IAS 27.30   A subsidiary is consolidated from its date of acquisition, the date on which the
IFRS 3.Appx A acquirer effectively obtains control, until the entity ceases to have control.

IAS 27.12   Where a subsidiary is classified as held for sale under IFRS 5 *Non-current Assets Held for Sale and Discontinued Operations*, the results and net assets of the subsidiary are consolidated but the subsidiary is measured, presented and disclosed in accordance with IFRS 5 (see section 1.9).

2.3   DEFINITION OF A SUBSIDIARY

IAS 27.4,IG2,IG4   A subsidiary is an entity (including an unincorporated entity) that is controlled by another entity, the parent.   The parent has control when it has the power to govern the financial and operating policies of an entity so as to obtain benefits from its activities.   It may be active or passive in nature and only one party will be the parent.

IAS 27.13   Control exists when the parent holds:

- directly or indirectly through subsidiaries, more than half of the voting power of an entity unless, in exceptional circumstances, it can be clearly demonstrated that such ownership does not constitute control;

- power over more than one half of the voting rights by virtue of an agreement with other investors;

- power to govern the financial and operating policies of the entity under a statute or an agreement;

- power to appoint or remove the majority of the members of the board of directors or equivalent governing body; or

- power to cast the majority of votes at meetings of the board of directors or equivalent governing body.

COMMENT

The IASB is engaged in a Consolidation Project will lead to a new IFRS to replace IAS 27 and SIC-12.   It is likely to contain significant changes to the criteria giving rise to a presumption of control.   The IASB has tentatively agreed that control should be based on satisfaction of all of the following:

- power criterion – the ability to set strategic direction and to direct operating policy and strategy.   In particular, the IASB have tentatively agreed that there should be a rebuttable presumption that the holdings of de facto agents of the company (such as senior employees, related parties etc) are available to the entity in assessing the power criterion.   There will also be additional clarification on potential voting rights;

- benefit criterion – the ability to access benefits; and

- the link – the ability to use power so as to protect or maintain benefits.

IAS 27.14-15   The existence and effect of potential voting rights (e.g. those arising from the
IAS 27.IG1-IG8   exercise of share options or conversion of convertible debt or equity) that are currently exercisable or currently convertible are also considered when assessing whether an entity controls another entity.   Potential voting rights are not currently exercisable or currently convertible when they cannot be exercised or converted

2.3   DEFINITION OF A SUBSIDIARY

'Subsidiary' refers to a corporation that is controlled, directly or indirectly, by another corporation.   The usual condition for control is ownership of a majority (over 50%) of the outstanding voting stock.   However, the power to control may also exist with a lesser percentage of ownership, for example, by contract, lease, and agreement with other stockholders or by court decree.   This definition excludes entities that are controlled through only significant minority ownership of the outstanding voting stock.   *APB 18.3(c)*

A   *SEC registrants*

In its rules on consolidation policy, the SEC emphasises the need to consider substance over form to determine the appropriate consolidation policy.   The SEC notes that there may be situations where consolidation of an entity, notwithstanding the lack of technical majority ownership, is necessary to present fairly the financial position and results of operations of the registrant, because of the existence of a parent/subsidiary relationship by means other than record, i.e. greater than 50%, ownership of voting stock.   *S-X 3A-02(a)*

The definition of a subsidiary contained in Regulation S-X is based on control and risk:

- Subsidiary – a subsidiary of a specified person is an affiliate (individual, corporation, partnership, trust or unincorporated organisation) controlled by such person directly or indirectly through one or more intermediaries.   *S-X 1-02(x)*

- Control – means the possession, direct or indirect, of the power to direct or cause the direction of management and policies of a person, whether through the ownership of voting shares, by contract or otherwise.   *S-X 1-02(g)*

- Voting shares – means the sum of all rights to vote for the election of directors.   *S-X 1-02(z)*

An entity may establish a controlling financial interest in another entity with little or no equity investment through either a nominee structure or other contractual arrangement.   EITF 97-2 relates to contractual arrangements between physician practices and entities established to manage the operations of those practices but the SEC has concluded that the guidance should be applied to similar arrangements in other industries.   Under the consensus, if all of the following requirements are met, then the management entity (entity 'A') has a controlling financial interest in the physician practice (entity 'B'):   *EITF 97-2*

145

until a future date or upon the occurrence of a future event. All potential voting rights should be considered, including potential voting rights held by other entities. All facts and circumstances should be considered including the terms of exercise of the potential voting rights and possible linked transactions. However, in making the assessment the intention of management and the financial ability to exercise or convert should not be taken into account.

2.4   EXCLUSION OF SUBSIDIARIES FROM CONSOLIDATED FINANCIAL STATEMENTS

IAS 27.12,19 Consolidated financial statements include all subsidiaries. A subsidiary is not excluded from consolidation simply because the investor is a venture capital organisation, mutual fund, unit trust or similar entity.

Where a subsidiary is classified as held for sale under IFRS 5 *Non-current Assets Held for Sale and Discontinued Operations*, the results and net assets of the subsidiary are consolidated but the subsidiary is measured, presented and disclosed in accordance with IFRS 5 (see section 1.9).

2.4.1   Unconsolidated subsidiaries

IAS 27.12 Consolidated financial statements include all subsidiaries.

- The arrangement term is either (a) the entire remaining legal life of entity A or (b) a period of 10 years or more; and is not terminable by entity B except in the case of gross negligence, fraud, or other illegal acts by entity A.

- Entity A Controls all major, or central operations of entity B including employee selection, hiring and firing and compensation arrangements.

- Entity A has a significant financial interest in entity B that is (a) unilaterally saleable or transferable; and (b) provides entity A with the right to receive income in an amount that fluctuates based on the performance, and therefore fair value, of entity B.

Based on this guidance, a contractual arrangement with a term of less than 10 years may not establish a controlling financial interest.

2.4   EXCLUSION OF SUBSIDIARIES FROM CONSOLIDATED FINANCIAL STATEMENTS

Consolidation is required of all majority-owned subsidiaries, i.e. all companies in which a parent has a controlling financial interest directly or indirectly, except: *FAS 94.13*

- if control does not rest with the majority owner; or

- if the subsidiary operates under foreign exchange restrictions, controls or other governmental imposed uncertainties which cast significant doubt on the parent's ability to control the subsidiary.

The exemption from consolidation where control is likely to be temporary, in ARB 51 *Consolidated Financial Statements*, as amended by FAS 94 *Consolidation of All Majority-Owned Subsidiaries an amendment of ARB No. 51*, with related amendments of APB Opinion No. 18 and ARB No. 43, Chapter 12, was removed by FAS 144 *Accounting for the Impairment or Disposal of Long-Lived Assets*. All long-lived assets or groups of assets classified as held for sale, even where recently acquired, should be recorded at the lower of carrying amount or fair value less cost to sell. FAS 144 also requires the results of operations classified as held for sale to be recognised in the period in which those operations occur.   *FAS 144.App C2*   *FAS 144.App B87*

FAS 144 governs the accounting for all planned dispositions of operations, including planned dispositions of subsidiaries and supersedes APB 30 *Reporting the Results of Operations – Reporting the Effects of Disposal of a Segment of a Business, and Extraordinary, Unusual and Infrequently Occurring Events and Transactions* (see section 1).

The presumption that all majority-owned investees should be consolidated may be overcome in cases where the minority shareholders have substantive participating rights that allow the minority shareholders to select management and establish operating and capital decisions of the investee.   *EITF 96-16*

2.4.1   Unconsolidated subsidiaries

The equity method should not be used as a substitute for consolidation. However, the equity method will generally be appropriate when conditions under which a subsidiary would not be consolidated prevail – namely where the investee is in legal reorganisation, bankruptcy or operates under foreign exchange restrictions etc.   *APB 18.14 fn4*   *FAS 94.15(c)*

2.5   CONSOLIDATION PROCEDURES

2.5.1   Intragroup transactions

IAS 27.22   Preparation of consolidated financial statements requires the financial statements of the parent and its subsidiaries to be combined on a line-by-line basis by adding together like items of assets, liabilities, equity, income and expenses.   In order to present financial information about the group as if it were that of a single economic entity, the following adjustments are required.

IAS 27.24-25   Intragroup balances, transactions, income and expenses and profits and losses arising from intragroup transactions must be eliminated in full.   Intragroup losses may indicate that the asset involved is impaired.

IAS 27.22   The carrying amount of the parent's investment in each subsidiary and the parent's portion of equity of each subsidiary must be eliminated, and the minority interests in the profit or loss for the period and net assets of the subsidiary identified (see section 2.5.5).   The treatment of goodwill or the excess of the acquirer's interest in the net fair value of the acquiree's identifiable assets, liabilities and contingent liabilities is dealt with in IFRS 3 *Business Combinations* (see section 3).

2.5.2   Non-coterminous financial statements

IAS 27.26-27   When the financial statements of a subsidiary are drawn up to a different reporting date from that of the parent, additional financial statements should be prepared by the subsidiary drawn up to the parent's reporting date.   If this is impracticable, the financial statements of the subsidiary at a different date may be used (so long as the difference between the reporting dates is no more than three months, and the length of the reporting periods and any difference in reporting dates is the same from period to period).   It is necessary to make adjustments for the effects of significant transactions or other events that occur between the reporting dates of the subsidiary and that of the parent.

IAS 21.46   If the financial statements of a subsidiary with a different reporting date are expressed in a currency different from the parent's reporting currency, the assets and liabilities are included in the consolidated financial statements at the exchange rate ruling at the balance sheet date of that subsidiary.   Adjustments are made for significant changes in exchange rates up to the balance sheet date of the parent.

2.5.3   Different accounting policies

IAS 27.28   Consolidated financial statements are prepared using uniform accounting policies for comparable transactions and other events in similar circumstances.

2.5.4   Shareholdings in the parent company

IAS 32.33   Treasury shares ('own shares'), acquired by the parent or by other members of the consolidated group, are presented as a deduction from equity and the purchase, sale, issue or cancellation of an entity's own equity instruments do not result in gains or

2.5   CONSOLIDATION PROCEDURES

2.5.1   Intragroup transactions

ARB 51 *Consolidated Financial Statements* requires complete elimination of *ARB 51.6,14* intragroup profits or losses on assets remaining within the group.

Elimination is also required of: *S-X 3A-04*

- intragroup items and transactions between entities included in consolidated financial statements; as well as

- unrealised profits and losses on transactions between entities in the group and *APB 18.19(a)* those which are accounted for under the equity method.

If such eliminations are not made, an explanation of the reasons and the treatment of those transactions should be disclosed.

The amount of intragroup items and transactions is not affected by the existence of *ARB 51.14* a minority interest.   However, the complete elimination of the profit or loss may be allocated proportionately between the majority (group) and minority interests.

2.5.2   Non-coterminous financial statements

A difference in accounting year ends would not justify the exclusion of a subsidiary *ARB 51.4* from consolidation, but the subsidiary should prepare financial statements, for consolidation purposes, for a period which corresponds with the parent company's year end.   Financial statements of subsidiaries with accounting periods ending within three months before or after of that of the parent company are usually acceptable for consolidation.   In such cases, the effect of intervening events that materially affect the financial position or results of operations should be recognised by disclosure, or otherwise.

The SEC has similar requirements to those in ARB 51.   Where such differences in *S-X 3A-02(b)* fiscal years exist, the closing date of the entity should be disclosed and the necessity for the use of different closing dates should be briefly explained.

2.5.3   Different accounting policies

Although there is no specific guidance, the consolidated financial statements are *ARB 51.6* based on the assumption that they represent the financial position and operating results of a single business entity.   Consequently, adjustment may be required to conform the accounting policies of consolidated entities.

2.5.4   Shareholdings in the parent company

These should not be treated as outstanding stock in the consolidated balance sheet *ARB 51.13* but should be treated in a manner similar to treasury stock (see section 12.5.4).

losses recognised in profit or loss. Consideration paid or received is recognised directly in equity.

IAS 32.34 The amount of treasury shares held is disclosed separately either on the face of the balance sheet or in the notes. Disclosure in accordance with IAS 24 *Related Party Disclosures* is given if the entity acquires its own shares from related parties.

2.5.5   Minority interests

IAS 27.4,22-23 Minority interest is the portion of the net assets and profit or loss of a subsidiary
IAS 27.IG5-7   attributable to equity interests that are not owned, directly or indirectly by the parent, and is therefore based on the fair values of assets and liabilities included in the consolidation. When potential voting rights exist, the proportion attributable to the minority interest is determined on the basis of present ownership interests and does not reflect the possible exercise or conversion of potential voting rights (except for the eventual exercise of potential voting rights and other derivatives that in substance give access at present to the economic benefits associated with an ownership interest). Interests in potential voting rights and other derivatives which do not in substance give a present ownership interest, are accounted for in accordance with IAS 39 *Financial Instruments: Recognition and Measurement.*

IAS 27.35 However, the minority's share in the losses may exceed the minority's share in the equity of the subsidiary. Where this is the case, the excess is charged against the majority interest except to the extent that the minority has a binding obligation and is able to make an additional investment to cover the losses. If the subsidiary later reports profits, such profits are allocated to the majority interest until the minority share of losses previously absorbed by the majority interest are recovered.

IAS 27.36 If a subsidiary has outstanding cumulative preference shares held by minority interests and classified as equity, the parent computes its share of profits or losses after adjusting for the dividends on such shares, whether or not dividends have been declared.

IAS 27.33-34 The minority interest in any financial instrument classified as an equity instrument by a subsidiary is presented by the parent in the consolidated balance sheet within equity, separate from the parent shareholders' equity. Minority interest in the profit or loss of the group is not income or expense and is also disclosed separately.

IAS 32.AG29 A financial instrument classified as a financial liability by a subsidiary remains a liability in the consolidated balance sheet unless eliminated on consolidation as an intragroup balance. However, when classifying a financial instrument in the consolidated financial statements, an entity considers all terms and conditions agreed between members of the group and holders of the instrument in determining whether the group as a whole has an obligation or settlement provision, and a financial liability. Consequently, financial instruments correctly classified as equity by a subsidiary may be classified as a financial liability in the consolidated balance sheet.

> **COMMENT**
>
> It is expected that Phase II of the Business Combinations project on application of the purchase method which is conducted jointly with the FASB will amend the treatment of minority interest.

2.5.5   Minority interests

Minority interests should be disclosed separately in the balance sheet, but not as part   *S-X 5-02.27*
of stockholders' equity.   Similarly, the minority interest in income of consolidated   *S-X 5-03.12*
subsidiaries should be separately disclosed.   Most companies reflect minority
interests as part of non-current liabilities or between liabilities and stockholders'
equity (the 'mezzanine') in the balance sheet.

> **COMMENT**
>
> The FASB plans to expose its proposals related to the accounting for non-
> controlling (minority) interests by issuing a proposed Statement that would amend
> and replace ARB 51, as amended by FAS 94.   This project is another phase of the
> Board's project on business combinations.   The Board expects to issue an exposure
> draft in the second quarter of 2005 and a final Statement in the second quarter of
> 2006.

A   Minority interests

Minority interests are generally presented in the consolidated balance sheet at an
amount equal to the minority's share of the carrying amount of the subsidiary's net
assets.   When consolidating the assets and liabilities of an acquired subsidiary that is
not wholly owned, the fair value adjustments are limited to the amount attributable to
the parent company's ownership percentage.   As a result, the assets and liabilities of
the subsidiary are included on a 'mixed' basis in the consolidated financial statements.

Profits or losses of the subsidiary undertaking should be consolidated in full, with an
allocation for equity minority interest based on the proportion held by the minority
shareholders.

In the case in which losses applicable to the minority interest in a subsidiary exceed   *ARB 51.15*
the minority interest in the equity capital of the subsidiary, the minority interest
should be reported as zero, as there is no obligation of the minority interest to make
good such losses (unless there is evidence indicating otherwise).   Any loss in excess
of the minority balance should be charged against the majority interest.   In the
event of future earnings, the majority interest should be credited for all those
earnings up to the amount of those losses previously absorbed.

B   Minority interests included in debt

Statement of Financial Accounting Concepts No. 6 *Elements of Financial
Statements* states that minority interests in the net assets of consolidated subsidiaries
do not represent present obligations of the consolidated company to pay cash or
distribute other assets to minority stockholders.   Rather, those stockholders have
ownership or residual interests in components of a consolidated company.

However, it is possible that minority interests do represent present obligations of the
consolidated company to pay cash or distribute other assets to minority stockholders,

The project's proposals are expected to require that:

- consolidated goodwill would include the minority's share of goodwill;
- the minority would bear their proportionate share of losses, even if these reduced the minority interest (to be known as non-controlling interest) below zero; and
- transactions between majority and minority shareholders, not resulting in a loss of control over the subsidiary, would be treated as equity transactions not giving rise to a profit or loss.

An Exposure Draft is expected in 2005 (with an IFRS to follow later in that year, likely to be effective for periods beginning on or after 1 January 2007).

2.5.6   Accounting for changes of ownership in a subsidiary

A   *Increasing an interest*

Step-by-step acquisitions of subsidiaries are discussed in section 3.4.4A.   However, there is no specific guidance on increases in interest subsequent to acquisition.

B   *Reducing an interest*

A reduction can arise either because the parent sells shares or the subsidiary issues additional shares to others.

IAS 27.30 When the parent sells shares of the subsidiary, the gain or loss – which is calculated
IAS 21.48-49 as the difference between the proceeds from the disposal of the subsidiary and its carrying amount (including allocated goodwill) as of the date of disposal, including the cumulative amount of any exchange differences that relate to the subsidiary recognised in equity in accordance with IAS 21 *The Effects of Changes in Foreign Exchange Rates* – is recognised in the consolidated income statement.

IAS 36.81,86 If goodwill has been allocated to a cash-generating unit (or group of units) and the entity disposed of an operation within that unit (or group of units), the goodwill associated with the operation disposed of is included in the carrying amount of the operation when determining the gain or loss on disposal, and is measured on the basis of the relative values of the operation disposed of and the portion of the cash-generating unit retained, unless the entity can demonstrate that some method better reflects the goodwill associated with the operation disposed of.   See section 9.

IFRS 3.80 If goodwill was previously recognised as a deduction from equity, this goodwill is not recognised in profit or loss when all or part of the business to which the goodwill relates is disposed of, or when a cash-generating unit to which the goodwill relates becomes impaired.

IAS 21.48-49 No guidance is provided under IFRSs regarding accounting for the effects of a reduction in the parent's interest due to a public offering by the subsidiary to external investors or indeed a partial disposal (while retaining control), although for a partial disposal, the appropriate portion of cumulative exchange differences would be recycled in profit or loss.   Minority interests would be adjusted.

C   *Cessation of subsidiary relationship*

IAS 27.31-32 If an investment no longer meets the definition of a subsidiary, it is accounted for in accordance with IAS 28 *Accounting for Investments in Associates* if it becomes an associate, IAS 31 *Financial Reporting of Interests in Joint Ventures* if it becomes a joint venture; otherwise IAS 39 is applied.   The carrying amount of the investment

e.g. a minority interest in stock with guaranteed mandatory redemption requirements. If such minority interests are classified between liabilities and equity (the 'mezzanine'), the SEC Staff have insisted on specific descriptive language.   The SEC Staff also believe that as an alternative to classification as minority interest in the mezzanine, it is acceptable to present these instruments within the debt caption in the balance sheet, with an appropriate description in the footnotes.   The income statement classification of the dividends on preferred redeemable securities should be presented in a manner consistent with the balance sheet treatment.

2.5.6   Accounting for changes of ownership in a subsidiary

A   Increasing an interest

Where the parent company acquires additional stock held by minority stockholders, the acquisition should be accounted for under the purchase method.   Goodwill is calculated as the difference between the consideration for the additional stock and proportionate share of the net assets acquired as a result, based on fair values at the date of acquisition.   Step-by-step acquisitions of subsidiaries are addressed in section 3.4.4A.

AIN-APB 16.26

B   Reducing an interest

A reduction can arise either because the parent sells shares or the subsidiary issues additional stock to others.   When the parent company sells shares of the subsidiary, the gain or loss should be calculated by comparing the carrying amount of the net assets of that subsidiary undertaking attributable to the group's interest before the sale with the carrying amount attributable to the group's interest after the sale together with any proceeds received.   The net assets compared should include any related goodwill not previously written-off through the profit and loss account and any related translation adjustment component.   Gain recognition is permitted only where the value of the proceeds can be objectively determined.

SAB 51
(Topic 5-H)
SAB 84
(Topic 5-H)

If the reduction in the parent company's interest occurs due to a public offering by the subsidiary to external investors, gain recognition is permitted provided the transaction is not 'a part of a broader corporate reorganisation' planned by the parent.   Gains or losses arising from issuances by a subsidiary of its own stock should be presented as a separate line item in the consolidated income statement (unless the amount is trivial) and clearly be designated as non-operating income.

Examples of situations where gain recognition would not be appropriate are:

- where subsequent capital transactions are contemplated that raise concerns about the parent company realising the gain that arises; or

- where the subsidiary is a start-up company, a research and development company or an entity with going concern problems.

In such cases, realisation is not assured and so the change in the parent's proportionate share of a subsidiary's equity should be accounted as an equity transaction, i.e. through reserves.

at the date the entity ceases to be a subsidiary is the cost on initial measurement of a financial asset in accordance with IAS 39.

IAS 27.30
IAS 21.48-49

The difference between the proceeds from disposal of the subsidiary and its carrying amount at the disposal date, including any cumulative exchange differences relating to the subsidiary recognised in equity, are recognised as part of the gain or loss on disposal in the consolidated income statement. An impairment, unless related to an actual disposal (or partial disposal), does not constitute a disposal requiring recycling of exchange differences, and it appears that classification as held for sale in accordance with IFRS 5 does not give rise to recycling of exchange differences.

IAS 27.21,IN9

Loss of control can occur without a change in absolute or relative ownership levels, e.g. when a subsidiary becomes subject to the control of a government, court, administrator or regulator or as a result of a contractual arrangement. An entity shall not exclude from consolidation an entity which operates under severe long-term restrictions that significantly impair the ability to transfer funds to the parent, without loss of control.

> **COMMENT**
>
> In February 2005, the IASB considered the following issues arising in developing an Exposure Draft of amendments to IAS 27. The IASB concluded that the gain or loss on disposal of a subsidiary should include cumulative gains and losses reflected in equity that relate to the subsidiary and that are 'recycled' on loss of control of that subsidiary. However, the portion of cumulative gains and losses attributed to and reflected in the non-controlling interest should not be recycled on loss of control.

2.6 SPECIAL PURPOSE ENTITIES

SIC-12.1-10, Appx

SIC-12 describes the main characteristics of a special purpose entity ('SPE') as follows:

- some SPEs may be created to accomplish a narrow and well-defined objective;
- SPEs may take the form of a corporation, trust, partnership or unincorporated entity; and
- SPEs are often created with legal arrangements that impose strict and sometimes permanent limits on the decision-making powers of their governing boards, trustees or managements over the SPE's operations. The SPE may operate on 'autopilot'.

SIC-12.2

The sponsor, on whose behalf an SPE was created, frequently transfers assets to the SPE, obtains the right to use assets held by the SPE or performs services for the SPE, while other parties may provide funding to the SPE. An entity engaging in transactions with the SPE may in substance control it. In most cases, the sponsor retains a significant beneficial interest in the SPE, even if it owns little or no equity in the SPE. Where an entity in substance controls the SPE, even where control arises through the predetermination of the SPE's activities (which operate on 'autopilot'), the entity must consolidate that SPE.

SIC-12.10
IAS 27.13

The following circumstances, in addition to those in IAS 27.13 (see section 2.3) may indicate that an entity controls an SPE and should consolidate that SPE:

- in substance, the activities of the SPE are being conducted on behalf of the entity according to its specific business needs so that the entity obtains benefits from the SPEs operation;

2.6   SPECIAL PURPOSE ENTITIES

In January 2003, the FASB issued FIN 46 *Consolidation of Variable Interest Entities, an Interpretation of Accounting Research Bulletin (ARB) No. 51*.   The FASB revised FIN 46 in December 2003 to address certain technical corrections and to clarify many of the implementation issues that had arisen.   FIN 46(R) provides guidance on how to apply the controlling financial interest criteria in ARB 51 to variable interest entities.

FIN 46(R) introduces a new consolidation model—the variable interests model— which determines control (and consolidation) of a variable interest entity based on the potential variability in its variable interest holders' gains and losses.   Variable interest entities (VIEs) include many entities referred to as special purpose entities (SPEs), but also may include many other entities not previously thought of as SPEs.

FIN 46(R) applies to all entities, with the following exceptions: *FIN 46.4*

*   Not-for-profit organisations as defined in FAS 117 *Financial Statements of Not-for-Profit Organizations* are not subject to FIN 46(R), except that they may be related parties for the purposes of considering the interests held by related party groups.

*   Separate accounts of life insurance enterprises, as described in the AICPA Audit and Accounting Guide, *Life and Health Insurance Entities* are not subject to FIN 46(R).

*   Regulated Investment Companies and other entities subject to SEC Regulation S-X Rule 6-03(c)(1), are not to consolidate any entity under FIN 46(R) that is not also subject to that same rule.

- in substance, the entity has the decision-making powers to obtain the majority of the benefits of the activities of the SPE or, by setting up an 'autopilot' mechanism, the entity has delegated these decision making powers;

- in substance, the entity has rights to obtain the majority of the benefits of the SPE and therefore may be exposed to risks incident to the activities of the SPE; or

- in substance, the entity retains the majority of the residual or ownership risks related to the SPE or its assets, in order to obtain benefits from its activities.

The Appendix to SIC-12 provides additional guidance and explains how the Interpretation should be applied.

SIC-12 (revised 2004) removed the scope exclusion for equity compensation plans and introduced a scope exclusion for other long-term employee benefit plans covered by IAS 19 *Employee Benefits*, in addition to post-employment benefits covered by IAS 19 which were excluded under the previous Interpretation. The revised Interpretation is effective for periods beginning on or after 1 January 2005, but will apply in earlier periods where IFRS 2 *Share-based Payment* is also adopted in those periods.

COMMENT

SPEs are common in securitisation vehicles. The effect of SIC-12 combined with IAS 39 may be that a securitisation transaction qualifies as a sale of the financial asset, but that the buyer is an SPE, which is consolidated.

The IASB is engaged in a Consolidation Project will lead to a new IFRS to replace IAS 27 and SIC-12. It is likely to contain significant changes to the criteria giving rise to a presumption of control. The IASB has tentatively agreed that control should be based on satisfaction of all of the following:

- power criterion – the ability to set strategic direction and to direct operating policy and strategy. In particular, the IASB have tentatively agreed that there should be a rebuttable presumption that the holdings of de facto agents of the company (such as senior employees, related parties etc) are available to the entity in assessing the power criterion. There will also be additional clarification on potential voting rights;

- benefit criterion – the ability to access benefits; and

- the link – the ability to use power so as to protect or maintain benefits.

The Project will also deal with Special Purpose Entities ('SPEs') but the discussion here is not advanced. The intention is to adapt and apply the control model above to SPEs. When the treatment of SPEs is resolved, an Exposure Draft of amendments to IAS 27 will be published, possibly in 2005.

COMMENT

FSP FIN 46-6 defers the applicability of FIN 46(R) to all investment companies until the AICPA's project to clarify the scope of the Audit and Accounting Guide *Audits of Investment Companies* is finalised.

- Employee benefit plans that are subject to the provisions of FAS 87 *Employers' Accounting for Pensions*, FAS 106 *Employers' Accounting for Postretirement Benefits Other Than Pensions*, or FAS 112 *Employers' Accounting for Postemployment Benefits*, should not be consolidated by a sponsoring employer applying FIN 46(R). Other parties with variable interests in employee benefit plans (for example, trustees, administrators, etc.) should evaluate these entities as potential VIEs.

- A qualifying special-purpose entity (SPE) is not to be consolidated in the financial statements of a transferor or its affiliates, consistent with FAS 140 *Accounting for Transfers and Servicing of Financial Assets and Extinguishments of Liabilities*. An investor in a qualifying SPE should not consolidate that entity unless the investor has the unilateral ability to cause the entity to liquidate or to change the entity so that it no longer meets the FAS 140 conditions for a qualifying SPE.

- A governmental organisation, or a financing entity established by a governmental organisation, should not be consolidated under FIN 46(R).

FIN 46(R) is not required to be applied to entities created before 31 December 2003, if information necessary to (a) determine whether the entity is a VIE, (b) determine whether the enterprise is the entity's primary beneficiary, or (c) perform the accounting required to consolidate the entity, cannot be obtained. The FASB believes situations to which this scope exception will apply will be infrequent, particularly when the company considering the scope exemption was involved in creating the entity.

As a further exemption, an entity that is deemed to be a business under the definition in Appendix C of FIN 46(R) (which is broadly consistent with the definition of a business in EITF 98-3) need not be evaluated to determine if it is a VIE unless one or more of the following conditions exist:

- the reporting company, its related parties, or both, participated significantly in the design or redesign of the entity (unless the entity is an operating joint venture under joint control of the reporting enterprise and one or more independent parties or a franchisee);

- the entity is designed so that substantially all of its activities either involve or are conducted on behalf of the reporting company and its related parties;

- the reporting company and its related parties provide more than half of the total of the equity, subordinated debt, and other forms of subordinated financial support to the entity, based on an analysis of the fair values of the interests in the entity; or

- the activities of the entity are primarily related to securitisations or other forms of asset-backed financings or single-lessee leasing arrangements.

An entity is a VIE and subject to consolidation under FIN 46(R) if, by design, the conditions in a, b, or c exist: *FIN 46.5*

a.   The total equity investment at risk is not sufficient to permit the entity to

finance its activities without additional subordinated financial support provided by any parties, including equity holders.

b. As a group, the holders of the equity investment at risk lack any one of the following three characteristics of a controlling financial interest:

   (1) The direct or indirect ability through voting rights or similar rights to make decisions about an entity's activities that have a significant effect on the success of the entity.

   (2) The obligation to absorb the expected losses of the entity.

   (3) The right to receive the expected residual returns of the entity.

c. The equity investors as a group also are considered to lack characteristic (b)(1) if (i) the voting rights of some investors are not proportional to their obligations to absorb the expected losses of the entity, their rights to receive the expected residual returns of the entity, or both and (ii) substantially all of the entity's activities either involve or are conducted on behalf of an investor that has disproportionately few voting rights.

The initial determination of whether an entity is a VIE and its primary beneficiary, if any, is to be made on the date on which an enterprise becomes involved with the entity, based on the circumstances that exist at the date of the assessment. A reporting company is not required to determine whether an entity with which it is involved is a VIE if (1) it is apparent that the company's interest would not be a significant variable interest and (2) the company, its related parties, and its de facto agents (as defined) were not significantly involved in the design or redesign of the entity. *FIN 46.6*

An entity that previously was not subject to FIN 46(R) does not become subject to it simply because of losses that reduce the equity investment, even if they are in excess of expected losses, and even if the equity investment is reduced to zero. *FIN 46.7*

When revising FIN 46(R), the Board retained a list of events that require reconsideration of whether an entity is a VIE, but clarified that only significant events need be considered. An event is significant if it changes the design of the entity in a fashion that calls into question (1) whether the entity's equity investment at risk is sufficient or (2) whether the rights and obligations provided to holders of the entity's at-risk equity investment are characteristic of a controlling financial interest. Additionally, the FASB agreed that a troubled debt restructuring, as defined in FAS 15 *Accounting by Debtor and Creditor for Troubled Debt Restructurings*, as amended, does not require a reconsideration of whether the entity involved is a VIE.

Under FIN 46(R), VIEs are evaluated for consolidation based on all contractual, ownership, or other interests that expose their holders to the risks and rewards of the entity. These interests are termed variable interests. The holder of a variable interest that receives the majority of the potential variability in expected losses or expected residual returns of the VIE is the VIE's primary beneficiary, and is required to consolidate the VIE. *FIN 46.14*

Expected losses and expected residual returns represent the potential variability from the expected cash flows of an entity. All entities, even entities that have a history of profitable operations and are projected to be profitable in the future, will have expected losses. *FIN 46.8*

There is a rebuttable presumption that an equity investment at risk of less than 10 % of an entity's total assets is not sufficient to allow the entity to finance its activities. Determination of sufficiency of equity investment at risk is required for all potential VIEs and some entities may require an equity investment at risk greater than 10 %. The determination should consider qualitative assessments, including but not limited to whether (1) the entity has demonstrated that it can finance its activities without additional subordinated financial support or (2) the entity has at least as much equity invested as other entities that hold similar assets and operate without additional subordinated financial support.

FIN 46.9

If a qualitative assessment proves inconclusive, a quantitative assessment that requires the amount of equity invested to exceed the entity's estimated expected losses should be applied either instead of, or together with, the qualitative assessments.

A company is required to determine whether it is a VIE's primary beneficiary, and therefore required to consolidate the VIE, at the time it becomes involved with the VIE. The primary beneficiary of a VIE should reconsider whether it remains the primary beneficiary whenever a change to the design of the VIE or the ownership of the variable interests in the VIE significantly changes the manner in which expected losses and expected residual returns are allocated.

FIN 46.15

A company with a variable interest in a VIE is required to treat other variable interests held by its related parties and parties acting as de facto agents as its own interests for purposes of determining whether it is the primary beneficiary of the VIE. FIN 46(R) defines related parties as those identified by FAS 57 *Related Party Disclosures* and certain other parties acting as de facto agents or principals. De facto agents include, among others, officers and employees of the company or a party that cannot sell, transfer or encumber its interests in the VIE without the company's prior approval. If the aggregate variable interest held by a related party group identify that group as the primary beneficiary of a VIE, the member of the related party group that is most closely associated with the VIE should consolidate it as the primary beneficiary.

FIN 46.16-17

Initial accounting for the assets, liabilities and non-controlling interests of a newly consolidated VIE generally should follow GAAP for business combinations, but goodwill may not be reported if the VIE is not a business. After initial measurement, the consolidation principles of ARB 51 should be followed as if the VIE were consolidated based on voting interests. Intragroup fees or other sources of income or expense should be eliminated against the related expense or income of the VIE, but the effect of that elimination in the net revenue or expense of the VIE should be allocated to the primary beneficiary – not to the non-controlling interest.

FIN 46.18

FAS 140 *Accounting for Transfers and Servicing of Financial Assets and Extinguishments of Liabilities* provides guidance for determining whether a transfer of financial assets constitutes a sale. FAS 140 is based on a financial-components approach for securitisation transactions that focuses on control, however, the FAS 140 definition of control should only be applied when assessing whether an SPE should be consolidated when all of the following criteria are met:

- the entity being considered is a 'qualifying SPE' (see below);
- the assets held by the qualifying SPE are financial assets or securities that represent a contractual right to cash from, or an ownership interest in, an entity that is unrelated to the transferor; and

161

- the financial assets held by the qualifying SPE are not the result of a structured transaction that has the effect of (1) converting non-financial assets into a financial asset, or (2) recognising previously unrecognised financial assets.

The concept of a qualifying SPE is intended to be restrictive. Under FAS 140, a qualifying SPE is a trust or other legal vehicle that meets all of the following conditions:

FAS 140.35

Q&A FAS 140

- the SPE is demonstrably distinct from the transferor;
- the SPE's permitted activities (1) are significantly limited, (2) were entirely specified in the legal documents that established the SPE or created the beneficial interests in the transferred assets that it holds, and (3) may be significantly changed only with the approval of the holders of at least a majority of the beneficial interests held by entities other than any transferor, its affiliates, and its agents;
- the SPE may hold only:
  - financial assets transferred to it that are passive in nature;
  - passive derivative financial instruments that pertain to beneficial interests (other than another derivative financial instrument) issued or sold to parties other than the transferor, its affiliates, or its agents;
  - financial assets, e.g. guarantees or rights to collateral, that would reimburse it if others were to fail to adequately service financial assets transferred to it or to timely pay obligations due to it and that it entered into when it was established, when assets were transferred to it, or when beneficial interests (other than derivative financial instruments) were issued by the SPE;
  - servicing rights related to financial assets that it holds:
  - temporarily, non-financial assets obtained in connection with the collection of financial assets that it holds; and
  - cash collected from assets that it holds and investments purchased with that cash pending distribution to holders of beneficial interests that are appropriate for that purpose, i.e. money-market or other relatively risk-free instruments without options and with maturities no later than the expected distribution date; and
- if the SPE can sell or otherwise dispose of non-cash financial assets, it can do so only in automatic response to one of the following conditions:
  - occurrence of an event or circumstance that (1) is specified in the legal documents by which it was established or created the beneficial interests in the transferred assets that it holds; (2) is outside the control of the transferor, its affiliates, or its agents; and (3) causes, or is expected at the date of transfer to cause, the fair value of those financial assets to decline by a specified degree below the fair value of those assets when the SPE obtained them;
  - exercise by a beneficial interest holder (other than the transferor, its affiliates, or its agents) of a right to put that holder's beneficial interest back to the SPE;
  - exercise by the transferor of a call or removal-of-accounts provision specified in the legal documents that established the SPE, transferred assets to the SPE, or created the beneficial interests in the transferred assets that it holds; and

2.7 COMBINED FINANCIAL STATEMENTS

IFRS 3.3   International Financial Reporting Standards do not address this subject. In addition, business combinations among entities under common control are specifically scoped out of IFRS 3.

2.8 SEPARATE FINANCIAL STATEMENTS

IAS 1.2
IAS 27.1,3-7,38
IAS 31.3,5,46-47
IAS 28.2-4,35-36

Though IAS 27 does not mandate presentation of separate financial statements available for public use, it applies to both separate and consolidated financial statements that comply with IFRS. Separate financial statements are those that are presented by a parent, investor in an associate or venturer in which the investments are accounted for on the basis of the direct equity interest rather than on the basis of reported results and net assets of the investees.

IAS 27.8
IAS 31.6
IAS 28.5

An entity may prepare separate financial statements as its only financial statements, if exempted from the preparation of consolidated financial statements by paragraph 10 of IAS 27, paragraph 2 of IAS 31 or paragraph 13(c) of IAS 28 (see sections 2.2 and 4.2A). IAS 31, as drafted has an apparently wider exemption, but again this inconsistency may be unintentional.

IAS 27.37
IAS 28.4,35
IAS 31.46

In separate financial statements presented under IFRS, investments in subsidiaries, jointly controlled entities and associates that are not classified as (or included in a disposal group classified as) held for sale in accordance with IFRS 5 (which are accounted for under that standard – see section 1.9) are accounted for either:

- at cost; or
- in accordance with IAS 39 (see section 11).

IAS 27.39   The same accounting shall be applied for each category of investment. If an investment in a jointly controlled entity or an associate is accounted for in accordance

    –   termination of the SPE or maturity of the beneficial interests in those financial assets on a fixed or determinable date that is specified at inception.

COMMENT

In June 2003, the FASB issued an exposure draft for a proposed Statement of Financial Accounting Standards *Qualifying Special-Purpose Entities and Isolation of Transferred Assets an amendment of FASB Statement No. 140.* The proposed Statement would clarify and expand certain conditions and limitations above. The Board expects to issue a revised exposure draft in the third quarter of 2005 and a final Statement in 2006.

2.7　COMBINED FINANCIAL STATEMENTS

To justify the preparation of consolidated financial statements, the controlling financial interest should rest directly or indirectly in one of the entities included in the consolidation. There are circumstances, however, where combined financial statements (as distinct from consolidated statements) of commonly controlled enterprises are likely to be more meaningful than their separate statements. For example, in the case where one individual owns a controlling interest in several enterprises that are related in their operations.

ARB 51.21-23

In preparing such statements, certain matters (i.e. minority interests, foreign operations, different accounting periods) should be treated as in consolidated financial statements.

2.8　SEPARATE FINANCIAL STATEMENTS

Because consolidated, rather than parent company, financial statements are regarded as the appropriate general-purpose financial statements of an entity having subsidiaries; there is no requirement to include parent company statements in a set of consolidated financial statements. However, the SEC requires 'condensed financial information' for the parent company (i.e. the registrant) where the amount of the registrant's share of net assets of consolidated subsidiaries (after intragroup eliminations) may not be transferred to the parent company in the form of loans, advances or cash dividends without the consent of a third party (i.e. lender, regulatory agency, foreign government, etc.) exceeds 25 % of consolidated net assets.

FAS 94.61
ARB 51.24
S-X 3-10,4-08
S-X 5-04,12-04

Investments in subsidiaries may be presented either using the cost or equity method when separate parent-only financial statements are prepared.

with IAS 39 in the consolidated financial statements, it must also be accounted for in accordance with IAS 39 in the separate financial statements.

IAS 27.4   Under the cost method, the investor recognises income only to the extent the distributions are received from post acquisition accumulated profits. Distributions received in excess of these are recognised as a reduction in the cost of investment.

2.9   DISCLOSURE

A   Consolidated financial statements

IAS 27.40   The following disclosures are required in the consolidated financial statements:

- the nature of the relationship between the parent and a subsidiary where the parent does not own more than one half of the voting power, directly or indirectly through subsidiaries;

- the reasons why the ownership, directly or indirectly through subsidiaries, of more than half of the potential voting power of an investee does not constitute control;

- the reporting date of the financial statements of a subsidiary used to prepare consolidated financial statements, where the reporting date or periods for the subsidiary differ from those of the parent, together with the reasons for using a different reporting date or period; and

- the nature and extent of any significant restrictions (e.g. from borrowing arrangements or regulatory requirements) on the ability of subsidiaries to transfer funds to the parent in the form of cash dividends or to repay loans or advances.

B   Separate financial statements

IAS 27.41-42   The separate financial statements of a parent, venturer in a jointly controlled entity or investor in an associate shall disclose:

- the fact that these are separate financial statements;

- a list of significant investments in subsidiaries, jointly controlled entities and associates, including the name, country of incorporation or residence, proportion of ownership interest and if different, proportion of voting power held; and

- a description of the method used to account for these investments.

Where separate financial statements are prepared for a parent that, in accordance with the exemption in IAS 27.10 from the preparation of consolidated financial statements (see section 2.2) elects not to prepare consolidated financial statements, the separate financial statements shall additionally disclose:

- that the exemption from consolidation has been used; and

- the name and country of incorporation or residence of the entity whose consolidated financial statements complying with IFRSs have been produced for public use and the address from where those consolidated financial statements are obtainable.

Where separate financial statements are prepared for (1) a parent preparing separate financial statements in addition to consolidated financial statements, or (2) by an

2.9   DISCLOSURE

The following is a summary of disclosure requirements (see section 4 for disclosures in respect of associated undertakings).

A   Entities included in consolidated financial statements

There is no requirement to disclose information on subsidiaries that have been included in the consolidated financial statements.   *S-X 4-10*

The SEC requires condensed consolidating financial information to be included in the financial statements of a group with issued securities guaranteed by an affiliated guarantor.   *S-X 3-10*

The term 'condensed consolidating financial information' means audited condensed consolidated financial statements of the group presented in a columnar format to disclose condensed financial information, if applicable, for each of the following:

- the parent company;
- each subsidiary issuer;
- the guarantor subsidiaries on a combined basis, excluding any guarantor subsidiaries which should be presented separately (see below);
- each separately presented guarantor subsidiary;
- any other subsidiaries on a combined basis;
- consolidating adjustments;
- total consolidated amounts.

The financial information should be audited and presented for the same periods that the parent company financial statements are required to be audited, and the financial information should present investments in all subsidiaries under the equity method.

B   Entities excluded from consolidated financial statements

Separate financial statements should be filed for any non-consolidated majority-owned subsidiary where, in respect of any such subsidiary (1) the group's investment or share of total assets exceeds 20% of group consolidated total assets, or (2) the group's share of net income before taxes exceeds 20% of group consolidated net income before taxes.   *S-X 3-09(a)*

Additional disclosures described below should be given for any non-consolidated majority-owned subsidiary where, individually or in aggregate, (1) the group's investment exceeds 10% of group consolidated total assets, or (2) the group's proportionate share of the total assets of the subsidiary exceeds 10% of the group consolidated total assets, or (3) the group's share of net income before taxes exceeds 10% of group consolidated net income before taxes.   *S-X 4-08(g)*
    S-X 1.02(w)

entity (not being a parent) that is a venturer in a jointly controlled entity or an investor in an associate, the separate financial statements shall additionally disclose:

- the reasons why separate financial statements are prepared, if not required by law; and

- identification of the consolidated financial statements or those which include the jointly controlled entity or associates through proportionate consolidation or the equity method, as appropriate.

C   *Held for sale*

IFRS 5.32   The presentational and disclosure requirements for disposal groups classified as held for sale in accordance with IFRS 5 are discussed in section 1.9. A subsidiary acquired exclusively with a view to resale and classified as held for sale is always a discontinued operation.

The following summarised information should be disclosed in a note to the financial statements:

S-X 1-02(bb)

- current and non-current assets;
- current and non-current liabilities;
- (if applicable) redeemable stock and minority interests;
- net sales or gross revenues;
- gross profit (or costs and expenses applicable to net sales or gross revenues);
- income or loss from continuing operations (before extraordinary items and the cumulative effect of accounting change); and
- net income or loss.

The above disclosures may be made on a combined basis.

When the significance test is applied for combined entities, entities reporting losses should not be aggregated with entities reporting income.

S-X 1.02(w)

C   *Consolidation of variable interest entities*

In addition to disclosures required by other standards, the primary beneficiary of a variable interest entity should disclose the following:

FIN 46.23

- the nature, purpose, size, and activities of the variable interest entity;
- the carrying amount and classification of consolidated assets that are collateral for the variable interest entity's obligations;
- lack of recourse if creditors (or beneficial interest holders) of a consolidated variable interest entity have no recourse to the general credit of the primary beneficiary.

A company that holds a significant variable interest in a variable interest entity but is not the primary beneficiary should disclose:

FIN 46.24

- the nature of its involvement with the variable interest entity and when that involvement began;
- the nature, purpose, size, and activities of the variable interest entity;
- the reporting company's maximum exposure to loss as a result of its involvement with the variable interest entity.

A company that does not apply FIN 46(R) to one or more variable interest entities or potential variable interest entities created before 31 December 2003, because information required to apply the Interpretation cannot be obtained, should disclose:

FIN 46.26

- the number of entities to which FIN 46(R) is not being applied and the reason why the information is not available;
- the nature, purpose, size (if available), and activities of the entity(ies) and the nature of the company's involvement with the entity(ies);
- the reporting company's maximum exposure to loss as a result of its involvement with the entity(ies);
- the amount of income, expense, purchases, sales, or other measure of activity between the reporting enterprise and the entity(ies) for all periods presented.

D   *Held for sale*

The disclosure requirements for a component of an entity that is either disposed of, or is held for sale are provided under section 1.9.

Section 3   Business combinations

3.1   AUTHORITATIVE PRONOUNCEMENTS

- IFRS 3

COMMENT

Phase I of the Business Combinations project resulted in the publication of IFRS 3 *Business Combinations*.

Phase II of the Business Combinations project on application of the purchase method is conducted jointly with the FASB.   An Exposure Draft is expected in 2005 (with an IFRS to follow later in that year, likely to be effective for periods beginning on or after 1 January 2007).   It is expected that the guidance in the exposure drafts issued by the FASB and the IASB will differ only to the extent of differing decisions reached in Phase 1 or in the course of the joint project, or as a result of inherited differences arising from other Standards.   Application is expected to be prospective, with the inclusion of special transitional arrangements. The expected proposals are discussed later in this section, and also in section 2.

Having issued that Exposure Draft, the IASB is expected to consider:

- business combinations in which separate entities or operations of entities are brought together to form a joint venture; and
- business combinations between entities under common control.

3.2   GENERAL APPROACH

A   Scope

IFRS 3.78-84, Appx A   For existing IFRS reporters, IFRS 3 applies to the accounting for business combinations, goodwill and any excess of the acquirer's interest in the net fair value of the acquiree's identifiable assets, liabilities and contingent liabilities over the cost of a business combination, for which the agreement date is on or after 31 March 2004.   The agreement date is the date that a substantive agreement between the combining parties is reached and in the case of publicly listed entities, announced to the public.   In the case of a hostile takeover, the earliest date this can be is the date that a sufficient number of the acquiree's owners have accepted the acquirer's offer for the acquirer to obtain control of the acquiree.

For business combinations for which IFRS 3 is not applied retrospectively (see section 3.2B), there are transitional rules for existing IFRS reporters in relation to the treatment of previously recognised goodwill (see section 3.4.6A), previously recognised negative goodwill (see section 3.4.6B), previously recognised intangible assets (see sections 3.4.6A and 6.2.1) and equity accounted investments (see section 4.4.1).

IFRS 1.Appx B   The transitional arrangements for first-time adopters are discussed in Chapter 2.

Section 3   Business combinations

3.1   AUTHORITATIVE PRONOUNCEMENTS

- FAS 72
- FAS 79
- FAS 87

- FAS 106
- FAS 141
- FAS 142

There is considerable guidance in the US on the subject of accounting for business combinations. In addition to the accounting standards listed above, there are several interpretations issued by the AICPA and the FASB, a number of EITF consensuses and SEC Staff Accounting Bulletins.

> **COMMENT**
>
> Currently, the FASB is partnering with the IASB on a joint project which represents the second phase of the Board's overall project on business combinations – reconsidering aspects of the purchase method of accounting that were not deliberated in FAS 141. The FASB has issued a summary of tentative decisions on phase II of the business combinations project as of July 2004. Phase I of the business combinations project resulted in FAS 141 which requires all business combinations to be accounted for under the purchase method (eliminating the pooling-of-interest method). Phase II will revise FAS 141 to require all acquisitions of businesses to be measured at the fair value of the business acquired and provide specific guidance for applying the purchase method. The FASB expects to issue an exposure draft in the first half of 2005 and a final standard (FAS 141(R)) in the first half of 2006.

3.2   GENERAL APPROACH

Under FAS 141 *Business Combinations* all business combinations are to be accounted for using the purchase method. For the purposes of applying FAS 141, a business combination occurs when an entity acquires net assets that constitute a business or obtains control over an entity through the acquisition of equity interests in that entity. EITF 98-3 *Determining Whether a Nonmonetary Transaction Involves Receipt of Productive Assets or of a Business* provides guidance on determining whether an asset group constitutes a business. *FAS 141.13* *FAS 141.9* *EITF 98-3*

The term business combination as used in FAS 141 excludes transfers of net assets or exchanges of equity interests between entities under common control. The accounting for transfers of net assets or exchanges of equity interests between entities under common control is discussed in section 3.3.

> **COMMENT**
>
> It is expected that Phase II of the FASB Business Combinations project will provide a new definition of a business that will replace the definition in EITF 98-3. The proposed statement would define a business as an integrated set of activities and assets that is capable of being conducted and managed for the purpose of providing (a) a return to investors or (b) lower costs or other economic benefits directly and proportionately to owners, members, or participants.

IFRS 3.3   IFRS 3 excludes from its scope business combinations in which separate entities or businesses are brought together to form a joint venture, business combinations involving entities or businesses under common control, business combinations involving two or more mutual entities and business combinations in which separate entities or businesses are brought together to form a reporting entity by contract alone without obtaining of an ownership interest (e.g. dual listed corporations).

COMMENT

It is expected that Phase II of the Business Combinations project on application of the purchase method which is conducted jointly with the FASB will address the application of the purchase method to business combinations involving two or more mutual entities and business combinations involving the formation of a reporting entity by contract only without the obtaining of an ownership interest. An Exposure Draft is expected in 2005 (with an IFRS to follow later in that year, likely to be effective for periods beginning on or after 1 January 2007).

IFRS 3.10-13   IFRS 3 states that a business combination involving entities or businesses under common control is one in which all of the combining entities or businesses are ultimately controlled by the same party or parties before and after the business combination and that control is not transitory. The extent of minority interests in the combining entities is not relevant to determining whether the combination involves entities under common control.

B   Limited retrospective application of IFRS 3

IFRS 3.85   Existing IFRS reporters may apply IFRS 3 to goodwill existing at or acquired after, and to business combinations occurring from any date before the effective dates provided:

- the valuations and other information necessary to apply the standard to past business combinations were obtained at the time those business combinations were initially accounted for; and

- IAS 36 (revised 2004) *Impairment of Assets* and IAS 38 (revised 2004) *Intangible Assets* (see sections 9 and 6 respectively) are also applied from the same date, and valuations and other information necessary to apply these standards from that date were previously obtained by the entity so that there is no need to determine estimates that would need to have been made at a prior date.

C   Definition of a 'business combination'

IFRS 3.4,Appx A   A business combination is defined as 'the bringing together of separate entities or businesses into one reporting entity'. A business, which generally consists of inputs, processes applied to those inputs and outputs used to generate revenues, is defined as 'an integrated set of activities and assets conducted and managed for the purpose of providing:

- a return to investors; or

- lower costs or other economic benefits directly and proportionately to policyholders or participants.'

If goodwill is present in a transferred set of activities and assets, the transferred set shall be presumed to be a business.

An entity should account for an exchange of securities in which it acquires control of a subsidiary that constitutes a business as a business combination. This requires the transaction to be measured at fair value rather than at the cost of the investment transferred. However, full gain recognition is not always appropriate – for example, if a company (A) transfers an asset to another company (B) in exchange for shares in company B and, as a result, B becomes a subsidiary of A, gain recognition should be limited to that portion of the asset that is considered as sold, i.e. the transaction is accounted for as a partial sale to the minority shareholders in B.

EITF 01-2

FAS 153 amends APB 29 and partially nullifies EIFT 01-2. The general rule of the amended APB 29 requires non-monetary transactions to be accounted for at fair value. Exceptions to the general rule are described in section 19.4.4. FAS 153 is effective for transactions occurring in fiscal periods beginning after 15 June 2005.

APB 29.18

IFRS 3.4 If an entity obtains control of one or more entities that are not businesses, the bringing together of those entities is not a business combination. The cost is allocated between the individual identifiable assets and liabilities in the net assets acquired based on their relative fair values at the date of acquisition.

IFRS 3.8 Business combinations arise even if the date of obtaining control does not coincide with the date(s) of exchange.

IFRS 3.14 All business combinations within the scope of IFRS 3 are accounted for by applying the purchase method.

3.3   UNITING OF INTERESTS

IFRS 3.1,4,14 Nearly all business combinations involve one entity, the acquirer, obtaining control of one or more other businesses, the acquiree.   All business combinations within the scope of IFRS 3 are accounted for by applying the purchase method.

> **COMMENT**
>
> IFRS 3 excludes from its scope business combinations in which separate entities or businesses are brought together to form a joint venture, business combinations involving entities or businesses under common control, business combinations involving two or more mutual entities and business combinations in which separate entities or businesses are brought together to form a reporting entity by contract alone without obtaining of an ownership interest (e.g. dual listed corporations).

3.3   COMMON CONTROL TRANSACTIONS

The provisions of FAS 141 prohibit the use of the pooling-of-interests method for all business combinations initiated after 30 June 2001.   However, FAS 141 does not apply to transfers of net assets or exchanges of shares between entities under common control.

FAS 141.11

When accounting for a transfer of assets or exchange of shares between entities under common control, the net assets or equity interests received should initially be recognised at their carrying amounts in the transferring entity at the date of transfer.

FAS 141.App D12

Where transfers of net assets or exchanges of shares between entities under common control result in a change in the reporting entity, in practice, the accounting is similar to the pooling method.   Consequently, certain provisions in APB 16 relating to the application of the pooling method will continue to provide guidance for accounting for transactions between entities under common control.

FAS 141.App D14

A   Application of pooling-of-interests method

The accounting for transfers of net assets or exchanges of shares between entities under common control, which result in a change in the reporting entity, is in practice similar to the pooling-of-interests method.

Under the pooling method, the recorded assets and liabilities of the separate entities should be combined in the financial statements.   Adjustments may have to be made to eliminate differences in accounting policies adopted by the separate entities if the change in policy would otherwise have been appropriate.   Such changes in accounting policy should be applied retroactively and financial statements presented for prior periods should be restated.

FAS 141.App D15

The consolidated financial statements should report results of operations for the period in which the combination occurs as though the companies had been combined as of the beginning of the earliest period presented.

FAS 141.App D16

The consolidated financial information as of the beginning of the period should be presented as though the assets and liabilities had been transferred at that date. Financial statements presented for prior years should be restated to present comparative information.   All restated financial statements and summaries should indicate that financial data of previously separate entities are combined.

FAS 141.App D17

3.4   THE PURCHASE METHOD

IFRS 3.16   The purchase method involves the following steps:

- identifying an acquirer (see section 3.4.1);

- measuring the cost of the business combination (see section 3.4.3);

- allocating, at the acquisition date, the cost of the business combination to the assets acquired and liabilities and contingent liabilities assumed at their fair values at that date (see section 3.4.4); and

IAS 27.22   - identifying the minority interest in the net fair value of the identifiable assets acquired less liabilities and contingent liabilities assumed (see section 2.5.5).

IFRS 3.51,56   The excess of the cost of the business combination over the acquirer's interest in
IFRS 3.Appx A   the net fair value of the identifiable assets acquired less liabilities and contingent liabilities assumed is goodwill (see section 3.4.6A).   The excess of the acquirer's share of the identifiable assets, liabilities and contingent liabilities, if any, over the cost of the business combination is recognised immediately in the income statement (see section 3.4.6B).

IFRS 3.38-40   Application of the purchase method commences at the acquisition date (see
IAS 27.22   section 3.4.2) and the acquirer shall:

- incorporate the results of operations of the acquiree after the acquisition date in its own income statement (but based on the cost of the business combination to the acquirer, e.g. depreciation based on fair values of assets acquired), recognising separately any minority interest in those results;

- recognise in the balance sheet, the fair value of the identifiable assets, liabilities and contingent liabilities of the acquiree, and any goodwill on the acquisition, then accounted for as in section 3.4.6A; and

- recognise as a separate component of equity, the minority interest in the net assets of the acquiree.   This consists of the amount of the minority interests at acquisition date (based on fair values at the acquisition date); together with the minority's share of changes in equity post the business combination.

3.4.1   Identifying an acquirer

A   *General*

IFRS 3.3,4,17   Nearly all business combinations involve one entity, the acquirer, obtaining control of one or more other businesses, the acquiree.   An acquirer, which is the combining entity that obtains control (see section 2.3) of the other combining entities or businesses, must be identified for all business combinations.

IFRS 3.22-23   When a new entity is formed to effect the combination, or several entities combine, one of the pre-existing combining entities is identified as the acquirer, on the basis

B   *Disclosure*

For the period in which the transfer of net assets or exchange of equity interests   *FAS 141.App D18*
occurred, the financial statements should disclose the name and a brief description
of the entity combined and the method of accounting for the transfer of net assets
or exchange of equity interests.

3.4   THE PURCHASE METHOD

Under FAS 141, all business combinations on or after 1 July 2001 are to be   *FAS 141.13*
accounted for using the purchase method.

The purchase method follows principles normally applicable under historical cost   *FAS 141.3-7*
accounting when recording acquisitions of assets for cash, by exchanging other assets,
or by issuing shares.   Acquiring a business requires ascertaining the cost of the assets
acquired as a group and then allocating the cost to the individual assets that comprise
the group.   FAS 141 provides guidance on determining the cost of a group and on
assigning a portion of the total cost to each individual asset acquired and liability
assumed on the basis of its fair value.   A difference between the sum of the assigned
costs of the tangible and identifiable intangible assets acquired less liabilities assumed
and the cost of the group is evidence of unspecified intangible values, i.e. goodwill.

3.4.1   Identifying an acquirer

A   *General*

Application of the purchase method requires the identification of the acquiring   *FAS 141.15-17*
entity.   In a business combination effected solely through the distribution of cash
or other assets or by incurring liabilities, the entity that distributes cash or other
assets or incurs liabilities is generally the acquiring entity.   In a business
combination effected through an exchange of equity, the entity that issues the equity
interests is generally the acquiring entity.

of evidence available. The evidence includes consideration of which entity initiated the combination and whether the assets or revenues of one of the entities significantly exceed the others.

COMMENT

At its September 2004 meeting, the IASB clarified that where an entity has identified an acquirer under IFRS 3, that acquirer is the parent for the purposes of IAS 27 *Consolidated and Separate Financial Statements.*

IFRS 3.20-21 Although it may sometimes be difficult to identify an acquirer, there are usually indications that one exists, e.g.:

- the fair value of one entity is significantly greater than that of the other combining entity. In such cases, the larger entity is likely to be the acquirer;

- the business combination is effected through an exchange of voting ordinary equity instruments for cash or other assets. In such cases, the entity giving up cash or other assets is likely to be the acquirer;

- the business combination results in the management of one entity being able to dominate the selection of the management team of the resulting combined entity. In such cases, the entity whose management is able to dominate is likely to be the acquirer; and

- in a business combination effected through an exchange of equity interests, the entity issuing the equity interests is normally the acquirer. However, all pertinent facts and circumstances are considered to determine which entity has control.

COMMENT

It is expected that Phase II of the Business Combinations project on application of the purchase method which is conducted jointly with the FASB will provide further application guidance on assessing whether a business is acquired and identifying the acquirer. An Exposure Draft is expected in 2005 (with an IFRS to follow later in that year, likely to be effective for periods beginning on or after 1 January 2007).

B Reverse acquisitions

IFRS 3.21,BC59,
Appx B1-B15 In some business combinations, however, known as reverse acquisitions, the acquirer is the entity whose equity interests have been acquired and the issuing entity is the acquiree. The legal subsidiary is the acquirer if it has the power to govern the financial and operating policies of the legal parent so as to obtain benefits from its activities. This could arise, for example, where in order to obtain a listing, an unlisted entity allows itself to be taken over by a listed entity which issues voting shares and, as part of the agreement, the directors of the public entity resign and are replaced with directors appointed by the private entity and its former owners. In such a case, the acquirer (legal subsidiary) applies the purchase method to the assets and liabilities of the acquiree (legal parent) issuing the shares. Reverse acquisition accounting determines the allocation of the cost of the business combination as at the acquisition date and does not apply to transactions after the combination. It applies only in the consolidated financial statements which are issued in the name of the legal parent, not the legal parent's separate financial statements. IFRS 3, Appendix B provides detailed guidance concerning the accounting of reverse acquisitions.

B   *Reverse acquisitions*

In some business combinations (often referred to as reverse acquisitions), however, the acquired entity issues the equity interests. Usually, the acquiring entity is the larger entity. In identifying the acquiring entity in a combination effected through an exchange of equity interests, all pertinent facts and circumstances should be considered. APB 16 states that presumptive evidence of the acquiring corporation *FAS 141.17* is obtained by identifying the former common stockholder of a combining company which either retains or receives the larger portion of the voting rights in the combined entity.

3.4.2   Acquisition date

IFRS 3.25,39 The acquisition date is the date on which the acquirer effectively obtains control of
IFRS 3.Appx A the acquiree. It is not necessary for a transaction to be closed or finalised at law
before the acquirer obtains control. When this is achieved through a single
exchange transaction, the date of exchange coincides with the acquisition date.

3.4.3   The cost of a business combination

IFRS 3.24 The cost of a business combination is the aggregate of:

- the fair values at the date of exchange, of assets given, liabilities incurred or
assumed and equity instruments issued by the acquirer, in exchange for
control of the acquiree; plus

- any costs directly attributable to the business combination.

Therefore, although accounting for the acquisition commences at the acquisition date,
the cost of the combination is determined at the date of each exchange transaction.

IFRS 3.25 When an acquisition is achieved in one exchange transaction, the date of exchange
and the acquisition date coincide. When an acquisition is achieved in stages, the
cost of the combination is the aggregate cost of the individual transactions, and the
date of exchange is the date of each exchange transaction (i.e. the date that each
individual investment is recognised in the financial statements of the acquirer).

IFRS 3.32,34 Any adjustment to the cost of the combination contingent on future events that is
probable and can be measured reliably is recognised in the cost of the combination
at the acquisition date. If, subsequent to the acquisition date, any contingent
adjustment becomes probable and can be measured reliably, it is recorded as an
adjustment to the cost of the combination.

IFRS 3.27 The published price at the date of exchange of a quoted equity instrument provides
the best evidence of the instrument's fair value and shall be used, except in rare
circumstances when it can be demonstrated that the published price at that date is
an unreliable indicator (this will only be when it is affected by the thinness of the
market), and that other evidence and valuation methods provide a more reliable
measure of the equity instrument's fair value.   Further guidance on determining the
fair value of equity instruments in such circumstances, or when published prices are
not available, is discussed in IFRS 3, which also refers to guidance given in IAS 39
Financial Instruments: Recognition and Measurement.

3.4.2   Acquisition date

The date of acquisition is ordinarily the date assets are received and other assets are   *FAS 141.48*
given up or securities are issued.   However, the parties to an acquisition may
designate the end of an accounting period between the date of initiation and
consummation of the transaction as the effective date.   This may be used as the date
of acquisition for accounting purposes if a written agreement provides that effective
control of the acquired enterprise is transferred to the acquiring entity on that date
without restrictions, except those required to protect the shareholders or other owners
of the acquired entity, e.g. restrictions on significant changes in the operations.   In
such cases, interest should be imputed into the value of the consideration.

FAS 142 requires that certain assets acquired and liabilities assumed, including
goodwill, be assigned to a reporting unit as of the date of acquisition.   To assist in   *FAS 141.50*
making those assignments, the basis for and method of determining the purchase
price, and other factors related to the acquisition, should be documented at the date
of acquisition.

3.4.3   The cost of a business combination

The cost of an acquired entity should be measured by taking into account the fair   *FAS 141.20-22*
values of other assets distributed and the fair value of liabilities incurred by the
acquiring entity.   In the case of quoted equity securities, the market price for a   *EITF 99-12*
reasonable period before and after the date the terms of the acquisition are agreed
to and announced should be considered in determining the fair value of securities
issued.   A premium or discount should be recorded for a debt security issued with
an interest rate fixed materially above or below the effective rate or current yield for
an otherwise comparable security.

> **COMMENT**
>
> It is expected that Phase II of the FASB Business Combinations project will nullify
> EITF 99-12 as the revised standard would require that equity securities issued as
> consideration in a business combination be measured at their fair value on the
> acquisition date.

If the quoted market price is not the fair value of the equity securities issued, the   *FAS 141.23*
consideration received (including goodwill) should be estimated notwithstanding the
difficulty in measuring directly the fair values of net assets received.   Both the fair
value of net assets received and the extent of the adjustments of the quoted market
price of the shares issued should be weighed to determine the amount to be
recorded.   Independent appraisals can be used to help determine the fair value of
the securities issued.   Consideration other than equity securities distributed to
effect an acquisition may provide evidence of the total fair value received.

Cash and other assets distributed, securities issued unconditionally and amounts of   *FAS 141.26*
contingent consideration that are determinable, i.e. where the outcome of the
contingency is determinable beyond reasonable doubt, at the date of acquisition
should be included in determining the cost of an acquired entity and recorded at
that date.

IFRS 3.26,28   Where settlement of all or part of a business combination is deferred, the fair value of the deferred part is determined by discounting the amounts payable to its present value at the date of exchange, taking into account any premium or discount likely to be incurred in settlement. Future losses or other costs expected to be incurred or assumed by the acquiree are not part of the cost of the combination.

IFRS 3.35   Where an acquirer is required to make a subsequent payment to the seller as compensation for a reduction in the value of the purchase consideration, e.g. the acquirer has guaranteed the market price of equity instruments or debt issued as part of the cost of the business combination, and is required to issue additional equity or debt to restore the originally determined cost, the cost of the combination and goodwill are not adjusted. The fair value of the additional equity instruments issued is offset by an equal reduction in the value attributed to the original equity instruments. For debt instruments, the additional payment is regarded as a reduction in the premium or increase in the discount on the initial issue (and hence will be taken to income as increased interest expense over the period of the debt).

IFRS 3.29-31   The cost of the business combination includes directly attributable costs such as professional fees paid. General administrative costs, the costs of maintaining an acquisitions department and other costs not directly attributable to the particular business combination are expensed as incurred. Costs of arranging and issuing financial liabilities or equity instruments, even where these are issued to effect a business combination, are not part of the cost of the business combination. These costs are an integral part of the liability or equity issue transaction and are included in the initial measurement of the liability or deducted from the proceeds of the equity issue respectively in accordance with IAS 39 and IAS 32 *Financial Instruments: Disclosure and Presentation* respectively.

> **COMMENT**
>
> It is expected that Phase II of the Business Combinations project on application of the purchase method which is conducted jointly with the FASB will provide further application guidance on the treatment of contingent consideration, accounting for pre-existing relationships between the parties to a business combination and directly attributable costs. An Exposure Draft is expected in 2005 (with an IFRS to follow later in that year, likely to be effective for periods beginning on or after 1 January 2007).
>
> The project's proposals are expected to incorporate the guidance in EITF 95-8 and EITF 04-1 from US GAAP on contingent consideration and accounting for pre-existing relationships, and are expected to require that directly attributable costs should be expensed as incurred.

IFRS 3 does not provide any guidance regarding the recognition of employee stock options nor the exchange of options in a business combination.

IFRS 2.5   IFRS 2 *Share-based Payment* does not apply to transactions in which an entity acquires goods as part of the net assets in a business combination to which IFRS 3 applies. Hence, equity instruments issued in exchange for control of the acquiree in such a business combination are not within the scope of IFRS 2. However, equity instruments granted to employees (e.g. in return for continued service) or the cancellation, replacement or other modification of share-based payment arrangements because of a business combination or other equity restructuring are within the scope of IFRS 2 (see section 22).

Contingent consideration is usually recorded when the contingency is resolved and consideration is issued or becomes issuable.

FAS 141.27

The issuance of additional securities or other consideration at the resolution of contingencies based on earnings results in an addition to the cost of an acquired company (usually goodwill).

FAS 141.28

Additional consideration may be contingent on the market price of a specified security issued; in which case the securities issued unconditionally at the date of the combination should be recorded at that date at the specified amount.

FAS 141.29

Additional securities or other consideration issued at the resolution of contingencies based on security prices do not change the recorded cost of an acquired company. When the contingency is resolved and additional consideration is distributable, the fair value of the additional consideration is recorded. However, the amount previously recorded for securities issued at the date of acquisition should simultaneously be reduced to the lower current value of those securities. Reducing the values of debt securities results in recording a discount that should be amortised from the date the additional securities are issued.

FAS 141.30

If contingent consideration in a purchase business combination is based on earnings or other performance measures, and the selling shareholders have positions as 'employees' that could affect the financial results of the acquired entity subsequent to the acquisition, the acquirer needs to analyse the relevant facts and circumstances to determine whether the contingent consideration should be accounted for as an adjustment of the purchase price or as compensation for services.

EITF 95-8

COMMENT

It is expected that Phase II of the FASB Business Combinations project will require the fair value of consideration exchanged for the acquired business to include the fair value of obligations for future payments of contingent consideration.

The direct costs of acquisition of an entity should be included as part of the cost of the acquisition. Indirect and general expenses related to business combinations should be expensed as incurred. Costs of registering and issuing equity securities are a reduction of the otherwise determinable fair value of the securities. Debt issue costs are an element of the effective interest cost of debt and not a direct cost of acquisition.

FAS 141.24
AIN-APB 16.33
SAB 77
(Topic 2-A)

3.4.4   Determining fair values of identifiable assets and liabilities assumed

A   General approach

IFRS 3.36-37   The identifiable assets, liabilities and contingent liabilities of the acquiree shall be recognised separately at the acquisition date at their fair value at that date (except for non-current assets, or disposal groups classified as held for sale in accordance with IFRS 5 *Non-current Assets Held For Sale and Discontinued Operations*, which are recognised at fair value less costs to sell) if and only if they meet the following recognition criteria:

- in the case of an asset, other than an intangible asset (see section 3.4.4C), it is probable that any associated future economic benefits will flow to the acquirer;

- in the case of a liability, other than a contingent liability, it is probable that an outflow of resources embodying economic benefits will be required to settle the obligation; and

- the fair value of the asset, liability, intangible asset (which can include in-process research and development) or contingent liability can be measured reliably (i.e. the probability tests are not required for an intangible asset or a contingent liability).

IFRS 3.41-44   Identifiable assets and liabilities over which the acquirer obtains control may not necessarily have been recognised in the financial statements of the acquiree.

A payment that an entity is contractually required to make, in the event it is acquired in a business combination, is recognised as an identifiable liability.   However, no liability is recognised for an acquiree's restructuring plan whose execution is conditional upon it being acquired as it constitutes neither a present obligation nor a contingent liability in accordance with IAS 37 *Provisions, Contingent Liabilities and Contingent Assets* immediately before the combination.   A liability for terminating or reducing the activities of the acquiree is recognised only where the acquiree has, at the acquisition date, an existing liability recognised in accordance with IAS 37. Liabilities for future losses or other costs expected to be incurred as a result of the business combination may not be recognised.

IFRS 3.58-59   Where a business combination involves more than one exchange transaction, each exchange transaction is treated separately by the acquirer, using the cost of the transaction and the fair value information at the date of each exchange transaction, to determine the amount of any goodwill associated with that transaction.   This results in a step-by-step comparison of the cost of the individual investments with the acquirer's interest in the fair values of the acquiree's assets, liabilities and contingent liabilities acquired at each step.   As the identifiable assets, liabilities and contingent liabilities are restated to fair values at the time of successive purchases to determine the amount of any goodwill associated with each transaction, and the acquiree's identifiable assets, liabilities and contingent liabilities are recognised by the acquirer at their fair values at the acquisition date, any adjustment to those fair values relating to the previously held interest of the acquirer is a revaluation and is accounted for as such.   This does not, however, imply that the acquirer has elected to apply a policy of revaluation after initial recognition.

Accounting for minority interest is addressed in section 2.5.5.

3.4.4   Determining fair values of identifiable assets and liabilities assumed

A   General approach

An acquiring entity should allocate the cost of an acquired company to all identifiable *FAS 141.35*
assets acquired and liabilities assumed in a business combination by reference to their
fair values at date of acquisition, regardless of whether those assets or liabilities had
been recorded in the financial statements of the acquired entity.

Independent appraisals and actuarial or other valuations may be used as an aid in   *FAS 141.36*
determining estimated fair values.   The tax basis of an asset or liability shall not be
a factor in determining its estimated fair value.

It is appropriate to take account of the acquirer's intentions when identifying and   *EITF 95-3*
allocating fair values to the assets acquired and liabilities assumed.   For example, it
is appropriate to recognise obligations for costs of a plan to exit an activity, or to
terminate or relocate employees, of an acquired company as liabilities assumed in a
purchase business combination if certain conditions are met (see section 3.4.4K).

> **COMMENT**
>
> It is expected that Phase II of the FASB Business Combinations project will nullify
> EITF 95-3 as under the revised standard costs expected to be incurred by the
> acquiring entity pursuant to its plan to exit an activity, or to terminate or relocate
> employees, of an acquired entity would not be considered liabilities of the acquired
> entity and would not be recognised as liabilities assumed by the acquiring entity
> when the business combination is initially recorded.

When a company acquires a subsidiary which is consolidated in a series of purchases   *AIN-APB 17.2*
on a step-by-step basis, the company should identify the cost of each investment, the
fair value of the underlying assets acquired and the goodwill for each step purchase.

Accounting for minority interests is addressed in section 2.5.5.

IFRS 3.Appx A,   Further guidance on fair valuing the identifiable assets and liabilities is given below.
Appx B16-17   Where fair values need to be estimated, present value techniques may be used even
if not specifically mentioned in the guidance for a particular item.   Fair values are
the amounts for which assets could be exchanged, or liabilities settled between
knowledgeable, willing parties in an arm's length transaction.

COMMENT

It is expected that Phase II of the Business Combinations project on application of
the purchase method which is conducted jointly with the FASB will provide further
application guidance determining the fair values of identifiable assets and liabilities.
An Exposure Draft is expected in 2005 (with an IFRS to follow later in that year,
likely to be effective for periods beginning on or after 1 January 2007).

The project's proposals are expected to include:

- revisions to the definitions of contingent assets and liabilities, and their
treatment in a business combination;

- guidance on determining whether assets and liabilities should be included in
the business combination accounting, or whether they are post-combination;

- a requirement that identifiable assets and liabilities must all be included at fair
values, whether or not the probability criterion is met, unless this is not
reliable, on which more guidance is to be provided;

- to remove the requirement that an intangible asset acquired in a business
combination must be reliably measurable in order to be recognised separately
from goodwill; and

- the introduction of a fair value hierarchy principle and application guidance
for measuring fair values of acquired assets and assumed liabilities.

B   Property, plant and equipment

IFRS 3.Appx B16   Land, buildings, plant and equipment are valued using market values.   Where there
is no market value available, because of the item's specialised nature and the item is
rarely sold except as part of a continuing business, estimates of fair value using an
income or depreciated replacement cost may need to be made.

C   Intangible assets (including in-process research and development)

IFRS 3.45-46   An intangible asset is a non-monetary asset without physical substance which is
IFRS 3.IE   identifiable, i.e. it is separable, or arises from contractual or other legal rights
whether or not those rights are transferable or separable from the entity or from
other rights and obligations.   The illustrative examples to IFRS 3 give numerous
but not exhaustive examples of items meeting the definition of an intangible asset.
In addition to more conventional intangible assets, these include databases, trade
secrets, and customer-related intangibles such as customer lists, order backlogs,
customer contracts and non-contractual customer relationships.   In process
research and development is recognised as an asset separately from goodwill in the
same way as for other intangible assets, i.e. the project meets the definition of an
intangible asset and its fair value can be measured reliably.

B   *Property, plant and equipment*

The fair values of tangible fixed assets should be determined as follows:

- plant and equipment that is to be;   *FAS 141.37(d)*
    - used – at current replacement cost for similar capacity unless the expected future use of the assets indicates a lower value to the acquirer. Replacement cost may be determined directly if a used-asset market exists for the assets acquired.   Otherwise, it should be approximated from replacement cost new less estimated accumulated depreciation;
    - sold – at fair value less costs to sell;
- assets such as land and non-marketable securities at appraised values.   *FAS 141.37(f)*

C   *Intangible assets (including in-process research and development)*

Intangible assets, other than goodwill, should be included at estimated fair values.   *FAS 141.37(e)*
An intangible asset is recognised apart from goodwill if it (1) arises from contractual or other legal rights (regardless of whether those rights are transferable or separable) or (2) is separable (regardless of intent).

An intangible asset is considered separable if it is capable of being sold, transferred,   *FAS 141.39*
licensed, rented or exchanged (regardless of whether there is intent to do so) even when it can only be sold, transferred, licensed, rented or exchanged in combination with a related contract, asset or liability.   An assembled workforce should not be recognised as an intangible asset apart from goodwill.   Appendix A to FAS 141 provides additional guidance on, and examples of, acquired intangibles apart from goodwill.

IFRS 3.Appx B16 Intangible assets are most reliably valued by reference to quoted market prices (bid)
IAS 38.35-41 in an active market as defined in IAS 38 *Intangible Assets* (see section 6).   If
current bid prices are unavailable, the price of the most recent similar transaction
may provide a basis for estimating fair value, provided there has not been a
significant change in economic circumstances between the transaction date and the
date at which fair values are estimated.

In practice, often no active market exists, and the intangible asset is then valued on a
basis reflecting the amount the acquirer would have paid for the asset in an arm's
length transaction between knowledgeable willing parties, based on the best
information available.   In determining this, an entity considers recent transactions
in similar assets.   Techniques for estimating fair values indirectly include multiples
applied to revenue, market shares or operating profit, or to the royalty stream
obtainable from licensing the intangible asset to another party in an arms length
transaction ('relief from royalty' method); or discounting expected future net cash
flows.   Indirect techniques may be used if their objective is to estimate fair value
and if they reflect current transactions and practices in the industry to which the
asset belongs.

Where an acquired intangible asset is separable but only together with a related
tangible asset or intangible asset, the group of assets is recognised as a single asset if
the individual fair values are not reliably measurable.   The acquirer also recognises
as a single asset a group of complementary intangible assets comprising a brand (e.g.
trademarks and related trade names and formulae) if the individual values are not
reliably measurable or if they are reliably measurable but have similar useful lives.

The fair value of intangible assets acquired in a business combination can normally
be measured with sufficient reliability, and where the intangible asset has a finite life
there is a rebuttable presumption that its fair value can be measured reliably.   When
there is a range of possible outcomes with different probabilities in the estimates
used to measure fair value, that uncertainty enters the measurement of fair value
rather than demonstrates that fair value can not be measured reliably.

The only circumstances where it may not be possible to measure reliably the fair
value of an intangible asset acquired in a business combination are when the
intangible asset arises from legal or other contractual rights and either (1) is not
separable; or (2) is separable, but there is no history or evidence of exchange
transactions for the same or similar assets and otherwise estimating fair value would
be dependent on immeasurable variables.

D   Inventories

IFRS 3.Appx B16 Finished goods and merchandise are valued at selling prices less the sum of the costs
of disposal and a reasonable profit allowance for the selling effort of the acquirer
(based on profit for similar finished goods and merchandise).   Work in progress is
valued at selling prices less the sum of the costs to complete, costs of disposal and a
reasonable profit allowance for the completing and selling effort of the acquirer
(based on profit for similar finished goods).   Raw materials are valued at current
replacement costs.

Costs assigned to intangible assets to be used in a particular research and development project and that have no alternative future use should be charged to expense at the acquisition date. An overview of the accounting for acquired in-process research and development is included in section 6.2.3B.

D   Inventories

The fair values of inventories should be determined as follows: *FAS 141.37(c)*

- finished goods at estimated selling price less costs of disposal and less a reasonable profit allowance for the selling effort of the acquiring company;

- work in progress at estimated selling price less any future costs to complete, costs of disposal and less a reasonable profit allowance for the completing and selling effort of the acquiring entity; and

- raw materials at current replacement costs.

E   Investments

IFRS 3.Appx B16 Financial instruments traded in an active market are valued at current market values.

Financial instruments not traded in an active market are valued using estimated values which may (particularly for securities) take into consideration features such as price-earnings ratios, dividend yields and expected growth rates of comparable instruments of entities with similar characteristics.   IAS 39 has more guidance on estimating fair values for financial instruments.

F   Monetary assets and liabilities

IFRS 3.Appx B16 Receivables, beneficial contracts and other identifiable assets are valued at the present values of the amounts to be received less any allowances for uncollectibility and collection costs.   Accounts and notes payable, long-term debt, liabilities, accruals and other claims payable are valued at the present values of amounts to be disbursed.   Present values are determined at appropriate current interest rates but discounting is not required for short-term items where the impact is not material.

G   Non-current assets and disposal groups held for sale

IFRS 5
IFRS 3.36   Non-current assets or disposal groups classified as held for sale in accordance with IFRS 5 are recognised at fair value less costs to sell (see section 1.9).

H   Pre-acquisition contingencies

IFRS 3.42   A payment that an entity is contractually required to make, in the event it is acquired in a business combination is recognised as an identifiable liability.

IFRS 3.41   Liabilities for future losses or other costs expected to be incurred as a result of the business combination may not be recognised.

IFRS 3.Appx B16 Contingent liabilities of the acquiree are valued at the amounts that a third party would charge to assume these contingent liabilities, which shall reflect all expectations about possible cash flows and not the single most likely or expected maximum or minimum cash flow.

E   Investments

Marketable securities should be included at fair values.   *FAS 141.37(a)*

F   Monetary assets and liabilities

Receivables should be recorded at the present values of amounts to be received   *FAS 141.37(b)*
determined at appropriate current interest rates, less allowance for bad debts.

> **COMMENT**
>
> The SEC Staff are likely to raise questions where bad debt provisions raised during   *SAB 61*
> the fair value exercise are materially different from those made by the acquired   *(Topic 2-A)*
> company prior to its acquisition (the same applies to extra provisions that are made
> against the value of stock).

All liabilities (including notes and accounts payable and long-term debt), and   *FAS 141.37(g)*
accruals, e.g. accruals for warranties, vacation pay, deferred compensation, should   *FAS 141.37(j)-(k)*
be recorded at their present value determined at appropriate current interest rates.
Similarly, other liabilities and commitments (including unfavourable leases, contracts
and commitments and plant closing expense incidental to the acquisition) should be
recorded at present values of amounts to be paid determined at appropriate current
interest rates.

G   Businesses sold or held exclusively with a view to subsequent resale

Under FAS 144 *Accounting for the Impairment or Disposal of Long-Lived Assets,*   *FAS 144.32,34*
a long-lived asset, or component of an entity, that was acquired for resale rather
than to be 'held and used' would be classified as held for sale at the acquisition date
only if the sale is expected to be completed within one year and satisfaction of all
other criteria for 'held for sale' classification is probable within a short period
following the acquisition (usually within three months). A newly acquired long-
lived asset, or component of an entity, classified as held for sale should be measured
at fair value less cost to sell. As a result, operating losses during the period from
the date of acquisition to the date of sale would be recognised as incurred.

H   Pre-acquisition contingencies

A pre-acquisition contingency should be included in the purchase price allocation   *FAS 141.40*
either at fair value, where fair value can be determined during the allocation period,
or at an estimated amount where information available during the allocation period
indicates that a contingent asset, liability or impairment is probable and the amount
can be reasonably estimated.

The SEC Staff have stated that there is an assumption that contingencies, e.g. product   *SAB 100*
warranties and environmental costs, of the acquired entity, will not be materially
changed in the purchase price allocation, unless the acquiring entity intends to settle
the liability in a demonstrably different manner from the acquired entity.

IFRS 3.48 After initial recognition, the acquirer measures contingent liabilities that are recognised separately at the higher of:

- the amount that would be recognised in accordance with IAS 37; and

- the amount initially recognised less, when appropriate, cumulative amortisation recognised in accordance with IAS 18 *Revenue.*

IFRS 3.49 This does not apply to contracts accounted for in accordance with IAS 39. However, loan commitments excluded from the scope of IAS 39 (other than commitments to provide loans at below-market interest rates) are accounted for as contingent liabilities of the acquiree if at the acquisition date, an outflow of resources embodying economic benefits is not probable or the amount of the obligation cannot be measured reliably. Such loan commitments are recognised separately only if fair value can be measured reliably in accordance with the general recognition criteria.

I   *Pensions and post retirement/employment benefits*

IFRS 3.Appx B16
IAS 19.108 Net employee benefit assets or liabilities for defined benefit plans are valued at the present value of the full defined benefit obligation less the fair value of any plan assets. An asset is only recognised to the extent that it is probable that it will be available to the acquirer in the form of refunds from the plan or a reduction in future contributions.

J   *Taxation*

IFRS 3.Appx B16
IAS 12.19 Deferred tax assets and liabilities are recognised on an undiscounted basis for temporary differences resulting from a difference between the tax bases and the fair values of identifiable assets, liabilities and contingent liabilities. Tax assets and liabilities are determined, assessed from the perspective of the combined entity.

IAS 12.67 If as a result of a business combination, an acquirer considers it probable that it will recover its own deferred tax asset that was not recognised before the business combination, the acquirer recognises a deferred tax asset, but does not include this in determining the amount of any goodwill (or any excess of the acquirer's interest in the net fair value of the acquiree's identifiable assets, liabilities and contingent liabilities over the cost of the combination).

IFRS 3.44 A tax benefit arising from the acquiree's tax losses that was not recognised by the acquiree before the business combination, is recognised as an identifiable asset if it is probable that the acquirer will have future taxable profits against which the unrecognised tax benefit can be applied.

If the estimated costs of settling the liabilities are materially different from the amounts recognised by the acquired entity and if the manner of settlement is not demonstrably different this could indicate that the financial statements of the acquired entity are materially misstated or that the acquiring entity's estimates of fair value are not appropriate.

If it is determined that the acquired entity's financial statements as of the acquisition date are not fairly stated the correction should not be made through the purchase price allocation but the acquired entity's financial statements should be restated with the adjustment applied to the income statement in the period that the change in estimate occurred.

I   Pensions and post-retirement/employment benefits

When accounting for an acquisition under the purchase method, liabilities assumed   *FAS 87.74*
should include a liability for any projected benefit obligation in excess of plan assets (or an asset for plan assets in excess of the projected benefit obligation), thereby eliminating any previously existing unrecognised net gain or loss, unrecognised prior service cost or unrecognised net transitional obligation.

There are similar requirements for post-retirement benefits other than pensions.   *FAS 106.86-87*

The measurement of such assets or liabilities should reflect the effect of:

- any changes in assumptions based on the purchaser's assessment of relevant future events;

- changes to benefit plans of the acquired entity in compliance with the conditions of the business combination. If improvements were not a condition of the combination, credit granted for prior service should be treated as a plan amendment, i.e. impacting post acquisition earnings; and

- terminating or curtailing the acquired entity's benefit plans, if those actions are expected.

J   Taxation

A deferred tax liability or asset should be recognised for differences between the   *FAS 109.30*
assigned values and the tax bases of the assets and liabilities recognised in a purchase business combination except the portion of goodwill for which amortisation is not deductible for tax purposes and leveraged leases.

In some business combinations, the acquirer has cumulative losses or other negative   *FAS 109.266*
evidence, which resulted in a valuation allowance on its deferred tax assets immediately prior to the acquisition, and deferred tax liabilities arise in the business combination that are available to offset the reversal of the acquirer's pre-existing deferred tax assets. As a result of the business combination, the acquiring company may consider the pre-existing deferred tax assets are more-likely-than-not to be realised by the combined entity and the valuation allowance should be reduced or eliminated. FAS 109 requires any resulting reduction in the acquirer's valuation allowance to be accounted for as part of the business combination, as part of the purchase price allocation, impacting goodwill.

IAS 12.15   An entity shall not recognise deferred tax liabilities arising from the initial recognition of goodwill or arising from goodwill that is not tax deductible (see section 17.2.2).

IAS 12.68   The potential benefit of income tax loss carry forwards, or other deferred tax assets of
IFRS 3.65   an acquired entity, which were not recognised as an identifiable asset by the acquirer at the date of acquisition, may subsequently be realised.   When this occurs, the acquirer recognises the benefit as income under IAS 12 *Income Taxes*, and the acquirer:

- reduces the carrying amount of the goodwill to the amount that would have been recorded if the deferred tax asset had been recognised as an identifiable asset at the date of the business combination; and

- recognises the reduction in the carrying amount of the goodwill as an expense.

This procedure shall not result in the creation of excess of the acquirer's interest in the net fair value of the acquiree's identifiable assets, liabilities and contingent liabilities over the cost of the combination, nor shall it increase the amount previously recognised for any such excess.

COMMENT

It is expected that Phase II of the Business Combinations project on application of the purchase method which is conducted jointly with the FASB will amend the treatment of deferred tax assets.   An Exposure Draft is expected in 2005 (with an IFRS to follow later in that year, likely to be effective for periods beginning on or after 1 January 2007).

The project's proposals are expected to require that if deferred tax assets are not recognised at acquisition, but are subsequently realised, the deferred tax assets would be recognised in income.   However, if the benefit is realised within 12 months of the acquisition, there would be a rebuttable presumption that this is an initial accounting adjustment and the carrying amount of goodwill would be adjusted.

K   Provisions for reorganisations and future losses

IFRS 3.41,43   A liability for terminating or reducing the activities of the acquiree is recognised only
IFRS 3.BC85   where the acquiree has, at the acquisition date, an existing liability recognised in accordance with IAS 37 (see section 18.8).

No liability is recognised for an acquiree's restructuring plan whose execution is conditional upon it being acquired in a business combination.

Liabilities for future losses or other costs expected to be incurred as a result of the business combination are not recognised.

IFRS 3.Appx B16   Onerous contracts and other identifiable liabilities of the acquiree are valued at the present values, determined at appropriate current interest rates, of amounts to be disbursed in settling the obligations.

If the tax benefits of an acquired entity's operating loss or tax credit carryforward for financial reporting are not recognised at the acquisition date, i.e. a valuation allowance is made under FAS 109, subsequent recognition should first be applied to eliminate any goodwill and other non-current intangible assets related to the acquisition and next be recognised as a reduction of the tax expense. *EITF 93-7*

Additional guidance is provided for taxable business combinations in which the purchase price assigned to the assets and liabilities is recognised for tax purposes as well as for financial reporting, but at different amounts. *FAS 109.261*

K   Provisions for reorganisations and future losses

Consideration of the acquirers' intentions is permitted when recognising liabilities assumed in a purchase business combination, e.g. the costs of a plan to exit an activity or involuntarily terminate employees of an acquired entity, where the following conditions are met: *EITF 95-3*

- as of the acquisition date, management with the appropriate level of authority begins to assess and formulate a plan;
- as soon as possible (and within a year) after the acquisition date, management completes its assessment of which activities are to be ceased or which employees are to be affected and commits itself to the plan and communicates the arrangements to those employees affected;
- the plan identifies the actions to be taken to complete the plan, including the method of disposition and location of activities or the number, function and location of employees who are to be made redundant or relocated; and
- actions required by the plan will begin as soon as possible after the plan is finalised and the period of time to complete the plan indicates that significant changes are unlikely.

The costs or liabilities recognised cannot relate to activities or employees of the acquiring entity as the cost of the acquisition is not allocated to the assets and liabilities of the acquirer.

L   *Deferred revenue*

No specific guidance is provided regarding the valuation of deferred revenue. However, the general rule that identifiable assets and liabilities should be recognised at their fair values applies.

M   *Employee stock options exchanged*

IFRS 3 does not provide any guidance regarding the recognition of employee stock options nor the exchange of options in a business combination.

IFRS 2.5   IFRS 2 *Share-based Payment* does not apply to transactions in which an entity acquires goods as part of the net assets in a business combination to which IFRS 3 applies.   Hence, equity instruments issued in exchange for control of the acquiree in such a business combination are not within the scope of IFRS 2.   However, equity instruments granted to employees (e.g. in return for continued service) or the cancellation, replacement or other modification of share-based payment arrangements because of a business combination or other equity restructuring are within the scope of IFRS 2 (see section 22).

3.4.5   The allocation period

IFRS 3.62   If the initial accounting can be determined only provisionally by the end of the period in which the business combination is effected, provisional fair values are used.

The acquiree shall recognise any adjustments, as a result of completing the initial accounting, within twelve months of the acquisition date.   Such adjustments shall be calculated as if the adjusted fair values had been applied from the acquisition date.   They include both the effect of the change to the fair values initially assigned, and the effect of depreciation and other changes which would have resulted if the adjusted fair values had been applied from the date of acquisition.   The amount assigned to goodwill or any excess of the acquirer's interest in the net fair value of the acquiree's identifiable assets, liabilities and contingent liabilities over the cost of the combination (to be recognised as a gain) is adjusted from the acquisition date by an amount equal to the adjustment to the fair value at the acquisition date of the identifiable asset, liability or contingent liability.

Comparative information for the periods before the initial accounting is complete is presented as if the initial accounting had been completed from the acquisition date, including additional depreciation, amortisation or other profit or loss effect.

IFRS 3.63-64 Except for adjustments for contingent adjustments to the cost of the business combination (see section 3.4.3) and the subsequent recognition of deferred tax

COMMENT

It is expected that phase II of the FASB Business Combinations project will nullify EITF 95-3 as under the revised standard costs expected to be incurred by the acquiring entity pursuant to its plan to exit an activity, or to terminate or relocate employees, of an acquired entity would not be considered liabilities of the acquired entity and would not be recognised as liabilities assumed by the acquiring entity when the business combination is initially recorded.

L   *Deferred revenue*

The acquiring entity should recognise a liability related to the deferred revenue of an acquired entity only if that deferred revenue represents a legal obligation assumed by the acquiring entity (a legal performance obligation).   The amount assigned to that liability should be based on its fair value at the date of acquisition.

FAS 141.37(k)
EITF 01-3

M   *Employee stock options exchanged*

Under FAS 123R, exchanges of share options or other equity instruments or changes to their terms in connection with a business combination are treated as modifications.

FAS 123R.53-54

Accounting for a modification in connection with a business combination required a comparison of the fair value of the modified award with the fair value of the original award immediately before the modification (see section 22.3).

3.4.5   The allocation period

The allocation period should usually not exceed one year from consummation of a business combination.   Adjustments should be made to fair values (if necessary) when uncertainties existing at the date of acquisition have been resolved prior to the close of the 'allocation' period.   However, (1) adjustments resulting from economic events that clearly occurred subsequent to the acquisition date should be recognised in the income statement, and (2) adjustments to deferred tax should be accounted for in accordance with FAS 109 and EITF 93-7 (see section 3.4.3J).

FAS 141.App F1

assets of the acquiree (see section 3.4.4J), adjustments to the initial accounting for a business combination, once complete, are recognised only to correct an error in accordance with IAS 8 *Accounting Policies, Changes in Accounting Estimates and Errors*. This requires errors to be adjusted retrospectively by restating comparative periods in which the error occurred. The effects of changes in estimates, however, are recognised in the current and future periods.

3.4.6   Accounting for goodwill

A   Goodwill

IFRS 3.51,Appx A Goodwill is defined as 'future economic benefits arising from assets that are not capable of being individually identified and separately recognised'. It is recognised as an asset, and initially measured at cost, being the excess of the cost of the business combination over the acquirer's interest in the net fair value of the identifiable assets, liabilities and contingent liabilities.

IFRS 3.58-59 A business combination may involve more than one exchange transaction. Each exchange transaction is treated separately by the acquirer, using the cost of the transaction and the fair value information at the date of each exchange transaction, to determine the amount of any goodwill associated with that transaction. See section 3.4.4A). This results in a step-by-step comparison of the cost of the individual investments with the acquirer's interest in the fair values of the acquiree's assets, liabilities and contingent liabilities acquired at each step.

> **COMMENT**
>
> It is expected that Phase II of the Business Combinations project on application of the purchase method which is conducted jointly with the FASB will amend the definition and treatment of goodwill, and step-by-step acquisitions. An Exposure Draft is expected in 2005 (with an IFRS to follow later in that year, likely to be effective for periods beginning on or after 1 January 2007).
>
> Under the project's expected proposals, consolidated goodwill would include any minority's share of goodwill. In addition, if an acquirer obtains control of an acquiree in a step-by-step acquisition, the carrying amount of the previous investment would be revalued to fair value on the acquisition date, and any gain or loss recognised in profit or loss (or recycled from equity, if the interest was previously an available-for-sale asset). This would be the case, even if the acquisition date does not coincide with the date(s) of exchange transactions. If there are changes in ownership after control is obtained, that do not lead to a loss of control, no goodwill would be recognised. Any difference between the change in minority interest and consideration paid would be treated as an equity transaction, and attributed to the equity holders of the parent.

Increases in interest subsequent to acquisition are dealt with in section 2.5.6.

IFRS 3.54 Goodwill is subsequently carried at cost less any accumulated impairment losses.

IFRS 3.51,54-55 Goodwill is not amortised. However, the acquirer should test it for impairment annually, or more frequently if events or changes in circumstances indicate impairment, in accordance with IAS 36 *Impairment of Assets*.

Sections 9 and 6.4 address the impairment and disposal of goodwill, respectively.

IAS 21.47,58-59 Goodwill and fair value adjustments relating to the acquisition of a foreign operation are treated as assets and liabilities of the foreign operation, and are

3.4.6   Accounting for goodwill

A   Goodwill

The excess of the cost of the acquired entity over the net of the amounts assigned   *FAS 141.43*
to assets acquired and liabilities assumed should be recognised as an asset referred   *FAS 142.App F1*
to as goodwill.   An acquired intangible asset that does not meet the criteria in
section 3.4.3 C should be included in the amount recognised as goodwill.

Goodwill arising on the purchase of a foreign enterprise is a currency asset that   *FAS 52.101*
should be translated at closing rates.   Exchange differences arising upon
retranslation are reported in other comprehensive income.

Under FAS 142, goodwill is not amortised, but is tested for impairment.   Impairment   *FAS 142.18*
arises when the carrying amount of goodwill exceeds its implied fair value.

Impairment of goodwill is covered in section 9.   *APB 17.30*
FIN 9.9

therefore expressed in the functional currency of the foreign operation, and retranslated at the closing rate. For existing IFRS reporters, this requirement in IAS 21 is applied prospectively to all acquisitions occurring after the beginning of the financial reporting period in which IAS 21 is applied (mandatory for periods beginning on or after 1 January 2005, with early adoption encouraged). Retrospective application to earlier acquisitions is permitted. For an acquisition treated prospectively, but which occurred before the date on which IAS 21 is first applied, the entity shall not restate prior years and may, when appropriate, treat goodwill and fair value adjustments as assets and liabilities of the entity rather than of the foreign operation. Therefore, those goodwill and fair value adjustments either are already expressed in the entity's functional currency or are non-monetary foreign currency items, reported using the exchange rate at acquisition date.

For business combinations to which IFRS 3 is not applied retrospectively (see section 3.2B), there are transitional rules for existing IFRS reporters in relation to the treatment of previously recognised goodwill and previously recognised intangible assets (see also section 6.2.1).

IFRS 3.79 IFRS 3 applies prospectively from the beginning of the first annual period beginning on or after 31 March 2004, to goodwill acquired in a business combination for which the agreement date was before 31 March 2004, and to goodwill arising from an interest in a jointly controlled entity obtained before 31 March 2004 and accounted for applying proportionate consolidation.

Therefore, from the beginning of the first annual period beginning on or after 31 March 2004:

- amortisation of goodwill is discontinued;

- the carrying amount of the related amortisation of goodwill is eliminated with a corresponding decrease in the cost of the goodwill; and

- the goodwill is tested for impairment in accordance with IAS 36 (revised 2004).

IFRS 3.80 If goodwill was previously recognised as a deduction from equity, this goodwill is not recognised in profit or loss when all or part of the business to which the goodwill relates is disposed of, or when a cash-generating unit to which the goodwill relates becomes impaired.

IFRS 3.82 The carrying amount of an intangible asset which was (1) acquired in a business combination for which the agreement date was before 31 March 2004 or (2) arises from an interest in a jointly controlled entity obtained before 31 March 2004 and accounted for by applying proportionate consolidation, shall be reclassified as goodwill at the beginning of the first annual period beginning on or after 31 March 2004, if that intangible asset does not at that date meet the identifiability criterion in IAS 38 (see section 6.2.1).

B   *Excess of the acquirer's interest in the fair value of the identifiable assets, liabilities and contingent liabilities over the cost of the combination*

IFRS 3.56 Where the acquirer's interest in the fair value of the identifiable assets and liabilities exceeds the cost of the combination, the acquirer must reassess the identification and measurement of the cost of the combination. Any excess remaining after that reassessment is recognised immediately in profit or loss.

B   *Negative purchased goodwill*

Negative goodwill is the excess that arises when the net of the amounts assigned to   *FAS 141.44-45*
assets acquired and liabilities assumed exceeds the cost of the acquired entity.
Negative goodwill should be allocated to reduce proportionately the values assigned
to the acquired assets, including research and development assets acquired and

IFRS 3.57   IFRS 3 notes that such a gain recognised could represent errors in measuring fair values of either the cost of the combination or the identifiable assets, liabilities, or contingent liabilities; a requirement in an accounting standard to measure fair value of particular items acquired in a particular way, which is not true fair value (e.g. deferred tax is not discounted) or a bargain purchase.

For business combinations for which IFRS 3 is not applied retrospectively (see section 3.2B) there are transitional rules for existing IFRS reporters in relation to equity accounted investments.

IFRS 3.81   The carrying amount of negative goodwill at the beginning of the first annual period beginning on or after 31 March 2004 that arose from either (1) a business combination for which the agreement date was before 31 March 2004 or (2) an interest in a jointly controlled entity obtained before 31 March 2004 and accounted for by applying proportionate consolidation, is derecognised at the beginning of that period with a corresponding adjustment to the opening balance of retained earnings.

3.4.7   Disclosure

IFRS 3.66   An acquirer is required to disclose information that enables users of its financial statements to evaluate the nature and financial effect of business combinations effected during the period and after the balance sheet date but before the financial statements are authorised for issue.

IFRS 3.67-68   Therefore, the following disclosures are required to be made in the financial statements for each business combination effected during the period (or in aggregate for business combinations effected during the reporting period that are individually immaterial):

- the names and descriptions of the combining entities or businesses;
- the acquisition date;
- the percentage of voting equity instruments acquired;
- the cost of the combination and a description of its components, including any directly attributable costs.   When equity instruments are issued, or issuable as part of the cost, the following disclosures must also be made:
    - the number of equity instruments issued or issuable; and
    - the fair value of those instruments and the basis for determining their value.   If there is no published price, the significant assumptions must be disclosed.   If a published price exists but was not used, that fact, the reasons, method and assumptions used to attribute the value of the equity instruments, and the aggregate amount of the difference between the value attributed to and the published price of the equity instruments must be disclosed;
- details of any operations which the entity has decided to dispose of resulting from the business combination;
- the amounts recognised at the acquisition date for each class of the acquiree's assets, liabilities and contingent liabilities, and, unless disclosure would be impracticable, the carrying amounts of these classes, determined in accordance with IFRSs immediately before the combination.   If this would be impracticable, this fact, with reasons should be disclosed;

charged to expense, except (a) financial assets other than equity method investments, (b) assets to be disposed of by sale, (c) deferred tax assets, (d) prepaid assets relating to pension or other post-retirement benefit plans, and (e) any other current assets. Any remainder should be recognised as an extraordinary gain.

If a business combination involves contingent additional consideration, an amount equal to the lesser of the maximum contingent consideration or the balance of negative goodwill should be recognised as a liability on acquisition.   *FAS 141.46*

3.4.7 Disclosure

FAS 141 requires the following disclosures in the period in which a material business combination is completed: *FAS 141.51*

- name and a brief description of the acquired entity and the percentage of voting equity interests acquired;   *FAS 141.51(a)*

- the primary reasons for the acquisition, including a description of the factors that contributed to a purchase price that results in recognition of goodwill;   *FAS 141.51(b)*

- period for which results of operations of the acquired entity are included in the income statement of the acquiring entity;   *FAS 141.51(c)*

- cost of the acquired entity and, if applicable, the number of shares of stock issued or issuable, the value assigned to those interests, and the basis for determining that value;   *FAS 141.51(d)*

- a condensed balance sheet disclosing the amount assigned to each major asset and liability caption of the acquired entity at the acquisition date;   *FAS 141.51(e)*

- contingent payments, options, or commitments specified in the acquisition agreement and their proposed accounting treatment;   *FAS 141.51(f)*

- the amount of purchased research and development assets acquired and written off in the period, the basis of determining the fair value, and the line item in the income statement in which the amounts written off are aggregated;   *FAS 141.51(g)*
FIN 4

- if applicable, the fact that the purchase price allocation has not been finalised, and the reasons therefore – in subsequent periods, the nature and amount of any material adjustments to the initial allocation should be disclosed.   *FAS 141.51(h)*

The notes to the financial statements also should disclose the following in the period in which a material business combination is completed if the amounts assigned to goodwill or other intangible assets are significant in relation to the total cost of the acquired entity:

- for intangible assets subject to amortisation:
    - the total amount assigned and the amount assigned to any major class of intangible asset;

- the amount of any excess of the acquirer's interest in the fair value of the identifiable assets and liabilities over the cost of the combination, and the line item in the income statement in which the excess is recognised;

- a description of the factors that contributed to a cost resulting in the recognition of goodwill including a description of each intangible asset not recognised separately and an explanation as to why its fair value could not be measured reliably;

- a description of the nature of any excess of the acquirer's interest in the fair value of the identifiable assets and liabilities over the cost of the combination recognised in profit or loss; and

- the amount of the acquiree's profit or loss since the acquisition date included in the acquirer's profit or loss for the period, unless the disclosure would be impracticable. If such disclosure would be impracticable, that fact should be disclosed with reasons.

IFRS 3.71   In addition, the information above is required for each business combination effected after the balance sheet date but before the financial statements are authorised for issue, unless impracticable (in which case, this fact and reasons must be disclosed).

IFRS 3.69   If the initial accounting for a business combination effected during the period was determined only on a provisional basis, this should be stated and reasons given.

IFRS 3.70   The acquirer shall disclose, unless impracticable (in which case, this fact with reasons must be disclosed):

- the revenue of the combined entity for the period as though the acquisition date for all business combinations effected during the period had been the beginning of the period; and

- the profit or loss of the combined entity for the period as though the acquisition date for all business combinations effected during the period had been the beginning of the period.

IFRS 3.72   The acquirer should disclose information that enables users of its financial statements to evaluate the financial effects of gains, losses, error corrections and other adjustments recognised in the current period relating to business combinations.

IFRS 3.73   Therefore, the following disclosures shall be made:

- the amount and an explanation of any gain or loss recognised in the current period that:

  - relates to the identifiable assets acquired or liabilities or contingent liabilities assumed in a business combination effected in the current or previous period; and

  - which is of such size, nature or incidence that disclosure is relevant to an understanding of the combined entity's financial performance;

- amounts and explanations of adjustments during the period to the provisional values recognised in the initial accounting for a business combination in the prior period; and

- information about error corrections required by IAS 8 for any of the acquiree's identifiable assets, liabilities or contingent liabilities, or changes in the values assigned to those items recognised during the current period.

- the amount of any significant residual value, in total and by major class of intangible asset;
- the weighted-average amortisation, in total and by major class of intangible asset;
- for intangible assets not subject to amortisation, the total amount assigned and the amount assigned to any major class of intangible asset;
- for goodwill;
  - the total amount of goodwill and the amount that is expected to be deductible for tax purposes;
  - the amount of goodwill by reportable segment, unless not practicable.

The notes to the financial statements also should disclose the following if a series of individually immaterial business combinations completed during the period are material in aggregate:
- the number of entities acquired and a brief description of those entities;
- the aggregate cost of the acquired entities, the number of equity interests issued or issuable, and the value assigned to those interests;
- the aggregate amount of any contingent payments, options, or commitments and the proposed accounting treatment, if potentially significant;
- the information described above in respect of goodwill or other intangible assets if the aggregate amount assigned to goodwill or other intangible assets acquired is significant in relation to the costs of the acquired entities.

If the combined entity is a public enterprise, the notes to the financial statements should include the following supplemental pro forma information for the period in which a material acquisition occurs: *FAS 141.54*
- results of operations for the current period as though the businesses combination had been completed at the beginning of the period;
- results of operations for the immediately preceding period as though the businesses combination had been completed at the beginning of that period if comparative financial statements are presented;
- details of any operations identified as acquired for resale; and   *EITF 87-11*
- details of liabilities recognised for any plan to exit from or restructure the   *EITF 95-3* activities of an acquired entity (disclosures are required for the period in which the acquisition occurs and for all subsequent periods until its plan is fully executed).

The aggregate amount of goodwill should be presented as a separate line item in the   *FAS 142.43* statement of financial position. The aggregate amount of goodwill impairment losses associated with continuing operations should be presented as a separate line item in the income statement before the subtotal 'income from continuing operations' (or similar caption). A goodwill impairment loss associated with a discontinued operation shall be included (on a net-of-tax basis) within the results of discontinued operations.

The following information should be disclosed in the financial statements or the notes   *FAS 142.45* to the financial statements for each period for which a balance sheet is presented:
- The changes in the carrying amount of goodwill during the period including:
  - The aggregate amount of goodwill acquired.

IFRS 3.74   An entity shall disclose information enabling users of the financial statements to evaluate changes in the carrying amount of goodwill during the period.

IFRS 3.75   Accordingly, the financial statements shall disclose a reconciliation of the carrying amount of goodwill at the beginning and end of the period showing:

- the gross amount and the accumulated impairment losses, at the beginning of the period;
- additional goodwill recognised during the period except for goodwill included in a disposal group that, on acquisition, meets the criteria to be classified as held for sale in accordance with IFRS 5;
- goodwill included in a disposal group classified as held for sale in accordance with IFRS 5 and goodwill derecognised during the period without having previously been included in a disposal group classified as held for sale;
- adjustments resulting from the subsequent recognition of the acquiree's deferred tax assets during the period;
- impairment losses recognised during the period in accordance with IAS 36;
- net exchange differences arising during the period in accordance with IAS 21;
- any other changes in the carrying amount during the period; and
- the gross amount and the accumulated impairment losses, at the end of the period.

IFRS 3.76
IAS 36.126-137   In addition, IAS 36 requires further disclosures about the recoverable amount and impairment of goodwill (see section 9.7).

IFRS 3.77   If the information required to be disclosed by IFRS 3 does not satisfy the general objectives in paragraphs 66, 72 and 74, additional information necessary to meet those objectives must be disclosed.

IFRS 3.50   Although contingent liabilities recognised separately as part of allocating the cost of a business combination are excluded from the scope of IAS 37, the information required by IAS 37 for each class of provision is required to be disclosed (see section 18.9).

Where the business combination includes non-current assets classified or held for sale under IFRS 5, the disclosures of that Standard are required (see section 1.9).

- The aggregate amount of impairment losses recognised.
- The amount of goodwill included in the gain or loss on disposal of all or a portion of a reporting unit.

Entities that report segment information in accordance with FAS 131 should provide this disclosure in total and for each reportable segment and should disclose any significant changes in the allocation of goodwill by reportable segment. If any portion of goodwill has not yet been allocated to a reporting unit at the date the financial statements are issued, that unallocated amount and the reasons for not allocating that amount should be disclosed.

For each goodwill impairment loss recognised, the following information should be disclosed in the notes to the financial statements that include the period in which the impairment loss is recognised: *FAS 142.47*

- a description of the facts and circumstances leading to the impairment;
- the amount of the impairment loss and the method of determining the fair value of the associated reporting unit; and
- if applicable, the fact that a recognised impairment loss is an estimate that has not yet been finalised and the reasons therefore and, in subsequent periods, the nature and amount of any significant adjustments made to the initial estimate of the impairment loss.

In the period of initial application of FAS 142 and thereafter until FAS 142 has been applied, in full, to all periods presented, the income before extraordinary items and net income should be disclosed either on the face of the income statement or in the notes for all periods presented adjusted to exclude amortisation of: *FAS 142.61*

- goodwill;
- negative goodwill; and
- intangible assets no longer being amortised,

and to reflect any adjustments for changes in amortisation periods for intangible assets that will continue to be amortised.

The notes to the financial statements should disclose a reconciliation of reported net income to the adjusted net income.

Adjusted earnings per share amounts for all periods presented should be presented either on the face of the income statement or in the notes to the financial statements.

Section 4   Associates and joint ventures

4.1   AUTHORITATIVE PRONOUNCEMENTS

- IAS 27
- IAS 28
- IAS 31

- IAS 39
- IFRS 5
- SIC-13

4.2   SCOPE

A   General

IAS 28.1
IAS 31.1
IAS 28 *Investments in Associates* is applied in accounting by an investor for investments in associates and IAS 31 *Interest in Joint Ventures* is applied to joint ventures. Neither Standard applies to investments in associates or interests in jointly controlled entities (see sections 4.3.1 and 4.3.2) held by venture capital organisations, or mutual funds, unit trusts and similar entities including investment-linked insurance funds, that on initial recognition are designated as at fair value through profit or loss, or classified as held for trading, and are accounted for in accordance with IAS 39 *Financial Instruments: Recognition and Measurement* (see section 11.6B).

IAS 31.7
IAS 31 addresses three different types of joint ventures:
- jointly controlled operations;
- jointly controlled assets; and
- jointly controlled entities.

IAS 28.13-14
IAS 31.2,30,38,42
Investments in associates are accounted for using the equity method and investments in jointly controlled entities are accounted for under the equity method or proportionate consolidation, except when:
- the investment is classified as held for sale in accordance with IFRS 5 *Non-current Assets Held for Sale and Discontinued Operations* – the associate or jointly controlled entity(or the disposal group of which it is a part) is accounted for in accordance with IFRS 5 (see section 1.9);

IAS 27.10
- the reporting entity is also a parent company, and is exempt from preparing consolidated financial statements under IAS 27 *Consolidated and Separate Financial Statements* (see section 2.2); or
- where the reporting entity is not a parent, all of the following apply:
  - the investor or venturer is a wholly owned subsidiary itself (or is a partially-owned subsidiary, and its other owners, including those not entitled to vote, have been informed about and do not object to the investor or venturer not applying proportionate consolidation or the equity method);

Section 4

Associates and joint ventures

4.1 AUTHORITATIVE PRONOUNCEMENTS

- APB 18
- APB 29
- FAS 58

4.2 SCOPE

The equity method of accounting for an investment in common stock should be followed by an investor where its investment in voting stock gives it the ability to exercise significant influence over operating and financial policies of an investee even though the investor holds 50% or less of the voting stock. This includes investments in common stock of corporate joint ventures. *APB 18.17 FIN 35.4*

The ability to exercise significant influence is presumed to exist for investments of 20% or more and is presumed not to exist for investments of less than 20%. Both presumptions may be overcome by predominant evidence to the contrary.

Examples of indicators that an investor may be unable to exercise significant influence are provided in FIN 35 *Criteria for Applying the Equity Method of Accounting for Investments in Common Stock – an interpretation of APB Opinion No. 18.*

The equity method should also be used by investors to account for interests in limited partnerships, unless the investor's interest 'is so minor that the limited partner may have virtually no influence over the partnership operating and financial policies'. In practice, investments of more than 3-5% are viewed to be more than minor. *EITF D-46*

Investments in a limited liability corporation (LLC) that maintains a 'specific ownership account' for each investor, similar to a partnership structure, should be viewed as similar to an investment in a limited partnership for purposes of determining whether a non-controlling investment in an LLC should be accounted for using the cost method or equity method. *EITF 03-16*

The powers of a shareholder with a majority voting interest to control the operations or assets of an investee may be restricted as a result of substantive participating rights of the minority investor. In such cases, the investee should not be consolidated but should be accounted for under the equity method. *EITF 96-16*

- the investor's or venturer's debt or equity instruments are not traded in a public market;
- the investor or venturer did not file, nor is in the process of filing, its financial statements with a securities commission or other regulatory organisation for the purpose of issuing any class of instruments in a public market; and
- the ultimate or any intermediate parent of the investor or venturer produces consolidated financial statements available for public use that comply with IFRS.

Where the reporting entity is not a parent, but has associates or jointly controlled entities, it will need to equity account for its associates or equity account for or apply proportionate consolidation to jointly controlled entities in its own financial statements, if the above exemptions do not apply. These are not separate financial statements, as defined (see section 2.8).

COMMENT

While IAS 28 appears to prohibit use of equity method where the above exceptions apply (as it requires the equity method except when the criteria above are met), both IAS 27 and IAS 31 are drafted as permissive (IAS 31 states that a venturer is exempted from proportionate consolidation or the equity method when the above criteria are met); this inconsistency may be unintentional. An entity may prepare separate financial statements as its only financial statements, if it meets all the conditions for the final exemption. IAS 31, as drafted has an apparently wider exemption, but this inconsistency may be unintentional.

There are no exemptions from applying IAS 31 to jointly controlled operations or jointly controlled assets.

B   Separate financial statements

IAS 28.35
IAS 31.46
IAS 27.37-42
In separate financial statements (which are those that account for investments in associates, subsidiaries or joint ventures on the basis of the direct equity interest, rather than consolidation, equity accounting or proportionate consolidation), an investment in an associate or jointly controlled entity is accounted for in accordance with IAS 27 (see section 2.8).

C   Taxation

Income taxes arising from investments in associates and joint ventures are accounted for in accordance with IAS 12 *Income Taxes* (see section 17.2.2) which has specific rules for associates and joint ventures. The temporary differences in question for the purposes of deferred tax may differ, depending on whether the financial statements include the investees under the equity method (or proportionate consolidation), or are separate financial statements.

4.3   DEFINITIONS AND METHOD OF ACCOUNTING

4.3.1   Associates

IAS 28.2
An associate is an entity (including an unincorporated entity) in which the investor has significant influence, and that is neither a subsidiary nor a joint venture.

4.3   DEFINITIONS AND METHOD OF ACCOUNTING

4.3.1   Associates

The equity method of accounting should be applied when the investor has the   *APB 18.17*
ability to exercise significant influence over the operating and financial policies of

Significant influence is the power to participate in the financial and operating policy decisions of the investee, but not control or joint control over those policies. See sections 2.3 and 4.3.2 on control and joint control.

IAS 28.8-9
IAS 27.IG1-IG8

The existence and effect of potential voting rights (e.g. those arising from the exercise of share options or conversion of convertible debt or equity) that are currently exercisable or currently convertible are also considered when assessing whether an entity controls another entity. Potential voting rights are not currently exercisable or currently convertible when they cannot be exercised or converted until a future date or upon the occurrence of a future event. All potential voting rights should be considered, including potential voting rights held by other entities. All facts and circumstances should be considered including the terms of exercise of the potential voting rights and possible linked transactions. However, in making the assessment the intention of management and the financial ability to exercise or convert should not be taken into account.

IAS 28.6

There is a rebuttable presumption that the investor has significant influence when the investor (directly, or indirectly, via subsidiaries) holds 20% or more of the voting power of the investee unless it can be clearly demonstrated that this is not the case. A substantial or majority ownership by another investor does not necessarily preclude an investor from having significant influence.

IAS 28.6

There is a rebuttable presumption that the investor does not have significant influence when the investor (directly or indirectly, via subsidiaries) holds less than 20% of the voting power of the investee, unless such influence can be clearly demonstrated.

IAS 28.7

The existence of significant influence is usually evidenced by Board representation (or representation on an equivalent governing body), participation in policy-making processes (including decisions about dividends or distributions), material transactions between investor and investee, interchange of management personnel, or provision of essential technical information.

4.3.2   Joint ventures

IAS 31.3,7

Joint ventures are contractual arrangements whereby two or more parties undertake an economic activity that is subject to joint control, i.e. over which there is contractually agreed sharing of the power to govern the financial and operating policies so as to obtain benefits. This exists only where the strategic financial and operating decisions require unanimous consent of the parties sharing control ('the venturers').

IAS 31.10

The contractual arrangement that establishes joint control is usually in writing and addresses subjects such as:

- the activity, duration and reporting obligations of the joint venture;
- the appointment of the board of directors or equivalent governing body of the joint venture and the voting rights of the venturers;
- capital contributions by the venturers; and
- the sharing by the venturers of the output, income, expenses or results of the joint venture.

The contractual arrangement may identify one venturer as the operator or manager of the joint venture. The operator does not control the joint venture but acts

the investee and has an investment in common stock and/or in-substance common stock of the investee, albeit less than 50% of the voting stock.

EITF 02-14 provides guidance to determine whether an investor's investment is 'in-substance common stock'. The initial determination under EITF 02-14 should be made based on circumstances that exist on the date of adoption, rather than the date of original investment. The consensus should be applied for periods beginning after 15 September 2004 with the effect of adoption reported as for a cumulative effect of a change in accounting principle.

EITF 02-14

4.3.2   Joint ventures

APB 18 defines a corporate joint venture as an entity owned and operated by a small group of businesses as a separate and specific business or project for their mutual benefit. The purpose of a joint venture frequently is to share risks and rewards in developing a new market, product or technology; to combine complementary technological knowledge; or to pool resources in developing production or other facilities. A joint venture also usually provides an arrangement under which each investor may participate, directly or indirectly, in the overall management of the entity. Accordingly, the investors in the entity should have an interest or relationship other than as passive investors. An entity that is a subsidiary of one of the investors through voting control is not a joint venture. The ownership interests in a joint venture seldom change, and equity or other interests in an operating joint venture are usually not traded publicly. A minority public ownership interest, however, does not preclude an entity from being a joint venture.

APB 18.3

Investors should account for investments in common stock of corporate joint ventures by the equity method – as for associates.

within the financial and operating policies agreed by the joint venturers, in accordance with the contractual arrangement, and delegated to the operator. If the operator has the power to govern the financial and operating policies, it has control, and the venture is its subsidiary, and not a joint venture.

IAS 31 addresses three different types of joint ventures:

- jointly controlled operations;
- jointly controlled assets; and
- jointly controlled entities.

A   Jointly controlled operations

IAS 31.13,15-16 Jointly controlled operations are joint ventures that involve the use of assets and other resources of the venturers rather than the establishment of a separate corporation, partnership or other entity. Each venturer uses its own assets, incurs its own expenses and liabilities and raises its own finance. Usually, revenue from the sale of the joint product and expenses incurred in common are shared among the venturers. A venturer recognises in its (own and consolidated) financial statements:

- the assets that it controls and the liabilities that it incurs; and
- the expenses that it incurs and its share of the income that it earns from the sale of goods or services by the joint venture.

B   Jointly controlled assets

IAS 31.18-19 A joint venture may involve the joint control, and often joint ownership by the
IAS 31.21-22 venturers of certain assets that are dedicated to the purposes of the joint venture, and used to obtain benefits for the venturers. Each venturer may take a share of the output from the assets and bear an agreed share of expenses incurred. These joint ventures do not involve the establishment of a corporation, partnership or other entity, or a financial structure separate from the venturers themselves. Each venturer has a share of the jointly controlled asset. A venturer recognises in its (own and consolidated) financial statements:

- its share of the jointly controlled assets, classified according to the nature of the assets;
- any liabilities that it has incurred;
- its share of any liabilities incurred jointly with the other venturers in relation to the joint venture;
- any income from the sale or use of its share of joint venture output, together with its share of any expenses incurred by the joint venture; and
- any expenses that it has incurred in respect of its interest in the joint venture.

C   Jointly controlled entities

IAS 31.24-25 A jointly controlled entity is a joint venture that involves the establishment of a
IAS 31.27-28 corporation, partnership or other entity in which each venturer has an interest. The entity controls the joint venture assets, incurs liabilities and expenses and earns income. It may enter contracts in its own name and raise finance for the joint venture activity. Each venturer shares the profits of the jointly controlled entity, although some jointly controlled entities involve also sharing of output. Many jointly controlled entities are similar in substance to jointly controlled operations or assets.

Proportionate gross financial statement presentation (proportionate consolidation)   *EITF 00-1*
should not be used to account for investments in the common stock of corporate
entities when the investor has significant influence over the investee.

Proportionate consolidation is not appropriate for an investment in a an
unincorporated entity accounted for by the equity method unless the investee is in
either the construction industry or an extractive industry where there is a
longstanding practice of its use.   This was intended to be a narrow exception for
practical purposes.   For purposes of this consensus, an entity is in an extractive
industry only if its activities are limited to the extraction of mineral resources (such
as oil and gas exploration and production) and not if its activities involve related
activities such as refining, marketing or transporting extracted mineral resources.

The jointly controlled entity keeps its own accounting records and prepares its own financial statements in accordance with International Financial Reporting Standards.

IAS 27.IG1 While IAS 31 does not explicitly address potential voting rights, the guidance above for associates (see section 4.3.1) is also relevant to the determination of joint control although the Implementation Guidance to IAS 27 notes that the contractual aspect is likely to be the critical determinant.

IAS 31.30-31,34 A venturer shall recognise its interest in the jointly controlled entity (irrespective of whether it also has investments in subsidiaries) by either applying:

- the benchmark treatment of proportionate consolidation of the financial statements of the jointly controlled entity. Proportionate consolidation may be given effect by either:
  - combining the venturer's share of each of the assets, liabilities, income and expenses of the jointly controlled entity with the similar items in its own financial statements on a line-by-line basis; or
  - including separate line items for the venturer's share of the assets, liabilities, income and expenses of the jointly controlled entity in its own financial statements.

IAS 31.35 It is inappropriate to offset assets and liabilities, or income and expenses, unless a legal right of offset exists and there is an intention to settle net; or

IAS 31.38-39 • alternatively, the equity method.

COMMENT

In many cases, the difference between these methods is one of presentation, on a line-by-line basis or as a one-line item under the equity method. However, there may be differences where the jointly controlled entity is loss making, where waterline accounting is adopted under the equity method so that the carrying amount never fall below zero (see section 4.4.4), except to the extent that the investor has incurred legal or constructive obligations or made payments on behalf of the joint venture.

IAS 31.52-53 However, operators or managers of a joint venture shall account for any management fees in accordance with IAS 18 *Revenue*. These management fees are expensed by the joint venture.

IAS 31.51 An investor in a joint venture that does not have joint control shall account for the investment in accordance with IAS 39 unless it has significant influence when IAS 28 is applied.

4.4   APPLICATION OF EQUITY METHOD

4.4.1   General

IAS 28.2,13,20 Associates are accounted for under the equity method. The detailed requirements
IAS 31.40 of the equity method are included in IAS 28, and must also be followed where a venturer accounts for its interest in a jointly controlled entity using the equity method. IAS 28 notes that many of the procedures used in the equity method are similar to consolidation procedures.

IAS 28.2,11,23 Under this method, the investment is initially recorded at cost. On acquisition, any difference between the cost of the investment and the investor's share of the net fair

4.4 APPLICATION OF EQUITY METHOD

4.4.1 General

Under the equity method, the investing group's share of after tax profits or losses of the investee company should be included in the group's income statement as a single line item except that, if material, the investing group's share of extraordinary items and prior period adjustments should be classified separately in the group income statement.

APB 18.19(c),(d)

Under the equity method the investment is included in the balance sheet at cost plus appropriate share of post-acquisition profits, less dividends received from the investee.

value of the associate's identifiable assets, liabilities and contingent liabilities is accounted for in accordance with IFRS 3 *Business Combinations*. Therefore, goodwill is included within the carrying amount of the investment but not amortised. Any excess of the investor's or venturer's share of the net fair value of the associate's or jointly controlled entity's identifiable assets, liabilities and contingent liabilities over the cost of investment is included as income in determining the investor's or venturer's share of the investee's profit or loss in the period the investment is acquired. The carrying amount is subsequently adjusted to recognise the investor's or venturer's share in the post-acquisition profits or losses of the investee (which are recognised in the investor's or venturer's profit or loss) and to recognise the investor's or venturer's share in post-acquisition changes in the investee's equity that have not been recognised in profit or loss (e.g. revaluations, which are recognised directly in equity of the investor or venturer). Distributions received from an investee reduce the carrying amount of the investment.

For business combination for which IFRS 3 is not applied retrospectively (see section 3.2B), there are transitional rules for existing IFRS reporters in relation to equity accounted investments.

IFRS 3.83 IFRS 3 is applied by existing IFRS reporters in accounting for investments accounted for by applying the equity method and acquired on or after 31 March 2004. Accordingly, acquired goodwill included in the carrying amount of the investment is not amortised, and the excess of the entity's interest in the net fair value of the investee's identifiable assets, liabilities and contingent liabilities over the cost of the investment is included as income in determining the entity's share of the investee's results in the period in which the investment is acquired.

For business combinations for which IFRS 3 is not applied retrospectively (see section 3.2B) there are transitional rules for existing IFRS reporters in relation to equity accounted investments.

IFRS 3.84 IFRS 3 is applied prospectively by existing IFRS reporters from the beginning of the first annual period beginning on or after 31 March 2004 to any such acquired goodwill or excess included in the carrying amount of investments accounted for by applying the equity method and acquired before 31 March 2004. Accordingly, from the beginning of this period, amortisation of the goodwill is discontinued, and the negative goodwill is derecognised with a corresponding adjustment to the opening balance of retained earnings.

IFRS 3.85 IFRS 3 permits limited retrospective application (see section 3.2B). The transitional rules for first-time-adopters are in Chapter 2.

IAS 28.12 The investor's and venturer's share that is equity accounted is determined based on
IAS 39.2 present ownership interests without reflecting the possible exercise or conversion of
IAS 27.IG6-IG7 potential voting rights (although, it does take into account the eventual exercise of rights and other derivatives that in substance give access at present to the economic benefits associated with an ownership interest). Interests in potential voting rights and other derivatives which do not in substance give a present ownership interest, are accounted for in accordance with IAS 39.

IAS 28.28 If an associate or jointly controlled entity has outstanding cumulative preference shares held by other parties than the investor and classified as equity, the investor's

If cost differs from the amount of underlying equity in net assets of an investee at the date of acquisition, the difference should be accounted for as if the investee were a consolidated subsidiary.

APB 18.19(b)

In certain situations, an investor may capitalise interest costs it incurs related to the activities of an equity method investee.

FAS 58.5

or venturer's share of the investee's profits is adjusted for the preference dividends, even if not declared.

IAS 28.21   The group's share in an associate or jointly controlled entity is the aggregate of the holdings in that investee by the parent and its subsidiaries only.   When the investee itself has subsidiaries, associates or joint ventures, the results and net assets taken into account in applying the equity method are those recognised in the investee's financial statements (i.e. including the subsidiaries, and the investee's share of its associates and joint ventures after any adjustments necessary to give effect to uniform accounting policies).

IAS 28.26-27   In applying the equity method, the financial statements of the associate or jointly controlled entity are prepared using the same accounting policies as the investor or venturer.

Additional detail regarding the application of the equity method is provided in sections 4.4.2 to 4.4.5 below.

4.4.2   Transactions between the reporting entity and associates and jointly controlled entities

IAS 28.22   Profits and losses resulting from transactions between an investor and an associate are recognised in the investor's financial statements only to the extent of unrelated investors' interests in the associate.   Therefore, the investor's share in the associate's profits and losses resulting from these transactions is eliminated.

IAS 31.48   A venturer may contribute or sell assets to a joint venture, while the assets are retained by the joint venture; the venturer recognises only the portion of the gain or loss attributable to the interests of the other venturers.

IAS 31.49   When a venturer purchases assets from a joint venture, the venturer shall not recognise its share of the profits or losses of the joint venture from the transaction until it resells the assets to an independent party.

IAS 31.48-49   IAS 31 further notes that the full loss is recognised when the loss (1) provides evidence of a reduction in the net realisable value of current assets or an impairment loss or (2) represents a reduction in the net realisable value of current assets or an impairment loss.

> **COMMENT**
>
> It is unlikely that the requirement to eliminate unrealised profits or losses extends to interest paid on loans between the venturer or investor, and the associate or jointly controlled entity which is equity accounted.

SIC-13.5-7   A venturer may make a non-monetary contribution to a jointly controlled entity in exchange for an equity interest in that entity.   The venturer shall recognise in profit or loss the proportion of the gain or loss corresponding to the equity interests of the other venturers except when:

- the significant risks and rewards of ownership of the contributed non-monetary assets have not been transferred to the jointly controlled entity; or

- the gain or loss on the non-monetary contribution cannot be measured reliably; or

- the contribution transaction lacks commercial substance as described in IAS 16 *Property, Plant and Equipment* (see section 7.2).

4.4.2   Transactions between the reporting entity and associates and jointly controlled entities

Intragroup profits and losses should be eliminated until realised by the investor or investee as if a corporate joint venture or investee company were consolidated.

APB 18.19(a)
AIN-APB 18.1

The accounting for non-monetary exchanges is described in APB 29. In general, non-monetary exchanges are accounted for at fair value. However, one exception to the use of fair value is in an exchange of 'similar' productive assets'. EITF 01-2 provides interpretive guidance to determine if a non-monetary transaction should be recorded at fair value or historical cost.

EITF 01-2

The EITF considered two basic transactions involving transfers of assets by an enterprise to a newly created entity in exchange for a noncontrolling ownership interest in that entity. The EITF reached a consensus that (1) a gain should be recognised based on the fair values of the assets transferred if the entity accounts for the ownership interest received using the cost method, or (2) a partial gain should be recognised if the entity accounts for the ownership interest received using the equity method. The partial gain should be calculated as the amount described in (1) above, less the portion of that gain represented by the economic interest (which may be different from the voting interest) retained.

The EITF observed that accounting for a nonmonetary transaction subject to APB 29 should not be based on the fair values of the assets transferred unless those fair values are determinable within reasonable limits.

The SEC observer (1) stated that the exchange of a consolidated business for an interest in a joint venture would typically not result in gain recognition, absent the receipt of cash or near cash consideration, and (2) emphasised that gain recognition would not be appropriate if a significant uncertainty exists regarding realisation or the enterprise has an actual or implied commitment to support the operations of the new entity in any manner.

FAS 153 amends APB 29 and partially nullifies EITF 01-2. The general rule of the amended APB 29 requires non-monetary transactions to be accounted for at fair value. Exceptions to the general rule are described in section 19.4.4. FAS 153 is

APB 29.18

If any of the above conditions applies, the gain or loss arising would be considered 'unrealised' (and therefore not recognised in profit or loss) unless in addition to receiving an equity interest in the entity, a venturer receives monetary or non-monetary assets, in which case an 'appropriate portion' of the gain or loss on the transaction should be recognised by the venturer. Where the venturer accounts for the jointly controlled entity using proportionate consolidation, any unrealised gains or losses should be eliminated against the venturer's share of the underlying assets of the entity. Where equity accounting is used, the elimination should be against the carrying amount of the investment in the entity. Unrealised gains or losses are not accounted for as deferred income or expenditure in the venturer's consolidated balance sheet. Where 'unrealised' losses are eliminated in this way, the carrying amount of the investment in the jointly controlled entity will be the same as the carrying amount of the non-monetary assets transferred in exchange for it, subject of course to any necessary provision for impairment uncovered by the transaction.

COMMENT

While SIC-13 *Jointly Controlled Entities – Non-Monetary Contributions by Venturers* does not explicitly address associates, it provides appropriate guidance. Similarly applicable for associates would be the guidance in IAS 31 that where a transaction between a venturer and joint venture indicates impairment of the asset that is the subject of the transaction, the full impairment loss should be recognised.

4.4.3 Non-coterminous financial statements

IAS 28.24-25   The most recent financial statements of the associate or jointly controlled entity are used in applying the equity method. Where the reporting dates of the investor or venturer and the investee are different, the financial statements are prepared by the investee as at the date of the investor's or venturer's financial statements. When it is impracticable to do so, the investor or venturer may use financial statements drawn up to a different reporting date. The length of the financial reporting periods and any difference between reporting dates should be the same from period to period, and may not exceed three months. However, adjustments should be made for the effects of any significant events or transactions that occur between the date of the associate's or jointly controlled entity's financial statements and the date of the investor's or venturer's financial statements.

4.4.4 Deficiency of net assets and impairment

IAS 28.29   If, under the equity method, the investor's or venturer's share of losses in the associate or jointly controlled entity equals or exceeds its interest in the investee, the investor's or venturers share of further losses is not recognised and the investment is reported at nil value. The interest in the investee is the carrying amount of the investment under the equity method together with long term interests that in substance form part of the net investment (e.g. items for which settlement is neither planned nor likely to occur in the foreseeable future such as preference shares or long-term receivables and loans, but not trade receivables and payables or secured long-term receivables). Losses recognised under the equity method in excess of the investment in ordinary shares are applied to other components in reverse order of their priority in liquidation.

IAS 28.30   However, after the interest is reduced to nil, additional losses are provided for only to the extent the investor or venturer has incurred legal or constructive obligations

effective for transactions occurring in fiscal periods beginning after 15 June 2005.

4.4.3   Non-coterminous financial statements

If the financial statements of an investee are not sufficiently timely, the investor   *APB 18.19(g)*
should normally record its share of the earnings or losses of an investee from the
most recent available financial statements, which may be its audited year-end
financial statements.   The investor could base its proportionate share of the results
of operations of an investee on the investee's unaudited interim financial statements.
Where there is a time lag in reporting, this time lag should be consistent from period
to period.

For SEC registrants, a 93-day rule operates as for subsidiaries (see section 2.5.2).

4.4.4   Deficiency of net assets and impairment

The investor should normally discontinue applying the equity method when the   *APB 18.19(i)*
investment accounted for by the equity method plus net advances made by the   *EITF D-68*
investor is reduced to zero and should not provide for additional losses unless the
investor has guaranteed obligations of the investee or is otherwise committed to
provide further financial support for the investee.   If the investee subsequently
reports net income, the investor should resume applying the equity method only
after its share of that net income equals the share of net losses not recognised
during the period the equity method was suspended.

Where the investor has loans to and investments in other securities of the investee,   *EITF 98-13*
the basis of the other investments should be adjusted for the amount of the equity   *EITF 99-10*
method loss, based on their seniority.

or has made payments on behalf of the investee. If the investee subsequently reports profits, the investor or venturer recognises its share only where the share of profits exceeds the share of losses not recognised previously.

IAS 28.31-34
IAS 39.2,58-62
After applying the equity method, the investor or venturer applies IAS 39 to determine whether additional impairment should be recognised in respect of the investor's or venturer's net investment (see section 11.6.3), and if this is the case, the entire carrying amount of the investment (including goodwill) is tested for impairment under IAS 36 *Impairment of Assets*. The value in use may be determined using the present value of either (1) the share of the present value of estimated cash flows expected to be generated by the investee and the proceeds on ultimate disposal, or (2) the present value of estimated dividend receipts and the proceeds on ultimate disposal. The recoverable amount is assessed for each investee, unless the investee does not generate cash inflows largely independent of those from other assets. Even though the carrying amount of an associate or joint venture effectively includes goodwill, impairment testing under IAS 36 is only required when there is an indication of impairment under IAS 39.

IAS 39.58-70
The investor or venturer applies IAS 39 to determine whether any additional impairment loss is required, and the amount of that loss, in respect of the investor's or venturer's interest in the investee which does not form part of the net investment.

4.4.5   Commencement and cessation of relationship

IAS 28.23
The investor accounts for its investment in an associate using the equity method from the date it obtains significant influence. A venturer accounts for its interest in a jointly controlled entity from the date it obtains joint control. Exemptions from applying the equity method or proportionate consolidation are detailed in section 4.2.

IAS 28.13,15
IAS 31.42-43
Interests in associates and jointly controlled entities classified as held for sale (or included in a disposal group held for sale) in accordance with IFRS 5 shall be accounted for in accordance with that standard, from the date the 'held for sale' criteria are met. When an investment in an associate or jointly controlled entity, previously classified as held for sale under IFRS 5 no longer meets those criteria, it is accounted for under the equity method from the date of its classification as held for sale, with restatement of prior financial statements (see section 1.9).

IAS 28.18-19
An investor shall discontinue the application of the equity method from the date it ceases to have significant influence in an associate. It thereafter accounts for the investment in accordance with IAS 39. The carrying amount of the investment, at this date is regarded thereafter as its cost, on initial measurement as a financial asset in accordance with IAS 39. However, if the investee becomes a subsidiary or jointly controlled entity, it shall be accounted for in accordance with IAS 27 or IAS 31 respectively.

IAS 28.10
An entity loses significant influence when it loses the power to participate in the financial and operating policy decisions of that investee. The loss of significant influence can occur with or without a change in absolute or relative ownership levels, e.g. when an associate becomes subject to the control of a government, court, administrator or regulator, or as a result of a contractual agreement.

When subsequent investments in an investee are made after suspension of equity method loss recognition, those investments may represent, in substance, the funding of prior losses.   In that case, previously suspended losses (up to the amount of additional investment) should be recognised.

EITF 02-18

A loss in value which is other than a temporary decline should be recognised. Evidence of a loss in value might include a current fair value which is less than the carrying amount, but a decline in the quoted market price or the existence of operating losses would not necessarily indicate a loss in value which is other than temporary.

APB 18.19(h)

4.4.5   Commencement and cessation of relationship

When an investment qualifies for use of the equity method, the investor should adopt the equity method of accounting.

APB 18.19(m)

An investment may qualify for use of the equity method as a result of the acquisition of additional voting stock by the investor, acquisition or retirement of voting stock by the investee, or other transactions.   When an investor adopts the equity method of accounting, the carrying amount of the investment, the results of operations (current and prior periods presented), and retained earnings of the investor should be adjusted retroactively in a manner consistent with the accounting for a step-by-step acquisition of a subsidiary (see section 3.4.4).

The carrying amount of an investment in an equity method investee may differ from the underlying equity in net assets of the investee.   If the investor is unable to relate the difference to specific accounts of the investee, the difference should be considered to be goodwill (see section 6.3).

An investment in voting stock of an investee company may fall below the level of ownership at which significant influence exists from sale of a portion of an investment, sale of additional stock by an investee, or other transactions and the investor may thereby lose the ability to influence policy.   The equity method of accounting should be applied from the date significant influence exists until the date it is lost.

APB 18.19(l)

The earnings or losses that relate to the stock retained by the investor and that were previously accrued should remain as a part of the carrying amount of the investment.

To the extent that dividends received by the investor in subsequent periods exceed the investor's share of earnings for such periods the excess dividend should be applied to reduce the carrying amount of the investment.

IAS 31.8,36,41,45   A venturer shall discontinue application of proportionate consolidation or the equity method from the date on which it ceases to have joint control over the jointly controlled entity (unless in the latter case it becomes an associate). Joint control may be precluded when an investee is in legal reorganisation or bankruptcy or operates under severe restrictions on its ability to transfer funds to the venturer, but if joint control continues, these events are not enough in themselves not to account for joint ventures in accordance with IAS 31. From the date it becomes a subsidiary or an associate, the venturer should account for its interest in accordance with IAS 27 or IAS 28 respectively.

IAS 31.51   An investor in a joint venture that does not have joint control shall account for the investment in accordance with IAS 39 unless it has significant influence when IAS 28 is applied.

COMMENT

While IAS 31 does not explicitly address the treatment of a former jointly controlled entity that does not become an associate or subsidiary, equivalent guidance is addressed in IAS 27 and IAS 28. Consequently, the entity should thereafter account for the investment in accordance with IAS 39. The carrying amount of the investment at this date should be regarded thereafter as its cost on initial measurement as a financial asset in accordance with IAS 39.

IAS 21 *The Effects of Foreign Exchange Rates* requires recycling of foreign exchange differences recognised in equity, in profit or loss on disposal (but not impairment) of a foreign operation. While not explicitly addressed, the same principle should apply to an investment in an associate or a jointly controlled entity.

4.5   DISCLOSURE

IAS 1.68,81   Investments accounted for using the equity method and the share of the profit or loss of associates and joint ventures accounted for using the equity method, are required to be disclosed on the face of the balance sheet and income statement.

A   Associates

IAS 28.38
IAS 1.68,81   Investments in associates accounted for using the equity method are classified in the balance sheet as non-current assets. The carrying amount of the investments in associates, the investor's share in the results of associates, and its share of any discontinued operations of such associates are separately disclosed.

IAS 28.39
IAS 1.96-101   The investor's share of changes in the associate's equity recognised directly in equity by the investor are disclosed in the statement of changes in equity as required by IAS 1 *Presentation of Financial Statements.*

IAS 28.40   The investor shall disclose in accordance with IAS 37 *Provisions, Contingent Liabilities and Contingent Assets:*

- its share of the associate's contingent liabilities incurred jointly with other investors; and

- those contingent liabilities that arise because the investor is severally liable for all or part of the liabilities of the associate.

4.5　DISCLOSURE

The following should be disclosed, when material, in the financial statements:　　*APB 18.20(a)-(b)*

- the name of each investee and percentage of common stock held;
- the accounting policies of the investor with respect to investments in common stock;
- the difference, and the accounting treatment for the difference, if any, between the amount at which an investment is carried and the amount of underlying equity in net assets; and
- for quoted investments, the aggregate value of each identified investment based on the quoted market price.

The amount of consolidated retained earnings which represents undistributed earnings of 50% or less owned persons accounted for by the equity method should be disclosed.　　*S-X 4-08(e)(2)*

Investments in common stock should be shown in the balance sheet of an investor as a single amount, and the investor's share of earnings or losses of investees usually should be shown in the income statement as a single amount (except for certain items, e.g. extraordinary items, prior year adjustments).

If a 20% or more investee is not equity accounted, disclosure should be made of the name of the investee and the reasons why the equity method is not considered appropriate.　Similar disclosure is required if less than 20% is held but is accounted for under the equity method.　　*APB 18.19 fn13*

IAS 28.37 The following disclosures shall be made:

- the fair value of investments in associates for which there are published price quotations;

- summarised financial information of associates, including the aggregated amounts of assets, liabilities, revenues and profit or loss;

- the reasons why the presumption that an investor does not have significant influence is overcome if the investor holds, directly or indirectly through subsidiaries, less than 20 per cent of the voting or potential voting power of the investee but concludes that it has significant influence;

- the reasons why the presumption that an investor has significant influence is overcome if the investor holds, directly or indirectly through subsidiaries, 20 per cent or more of the voting or potential voting power of the investee but concludes that it does not have significant influence;

- the reporting date of the financial statements of an associate, when such financial statements are used in applying the equity method and are as of a reporting date or for a period that is different from that of the investor, and the reason for using a different reporting date or different period;

- the nature and extent of any significant restrictions on the ability of associates to transfer funds to the investor in the form of cash dividends, or repayment of loans or advances;

- the unrecognised share of losses of an associate, both for the period and cumulatively, if an investor has discontinued recognition of its share of losses of an associate;

- the fact that an associate is not accounted for using the equity method in accordance with paragraph 13 of IAS 28; and

- summarised financial information of associates, either individually or in groups, that are not accounted for using the equity method, including the amounts of total assets, total liabilities, revenues and profit or loss.

IAS 27.41-42 Where separate financial statements are prepared, the disclosures required by IAS 27 (see section 2.8) must be given.

B   Joint ventures

IAS 31.54 A venturer shall disclose the aggregate amount of the following contingent liabilities, unless the probability of loss is remote, separately from the amount of other contingent liabilities:

- any contingent liabilities that the venturer has incurred in relation to its interests in joint ventures and its share in each of the contingent liabilities that have been incurred jointly with other venturers;

- its share of the contingent liabilities of the joint ventures themselves for which it is contingently liable;

- those contingent liabilities that arise because the venturer is contingently liable for the liabilities of the other venturers of a joint venture.

A   Additional disclosures for significant investees

Separate financial statements should be filed for any 50% or less owned entities where, in respect of any such entity (1) the group's investment exceeds 20% of group consolidated total assets, or (2) the group's share of net income before taxes exceeds 20% of group consolidated net income before taxes.

S-X 3-09(a)

Where financial statements are required for two or more non-consolidated subsidiaries, or two or more 50% or less owned entities, combined or consolidated statements may be filed, provided that the basis of preparation clearly shows the financial position, cash flows and results of operations of the combined or consolidated sub-group.

S-X 3-09(c)

Additional disclosures should be given for unconsolidated investees accounted for by the equity method where, individually or in aggregate, (1) the group's investment exceeds 10% of group consolidated total assets, or (2) the group's proportionate share of the total assets of the investee exceeds 10% of the group consolidated total assets, or (3) the group's share of net income before taxes exceeds 10% of group consolidated net income before taxes.

S-X 4-08(g)
S-X 1.02(w)

The following summarised information should be disclosed in a note to the financial statements:

S-X 1-02(bb)

*   current and non-current assets;
*   current and non-current liabilities;
*   (if applicable) redeemable stock and minority interests;
*   net sales or gross revenues;
*   gross profit;
*   income or loss from continuing operations (before extraordinary items and the cumulative effect of accounting change); and
*   net income or loss.

The above disclosures may be made on a combined basis.

When the significance test is applied for combined entities, entities reporting losses should not be aggregated with entities reporting income.

S-X 1.02(w)

Dividends received from a significant investee should also be disclosed.

S-X 5-03.13

Where material to an investee's share of reported earnings or losses, effects of possible stock conversions, exercises or contingent issuances of an investee should be disclosed.

APB 18.20(e)

When assessing significance, if the group's income for the most recent fiscal year is 10% or more lower than the average of the last five fiscal years, average income of the group may be used for this assessment. Loss years should be assigned a value of zero in computing the numerator for this average, but the denominator should always be '5'. This rule is not applicable if the group reported a loss, rather than income, in the latest fiscal year. The acquiree's income is never averaged.

IAS 31.55 A venturer shall disclose the aggregate amount of the following commitments in respect of its interests in joint ventures separately from other commitments:

- any capital commitments of the venturer in relation to its interests in joint ventures and its share in the capital commitments that have been incurred jointly with other venturers; and

- its share of the capital commitments of the joint ventures themselves.

IAS 31.56 A venturer shall disclose the following information:

- a listing and description of interests in significant joint ventures and the proportion of ownership interest held in jointly controlled entities; and

- the aggregate amounts of each of current assets, long-term assets, current liabilities, long-term liabilities, income and expenses related to its interests in joint ventures, where jointly controlled entities are reported using the line-by-line reporting format for proportionate consolidation or the equity method.

IAS 31.57 A venturer shall disclose the method used to recognise its interests in jointly controlled entities.

Section 5   Foreign currency translation

5.1   AUTHORITATIVE PRONOUNCEMENTS

• IAS 1	• IAS 29
• IAS 10	• IAS 39
• IAS 21	• SIC-7
• IAS 23	

COMMENT

SIC-7 provides additional guidance on the application of the requirements of IAS 21 in accounting for the introduction of the euro.

5.2   FUNCTIONAL CURRENCY AND PRESENTATION CURRENCY

IAS 21.8-9,17   IAS 21 requires each individual entity to determine its functional currency and to measure its results and financial position in that currency. The functional currency is the currency of the primary economic environment in which the entity operates; normally the one in which it primarily generates and expends cash.

IAS 21.9   The primary factors to be considered in determining the functional currency are:
- the currency that influences its sales prices which will often be the currency in which the sales prices for its good and services are denominated and settled and the currency of the country whose competitive forces and regulations determine these sales prices; and
- the currency that mainly influences labour, material and other costs of providing goods or services.

IAS 21.10   The following factors may also provide evidence of the functional currency:
- the currency of financing; and
- the currency in which operating cash flows are retained.

IAS 21.11   Additional factors to be taken into account in determining the functional currency of a foreign operation (be it a subsidiary, associate, joint venture or branch of the reporting entity) and whether this functional currency is the same as that of the reporting entity include:
- whether the activities of the foreign operation are carried out as an extension of the reporting entity, rather than being carried out with a significant degree of autonomy;
- whether transactions with the reporting entity are a high or a low proportion of the foreign operation's activities;
- whether cash flows from the activities of the foreign operation directly affect the cash flows of the reporting entity and are readily available for remittance to it; and

Section 5   Foreign currency translation

5.1   AUTHORITATIVE PRONOUNCEMENTS

- FAS 52
- FAS 133

5.2   FUNCTIONAL CURRENCY AND PRESENTATION CURRENCY

Assets, liabilities and operations of an entity should be recorded using the functional currency of that entity.   This is defined as the currency of the primary economic environment in which the entity operates; normally it is the currency of the environment in which it generates and expends cash.   *FAS 52.5*

FAS 52 *Foreign Currency Translation* provides general guidance on how to identify the functional currency.   The following economic factors, and possibly others, should be considered both individually and collectively when determining the functional currency: *FAS 52 App A*

- Cash flow;
- Sales price;
- Sales market;
- Expenses;
- Financing; and
- Intragroup transactions and arrangements.

Where the indicators are inconclusive, management's judgement will be required to determine the functional currency, provided only that it is not contradicted by the facts.

Parent company control over the management decision-making process of foreign investments that are consolidated or accounted for by the equity method may reflect, indicate or create economic factors.   However, the exercise of significant management control and the use of the parent's currency for decision-making purposes do not determine, per se, that the parent's currency is the functional currency for foreign operations.

Once the functional currency is determined, it can only be changed where significant changes in economic factors indicate clearly that the functional currency has changed.

- whether cash flows from the activities of the foreign operation are sufficient to service existing and normally expected debt obligations without funds being made available by the reporting entity.

IAS 21.12   When the above indicators are mixed and the functional currency is not obvious, management uses its judgement to determine the functional currency that most faithfully represents the economic effects of the underlying transactions, events and conditions, giving priority to the primary factors detailed above.

IAS 21.14   If the functional currency is the currency of a hyperinflationary economy then the financial statements require restatement in accordance with IAS 29 *Financial Reporting in Hyperinflationary Economies.*

IAS 21.13,35   The functional currency of an entity is only changed when there is a change in these underlying factors that determine this currency. When there is change in the functional currency of an entity the change should be accounted for prospectively from the date of the change.

IAS 21.34   When an entity keeps its books and records in a currency other than its functional currency, then IAS 21 requires that at the time the entity prepares its financial statements all amounts are translated into the functional currency in accordance with paragraphs 20-26 of the standard (see below). This produces the same amounts in the functional currency as would have occurred had the items been recorded initially in the functional currency. For example, monetary items are translated into the functional currency using the closing rate, and non-monetary items that are measured on a historical cost basis are translated using the exchange rate at the date of the transaction that resulted in their recognition.

IAS 21.38-40   The standard permits an entity to present its financial statements in any currency. If this presentation currency is different to the entity's functional currency then it must retranslate its results and position (this is what has to be done for many individual companies within a multinational group for inclusion in the consolidated financial statements). This method of retranslation from functional currency to presentation currency is dependent upon whether the functional currency is the currency of a hyperinflationary economy or not and whether the presentation currency is the currency of a hyperinflationary economy or not. This method is the same as the method required for translating a foreign operation for inclusion in a reporting entity's financial statements (even if the purpose of the retranslation is just to change the currency of the presentation of the individual company's results and financial position and not for purposes of consolidation). These methods are detailed at section 5.4.1 below.

If the entity's accounting records have not been maintained in the functional currency, the standard requires the use of the temporal method to translate the entity's financial statements from the currency in which the accounting records are kept into its functional currency. The translation should produce the same result as if the accounting records had been initially recorded in the functional currency. Consequently, historical exchange rates should be used to translate certain non-monetary balance sheet items and related revenue, expense, gain and loss accounts; current rates should be used for all other items.

FAS 52.10
FAS 52 App B

If an entity's reporting currency is not the same as its functional currency then all elements of the financial statements should be translated using a current exchange rate. Assets and liabilities should be translated at the exchange rate at the balance sheet date. Revenues, expenses, gains and losses should be translated at actual exchange rates or at an appropriately weighted average exchange rate (see 5.4.1 below).

FAS 52.12

5.3   REPORTING FOREIGN CURRENCY TRANSACTIONS IN THE FUNCTIONAL CURRENCY

5.3.1   Basic requirements

IAS 21.21-22   Foreign currency transactions should be translated into the functional currency using the spot exchange rate between the foreign currency and the functional currency on the date of the transaction. For convenience, an average rate for a week or month may be used for all foreign currency transactions occurring during that period, if the exchange rate does not fluctuate significantly.

IAS 21.23   At each balance sheet date:

- foreign currency monetary items should be translated using the exchange rate at the end of the period (the 'closing rate');

- non-monetary items that are measured in terms of historical cost in a foreign currency should be translated using the exchange rate at the date of the transaction; and

- non-monetary items that are measured at fair value in a foreign currency should be translated using the exchange rate at the date when the fair value was determined.

IAS 21.28   Exchange differences arising both on transactions settled during the period and upon retranslation of monetary items at the balance sheet date should be recognised in profit or loss in the period in which they arise, except as noted in section 5.3.2.

IAS 21.30-31   When a gain or loss on a non-monetary item is recognised directly in equity, any exchange component of that gain or loss should be recognised directly in equity. For example, IAS 16 *Property, Plant and Equipment* requires some gains and losses arising on a revaluation of property, plant and equipment to be recognised directly in equity. When such an asset is measured in a foreign currency, the revalued amount has to be translated using the rate at the date the value is determined, resulting in an exchange difference that is also recognised in equity.

IAS 21.30   Conversely, when a gain or loss on a non-monetary item is recognised in profit or loss, any exchange component of that gain or loss should be recognised in profit or loss.

5.3.2   Exceptions

A   Intragroup long-term loans

IAS 21.15,32-33   The first exception to the general rule identified in IAS 21 relates to exchange differences arising on a monetary item that, in substance, forms part of an entity's net investment in a foreign operation. An entity may have a monetary item that is receivable from or payable to a foreign operation for which settlement is neither planned nor likely to occur in the foreseeable future. In this situation the exchange differences should be recognised initially in a separate component of equity until the disposal of the investment. However, this treatment only applies in the financial statements that include the foreign operation and the reporting entity (i.e. financial statements in which the foreign operation is consolidated, proportionately consolidated or accounted for using the equity method) and if the item is denominated in the functional currency of either the foreign operation or the

5.3   REPORTING FOREIGN CURRENCY TRANSACTIONS IN THE FUNCTIONAL CURRENCY

5.3.1   Basic requirements

Foreign currency transactions are transactions denominated in a currency other than the entity's functional currency.   They may produce receivables or payables that are fixed in terms of the amount of foreign currency that will be received or paid.   For all foreign currency transactions, other than derivative instruments, the following rules apply:

FAS 52.15

- at the date the transaction is recognised, each balance sheet and income statement item arising from the transaction should be translated into the functional currency using exchange rates in effect at the transaction date – it is acceptable to use averages or other methods of approximation;

- at each balance sheet date, recorded foreign currency monetary balances should be translated into the functional currency to reflect current exchange rates; and

- an increase or decrease in the expected amount of functional currency cash flows on settlement of a transaction as a result of changes in exchange rates is a foreign currency transaction gain or loss which generally should be included in determining net income for the period in which the exchange rate changes.   A transaction gain or loss realised upon settlement of a foreign currency transaction generally should be included in net income for the period in which the transaction is settled.   The exceptions to the requirement for inclusion in net income of transaction gains and losses are noted in sections 5.3.2 and 5.3.4.

5.3.2   Exceptions

A   Intragroup long-term loans

Transaction gains and losses arising on intragroup foreign currency transactions of a long-term-investment nature, i.e. settlement is not planned or anticipated in the foreseeable future, are considered to be part of the net investment.

FAS 52.131

Such gains and losses should not be included in determining net income but should be reported and accumulated in the same manner as translation adjustments when the entities to the transaction are consolidated, combined, or accounted for by the equity method in the reporting entity's financial statements.

FAS 52.20

B   Hedges of a net investment in a foreign entity

A derivative instrument or a non-derivative financial instrument that may give rise to a foreign currency transaction gain or loss can be designated as hedging the

FAS 133.42

reporting entity. It does not apply to the reporting entity's separate financial statements or the financial statements of the foreign operation; the exchange differences will be recognised in profit or loss in the period in which they arise in the financial statements of the entity that has the foreign currency exposure.

B   Hedges

IAS 21.27
IAS 39.102

The second exception relates to hedge accounting. IAS 39 applies to hedge accounting for foreign currency items. The application of hedge accounting requires an entity to account for some exchange differences differently from the treatment of exchange differences required by IAS 21. For example, IAS 39 requires that exchange differences on monetary items that qualify as hedging instruments in a cash flow hedge or a hedge of a net investment in a foreign operation are reported as follows:

- the portion of the gain or loss on the hedging instrument that is an effective hedge is recognised directly in equity; and

- the ineffective portion is recognised in profit or loss.

The effective portion recognised in equity is either recognised when the foreign operation is disposed of (for a hedge of a net investment in a foreign entity) or in accordance with section 13.3 (for a cash flow hedge).

> **COMMENT**
>
> This exception relating to the hedge of a net investment in a foreign operation is only applicable to the group financial statements. In the entity's individual financial statements, the investment will be accounted for as an asset measured at cost or as a financial asset in accordance with IAS 39. However, hedge accounting for a fair value hedge of the currency risk on this investment may be possible in the individual financial statements of the entity.

C   Exchange differences adjusting interest costs

IAS 23.5,11

Exchange differences arising from foreign currency borrowings may be capitalised to the extent that they are regarded as an adjustment to interest costs.

5.4   USE OF A PRESENTATION CURRENCY OTHER THAN THE FUNCTIONAL CURRENCY

5.4.1   Basic methods of translating to the presentation currency

IAS 21.38

An entity may present its financial statements in any currency (or currencies). If the presentation currency differs from the entity's functional currency, it translates its results and financial position into the presentation currency. For example, when a group contains individual entities with different functional currencies, the results and financial position of each entity are expressed in a common currency so that consolidated financial statements may be presented.

IAS 21.39

The results and financial position of an entity whose functional currency is not the currency of a hyperinflationary economy should be translated into a different presentation currency using the following procedures:

foreign currency exposure of a net investment in a foreign operation (the applicable hedge criteria are addressed in section 11). The gain or loss on a hedging derivative instrument (or the foreign currency transaction gain or loss on the non-derivative hedging instrument), to the extent it is effective as an economic hedge of the net investment in a foreign operation, should be reported in the same manner as a translation adjustment from the designation date. The hedged net investment should be accounted for in accordance with section 5.3.

C   Other hedges

An entity may designate the following types of foreign currency hedges other than hedges of a foreign net investment: *FAS 133.36*

- Fair value hedges of unrecognised firm commitments.   *FAS 133.37,39*

  If the firm commitment meets the criteria for a hedged item, a derivative or a non-derivative instrument may be designated as a hedging instrument. Gains or losses on such hedges should be accounted in income, in accordance with the rules on fair value hedges.

- Fair value hedges of available-for-sale securities.   *FAS 133.38*

  Derivative instruments may be designated as a hedging instrument in a fair value hedge of available-for-sale securities. Changes in the value of the available-for-sale securities should be recorded in earnings and not in comprehensive income. Gains or losses on the hedging instrument should be accounted for in income, in accordance with the rules on fair value hedges.

- Cash flows hedges of forecasted (intragroup) foreign currency denominated transactions should be accounted for in accordance with the rules on cash flow hedges.   *FAS 133.40-41*

See section 11 for a description of the applicable hedge criteria.

D   Exchange differences adjusting interest costs

Only amounts recorded in an entity's income statement as interest costs should be reflected in the rate applied for capitalisation of interest where appropriate. This amount would not include exchange differences on foreign currency borrowings.   *FAS 34.12-14*
EITF 99-9

5.4   USE OF A PRESENTATION CURRENCY OTHER THAN THE FUNCTIONAL CURRENCY

5.4.1   Basic methods of translating to the presentation currency

All elements of financial statements of a foreign entity having a functional currency that is different from the reporting currency of the investing entity should be translated using a current exchange rate.   *FAS 52.12*

Assets and liabilities should be translated by using the exchange rate at the balance sheet date.   *FAS 52.12*

Amounts in the income statement of foreign entities should be translated at the exchange rates ruling when those elements are recognised or at an appropriate weighted average rate for the period.   *FAS 52.12*

- assets and liabilities for each balance sheet presented (i.e. including comparatives) should be translated at the closing rate at the date of that balance sheet;

- income and expenses for each income statement (i.e. including comparatives) should be translated at exchange rates at the dates of the transactions; and

- all resulting exchange differences should be recognised as a separate component of equity.

IAS 21.40   For convenience reasons, the reporting entity may use an average exchange rate for the period to translate income and expense items unless the exchange rate has fluctuated significantly.

The results and financial position of an entity whose functional currency is the currency of a hyperinflationary economy should be translated into a different presentation currency using the procedures detailed at section 5.4.2 below.

5.4.2   Hyperinflation

IAS 29.3   Hyperinflation is indicated by a number of characteristics:

- the general population prefers to keep its wealth in non-monetary assets or in a relatively stable foreign currency;

- the general population regards monetary amounts not in terms of the local currency but in terms of a relatively stable foreign currency;

- sales and purchases on credit take place at prices that take into account the expected inflation during the credit period;

- interest rates and wages are linked to a price index; and

- cumulative inflation over a three-year period is approaching, or exceeds, 100%.

An entity should determine its functional currency in accordance with IAS 21. If this functional currency is the currency of a hyperinflationary economy the entity's own financial statements should be restated under IAS 29 *Financial Reporting in Hyperinflationary Economies*.

COMMENT

IAS 21 makes it clear that, where an entity operates in a hyperinflationary environment, it must determine its functional currency strictly in accordance with the criteria laid down in the standard. It is not permitted for the entity to simply select a hard currency as its functional currency, merely to avoid the restatement requirements of IAS 29.

IAS 29.8   Financial statements of an entity whose functional currency is the currency of a
IAS 21.42   hyperinflationary economy should be stated in terms of the measuring unit current at the balance sheet date. Comparative figures for any previous period should also be stated in terms of the measuring unit current at the balance sheet date. For the purposes of presenting amounts in a different presentation currency, comparative amounts should be those that were presented as current year amounts in the relevant prior year financial statements (see below). The principal procedures to be applied in restating the financial statements are as follow:

IAS 29.11,25,29   • balance sheet amounts, including the components of shareholders' equity, not expressed in terms of the measuring unit current at the balance sheet date,

The rate to be used for translation purposes is generally the rate applicable to conversion of the foreign currency for the purposes of dividend remittances.   *FAS 52.27(b)*

5.4.2   Hyperinflation

A highly inflationary economy is defined as one that has cumulative inflation of approximately 100% or more over a three-year period. The temporal method should be used to translate the financial statements of subsidiaries and equity accounted investees where they are denominated in currencies of highly-inflationary economies, i.e. remeasurement of the financial statements as if the reporting currency of the parent had been the functional currency.   *FAS 52.11* *EITF D-55*

When an economy ceases to be considered 'highly inflationary', the amounts recorded using the temporal method as at the date of change should be translated into the local currency at current exchange rates and those amounts should become the new functional currency accounting bases for the non-monetary assets and liabilities.   *EITF 92-4*

The FASB staff believes that the determination of a highly inflationary economy requires a calculation of the cumulative inflation rate for the three years that precede the beginning of the reporting period, including interim reporting periods. If that calculation results in a cumulative inflation rate in excess of 100%, the economy should be considered highly inflationary in all instances. However, if that calculation results in the cumulative rate being less than 100%, the staff believes that historical inflation rate trends (increasing or decreasing) and other pertinent economic factors should be considered to determine whether such information suggests that classification of the economy as highly inflationary is appropriate. The staff believes that projections of future inflation rates were not contemplated by the language in paragraph 109 and thus projections cannot be used to overcome the presumption that an economy is highly inflationary if the 3-year cumulative rate exceeds 100%.   *EITF D-55*

COMMENT

The AICPA International Practices Task Force regularly monitors inflation rates to identify cases where the Task Force could discuss and assess a country's inflationary status. The Task Force periodically publishes a complete list of those countries it considers to be highly inflationary and those to be monitored.

should be restated by applying a general price index.   However, balance sheet amounts stated at current cost should not be restated;

IAS 29.12 • monetary balance sheet items should not be restated as they are already expressed in the measuring unit current at the balance sheet date;

IAS 29.26 • all items in the income statement need to be restated by applying the change in the general price index from the dates when the items of income and expense were initially recorded; and

IAS 29.9,27 • the gain or loss on the net monetary position of the entity, should be included in income, separately disclosed, and may be estimated by applying the change in the general price index to the weighted average net monetary position for the period.

IAS 29.38 When an economy ceases to be hyperinflationary, entities should treat amounts expressed in the measuring unit current at the end of the reporting period as the basis for the carrying amounts in its subsequent financial statements.

IAS 29.39 If an entity has a functional currency that is the currency of a hyperinflationary economy and therefore applies IAS 29 it needs to disclose the fact that the financial statements and the corresponding figures for previous periods have been restated for the changes in the general purchasing power of the functional currency and, as a result, are stated in terms of the measuring unit current at the balance sheet date.   It must also disclose whether the financial statements are based on a historical cost approach or a current cost approach and the identity and level of the price index used and the movement in the index during the current and the previous reporting period.

IAS 21.42-43 When financial statements of an entity whose functional currency is the currency of a hyperinflationary economy are presented in a different presentation currency the following translation procedures should be applied after applying the procedures of restatement under IAS 29 outlined above:

• all amounts (i.e., assets, liabilities, equity items, income and expenses, including comparatives) should be translated at the closing rate existing at the date of the most recent balance sheet presented; except that

• when amounts are translated into the currency of a non-hyperinflationary economy, comparative amounts should be those that were presented as current year amounts from the relevant prior year financial statements (i.e., not adjusted for subsequent changes in price levels or exchange rates).

COMMENT

In March 2004, IFRIC issued Draft Interpretation D5 – *Applying IAS 29 Financial Reporting Hyperinflationary Economies for the First Time*, which proposes specific guidance to facilitate the first time application of IAS 29.   IFRIC D5 is best described as an omnibus interpretation and it deals with a number of unrelated practical problems that entities applying IAS 29 for the first time might experience.

5.4.3   Foreign currency translation reserve

IAS 21.52 Net exchange differences classified in a separate component of equity should be disclosed along with a reconciliation of the amount at the beginning and end of the period.

5.4.3   Foreign currency translation reserve

The translation adjustments resulting from translating the foreign entity's financial   *FAS 52.13*
statements should not be included in determining net income but should be   *FAS 130.29*
reported separately in other comprehensive income and as a separate component of
shareholders' equity.

5.4.4   Disposal of a foreign operation

IAS 21.48   When the reporting entity disposes of its investment in a foreign operation, the cumulative amount of the exchange differences deferred in the separate component of equity, which relate to that operation, should be recognised as profit or loss in the same period in which the gain or loss on disposal is recognised.

IAS 21.49   An entity may dispose of its interest in a foreign entity through sale, liquidation, repayment of share capital, or abandonment of that entity. The payment of a dividend is part of a disposal only when it constitutes a return of the investment, for example when the dividend is paid out of pre-acquisition profits.   In the case of a partial disposal, only the proportionate share of the related accumulated exchange differences is included in the gain or loss.   A write-down of the carrying amount of a foreign entity does not constitute a partial disposal, therefore no deferred exchange difference should be recognised in income at the time of the write-down.

5.4.5   Goodwill and fair value adjustments on consolidation

IAS 21.39,47   Goodwill and any fair value adjustments arising on the acquisition of a foreign entity are treated as assets and liabilities of the foreign operation and therefore should be expressed in the functional currency of the foreign operation and translated at the closing rate.   Exchange differences arising upon retranslation are taken to the foreign currency translation reserve.

5.5   DISCLOSURE

IAS 1.111   Entities that have significant foreign operations or transactions in foreign currencies should disclose their accounting policies for foreign currency translation.

IAS 21.52   An entity should disclose:

*   the amount of exchange differences recognised in profit or loss except for those arising on financial instruments measured at fair value through profit or loss in accordance with IAS 39; and

*   net exchange differences classified in a separate component of equity, and a reconciliation of the amount of such exchange differences at the beginning and end of the period.

IAS 21.53   When the presentation currency is different from the functional currency (in the case of a group, that of the parent), that fact should be stated, together with disclosure of the functional currency and the reason for using a different presentation currency.

IAS 21.54   When there is a change in the functional currency of either the reporting entity or a significant foreign operation, that fact and the reason for the change in functional currency should be disclosed.

IAS 21.55   When an entity presents its financial statements in a currency that is different from its functional currency (in the case of a group, that of the parent), it should describe the financial statements as complying with International Financial Reporting Standards only if they comply with all the requirements of each applicable Standard including the translation method set out in IAS 21.

5.4.4   Disposal of a foreign operation

Where all or part of an investment in a foreign entity is sold, or it is substantially liquidated, the cumulative foreign currency translation differences included in the separate component of equity relating to the part which is sold or liquidated should be included in the net profit for the period as part of the gain or loss on sale or liquidation.

FAS 52.14
FIN 37
FAS 130.19

The EITF reached consensuses that accumulated foreign currency translation adjustments, including those that represent hedging gains or losses, should be included as part of the carrying amount when evaluating impairment of an equity method or consolidated investment, or the net investment in a foreign operation, if the entity has committed to a plan to dispose of the investment that will cause the translation adjustments to be reclassified to earnings.

EITF 01-5

5.4.5   Goodwill and fair value adjustments on consolidation

Goodwill and any fair value adjustments arising on the purchase of a foreign entity are currency assets and liabilities of the foreign operation that should be translated at closing rates. Exchange differences arising upon retranslation are taken to the foreign currency translation reserve (see section 5.4.3).

FAS 52.101

5.5   DISCLOSURE

The aggregate transaction gain or loss included in determining net income for the period should be disclosed.

FAS 52.30

The following should be disclosed for changes during the period in the cumulative translation adjustments included as a separate component of shareholders' equity (other comprehensive income):

FAS 52.31

- beginning and ending amounts of cumulative translation adjustments;
- the aggregate adjustment for the period resulting from translation adjustments and gains and losses from certain hedges and intragroup balances (additional disclosure requirements for derivative instruments and hedging activities are described in section 14.3);
- the amount of income taxes for the period allocated to translation adjustments; and
- the amounts transferred from cumulative other comprehensive income and included in income for the period because of the sale or complete, or substantially complete, liquidation of an investment in a foreign entity.

An entity's financial statements should not be adjusted for a rate change that occurs after the date of the financial statements or after the date of the foreign currency financial statements of a foreign entity if they are consolidated, combined, or accounted for by the equity method. However, disclosure of the rate change and its effects on unsettled foreign currency amounts may be necessary, if significant.

FAS 52.143

IAS 21.57 When an entity displays its financial statements or other financial information in a currency that is different from either its functional currency (in the case of a group, that of the parent) or its presentation currency and the requirements in the paragraph immediately above are not met, it should:

- clearly identify the information as supplementary information to distinguish it from the information that complies with International Financial Reporting Standards;

- disclose the currency in which the supplementary information is displayed; and

- disclose the entity's functional currency and the method of translation used to determine the supplementary information.

IAS 10.21-22 Abnormally large changes in foreign exchange rates after the balance sheet date require disclosure, including if possible an estimate of their financial effect, if they are material.

Section 6

Intangible assets and goodwill

6.1   AUTHORITATIVE PRONOUNCEMENTS

- IFRS 3
- IAS 38

- IFRIC 3
- SIC-32

6.2   ACCOUNTING FOR INTANGIBLE ASSETS

6.2.1   Scope and definition

IAS 38.8,12-13   An intangible asset is defined as 'an identifiable non-monetary asset without physical substance.' An intangible asset is therefore an asset controlled by an entity as a result of past events and from which future economic benefits are expected to flow to the entity. In addition, it is identifiable when (1) it is separable, i.e. is capable of being separated or divided from the entity and sold, transferred, licensed, rented or exchanged, either individually or together with a related contract, asset or liability, or (2) arises from contractual or other legal rights, regardless of whether those are transferable or separable from the entity or from other rights and obligations. Legally enforceable rights are not necessary for control, although in their absence, it is more difficult to demonstrate control.

IAS 38.2-3   The general Standard on accounting for intangible assets – IAS 38 *Intangible Assets* – excludes the following from its scope:

- intangible assets covered by other Standards. In particular, other Standards address intangible assets held for sale in the ordinary course of business (IAS 2 *Inventories* and IAS 11 *Construction Contracts* – see section 15), leases in the scope of IAS 17 *Leases* (see section 16), and non-current intangible assets held for sale or included in a disposal group held for sale (IFRS 5 *Non-Current Assets Held for Sale and Discontinued Operations* – see section 1.9), and goodwill (IFRS 3 *Business Combinations* – see section 3);
- financial assets as defined in IAS 39 *Financial Instruments: Recognition and Measurement* (see section 11);
- the recognition and measurement of exploration and evaluation assets (see IFRS 6 *Exploration for and Evaluation of Mineral Resources*); and
- expenditure on the development and extraction of minerals, oil, natural gas and similar non-regenerative resources.

Section 6

Intangible assets and goodwill

6.1 AUTHORITATIVE PRONOUNCEMENTS

- FAS 2
- FAS 68
- FAS 86
- FAS 141

- FAS 142
- FAS 144
- SOP 98-1

6.2 ACCOUNTING FOR INTANGIBLE ASSETS

6.2.1 Scope and definition

The initial recognition and measurement provisions of FAS 142 *Goodwill and Other Intangible Assets* apply to intangible assets acquired individually and as part of a group. FAS 141 *Business Combinations* addresses the recognition and measurement of intangible assets acquired in a business combination or the purchase of the minority interest in a subsidiary. FAS 142 addresses the subsequent accounting for goodwill and intangible assets and the impairment of goodwill and intangible assets that are not amortised. FAS 144 addresses the impairment of intangible assets that are amortised. Equity method goodwill is not tested for impairment under FAS 142. Instead, the carrying amount of the investment as a whole is tested for impairment under APB 18.

Intangible assets are defined as assets (not including financial assets) that lack physical substance.   *FAS 142.App F*

IAS 38.129-132   An entity shall apply IAS 38:

- to the accounting for intangible assets acquired in business combinations for which the agreement date is on or after 31 March 2004 (see section 3.2); and

- to the accounting for all other intangible assets prospectively from the beginning of the first annual period beginning on or after 31 March 2004. The carrying amount of such intangible assets recognised at that date is not therefore adjusted. However, the carrying amount of an intangible asset which was (1) acquired in a business combination for which the agreement date was before 31 March 2004 or (2) arises from an interest in a jointly controlled entity obtained before 31 March 2004 and accounted for by applying proportionate consolidation, shall be reclassified as goodwill at the beginning of the first annual period beginning on or after 31 March 2004, if that intangible asset does not at that date meet the identifiability criterion in IAS 38.

  In addition, the entity shall, at that date, apply IAS 38 to reassess the useful lives of such intangible assets. If, as a result of that reassessment, the entity changes its assessment of the useful life of an asset, that change shall be accounted for as a change in an accounting estimate in accordance with IAS 8 *Accounting Policies, Changes in Accounting Estimates and Errors*.

An entity is encouraged to apply the requirements of IAS 38 before the effective dates specified above but if it does so, it also shall apply IFRS 3 (see section 3) and IAS 36 (revised 2004) *Impairment of Assets* (see section 9) at the same time. If an entity elects to apply IFRS 3 from a date earlier than 31 March 2004 (see section 3.2B), it shall apply IAS 38 prospectively from that same date.

The transitional arrangements for first-time adopters are discussed in Chapter 2.

IAS 38.4   Some intangible assets may be contained in or on a physical substance such as a compact disc (in the case of computer software), legal documentation (in the case of a licence or patent) or film. Judgement is used in assessing whether the tangible or intangible elements are more significant, e.g. computer software for a computer-controlled machine tool that can not operate without that specific software or a computer's operating system is an integral part of the related hardware and is treated as property, plant and equipment. When the software is not an integral part of the related hardware, computer software is treated as an intangible asset.

6.2.2 Recognition and measurement

IAS 38.21-22   An intangible asset shall be recognised if and only if (1) it is probable that the expected future economic benefits attributable to the asset will flow to the entity and (2) the cost of the asset can be measured reliably. The assessment of the probability of future economic benefits shall be based on reasonable and supportable assumptions that reflect management's best estimate of the economic conditions that will exist over the useful life of the asset.

IAS 38.25,33   The probability criterion is always met for separately acquired intangible assets or intangible assets acquired as part of a business combination.

IAS 38.8,24   When an intangible asset is initially recognised, it is measured at cost. Cost is defined as 'the amount of cash or cash equivalents paid or the fair value of other consideration given to acquire an asset at the time of its acquisition or construction, or, when

6.2.2   Recognition and measurement

An intangible asset acquired either individually or with a group of other assets, other than when acquired in a business combination, should be initially recognised and measured based on its fair value.
FAS 142.9

In a business combination, an intangible asset should be recognised as an asset apart from goodwill if it arises from contractual or other legal rights (regardless of whether those rights are transferable or separable from the acquired entity or from other rights and obligations).   If an intangible asset does not arise from contractual or other legal rights, it should be recognised as an asset apart from goodwill only if it is separable.   An intangible asset is considered separable if it is capable of being separated or divided from the acquired entity and sold, transferred, licensed, rented or exchanged (regardless of whether there is an intent to do so) even when it can
FAS 141.39

applicable, the amount attributed to that asset when initially recognised in accordance with the specific requirements of other IFRSs, e.g. IFRS 2 *Share-based Payment.*'

6.2.3   Acquired

A   Acquired separately

The cost of intangible assets is determined as follows:

IAS 38.27-28 • if the intangible asset is acquired separately, the cost is the sum of (1) its purchase price (at cash price equivalent, if payment is deferred), including import duties, non-refundable purchase taxes, and after deducting trade discounts and rebates plus (2) any directly attributable cost of preparing the asset for its intended use.   The latter include costs of employee benefits and professional fees arising directly from bringing the asset to its working condition, and costs of testing the asset is functioning properly.   IAS 23 *Borrowing Costs* contains the criteria for capitalisation of borrowing costs for a 'qualifying asset', i.e. one that necessarily takes a substantial period of time to get ready for its intended use or sale (see section 10);

IAS 38.44 • an intangible asset acquired by way of a government grants may be measured at either fair value or at nominal value, plus any expenditure directly attributable to preparing the asset for its intended use, in accordance with IAS 20 *Accounting for Government Grants and Disclosure of Government Assistance* (see section 20);

IAS 38.6 • an intangible asset held under a finance lease, within the scope of IAS 17, is measured on initial recognition in accordance with that Standard, but IAS 38 is applied thereafter; or

IAS 38.45-47,131 • if the intangible asset is acquired in exchange for a non-monetary asset, or a combination of monetary and non-monetary assets, it is recognised at its fair value unless (1) the exchange transaction lacks commercial substance or (2) the fair value of neither the asset received nor the asset given up is reliably measurable.   The acquired item is measured in this way even if an entity cannot immediately derecognise the asset given up.   The fair value of the asset given up is used, unless the fair value of the asset received is more clearly evident.   If the acquired item is not measured at fair value, its cost is measured at the carrying amount of the asset given up.

IAS 38 contains more guidance on the circumstances when fair value is reliably measurable and when an exchange transaction lacks commercial substance.

An entity determines whether an exchange transaction has commercial substance by considering the extent to which its future cash flows are expected to change as a result of the transaction.   An exchange transaction has commercial substance if:

• the configuration (risk, timing and amount) of the cash flows of the asset received differs from the configuration of the cash flows of the asset transferred; or

only be sold, transferred, licensed, rented or exchanged in combination with a related contract, asset or liability.

Examples of intangible assets which are recognised in practice include patents, franchise agreements, trademarks, covenants not to compete, management contracts, subscription and customer lists, air rights, favourable leases or financing, player contracts and supply contracts. An assembled workforce should not be recognised as a separable intangible asset acquired in a business combination.

6.2.3   Acquired

A   Acquired separately

The cost of a group of assets, including intangible assets, acquired in a transaction other than a business combination should be allocated to the individual assets acquired based on their relative fair values and should not result in the recognition of goodwill. This could result in acquired assets being valued in excess of or less than their individual fair values.   *FAS 142.9*

In exchange transactions, the consideration paid is generally assumed to be equal to the fair value of net assets acquired. Where consideration is given in cash the exchange is measured by the amount of cash paid. For non-cash transactions, measurement is based on the fair value of the consideration or the fair value of the net assets acquired, whichever is more reliably measurable.

Intangible assets that are acquired separately might meet the asset recognition criteria under CON 5 but not satisfy the contractual-legal or separability criteria in FAS 141 for separate recognition apart from goodwill. In this case, provided there is reliable evidence for existence and fair value, those assets should be recognised as intangible assets. Examples of intangible assets that do not meet the contractual-legal or separability criteria in FAS 141 but would meet the recognition criteria if acquired individually or as part of an asset group are an assembled workforce or a customer base.

B   Business combinations

Intangible assets acquired in a business combination are initially recognised and measured in accordance with FAS 141 (section 3.4.3 C).

Costs should be assigned to all identifiable tangible and intangible assets of an acquired entity, including any resulting from research and development activities of the acquired entity or to be used in research and development activities of the combined entity, in accordance with FAS 141 *Business Combinations*.   *FAS 2.34*

FIN 4 *Applicability of FASB Statement No. 2 to Business Combinations Accounted for by the Purchase Method* addresses the accounting treatment for identifiable tangible and intangible assets to be used in research and development activities that are acquired in a purchase business combination. Costs assigned to assets to be used in a particular research and development project and that have no alternative future use should be charged to expense at the date of consummation of the combination.   *FIN 4.4-5*

- the entity-specific value of the portion of the entity's operations affected by the transaction changes as a result of the exchange; and

- the difference in either of the above two items is significant relative to the fair value of the assets exchanged.

The entity-specific value is the present value of the post-tax cash flows an entity expects to arise from the continuing use of an asset and from its disposal at the end of its life or expects to incur when settling a liability. The result of these analyses may be clear without an entity having to perform detailed calculations.

The fair value of an asset for which comparable market transactions do not exist is reliably measurable if (1) the variability in the range of reasonable fair value estimates is not significant for that asset or (2) the probabilities of the various estimates within the range can be reasonably assessed and used in estimating fair value.

The requirement to apply IAS 38 prospectively means that if an exchange of assets was measured before the effective date of IAS 38 on the basis of the carrying amount of the asset given up, the entity does not restate the carrying amount of the asset acquired to reflect its fair value at the acquisition date.

B   Business combinations

IAS 38.33-34 If the intangible asset (including in-process research and development) is acquired in a business combination, it is measured at its fair value at the date of acquisition in accordance with IFRS 3 (see section 3.4.4C). It is separately recognised if its fair value can be measured reliably, irrespective of whether it was recognised by the acquiree prior to the business combination.

C   Emission rights

IFRIC 3.1-11 IFRIC published, in December 2004, IFRIC 3 *Emission Rights* which addresses the accounting by a participant for emission rights that arise from an operational 'cap and trade' scheme. For IFRS reporters, the Interpretation applies to periods beginning on or after 1 March 2005. A cap and trade scheme gives rise to:

- an intangible asset in accordance with IAS 38 for allowances held (whether purchased, or issued by the Government). If issued for less than fair value, the intangible asset is initially recognised at fair value;

- a government grant in accordance with IAS 20, where allowances are issued for less than fair value. The difference between the amount paid and the fair value of the allowances is initially recognised as deferred income in the balance sheet and recognised subsequently in income on a systematic basis over the compliance period for which allowances were issued (regardless of whether these are held or sold); and

- a liability for the obligation to deliver allowances equal to the emissions made, in accordance with IAS 37 *Provisions, Contingent Liabilities and Contingent Assets.* The best estimate of this liability will usually be the present market price of the number of allowances required to cover the emissions made up to the balance sheet date.

These items shall not be presented as a net asset or liability.

COMMENT

The SEC Staff have raised concerns about excessive write-offs of acquired in-process research and development in business combinations and have presented their views on a number of valuation issues, including:

- In-process research and development cannot be considered as a residual amount, similar to goodwill, in a purchase price allocation.

- Allocations to in-process research and development which differ significantly from estimated replacement cost to the acquiring company will be challenged.

- The policy applied for determining when the research and development cycle is complete and whether technology has alternative use should be the same for acquired in-process research and development as for internally developed products.

- The same definition for technical feasibility should be used for both acquired and internally developed products.

emissions scheme may cause a reduction in the cash flows expected to be generated by certain assets; those assets are required to be tested for impairment in accordance with IAS 36.

COMMENT

IFRIC initially deferred issuance of IFRIC 3, given the IASB's project to amend IAS 20. Since the EU Emissions Trading Scheme was to commence at the beginning of 2005, IFRIC finalised the proposals, but noted that the accounting may subsequently change as a result of the IASB project on government grants.

In April 2005, IFRIC considered a proposed amendment to require a narrowly specified subset of intangible assets (including emission allowances traded in an active market as defined in IAS 38) to be measured after initial recognition at fair value with the gains or losses arising from changes in fair value recognised in profit or loss. This would amend the accounting in IFRIC 3 and result in the allowances and emission liability being measured on a consistent basis by reference to the fair value of the allowances and changes in both being recognised in profit or loss.

6.2.4 Internally developed

IAS 38.52   In determining the costs to be capitalised in respect of internally generated intangible assets, the entity needs to draw a distinction between the research phase and the development phase of the generation of the asset. Although the terms 'research' and 'development' are defined, the terms 'research phase' and 'development phase' have broader meanings for the purpose of IAS 38.

IAS 38.8   Research is defined as 'original and planned investigation undertaken with the prospect of gaining new scientific or technical knowledge and understanding.'

Development is defined as 'the application of research findings or other knowledge to a plan or design for the production of new or substantially improved materials, devices, products, processes, systems or services before the start of commercial production or use.'

IAS 38.53-54   Costs of research (or the research phase of an internal project) may not be recognised as an intangible asset, but should be expensed when incurred. If an entity cannot distinguish the research phase from the development phase of an integral project to create an intangible asset, the entity treats the expenditure on that project as if it were incurred in the research phase only.

IAS 38.57   The costs of development may be recognised as an intangible asset if and only if the entity can demonstrate all of the following (in addition to meeting the general recognition criteria in IAS 38, para. 21 above):

- the technical feasibility of completing the intangible asset so that it will be available for use or sale;
- its intention to complete the intangible asset and use or sell it;
- its ability to use or sell the intangible asset;
- how the intangible asset will generate probable future economic benefits (including the existence of a market for the output of the intangible asset or the intangible asset itself, or if it is to be used internally, the intangible asset's usefulness) using the principles of IAS 36 to assess the benefits;

6.2.4   Internally developed

FAS 2 *Accounting for Research and Development Costs* defines 'research' and 'development' as follows: *FAS 2.8*

- *Research:* planned search or critical investigation aimed at discovery of new knowledge with the hope that such knowledge will be useful in developing a new product or service or a new process or technique or in bringing about a significant improvement to an existing product or process.

- *Development:* the translation of research findings or other knowledge into a plan or design for a new product or process or for a significant improvement to an existing product or process whether intended for sale or use. It includes the conceptual formulation, design, and testing of product alternatives, construction of prototypes and operation of pilot plants. It does not include routine or periodic alterations to existing products, production lines, manufacturing process, and other on-going operations even though those alterations may represent improvements and it does not include market research or market testing activities.

If an entity enters into an arrangement with other parties for the funding of that entity's research and development, the entity must determine whether it is obligated only to perform research and development for others or has an obligation to repay any of the funds provided, regardless of the outcome of the research and development (and hence should record a liability and expense research and development as incurred). *FAS 68.4-6*

FAS 68 *Research and Development Arrangements* provides guidance on determining the nature of the obligation in such arrangements and indicates that a critical factor is whether the financial risks involved in the research and development arrangement have been substantively and genuinely transferred to the other parties. It provides examples of conditions (other than a written agreement) that create a presumption that the entity will repay the funds provided by the other parties under the arrangement. *FAS 68.7-8* *SAB 63* *(Topic 5-O)*

- the availability of adequate technical, financial and other resources to complete the development and to use or sell the intangible asset; and

- its ability to measure reliably the expenditure attributable to the intangible asset during its development.

IAS 38.65-66,71 Costs of intangible assets that were initially expensed shall not be recognised as part of the cost of an intangible asset at a later date – even if the criteria for capitalisation are later met. The cost of internally developed intangible assets comprises all directly attributable costs necessary to create, produce and prepare the asset to be capable of operating in the manner intended by management. IAS 23 contains the criteria for capitalisation of borrowing costs for qualifying assets (see section 10). Costs are capitalised only from the date the recognition criteria are met.

IAS 38.66-70 Additional guidance is provided on which cost components are capable of being capitalised. Expenditure on an intangible item should be recognised as an expense when it is incurred unless it forms part of the cost of an intangible asset that meets the recognition criteria.

IAS 38.29,67,69 Examples of expenditure that is not recognised as part of the cost of an internally generated intangible asset and is recognised as an expense when incurred include:

- certain start-up costs (see section 6.2.8 below);

- training costs;

- advertising and promotion costs;

- relocation and reorganisation costs; and

- administration and other general overhead costs (unless directly attributable to preparing an internally generated asset for use).

IAS 38.31 Revenue and related costs from incidental operations, which occur in connection with an intangible asset's development but are not necessary to bringing the asset to the location and condition necessary for it to be capable of operating in the manner intended by management, are recognised immediately in profit or loss.

No specific guidance exists regarding the accounting for research and development arrangements of the type where other parties fund the research and development efforts of the entity. Where applicable, IAS 2 or IAS 20 are followed.

IAS 38.20 Capitalisation of subsequent expenditure on an intangible asset will be rare since most subsequent expenditures are likely to maintain the expected future economic benefits of the existing intangible asset and it is often difficult to attribute subsequent expenditure directly to a particular intangible asset rather than the business as a whole. Capitalisation of subsequent expenditure on brands, mastheads, publishing titles, customer lists and similar items is expressly forbidden.

IAS 38.42-43 Research or development expenditure relating to an in-process research and development project acquired separately or in a business combination, but incurred subsequent to its acquisition, is expensed unless it is development expenditure satisfying the recognition criteria above, when it is added to the carrying amount of the acquired in-process research and development project.

IAS 38.63 Internally generated brands, mastheads, publishing titles, customer lists and similar items shall not be recognised as intangible assets.

FAS 2 provides examples of activities that typically would be included in research *FAS 2.9-11* and development and also describes the following elements of costs that should be identified with research and development activities:

- materials, equipment and facilities;
- personnel;
- intangible assets purchased from others;
- contract services; and
- indirect costs.

The costs of materials, equipment and facilities that are acquired or constructed for *FAS 2.11* research and development activities and that have alternative future uses (in other research and development projects or otherwise) should be capitalised and the cost/depreciation of such material, equipment or facilities used in those activities accounted for as research and development costs. If the materials, equipment, facilities or intangibles acquired for a specific research and development project have no alternative future use, their cost should be classified as research and development upon acquisition.

Costs incurred to develop identifiable intangible assets through internal research *FAS 2.12* efforts should be written off as incurred.

Costs of internally developing, maintaining, or restoring intangible assets (including *FAS 142.10* goodwill) which are not specifically identifiable, have indeterminate lives, or are inherent in a continuing business and related to an entity as a whole should be charged to expense when incurred.

The allocation of interest to research and development activities was not included in the scope of FAS 2. Capitalisation of interest is covered in section 10.

6.2.5   Subsequent measurement

IAS 38.74 Subsequent to initial recognition, under the cost model, the intangible asset shall be carried at cost less any accumulated amortisation and impairment losses.

IAS 38.75 Subsequent to initial recognition at cost, under the revaluation model, the intangible asset is carried at a revalued amount, being fair value at the date of revaluation, less any subsequent accumulated amortisation and impairment losses, where:

- fair value is determined by reference to an active market;

- revaluations are made with such regularity that the carrying amount at balance sheet date does not differ materially from its fair value at that date;

IAS 38.76-77
- an intangible asset that has not been recognised previously as an asset may not be revalued. However, if only part of the cost of the intangible asset is recognised as it did not meet the recognition criteria until part of the way through the process, the whole asset may be revalued. An asset received via a government grant and recognised at a nominal amount may also be revalued;

IAS 38.72-73,81
- all other assets in its class, being a grouping of assets of a similar nature and use in the entity's operations, should also be accounted for using the same model unless there is no active market for those assets, in which case those assets are carried at cost less any accumulated amortisation or impairment;

IAS 38.82,84
- if the fair value of a revalued intangible asset can no longer be determined by reference to an active market, the carrying amount shall be the revalued amount at the date of last revaluation by reference to the active market less any subsequent accumulated amortisation and impairment losses. If, at a later date, the fair value can be determined by reference to an active market, the asset is revalued from that later date;

IAS 38.85
- any increase in the carrying amount of an intangible asset resulting from a revaluation is credited to the revaluation surplus in equity. However, to the extent that the revaluation increase reverses a previous revaluation decrease that was recognised in profit or loss, the increase is also recognised in profit or loss;

IAS 38.86
- any decrease in the carrying amount of an intangible asset resulting from a revaluation is recognised in profit or loss, after any revaluation surplus in equity related to the same asset has been reduced to zero; and

IAS 38.87
IAS 12.64
- the cumulative revaluation surplus recognised in equity may be transferred directly to retained earnings when the surplus is realised, through use of the asset (excess amortisation based on the revalued amount rather than cost) or on disposal, in both cases net of related deferred tax.

IAS 8.17 The initial application of a policy to revalue assets is dealt with as a revaluation in accordance with the Standard, rather than retrospectively in accordance with IAS 8.

COMMENT

IAS 38.8 The term 'active market' is defined extremely narrowly in IAS 38 as being a market where all the following conditions exist:

- the items traded in the market are homogeneous;

- willing buyers and sellers can normally be found at any time; and

- prices are available to the public.

In view of this restrictive definition, it is highly unlikely that many intangible assets will qualify for the revaluation model.

6.2.5   Subsequent measurement

Under FAS 142, the accounting for a recognised intangible asset is based on its useful life to the reporting entity.   An intangible asset with a finite useful life is amortised; an intangible asset with an indefinite useful life is not amortised.   (See section 6.3). *FAS 142.11*

An intangible asset that is subject to amortisation should be reviewed for impairment in accordance with FAS 144.   An impairment loss should be recognised if the carrying amount of an intangible asset is not recoverable and its carrying amount exceeds its fair value. *FAS 142.15*

An intangible asset that is not subject to amortisation should be tested for impairment annually, or more frequently if events or changes in circumstances indicate impairment. *FAS 142.17*

After an impairment loss is recognised, the adjusted carrying amount is the new accounting basis and subsequent reversal of a previously recognised impairment loss is prohibited. *FAS 142.15,17*

Impairment of intangible assets is discussed in section 9.

6.2.6   Goodwill

IFRS 3.51,54-55
IFRS 3.Appx A
IAS 38.11,15,48

Goodwill is defined as 'future economic benefits arising from assets that are not capable of being individually identified and separately recognised.' It is measured initially at cost, being the excess of the cost of the business combination over the acquirer's interest in the net fair value of the identifiable assets, liabilities and contingent liabilities recognised. Intangible assets (including in-process research and development) meeting the definition in IAS 38 are recorded separately from goodwill, at their fair value, where this can be measured reliably. The Illustrative Examples to IFRS 3 contain extensive examples of items acquired in a business combination that meet the definition of an intangible asset including, inter alia, items such as customer lists, customer contracts and related customer relationships, order backlogs, databases and trade secrets. A team of skilled staff, however, is unlikely to qualify as an intangible asset. After initial recognition, acquired goodwill should be capitalised in accordance with IFRS 3. It is not amortised but is tested for impairment under IAS 36 (see sections 3.4.6A and 9), both annually and whenever there are indications of impairment. After initial recognition, it is therefore measured at cost less any accumulated impairment losses. It is not permitted to capitalise internally generated goodwill.

IFRS 3.56

If the acquirer's interest in the net fair value of the identifiable assets, liabilities and contingent liabilities recognised exceeds the cost of the business combination, any excess remaining, after the acquirer has reassessed the identification and measurement of the acquiree's identifiable assets, liabilities and contingent liabilities and the measurement of the cost of the combination, is recognised immediately in profit or loss (see section 3.4.6B).

The transitional rules in IFRS 3 are addressed in sections 3.2 and 3.4.6.

6.2.7   Computer software costs

IAS 38.52

A project for the development of computer software should be classified into a research phase and a development phase.

The costs of the research phase must be expensed when incurred, while the costs of the development phase should be capitalised in accordance with the conditions outlined in section 6.2.2.

A   *Web site development*

SIC-32.7-9

A web site developed by an entity is an internally generated intangible asset subject to the requirements of IAS 38. An entity shall capitalise the costs of developing a web site if and only if the web site will result in probable future economic benefits, can be measured reliably and meets the specific criteria for capitalisation in paragraph 57 of IAS 38 (see section 6.2.4). Costs associated with developing a web site solely or primarily for promoting and advertising the entity's products or services are expensed when incurred. SIC-32 *Intangible Assets – Web Site Costs* provides specific guidance on identifying various stages in the development of web sites and accounting for each of these stages:

- Planning – expenditure is expensed as incurred;
- Application and Infrastructure Development, Graphical Design and Content

6.2.6   Goodwill

In a business combination, the excess of the cost of the acquired entity over the net   *FAS 141.43*
of the amounts assigned to assets acquired and liabilities assumed should be
recognised as an asset referred to as goodwill (see section 3.4.6).

Under FAS 142, goodwill is not amortised, but is tested for impairment.   Impairment   *FAS 142.18*
arises when the carrying amount of goodwill exceeds its implied fair value.
Impairment of goodwill is covered in section 9.

Negative goodwill arises when the net of the amounts assigned to assets acquired   *FAS 141.44*
and liabilities assumed exceeds the cost of the acquired entity.   Negative goodwill
should be allocated to reduce proportionately the values assigned to the acquired
assets, including research and development assets acquired and charged to expense,
except (a) financial assets other than equity method investments, (b) assets to be
disposed of by sale, (c) deferred tax assets, (d) prepaid assets relating to pension or
other post-retirement benefit plans, and (e) any other current assets.   Any
remainder should be recognised as an extraordinary gain.

6.2.7   Computer software costs

A   Computer software products for sale

All costs incurred to establish the technological feasibility of a computer software   *FAS 86.3-4*
product that is to be sold, leased or otherwise marketed are research and
development costs.   These costs should be charged to expense as incurred as
required by FAS 2.   Technological feasibility of a computer software product is
established when the enterprise has completed all planning, designing, coding, and
testing activities that are necessary to establish that the product can be produced to
meet its design specifications including functions, features, and technical
performance requirements.   At a minimum, the entity should have completed and
tested a detailed program design or, in its absence, completed a working model as
evidence that technological feasibility has been established.

Capitalised software costs should be amortised on a product-by-product basis.   *FAS 86.8*
The annual amortisation should be the greater of the amount computed using
(1) the ratio of current gross revenues for a product to the total of current and
anticipated future gross revenues for that product or (2) the straight-line method
over the remaining estimated economic life of the product including the period
being reported on.   Amortisation should start when the product is available for
general release to customers.

Development (other than content developed to advertise and promote an entity's own products and services, which is expensed as incurred) – directly attributable expenditure necessary to creating, producing or preparing the website to be capable of operating in the manner intended by management, and which meets the criteria for capitalisation of development costs in paragraph 57 of IAS 38, is capitalised. Expenditure initially recognised as an expense is not reinstated as an intangible asset at a later date; and

- Operating – when website development is complete, expenditure is expensed as incurred unless it meets the definition of an intangible asset and the recognition criteria in paragraph 18 of IAS 38. However, only rarely will subsequent expenditure be recognised in the carrying amount of an asset.

B   Computer software for internal use

Guidance on accounting for the costs of computer software developed or obtained   *SOP 98-1*
for internal use is provided by SOP 98-1 *Accounting for the Costs to Develop or
Obtain Software for Internal Use.*   Internal use software is software which is:

- acquired, internally developed, or modified solely to meet the entity's internal
  needs; and

- during the software's development or modification, no substantive plan exists
  or is being developed to market the software externally.

An entity's past practices may help determine whether software is for internal use or
to be marketed externally, e.g. an entity in the business of selling computer software
often both uses and sells its own software products.   Such a past practice creates a
rebuttable presumption that any software developed is intended for sale.

The SOP identifies three stages of computer software development:

- *preliminary project stage* – allocating resources between projects, determining
  performance requirements of the software, determining alternatives to meet
  performance requirements, and meeting and selecting software vendors and
  consultants.   Costs incurred during the preliminary project stage should be
  expensed as incurred;

- *application development stage* – designing software configuration and
  interfaces, coding, installing software, and testing.   Costs incurred to develop
  internal use computer software during the application development stage
  should be capitalised; and

- *post-implementation/operation stage* – training employees or performing
  maintenance activities.   Training costs and maintenance costs should be
  expensed as incurred.

Costs for upgrades and enhancements should be expensed or capitalised as separate
projects depending on the nature of the costs.   Upgrades and enhancements are
modifications to enable the software to perform tasks that it previously was not
capable of performing.   A modification that only extends the useful life without
adding additional functionality is a maintenance activity, the costs of which should
be expensed as incurred.   Where internal costs cannot be separated on a reasonable
basis between maintenance and relatively minor upgrades and enhancements the
costs should be expensed as incurred.

Once the capitalisation criteria have been met, external direct costs of materials and
services consumed in developing or obtaining internal use computer software;
payroll and related costs for employees who are directly associated with the internal
use computer software project (to the extent of the time spent directly on the
project); and associated interest costs incurred should be capitalised.

The capitalised costs of computer software developed or obtained for internal use
should be amortised on a straight-line basis unless another systematic and rational
basis is more representative of the software's use.   Impairment should be
recognised and measured in accordance with FAS 144 *Accounting for the
Impairment or Disposal of Long-Lived Assets.*

6.2.8   Start up costs

IAS 16.19-20   Start-up costs are capitalised only when directly attributable to bringing an item of
IAS 38.29-30   property, plant and equipment to the location and condition necessary to be capable
IAS 38.69-70   of operating in the manner intended by management in accordance with IAS 16.
All other start-up costs, e.g. establishment costs, costs of opening a new facility or
business; costs of introducing new operations, products or services (including a new
location or class of customer); relocation and reorganisation costs; and training,
advertising and promotion costs are expensed.

Identified inefficiencies, operating losses while initial demand builds up, and costs
incurred while an item is capable of operating in the intended manner, but is not yet
brought into use or operated below capacity, are recognised as an expense when
incurred.

IAS 11.21   IAS 11 addresses the treatment of contract costs.   These include the costs
attributable to a contract from the date of securing the contract to final completion.
Direct costs incurred in securing a contract may also be included if they are
separately identifiable, may be measured reliably and it is probable that the contract
will be obtained.   However, if costs incurred in obtaining a contract are expensed,
they must not be reinstated as a contract cost if the contract is secured in a
subsequent period (see section 15.3.2B).

C   Web site development

The EITF has considered web site development costs and concluded that the   *EITF 00-2*
accounting should generally follow the guidance in SOP 98-1, where the web site is
for internal use, or FAS 86 *Accounting for the Costs of Computer Software to Be
Sold, Leased, or Otherwise Marketed* where the web site is to be sold.

The various stages of web site development should be dealt with as follows:

- *Planning stage* – all costs should be expensed as incurred.

- *Application and infrastructure development* – all costs relating to software
  used to operate a web site should be accounted for under SOP 98-1, or
  FAS 86 where a plan exists to market the software externally.   Fees incurred
  for web site hosting generally should be expensed over the period expected to
  benefit.

- *Graphics development* – costs of developing initial graphics should be
  accounted for under SOP 98-1 for internal use software or FAS 86 for
  software to be marketed externally.   Modifications to graphics after a web
  site is launched are dealt with under operating stage costs below.

- *Content development* – the EITF did not reach a consensus for content
  development costs.

Operating stage – operating costs include training, administration, maintenance and
other costs of operating a web site.   General operating costs should be expensed as
incurred.   However, costs of upgrades and enhancements should be expensed, unless
it is probable that they will add functionality when they should be capitalised under the
general model of SOP 98-1; or for software that is marketed, under FAS 86.

6.2.8   Start-up costs

SOP 98-5 *Reporting on the Costs of Start-up Activities* requires the costs of   *SOP 98-5*
start-up activities, both of development-stage entities and established operating
entities, to be expensed as incurred.

Start-up activities are defined broadly as one-time activities related to opening a new
facility, introducing a new product or service, conducting business in a new territory,
conducting business with a new class of customer or beneficiary, initiating a new
process in an existing facility, or commencing some new operation.   Examples of
start-up activities include organising a new entity; opening a new plant or retail site;
designing, developing or launching a new product or marketing an existing product
to a new market segment; and implementing a new manufacturing process.   Costs
associated with start-up activities could include training costs, consulting fees,
utilities and related expenses during the pre-opening period, and operating losses
incurred before a project reaches normal productive capacity.

The SOP also provides examples of items which are outside of, or excluded from,
start-up costs but an entity should not infer that costs outside the scope of the SOP
should be capitalised, unless those costs specifically qualify for capitalisation under
GAAP.   For example, property plant and equipment, and related costs, would be
accounted for in accordance with existing GAAP for non-current assets (see
section 7.2.1), while research and development costs would be accounted for in
accordance with FAS 2 *Accounting for Research and Development Costs*, and

6.3   AMORTISATION OF INTANGIBLE ASSETS

A   Intangible assets – subject to amortisation

IAS 38.74,88   Intangible assets are amortised on a systematic basis, reflecting the pattern of use,
IAS 38.97,117   (where the pattern of use can not be determined reliably, a straight-line basis is used)
over their estimated useful life, where finite.   Amortisation commences when the
asset is available for use, and ceases at the earlier of the date the asset is (or is
included in a disposal group) classified as held for sale in accordance with IFRS 5
and the date the asset is derecognised.   It does not cease just because the asset is
no longer used.   Amortisation is recognised in profit or loss unless a Standard
permits or requires its inclusion in the carrying amount of another asset.

IAS 38.104   The amortisation period and method shall be reviewed at least at each financial year-
end, with any changes accounted for as changes in estimates in accordance with IAS 8.

IAS 38.129-130   The transitional arrangements for existing IFRS reporters are detailed in
section 6.2.1 and for first-time adopters in Chapter 2.

IAS 38.100   The residual value of an intangible asset with a finite useful life is assumed to be
zero, unless (1) there is a commitment by a third party to acquire the asset at the end
of its useful life or (2) residual value can be determined by reference to an active
market for the asset, and it is probable that such a market will exist at the end of the
asset's useful life.

IAS 38.102-103   Residual values are based on the amount recoverable from disposal using prices
prevailing at the date of the estimate for the sale of a similar asset that has reached
the end of its useful life and operated under similar conditions to those in which the
asset will be used.   It is reviewed at least at each financial year-end.   If the residual
amount equals or exceeds the carrying amount, no amortisation is charged.

advertising costs, other than direct response advertising under SOP 93-7 *Reporting on Advertising Costs*, would continue to be expensed.

Manufacturers often incur pre-production costs related to products they will supply under long-term supply arrangements. Pre-production costs could include costs to perform certain services related to the design and development of the products or services as well as costs to build moulds, dies and other tools that will be used in production.

EITF 99-5 *Accounting for Pre-Production Costs Related to Long-Term Supply Arrangements* concluded that pre-production costs related to long-term supply arrangements should be treated as follows:

EITF 99-5

- pre-production design and development costs should be expensed as incurred, unless a legally enforceable reimbursement is explicitly stated in the contract when they may be capitalised; and

- design and development costs relating to production moulds, dies, and other tools that are not owned by the supplier may only be capitalised if the supplier has the non-cancellable right to use the moulds, dies, and other tools during the supply arrangement.

6.3   AMORTISATION OF INTANGIBLE ASSETS

A   Intangible assets – subject to amortisation

Under FAS 142, the accounting for a recognised intangible asset is based on its useful life to the reporting entity. An intangible asset with a finite useful life is amortised; an intangible asset with an indefinite useful life is not amortised. The useful life of an intangible asset to an entity is the period over which the asset is expected to contribute directly or indirectly to the future cash flows of that entity. If no factors limit the useful life of an intangible asset to the reporting entity, the useful life is considered to be indefinite. Indefinite is not the same as infinite.

FAS 142.11

A recognised intangible asset should be amortised over its useful life unless that life is indefinite. If the useful life is finite but the actual length of life is not known then amortisation should be based on the best estimate of useful life. The method of amortisation should reflect the pattern of depletion of economic benefits from the intangible asset. If that pattern cannot be reliably determined, a straight-line amortisation should be used.

FAS 142.12

The amount of an intangible asset to be amortised should be the amount initially assigned to that asset less any residual value. The residual value is assumed to be zero unless at the end of its useful life to the reporting entity the asset is expected to have a further useful life to another entity and;

FAS 142.13

- the reporting entity has a commitment from a third party to purchase the asset at the end of its useful life; or

- the residual value can be determined by reference to an exchange transaction in an existing market which is expected to exist at the end of the asset's useful life.

The periods of amortisation should be continually reviewed and the unamortised amount should be allocated to the increased or reduced number of remaining

FAS 142.14

IAS 38.94 The useful life of an intangible asset that arises from contractual or other legal rights shall not exceed the period of the contractual or legal rights but may be shorter depending on the period over which the entity expects to use the asset. If the contractual or other legal rights are conveyed for a limited but renewable term, the useful life shall include the renewal period(s) only if there is evidence to support renewal by the entity without significant cost.

IAS 36.63,121 An intangible asset subject to amortisation is reviewed for impairment whenever
IAS 38.111 there are indications of impairment in accordance with IAS 36 (see section 9 for a description of that method). After the recognition of an impairment loss, the amortisation charge is adjusted in future periods to allocate the asset's revised carrying amount less its residual value, if any, on a systematic basis over its remaining useful life. Where an impairment is later reversed, again the amortisation charge is adjusted prospectively in the same way.

B   *Intangible assets – not subject to amortisation*

IAS 38.88,91 An intangible asset shall have an indefinite useful life (which does not mean an infinite life) when, based on an analysis of all the relevant factors, there is no foreseeable limit to the period over which the asset is expected to generate net cash inflows for the entity. The useful life reflects only that level of future maintenance expenditure required to maintain the asset at the assessed standard of performance at the time of estimating its useful economic life, and the entity's ability and intention to reach such a level.

IAS 38.107-111 An intangible asset with an indefinite life or which is not yet available for use is not
IAS 36.10,114 amortised, and is evaluated for impairment in accordance with IAS 36 both annually and whenever there are indications of impairment (see section 9 for a description of that method). An impairment loss recognised in prior periods for an asset other than goodwill is reversed if, and only if, there has been a change in the estimates used to determine the asset's recoverable amount.

The useful life shall be reviewed at least at every financial year end with any change accounted for as a change in estimate in accordance with IAS 8. If the life is reassessed as finite, the entity shall test the asset for impairment.

6.4   DISPOSAL OF GOODWILL AND INTANGIBLE ASSETS

IAS 38.112-114 An intangible asset is derecognised on disposal or when no future economic benefits
IAS 38.116 are expected from its use or disposal.   The difference between the carrying amount of the intangible asset and any net disposal proceeds (at fair value, i.e. cash price equivalent, if consideration is deferred) is recognised in profit or loss for the period (unless it is a sale and leaseback when IAS 17 applies – see section 16.7).   Gains are not classified as revenue.   See IAS 18 *Revenue* for guidance on the date of disposal – see section 19.2.

The treatment of intangible assets (and disposal groups) classified as held for sale and the transitional provisions in IFRS 5 are included in section 1.9.

IAS 38.115 If an entity capitalises the cost of a replacement for part of an intangible asset, it derecognises the carrying amount of the replaced part.   Where this is not

periods in the revised useful life. If a finite useful life is subsequently determined to be indefinite the asset should no longer be amortised but should be tested for impairment and accounted for as an asset not subject to amortisation.

An intangible asset that is subject to amortisation should be reviewed for impairment in accordance with FAS 144 (section 9.4) and an impairment loss should be recognised if the carrying amount is not recoverable and exceeds fair value. After an impairment loss is recognised, the adjusted carrying amount is the new accounting basis. Subsequent reversal of a recognised impairment loss is prohibited.   *FAS 142.15*

B   Intangible assets – not subject to amortisation

Under FAS 142, an intangible asset with an indefinite life is not amortised until its useful life is determined to be no longer indefinite. The remaining useful life should be evaluated each period. If an intangible asset that is not amortised is subsequently determined to have a finite life, the asset should be tested for impairment and accounted for as an asset subject to amortisation.   *FAS 142.16*

An intangible asset that is not subject to amortisation should be tested for impairment annually, or more frequently if there is indication of impairment, see section 9.4. If the carrying amount exceeds fair value, an impairment loss should be recognised. After an impairment loss is recognised, the adjusted carrying amount is the new accounting basis. Subsequent reversal of a recognised impairment loss is prohibited.   *FAS 142.17*

6.4   DISPOSAL OF GOODWILL AND INTANGIBLE ASSETS

Goodwill attributable to a reporting unit to be disposed of should be included in the carrying amount in determining the gain or loss on disposal.   *FAS 142.39*

When a business representing a portion of a reporting unit is to be disposed of, goodwill and other intangible assets associated with that business should be included in the carrying amount in determining the gain or loss on disposal. The amount of goodwill to be included in the carrying amount of the business should be based on the relative fair values of the business to be disposed of and the portion of the reporting unit that will be retained. However, if the business to be disposed of was never integrated into the reporting unit after its acquisition, the current carrying amount of that acquired goodwill should be included in the carrying amount of the business to be disposed of.

practicable to determine, the cost of the replacement may be used as an indication of the cost of the replaced part when originally acquired or internally generated.

IAS 36.86   If goodwill has been allocated to a cash-generating unit and the entity disposed of an operation within that unit, the goodwill associated with the operation disposed of is included in the carrying amount of the operation when determining the gain or loss on disposal, and is measured on the basis of the relative values of the operation disposed of and the portion of the cash-generating unit retained, unless the entity can demonstrate that some method better reflects the goodwill associated with the operation disposed of.

IFRS 3.80   If goodwill was previously recognised as a deduction from equity, this goodwill is not recognised in profit or loss when all or part of the business to which the goodwill relates is disposed of, or when a cash-generating unit to which the goodwill relates becomes impaired.

See section 5.4.4 for the treatment of cumulative foreign exchange translation differences on disposal of a foreign operation.

6.5   DISCLOSURE

IAS 38.118   The following information shall be disclosed for each class of intangible assets, distinguishing between internally generated intangible assets and other intangible assets (see section 3.4.7 for disclosure requirements relating to goodwill):

- whether the useful lives are indefinite or finite and, if finite, the useful lives or the amortisation rates used;
- the amortisation methods used for intangible assets with finite lives;
- the gross carrying amount and the total of accumulated amortisation and impairment losses at the beginning and end of the period;
- the line items of the income statement in which the amortisation of intangible assets is included;
- a reconciliation of the carrying amount at the beginning and end of the period showing the following items for the period:
  - additions, indicating separately those from internal development, those acquired separately, and those through business combinations;
  - assets classified as held for sale or included in a disposal group classified as held for sale in accordance with IFRS 5 and other disposals;
  - increases or decreases during the period resulting from revaluations and from impairment losses recognised or reversed directly in equity;
  - impairment losses recognised in profit or loss;
  - impairment losses reversed in profit or loss;
  - amortisation recognised;
  - net exchange differences arising on the translation of the financial statements into the presentation currency, and on the translation of a foreign operation into the presentation currency of the entity; and
  - other changes in the carrying amount.

Comparatives are required.

When only a portion of goodwill is allocated to a business to be disposed of, the goodwill remaining in the portion of the reporting unit to be retained should be tested for impairment.

A component of an entity to be disposed of that satisfies certain criteria should be classified as held-for-sale and measured at the lower of its carrying amount or fair value less costs to complete the disposal. The carrying amount of goodwill included within a disposal group classified as held-for-sale should be adjusted (i.e. impaired) in accordance with FAS 142 prior to measuring the fair value less cost to sell of the disposal group.

FAS 144.34-36

Further details on accounting for and disclosures related to discontinued operations are included in section 1.9.

6.5 DISCLOSURE

At a minimum, all intangible assets should be aggregated and presented as a separate line item in the statement of financial position. The amortisation expense and impairment losses for intangible assets should be presented in the appropriate income statement line items within continuing operations.

FAS 142.42

Disclosure is required of each class of intangible assets which is in excess of 5% of total assets, the carrying basis and any significant additions or deletions. The amortisation and accumulated amortisation of intangible assets should be given either in the balance sheet or in the notes.

S-X 5-02.15-16

Unamortised capitalised computer software costs and the amounts charged to income in respect of amortisation and write down of capitalised software costs must be disclosed. Amortisation of capitalised computer software costs should not be disclosed as part of research and development.

FAS 86.11

For intangible assets acquired either individually or with a group of assets, the following information should be disclosed in the notes to the financial statements in the period of acquisition:

FAS 142.44

- for intangible assets subject to amortisation:
    - the total amount assigned and the amount assigned to any major class of intangible asset;
    - the amount of any significant residual value, in total and by major class of intangible asset; and
    - the weighted-average amortisation period, in total and by major class of intangible asset;
- for intangible assets *not* subject to amortisation, the total amount assigned and the amount assigned to any major class of intangible asset; and
- the amount of research and development assets acquired and written off in the period and the line item in the income statement in which the amounts written off are aggregated.

IAS 38.120-121   IAS 8 and IAS 36 may also require further disclosures in relation to changes in estimates arising from reassessment of useful lives, residual values or amortisation method; and impairment respectively.

IAS 38.122-123   The financial statements shall also disclose:

- for an intangible asset with an indefinite life, its carrying amount and the reasons and significant factors supporting the assessment of an indefinite useful life;

- a description, the carrying amount and remaining amortisation of any material individual intangible asset;

- for intangible assets acquired by way of a government grant and initially recognised at fair value:
  - the fair value initially recognised for these assets;
  - their carrying amount; and
  - whether measured on the cost (or revaluation) model;

- the existence and carrying amounts of intangible assets whose title is restricted and the carrying amounts of intangible assets pledged as security for liabilities;

- the amount of contractual commitments for the acquisition of intangible assets; and

IAS 38.126   - the aggregate amount of research and development expenditure expensed in the period.

IAS 38.124   If intangible assets are carried at revalued amounts, the following shall be disclosed:

- by class of intangible assets:
  - the effective date of the revaluation;
  - the carrying amount of revalued intangible assets; and
  - the carrying amount that would have been recognised had the revalued intangible assets been measured using the cost model;

- the amount of the revaluation surplus that relates to intangible assets at the beginning and end of the period, indicating the changes during the period and any restrictions on the distribution of the balance to shareholders; and

- the methods and significant assumptions applied in estimating the assets' fair values.

Where an intangible asset is classified as (or included in a disposal group) held for sale in accordance with IFRS 5, the disclosure requirements of that Standard apply (see section 1.9).

The following information should be disclosed in the financial statements or the notes to the financial statements for each period for which a statement of financial position is presented:

FAS 142.45

- for intangible assets subject to amortisation:
    - the gross carrying amount and accumulated amortisation, in total and by major class of intangible asset;
    - the aggregate amortisation expense for the period; and
    - the estimated aggregate amortisation expense for each of the five succeeding fiscal years;
- for intangible assets *not* subject to amortisation, the total carrying amount and the carrying amount for each major intangible asset class.

The following disclosures should be made by an entity which recognises an impairment loss:

FAS 142.46
FAS 144.26

- a description of the impaired assets and the facts and circumstances leading to the impairment;
- the amount of the impairment loss and how fair value was determined;
- the caption in the income statement in which the impairment loss is reported if the loss is not presented as a separate caption; and
- if applicable, the business segment(s) affected.

The total research and development costs charged to expense presented in each period should be disclosed.

FAS 2.13

Where an enterprise has entered into a contract to perform research and development for others on the basis that repayment of any of the funds provided by the other parties depends solely on the outcome of the research and development having economic benefit, the following disclosures should be made:

FAS 68.14

- the terms of significant agreements relating to the research and development arrangement, including purchase provisions, license agreements, royalty arrangements and commitments to provide additional funds; and
- the amount of research and development costs incurred and compensation earned during the period for such research and development arrangements.

Section 7   Property, plant and equipment

7.1   AUTHORITATIVE PRONOUNCEMENTS

- IAS 16
- IFRS 5
- IFRIC 1

7.2   ACCOUNTING FOR PROPERTY, PLANT AND EQUIPMENT

7.2.1   Cost

IAS 16.6   Property, plant and equipment are defined as tangible assets that (1) are held for use in the production or supply of goods or services, for rental to others, or for administrative purposes and (2) are expected to be used during more than one period.

IAS 16.8   Major spare parts and stand-by equipment qualify as property, plant and equipment, as do spares and equipment used only in connection with an item of property, plant and equipment.

IAS 38.4   Some intangible assets may be contained in or on a physical substance such as a compact disc (in the case of computer software), legal documentation (in the case of a licence or patent) or film.   Judgement is used in assessing whether the tangible or intangible elements are more significant, e.g. computer software for a computer-controlled machine tool that cannot operate without that specific software or a computer's operating system is an integral part of the related hardware and is treated as property, plant and equipment.   When the software is not an integral part of the related hardware, computer software is treated as an intangible asset.

IAS 16.2,5   IAS 16 *Property, Plant and Equipment* is applied in accounting for property, plant and equipment except where another Standard requires or permits a different treatment, e.g. land and buildings accounted for as investment property in accordance with IAS 40 *Investment Property* (see section 8).   However, IAS 16 applies to property being constructed or developed for future use as investment property until it is complete (although it does not apply to investment property being redeveloped for continuing use as investment property).   Where the cost model for investment property is used, the cost model in IAS 16 should be used.

IAS 16.3   Biological assets related to agricultural activity (covered by IAS 41 *Agriculture*); the recognition and measurement of exploration and evaluation assets (see IFRS 6 *Exploration for and Evaluation of Mineral Resources*); mineral rights and mineral reserves such as oil, natural gas and similar non-regenerative resources; and property, plant and equipment classified as held for sale in accordance with IFRS 5 *Non-current Assets Held for Sale and Discontinued Operations* (see section 1.9) are excluded from the scope of IAS 16.

Section 7 Property, plant and equipment

7.1 AUTHORITATIVE PRONOUNCEMENTS

- ARB 43
- APB 6
- APB 12
- FAS 144

7.2 ACCOUNTING FOR PROPERTY, PLANT AND EQUIPMENT

7.2.1 Cost

Property, plant and equipment should be reported at historical cost, which is the   *CON 5.67*
amount of cash, or its equivalent, paid to acquire an asset, adjusted after acquisition
for amortisation or other allocations.

Interest capitalisation is required in certain circumstances (see section 10).

There are no special transitional arrangements for first-time adopters. However, the reliefs available for recording property, plant band equipment at transition date are described in Chapter 2.

A   Initial recognition

IAS 16.7,11,15 An item of property, plant and equipment shall be recognised as an asset – measured at cost – if, and only if (1) it is probable that future economic benefits associated with the item will flow to the entity and (2) the cost of the item can be measured reliably. Property, plant and equipment necessary to meet safety and environmental regulations qualify as assets and are capitalised, but the resulting carrying amount of such assets (together with related assets) must be reviewed for impairment in accordance with IAS 36 *Impairment of Assets.*

IAS 16.6,16-17 The cost of an item of property, plant and equipment is the amount of cash and
IAS 16.22-23 cash equivalents paid or fair value of other consideration given to acquire the asset at the time of its acquisition or construction, or where applicable, the amount attributed to the asset on initial recognition in accordance with the specific requirements of other International Financial Reporting Standards. It is determined as follows:

- the cost comprises the purchase price (less any trade discounts and rebates), import duties, non-refundable purchase taxes, and any directly attributable costs of bringing the asset to the location and condition necessary for it to be capable of operating in the manner intended by management;

- the cost of an item of property, plant and equipment is the cash price equivalent at the recognition date, and the difference between that and the total payment is recognised as interest, unless capitalised in accordance with IAS 23 *Borrowing Costs;*

- directly attributable costs include costs of employee benefits arising directly from the construction or acquisition of the asset, costs of site preparation, initial delivery and handling costs, installation and assembly costs, costs of testing the equipment (less net sales proceeds of items produced) while bringing the asset to that location and condition, and professional fees. The cost of abnormal amounts of wasted materials, labour or other resources incurred in self-constructing an asset are excluded;

IAS 23.4,11 - borrowing costs incurred in the period that are directly attributable to the acquisition, construction or production of a 'qualifying asset' (i.e. one that necessarily takes a substantial period of time to get ready for its intended use or sale) may be capitalised in accordance with the requirements of IAS 23 (see section 10);

IAS 16.16,18 - the initial estimate of the costs of dismantling and removing the item and
IFRIC 1.1 restoring the site on which it is located, the obligation for which is incurred on acquisition of the item or as a result of its use in the period (except in producing inventories during the period – which would be included within the cost of inventory – see IAS 2 *Inventories*, section 15), is capitalised;

IAS 16.21 - revenue and related costs from incidental operations in connection with the asset's construction or development, are recognised in profit or loss if they are not necessary to bringing the asset to the location and condition necessary for it to be capable of operating in the manner intended by management;

A   Initial recognition

Property, plant and equipment should be reported at historical cost, which is the   *CON 5.67*
amount of cash, or its equivalent, paid to acquire an asset, adjusted after acquisition
for amortisation or other allocations.

Interest capitalisation is required in certain circumstances (see section 10).

IAS 16.19-20 • general and administrative overheads, start-up costs, and costs incurred in using or redeploying an item are not capitalised;

IAS 16.28 • government grants related to the acquisition of property, plant and equipment may be deducted from the carrying amount of the asset in accordance with the requirements of IAS 20 *Accounting for Government Grants and Disclosure of Government Assistance* (see section 20);

IAS 39.98 • if a hedge of a forecast transaction subsequently results in recognition of a non-financial asset, such as property, plant and equipment, an entity may choose as its accounting policy either to (1) reclassify the associated gains and losses on the cash-flow hedge that were recognised in equity into profit or loss in the same period as the asset acquired affects profit or loss (e.g. as depreciation or impairment is charged), although if all or part of a loss recognised directly in equity is not expected to be recovered, the amount not expected to be recovered is recognised in the income statement or to (2) remove the associated gains and losses recognised in equity and include them in the initial carrying amount of the asset (see sections 11 and 13.3.6C);

IAS 16.27 • property, plant and equipment held under a finance lease should be capitalised in accordance with the requirements of IAS 17 *Leases* (see section 16); and

IAS 16.6,24-26,80 • where property, plant and equipment is acquired in exchange for a non-monetary asset or assets, or a combination of non-monetary and monetary assets, the cost of the property, plant and equipment is measured at fair value unless (1) the exchange transaction lacks commercial substance or (2) the fair value of neither the asset received nor the asset given up is reliably measurable. The acquired item is measured in this way even if an entity cannot immediately derecognise the asset given up. The fair value of the asset given up is used, unless the fair value of the asset received is more clearly evident. If the acquired item is not measured at fair value, its cost is measured at the carrying amount of the asset given up.

COMMENT

IAS 16 contains more guidance on the circumstances when fair value is reliably measurable and when an exchange transaction lacks commercial substance.

An entity determines whether an exchange transaction has commercial substance by considering the extent to which its future cash flows are expected to change as a result of the transaction. An exchange transaction has commercial substance if:

• the configuration (risk, timing and amount) of the cash flows of the asset received differs from the configuration of the cash flows of the asset transferred; or

• the entity-specific value of the portion of the entity's operations affected by the transaction changes as a result of the exchange; and

• the difference in either of the above two items is significant relative to the fair value of the assets exchanged.

The entity-specific value is the present value of the post-tax cash flows an entity expects to arise from the continuing use of an asset and from its disposal at the end of its life or expects to incur when settling a liability. The result of these analyses may be clear without an entity having to perform detailed calculations.

The fair value of an asset for which comparable market transactions do not exist is reliably measurable if (1) the variability in the range of reasonable fair value estimates is not significant for that asset or (2) the probabilities of the various estimates within the range can be reasonably assessed and used in estimating fair value.

The requirement to apply paragraphs 24 to 26 of IAS 16 prospectively means that if an exchange of assets was measured before the effective date of IAS 16 (i.e. 1 January 2005, or earlier date of adoption) on the basis of the carrying amount of the asset given up, the entity does not restate the carrying amount of the asset acquired to reflect its fair value at the acquisition date.

IAS 16.29,37   After recognition, an entity must choose either the cost model or the revaluation model (see section 7.2.2) as its accounting policy and apply that policy to an entire class of property, plant and equipment, which is a grouping of assets of a similar nature and use in an entity's operations.

IAS 16.30,63   Under the cost model, an item of property, plant and equipment is carried at cost less any accumulated depreciation (see section 7.2.3) and any accumulated impairment losses.   Impairment is determined in accordance with the provisions of IAS 36 as described in section 9.

B   Subsequent expenditure

IAS 16.7,10   Subsequent expenditure on an item of property, plant and equipment is capitalised using the same criteria as on initial recognition, i.e. when it is probable that future economic benefits associated with the item will flow, and the cost of the expenditure can be measured reliably.

IFRIC 1.4-5,8   Changes in a decommissioning liability may arise from changes in the estimated timing or amount of the outflow of resources required to settle the obligation or the discount rate.   If the asset is carried at cost, changes in the liability are added to, or deducted from the cost of the asset.   This deduction may not exceed the carrying amount of the asset and any excess over the carrying amount is taken immediately to profit or loss. If the change increases the carrying amount, the entity must consider whether this is an indication of impairment, and if so, test for impairment in accordance with IAS 36. The unwinding of the discount on the provision is recognised as a finance cost in profit or loss.   Additional guidance is provided in IFRIC 1 *Changes in Existing Decommissioning, Restoration and Similar Liabilities* in respect of revalued assets.

C   Servicing and replacement costs

IAS 16.13-14,70   Parts of some items of property, plant and equipment may require replacement. Where the recognition criteria are met, the cost of replacement is capitalised and the carrying amount of the part that is replaced is derecognised (regardless of whether it had been depreciated separately).   If it is not practicable to determine the carrying amount of the replaced part, the cost of replacement may be used as an indication of what the cost of the replaced part was when the item was acquired or constructed.

Where the recognition criteria are met, the cost of a regular major inspection is capitalised as a replacement, and any remaining carrying amount of the cost of the previous inspection (as distinct from the physical parts which may or may not have been replaced) is derecognised, even if the cost of the previous inspection was not identified when the item was acquired or constructed.   If necessary, the estimated cost of a future similar inspection may be used as an indication of what the cost of the existing inspection component was when the item was acquired or constructed.

IAS 16.12   Costs of day-to-day servicing are recognised in profit or loss as incurred.

B   Subsequent expenditure

Subsequent or replacement expenditure may be capitalised in accordance with an   *EITF D-88*
entity's disclosed accounting policy.

C   Servicing and replacement costs

The cost of planned major maintenance, inspection or overhaul may be capitalised   *EITF D-88*
and amortised over the period to the next planned, inspection and any carrying
amount remaining from a previous inspection should be written off.   Other
accounting methods permitted include accruing in advance the costs expected to be
incurred in the next planned major maintenance activity or expensing maintenance
expenditure as incurred (see section 18.4).

> **COMMENT**
> AcSEC added a project to its agenda in January 1999 to develop a SOP to address
> accounting and disclosure for costs related to property, plant, and equipment to be
> capitalized as improvements and expensed as repairs and maintenance and the
> accrual of a liability in advance of a planned major maintenance activity. No
> exposure draft has been issued to date.
> The SEC staff believes that if a registrant that is currently accruing in advance the
> costs expected to be incurred in the next planned major maintenance activity wants
> to change from that method to some other method permitted under US GAAP, the
> SEC staff would not object to a conclusion that a change from the accrue-in-
> advance method is preferable.

Servicing and maintenance costs are generally expensed as incurred.

D   *Disposal or retirement and items held for disposal*

IAS 16.41-42   The carrying amount of an item (or part of an item) of property, plant and equipment
IAS 16.67-69   is derecognised upon disposal or when no future economic benefits are expected from
IAS 16.71-72   its use or disposal.   The difference between the carrying amount of the asset and any
IAS 12.64   net disposal proceeds, measured at fair value (cash price equivalent where deferred), is
recognised in profit or loss for the period (unless required otherwise by IAS 17 for a
sale and leaseback), but not classified as revenue.   See IAS 18 *Revenue* gives guidance
on the date of disposal – see section 19.3.4.   If the consideration is deferred, the
difference between the nominal amount of the consideration and cash price equivalent
is recognised as interest income using the effective interest method.   The revaluation
surplus, net of any deferred tax liability recognised on the revaluation arising on a
revalued asset is transferred to retained earnings on disposal of the asset.

IAS 16.65-66   Compensation from third parties for items of property, plant and equipment that
were impaired, lost or given up shall be included in profit or loss when the
compensation becomes receivable.   The derecognition or impairment of the items
and the cost of their replacement or restoration are accounted for separately.

The treatment of property, plant and equipment (and disposal groups) held for sale
and the transitional provisions in IFRS 5 are included in section 1.9.

7.2.2   Valuation

IAS 16.29   An entity must choose either the cost model (see section 7.2.1) or the revaluation
model as its accounting policy and apply that policy to an entire class of property,
plant and equipment.

The discussion in section 7.2.1 on initial recognition, subsequent expenditure,
disposal or retirement and held for disposal also apply to revalued assets.

IAS 8.17   The initial application of a policy to revalue assets is dealt with as a revaluation in
accordance with the Standard, rather than retrospectively in accordance with IAS 8
Accounting Policies, Changes in Accounting Estimates and Errors.

IAS 16.31   Under the revaluation model, an item of property, plant and equipment whose fair
value can be measured reliably is carried at a revalued amount as follows:

IAS 16.31-34   • the revalued carrying amount is equal to the item's fair value at the date of
revaluation less any subsequent depreciation and impairment losses;

• property, plant and equipment shall be revalued with sufficient regularity to
ensure that the carrying amount at balance sheet date does not differ materially
from the fair value at that date.   The fair value of land and buildings is usually
determined from market-based evidence by appraisal, normally undertaken by
professionally qualified valuers, although where there is no such evidence
because of the specialised nature of the items and the item is rarely sold, except
as part of a continuing business, fair value may need to be estimated using an
income or depreciated replacement cost approach.   Some items may
experience significant and volatile movements in fair value thus necessitating
annual revaluation.   Where there are insignificant movements in fair value,
revaluation every three or five years may be sufficient;

IAS 16.36,38   • property, plant and equipment in the same class shall be revalued
simultaneously, although rolling revaluations are permitted where completed
within a short period and revaluations are kept up to date;

D *Disposal or retirement and items held for disposal*

A component of an entity to be disposed of that satisfies certain criteria should be classified as held-for-sale and measured at the lower of its carrying amount or fair value less indirect costs to complete the disposal. *FAS 144.34-35*

Further details on accounting for and disclosures related to discontinued operations are included in section 1.9.

7.2.2 Valuation

Property, plant and equipment should not be written up to reflect appraisal, market or current values that are above cost to the entity except in certain specific cases, for example in quasi-reorganisations or push down accounting.

APB 6.17
SAB 54
Topic 5J

IAS 16.39-40 • any increase in the carrying amount of an item of property, plant and equipment resulting from a revaluation shall be credited to the revaluation surplus in equity. However, to the extent that the revaluation increase reverses a previous revaluation decrease that was previously recognised in profit or loss, the increase shall also be recognised in profit or loss;

• any decrease in the carrying amount of an item of property, plant and equipment resulting from a revaluation should be recognised in profit or loss, after any revaluation surplus in equity related to the same asset has been reduced to zero; and

IAS 16.41-42
IAS 12.64 • the revaluation surplus included in equity, net of deferred tax, in respect of an item of property, plant and equipment may be transferred directly to retained earnings when the asset is derecognised.

7.2.3 Depreciation

IAS 16.6,48,50,52 The cost (or revalued amount) less residual value is allocated on a systematic basis over the estimated useful life to the entity. The residual value is the estimated amount, net of estimated disposal costs, that the entity would currently obtain from disposal of the asset, if the asset were already of the age and in the condition expected at the end of its useful life. The depreciation charge is recognised in profit or loss unless it has to be included in the carrying amount of another asset. A depreciation charge must be recognised even if the fair value of the asset exceeds its carrying amount, as long as its residual value does not exceed the carrying amount (when the depreciation charge is zero). Repairs and maintenance do not negate the need to depreciate.

IAS 16.43-48
IAS 16.58-59 Each part of an item of property, plant and equipment with a cost significant in relation to the total cost of the item shall be depreciated separately. An entity also depreciates separately the remainder of the item and may use approximation techniques or choose to depreciate separately the other parts. For accounting purposes, land and buildings are considered separable assets that should be accounted for separately. Normally, land has an unlimited life and is not depreciated. Where the land includes an element for site dismantlement or restoration, this element is depreciated over the period of benefits. However, buildings have a limited life and should be depreciated, independent of the value of the land they are built on.

IAS 16.60-62 While IAS 16 permits a range of depreciation methods that allocate the depreciation charge on a systematic basis over the useful life of an asset, the following methods are specifically listed as permissible: the straight-line method, the diminishing balance method and the unit-of-production method. An entity shall select the method that most closely reflects the expected pattern of consumption of future economic benefits by the entity, and apply it consistently from period to period. The method must be changed if there is a significant change in the expected pattern of consumption of the future economic benefits.

IAS 16.51,61 The residual value, useful life and depreciation method applicable to an asset shall be reviewed at least at each financial year-end. Changes are accounted for as changes in accounting estimates, in accordance with IAS 8 by adjusting the depreciation charge for the current and future periods.

IAS 16.55
IFRS 5.25 Depreciation of an asset begins when it is available for use, i.e. it is in the location and condition necessary for it to be capable of operating in the manner intended by

7.2.3   Depreciation

The cost of a productive facility (less any salvage value) to be spread over its   *ARB 43 Ch 9C.5*
expected useful life in such a way as to allocate it as equitably as possible to the
periods during which services are obtained from the use of the facility.

A change in amortisation method for a class of identifiable assets is a change in   *APB 20.23-24*
accounting principle and requires an adjustment for the cumulative effect of the
change in the income statement of the period of the change (see section 1.10.2).

> **COMMENT**
>
> SAB 100 *Restructuring and Impairment Charges* provides the SEC staff's views on
> the need to challenge depreciable lives, amortisation periods and salvage values of
> non-current assets.
>
> The SAB emphasises that registrants should continually evaluate the appropriateness
> of useful lives assigned to long-lived assets, including identifiable intangible assets
> and goodwill.   The SAB indicates that the SEC staff may challenge impairment
> charges for which the timely evaluation of useful life and residual value cannot be
> demonstrated.

Buildings must be depreciated.   Land is not depreciated.

management. Depreciation ceases at the earlier of the date that the asset is classified as held for sale (or included in a disposal group that is classified as held for sale) in accordance with IFRS 5 and the date that the asset is derecognised. It does not cease when the asset is retired from active use or becomes idle.

IAS 16.41
IAS 12.64
As a revalued asset is depreciated, an amount equal to the difference in depreciation based on the revalued asset and that based on cost (net of the appropriate portion of related deferred tax arising on the revaluation) may be transferred to retained earnings from the revaluation surplus.

IAS 36.63,121
Property, plant and equipment is reviewed for impairment whenever there are indications of impairment in accordance with IAS 36 (see section 9 for a description of that method). After the recognition of an impairment loss, the depreciation charge is adjusted in future periods to allocate the asset's revised carrying amount less its residual value, if any, on a systematic basis over its remaining useful life. Where an impairment is later reversed, again the depreciation charge is adjusted prospectively in the same way.

7.3   DISCLOSURE

IAS 16.73
The entity shall disclose for each class of property, plant and equipment:
- the measurement bases used for determining the gross carrying amount;
- the depreciation methods used;
- the useful lives or the depreciation rates used;
- the gross carrying amount and the aggregate of accumulated depreciation and accumulated impairment losses at the beginning and end of the period;
- a reconciliation of the carrying amount at the beginning and end of the period showing:
  - additions;
  - assets classified as held for sale or included in a disposal group classified as held for sale in accordance with IFRS 5 and other disposals;
  - acquisitions through business combinations;
  - increases or decreases resulting from revaluations and from impairment losses recognised or reversed directly in equity;
  - impairment losses recognised in profit or loss;
  - impairment losses reversed in profit or loss;
  - depreciation;
  - the net exchange differences arising on the translation of the financial statements from the functional currency into a different presentation currency, including the translation of a foreign operation into the presentation currency of the reporting entity; and
  - other changes.

There is no exemption from providing comparative information for the reconciliation.

IAS 36 has further disclosures on impairment (see section 9.7).

7.3　DISCLOSURE

Disclosure should be made of:

- the method or methods used in computing depreciation for major classes of depreciable assets;
- the cost of depreciable assets by major class;
- accumulated depreciation either by major class of depreciable asset or in total; and
- the depreciation expense for the period.

S-X 5-02.13(a),14
APB 12.4-5

The aggregate carrying amount of mineral rights should be disclosed as a separate component of property, plant, and equipment either on the face of the financial statements or in the notes to the financial statements.

EITF 04-2

An impairment loss should be reported as a component of income from continuing operations before taxes and, where applicable, should be included in operating income.

FAS 144.25-26
FAS 144.47

An entity that recognises an impairment loss should disclose the following information:

- a description of the impaired assets and the facts and circumstances leading to the impairment;
- the amount of the impairment loss and how fair value was determined;
- the location of the impairment loss in the income statement;
- if applicable, the business segment(s) affected; and
- the gain or loss, if any, resulting from changes in the carrying amounts of assets to be disposed of.

IAS 16.74   The entity shall also disclose in its financial statements:

- the existence and amounts of restrictions on title, and property, plant and equipment pledged as security for liabilities;

- the amount of expenditures recognised in the carrying amount of an item of property, plant and equipment in the course of construction;

- the amount of contractual commitments for the acquisition of property, plant and equipment;

- if it is not disclosed separately on the face of the income statement, the amount of compensation from third parties for items of property, plant and equipment that were impaired, lost or given up that is included in profit or loss; and

IAS 16.76
IAS 8.39-40
- the nature and effect of a change in accounting estimate, e.g. in respect of residual values, useful lives, depreciation methods, or the estimated costs of dismantling, removing or restoring items of property, plant and equipment, that has an effect in the current period or, is expected to have an effect in subsequent periods, in accordance with IAS 8. If the effect on future periods is not disclosed, as impracticable, this fact shall be stated.

IAS 16.77   If items of property, plant and equipment are stated at revalued amounts, the following shall be disclosed:

- the effective date of the revaluation;

- whether an independent valuer was involved;

- the methods and significant assumptions applied in estimating the fair values;

- the extent to which the items' fair values were determined directly by reference to observable prices in an active market or recent market transactions on arm's length terms or were estimated using other valuation techniques;

- for each revalued class of property, plant and equipment, the carrying amount that would have been recognised had the assets been carried under the cost model; and

- the revaluation surplus, indicating the change for the period and any restrictions on the distribution of the balance to shareholders.

IFRIC 1.6   A change in the revaluation surplus on a revalued asset arising from a change in a decommissioning, restoration or similar liability shall be separately identified and disclosed as such in equity.

Where an asset is (or is included in a disposal group) held for sale, the disclosures required by IFRS 5 are required (see section 1.9).

Section 8   Investment property

8.1   AUTHORITATIVE PRONOUNCEMENTS

- IAS 16
- IAS 17
- IAS 40

8.2   SCOPE AND INITIAL RECOGNITION

IAS 40.5,7   Investment property is property – land and/or buildings – held (by the owner or by the lessee under a finance lease) to earn rentals or for capital appreciation or both, rather than for:

- use in the production or supply of goods or services or for administrative purposes; or
- sale in the ordinary course of business.

It generates cash flows largely independently from an entity's other assets.

IAS 40.6,32A   A property interest held by a lessee under an operating lease may be classified and accounted for as an investment property if and only if the property would otherwise meet the definition of an investment property and the lessee uses the fair value model for all its investment property (with the exception of investment property backing liabilities that pay a return linked directly to the fair value of, or returns from, specified assets including that investment property, which can be accounted for either under the cost or the fair value model, regardless of the model adopted for other investment property) – see section 8.3. This classification alternative is available on a property-by-property basis.

COMMENT

An entity that has previously applied IAS 40 (2000) *Investment Property* and elects for the first time to classify and account for some or all eligible property interests held under operating leases as investment property shall recognise the effect of that election as an adjustment to the opening balance of retained earnings for the period in which the election is first made.

If the entity has previously disclosed publicly (in financial statements or otherwise) the fair value of those property interests in earlier periods (determined on a basis that satisfies the definition of fair value in paragraph 5 and the guidance in paragraphs 36-52 of IAS 40), the entity is encouraged, but not required:

- to adjust the opening balance of retained earnings for the earliest period presented for which such fair value was disclosed publicly; and
- to restate comparative information for those periods.

If the entity has not previously disclosed publicly the information described above, it shall not restate comparative information and shall disclose that fact.

Section 8   Investment property

8.1   AUTHORITATIVE PRONOUNCEMENTS

Under US GAAP, there is no specific guidance concerning accounting for investment property directly held by the reporting entity. However, accounting guidance does exist regarding accounting by real estate investment entities qualifying as investment companies under the Investment Companies Act of 1940 and transactions involving real estate held through an intermediate entity.

8.2   SCOPE AND INITIAL RECOGNITION

See section 8.1.

IAS 40.8   Investment properties include:

- buildings, owned by the entity (or held under a finance lease) leased or held to be leased out under operating leases (even if currently vacant);

- land held for long-term capital appreciation rather than short term sale in the ordinary course of business; and

- land held for currently undetermined future use.

IAS 40.9   Investment properties exclude:

- property intended for sale in the ordinary course of business, or in construction or development for such sale (see IAS 2 *Inventories* – section 15)

- property being constructed or developed on behalf of third parties (see IAS 11 *Construction Contracts* – section 15);

- owner-occupied property (including such property awaiting disposal, property occupied by employees, property held for future use as, or for future development and subsequent use as owner occupied property) (see IAS 16 *Property, Plant and Equipment* – section 7);

- property leased to another entity under a finance lease; and

- property being constructed or developed for future use as investment property. IAS 16 applies to such property, although IAS 40 applies to existing investment property that is being redeveloped for continued future use as an investment property.

IAS 40.10   Some properties comprise a portion held to earn rentals or for capital appreciation, and another portion held for use in the production or supply of goods or services, or for administrative purposes. If the portions could be sold separately (or leased under a finance lease), the portions are accounted for separately. If they cannot be sold separately, then the property is an investment property only if an insignificant portion is held for use.

IAS 40.11-14   Where ancillary services are provided by the entity to the occupants of the property, an entity treats the property as investment property if the services are insignificant, to the arrangement. Judgement is needed to determine whether the property is an investment property.

IAS 40.15   Where an entity owns property that is leased to, and occupied by, its parent or another subsidiary, the property is not investment property in the consolidated financial statements, but if it meets the definition of an investment property, is treated as such in the individual financial statements.

IAS 40.16   Investment property is recognised as an asset when and only when it is probable that future economic benefits will flow to the entity, and the cost of the investment property can be measured reliably.

IAS 40.20-24   Initially, investment property meeting the recognition criteria should be measured at cost, which includes transaction costs. This will be the cash price equivalent, if payment is deferred, with any difference between that amount and the total payments recognised as interest expense on the effective interest method. Where the investment property is self-constructed, the initial cost is its cost at completion of construction or development, as recognised in accordance with IAS 16. It is not increased by start-up costs, operating losses before the planned level of occupancy is achieved, or abnormal wastage costs of construction or development.

IAS 40.25
IAS 17.20 The initial cost of a property interest held under a lease (operating or finance) and classified as an investment property is the lower of the fair value of the property and the present value of the minimum lease payments, determined at lease inception. An equivalent amount is recognised as a liability. Initial direct costs are capitalised.

IAS 40.27-29,84 Where investment property is acquired in exchange for non-monetary assets, or a combination of monetary and non-monetary assets, the cost of the investment property is measured at fair value unless (1) the exchange transaction lacks commercial substance, or (2) the fair value of neither the assets received nor the assets given up is reliably measurable. The acquired item is measured in this way even if an entity cannot immediately derecognise the asset given up. The fair value of the asset given up is used, unless the fair value of the asset received is more clearly evident. If the acquired item is not measured at fair value, its cost is measured at the carrying amount of the asset given up.

COMMENT

IAS 40 contains more guidance on the circumstances when fair value is reliably measurable and when an exchange transaction lacks commercial substance.

An entity determines whether an exchange transaction has commercial substance by considering the extent to which its future cash flows are expected to change as a result of the transaction. An exchange transaction has commercial substance if:

- the configuration (risk, timing and amount) of the cash flows of the asset received differs from the configuration of the cash flows of the asset transferred; or

- the entity-specific value of the portion of the entity's operations affected by the transaction changes as a result of the exchange; and

- the difference in either of the above two items is significant relative to the fair value of the assets exchanged.

The entity-specific value is the present value of the post-tax cash flows an entity expects to arise from the continuing use of an asset and from its disposal at the end of its life or expects to incur when settling a liability. The result of these analyses may be clear without an entity having to perform detailed calculations.

The fair value of an asset for which comparable market transactions do not exist is reliably measurable if (1) the variability in the range of reasonable fair value estimates is not significant for that asset or (2) the probabilities of the various estimates within the range can be reasonably assessed and used in estimating fair value.

The requirement to apply paragraphs 27 to 29 of IAS 40 prospectively means that if an exchange of assets was measured before the effective date of IAS 40 (i.e. 1 January 2005, or earlier date of adoption) on the basis of the carrying amount of the asset given up, the entity does not restate the carrying amount of the asset acquired to reflect its fair value at the acquisition date.

IAS 40.17-19,68 Subsequent expenditure may be capitalised where it meets the recognition criteria. Costs of day-to-day servicing are recognised in profit or loss as incurred. Where parts of investment properties are replaced, an entity should recognise the cost of replacing that part, where it meets the recognition criteria, and the carrying amount of the parts that are replaced is derecognised, whether or not the replaced part was depreciated separately (see section 8.5).

There are no special transitional arrangements for first-time adopters. However, the reliefs available for recording property, plant band equipment at transition date extend to investment property and are described in Chapter 2.

8.3   VALUATION

IAS 40.6,30,32A   An entity shall choose to apply either the fair value model or the cost model.
IAS 40.32B,33-34   However, when a property interest held by a lessee under an operating lease is classified as an investment property (see section 8.2), the fair value model must be adopted.

An entity should apply the model adopted to all of its investment property except that an entity may choose either:

- the fair value model or the cost model for all investment property backing liabilities that pay a return linked directly to the fair value of, or returns from, specified assets including that investment property (e.g. funds held by some insurers); and

- the fair value model or the cost model for all other investment property, regardless of the choice made above.

IAS 40.32C   Where different models are used for the above two categories, sales of investment property between pools of assets measured using different models shall be recognised at fair value, with the cumulative change recognised in profit or loss.

IAS 40.31   It is highly unlikely that a change from the fair value model to the cost model will result in a more appropriate presentation, as required for a change under IAS 8 *Accounting Policies, Changes in Accounting Estimates and Errors.*

COMMENT

IAS 40.82-83   When an entity first applies IAS 40 (revised 2004) (and the fair value model), the adjustment to the opening balance of retained earnings includes the reclassification of any amount held in revaluation surplus for investment property.

IAS 8 applies to any change in accounting policies that is made when an entity first applies IAS 40 (revised 2004) and chooses to use the cost model. The effect of the change in accounting policies includes the reclassification of any amount held in revaluation surplus for investment property.

A   *Fair value model*

IAS 40.32-34   All investment property (with the exception for investment property backing
IAS 40.38   liabilities that pay a return linked to specified assets including that investment property, if measured under the cost model) should be measured at fair value, reflecting market conditions at the balance sheet date.

IAS 40.5,32,36   Fair value is 'the amount for which an asset could be exchanged between
IAS 40.37,41   knowledgeable, willing parties in an arm's length transaction' without deduction of transaction costs. Considerable guidance is included in IAS 40 concerning fair value measurement. IAS 40 notes that for a lease negotiated at market rates, the fair value of an interest in a leased property at acquisition, net of all expected leased payments is nil, so remeasurement to fair value at acquisition will not give rise to a gain or loss. Use of an independent valuer with a recognised qualification and recent experience is encouraged but not required.

IAS 40.35   Gains or losses arising from a change in fair value are recognised in profit or loss for the period in which they arise. No depreciation is charged on investment properties accounted for under the fair value model.

8.3   VALUATION

See section 8.1.

IAS 40.48,53   There is a rebuttable presumption that an entity can reliably determine the fair value of an investment property on a continuing basis.   In exceptional cases, there is clear evidence when an investment property is first acquired or an existing property is first classified as an investment property, that its fair value is not reliably determinable on a continuing basis.   Such cases arise when and only when comparable market transactions are infrequent and alternative reliable estimates of fair value are not available.   In such cases, an entity should measure the investment property in question using the cost model in IAS 16 (see section 7.2.1) even where the fair value model is adopted for the other investment properties.   The residual value of the investment should be assumed to be zero and the entity should continue to apply IAS 16 until disposal of the investment property.

IAS 40.55   If an entity has previously measured an investment property at fair value, it should continue to measure the investment property at fair value until disposal even if comparable market transactions become less frequent or market prices become less readily available.   The entity should not continue to measure the investment property at fair value when it becomes owner-occupied property or the entity begins to develop the property for subsequent sale in the ordinary course of business.

IAS 17.18   Separate measurement of the land and buildings element of an investment property held under a lease and accounted for under the fair value model is not required.

IAS 40.50   In determining fair value, assets or liabilities recognised separately must not be double-counted.   For instance, equipment and furniture that is included within the valuation should not also be separately recognised.   Prepaid or accrued operating lease income should be treated as separate assets and not subsumed within the fair value of investment property.   The fair value of investment property held under a lease reflects expected cash flows, including contingent rentals, and therefore if the valuation is made net of all payments expected to be made, it will be necessary to add back any recognised lease liability to arrive at the investment property valuation for accounting purposes.

B   Cost model

IAS 40.32A,56   Under the cost model, an entity should measure all of its investment property (with
IAS 16.30   the exception noted above for investment property backing liabilities paying a return linked directly to the fair value of, or returns from, specified assets including that investment property) using the cost model under IAS 16 (see section 7.2.1), i.e. at cost less any accumulated depreciation and any accumulated impairment losses. This will require the analysis of investment properties into parts, for depreciation purposes.   Impairment is covered by IAS 36 *Impairment of Assets* (see section 9).

IAS 40.32   Fair value measurements are also required for disclosure purposes.

8.4   TRANSFERS

IAS 40.57   Transfers to or from investment property should be made when and only when there is a change of use, evidenced by:

- commencement of owner-occupation, for a transfer from investment property to owner-occupied property;
- commencement of development with a view to sale, for a transfer from investment property to inventories;

8.4   TRANSFERS

See section 8.1.

- end of owner-occupation, for a transfer from owner-occupied property to investment property;

- commencement of an operating lease to another party, for a transfer from inventories to investment property; or

- end of construction or development, for a transfer from property in the course of construction or development to investment property.

IAS 40.58   Consequently, if an investment property is disposed of, without development, or is redeveloped for continued future use as an investment property, the property remains an investment property (until derecognised).

IAS 40.59   When an entity uses the cost model, transfers between investment property, owner-occupied property and inventories do not change the carrying amount of the property transferred nor its cost for measurement or disclosure purposes.

IAS 40.60   If a property is transferred from investment property (under the fair value model) to owner-occupied property or inventories, the property's deemed cost for subsequent accounting under IAS 16 or IAS 2 should be its fair value at the date of change in use.

IAS 40.61,63,65   If an owner-occupied property becomes an investment property, carried at fair value, the entity should treat any difference between the carrying amount under IAS 16 at the date of change in use and its fair value at that date in the same way as a revaluation in accordance with IAS 16. When inventories or self-constructed investment properties (on completion of construction or development) are transferred to investment property, which is carried at fair value, any difference between the carrying amount and the fair value at that date should be recognised in profit or loss.

IAS 17.19   If an investment property held under an operating lease ceases to be so classified, the property interest continues to be treated as if it were a finance lease. If it becomes owner-occupied, it is transferred at a deemed cost equal to fair value at the date of change of use. If a sublease is granted that transfers substantially all the risks and rewards of the property interest to an unrelated third party, the sublease is treated as a finance lease by the entity.

8.5   DISPOSALS AND HELD FOR DISPOSAL

IAS 40.66-67
IAS 40.69-70   Investment property should be derecognised on disposal (via sale, finance lease, or sale-and-leaseback) or when it is permanently withdrawn from use and no future economic benefits are expected from its disposal. Gains or losses from retirement or disposal of investment property are determined as the difference between (1) the fair value of the net disposal proceeds (at cash price equivalent, if receipt is deferred, with any difference between that amount and total proceeds recognised as interest income using the effective interest method) and (2) the carrying amount of the asset. Gains and losses are recognised in profit or loss in the period of the retirement or disposal (unless IAS 17 *Leases* rules on sale-and-leaseback transactions apply). See guidance in IAS 18 *Revenue* (section 19.3.4) and IAS 17 (section 16.7).

IAS 40.68   Where part of an investment property is replaced, the cost of the replacement should be recognised and the carrying amount of the replaced part derecognised. Under the cost model, where the part was not depreciated separately, the cost of the replacement may be used as an indication of the original cost of the replaced part,

8.5   DISPOSALS AND HELD FOR DISPOSAL

See section 8.1.

where it is not practicable to determine the carrying amount of the replaced part. Under the fair value model, the fair value of the investment property may already reflect that the part to be replaced has lost its value. Where it is not practical to reduce fair value for the part being replaced, the cost of the replacement asset could be capitalised, and then fair value reassessed.

IAS 40.72-73 Compensation from third parties for investment property that was impaired, lost or given up should be recognised in profit or loss when the compensation becomes receivable. Impairment or losses of investment property, compensation from third parties and the purchase or construction of replacement assets are accounted for separately.

IAS 40.56 Where an investment property is (or is included within a disposal group) classified
IFRS 5.2,5 as held for disposal, IFRS 5 is applied. However, its measurement provisions do not apply to investment property under the fair value model, whether as an individual asset or as part of a disposal group. They do apply to investment property under the cost model and such investment property (or where it is part of a disposal group, the disposal group) is measured at the lower of its carrying amount and fair value less costs to sell. The disclosure and presentation requirements apply to all non-current assets or disposal groups classified as held for sale. See section 1.9 for details on the accounting, disclosure and transitional rules of IFRS 5.

8.6   DISCLOSURE

IAS 40.75 An entity (regardless of which model is followed) should disclose:
- whether it applies the fair value or the cost model;
- if it applies the fair value model, whether, and in what circumstances, property interests held under operating leases are classified and accounted for as investment property;
- when classification is difficult, the criteria used by the entity to distinguish investment property from owner-occupied property, and from property held for sale in the ordinary course of business;
- the methods and significant assumptions applied in determining the fair value of investment property, including a statement whether the determination of fair value was supported by market evidence or was more heavily based on other factors (which should be disclosed) because of the nature of the property and lack of comparable market data;
- the extent to which the fair value of investment property is based on a valuation by an independent valuer who holds a recognised and relevant professional qualification and who has recent experience in the location and category of the investment property being valued. If there has been no such valuation, that fact should be disclosed;
- the amounts recognised in profit or loss for:
  - rental income from investment property;
  - direct operating expenses (including repairs and maintenance) arising from investment property that generated rental income during the period;

8.6   DISCLOSURE

See section 8.1.

              –   direct operating expenses (including repairs and maintenance) arising from investment property that did not generate rental income during the period; and

              –   the cumulative change in fair value recognised in profit or loss on a sale of investment property from a pool of assets in which the cost model is used into a pool in which the fair value model is used (see section 8.3);

- the existence and amounts of restrictions on the realisability of investment property or the remittance of income and proceeds of disposal; and
- contractual obligations to purchase, construct or develop investment property or for repairs, maintenance or enhancements.

IAS 40.74   In addition, the disclosures required by IAS 17 (see sections 16.4 and 16.5) as lessor and/or lessee are required.

IAS 40.76   When the entity applies the fair value model it should also disclose a reconciliation between the carrying amounts of investment property at the beginning and end of the period showing the following:

- additions, disclosing separately those additions resulting from acquisitions and those resulting from subsequent expenditure recognised in the carrying amount of the asset;
- additions resulting from acquisitions through business combinations;
- assets classified as held for sale or included in a disposal group classified as held for sale in accordance with IFRS 5 and other disposals;
- net gains or losses from fair value adjustments;
- the net exchange differences arising on the translation of the financial statements into a different presentation currency, and on translation of a foreign operation into the presentation currency of the reporting entity;
- transfers to and from inventories and owner-occupied property; and
- other changes.

IAS 40.77   When a valuation obtained for investment property is adjusted significantly for use in the financial statements (e.g., to avoid double-counting of assets or liabilities recognised separately), the entity should disclose a reconciliation between the valuation and the adjusted valuation included in the financial statements, showing separately the aggregate amount of any recognised lease obligations added back and any other significant adjustments.

IAS 40.78   When an entity, applying the fair value method, measures investment property using the cost model in IAS 16, because a reliable fair value is not available (see section 8.3A), it should disclose:

- a reconciliation of the opening and closing carrying amount (as required by paragraph 76 of IAS 40) for that investment property, separately from amounts relating to other investment property;
- a description of the investment property;
- an explanation of why fair value cannot be determined reliably;
- if possible, the range of estimates within which fair value is highly likely to lie; and

- on disposal of investment property not carried at fair value:
    - the fact that the entity has disposed of investment property not carried at fair value;
    - the carrying amount of that investment property at the time of sale; and
    - the amount of gain or loss recognised.

IAS 40.79   When the entity applies the cost model it should also disclose the following:
- the depreciation methods used;
- the useful lives or the depreciation rates used;
- the gross carrying amount and the accumulated depreciation (aggregated with accumulated impairment losses) at the beginning and end of the period;
- a reconciliation of the carrying amount of investment property at the beginning and end of the period, showing the following:
    - additions, disclosing separately those additions resulting from acquisitions and those resulting from subsequent expenditure recognised as an asset;
    - additions resulting from acquisitions through business combinations;
    - assets classified as held for sale or included in a disposal group classified as held for sale in accordance with IFRS 5 and other disposals;
    - depreciation;
    - the amount of impairment losses recognised, and the amount of impairment losses reversed, during the period in accordance with IAS 36;
    - the net exchange differences arising on the translation of the financial statements into a different presentation currency, and on translation of a foreign operation into the presentation of the reporting entity;
    - transfers to and from inventories and owner-occupied property; and
    - other changes; and
- the fair value of investment property.   If an entity cannot determine the fair value of the investment property reliably (see section 8.3A), the entity should disclose the following:
    - a description of the investment property,
    - an explanation of why fair value cannot be determined reliably; and
    - if possible, the range of estimates within which fair value is highly likely to lie.

Where an investment property is classified as (or included in a disposal group classified as) held for sale in accordance with IFRS 5, the disclosure requirements of that Standard apply (see section 1.9).

Section 9   Impairment

9.1   AUTHORITATIVE PRONOUNCEMENTS

- IAS 36
- IAS 16

9.2   GENERAL PRINCIPLE

IAS 36.6,8,31   An asset is impaired when its carrying amount exceeds its recoverable amount – the higher of the asset's fair value less costs to sell and its value in use.   The value in use of an asset is the present value of the future cash flows expected to be derived from the asset through its continued use over its remaining useful life and from its disposal.   Fair value less costs to sell is defined as 'the amount obtainable from the sale of an asset in an arm's length transaction between knowledgeable, willing parties, less the costs of disposal.'

IAS 36.59-60
IAS 16.39-40
IAS 38.85-86   The carrying amount of an asset is reduced to its recoverable amount, and an impairment loss recognised for this reduction, if and only if the recoverable amount of an asset is less than its carrying amount.   The impairment loss is recognised immediately in profit or loss, unless the asset is carried at a revalued amount in accordance with another Standard.   The impairment loss on a revalued asset is treated as a revaluation decrease and is recognised against any revaluation surplus held for the same asset to the extent that the impairment loss does not exceed the amount held in the revaluation surplus for that same asset.   Any impairment loss over and above the amount held in the revaluation surplus is recognised as an expense in the income statement.

IAS 36.17,113-114   If there is an indication of impairment or its reversal, this may indicate that the remaining useful life, depreciation (or amortisation) method or residual value needs to be reviewed.

IAS 36.2   Non-current assets (or disposal groups) classified as 'held for sale' are accounted for in accordance with IFRS 5 *Non-current Assets Held for Sale and Discontinued Operations* (see section 1.9).

IAS 21.49   Where a foreign operation is impaired, no part of the foreign exchange gains or losses deferred in equity relating to the foreign operation (see section 5.4.4) are recognised in profit or loss.

IAS 36.138-140   For existing IFRS reporters, if an entity elects to apply IFRS 3 *Business Combinations* from any date before the effective dates in that Standard – see section 3.2B – which are the same as for IAS 36 *Impairment of Assets* below, it shall also apply IAS 36 prospectively from that date.   Otherwise, IAS 36 should be applied to goodwill and intangible assets acquired in business combinations for which the agreement date is on or after 31 March 2004, and to all other assets prospectively from the beginning of the first annual period beginning on or after 31 March 2004.   The entity is encouraged to

Section 9 Impairment

9.1 AUTHORITATIVE PRONOUNCEMENTS

- FAS 142
- FAS 144

9.2 GENERAL PRINCIPLE

An impairment loss should be recognised only where an impairment review *FAS 144.7* indicates that the sum of future cash flows (undiscounted and without interest charges) expected to result from the use of the asset (or asset group) and its eventual disposition is less than the carrying amount of the asset (or asset group). An impairment loss is measured as the amount by which the carrying amount of the asset exceeds its fair value.

The fair value is the amount at which an asset could be bought or sold in a current *FAS 144.22* transaction between willing parties, that is, other than in a forced or liquidation sale. The fair value may be determined by reference to:

- quoted market prices in active markets;
- estimates based on the values of similar assets; or
- estimates based on the results of valuation techniques.

> ### COMMENT
> In June 2004 the FASB issued an exposure draft of a Proposed Statement of Financial Accounting Standards *Fair Value Measurements*. The proposed Statement provides guidance for how to measure fair value and would supersede the fair value measurement guidance in FAS 144. The proposed statement would be effective for financial statements issued for fiscal years beginning after June 15, 2005. The FASB expect to issue a final statement in the third quarter of 2005.

If an impairment loss is recognised, the adjusted amount becomes the new cost basis *FAS 144.15* which, for a depreciable long-lived asset should be depreciated over its remaining useful life. Restoration of a previously recognised impairment loss is prohibited.

When an asset (or asset group) is tested for impairment a review of depreciation *FAS 144.9* policies also may be appropriate.

A long-lived asset classified as 'held for sale' is initially measured at the lower of *FAS 144.34-37* carrying amount or fair value less cost to sell (see criteria for classification as 'held for sale' in Section 1.9.1A). Subsequent changes in fair value less cost to sell should be reported as adjustments to the carrying amount, except that the adjusted carrying amount should not exceed the carrying amount at the time the asset was classified as 'held for sale'. Long-lived assets classified as 'held for sale' should not be depreciated. Costs to sell are restricted to the incremental costs that result directly from and are essential to a sale transaction, such as broker commissions, legal and title transfer fees.

apply IAS 36 before the effective date, but if it does so, it must also apply IFRS 3 (and IAS 38 *Intangible Assets*) from that same date.

IFRS 1.Appx B2(l) Under IAS 36, for both existing IFRS reporters and first-time adopters, goodwill
IFRS 3.80 previously recognised as a deduction in equity is not subsequently recognised in the income statement on disposal or impairment of the subsidiary to which it relates.

Transitional arrangements for first-time adopters are addressed in Chapter 2.

9.3   ASSETS SUBJECT TO IMPAIRMENT REVIEW

IAS 36.2,4 The Standard, IAS 36, dealing with impairment of assets shall be applied in accounting for the impairment of all assets, other than:

- inventories (see IAS 2 *Inventories* – section 15);
- assets arising from construction contracts (see IAS 11 *Construction Contracts* – section 15);
- deferred tax assets (see IAS 12 *Income Taxes* – section 17);
- assets arising from employee benefits (see IAS 19 *Employee Benefits* – see sections 23 to 25);
- financial assets within the scope of IAS 39 *Financial Instruments: Recognition and Measurement*. Investments in subsidiaries, associates and joint ventures are within the scope of IAS 36 (see section 4.4.4);
- investment property measured at fair value (see IAS 40 *Investment Property* – section 8);
- biological assets related to agricultural activity that are measured at fair value less estimated point-of-sale costs (see IAS 41 *Agriculture*);
- deferred acquisition costs and intangible assets, arising from an insurer's contractual rights under insurance contracts within the scope of IFRS 4 *Insurance Contracts*; and
- non-current assets (or disposal groups) classified as held for sale in accordance with IFRS 5 *Non-current Assets Held for Sale and Discontinued Operations* (see section 1.9).

9.4   WHEN IS AN IMPAIRMENT REVIEW REQUIRED?

A   Assets other than intangible assets not subject to amortisation and goodwill

IAS 36.9 An entity shall assess at each reporting date whether there is any indication that an asset may be impaired. If any such indication exists, the entity shall estimate the recoverable amount of the asset.

The EITF reached consensuses that accumulated foreign currency translation adjustments, including those that represent hedging gains or losses, should be included as part of the carrying amount when evaluating impairment of an equity method or consolidated investment, or the net investment in a foreign operation, if the entity has committed to a plan to dispose of the investment that will cause the translation adjustments to be reclassified to earnings.

EITF 01-5

Long-lived assets to be disposed of which do not qualify for classification as 'held for sale' or discontinued operations presentation (see section 1.9) should continue to be classified as held and used, and measured for impairment accordingly. Assets to be abandoned before the end of their previously estimated useful lives should be depreciated over their shortened lives. The salvage value of a long-lived asset should not be reduced below zero.

FAS 144.27-28

9.3   ASSETS SUBJECT TO IMPAIRMENT REVIEW

FAS 144 applies to all long-lived assets, e.g. property, plant, equipment, capital leases of lessees, long-lived assets of lessors subject to operating leases, certain identifiable intangibles being amortised and long-term prepaid assets, including similar assets that are held for disposal, other than by sale.

FAS 144.3-5

FAS 144 also applies to assets held for sale (see section 9.2) and components of an entity held for sale (covered under discontinued operations in section 1.9).

FAS 144 does not apply to goodwill, intangible assets not being amortised, long-term customer relationships of financial institutions, financial instruments, including investments in equity securities accounted for under the cost or equity method (see section 11), deferred policy acquisition costs, unproved oil and gas properties accounted for under the successful-efforts method, or deferred tax assets.

Goodwill related to equity method investments is within the scope of FAS 142 and is not amortised, but it is not reviewed for impairment in accordance with the standard. Equity method investments should continue to be reviewed for impairment in accordance with APB 18 (see section 4.4.4).

FAS 142.40

APB 18.19(h)

9.4   WHEN IS AN IMPAIRMENT REVIEW REQUIRED?

A   Long-lived assets and intangible assets that are subject to amortisation

An entity should review long-lived assets to be held and used for impairment whenever events or changes in circumstances indicate that the carrying amount of an asset may not be recoverable.

FAS 144.8

IAS 36.12-14   In assessing whether there is any indication of impairment, the entity should at a minimum consider the following:

- a significant decline in the asset's market value;

- significant changes with an adverse effect on the entity have taken place during the period (or will in the near future) in the technological, market, economic or legal environment in which the entity operates, or in the market to which an asset is dedicated;

- market interest rates or other market rates of return on investments have increased during the period, and these are likely to affect the discount rate used in calculating the asset's value in use and materially reduce the recoverable amount;

- the carrying amount of the net assets of the entity is more than its market capitalisation;

- evidence is available of obsolescence or physical damage of an asset;

- significant adverse changes have taken place during the period (or are expected in the near future) in the extent to which an asset is used or is expected to be used. These changes include the asset becoming idle, plans to discontinue or restructure the operation to which an asset belongs, or to dispose of an asset before the previously expected date, and reassessing the asset's useful life as finite rather than indefinite; and

- evidence is available from internal reporting that the economic performance of an asset is worse than expected.

The above list is not exhaustive, and an entity needs to evaluate all other indications that the value of an asset may be impaired.

IAS 36.15-16   A previous calculation may have shown that an asset's recoverable amount was significantly greater than its carrying amount, and it may be clear that subsequent events have been insufficient to eliminate the headroom, or previous analysis may show that the recoverable amount is not sensitive to certain indicators, e.g. market interest rates. In such cases, the recoverable amount need not be re-estimated.

B   Goodwill and intangible assets that are not subject to amortisation

IAS 36.9   An entity shall assess at each reporting date whether there is any indication that an asset may be impaired (see discussion above). If any such indication exists, the entity shall estimate the recoverable amount of the asset.

IAS 36.10
IAS 38.108   Irrespective of whether there is any indication of impairment, an entity shall also test annually for impairment:

- goodwill acquired in a business combination (see sections 9.5C and 9.5D); and

- an intangible asset either (1) not yet available for use or (2) with an indefinite useful life. This impairment test may be performed at any time during an annual period, but at the same time each year. Different intangible assets may be tested at different time, but an intangible asset shall be tested for impairment before the end of the first annual period in which it was initially recognised.

The following are examples of events or changes in circumstances that indicate that the recoverability of the carrying amount should be assessed:

- a significant decrease in the market value of an asset;

- a significant adverse change in the extent or manner in which an asset is used or a significant change in an asset;

- a significant adverse change in legal factors or in the business climate that could affect the value of an asset or an adverse action or assessment by a regulator;

- an accumulation of costs significantly in excess of the amount originally expected to acquire or construct an asset;

- a current period operating or cash flow loss combined with a history of operating or cash flow losses or a projection or forecast that demonstrates continuing losses associated with the use of a long-lived asset; and

- a current expectation that, more likely than not, a long-lived asset will be sold or otherwise disposed of significantly before the end of its previously estimated useful life.

COMMENT

The SEC Staff issued SAB 100 *Restructuring and Impairment Charges*, which provides the Staff's views on the recognition and disclosure of asset impairment charges, including the accounting for enterprise-level goodwill, and the need to challenge depreciable lives. A significant portion of the SAB consists of examples that illustrate when the SEC Staff believe it is too early to recognise a charge because the criteria of the applicable authoritative literature have not been met.

B   *Goodwill and intangible assets that are not amortised*

Under FAS 142, goodwill of a reporting unit should be tested for impairment on an annual basis and between annual tests if an event occurs or circumstances change that would more likely than not reduce the fair value of a reporting unit below its carrying amount. Examples of such events or circumstances include: *FAS 142.26-28*

- a significant adverse change in legal factors or in the business climate;

- an adverse action or assessment by a regulator;

- unanticipated competition;

- a loss of key personnel;

- a more-likely-than-not expectation that a reporting unit or a significant portion of a reporting unit will be sold or otherwise disposed of;

- the testing for recoverability under FAS 144 of a significant asset group within a reporting unit;

- recognition of a goodwill impairment loss in the financial statements of a subsidiary undertaking that is a component of a reporting unit.

The annual impairment test may be performed at any time during the year but must be performed at the same time each year. Different reporting units may be tested at different times.

IAS 36.24,99 However, for goodwill, or an intangible asset with an indefinite life, the most recent detailed calculation made in a prior period may be used for the annual impairment test where:

- if the goodwill or intangible asset is tested for impairment as part of a cash-generating unit, the assets and liabilities making up that unit have not changed significantly since that calculation;

- that calculation resulted in an amount that exceeded the carrying amount of the asset or cash-generating unit (where tested) by a substantial margin; and

- based on an analysis of subsequent events and circumstances since that calculation, the likelihood of a current impairment is remote.

9.5   HOW TO PERFORM AN IMPAIRMENT REVIEW

IAS 36.19-21 In measuring the recoverable amount, it is not always necessary to measure both fair value less costs to sell and value in use, when one of the two exceeds the carrying amount of the asset or if there is no reason to believe that the asset's value in use materially exceeds its fair value less costs to sell (as is often the case for an asset held for disposal).   Sometimes there will be no basis for making a reliable estimate of fair value less costs to sell, in which case, the value in use is used as the recoverable amount.

A   Fair value less costs to sell

IAS 36.25-28 Fair value less costs to sell shall be determined as follows:

- the price in a binding sale agreement in an arm's length transaction, adjusted for incremental costs that are directly attributable to the asset's disposal;

- if there is no binding sale agreement, the current bid price in an active market (see section 6.2.5), less any costs of disposal is used.   If current bid prices are unavailable, an estimate may be based on the price of the most recent transaction in an active market, provided there have been no significant changes in economic circumstances since that transaction date;

- if there is no binding sale agreement or active market, it is based on the best information available, including the outcome of recent transactions for similar assets in the same industry, to reflect the amount an entity, could obtain at the balance sheet date from the asset's disposal in an arms length transaction between knowledgeable, willing parties, after deducting costs of disposal. This does not reflect a forced sale unless management is compelled to sell immediately; and

- costs of disposal exclude termination benefits and reorganisation costs following the disposal of an asset.

IAS 36.29,78 Sometimes, where the disposal of an asset would require the buyer to assume a liability (e.g. restoration costs for a mine), only a single estimate of fair value less costs to sell is available for the asset and liability combined.

A goodwill impairment test may be carried forward from one year to the next if all   *FAS 142.27*
of the following criteria have been met;

- there has been no significant change in the assets and liabilities of the reporting unit;

- when last tested, the fair value of the reporting unit exceeded its carrying amount by a substantial margin; and

- the likelihood that the current fair value of the reporting unit would be less than its carrying amount is remote.

In addition, goodwill should be tested for impairment after a portion of goodwill has been allocated to a business to be disposed of.

9.5   HOW TO PERFORM AN IMPAIRMENT REVIEW

A   Long-lived assets and intangible assets that are subject to amortisation

A review for impairment requires an estimate of the future cash flows expected to   *FAS 144.7*
result from the use of the asset and its eventual disposition.   Only if the sum of the
expected future cash flows (undiscounted and without interest charges) is less than the
carrying amount of the asset, should an impairment loss be recognised.   The amount
of the impairment loss should be assessed as the amount by which the carrying
amount of the asset exceeds its fair value (i.e. the amount at which the asset could be
bought and sold between willing parties, other than in a forced liquidation or sale).

When estimating future cash flows, assets should be grouped at the lowest level for   *FAS 144.10*
which cash flows can be identified that are independent of cash flows of other
assets and liabilities.

Goodwill should be included in an asset group for impairment testing only if the   *FAS 144.12*
asset group includes a reporting unit (as defined in FAS 142 as the same level or one
level below an operating segment, as defined in FAS 131).   If goodwill is excluded
from an asset group the estimates of future cash flows used to test that asset group
for recoverability should not be adjusted for the effect of excluding goodwill.

B   Goodwill and intangible assets that are not amortised

To identify potential impairment, the fair value of a reporting unit should be   *FAS 142.19-20*
compared with its carrying amount.   If the carrying amount of a reporting unit,
including goodwill, exceeds its fair value the goodwill should be tested to measure
the amount of impairment loss, if any.   This second test compares the implied fair
value of the goodwill of the reporting unit with the carrying amount of that
goodwill.   An impairment loss should be recognised for any carrying amount in
excess of implied fair value.

For the purpose of determining the implied fair value of the goodwill of a reporting   *FAS 142.21*
unit, the fair value of the reporting unit should be allocated to all of the assets and
liabilities of that unit as if the reporting unit had been acquired in a business
combination and its fair value was the purchase price.   Section 3.4.3 provides guidance
on the allocation of fair value.   The excess of the fair value of a reporting unit over
the amount assigned to its assets and liabilities is the implied fair value of goodwill.

B   *Value in use*

IAS 36.30-31   Determining the value in use of an asset involves estimating the expected future cash flows to be derived from continuing use of the asset and its ultimate disposal and applying the appropriate discount rate to those cash flows.

The value in use calculation shall reflect:

- an estimate of the future cash flows the entity expects to derive from the asset;
- the time value of money, being the current market risk-free rate of interest;
- expectations about possible variations in the amount or timing of those future cash flows;
- the price for bearing the uncertainty inherent in the asset; and
- other factors, such as illiquidity, that market participants would reflect in pricing the future cash flows the entity expects to derive from the asset.

IAS 36.32   The last three items can be reflected either as adjustments to the future cash flows or as adjustments to the discount rates. Both approaches will result in the expected present value of the future cash flows.

IAS 36.33-34   The cash flow estimates made by the entity must:

- be based on reasonable and supportable assumptions that represent management's best estimate of the range of economic conditions that will exist over the remaining useful life of the asset, giving greater weight to external evidence. Management must ensure the assumptions used are consistent with past actual outcomes, provided the effects of subsequent events or circumstances still make this appropriate;

IAS 36.33,35   • be based on the most recent budgets or forecasts approved by management, which cover a maximum period of five years, unless a longer period can be justified;

IAS 36.33   • extrapolate budgets or forecasts to periods beyond those covered by those budgets or forecasts using a steady or declining growth rate for subsequent years. The growth rate used may not exceed the long-term average growth rate for the products, industries, or country in which the entity operates or for the market in which the asset is used. A higher or increasing rate may only be used if it can be justified;

IAS 36.39,41   • include projections for the following components:
IAS 36.49,52
  - cash inflows from continuing use of the asset (or cash-generating unit);
  - cash outflows necessary to generate the cash inflows from continuing use, which are directly attributed or allocated on a reasonable or consistent basis to the asset (or unit). These include cash outflows to prepare an asset for use, day-to-day servicing, replacement of components (or assets) with a shorter life than the remainder of the asset (or unit), and future direct overheads and overheads allocated on a consistent and reliable basis to the use of the asset (or unit); and
  - net cash flows to be received or paid for the disposal of the asset or unit at the end of its useful life in an arm's length transaction.

IAS 36.33,44-48   • be based on the current condition of the asset or unit and shall not take into account future restructuring to which the entity is not yet committed (i.e. no provision is recognised in accordance with IAS 37 *Provisions, Contingent*

If the second step of the impairment test is not complete before financial statements are issued, and goodwill impairment is probable and can be reasonably estimated, the best estimate of the loss should be recognised.   *FAS 142.22*

The fair value of an asset (or liability) is the amount at which that asset (or liability) could be bought (incurred) or sold (settled) in a current transaction between willing parties, i.e. other than in a forced or liquidation sale.   Quoted market prices are the best evidence of fair value and should be used if available.   However, the market price of an equity security may not be representative of the fair value of the entity as a whole as additional value may arise from synergy and other benefits of control. If quoted market prices are not available, estimated fair values should be based on the best information available or other valuation methods, such as present values of future cash flows or multiples of earnings or revenue.   *FAS 142.23*

> **COMMENT**
>
> In June 2004, the FASB issued an exposure draft of a Proposed Statement of Financial Accounting Standards *Fair Value Measurements*.   The proposed Statement provides guidance for how to measure fair value.   The proposed statement would be effective for financial statements issued for fiscal years beginning after 15 June 2005.   The FASB expect to issue a final statement in the second quarter of 2005.

If goodwill is tested at the same time as other assets of a reporting unit, the other assets should be tested, and any impairment loss recognised, before goodwill.   *FAS 142.29*

A reporting unit is an operating segment or a component of an operating segment. An operating segment is a segment of an entity: *FAS 142.30*
                                                                 FAS 131.10
- that engages in business activities from which it may earn revenues and incur expenses (including revenues and expenses relating to transactions with other segments of the same enterprise);

- whose operating results are regularly reviewed by the entity's chief operating decision maker to make decisions about resources to be allocated to the segment and assess its performance; and

- for which discrete financial information is available.

A component of an operating segment is a reporting unit if the component constitutes a business (as defined in EITF 98-3) for which discrete financial information is available and the results of the component are regularly reviewed by segment management.   Components of a segment with similar economic characteristics should be aggregated as a single reporting unit.   *FAS 142.30-31*

An operating segment is a reporting unit if all of its components are similar, if none of its components is a reporting unit, or if it comprises only one component.

For the purpose of testing goodwill, assets and liabilities acquired or assumed in a business combination or individually should be assigned to a reporting unit if the following criteria are met;   *FAS 142.32*
- the asset will be employed in or the liability relates to the operations of a reporting unit; and

- the asset or liability will be considered in determining the fair value of the reporting unit.

Reasonable and supportable bases should be applied consistently in assigning assets or liabilities, including goodwill, between multiple reporting units.   *FAS 142.33*

Assets and Contingent Liabilities) or future improvements or enhancements of the asset's performance not yet incurred;

IAS 36.50 ● exclude the effects of financing activities and income taxes; and

IAS 36.54,BCZ50
IAS 21.25 ● be determined in the currency in which they will be generated and discounted using a rate appropriate for that currency. The cash flows are translated into the reporting currency of the entity using the spot exchange rate at the date of the value-in-use calculation, often the reporting date.

IAS 36.40,43,79 Cash flows are determined on a basis consistent with the other assumptions made in arriving at the discounted cash flows, e.g. where the general rate of inflation is included in (or excluded from) the discount rate, the cash flow estimates are estimated in nominal (or real, but including future specific price changes) terms respectively. Cash inflows from assets generating cash inflows that are largely independent from those of the asset under review (e.g. receivables) and cash outflows relating to recognised liabilities, are excluded. However, where these cash flows are used in the calculation for practical reasons, the carrying amount of the cash-generating unit is increased (decreased) by the carrying amount of the assets (liabilities).

IAS 36.55-57,
Appx A15-A21 The discount rate used in calculating the present value of the cash flows shall be a pre-tax rate that reflects current market assessments of the time value of money for the periods until the end of the asset's useful life and the risks specific to the asset for which the future cash flow estimates have not been adjusted. This is the return that investors would require for an investment generating cash flows of amounts, timing and risk profile equivalent to those the entity expects to derive from the asset, and is independent of the entity's capital structure and the way in which it financed the purchase of the asset. This rate is estimated from the rate implicit in current market transactions for similar assets, or from the weighted average cost of capital of a listed entity with assets similar in terms of service potential and risks to the asset under review. When an asset-specific rate is not directly available from the market, surrogates are used to estimate the discount rate. Further detailed guidance is included in Appendix A to IAS 36, which forms part of the Standard.

C   Cash-generating units

IAS 36.22,66-67 The recoverable amount is measured for an individual asset, except for cases where the cash flows from the asset are not largely independent from those from other assets or groups of assets. In such cases, value in use and recoverable amount can not be estimated for the individual asset and is instead measured at the level of the cash-generating unit to which the asset belongs. There are two exceptions:

● either the asset's fair value less costs to sell exceeds its carrying amount; or

● fair value less costs to sell can be determined, and the asset's value in use can be estimated to be close to it.

IAS 36.6 A cash-generating unit is defined as 'the smallest identifiable group of assets that generates cash inflows that are largely independent of the cash inflows from other assets or groups of assets.'

IAS 36.68-72 Identifying cash-generating units involves judgement and factors such as how management monitors operations, or makes decisions about continuing or disposing of assets and operations are considered. Cash-generating units shall be defined consistently from period to period, unless a change is justified. A cash-generating

All goodwill acquired in a business combination should be assigned to reporting units of the acquiring entity that are expected to benefit from the synergies of the combination.

FAS 142.34

Assets and liabilities, including goodwill, should be reassigned if the composition of one or more reporting units is changed. Goodwill should be reassigned to reporting units based on the relative fair values of the reporting units prior to the change.

FAS 142.36

unit is presumed to exist where there is an active market for the output of an asset or group of assets, even if some or all of the output is used internally. The value-in-use test for assets or cash-generating units affected by internal transfer pricing shall use management's best estimate of future prices that could be achieved in arms length transactions in estimating the cash inflows (or outflows).

IAS 36.29,75-79 The carrying amount of a cash-generating unit is determined on a basis consistent with the unit's recoverable amount. It includes only assets that can be directly attributed or allocated on a reasonable and consistent basis, and which generate the future cash inflows used in determining value in use. The treatment of goodwill and corporate assets is discussed below. It excludes any recognised liability, unless the recoverable amount of the cash generating unit can not be determined without considering this liability. This may occur, for example, when the disposal of a cash-generating unit would require the buyer to assume the liability (e.g. restoration costs for a mine) and only a single fair value less costs to sell is available for the asset and liability.

IAS 36.80,82-83 Goodwill acquired in a business combination is, from the acquisition date, allocated to each of the acquirer's cash-generating units or groups of cash-generating units expected to benefit from the synergies of the combination. Each unit or group of units to which goodwill is allocated shall represent the lowest level within the entity at which the goodwill is monitored for internal management purposes, and not be larger than a segment based on either the entity's primary or secondary segments determined in accordance with IAS 14 *Segment Reporting*. This need not coincide with the level at which goodwill arising on acquisition of a foreign operation is allocated in accordance with IAS 21 *The Effects of Changes in Foreign Exchange Rates* (see section 5.4.5).

IAS 36.84-85 Where the initial accounting for the business combination is only provisional, it might also not be possible to complete the initial allocation of goodwill. If the initial allocation of goodwill can not be completed before the end of the annual period in which the business combination is effected, the initial allocation shall be completed before the end of the first annual period beginning after the acquisition date.

IAS 36.81,86 If goodwill has been allocated to a cash-generating unit (or group of units) and the entity disposed of an operation within that unit (or group of units), the goodwill associated with the operation disposed of is included in the carrying amount of the operation when determining the gain or loss on disposal, and is measured on the basis of the relative values of the operation disposed of and the portion of the cash-generating unit(s) retained, unless the entity can demonstrate that some method better reflects the goodwill associated with the operation disposed of.

IAS 36.81,87 If an entity reorganises its reporting structure in a way that changes the composition of one or more cash-generating units to which goodwill has been allocated, the goodwill shall be reallocated to the units affected, using a similar relative value approach to above, unless the entity can demonstrate that some method better reflects the goodwill associated with the reorganised units.

IAS 36.100-102 An entity may have corporate assets, e.g. its headquarters, that do not generate cash flows independently from other assets and cannot be fully attributed to the cash-generating unit under review. When testing a cash-generating unit for impairment, all corporate assets relating to the unit under review are treated as follows:

- if a portion of the carrying amount of a corporate asset can be allocated on a

reasonable and consistent basis to the unit, the carrying amount of the cash-generating unit including the allocated portion of the carrying amount of the corporate asset, is compared with the unit's recoverable amount.; or

- if this allocation is not possible, then:
  - the carrying amount of the unit excluding the corporate asset is compared with its recoverable amount and any impairment loss recognised;
  - the smallest group of cash-generating units including the unit under review, to which a portion of the corporate asset can be allocated on a reasonable and consistent basis is identified; and
  - the carrying amount of this group of cash-generating units, including the allocated portion of the carrying amount of the corporate asset is compared with the group's recoverable amount, and any impairment loss recognised.

If there is an indication that a corporate asset is impaired, the cash-generating units to which it belongs are tested for impairment.

D   Testing cash-generating units with goodwill for impairment

IAS 36.88-89 When goodwill relates to a cash-generating unit but has not been allocated to it, the unit is tested for impairment whenever there is an indication of impairment (and in addition, annually if it includes an intangible asset which is either not yet available for use or which has an indefinite life) by comparing its carrying amount excluding goodwill with its recoverable amount, and recognising any impairment loss.

IAS 36.81,90 When goodwill has been allocated to a cash-generating unit (or group of units), the cash-generating unit (or group of units) must be tested whenever there is an indication of impairment and also annually for impairment, by comparing the carrying amount including the goodwill to its recoverable amount, and recognising any impairment loss.

IAS 36.81,96 The annual test may be performed at any time during the annual period, but at the same time each year. Different cash-generating units may be tested at different times. However, if some or all of the goodwill allocated to a cash-generating unit (or group of units) was acquired in a business combination during the current annual period, the unit (or group of units) must be tested for impairment before the end of the current annual period.

IAS 36.81,97 If the assets constituting the cash-generating unit to which goodwill is allocated are tested for impairment at the same time as the unit containing the goodwill, the assets are tested for impairment prior to testing the unit containing the goodwill. Similarly, if the cash-generating units constituting a group of units to which goodwill is allocated are tested for impairment at the same time as the group of units containing the goodwill, the individual units are tested for impairment prior to testing the group of units containing the goodwill.

IAS 36.81,91-95, When testing a cash-generating unit (or group of units) to which goodwill is
I.E.,Example 7 allocated and which is not wholly-owned, the carrying amount of that unit (or group of units) – which comprises goodwill, but both the parent's interest and the minority interest in the identifiable net assets of the unit(s) – is notionally adjusted, by grossing up the carrying amount of the goodwill allocated to include the goodwill attributable to the minority interest.   The notionally adjusted carrying amount is

compared with the recoverable amount of the unit to determine any impairment. Any impairment loss relates first to goodwill and is apportioned between the parent and minority interest in the goodwill (with only the former recognised as a loss in the consolidated financial statements, since the goodwill attributable to the minority interest is not recognised in the consolidated financial statements) and secondly, is allocated to the other assets of the unit pro rata on the basis of the carrying amount of each asset in the unit.   If those assets are impaired, the minority interest in those assets will also generally be affected (see section 2.5.5).

9.6   ACCOUNTING FOR IMPAIRMENTS

IAS 36.59-61   If and only if the recoverable amount of an asset is lower than its carrying amount,
IAS 36.63-64   the entity shall recognise the difference as an impairment loss in profit or loss.
IAS 16.40,63   However, if the entity is applying the revaluation model under IAS 16 *Property,*
IAS 38.86,111   *Plant and Equipment* or IAS 38 then the impairment loss of the revalued asset is treated as a revaluation decrease under IAS 16 or IAS 38 to the extent that the impairment loss does not exceed the amount held in the revaluation surplus (see section 7.2.2).   The depreciation or amortisation charge for future periods is adjusted to allocate the remaining carrying amount to future periods.   Related deferred tax amounts are determined in accordance with IAS 12 by comparing the revised carrying amount with its tax base.

IAS 36.104-105,   An impairment loss on a cash-generating unit (or the smallest group of cash-
IE.Example 8   generating units to which goodwill or a corporate asset is allocated) because its carrying amount exceeds its recoverable amount should be allocated as follows:

- first reduce any allocated goodwill to zero; and
- then reduce the carrying amount of the other assets in the unit (group of units) pro rata on the basis of the carrying amount of each asset (including allocated corporate assets).   However, no individual asset may be reduced below the highest of (1) its fair value less costs to sell, if determinable, (2) value in use, if determinable and (3) zero.   The amount of any impairment loss that would otherwise have been allocated to the asset is allocated pro rata to the other assets of the unit (group of units).

IAS 36.60,104   The reduction in the carrying amount of individual assets is accounted for in profit or loss, or as a revaluation decrease, as for individual impaired assets.

IAS 36.62,108   If the impairment loss exceeds the carrying amount of an asset or cash-generating unit, the entity should recognise only a liability if and only if this is required by other Standards, i.e. an entity is not permitted to provide for future operating losses.

IAS 16.65,74(d)   If an entity will be compensated by third parties for the impairment of property,
IAS 40.72   plant and equipment, the impairment of the assets, receipt of the compensation (which is recognised in profit or loss when receivable), and purchase of replacement assets, are accounted for separately.

A   *Reversal of an impairment loss*

IAS 36.110-111   An entity shall assess at each balance sheet date whether indications exist that an impairment loss may no longer exist or may have decreased.   If there are any such indications, the entity should estimate the recoverable amount.

9.6　ACCOUNTING FOR IMPAIRMENTS

An impairment loss recognised for a long-lived asset, or group of assets, to be held and used should be reported as a component of income from continuing operations before taxes and, where applicable, should be included in operating income. *FAS 144.25*

After an impairment loss is recognised, the reduced carrying amount of the asset should be accounted for as its new cost, which for a depreciable long-lived asset should be depreciated over its remaining useful life. *FAS 144.15 FAS 142.20*

If goodwill and another asset (or group of assets) are tested for impairment at the same time, the other asset (or group of assets) should be tested for impairment before goodwill. If the asset (or group of assets) was impaired, the impairment loss would be recognised before testing goodwill for impairment. *FAS 142.29*

A　Reversal of an impairment loss

Restoration of a previously recognised impairment loss is prohibited. Subsequent reversal of a previously recognised goodwill impairment loss is prohibited once the measurement of that loss is completed. *FAS 144.15 FAS 142.20*

An entity shall consider, at a minimum whether:

- the asset's market value has significantly increased in the period;

- significant favourable changes have taken place in the period (or will take place in the near future) in the technological, market, economic or legal environment in which the entity operates or in the market to which the asset is dedicated;

- market interest rates or other market rates of return on investments have decreased during the period and these are likely to materially affect discount rates used and hence increase materially the asset's recoverable amount;

- significant favourable changes have taken place (or are expected to take place in the near future) in the extent and way in which the asset is used or expected to be used. These include costs incurred during the period to improve or enhance the asset's performance or restructure the operations to which the asset belongs; or

- evidence is available from internal reporting indicating that the economic performance of the asset is, or will be, better than expected.

IAS 36.114
IAS 36.116-117
A previously recognised impairment loss for an asset shall be reversed if and only if there has been a change in the estimates used to determine the recoverable amount since the last impairment loss was recognised. This is not the case if value in use has become greater simply as a result of the passage of time. Where the estimates have changed, the carrying amount of the asset is increased to its recoverable amount, not exceeding the carrying amount that would have resulted (net of depreciation or amortisation) had no impairment loss been recognised in prior years.

IAS 36.119,121
IAS 16.39,63
IAS 38.85,111
A reversal of an impairment loss shall be recognised in profit or loss immediately. However, if the entity applies the revaluation model under IAS 16 or IAS 38, it should recognise the reversal of impairment as a revaluation increase under that method of accounting. The depreciation or amortisation charge for the asset shall be adjusted for future periods after the reversal of the impairment loss.

IAS 36.122-123
When an entity recognises a reversal of an impairment loss on a cash-generating unit, the reversal shall be allocated to increase the carrying amount of the assets other than goodwill in the unit pro rata with the carrying amounts of those assets. These increases in carrying amounts are treated as reversals of impairment losses for individual assets as discussed above. However, the carrying amount of an individual asset is not increased above the lower of (1) its recoverable amount, if determinable, and (2) the carrying amount that would have resulted (net of depreciation and amortisation) had no impairment loss been recognised in prior periods. The amount of the reversal of impairment loss that would otherwise have been allocated to the asset is allocated pro rata to the other assets of the unit, except for goodwill.

IAS 36.124
An impairment loss on goodwill should not be reversed.

9.7   DISCLOSURE

IAS 36.126-127
The entity shall disclose for each class of asset (i.e. group of assets of similar nature and use in the entity's operations) the amount of impairment losses:

- recognised in profit or loss and the line items of the income statement in which those impairment losses are included;

9.7   DISCLOSURE

An impairment loss recognised for a long-lived asset, or group of assets, to be held   *FAS 144.25-26*
and used should be reported as a component of income from continuing operations   *FAS 142.46*
before taxes and, where applicable, should be included in operating income.

- reversed in profit or loss and the line items of the income statement in which those impairment losses are reversed;
- recognised directly in equity (re revalued assets) during the period; and
- reversed directly in equity (re revalued assets) during the period.

IAS 36.129   Entities applying IAS 14 *Segment Reporting* (see section 21) shall disclose for each of its reportable segments, based on its primary format, the amount of impairment losses:

- recognised in profit or loss and directly in equity during the period; and
- reversals recognised in profit or loss and directly in equity during the period.

IAS 36.130   For each material impairment loss for an individual asset or a cash-generating unit, recognised or reversed during the period, an entity shall disclose:

- the events and circumstances that led to the recognition or reversal of the impairment loss;
- the amount of the impairment loss recognised or reversed;
- for an individual asset:
  - the nature of the asset; and
  - the reportable segment to which the asset belongs, based on the entity's primary format;
- for a cash-generating unit:
  - a description of the cash-generating unit;
  - the amount of the impairment loss recognised or reversed by class of asset and by reportable segment based on the entity's primary format; and
  - if the aggregation of assets for identifying the cash-generating unit has changed since the previous estimate of the cash-generating unit's recoverable amount (if any), the entity should describe the current and former way of aggregating assets and the reasons for the change;
- whether the recoverable amount of the asset or cash-generating unit is its fair value less costs to sell or its value in use;
- if recoverable amount is fair value less costs to sell, the basis used to determine fair value less costs to sell; and
- if recoverable amount is value in use, the discount rates used in the current estimate and previous estimate (if any) of value in use.

IAS 36.131   For aggregate impairment losses recognised and reversed during the period for which the above information has not been disclosed, a brief description of the following should be given:

- the main classes of assets affected by impairment losses, or reversals of impairment losses; and
- the main events and circumstances that led to the recognition, or reversals, of these impairment losses.

IAS 36.133   If any portion of the goodwill acquired in a business combination during the period has not been allocated to a cash-generating unit (group of units) (see section 9.5C) at the reporting date, the amount of the unallocated goodwill shall be disclosed together with the reasons why that amount remains unallocated.

IAS 36.134   An entity shall disclose the following information for each cash-generating unit (group of units) for which the carrying amount of goodwill or intangible assets with

An entity that recognises an impairment loss should disclose the following information:

- a description of the impaired assets and the facts and circumstances leading to the impairment;
- if not separately presented, the amount of the impairment loss and the caption in the income statement that includes that loss;
- the method(s) for determining the fair value; and
- if applicable, the business segment(s) in which the impaired long-lived asset or group of assets, is reported under FAS 131.

When a goodwill impairment loss is recognised, the following information should be disclosed: *FAS 142.47*

- a description of the impaired assets and the facts and circumstances leading to the impairment;
- the amount of the impairment loss and how fair value of the associated reporting unit was determined; and
- if the impairment testing is not yet finalised but an impairment loss is probable and can be reasonably estimated, the fact that the recognised impairment loss is an estimate and the reasons therefore and, in subsequent periods, the nature and amount of any significant adjustments to the initial estimate.

The aggregate amount of goodwill impairment losses should be presented as a separate line item in the income statement as part of income from continuing operations, or discontinued operations if a goodwill impairment loss is associated with a discontinued operation.   *FAS 142.43*

The accounting policy for measuring impairment, including how reporting units are determined and how goodwill is allocated to those reporting units, should be disclosed for all intangible assets (including goodwill).   *S-X 5-02.15-16*

indefinite useful lives allocated to that unit (group of units) is significant in comparison with the entity's total carrying amount of goodwill or intangible assets with indefinite useful lives:

- the carrying amount of goodwill allocated to the unit (group of units);
- the carrying amount of intangible assets with indefinite useful lives allocated to the unit (group of units);
- the basis on which the unit's (group of units') recoverable amount has been determined (i.e. value in use or fair value less costs to sell);
- if the unit's (group of units') recoverable amount is based on value in use:
  - a description of each key assumption on which management has based its cash flow projections for the period covered by the most recent budgets/forecasts. Key assumptions are those to which the unit's (group of units') recoverable amount is most sensitive;
  - a description of management's approach to determining the value(s) assigned to each key assumption, whether those value(s) reflect past experience or, if appropriate, are consistent with external sources of information, and, if not, how and why they differ from past experience or external sources of information;
  - the period over which management has projected cash flows based on financial budgets/forecasts approved by management and, when a period greater than five years is used for a cash-generating unit (group of units), an explanation of why that longer period is justified;
  - the growth rate used to extrapolate cash flow projections beyond the period covered by the most recent budgets/forecasts, and the justification for using any growth rate that exceeds the long-term average growth rate for the products, industries, or country or countries in which the entity operates, or for the market to which the unit (group of units) is dedicated;
  - the discount rate(s) applied to the cash flow projections;
- if the unit's (group of units') recoverable amount is based on fair value less costs to sell, the methodology used to determine fair value less costs to sell. If fair value less costs to sell is not determined using an observable market price for the unit (group of units), the following information shall also be disclosed:
  - a description of each key assumption on which management has based its determination of fair value less costs to sell;
  - a description of management's approach to determining the value(s) assigned to each key assumption, whether those value(s) reflect past experience or, if appropriate, are consistent with external sources of information, and, if not, how and why they differ from past experience or external sources of information;
- if a reasonably possible change in a key assumption on which management has based its determination of the unit's (group of units') recoverable amount would cause the unit's (group of units') carrying amount to exceed its recoverable amount:
  - the amount by which the unit's (group of units') recoverable amount exceeds its carrying amount;
  - the value assigned to the key assumption;

      –   the amount by which the value assigned to the key assumption must change, after incorporating any consequential effects of that change on the other variables used to measure recoverable amount, in order for the unit's (group of units') recoverable amount to be equal to its carrying amount.

IAS 36.135   If some or all of the carrying amount of goodwill or intangible assets with indefinite useful lives is allocated across multiple cash-generating units (groups of units), and the amount so allocated to each unit (group of units) is not significant in comparison with the entity's total carrying amount of goodwill or intangible assets with indefinite useful lives, that fact shall be disclosed, together with the aggregate carrying amount of goodwill or intangible assets with indefinite useful lives allocated to those units (groups of units). In addition, if the recoverable amounts of any of those units (groups of units) are based on the same key assumption(s) and the aggregate carrying amount of goodwill or intangible assets with indefinite useful lives allocated to them is significant in comparison with the entity's total carrying amount of goodwill or intangible assets with indefinite useful lives, an entity shall disclose that fact, together with:

- the aggregate carrying amount of goodwill allocated to those units (groups of units);

- the aggregate carrying amount of intangible assets with indefinite useful lives allocated to those units (groups of units);

- a description of the key assumption(s);

- a description of management's approach to determining the value(s) assigned to the key assumption(s), whether those value(s) reflect past experience or, if appropriate, are consistent with external sources of information, and, if not, how and why they differ from past experience or external sources of information;

- if a reasonably possible change in the key assumption(s) would cause the aggregate of the units' (groups of units') carrying amounts to exceed the aggregate of their recoverable amounts:

  –   the amount by which the aggregate of the units' (groups of units') recoverable amounts exceeds the aggregate of their carrying amounts;

  –   the value(s) assigned to the key assumption(s);

  –   the amount by which the value(s) assigned to the key assumption(s) must change, after incorporating any consequential effects of the change on the other variables used to measure recoverable amount, in order for the aggregate of the units' (groups of units') recoverable amounts to be equal to the aggregate of their carrying amounts.

IAS 36.136   Where the most recent detailed calculation made in a preceding period of the recoverable amount of a cash-generating unit (group of units) is carried forward and used in the impairment test for that unit (group of units) in the current period because specified criteria are met, the disclosures for that unit (group of units) required by paragraphs 134 and 135 relate to the carried forward calculation of recoverable amount.

Example 9 in Appendix B to IAS 36 gives example disclosures.

Section 10

Capitalisation of borrowing costs

10.1   AUTHORITATIVE PRONOUNCEMENTS

- IAS 23

10.2   GENERAL APPROACH

Capitalisation of borrowing costs is not mandatory under IAS 23 *Borrowing Costs*. Two methods of accounting for borrowing costs exist:

- Benchmark treatment

IAS 23.7-8   Borrowing costs are recognised as an expense in the period in which they are incurred, irrespective of the use of the proceeds from the borrowings.

- Allowed alternative treatment

IAS 23.10-11,13   Borrowing costs are expensed as incurred, except to the extent they are
IAS 8.13   directly attributable to the acquisition, construction or production of a qualifying asset, in which case they are capitalised as part of the cost of that asset. Entities that adopt this treatment shall apply it consistently to all borrowing costs that are directly attributable to the acquisition, construction or production of all qualifying assets.

The allowed alternative treatment is covered in sections 10.3 to 10.5 below.

IAS 23.4-5   IAS 23 defines borrowing costs as 'interest and other costs incurred by an entity in connection with the borrowing of funds.' IAS 23 specifically states that borrowing costs may include interest; amortisation of discounts, premiums and arrangement costs relating to borrowings; finance charges in respect of finance leases; and exchange differences arising from foreign currency borrowings to the extent that they are regarded as an adjustment to interest costs.

IAS 23.3   IAS 23 does not deal with the actual or imputed costs of equity, including preferred capital not classified as a liability (see section 12).   Consequently, such costs would not qualify for capitalisation as borrowing costs under IAS 23.   Interest and dividends payable on financial liabilities are, by implication, within the scope of IAS 23.

10.3   QUALIFYING ASSETS

IAS 23.4,6   Qualifying assets are those assets that necessarily take a substantial period of time to get ready for their intended use or sale.

Qualifying assets exclude inventories routinely manufactured or produced in large quantities on a repetitive basis over a short period of time, other investments, and assets that are ready for their intended use or sale when acquired.

Section 10 Capitalisation of borrowing costs

10.1 AUTHORITATIVE PRONOUNCEMENTS

- FAS 34

10.2 GENERAL APPROACH

Interest cost should be capitalised as part of the historical cost of acquiring certain *FAS 34.6-8*
assets. In principle, if an asset requires a period of time in which to carry out the
activities necessary to bring it to the condition and location necessary for its
intended use, the interest cost incurred during that period as a result of expenditures
for the asset is a part of the historical cost of acquiring the asset. However, the
benefit in terms of disclosures about an entity's resources and earnings may not
always justify the additional accounting and administrative cost of providing the
information. If the net effect of interest capitalisation is not material, interest
capitalisation is not required.

10.3 QUALIFYING ASSETS

The types of assets for which interest should be capitalised are referred to as *FAS 34.9*
qualifying assets. The following examples have been identified:
- assets which are constructed or otherwise produced for an entity's own use
  (including assets constructed or produced for the entity by others for which
  deposits or progress payments have been made);

10.4   AMOUNT TO BE CAPITALISED

IAS 23.13   Borrowing costs are directly attributable and eligible for capitalisation if they would have been avoided if the expenditure on the qualifying assets had not been made.

IAS 23.15-16   If the entity can associate a specific new borrowing with a qualifying asset, the amount of borrowing cost eligible for capitalisation is determined as:

- the actual borrowing costs incurred on that borrowing; less
- any investment income on the temporary investment of those borrowings.

IAS 23.17   Where funds that have been used to finance a qualifying asset cannot be specifically identified, the amount of borrowing costs to be capitalised is determined by applying a capitalisation rate to the expenditures on that asset.   The capitalisation rate is the weighted average of the borrowing costs applicable to borrowings that are outstanding during the period, excluding those borrowings made specifically for obtaining a qualifying asset.

IAS 23.18   Depending on the circumstances, the capitalisation rate is determined either, based on group borrowings, or at the level of the borrowings of the individual subsidiaries.

IAS 23.17   The amount of borrowing costs capitalised shall not exceed the actual borrowing costs incurred during the period.

IAS 23.12,19   All borrowing costs should be capitalised even where the carrying amount of the asset exceeds its recoverable amount or net realisable value, as clarified and confirmed by SIC-2 *Consistency – Capitalisation of Borrowing Costs* (superseded 2003).   When the carrying amount or the expected ultimate cost of the qualifying asset exceeds its recoverable amount or net realisable value, the carrying amount is written down or written off in accordance with the requirements of other Standards.

- assets intended for sale or lease that are constructed or otherwise produced as discrete projects, e.g. ships or real estate developments;

- investments accounted for by the equity method while the investee has activities in progress necessary to commence its planned principal operations provided that the investee's activities include the use of funds to acquire qualifying assets for its operations.

Interest should not be capitalised for: *FAS 34.10*

- inventories that are routinely manufactured or otherwise produced in large quantities on a repetitive basis;

- assets that are in use or ready for their intended use in the entity's business;

- assets that are not being used in the earning activities of the entity and that are not undergoing the activities necessary to get them ready for use;

- assets that are not included in the consolidated balance sheet of the parent company and consolidated subsidiaries;

- investments accounted for by the equity method after the planned principal operations of the investee begin;

- certain assets in regulated investees; or

- assets acquired through restricted gifts and grants.

10.4   AMOUNT TO BE CAPITALISED

The amount to be capitalised is the interest cost that could theoretically have been   *FAS 34.12-14*
avoided if the expenditure on the qualifying asset were not made.

The interest cost is determined by applying an interest rate to the average amount of accumulated expenditure for the asset during the period.   The interest rate should be either based on borrowings outstanding during the year to finance the qualifying asset or a weighted average.

If an entity's financing plans associate a specific new borrowing with a qualifying   *FAS 34.13*
asset, the interest rate on that borrowing may be applied to that portion of the average accumulated expenditures for the asset that does not exceed the amount of that borrowing.   If the average accumulated expenditures for the asset exceed the amount of that borrowing, the weighted average of the interest rates applicable to other borrowings of the entity should be applied to the excess.

The total interest cost capitalised in a financial period should not exceed the total   *FAS 34.15*
amount of interest cost incurred by the entity in that period.   In consolidated financial statements, this test should be applied by reference to the total amount of interest cost incurred by the parent and consolidated subsidiaries on a consolidated basis.

The EITF reached a consensus that interest costs eligible for capitalisation could   *EITF 99-9*
include amortisation of the adjustments of the carrying amount of a hedged liability if an entity elects to begin amortisation of those adjustments during the period in which interest is eligible for capitalisation.   The EITF observed that any ineffective portion of the fair value hedge should not be reflected in the capitalisation rate.

In certain circumstances, the amount of the write-down or write-off is written back in accordance with those other Standards.

10.5   CAPITALISATION PERIOD

IAS 23.20   Capitalisation of borrowing costs commences when the following three conditions are present:

- expenditures for the assets are being incurred;
- borrowing costs are being incurred; and
- activities that are necessary to prepare the asset for its intended use or sale are in progress.

IAS 23.21   Expenditures on a qualifying asset include only those expenditures that have resulted in payments of cash, transfers of other assets or the assumption of interest-bearing liabilities, and are reduced by any progress payments and grants received in connection with the asset. The average carrying amount of the asset, including borrowing costs previously capitalised, is normally a reasonable approximation of the expenditures to which the capitalisation rate is applied in the period.

IAS 23.22   The activities necessary to prepare the asset for its intended use include technical and administrative work (e.g. obtaining permits) prior to the commencement of physical construction, but exclude the holding of an asset when no production or development that changes the asset's condition takes place (e.g. a land bank acquired for building purposes held without associated development).

IAS 23.23-24   Borrowing costs are not capitalised when incurred during an extended period in which the activities necessary to prepare an asset for its intended use or sale are interrupted. Capitalisation is not normally suspended during a period when substantial technical and administrative work is carried out, or where a temporary delay is a necessary part of the process of getting an asset ready for its intended use or sale.

IAS 23.25-26   Capitalisation of borrowing costs ceases when substantially all the activities necessary to prepare the asset for its intended use or sale are complete. If the asset is physically complete, but routine administrative work continues, or only minor modifications are outstanding, this indicates that substantially all the activities are complete.

IAS 23.27   When the construction of an asset is completed in parts, and each part is capable of being used, while construction continues on other parts, the capitalisation of borrowing costs ceases on each part, when substantially all the activities necessary to prepare that part for its intended use or sale are complete.

The EITF observed that FAS 133 prohibits the capitalisation of the gain or loss on the hedging instrument in a cash flow hedge as FAS 133 prohibits reporting such gains or losses as basis adjustments of the qualifying assets.

10.5   CAPITALISATION PERIOD

Capitalisation should begin when the following three conditions are present: *FAS 34.17*

- expenditures for the asset have been made;
- activities that are necessary to get the asset ready for its intended use are in progress; and
- interest cost is being incurred.

If an entity suspends substantially all activities related to acquisition of an asset interest capitalisation should cease until activities are resumed. Brief interruptions, externally imposed interruptions and delays inherent in the acquisition process should not require cessation of interest capitalisation.

Interest should continue to be capitalised as long as these three conditions are present and cease when the asset is substantially complete and ready for use. The term 'substantially complete' is used to prohibit capitalisation of interest where completion of the asset is intentionally delayed.   *FAS 34.18*

Some assets are completed in parts, and each part is capable of being used independently while work is continuing on other parts. In such cases, interest capitalisation should stop on each part when it is substantially complete and ready for use. In other cases, assets cannot be used effectively until a separate facility has been completed. For such assets, interest should continue to be capitalised until the separate facility is substantially complete and ready for use.   *FAS 34.58*

10.6   DISCLOSURE

A   Benchmark treatment

IAS 23.9,29   The financial statements shall disclose that the entity's policy is to expense all borrowing costs immediately.

B   Allowed alternative treatment

IAS 23.9,29   The financial statements shall disclose:

- that the entity capitalises borrowing costs in accordance with the allowed alternative treatment;
- the amount of borrowing costs capitalised during the period; and
- the capitalisation rate used to determine the amount of borrowing costs eligible for capitalisation.

10.6   DISCLOSURE

The total amount of interest cost incurred and the amount capitalised during the   *FAS 34.21*
financial year should be disclosed.

Section 11   Financial instruments: Recognition and measurement

11.1   AUTHORITATIVE PRONOUNCEMENTS

- Framework
- IAS 32
- IAS 36

- IAS 37
- IAS 39
- SIC-12

11.2   SCOPE AND DEFINITIONS

11.2.1   Scope

IAS 39.2 IAS 39 *Financial Instruments: Recognition and Measurement* applies to all types of financial instruments, except for:

- interests in subsidiaries, associates and joint ventures that are accounted for under IAS 27 *Consolidated and Separate Financial Statements*, IAS 28 *Investments in Associates* or IAS 31 *Interests in Joint Ventures* (unless required to by one of these standards or the interest is a derivative that does not meet the definition of an equity instrument of the entity in IAS 32);

- rights under leases to which IAS 17 *Leases* applies, although the derecognition, impairment and embedded derivative requirements are still applicable to some extent;

- employer's assets under employee benefit plans to which IAS 19 *Employee Benefits* applies;

- financial instruments issued by the entity that meet the IAS 32 definition of an equity instrument, although the holder of such instruments is generally required to apply the Standard;

- rights and obligations under insurance contracts as defined in IFRS 4 *Insurance Contracts* or under a contract that is within the scope of IFRS 4 because it contains a discretionary participation feature. However, this exclusion does not extend to certain derivatives embedded in such contracts and certain financial guarantee contracts;

- an acquirer's contingent consideration in business combinations;

- contracts between an acquirer and a vendor in a business combination to buy or sell an acquiree at a future date;

Section 11 Financial instruments: Recognition and measurement

11.1 AUTHORITATIVE PRONOUNCEMENTS

- APB 12
- APB 14
- APB 21
- ARB 26
- FAS 15
- FAS 64

- FAS 107
- FAS 114
- FAS 115
- FAS 116
- FAS 133
- FAS 140

11.2 SCOPE AND DEFINITIONS

11.2.1 Scope

FAS 107 *Disclosures about Fair Value of Financial Instruments* applies to all entities that have financial instruments.   *FAS 107.7*

FAS 115 *Accounting for Certain Investments in Debt and Equity Securities* applies to all investments in: *FAS 115.3-4*

- equity securities that have readily determinable fair values except investments in equity securities accounted for under the equity method and investments in consolidated subsidiaries; and

- debt securities, e.g. government bonds, corporate bonds, commercial paper, securitised debt instruments.

The standard does not apply to entities that currently account for all investments in securities at market value or fair value, e.g. investment companies, brokers and dealers in securities.

FAS 140 *Accounting for Transfers and Servicing of Financial Assets and Extinguishments of Liabilities a replacement of Statement No. 125*, provides revised accounting and financial reporting rules for sales, securitizations, and servicing of receivables and other financial assets, and for secured borrowing and collateral transactions.

- loan commitments that cannot be settled net and have not been designated as financial liabilities at fair value through profit or loss (although these are subject to the derecognition provisions); and

- most financial instruments, contracts and obligations under share-based payment transactions to which IFRS 2 *Share-based Payment* applies. However, the Standard does apply to contracts to buy or sell non-financial items in share-based transactions that can be settled net unless they are considered to be 'normal' sales and purchases (see below).

COMMENT

In July 2004, the IASB issued an exposure draft proposing amendments to IAS 39 Financial Instruments: Recognition and Measurement (and IFRS 4 *Insurance Contracts*) that would specify the accounting requirements for many financial guarantee contracts that are currently within the scope of IFRS 4. The proposals would require the issuer of such a financial guarantee contract to measure the contract:

- initially at fair value. If the financial guarantee contract was issued in a stand-alone arm's length transaction to an unrelated party, its fair value at inception is likely to equal the premium received, unless there is evidence to the contrary; and

- subsequently at the higher of:

    - the amount determined in accordance with IAS 37 Provisions, Contingent Liabilities, and Contingent Assets; and

    - the amount initially recognised less, when appropriate, cumulative amortisation recognised in accordance with IAS 18 Revenue.

These requirements would be mandatory for accounting periods commencing 1 January 2006, although earlier adoption would be encouraged.

IAS 39.5   IAS 39 also applies to contracts to buy or sell non-financial items (such as commodity contracts) that can be settled net in cash unless the contract was originally entered into and continues to be held for the purpose of the receipt or delivery of the non-financial item in accordance with the entity's expected purchase, sale or usage requirements (a 'normal' purchase or sale).

IAS 39.6   There are various ways in which a contract to buy or sell a non-financial item can be settled net, including when:

(a) the terms of the contract permit either party to settle it net;

(b) the ability to settle the contract net is not explicit in its terms, but the entity has a practice of settling similar contracts net (whether with the counterparty, by entering into offsetting contracts or by selling the contract before its exercise or lapse);

(c) for similar contracts, the entity has a practice of taking delivery of the underlying and selling it within a short period after delivery for the purpose of generating a profit from short-term fluctuations in price or dealer's margin; and

(d) the non-financial item that is the subject of the contract is readily convertible to cash.

IAS 39.6-7   Contracts to buy or sell non-financial items to which (b) or (c) apply cannot be considered 'normal' purchases or sales. In addition a written option to buy or sell a non-financial item that can be settled net in cash or another financial instrument, or by exchanging financial instruments, in accordance with (a) or (d) cannot be considered 'normal' purchases or sales.

11.2.2   What is a financial instrument?

IAS 32.11   A financial instrument is defined as any contract that gives rise to both a financial asset of one entity and a financial liability or equity instrument of another entity.

A financial asset is any asset that is:

* cash;

* an equity instrument of another entity;

* a contractual right to receive cash or another financial asset from another entity or to exchange financial assets or financial liabilities with another entity under conditions that are potentially favourable to the entity; or

* a contract that will or may be settled in the entity's own equity instruments and is:

  – a non-derivative for which the entity is or may be obliged to receive a variable number of the entity's own equity instruments; or

  – a derivative that will or may be settled other than by the exchange of a fixed amount of cash or another financial asset for a fixed number of the entity's own equity instruments.   For this purpose the entity's own equity instruments do not include instruments that are themselves contracts for the future receipt or delivery of the entity's own equity instruments.

A financial liability is any liability that is:

* a contractual obligation to deliver cash or another financial asset to another entity;

* a contractual obligation to exchange financial assets or financial liabilities with another entity under conditions that are potentially unfavourable; or

* a contract that will or may be settled in the entity's own equity instruments and is:

  – a non-derivative for which the entity is or may be obliged to deliver a variable number of the entity's own equity instruments; or

  – a derivative that will or may be settled other than by the exchange of a fixed amount of cash or another financial asset for a fixed number of the entity's own equity instruments.   For this purpose the entity's own equity instruments do not include instruments that are themselves contracts for the future receipt or delivery of the entity's own equity instruments.

An equity instrument is any contract that evidences a residual interest in the assets of an entity after deducting all of its liabilities.

11.3   RECOGNITION AND DERECOGNITION OF ASSETS AND LIABILITIES

11.3.1   Assets and liabilities

IAS F.49   An asset is defined as 'a resource controlled by the entity as a result of past events and from which future economic benefits are expected to flow to the entity.'

A liability is 'a present obligation of the entity arising from past events, the

11.2.2   What is a financial instrument?

A financial instrument is defined as: *FAS 107.3*

- cash;

- evidence of an ownership interest in an entity, e.g. common stock, warrants or options etc.; or

- a contract that both:

    - imposes on one entity a contractual obligation (1) to deliver cash or another financial instrument to a second entity or (2) to exchange financial instruments on potentially unfavourable terms with the second entity; and

    - conveys to that second entity a contractual right (1) to receive cash or another financial instrument from the first entity or (2) to exchange other financial instruments on potentially favourable terms with the first entity.

The above definition is recursive (because the term financial instrument is included   *FAS 107.3 fn2*
in it) but not circular.   A financial instrument may be a link in a contractual chain
with other financial instruments, but the chain must end eventually with the delivery
of cash or an ownership interest in an entity.

11.3   RECOGNITION AND DERECOGNITION OF ASSETS AND LIABILITIES

11.3.1   Assets and liabilities

Assets are 'probable future economic benefits obtained or controlled by a particular   *CON 6.25*
entity as a result of past transactions or events'.

Liabilities are 'probable future sacrifices of economic benefits arising from present   *CON 6.35*

settlement of which is expected to result in an outflow from the entity of resources embodying economic benefits.'

IAS F.53,57,59 The future economic benefit embodied in an asset is the potential to contribute to the flow of cash (or equivalents) to the entity. The capacity of an entity to control the benefits is usually the result of legal rights, but an item may satisfy the definition of an asset even when there is no legal control. Generally, there is a close association between incurring expenditure and generating assets, but the former does not guarantee the latter; similarly the absence of a related expenditure does not preclude an item from satisfying the definition of an asset and being recognised in the balance sheet.

11.3.2   Recognition of assets and liabilities

IAS F.83   An item that meets the definition of an asset or a liability should be recognised if:

IAS 37.14   • it is probable that any future economic benefit associated with the item will flow to or from the entity; and

   • the item has a cost or value that can be measured reliably.

IAS F.90   An asset should not be recognised in the balance sheet when expenditure has been incurred as a result of which it is improbable that economic benefits will flow to the entity beyond the current accounting period.

IAS F.91   A liability is recognised when it is probable that an outflow of resources embodying economic benefits will result from the settlement of a present obligation and the amount at which the settlement will be made can be measured reliably. In practice, obligations under contracts that are equally proportionately unperformed (e.g. executory contracts) are generally not recognised as liabilities in the financial statements. However, such obligations may meet the definition of liabilities and may qualify for recognition.

IAS 39.14   A financial asset or financial liability should be recognised by an entity on its balance
IAS 39.38   sheet when it becomes a party to the contractual provisions of the instrument.   A
IAS 39.AG53 'regular way' purchase or sale of financial assets should be recognised using either

obligations of a particular entity to transfer assets or provide services to other entities in the future as a result of past transactions or events'.

An asset has three essential characteristics: *CON 6.26*

- it embodies a probable future benefit that involves a capacity, singly or in combination with other assets, to contribute directly or indirectly to future net cash inflows;
- a particular entity can obtain the benefit and control others' access to it; and
- the transaction or other event giving rise to the entity's right to, or control of, the benefit has already occurred.

A liability has three essential characteristics: *CON 6.36*

- it embodies a present duty or responsibility to one or more other entities that entails settlement by probable future transfer or use of assets at a specified or determinable date, on occurrence of a specified event, or on demand;
- the duty or responsibility obligates a particular entity, leaving it little or no discretion to avoid the future sacrifice; and
- the transaction or other event obligating the entity has already happened.

A financial asset is defined as cash, evidence of an ownership interest in an entity, or   *FAS 140.364*
a contract that conveys to a second entity the contractual right (a) to receive cash or   *FAS 107.3(b)*
another financial instrument from a first entity of (b) to exchange other financial instruments on potentially favourable terms with the first entity.

A financial liability is defined as a contract that imposes on one entity a contractual   *FAS 140.364*
obligation (a) to deliver cash or another financial instrument to a second entity or   *FAS 107.3(a)*
(b) to exchange other financial instruments on potentially unfavourable terms with the second entity.

11.3.2   Recognition of assets and liabilities

An item and information about it should meet four fundamental recognition criteria   *CON 5.63*
to be recognised and should be recognised when the criteria are met. Those criteria are:

- definitions – the item meets the definition of an element of financial statements, e.g. asset or liability;
- measurability – it has a relevant attribute measurable with sufficient reliability;
- relevance – the information about it is capable of making a difference in user decisions; and
- reliability – the information is representationally faithful, verifiable, and neutral.

Generally, contributions received should be recognised as revenues or gains in the   *FAS 116.8*
period and as assets, decreases of liabilities, or expenses depending on the form of the benefits received.

Contributions made should be recognised as expenses in the period and as decreases   *FAS 116.18*
of assets or increases of liabilities depending on the form of the benefits given.

Contributions received and given should be measured at their fair values.

trade date accounting or settlement date accounting. The method used should be applied consistently for all purchases and sales of financial assets that belong to the same category as defined in IAS 39 (paragraph 9).

11.3.3   Derecognition of financial assets

A   Derecognition

The general rule is that derecognition of assets should occur only when substantially all the risks and rewards of ownership have been transferred to other parties.

IAS 39 *Financial Instruments: Recognition and Measurement* contains complicated and detailed guidance on the derecognition of financial assets and liabilities. The application guidance includes a flow chart that summarises the steps to be followed when evaluating derecognition.

IAS 39.16   IAS 39 requires an entity, before evaluating whether, and to what extent, derecognition is appropriate under the provisions of IAS 39, to determine whether these provisions should be applied to a part of the asset or to the asset in its entirety.

The derecognition principles will be applied to a part of the asset only when either:

- the part comprises only specifically identified cash flows from a financial asset;
- the part comprises only a fully proportionate shares of the cash flows from a financial asset; or
- the part comprises only a fully proportionate share of specifically identified cash flows from a financial asset.

IAS 39.17-20   An entity will derecognise a financial asset when, and only when:

- the contractual rights to the cash flows from the financial asset expire; or
- it transfers the contractual rights to receive the cash flows of the financial asset or it retains the right to these cash flows but assumes a contractual obligation to pay the cash flows to one or more recipients in an arrangement whereby (i) the entity has no obligation to pay amounts to these recipients unless it also collects equivalent amounts from the asset, (ii) the entity cannot otherwise sell or pledge the financial asset and (iii) the entity has to pass such amounts on to the recipients in a timely manner. Even if transfer has taken place, or is deemed to have taken place by the satisfaction of these three conditions, the entity must then assess whether:
  - substantially all of the risks and rewards of ownership have been transferred, in which case the asset will be derecognised and any right or obligation now created or retained will be separately recognised;
  - substantially all of the risks and rewards of ownership have been retained, in which case the asset will continue to be recognised; or
  - substantially all of the risks and rewards of ownership have neither been transferred nor retained, in which case the entity will assess whether it has retained control over the asset and will continue to recognise any continuing involvement if this control still exists and will derecognise the asset if this control has been lost (but separately recognising any rights and obligations now created or retained).

11.3.3   Derecognition of financial assets

A   Derecognition

The general rule is that derecognition of assets should occur only when substantially all the risks and rewards of ownership have been transferred to other parties.

FAS 140 *Accounting for Transfers and Servicing of Financial Assets and Extinguishments of Liabilities a replacement of FASB Statement 125* establishes the general rules for determining whether a transfer of financial assets constitutes a sale. Under the standard, the transfer of financial assets in which the transferor surrenders control over the transferred assets is accounted for as a sale.   A transferor is considered to have surrendered control over transferred assets if and only if all of the following three conditions are met: *FAS 140.9*   *Q&A FAS 140*

- the transferred assets have been isolated from the transferor – beyond the reach of the transferor and its creditors, even in bankruptcy or other receivership;

- each transferee (or if the transferee is a qualifying special purpose entity – see section 2.6 – each holder of its beneficial interest) has the right to pledge or exchange the transferred assets (or beneficial interests) it received, and no condition both constrains the transferee (or holder) from taking advantage of its right to pledge or exchange and provides more than a trivial benefit to the transferor; and

- the transferor does not retain effective control over the transferred assets through either (1) an agreement that both entitles and obligates the transferor to repurchase or redeem the assets before their maturity, or (2) the ability to unilaterally cause the holder to return specific assets, other than through a cleanup call to purchase an uneconomic residual asset or beneficial interest.

COMMENT

In June 2003 the FASB issued an exposure draft for a proposed Statement of Financial Accounting Standards *Qualifying Special-Purpose Entities and Isolation of Transferred Assets an amendment of FASB Statement No. 140.*   The proposed Statement would amend the first condition above to read; 'the transferred assets have been isolated from the transferor – beyond the reach of the powers of a bankruptcy trustee or other receiver for the transferor or any consolidated affiliate of the transferor that is not a special-purpose corporation or other entity designed to make remote the possibility that it would enter bankruptcy or other receivership'.

On completion of any transfer of financial assets, the transferor (seller) should: *FAS 140.10*

- continue to recognise any retained interest in the transferred assets; and

- allocate the previous carrying amount between the assets sold, if any, and the retained interests, if any, based on their relative fair values at the date of transfer.

On completion of a transfer of assets that satisfies the conditions to be accounted for as a sale, the transferor (seller) should: *FAS 140.11*

- derecognise all assets sold;

IAS 39.25   If, as a result of the transfer, a financial asset, or part thereof, is derecognised in its entirety (i.e., the situation in the first of the three dashed bullet points immediately above and the situation in the third bullet point so long as control has been lost) but that this transfer results in the transferor obtaining a new financial asset or servicing asset or assuming a new financial liability or servicing liability then the entity must recognise this new asset or liability at fair value.

IAS 39.26   On derecognition of a financial asset in its entirety, the amount to be recognised in profit and loss will be calculated as the difference between:
- the carrying amount of the asset; and
- the sum of the consideration received (including any new asset obtained less any new liability assumed) and any cumulative gain or loss that has been recognised directly in equity (such as on 'available for sale' assets).

IAS 39.27   If it is a part of a financial asset that is being derecognised in its entirety then in order to calculate the profit or loss on derecognition it is necessary to allocate the carrying amount of the previous asset of which this part relates between the part that is being derecognised in its entirety and the remainder that is continuing to be recognised.   This allocation will be based upon the relative fair values of those parts on the date of the transfer.

IAS 39.29   If the transfer did not qualify for derecognition because the entity has retained substantially all of the risks and rewards of ownership of the asset, the asset continues to be recognised in its entirety with any consideration received being recognised as a financial liability.

IAS 39.30   If substantially all of the risks and rewards of ownership have been neither transferred nor retained and control still exists then the entity must continue to recognise any continuing involvement.   The extent of this entity's continuing involvement in the transferred asset is the extent to which it is exposed to changes in the value of the transferred asset.   For example:
- when this continuing involvement is in the form of a guarantee the extent of the continuing involvement is the lower of the amount of the asset and the amount of the guarantee.
- when this involvement is in the form of a written or purchased option (including a cash settled option) on the transferred asset the extent of the continuing involvement is the amount of the transferred asset that the entity may repurchase.   However, in the case of a written put option on an asset measured at fair value, the extent of the continuing involvement is limited to the lower of the fair value of the transferred asset and the option exercise price.

IAS 39.31   When an entity continues to recognise an asset to the extent of its continuing involvement the entity should also recognise an associated liability.   The transferred asset and associated liability are measured in such a way that the net carrying amount is equal to:
- the amortised cost of the rights and obligations retained by the entity, if the transferred asset is measured at amortised cost; or
- the fair value of the rights and obligations retained by the entity when measured on a stand-alone basis, if the transferred asset is measured at fair value.

IAS 39.32   In addition, the entity continues to recognise any income or expense on the transferred asset and associated liability to the extent of its continuing involvement.

- recognise all assets obtained and liabilities incurred in consideration as proceeds of the sale, initially measured at fair value (if practicable); and
- recognise in earnings any gain or loss on the sale.

The transferee should recognise all assets obtained and any liabilities incurred and initially measure them at fair value.

IAS 39.36   If a transferred asset continues to be recognised, the entity must not offset either the asset with the associated liability and must not offset any income arising from the transferred asset with any expense incurred on the associated liability.

B   Continued recognition

IAS 39.29   If the transfer did not qualify for derecognition because the entity has retained substantially all of the risks and rewards of ownership of the asset, the asset continues to be recognised in its entirety with any consideration received being recognised as a financial liability.   In subsequent periods, the entity should recognise any income on the transferred asset and any expense incurred on the financial liability.

11.3.4   Extinguishment of financial liabilities

IAS 39.39   A financial liability is extinguished when the obligation in the contract has been
IAS 39.AG57 discharged, cancelled or has expired.   Financial liabilities are considered to have been extinguished when:

- the debtor discharges the liability by paying the creditor; or
- the debtor is legally released from primary responsibility for the liability, either by law or by the creditor.

IAS 39.AG59   Payment to a party other than the creditor, e.g. payment to a trust in an in-substance defeasance, does not, by itself, release the debtor from its primary obligation to the creditor.

IAS 39.AG60   If a debtor pays a third party to assume an obligation and notifies its creditor that the third party has assumed its debt obligation, the debtor does not derecognise the debt obligation unless the conditions above are met.   If the debtor pays a third party to assume an obligation and obtains a legal release from its creditor, the debtor has extinguished the debt.   However, if the debtor agrees to make payments on the debt to the third party, the debtor recognises a new debt obligation.

IAS 39.41   The difference between the carrying amount of a financial liability (or part of a financial liability) extinguished or transferred to another party and the consideration paid, including any non-cash assets transferred or liabilities assumed, is recognised in profit or loss.

IAS 39.40   An exchange between an existing borrower and lender of debt instruments with substantially different terms should be accounted for as an extinguishment of the original financial liability and the recognition of a new financial liability.   Similarly, a substantial modification (see below) of the terms of an existing financial liability or a part of it (whether or not attributable to the financial difficulty of the debtor) should be accounted for as an extinguishment of the original financial liability and the recognition of a new financial liability.

IAS 39.AG62   Terms are regarded as substantially different if the net present value of the cash flows under the new terms (including any fees paid net of any fees received) discounted using the original effective interest rate, is at least 10 per cent different from the net present value of the remaining cash flows of the original financial liability.

IAS 39.AG62   If an exchange of debt instruments or modification of terms is accounted for as an extinguishment, any costs or fees incurred are recognised as part of the gain or loss on the extinguishment.   However, if the exchange or modification is not accounted

B   Continued recognition

Where a transaction does not meet the above three criteria for sales recognition, the assets should continue to be recognised and accounted for as a secured borrowing. The transferor would recognise any proceeds received as a liability, and continue to account for the assets.   The transferee would record a receivable for the amount of the funds advanced.   *FAS 140.12*

11.3.4   Extinguishment of financial liabilities

Extinguishment is the term used to describe the circumstance when debt ceases to be a liability that warrants continued recognition in the balance sheet.   It is not to be confused with offsetting, which deals with how recognised assets and recognised liabilities should be presented in a balance sheet.   *FAS 140.16*   *Q&A FAS 140*

A debt is considered extinguished for financial reporting purposes only when:

- the debtor pays the creditor and is relieved of all its obligations with respect to the debt; or
- the debtor is legally released as the primary obligor under the debt, either judicially or by the creditor.

The exchange of existing debt instruments for new debt instruments with substantially different terms is a debt extinguishment and should be accounted for in accordance with paragraph 16 of FAS 140.   A modification to the terms of a debt instrument with a cash flow effect on a present value basis of less than 10% is not considered substantial.   *EITF 96-19*

The EITF Abstract provides guidance to be used to calculate the present values of cash flows for the purpose of applying the 10% test.

Gains and losses from all extinguishments of debt (including convertible debt) should be recognised in income of the period of extinguishment and identified as a separate item.   *APB 26.20*

If it is determined that the original and new debt instruments are substantially different, then the new debt instrument should be initially recorded at fair value and that amount should be used to determine the debt extinguishment gain or loss to be recognised and the effective rate of the new instrument.   *EITF 96-19*

If it is determined that the original and new debt instruments are not substantially different, then there is no extinguishment and a new effective interest rate is to be determined based on the carrying amount of the original debt instrument and the revised cash flows.

Fees paid or received between the debtor and creditor as part of the exchange or modification of debt instruments should be accounted for as follows:

- If the exchange or modification is accounted for as an extinguishment, the fees are associated with the extinguished debt instrument and included in the gain or loss recognised.
- If the exchange or modification is not accounted for as an extinguishment, the

for as an extinguishment, any costs or fees incurred are an adjustment of the carrying amount of the liability and are amortised over the remaining term of the modified liability.

IAS 39.AG63   A creditor may release a debtor from its present obligation to make payments, but with the debtor assuming a guarantee obligation to pay if the party assuming primary responsibility defaults.   In this circumstance the debtor recognises a new financial liability based on the fair value of its obligation for the guarantee and recognises a gain or loss based on the difference between (i) any proceeds paid and (ii) the carrying amount of the original financial liability less the fair value of the new financial liability.

11.4   TROUBLED DEBT RESTRUCTURINGS

The term 'troubled debt restructuring' is undefined under International Financial Reporting Standards, but guidance is provided on accounting for exchanges of debt instruments with substantially different terms and the accounting for such events is described above.

fees are associated with the replacement or modified debt instrument and amortised over the remaining term of the replacement or modified debt instrument.

Costs incurred with third parties directly related to the modification of debt instruments should be accounted for as follows:

- If the exchange or modification is accounted for as an extinguishment, the costs are associated with the new debt instrument and amortised over the term of the new debt instrument, as for debt issue costs.

- If the exchange or modification is not accounted for as an extinguishment, the costs should be expensed as incurred.

11.4   TROUBLED DEBT RESTRUCTURINGS

A restructuring of a debt constitutes a 'troubled debt restructuring' if the borrower is experiencing financial difficulties and the lender, in an attempt to protect as much of its investment as possible, grants concessions that it would not otherwise consider. Not all debt restructurings are troubled debt restructurings, e.g. a debt restructuring involving a borrower who is able to obtain funds from sources other than the existing lender, at market rates of interest at or near those for 'non-troubled' debt (as opposed to at rates of interest that are so high that the borrower cannot afford them).   *FAS 15.2,7*

There are different ways in which a lender can grant concessions to the borrower in a troubled debt restructuring. Although troubled debt that is fully satisfied by foreclosure, repossession, or other transfer of assets or by grant of equity securities is, in a technical sense, not restructured, that kind of event is included in the term troubled debt restructuring.

A   *Transfer of assets in full settlement*

The borrower should record a gain on restructuring payables where the carrying amount of the payable settled exceeds the fair value of the assets transferred. A difference between the fair value and carrying amounts of assets transferred to a creditor to settle a payable should be recognised as a gain or loss on transfer of assets in the normal way.   *FAS 15.13-14*

B   *Debt for equity swap*

The borrower should use the fair value of the equity interest granted to the lender to account for the shares that are issued. The difference between this and the carrying amount of the debt that is thereby settled should be recognised as a gain on restructuring of payables.   *FAS 15.15*

C   *Modification of debt agreement*

Where the lender agrees to modify the debt agreement, the effects of the modification should generally be accounted for prospectively from the time of the restructuring. If the carrying amount of the debt at the time of the restructuring is lower than the total future cash payments due under the revised agreement (including contingent payments), a new effective rate of interest should be calculated and applied to determine the finance costs in the period to maturity. The concession granted by the lender therefore is spread over the term to maturity.   *FAS 15.16-18*

11.5   SPECIFIC RECOGNITION ISSUES

11.5.1   Factoring of debts and transfers of receivables with recourse

A   Factoring of debts

Factoring is a long-established means of obtaining finance by selling trade debtors to accelerate the receipt of cash following a sale on credit.   Factoring arrangements that meet the criteria for derecognition under IAS 39 (see section 11.3.3) should be accounted for as sales of financial assets because the transferor will have substantially transferred the risks and rewards of these receivables.

B   Transfers of receivables with recourse

In a transfer of receivables with recourse, the transferor provides the transferee with full or limited recourse.   The transferor is obligated under the terms of the recourse provision to make payments to the transferee or to repurchase receivables sold under certain circumstances, typically for defaults up to a specified percentage.

IAS 39.17-31   A transfer of receivables with recourse may result in partial derecognition (see section 11.3.3 above).   It is unlikely to lead to complete derecognition since the recourse nature will mean that there is continuing involvement with the asset.   Any guarantee to the buyer to pay for any credit losses will be recognised as a financial liability.   If the criteria for partial or complete recognition were not met, transferred receivables would generally be accounted for to the extent of the transferor's continuing involvement together with an associated liability (see section 11.3.1 above).

11.5.2   Securitised assets

Securitisation is the process whereby financial assets are transformed into securities (often referred to as 'asset-backed securities').   Asset-backed securities entitle their holders to specified cash flows from a designated portfolio of financial assets.   The value of an asset-backed security derives from the underlying financial assets.

In order to conclude that securitised assets should be treated off-balance sheet, an entity must conclude:

SIC-12   •   that the transferee in the securitisation transaction is not a special-purpose entity that must be consolidated in accordance with the requirements of SIC-12 (see section 2.6); and

If, however, the total future cash payments are less than the carrying amount of the debt, the difference should be recognised as a gain on restructuring of payables. In subsequent periods, cash payments made to the lender simply reduce the carrying amount of the debt and no interest cost is reported.

FAS 15 also provides guidance on the accounting treatment where the troubled debt restructuring involves partial settlement of a payable by transferring assets or an equity interest (or both) and modification of terms of the remaining payable.

FAS 15.19

Additional disclosures should be provided in accounts about troubled debt restructurings that have occurred in a period.

FAS 15.25-26

11.5   SPECIFIC RECOGNITION ISSUES

11.5.1   Factoring of debts and transfers of receivables with recourse

A   Factoring of debts

Factoring arrangements are a means of discounting accounts receivable on a non-recourse, notification basis. Accounts receivable are sold outright, usually to a transferee (the factor) that assumes the full risk of collection, without recourse to the transferor in the event of a loss. Debtors are directed to send payments to the transferee.

FAS 140.112
Q&A FAS 140

Factoring arrangements that meet the criteria for sales recognition under FAS 140 (see section 11.3.3A) should be accounted for as sales of financial assets because the transferor surrenders control over the receivables to the factor.

FAS 140.9,11

B   Transfers of receivables with recourse

In a transfer of receivables with recourse, the transferor provides the transferee with full or limited recourse. The transferor is obligated under the terms of the recourse provision to make payments to the transferee or to repurchase receivables sold under certain circumstances, typically for defaults up to a specified percentage.

FAS 140.113

A transfer of receivables with recourse should be accounted for as a sale, with the proceeds of the sale reduced by the fair value of the recourse obligation, if the criteria for a sale under FAS 140 (see section 11.3.3A) are met. Otherwise, a transfer of receivables with recourse should be accounted for as a secured borrowing.

FAS 140.113

11.5.2   Securitised assets

Securitisation is the process whereby financial assets are transformed into securities (often referred to as 'asset-backed securities'). Asset-backed securities entitle their holders to specified cash flows from a designated portfolio of financial assets. The value of an asset-backed security is, therefore, derived from the underlying financial assets.

FAS 140.73
Q&A FAS 140

A securitisation, in its most simple form, can result in the sale of the underlying financial assets, i.e. derecognition from the balance sheet, the receipt of cash proceeds, and a resulting gain or loss. As such, securitisations often are thought of as providing a form of 'off-balance-sheet' financing. The criteria for sales

- that the assets underlying the securitisation transaction may be derecognised in accordance with the derecognition criteria of IAS 39, as described in section 11.3.3.

IAS 32.94   If an entity has transferred a financial asset in such a way that the arrangement does not qualify as a transfer of a financial asset and therefore either continues to recognise all of the asset or continues to recognise the asset to the extent of the entity's continuing involvement it should disclose for each class of financial asset:

- the nature of the assets;
- the nature of the risks and rewards of ownership to which the entity remains exposed;
- when the entity continues to recognise all of the asset, the carrying amounts of the asset and of the associated liability; and
- when the entity continues to recognise the asset to the extent of its continuing involvement, the total amount of the asset, the amount of the asset that the entity continues to recognise and the carrying amount of the associated liability.

11.6   FINANCIAL ASSETS

IAS 39.9   IAS 39 defines the accounting for and specifies the four different categories of financial assets: held-to-maturity investments, financial assets at fair value through profit or loss, available-for-sale financial assets, and loans and receivables.

A   Held-to-maturity investments

IAS 39.9   Held-to-maturity investments are defined as non-derivative financial assets with fixed or determinable payments and fixed maturity that an entity has the positive intention and ability to hold to maturity other than:

- those that the entity at upon initial recognition designates as at fair value through profit or loss;
- those that the entity designates as available-for-sale; and
- those that meet the definition of loans and receivables.

In certain circumstances an entity cannot classify a financial asset as held-to-maturity. These 'tainting' provisions apply if the entity has, during the current financial year or during the two preceding financial years, sold or reclassified more than an insignificant amount of held-to-maturity investments before maturity other than sales or reclassifications that:

- are so close to maturity or the financial asset's call date (for example, less than three months before maturity) that changes in the market rate of interest would not have a significant effect on the financial asset's fair value;
- occur after the entity has collected substantially all of the financial asset's original principal through scheduled payments or prepayments; or
- are attributable to an isolated event that is beyond the entity's control, is non-recurring and could not have been reasonably anticipated by the entity.

IAS 39.AG20   This held-to-maturity category is viewed as an exception that is only to be used in limited circumstances and consequently, its use is restricted by a number of detailed conditions, largely designed to test whether there is a genuine intention and ability to hold such investments to maturity.

recognition under FAS 140 (see section 11.3.3A) should be applied to determine whether derecogition of the assets is appropriate or whether the securitisation should be recorded as a secured borrowing.

Both financial assets (such as mortgage loans, automobile loans, trade receivables, credit card receivables, and minimum lease payments under financing lease receivables) and non-financial assets can be securitised, but securitisations of non-financial assets are outside of the scope of FAS 140.

11.6   FINANCIAL ASSETS

There are three categories for the classification of an investment in debt or marketable equity securities at acquisition: 'held-to-maturity', 'available-for-sale' or 'trading'. The accounting treatment of investments depends on the appropriate category rather than on whether the investment is a current or non-current asset. The appropriateness of the classification should be reassessed at each reporting date.   *FAS 115.6*

A company that presents a classified balance sheet should report investments as current or non-current based on the guidance contained in ARB 43 *Restatement and Revision of Accounting Research Bulletins*. Under ARB 43, classification between current and non-current depends upon whether or not the investment is reasonably expected to be realised in cash during the normal operating cycle of the business. A one-year time period is to be used as a basis for segregation of current assets in cases where several operating cycles occur within a year.

A   Held-to-maturity investments

The held-to-maturity category is available only for debt securities which the company has both the positive intent and ability to hold to maturity. It does not include securities which the company intends to hold for only an indefinite period. As a result, securities that are available to be sold in response to changes in market interest rates, management of the company's tax position or general liquidity needs would not qualify for the held-to-maturity category.   *FAS 115.7,9*

A security may not be classified as held-to-maturity if that security can contractually be prepaid or otherwise settled in such a way that the holder of the security would not recover substantially all of its recorded investment. A debt security with those characteristics should be evaluated to determine whether it contains an embedded derivative that must be accounted for separately (see section 13.3A).   *FAS 115.7*

Sales or transfers from the held-to-maturity category prior to maturity would be expected to be rare and difficult to justify. Such transactions would call into question the classification of other held-to-maturity securities and could require   *FAS 115.8-11*

IAS 39.AG16   The entity does not have the positive intent to hold to maturity an investment in a financial asset with a fixed maturity if any of the following conditions exist:

- the entity only has the intention to hold the financial asset for an undefined period;
- the entity stands ready to sell the financial asset in response to changes in market interest rates or risks, liquidity needs, changes in the availability of and the yield on alternative investments, changes in financing sources and terms, or changes in foreign currency risk; or
- the issuer has a right to settle the financial asset at an amount significantly below its amortised cost.

IAS 39.AG23   The entity does not have a demonstrated ability to hold an investment in a financial asset to maturity when:

- it does not have the financial resources available to continue to finance the investment until maturity; or
- it is subject to an existing legal or other constraint that could frustrate its intention to hold the financial asset to maturity.

B   *Financial assets at fair value through profit or loss*

IAS 39.9   Assets within this category must either:

- be classified as held for trading.   Such assets are:
  - acquired or incurred principally for the purpose of sale or repurchase in the near term;
  - part of a portfolio of identified financial instruments that are managed together and for which there is evidence of a recent actual pattern of short-term profit-taking; or
  - derivatives (except for designated and effective hedging instruments). See section 13.2.2 for the definition of a derivative;
- be designated as at fair value through profit or loss on initial recognition. This can include any financial asset that is within the scope of this standard that is designated as such upon initial recognition except for investments in equity instruments that do not have a quoted market price in an active market and whose fair value cannot be reliably measured.

COMMENT

In response to criticism, by various regulators, of certain aspects of IAS 39, the IASB, in April 2004, issued an exposure draft to IAS 39 *Financial Instruments: Recognition and Measurement, The Fair Value Option*.   In order to address these regulators' concerns this exposure draft proposed to limit the types of financial assets and financial liabilities to which the option may be applied.   This exposure draft has been extremely contentious and at the time this publication went to print there was still ongoing discussions to determine how these regulators' concerns would be alleviated.

C   *Available-for-sale financial assets*

IAS 39.9   Available-for-sale financial assets are those non-derivative financial assets that are not (1) loans and receivables, (2) held-to-maturity investments, or (3) financial assets at fair value through profit or loss.

transfer of the securities to the available-for-sale category. However, a sale or transfer of held-to-maturity securities in the following circumstances may not be considered inconsistent with the original classification:

- sales or transfers due to extremely remote circumstances, e.g. significant deterioration in the issuer's credit worthiness, or which have resulted from 'other events that are isolated, nonrecurring, and unusual for the reporting entity that could not have been reasonably anticipated'; or

- sales which occur near enough to maturity that interest rate risk is substantially eliminated as a pricing factor or which occur after a substantial portion (at least 85%) of the principal outstanding at acquisition has been collected.

B   *Trading securities*

Investments in debt and marketable equity securities that are acquired and held primarily for resale in the near term to make a profit from short-term movements in market prices should be classified as 'trading securities'.   The intent to trade (rather than the type of security or the period of time it is expected to be held) and the existence of active and frequent trading activity are generally key factors to be considered when determining whether a security should be included in this category. However, at acquisition an entity is not precluded from classifying a security as trading simply because it does not intend to sell it in the near term.

FAS 115.12

Q&A FAS 115.34
Q&A FAS 115.35

An available-for-sale security should not be transferred to trading because the passage of time has caused the maturity date to be within one year or because the company intends to sell it within one year.

FAS 115.81
Q&A FAS 115.36

C   *Available-for-sale securities*

This category is for:

- debt securities not classified as either held-to-maturity or trading; and
- equity securities not classified as trading.

D   Loans and receivables

IAS 39.9   Loans and receivables are non-derivative financial assets with fixed or determinable payments that are not quoted in an active market, do not qualify as trading assets and have not been designated as 'at fair value through profit or loss' or as 'available-for-sale'.

11.6.1   Measurement

IAS 39.43   A financial asset at fair value through profit or loss is initially measured at fair value. The initial measurement of other financial assets is also based on their fair value, but adjusted in respect of any transaction costs that are directly attributable to their acquisition.

IAS 39.AG64   This initial fair value of the financial instrument will normally be the transaction price. However, this will not be the case if part of the consideration was for something other than the financial instrument, in which case a valuation technique will be required to estimate the fair value of this instrument.

IAS 39.45-46   Subsequent measurement is determined by which of the four classifications detailed above the particular financial asset is included within. Loans and receivables and held-to-maturity investments are measured at amortised cost using the effective interest method (see below). Investments in equity instruments that do not have a quoted market price in an active market and whose fair value cannot be reliably measured (and linked derivatives that settle in such instruments) are measured at cost. All other financial assets are measured at fair value, with no deduction for disposal costs.

IAS 39.9   The amortised cost of a financial asset is defined as the amount at which it was measured at initial recognition minus principal repayments, plus or minus the cumulative amortisation using the 'effective interest method' of any difference between that initial amount and the maturity amount, and minus any write-down (directly or through the use of an allowance account) for impairment or uncollectibility.

IAS 39.9   The effective interest rate is the rate that exactly discounts estimated future cash payments or receipts over the expected life of the instrument or, when appropriate, a shorter period, to the instrument's net carrying amount. The calculation of the effective interest rate should include all fees and points paid or received between the contracting parties to the extent they are an integral part of the effective interest rate. The calculation should also include transaction costs, and all other premiums or discounts, but not the effect of future credit losses.

Financial assets that are designated as hedged items are subject to measurement under the hedge accounting requirements of IAS 39 and these can override these general measurement rules.

Except for those that are measured at fair value through profit or loss all financial assets are subject to review for impairment.

IAS 39.AG71-72   The existence of published price quotations in an active market is the best evidence of fair value. The appropriate quoted market price to be used in fair valuing an asset is the bid price. However, when an entity has offsetting market risks, it may use mid-market prices as a basis for establishing fair values for the offsetting risk positions and apply the bid price (or ask price) to the net long position (or short position).

11.6.1　Measurement

Investments in debt securities categorised as held-to-maturity should be measured at amortised costs.　Dividends and interest income (including amortisation of premium and discount) should be included in earnings.　Even though the investments are carried at amortised costs, an assessment should be carried out to determine whether a decline in fair value below amortised cost is 'other-than-temporary' (see section 11.6F).

FAS 115.7,14,16

Trading securities should be measured at fair value.　Dividends, interest income, and unrealised gains and losses should be included in earnings.

FAS 115.12-13

Available-for-sale securities should be stated at fair value.　Unrealised gains and losses, net of the related tax effect, are included as a separate component of shareholders' equity in other comprehensive income.　The deferred tax consequences of unrealised holding gains and losses reported as a separate component of shareholders' equity should be charged or credited directly to the related component of shareholders' equity in other comprehensive income.

FAS 115.12-13
FAS 109.36

If a decline in fair value below cost is 'other-than-temporary' (see section 11.6F), the unrealised loss should be accounted for as a realised loss and included in earnings.

Dividends and interest income, including amortisation of the premium and discount arising at acquisition, as well as realised gains and losses, should be included in earnings.

FAS 115.14

IAS 39.AG72   If there are no current quoted prices available, the price of the most recent transaction provides evidence of the current fair value unless there have been significant changes in economic circumstances since that transaction.

IAS 39.AG74   If the market for a financial asset is not active, an entity establishes fair value by using a valuation technique (apart from investments in equity instruments that do not have a quoted market price in an active market and whose fair value cannot be reliably measured and have to therefore be measured at cost as explained above).

IAS 39.55   All gains and losses arising from recognised changes in fair value of financial assets that are not part of a hedging relationship and that are classified at fair value through profit or loss are recognised in the income statement.

IAS 39.56   For financial assets carried at amortised cost (held-to-maturity investments and loans and receivables) that are not part of a hedging relationship, gains and losses are recognised in the income statement when the asset is derecognised or impaired, as well as through the amortisation process.

IAS 39.55   Accounting for available-for-sale assets is slightly more complex. Gains and losses arising from changes in fair value (after adjusting for interest accruals and certain foreign exchange gains and losses) are initially recognised directly in equity and reported in the statement of changes in equity. When an asset is derecognised, often by way of sale, or is impaired, the cumulative gain or loss previously recognised in equity is recycled and recognised in profit or loss. Where appropriate, interest receivable is recognised in the income statement using the effective interest method and dividends receivable are recognised in profit or loss when a right to receive payment is established. Again, if the asset is part of a hedging relationship other rules apply.

IAS 39.57   If an entity recognises financial assets using settlement date accounting, any change in the fair value of the asset to be received between the trade and settlement dates is not recognised for assets carried at cost or amortised cost. For assets carried at fair value, such a change in fair value is recognised in profit or loss or in equity as described above.

11.6.2 Transfers between categories

IAS 39.50   An entity should not reclassify a financial instrument into or out of the fair value through profit or loss category while it is held.

IAS 39.51,55   An investment will be reclassified as available-for-sale if, as a result of a change in intention or ability, it fails to meet the requirements for classification as held-to-maturity. In addition, if 'tainting' occurs (see section 11.6A above) any remaining held-to-maturity investments should be reclassified as available-for-sale. In such situations the assets will be remeasured to fair value and any associated gain or loss recognised in equity.

IAS 39.54   If as a result of a change of intention or ability, or because the tainting period has passed, it becomes appropriate to reclassify an available-for-sale investment as held-to-maturity then the fair value carrying amount on the date of reclassification becomes its new amortised cost. Any previous gain or loss on that asset that has been recognised in equity should be amortised over the remaining life of the investment using the effective interest method. Any difference between the new

11.6.2   Transfers between categories

Although the classification of each investment should be reassessed at each balance sheet date, transfers between the various categories of investments should be infrequent and, in the case of transfers from the held-to-maturity category, they should be rare.   Given the nature of a trading security, transfers into or from the trading category also should be rare.

FAS 115.15

Transfers are accounted for at fair value as of the transfer date but the accounting treatment of the unrealised holding gains and losses and related income tax effects on any temporary differences is determined by the category into which the security is transferred, as follows:

- for a security transferred from the trading category, the unrealised holding gain or loss at the date of transfer will already be recognised in earnings and should not be reversed;

- for a security transferred into the trading category, the unrealised portion of the holding gain or loss that has not been previously recognised in earnings should be recognised in earnings immediately;

amortised cost and maturity amount should be similarly amortised, akin to the amortisation of a premium or discount.

IAS 39.54   As mentioned at section 11.6.1 above, if the fair value of an equity instrument cannot be reliably measured it is measured at cost. If a reliable measure of fair value subsequently becomes available, the asset should be remeasured at that fair value and the gain or loss reported in the income statement or equity as appropriate. If a reliable measure ceases to be available, it should thereafter be measured at cost based on the fair value carrying amount on that date. Any gains or losses previously recognised in equity should be left there until the asset has been sold, otherwise disposed of or impaired, at which time it should be recognised in profit or loss.

11.6.3   Impairment of financial assets

A   Financial assets outside the scope of IAS 39

IAS 36   IAS 36 *Impairment of Assets* should be applied in accounting for the impairment of financial assets that are not included within the scope of IAS 39. Section 9 describes accounting for impairment in detail.

B   Financial assets covered by IAS 39 – General

IAS 39.46,58   All financial assets, except for those measured at fair value through profit or loss, are subject to review for impairment. Assessments should be made at each balance sheet date as to whether there is any objective evidence that a financial asset or group of financial assets is impaired.

IAS 39.59   A financial asset or a group of financial assets is impaired and impairment losses are incurred if, and only if, there is objective evidence of impairment as a result of one or more events that occurred after the initial recognition of the asset (a 'loss event') and that loss event (or events) has an impact on the estimated future cash flows of the financial asset or group of financial assets that can be reliably estimated. Losses expected as a result of future events, no matter how likely, are not recognised.

C   Financial assets held at amortised cost

IAS 39.63,65   If there is objective evidence that an impairment loss on loans and receivables or held-to-maturity investments carried at amortised cost has been incurred, the amount of the loss is measured as the difference between the asset's carrying amount and the present value of estimated future cash flows (excluding future credit losses that have not been incurred) discounted at the financial asset's original effective interest rate. The amount of the loss should be recognised in profit or loss. If, in a subsequent period, an event occurs that reduces the impairment loss, then this reversal should also be recognised in profit or loss. This reversal should not lead to a higher amortised cost, at the date of the reversal, than would have existed if there had not initially been any impairment.

D   Financial assets held at cost

IAS 39.66   Unquoted equity instruments and derivative assets that are linked to and must be settled by delivery of such instruments whose fair value cannot be reliably measured,

- for a debt security transferred into the available-for-sale category from the held-to-maturity category, the unrealised holding gain or loss should be reported in other comprehensive income; and

- for a debt security transferred into the held-to-maturity category from the available-for-sale category, the unrealised holding gain or loss should continue to be reported in a separate component of shareholders' equity, such as accumulated other comprehensive income, but should be amortised over the remaining life of the security.

COMMENT

The SEC Staff have stated that sales or transfers of held-to-maturity securities would taint the portfolio and the held-to-maturity classification would not be available for new purchases (or transfers of existing debt securities) for a period of two years.

11.6.3   Impairment of financial assets

For individual securities classified as either available-for-sale or held-to-maturity, a company should determine whether a decline in fair value below the amortised cost basis is 'other-than-temporary'. *FAS 115.16*

At present, there is little guidance on how to determine whether a decline in fair value below cost is 'other-than-temporary'. FAS 115 indicates that a debt security (not impaired at acquisition) should be considered to be impaired when the company determines that it is probable that all amounts due (principal and interest) will not be collected according to the security's contractual terms. SAB 59 notes that unless evidence exists to support a realisable value equal to or greater than the carrying amount of the investment, a write-down accounted for as a realised loss should be recorded. *SAB 59 (Topic 5-M)*

For securities classified as either held-to-maturity or available for sale, if a decline in fair value below cost is considered to be 'other-than-temporary', the cost basis of the security should be written down to fair value. The write-down should be included in earnings as a realised loss. The new cost basis for the security should not be changed for subsequent recoveries in fair value. For available-for-sale securities, subsequent increases in fair value should be included in other comprehensive income until realised (unless the security is designated as being hedged in a fair value hedge when the part or all of the unrecognised gain and loss is recognised in earnings). Subsequent decreases in fair value (provided they are not an other-than-temporary impairment) also should be included in other comprehensive income. *FAS 115.16* / *FAS 133.23* / *FAS 115.16*

FAS 114 provides guidance on how to measure impairment of a loan. For the purposes of the standard, a loan is a contractual right to receive money on demand or on fixed or determinable dates that is recognised as an asset in the creditor's balance sheet. *FAS 114.4*

The guidance applies to all creditors, i.e. lenders, and to all loans (uncollateralised as well as collateralised) except large groups of smaller-balance homogenous loans that are collectively evaluated for impairment, e.g. credit card and residential mortgage loans, loans that are measured at fair value or at the lower of cost or fair value, leases and debt securities as defined in FAS 115. *FAS 114.5-6*

A loan is impaired when, based on current information and events, it is probable that the lender will be unable to collect all amounts due according to the contractual *FAS 114.8*

are measured at cost. If there is objective evidence that an impairment loss has been incurred on such an asset, the amount of the impairment loss is measured as the difference between the carrying amount of the financial asset and the present value of estimated future cash flows discounted at the current market rate of return for a similar financial asset. Any such impairment loss cannot be reversed.

E   Financial assets classified as available-for-sale

IAS 39.67-70 If there has been a decline in the fair value of an available-for-sale asset that has been recognised directly in equity and there is objective evidence that the asset is impaired, the cumulative loss in equity should be recycled into profit or loss even though the asset has not been derecognised. The amount of the loss that should be recycled is the difference between its acquisition cost (net of any principal repayment and amortisation for assets measured using the effective interest method) and current fair value, less any impairment loss on that asset previously recognised in profit or loss. If, in a subsequent period, the fair value of an available-for-sale debt instrument increases and the increase can be objectively related to an event occurring after the loss was recognised in the income statement, the impairment loss should be reversed and recognised in profit or loss. However, in the case of equity instruments, impairments cannot be reversed through the income statement.

11.7   FINANCIAL LIABILITIES

IAS 39.43,47 Financial liabilities are classified as either:

- at fair value through profit or loss; or
- other financial liabilities (though not explicitly defined in the Standard).

Such liabilities are initially measured at fair value less, in the case of a financial liability not at fair value through profit or loss, transaction costs that are directly attributable to their issue.

> **COMMENT**
>
> In response to criticism, by various regulators, of certain aspects of IAS 39, the IASB, in April 2004, issued an exposure draft to IAS 39 *Financial Instruments: Recognition and Measurement, The Fair Value Option*. In order to address these regulators' concerns this exposure draft proposed to limit the types of financial assets and financial liabilities to which the option may be applied. This exposure draft has been extremely contentious and at the time this publication went to print there was still ongoing discussions to determine how these regulators' concerns would be alleviated.
>
> There has also been a recent development relating to IAS 39 that is of importance to many European companies. In November 2004 the European Commission, in response to criticism of some of the rules of the Standard, endorsed an amended version of IAS 39. One way that this differs to the unamended version is in removing the option available under the standard to designate any liabilities as held at fair value through profit or loss. However, entities are still permitted to measure financial liabilities at fair value through profit or loss if such measurement is allowable under the national legislation that the entity is subject to.

IAS 32.38 Transaction costs that relate to the issue of a compound financial instrument are allocated to the liability and equity components in proportion to the allocation of the proceeds.

terms of the loan agreement. There is no guidance on how to assess whether a loan is impaired – the creditor should apply its normal loan review procedures in making that judgement.

Impairment should be assessed on a loan-by-loan basis. If an impaired loan has risk characteristics in common with other impaired loans, the loans can be aggregated and historical statistics, e.g. average recovery period, average amount recovered, along with a composite effective interest rate used as a means of measuring those impaired loans.

FAS 114.12

Impairment should be calculated based on the present value of expected future cash flows discounted at the loan's effective interest rate. As a practical expedient, the observable market price for the loan or the fair value of the collateral if the loan is collateral dependent could be used as alternatives to discounted future cash flows.

FAS 114.13

11.7 FINANCIAL LIABILITIES

The initial carrying amount is determined by reference to the fair value of the consideration received or at an amount that reasonably approximates the market value of the debt, whichever is the more clearly determinable. The difference between the fair value and the face amount of debt should be treated as a discount or as interest expense or capitalised (see section 10). If the consideration is cash and some other unstated (or stated) rights or privileges, the value of those rights or privileges should be recognised by recording the debt at a discount or premium. Issue costs should be reported in the balance sheet as deferred charges.

APB 21.11-16

Where an entity issues debt instruments with both guaranteed and contingent payments, i.e. linked to the price of a specific commodity or a specific index, and the investor's right to receive the contingent payment is separable, the issuer should allocate the proceeds between the debt instrument and the investor's stated right to receive the contingent payment.

EITF 86-28

As the applicable index value increases, the issuer should recognise a liability for the amount that the contingent payment exceeds the amount, if any, originally attributed to the contingent payment feature. The liability for the contingent payment feature should be based on the applicable index value at the balance sheet date. The EITF discussed the appropriateness of hedge accounting to account for changes in the liability but expressed a number of concerns and reservations.

The proceeds of debt securities issued with detachable stock purchase warrants should be allocated based on the fair values of the two elements of the security at the date of issue. The portion relating to the warrants should be accounted for as paid-in capital.

APB 14.16

IAS 39.47   After initial recognition, an entity should measure all financial liabilities at amortised cost using the effective interest method, except for:

- financial liabilities at fair value through profit or loss. Such liabilities, including derivatives that are liabilities, should be measured at fair value except for a derivative liability that is linked to and must be settled by delivery of an unquoted equity instrument whose fair value cannot be reliably measured, which should be measured at cost;

- financial liabilities that arise when a transfer of a financial asset does not qualify for derecognition or is accounted for using the continuing involvement approach (see derecognition rules at section 11.3.3); and

- financial liabilities that are designated as hedged items and that are subject to measurement under the hedge accounting requirements which can override the general accounting requirements (see hedge accounting rules at section 13.3).

IAS 39.9   The amortised cost of a financial liability is the amount at which the liability is measured at initial recognition minus principal repayments, plus the cumulative amortisation, using the effective interest method (see below), of any difference between that initial amount and the maturity amount.

11.7.1   Allocation of finance costs

IAS 39.9   The amortisation of a financial liability and the interest expense is calculated using the effective interest method. The effective interest rate is the rate that exactly discounts estimated future cash payments or receipts through the expected life of the financial instrument or, when appropriate, a shorter period to the net carrying amount of the financial liability. When calculating the effective interest rate, an entity should estimate cash flows considering all contractual terms of the financial instrument. The calculation includes all fees and points paid or received between parties to the contract that are an integral part of the effective interest rate, transaction costs, and all other premiums or discounts.

IAS 39.AG8   If an entity revises its estimates of payments or receipts, the entity should adjust the carrying amount of the financial liability to reflect actual and revised estimated cash flows. The entity recalculates the carrying amount by computing the present value of estimated future cash flows at the financial instrument's original effective interest rate. The adjustment is recognised as income or expense in profit or loss.

IAS 39.55   A gain or loss on a financial liability classified as at fair value through profit or loss should be recognised in profit or loss. Some of this gain or loss is likely to include a component of accrued interest but there is no requirement to show this amount within the profit and loss caption for interest, or to disaggregate this component from the other changes in fair value that may be due to factors such as foreign currency retranslation, movements in the entity's credit rating and changes in market interest rates.

11.7.1   Allocation of finance costs

The borrower's periodic interest cost is calculated using the 'interest method' based on the estimated outstanding term of the debt. The difference between the present value and face amount should be treated as a premium and amortised as interest expense over the term of the debt. In estimating the term of the debt, the borrower would consider its plans, ability, and intent to service the debt.   *APB 21.15*   *APB 12.16*

Debt issue costs should be reported in the balance sheet as deferred charges and amortised (by the interest method) over the same period used in determining interest cost.   *APB 21.16*   *EITF 86-15*

Section 12   Financial instruments: Shareholders' equity

12.1   AUTHORITATIVE PRONOUNCEMENTS

- Framework
- IAS 1
- IAS 10
- IAS 16

- IAS 21
- IAS 32
- IAS 38

12.2   SHAREHOLDERS' EQUITY

IAS F.49,65   The Framework defines equity as the residual of assets minus liabilities. Occasionally instruments may be issued by an entity of a hybrid nature combining aspects of both debt and equity. The Framework recognises that equity may be sub-classified in the balance sheet. Such sub-classification – for example, funds contributed by shareholders, retained earnings, reserves representing capital appropriations or capital maintenance adjustments – can be relevant for the users of the financial statements as they may indicate legal or other restrictions on the entity's ability to apply its equity. The sub-classification may also reflect the differing rights of various parties in the distribution of dividends or repayment of equity.

IAS 1.75-76   Equity capital and reserves should be analysed on the face of the balance sheet, or in the footnotes, showing separately the various classes of share capital and reserves. However, the Standards do not specifically name the categories that should be identified at a minimum.

Section 12   Financial instruments: Shareholders' equity

12.1   AUTHORITATIVE PRONOUNCEMENTS

- ARB 43
- APB 6
- APB 12
- APB 14
- APB 29
- FAS 5
- FAS 52

- FAS 84
- FAS 87
- FAS 115
- FAS 129
- FAS 130
- FAS 150

In May 2003, the FASB issued FAS 150 *Accounting for Certain Financial Instruments with Characteristics of both Liabilities and Equity*. This Statement established standards for classifying and measuring as liabilities certain financial instruments that have characteristics of both liabilities and equity.

COMMENT

FAS 150 is the first phase of the FASB's Liabilities and Equity Project. This Statement deals only with certain freestanding financial instruments and does not address issues such as bifurcation of financial instruments with liability and equity components and accounting for instruments indexed both to the issuer's shares and another underlying. Phase II of the project will likely address these and other areas.

FAS 150 generally must be applied immediately to instruments entered into or modified after 31 May 2003 and to all other instruments as of the beginning of the first interim period beginning after 15 June 2003 as a cumulative effect of a change in accounting principle.

12.2   STOCKHOLDERS' EQUITY

The items that are normally shown under the caption 'stockholders' equity' are common stock, additional paid-in capital, other additional capital, retained earnings, and accumulated other comprehensive income.

Financial instruments issued in the form of shares that are mandatorily redeemable on a fixed or determinable date or upon an event certain to occur should be classified as liabilities.   *FAS 150.9*

The following must be shown on the balance sheet in the sequence presented below:

- non-redeemable preferred stocks;
- common stocks (see section 12.5);
- additional paid-in capital (or any other additional capital) (see section 12.6);
- retained earnings (see section 12.7); and
- cumulative other comprehensive income (see section 12.8).

IAS 32.15,26,28 All non-derivative financial instruments, including preferred shares and redeemable shares, issued by an entity should be analysed and the equity and liability components of those instruments should be accounted for separately. Derivative financial instruments that have settlement options that give one party the choice over how they are settled are classified as equity only if all possible settlement alternatives would result in them being equity instruments.

12.3   DISTINCTION BETWEEN DEBT AND EQUITY

IAS 32.15 The issuer of a financial instrument should classify it, or its component parts, as a financial liability or equity instrument, in accordance with its substance.

IAS 32.11 An equity instrument is any contract that evidences a residual interest in the assets of an entity after deducting all of its liabilities.

IAS 32.11 A financial liability is any liability that is:

- a contractual obligation:
    - to deliver cash or another financial asset to another entity; or
    - to exchange financial assets or financial liabilities with another entity under conditions that are potentially unfavourable to the entity; or
- a contract that will or may be settled in the entity's own equity instruments and is:
    - a non-derivative for which the entity is or may be obliged to deliver a variable number of the entity's own equity instruments; or
    - a derivative that will or may be settled other than by the exchange of a fixed amount of cash or another financial asset for a fixed number of the entity's own equity instruments. For this purpose, the entity's own equity instruments do not include instruments that are themselves contracts for the future receipt or delivery of the entity's own equity instruments.

IAS 32.18 In determining the classification between equity and liabilities substance takes precedence over legal form. For example a preference share that provides for a mandatory redemption by the issuer for a fixed or determinable amount at a fixed or determinable date in the future is a financial liability.

IAS 32.19,25 If the entity does not have the unconditional right to avoid delivering cash or another financial asset, the obligation is a financial liability. However, a contingent settlement provision that provides for settlement in cash or another financial asset only in the event of liquidation of the issuer does not make the instrument a financial liability.

IAS 32.22 An instrument is an equity instrument if it involves settlement of a fixed number of own equity instruments in exchange for a fixed amount of cash or another financial asset. Any consideration received is added directly to equity.

IAS 32.21,24 A contract is not an equity instrument solely because it results in delivery of an entity's own equity. For example a contract that requires delivery of a variable

Changes in stockholders' equity accounts should be presented in a statement or in the notes for the same periods that income statements are required. *S-X 5-03.04*

Individual classes of common shares must be identified on the face of the balance sheet (see section 12.5.3). If there is more than one issue of redeemable preferred stocks or non-redeemable preferred stocks outstanding, the details concerning each issue may be presented in the notes. However, the preferential rights of preferred stockholders in the event of liquidation must be shown in the equity section on the face of the balance sheet. *S-X 5-02.28-31*

FAS 129.6

12.3   DISTINCTION BETWEEN DEBT AND EQUITY

Under the definitions of assets and liabilities in the FASB's conceptual framework, liabilities are claims to the entity's assets while equity is the residual interest in the assets of an entity that remains after deducting its liabilities. Its key distinguishing feature is that equity does not carry 'an unconditional right to receive future transfers of assets from the entity except in liquidation, and then only after liabilities have been satisfied'. *CON 6.54,61*

When evaluating a capital instrument, this model first requires the issuer to determine whether the instrument qualifies as a liability; if it does not, it should be included in equity. In concept, this test requires all shares (irrespective of priority to participate in distributions) to be included as equity (see section 12).

FAS 150 generally requires liability classification for two broad classes of financial instruments: *FAS 150.9-12*

- instruments that represent, or are indexed to, an obligation to buy back the issuer's shares, regardless of whether the instrument is settled on a net-cash or gross physical basis (e.g. mandatorily redeemable equity instruments; written options that give the counterparty the right to require the issuer to buy back shares (written puts); and, forward contracts that require the issuer to purchase shares (forward purchases)); and
- obligations that can be settled in shares but meet one of the following conditions:
    (a) derive their value predominantly from some other underlying;
    (b) have a fixed value; or
    (c) have a value to the counterparty that moves in the opposite direction as the issuer's shares.

COMMENT

FAS 150 generally must be applied immediately to instruments entered into or modified after 31 May 2003 and to all other instruments as of the beginning of the first interim period beginning after 15 June 2003 as a cumulative effect of a change in accounting principle.

Some of the provisions of FAS 150 are consistent with FASB CON 6 *Elements of Financial Statements*. The remaining provisions are consistent with the FASB's plans to amend CON 6 although that amendment is deferred until the FASB has concluded its deliberations on the second phase of its liabilities and equity project. That next phase will deal with certain compound financial instruments including puttable shares, convertible bonds, and dual-indexed financial instruments.

number of own equity instruments for a fixed amount of cash or requires delivery of a fixed number of own equity instruments for a variable amount of cash is a financial liability.

IAS 32.26   If a derivative financial instrument has settlement options that give one party the choice over how it is settled, it is equity only if all possible settlement alternatives would result in it being an equity instrument.

IAS 32.28   The issuer of a non-derivative financial instrument must evaluate the instrument to determine whether it contains both a liability and equity component and, if so, the components of this compound financial instrument must be accounted for separately and shown separately on the balance sheet (commonly referred to as 'split accounting').

IAS 32.AG29   When classifying a financial instrument in the consolidated financial statements, an entity must consider all terms and conditions agreed between members of the group and holders of the instrument, e.g. a financial instrument that a subsidiary has correctly classified as equity may also be subject to a guarantee issued by the parent company to the instrument holder and in fact for the group as a whole be a liability, and should be disclosed as such in the consolidated financial statements.

IAS 32.35   Interest, dividends, losses and gains relating to a financial instrument, or a component part thereof, that is classified as a financial liability should be recognised as income or expense in profit or loss. Distributions to holders of equity instruments should be debited directly to equity.

IAS 32.36   The classification of the financial instrument between a financial liability and equity determines whether interest, dividends, losses and gains are recognised as income or expense in profit and loss. Thus dividend payments on shares wholly recognised as financial liabilities are recognised as an expense similar to interest on bonds, and gains and losses on refinancings of equity instruments are recognised as changes in equity.

The following freestanding financial instruments should be classified as liabilities (or assets in some circumstances):

- A financial instrument issued in the form of shares that is mandatorily redeemable (i.e. that embodies an unconditional obligation requiring the issuer to redeem it by transferring its assets at a specified or determinable date (or dates) or on an event that is certain to occur) unless the redemption is required to occur only on the liquidation or termination of the reporting entity.   *FAS 150.9*

- A financial instrument, other than an outstanding share, that, at inception, embodies an obligation to repurchase the issuer's equity shares, or is indexed to such an obligation, and that requires or may require the issuer to settle the obligation by transferring assets.   *FAS 150.11*

- A financial instrument that embodies an unconditional obligation, or a financial instrument other than an outstanding share that embodies a conditional obligation, that the issuer must or may settle by issuing a variable number of its equity shares, if, at inception, the monetary value of the obligation is based solely or predominantly on any of the following: *FAS 150.12*

  - A fixed monetary amount known at inception, e.g. a payable settleable with a variable number of the issuer's equity shares;

  - Variations in something other than the fair value of the issuer's equity shares (e.g. a financial instrument indexed to the S&P 500) and settleable with a variable number of the issuer's equity shares; or

  - Variations inversely related to changes in the fair value of the issuer's equity shares (e.g. a written put option that could be net share settled).

FAS 150 applies to freestanding financial instruments and does not apply to features embedded in a financial instrument that is not a derivative in its entirety.   *FAS 150.13-15*

FAS 150 does not affect the timing of recognition or measurement of financial instruments issued as contingent consideration in a business combination. However, the classification of a financial instrument, when recognised, would follow the guidance in FAS 150.   *FAS 150.16*

FAS 150 does not apply to obligations under stock-based compensation arrangements accounted for under APB 25 or FAS 123R but would apply to a freestanding financial instrument issued under a stock-based compensation arrangement but no longer subject to APB 25 or FAS 123R, e.g. mandatorily redeemable shares issued on exercise of an employee stock option.   *FAS 150.17*

Mandatorily redeemable financial instruments should be initially measured at fair value. Subsequent measurement should be in one of two ways: *FAS 150.20-22*

- If the settlement amount and date are fixed, subsequent measurement should be at the present value of the settlement amount with interest accrued at the implicit rate at inception.

- If either the settlement amount or date varies, subsequent measurement should be at the amount that would be paid if settlement occurred at the reporting date, recognising any resulting changes in that amount from the previous reporting date as interest cost.

All other financial instruments within the scope of FAS 150 should be initially measured at fair value. If a conditionally redeemable instrument becomes   *FAS 150.23-24*

12.4   CONVERTIBLE DEBT

IAS 32.29   An entity recognises separately the components of a financial instrument that (a) creates a financial liability of the entity and (b) grants an option to the holder of the instrument to convert it into an equity instrument of the entity.   For example, a bond or similar instrument convertible by the holder into a fixed number of ordinary shares of the entity is a compound financial instrument.   From the perspective of the entity, such an instrument comprises two components: a financial liability (a contractual arrangement to deliver cash or another financial asset) and an equity instrument (a call option granting the holder the right, for a specified period of time, to convert it into a fixed number of ordinary shares of the entity) and accordingly the entity presents the liability and equity components separately on its balance sheet.

IAS 32.30   Classification of the liability and equity components of a convertible instrument is not revised as a result of a change in the likelihood that a conversion option will be exercised, even when exercise of the option may appear to have become economically advantageous to some holders.

IAS 32.31   Equity instruments are instruments that evidence a residual interest in the assets of an entity after deducting all of its liabilities.   Therefore, when the initial carrying amount of a compound financial instrument is allocated to its equity and liability components, the equity component is assigned the residual amount after deducting from the fair value of the instrument as a whole the amount separately determined for the liability component.   The value of any derivative features (such as a call option) embedded in the compound financial instrument other than the equity component (such as an equity conversion option) is included in the liability component.   The sum of the carrying amounts assigned to the liability and equity components on initial recognition is always equal to the fair value that would be ascribed to the instrument as a whole.   No gain or loss arises from initially recognising the components of the instrument separately.

12.4.1   Convertible debt with a premium put

IAS 32.30   An entity may issue convertible bonds at par with a 'premium put' that allows the investor to redeem the bonds at a multiple of their par value before maturity.   At the date of issuance, the issuer will recognise the equity element and liability element of the financial instrument separately.   Subsequently, the classification is not revised because of a change in circumstances.

mandatorily redeemable, on reclassification the issuer should measure the liability initially at fair value with a corresponding reduction to equity, recognising no gain or loss. Otherwise, financial instruments should be measured subsequently at fair value with changes in fair value recognised in earnings.

Measurement of financial instruments within the scope of FAS 133 is covered in section 13.3 below.

12.4   CONVERTIBLE DEBT

The proceeds received from an issue of convertible debt (with a non-detachable conversion feature) should all be credited to a liability account, as an allocation of the proceeds to the conversion option is not permitted due to the inseparability of the debt and the conversion option. However, where the debt is issued with a non-detachable conversion feature that is in the money at the commitment date (a beneficial conversion feature), the beneficial conversion feature should be recognised separately at issuance. The conversion feature should be recognised by allocating a portion of the proceeds equal to the intrinsic value of the feature to additional paid-in capital. The intrinsic value should be measured as the difference between the conversion price and the fair value of the stock or securities into which the debt is convertible.

APB 14.12

EITF 98-5
EITF 00-27
EITF 01-1

On conversion, the principal carrying amount of the debt, together with accrued interest to the date of conversion should be credited to capital as the cost of securities issued. The rule applies in all situations even where the terms of conversion provide that the former debt holder forfeits any accrued but unpaid interest at the date of conversion.

EITF 85-17

If convertible debt is issued at a substantial premium over face value, i.e. the conversion option is priced at a discount, the premium should be accounted for as paid-in capital. This approach is necessary to avoid overstating the convertible debt and thereby producing an abnormally low (or even negative) finance cost.

APB 14.18

Where the terms of conversion of convertible debt have been altered for a limited period of time so as to induce holders to convert, an expense equal to the fair value of the additional securities or other consideration issued to induce the conversion should be recorded. This expense is measured to the date the inducement offer is accepted by the convertible debt holder and should not be reported as an extraordinary item.

FAS 84.2-4

12.4.1   Convertible debt with a premium put

The EITF has considered the accounting issues arising when a convertible bond is issued at par with a 'premium put'. Such instruments allow the investor to redeem the bonds for cash at a multiple of the bond's par value at a date or dates prior to maturity; if the put is not exercised, it expires.

EITF 85-29

The EITF reached a consensus that the issuer should accrue for the put premium over the period from issuance to the initial put date, regardless of changes in the market value of the debt or underlying common stock.

If the put expires unexercised and at that time the market value of the common stock under conversion exceeds the put price, the put premium should be credited

12.5   SHARE CAPITAL

IAS 32.16   An instrument is an equity instrument if, and only if, both conditions (a) and (b) below are met:

(a)   the instrument includes no contractual obligation:

    (i)   to deliver cash or another financial asset to another entity; or

    (ii)   to exchange financial assets or financial liabilities with another entity under conditions that are potentially unfavourable to the issuer;

(b)   if the instrument will or may be settled in the issuer's own equity instruments, it is:

    (i)   a non-derivative that includes no contractual obligation for the issuer to deliver a variable number of its own equity instruments; or

    (ii)   a derivative that will be settled only by the issuer exchanging a fixed amount of cash or another financial asset for a fixed number of its own equity instruments.   For this purpose the issuer's own equity instruments do not include instruments that are themselves contracts for the future receipt or delivery of the issuer's own equity instruments.

IAS 32 emphasises that a contractual obligation, including one arising from a derivative financial instrument, that will or may result in the future receipt or delivery of the issuer's own equity instruments, but does not meet conditions (a) and (b) above, is not an equity instrument.

IAS 32.22   An instrument is an equity instrument if it involves settlement of a fixed number of own equity instruments in exchange for a fixed amount of cash or another financial asset.   Any consideration received is added directly to equity.

IAS 32.21,24   A contract is not an equity instrument solely because it results in delivery of an entity's own equity.   For example a contract that requires delivery of a variable number of own equity instruments for a fixed amount of cash or requires delivery of a fixed number of own equity instruments for a variable amount of cash is a financial liability.

IAS 32.26   If a derivative financial instrument has settlement options that give one party the choice over how it is settled, it is equity only if all possible settlement alternatives would result in it being an equity instrument.

IAS 32.15,28,31   A non-derivative financial instrument may contain both a financial liability and an equity component.   The issuer of such a compound financial instrument should separate these parts and classify each separately, in accordance with their substance. The value that is prescribed to the equity component of a compound instrument is the residual amount after deducting from the fair value of the instrument the amount separately determined for the liability component.

to additional paid-in capital. If the put price exceeds the market value of the common stock under conversion, the put premium should be amortised as a yield adjustment over the remaining term of the debt.

Such bonds should not be included in equity.

12.5   CAPITAL STOCK

Under the FASB's conceptual framework, all shares (irrespective of priority to participate in distributions) should be included as 'equity'. Equity is the difference between assets and liabilities and its key distinguishing feature is that it does not carry 'an unconditional right to receive future transfers of assets from the enterprise except in liquidation, and then only after liabilities have been satisfied'.

FAS 150 generally requires liability classification for two broad classes of financial instruments: *FAS 150.9-12*

- instruments that represent, or are indexed to, an obligation to buy back the issuer's shares, regardless of whether the instrument is settled on a net-cash or gross physical basis (e.g. mandatorily redeemable equity instruments; written options that give the counterparty the right to require the issuer to buy back shares (written puts); and, forward contracts that require the issuer to purchase shares (forward purchases)); and

- obligations that can be settled in shares but meet one of the following conditions:

  (a)   derive their value predominantly from some other underlying;

  (b)   have a fixed value; or

  (c)   have a value to the counterparty that moves in the opposite direction as the issuer's shares.

In practice, most private companies include all shares within stockholders' equity. The SEC has expressed its concern that the traditional approach of showing all shares in stockholders' equity does 'not provide the most meaningful presentation' of the financial obligations attached to certain securities. As a result, public companies were required to present amounts in respect of mandatorily redeemable preferred stock separately on the face of the balance sheet between liabilities and stockholders' equity. This classification is sometimes referred to as 'temporary equity'.   *S-X 5-02.28*

This presentation is no longer permitted for instruments that must be classified as liabilities under FAS 150. However, for redeemable shares that are not accounted for as liabilities under FAS 150 (i.e. because they are contingently or optionally redeemable), public companies must continue to classify the redemption amount associated with those instruments outside of permanent equity in 'temporary equity').

COMMENT

FAS 150 generally must be applied immediately to instruments entered into or modified after 31 May 2003 and to all other instruments as of the beginning of the first interim period beginning after 15 June 2003 as a cumulative effect of a change in accounting principle.

12.5.1   Equity instruments

A   Accounting

IAS 32.22   The consideration received from the issue of equity instruments should be credited to equity.

IAS 32.31   Equity instruments are instruments that evidence a residual interest in the assets of an entity after deducting all of its liabilities. Therefore, when the initial carrying amount of a compound financial instrument is allocated to its equity and liability components, the equity component is assigned the residual amount after deducting from the fair value of the instrument as a whole the amount separately determined for the liability component. The sum of the carrying amounts assigned to the liability and equity components on initial recognition is always equal to the fair value that would be ascribed to the instrument as a whole. No gain or loss arises from initially recognising the components of the instrument separately.

IAS 32.37   The transaction costs of an equity transaction are accounted for as a deduction from equity (net of any related income tax benefit) to the extent they are incremental costs directly attributable to the equity transaction that otherwise would have been avoided. The costs of an equity transaction that is abandoned are recognised as an expense.

IAS 32.38   Transaction costs that relate to the issue of a compound financial instrument are allocated to the liability and equity components of the instrument in proportion to the allocation of proceeds. Transaction costs that relate jointly to more than one transaction (for example, costs of a concurrent offering of some shares and a stock exchange listing of other shares) are allocated to those transactions using a basis of allocation that is rational and consistent with similar transactions.

IAS 32.36   Changes in the fair value of an equity instrument are not recognised in the financial statements.

B   Cash dividends

IAS 10.12   Dividends to holders of equity instruments that are declared after the balance sheet date should not be recognised as a liability at the balance sheet date.

C   Stock dividends (scrip dividends)

IFRSs do not provide specific guidance on accounting for stock dividends. Timing of the recognition of stock dividends would be subject to the same rules as recognition of cash dividends. Typically, stock dividends will result at least in a transfer from retained earnings or similar free reserves to share capital for the nominal value of the shares issued.

D   Dividends-in-kind

IFRSs do not provide for specific guidance on accounting for dividends-in-kind.

12.5.1   Common stock

A   *Accounting*

Common stock issued by an entity is recorded at par value.   Differences between the fair value of the proceeds of the issue and the par value are recorded as additional paid-in capital, subject to any state corporation law.

When no-par value stock is issued, the common stock account is credited with the entire proceeds of the issue.   Some states permit the issue of no-par-value stock and either require or allow such stock to have a stated value, usually the minimum price at which the stock may be issued.   Any excess of proceeds received from the issue over stated value is credited to additional paid-in capital. *S-X 5-02.30*

If a company receives a note (rather than cash) as a contribution to its equity (from an issue of capital stock or a contribution to paid-in capital), the note receivable should be reported as a reduction of shareholders' equity.   It is not appropriate (except in very limited circumstances when there is substantial evidence of ability and intent to pay within a reasonably short period of time) for the receivable to be reported as an asset. *EITF 85-1 SAB 40 (Topic 4-E)*

For a number of business reasons, a company may enter into contracts that are indexed to, and sometimes settled in, its own stock.   Examples of these contracts include written put options, written call options (and warrants), purchased put options, purchased call options, forward sale contracts, and forward purchase contracts.   These contracts may be settled using a variety of settlement methods, or the issuing company or counterparty may have a choice of settlement methods and may be either freestanding or embedded in another financial instrument. EITF 96-13 and EITF 00-19 provide guidance for the classification and measurement of freestanding contracts that are indexed to, and potentially settled in, a company's own stock. *EITF 96-13 EITF 00-19*

B   *Cash dividends*

Dividends are an appropriation of retained earnings and are recognised at the point of time that they are formally declared by the board of directors.   Usually, common dividends are declared on a quarterly basis.

C   *Stock dividends*

Stock dividends should be accounted for by transferring from retained earnings to capital stock and additional paid-in capital an amount equal to the fair value of the additional shares issued.   However, if the number of additional shares issued as a stock dividend is so small in comparison with the shares previously outstanding, say 20% to 25%, that the share issue would not normally influence the unit market price of the stock, the transaction should be accounted for as a stock split and there is no need to capitalise retained earnings. *ARB 43 Ch 7B.10-13*

D   *Dividends-in-kind*

Dividends-in-kind are distributions of non-monetary assets (other than an enterprise's own capital stock) to stockholders.   They should be recorded at the fair value of the asset transferred and a gain or loss recognised on the disposition of the asset (see section 19.4.4 for exceptions to this rule). *APB 29.18*

12.5.2 Redeemable preferred shares

There are no specific rules under IFRSs regarding redeemable preferred shares. However, such instruments are discussed and the general rules that are applicable, as discussed above under section 12.5, will require separate recognition of the equity and liability components of such instruments. Where preferred shares are redeemable at the option of the holder, the issuing entity should recognise a liability.

12.5.3 Disclosure about shares

A   General

IAS 1.76   An entity should disclose the following on the face of the balance sheet or in the notes:

- for each class of share capital:
  - the number of shares authorised;
  - the number of shares issued and fully paid, and issued but not fully paid;
  - par value per share, or that the shares have no par value;

12.5.2   Redeemable preferred stocks

FAS 150 requires that any of various financial instruments that are issued in the   *FAS 150.9*
form of shares that are mandatorily redeemable on a fixed or determinable date or
upon an event certain to occur be classified as liabilities.   Shares are considered
mandatorily redeemable if they are subject to an unconditional obligation to be
redeemed by transferring assets (e.g. cash or other assets).   However, if the
instruments are redeemable only upon the liquidation or termination of the
reporting entity, those instruments are not considered mandatorily redeemable.

Mandatorily redeemable instruments initially should be recognised at their fair value.   *FAS 150.20-24*
In most cases, the fair value of an instrument at its issuance date will be the gross
proceeds received (we believe that issuance costs should be accounted for as a
separate deferred charge by analogy to APB 21).   A mandatorily redeemable
instrument that has a fixed redemption amount (that exceeds its initial fair value)
and a fixed redemption date should be accreted to the redemption amount using the
effective interest method, similar to the accounting for debt issued at a discount
under APB 21.   If the redemption amount varies or the redemption date is
unknown, the instrument should be carried at the amount of cash that would be
paid under the conditions specified in the contract (i.e. the settlement amount) if the
shares were repurchased or redeemed at the reporting date.

If the redemption amount is denominated in a foreign currency, mandatorily
redeemable shares should be measured as described above and then remeasured
under FAS 52.

Because mandatorily redeemable equity instruments are liabilities, any dividends or
accretion on such instruments are presented as interest expense.

Dividend costs of increasing rate preferred stock, e.g. non-redeemable preferred   *SAB 68*
stock with gradually increasing dividends in the first few years of issue preceding   *(Topic 5-Q)*
commencement of the perpetual dividend, should not be based on the stated
dividend schedule.   Instead, SAB 68 requires imputation of a market rate dividend
during the initial period.   A discount will be recorded at the date of issue of such
preferred stock (being the present value of the difference between the dividends in
the early years and the perpetual dividend for that same period, using a discount rate
based on the market rate for dividend yield on comparable preferred stocks) and
should be amortised directly to retained earnings over the period preceding the
commencement of the perpetual dividend using the interest method.   The   *S-X 4-07*
discount should be shown separately as a deduction from the applicable account.

12.5.3   Disclosure about stocks

A   General

For each type and class of stock the number of shares issued or outstanding, the   *S-X 5-02.30*
dollar amount thereof and if convertible, the fact that they are, should be disclosed
on the face of the balance sheet.

For each type and class of stock the following information should be disclosed on
the face of the balance sheet or in a note:

- the title of the issue, number of shares authorised and for convertible shares,
  the basis of conversion; and

- – a reconciliation of the number of shares outstanding at the beginning and at the end of the period;
- – the rights, preferences and restrictions attaching to that class including restrictions on the distribution of dividends and the repayment of capital;
- – shares in the entity held by the entity itself or by subsidiaries or associates of the entity; and
- – shares reserved for issue under options and contracts for the sale of shares, including the terms and amounts; and
- • a description of the nature and purpose of each reserve within equity.

IAS 1.77 An entity without share capital, such as a partnership, should disclose information equivalent to that required above, showing changes during the period in each category of equity interest and the rights, preferences and restrictions attaching to each category of equity interest.

IAS 1.96 An entity should present a statement of changes in equity showing on the face of the statement:

- • the profit or loss for the period;
- • each item of income and expense for the period that, as required by other Standards or by Interpretations, is recognised directly in equity, and the total of these items;
- • total income and expense for the period (calculated as the sum of the two above), showing separately the total amounts attributable to equity holders of the parent and to minority interest; and
- • for each component of equity, the effects of changes in accounting policies and corrections of errors recognised in accordance with IAS 8 *Accounting Policies, Changes in Accounting Estimates and Errors.*

A statement of changes in equity that comprises only the items above should be titled a statement of recognised income and expense.

IAS 1.97 In addition, an entity should present, either within this statement or in the notes:

- • the amounts of transactions with equity holders acting in their capacity as equity holders, showing separately distributions to equity holders;
- • the balance of retained earnings (i.e. accumulated profit or loss) at the beginning of the period and at the balance sheet date, and the changes during the period; and
- • a reconciliation between the carrying amount of each class of contributed equity and each reserve at the beginning and the end of the period, separately disclosing each change.

There are additional disclosures required by IAS 32 for financial instruments, including equity instruments, in general and these are detailed within section 14.

B *Dividends*

IAS 1.95 An entity should disclose, either on the face of the income statement or the statement of changes in equity, or in the notes, the amount of dividends recognised as distributions to equity holders during the period, and the related amount per share.

- the dollar amount of any common shares subscribed but unissued – the amounts receivable should be presented as a deduction from stockholders' equity.

In a note or separate statement disclose: *APB 12.10*

- for each period for which an income statement is presented, the changes in each type and class of stock; and

- changes in each type of stock (in aggregate) and in the number of shares outstanding for at least the most recent year.

An entity should explain, in summary within the financial statements, the rights and privileges of each type and class of stock outstanding.   Details of warrants or other rights to stock should also be disclosed (see section 12.5.5).   *FAS 129.4*

In addition to the general disclosures above, the income or loss applicable to common stock should be disclosed on the face of the profit and loss account when it is materially different from reported net income or loss.   The income or loss applicable to common stock is calculated by deducting the following amounts from net income or loss: *SAB 64 (Topic 6-B)*

- dividends on preferred stock (including arrears on cumulative preference stock); and

- periodic increases in the carrying amounts of instruments reported as redeemable preferred stock.

B   Preferred stocks

In addition to the general disclosures above, entities should disclose the aggregate preferential rights of preferred stockholders on involuntary liquidation, in the stockholders' equity section of the balance sheet.   Any restrictions on retained earnings that arise on such liquidations also should be disclosed.   *FAS 129.6 S-X 4-08(d)(1-2)*

Disclosure is also required of the following, either on the face of the balance sheet or in the notes: *FAS 129.4*

- any terms of conversion, if applicable;

- a general description of the voting rights;

- the dividend rate and whether participating cumulative or non-cumulative; and

- the aggregate or per share amounts at which preferred stock may be called or redeemed through sinking fund requirements or otherwise, and the dates when such events may occur.   *FAS 129.7(a)*

FAS 150 generally does not require additional disclosures beyond those required by existing accounting standards (this disclosure currently is required by FAS 129). Additionally, the following disclosures (which generally are consistent with the disclosures already required by ETF 00-19) are required for financial instruments within the scope of FAS 150:   *FAS 150.27*

- Settlement alternatives in the contract, if any, and the entity that controls the settlement alternatives.

- For each settlement alternative, issuers must disclose:

  (a)   the amount that would be paid, or the number of shares that would be issued and their fair value, determined under the conditions specified in the contract if the settlement were to occur at the reporting date;

IAS 1.125   An entity should also disclose the amount of dividends proposed or declared before the financial statements were authorised for issue but not recognised as a distribution to equity holders during the period, and the related amount per share, and the amount of any cumulative preference dividends not recognised.

C   Costs of an equity transaction

IAS 32.39   The amount of transaction costs accounted for as a deduction from equity in the period should be disclosed.   The related income tax recognised directly in equity should be included in the disclosure of the aggregate amount of current and deferred income tax credited or charged to equity that is disclosed under IAS 12 *Income Taxes.*

12.5.4   Treasury shares

IAS 32.33   If an entity reacquires its own equity instruments (treasury shares) these instruments should be deducted from equity by the amount of the consideration paid with no gain or loss recognised in the profit or loss on either the purchase, sale, issue or cancellation of own equity instruments.   Such treasury shares may either be acquired by the entity or by other companies within the consolidated group.

IAS 32.34   The amount of reduction to equity for treasury shares held should be disclosed separately either on the face of the balance sheet or in the notes.   An entity should provide disclosure, in accordance with IAS 24 *Related Party Disclosures,* if the entity or any of its subsidiaries reacquires its own shares from related parties.

(b)   how changes in the fair value of the issuer's equity shares would affect those settlement amounts;

(c)   the maximum amount that the issuer could be required to pay to redeem the instrument by physical settlement, if applicable;

(d)   the maximum number of shares that could be required to be issued, if applicable;

(e)   that a contract does not limit the amount that the issuer could be required to pay or the number of shares that the issuer could be required to issue, if applicable; and

(f)   for a forward contract or an option indexed to the issuer's equity shares, the forward price or option strike price, the number of issuer's shares to which the contract is indexed, and the settlement date or dates of the contract, as applicable.

C   *Dividends*

Dividends declared in a period are not disclosed in the income statement but are shown as a movement in shareholders' equity in a separate statement or note to the financial statements.   *S-X 3-04*

The per-share amount and aggregate amount should be disclosed by each class of stock and by type, e.g. cash or stock, for each period an income statement is presented.

The per-share and aggregate amounts of cumulative preferred dividends in arrears should be disclosed.   *FAS 129.7(a)*

Any restrictions that limit the payment of dividends by the registrant should be disclosed.   *S-X 4-08(e)*
FAS 5.18

12.5.4   Treasury stock

In the US, an enterprise may acquire shares of its own capital stock for purposes other than retirement, subject to state laws, and the requirements of listing agreements.   In such situations, the status of such shares is akin to that of authorised but unissued capital stock.

If treasury shares are reacquired for a purchase price significantly in excess of the current market price of the shares, it is presumed that the total purchase price includes amounts for stated/unstated rights or privileges (this will only apply when the shares are reacquired as a result of an offer to a limited group of shareholders as opposed to the whole class).   In such circumstances, the total purchase price should be allocated between the cost of the treasury shares and the cost of the rights/privileges (which is charged to income) based on their fair values at the date of the purchase agreement.   If no rights or privileges can be identified, the entire purchase price should be allocated to the cost of the treasury shares.   *FTB 85-6*

A   *Retirement of treasury stock*

When treasury stock is acquired with the intention of retiring the stock, the excess of the amount allocated to the price paid for the treasury stock over its par or stated value may either: *APB 6.12(a)*
ARB 43 Ch 1B

•   be charged entirely to retained earnings; or

12.5.5   Warrants

IAS 32.21,24 Warrants that allow the holder to subscribe for or purchase a fixed number of
IAS 32.AG13 nonputtable ordinary shares in the issuing entity in exchange for a fixed amount of
cash or another financial asset are equity instruments.   However, if the number of
ordinary shares to be issued is not fixed number or the amount of cash or other
financial assets receivable is not a fixed amount then the contract is a financial
liability and not an equity instrument.   In addition, if such a contract contains an
obligation for the entity to pay cash or another financial asset, it also gives rise to a
liability for the present value of the redemption amount.

12.6   SHARE PREMIUM

IAS 1.75,97 An entity should present a reconciliation between the carrying amount of each class
of contributed equity, separately disclosing each movement.

- allocated between additional paid-in capital arising from the same class of stock and retained earnings.

If the price paid is less than its par or stated value, the difference is credited to additional paid-in capital. The original capital balances relating to the shares acquired are eliminated.

If treasury stock is purchased at significantly above current market prices, amounts allocated to other elements of the transaction and the related accounting treatment should be disclosed.

FTB 85-6.3,16

B   Treasury stock acquired for purposes other than retirement

Treasury stock acquired for purposes other than retirement should be separately disclosed in the balance sheet as a deduction from stockholders' equity or alternatively accounted for as retired stock.

APB 6.12(b)

A gain on the sale of treasury stock should be credited to paid-in capital. Losses may be charged to paid-in capital but only to the extent of available net gains from previous sales or retirements of the same class of stock. Any excess should be charged against retained earnings.

ARB 43 Ch 1B

The dividends on treasury stock should not be credited to income.

ARB 43 Ch 1A

12.5.5   Warrants

The proceeds received on an issue of stock purchase warrants should be accounted for as paid-in capital. If the warrants are not exercised and lapse, the original treatment of the proceeds received is not changed.

APB 14.16

For warrants or rights outstanding as of the most recent balance sheet date, the following disclosures are required:

S-X 4-08(i)

- the title and aggregate amount of securities called for by warrants or rights outstanding;
- the period during which warrants or rights are exercisable; and
- the exercise price.

12.6   ADDITIONAL PAID-IN CAPITAL

The aggregate amount of additional paid-in capital should be disclosed as a separate item on the face of the balance sheet.

S-X 5-02.31(a)

An analysis of changes in additional paid-in capital should be presented in a note or separate statement in the form of a reconciliation of the beginning balance to the ending balance for each period for which an income statement is presented. All significant reconciling items should be described by appropriate captions.

S-X 3-04

Movements in additional paid-in capital arise due to:

- stock issued at amounts in excess of par or stated value or in a business combination;
- stock dividends;
- sale of treasury stock at a gain or loss;
- conversion of convertible preferred stock;

12.7   RETAINED EARNINGS

An entity should present, either on the face of the statement of changes in equity or in the notes, the balance of retained earnings at the beginning of the period and at the balance sheet date, and the change during the period.

12.8   OTHER RESERVES

A   Foreign currency translation reserve

IAS 21.52   Net exchange differences classified in a separate component of equity should be disclosed along with a reconciliation of the amount at the beginning and end of the period.

IAS 21.48   When the reporting entity disposes of its investment in a foreign operation, the cumulative amount of deferred exchange differences recorded in equity which relate to that entity should be recognised in profit or loss in the same period in which the gain or loss on disposal is recognised.

- issue and exercise of detachable stock warrants;
- donated assets from a related party, e.g. capital contributions;
- forgiveness of a debt from a stockholder; and
- expenses or liabilities paid by a principal stockholder.

Occasionally, common stock is issued at below par or stated value. The holder of shares issued at below par may nevertheless be required to pay the discount in the event of a liquidation where creditors will sustain a loss. The company may either create a 'discount on stock' account or charge such amount to additional paid-in capital to the extent available from the same class of stock.

12.7   RETAINED EARNINGS

Retained earnings should be disclosed separately on the balance sheet. Details of changes in retained earnings for each period presented should be presented either: *S-X 5-02.31(a)*
FAS 5.15
APB 12.10

- in a separate statement; or
- by combining the changes as part of the income statement.

The following is a list of events that may result in an entry to retained earnings:

- net income/loss for the year;
- dividends declared in the year;
- prior-period adjustments; and
- stock dividends.

Appropriated, e.g. for loss contingencies not accruable under FAS 5, and unappropriated retained earnings should be shown separately. *S-X 5-02.31(a)*

The nature and extent to which retained earnings is restricted should be disclosed. *APB 6.13*
Disclosure should also be made of significant restrictions on payment of dividends, *S-X 4-08(e)(1)* indicating their sources, pertinent provisions and the amount of retained earnings that is restricted or free of restrictions.

The amount of consolidated retained earnings represented by undistributed earnings *S-X 4-08(e)(2)* of 50% or less owned companies that are accounted for using the equity method should be disclosed.

12.8   CUMULATIVE OTHER COMPREHENSIVE INCOME

Cumulative other comprehensive income is a component of equity that is displayed *FAS 130.26* separately from additional paid-in capital and retained earnings. Accumulated balances for each classification in other comprehensive income should be presented on the face of the balance sheet, in a statement of changes in equity, or in notes to the financial statements. Items included in other comprehensive income should be classified based on their nature. Under existing accounting standards, other *FAS 130.17* comprehensive income should be classified separately into foreign currency items, unrealised gains and losses on derivative financial instruments and certain investments in debt and equity securities, and minimum pension liability adjustments.

Comprehensive income is discussed in section 1.6.6.

B   *Revaluation reserve*

IAS 16.39,41   Increases in the valuation of property, plant and equipment because of revaluation should be recorded in equity under the heading of revaluation surplus. The revaluation surplus included in equity may be transferred directly to retained earnings when the surplus is realised. The surplus may be realised on the retirement or disposal of the asset or as the asset is used by the entity. In the latter case, the amount of the surplus realised is the difference between depreciation based on the revalued carrying amount of the asset and depreciation based on the asset's original cost. The transfer from revaluation surplus to retained earnings is not made through profit or loss.

IAS 38.85,87   Increases in the valuation of intangible assets because of revaluation should be recorded in equity under the heading of revaluation surplus. The revaluation surplus may be transferred directly to retained earnings when it is realised.

IAS 16.77   A revaluation reserve should be disclosed separately.

C   *Gains and losses on remeasurement of certain financial assets to fair value*

IAS 32.94   Gains or losses on an available-for-sale financial asset should be recognised directly in equity until the financial asset is derecognised at which time the cumulative gain or loss previously recognised in equity should be recognised in the profit or loss for the period. Movements in such a reserve should be disclosed.

D   *Gains and losses on cash flow hedges recognised in equity*

IAS 32.59   Amounts recognised in equity and removed from equity (see hedge accounting rules at section 13.3) should be disclosed.

A   Foreign currency translation reserve

Where translation adjustments result from the translating an entity's financial statements from a foreign functional currency into the reporting currency, the translation adjustments should be reported in other comprehensive income and taken to a separate component of shareholders' equity.   On sale or liquidation of an investment in a foreign entity, the amount attributable to that entity and accumulated in the translation adjustment component of equity should be removed from the separate component of equity and reported as part of the gain or loss on sale or liquidation of the investment (see section 5.4.3).

FAS 52.13,14

B   Gains and losses on remeasurement to fair value

Where a designated cash flow hedge meets the hedge accounting criteria under FAS 133, to the extent that the hedge is effective, changes in the fair value of the derivative instrument are recognised in other comprehensive income and taken to a separate component of shareholders' equity until the hedged transaction affects earnings (see section 13.3).

FAS 133.30-31

Available-for-sale securities should be measured at fair value and unrealised gains and losses are included in other comprehensive income and taken to a separate component of shareholders' equity (see section 11.6).

FAS 115.12-13

C   Minimum pension liability

If the accumulated pension benefit obligation (value of accrued benefits without allowance for future salary increases) exceeds the fair value of the related pension scheme assets, an additional minimum liability may be required to be shown in the balance sheet.   If an additional minimum liability is recognised, an equal amount, but not to exceed the amount of unrecognised prior service cost, should be recognised as an intangible asset.   Any amount not recognised as an intangible asset should be reported in other comprehensive income and taken to a separate component of shareholders' equity (see section 23.4.7).

FAS 87.35-37

Section 13   Financial instruments: Derivatives and hedge accounting

13.1   AUTHORITATIVE PRONOUNCEMENTS

- IAS 39

13.2   SCOPE AND DEFINITIONS

13.2.1   Scope

IAS 39.2   IAS 39 *Financial Instruments: Recognition and Measurement* applies to all types of financial instruments, except for:

- interests in subsidiaries, associates and joint ventures that are accounted for under IAS 27 *Consolidated and Separate Financial Statements*, IAS 28 *Investments in Associates* or IAS 31 *Interests in Joint Ventures* (unless required to by one of these standards or the interest is a derivative that does not meet the definition of an equity instrument of the entity in IAS 32);

- rights under leases to which IAS 17 *Leases* applies are generally exempt although the derecognition, impairment and embedded derivative requirements are still applicable to some extent;

- employer's assets under employee benefit plans to which IAS 19 *Employee Benefits* applies;

- financial instruments issued by the entity that meet the IAS 32 definition of an equity instrument, although the holder of such instruments is generally required to apply the Standard;

- rights and obligations under insurance contracts as defined in IFRS 4 *Insurance Contracts* or under a contract that is within the scope of IFRS 4 because it contains a discretionary participation feature. However, this exclusion does not extend to certain derivatives embedded in such contracts and certain financial guarantee contracts;

- an acquirer's contingent consideration in business combinations;

- contracts between an acquirer and a vendor in a business combination to buy or sell an acquiree at a future date;

- loan commitments that cannot be settled net and have not been designated as financial liabilities at fair value through profit or loss (although these are subject to the derecognition provisions); and

Section 13   Financial instruments: Derivatives and hedge accounting

13.1   AUTHORITATIVE PRONOUNCEMENTS

- FAS 107
- FAS 130
- FAS 133

13.2   SCOPE AND DEFINITIONS

13.2.1   Scope

FAS 107 and FAS 133 apply to all entities that have financial instruments. The
FASB believe that certain contracts that otherwise meet the literal definition of a
derivative (see section 13.2.2) should not be accounted for as derivatives.
Accordingly, FAS 133 specifically excludes several types of contracts from the
scope.   These include:

FAS 107.7
FAS 133.5,10

- 'regular-way' (normal) securities trades, e.g. purchases or sales of securities that
  settle in the normal course for the particular security, however, a contract for
  an existing security that requires or permits net settlement is not a 'regular way'
  security trade;

- normal purchases and sales of non-financial instruments that are in quantities
  expected to be used or sold over a reasonable period in the normal course of
  business, e.g. the forward purchase of unleaded petrol by a rental car company
  for the quantity it expects to use in the next month.   Contracts that contain net
  settlement provisions may qualify as normal purchases/sales if it is probable, at
  inception and throughout the contract term, that the contract will not settle net
  and will result in physical delivery.   Option contracts and contracts that contain
  certain optionality features (other than power-related and capacity contracts) are
  not eligible for the normal purchases and sales exception;

- certain insurance contracts that compensate the holder only as a result of an
  identifiable insurable event;

- certain financial guarantee contracts that provide for payments to reimburse
  the guaranteed party for a loss because the debtor fails to pay by the due date
  and where the guaranteed party is exposed to the risk of non-payment both at
  inception of the financial guarantee and throughout its term.   Other financial
  guarantee contracts could be derivatives under FAS 133 if they provide for
  payments to be made in response to a change in an underlying, such as a
  decrease in a referenced entity's credit rating;

- most financial instruments, contracts and obligations under share-based payment transactions to which IFRS 2 *Share-based Payment* applies. However, the Standard does apply to contracts to buy or sell non-financial items in share-based transactions that can be settled net unless they are considered to be 'normal' sales and purchases (see below).

IAS 39.5 IAS 39 also applies to contracts to buy or sell non-financial items (such as commodity contracts) that can be settled net in cash unless the contract was originally entered into and continues to be held for the purpose of the receipt or delivery of the non-financial item in accordance with the entity's expected purchase, sale or usage requirements (a 'normal' purchase or sale).

IAS 39.6 There are various ways in which a contract to buy or sell a non-financial item can be settled net, including when:

- the terms of the contract permit either party to settle it net;

- the ability to settle the contract net is not explicit in its terms, but the entity has a practice of settling similar contracts net (whether with the counterparty, by entering into offsetting contracts or by selling the contract before its exercise or lapse);

- for similar contracts, the entity has a practice of taking delivery of the underlying and selling it within a short period after delivery for the purpose of generating a profit from short-term fluctuations in price or dealer's margin; and

- the non-financial item that is the subject of the contract is readily convertible to cash.

IAS 39.6,7 Contracts to buy or sell non-financial items to which b) or c) apply cannot take advantage of this 'normal' purchase or sale exemption. In addition a written option to buy or sell a non-financial item that can be settled net in cash or another financial instrument, or by exchanging financial instruments, in accordance with a) or d) cannot take advantage of this exemption.

13.2.2   What is a derivative?

IAS 39.9 A derivative is a financial instrument or other contract within the scope of IAS 39 with all three of the following characteristics:

- its value changes in response to the change in a specified interest rate, financial instrument price, commodity price, foreign exchange rate, index of prices or rates, a credit rating or credit index, or other variable, provided in the case of a non-financial variable that the variable is not specific to a party to the contract (sometimes called the 'underlying');

- it requires no initial net investment or an initial net investment that is smaller than would be required for other types of contracts that would be expected to have a similar response to changes in market factors; and

- it is settled at a future date.

IAS 39.AG9,12 Typical examples of derivatives are futures, forwards, swaps and options. A regular way purchase or sale gives rise to a derivative between trade and settlement date. However, because of the short duration of the commitment, IAS 39 does not recognise this as a derivative but instead provides special accounting provisions (see section 11.6.1 above).

- non-exchange traded contracts with underlyings based on the following:
    - climatic, geological, or other physical variables;
    - the price or value of a non-financial asset or liability of one of the parties that is not readily convertible to cash or does not require delivery of an asset that is readily convertible to cash; and
    - specified volumes of sales or service revenues of one of the parties;
- derivatives that serve as impediments to sales accounting, e.g. a residual value guarantee of a leased asset by the lessor that prevents the lease from being a sales-type lease or a call option that enables a transferor of financial instruments to repurchase the transferred assets and prevents sales accounting for the transfer;
- contracts issued or held by a reporting entity that are both (1) indexed to its own stock and (2) classified in stockholders' equity in its statement of financial position;   *FAS 133.11*
- contracts issued by an entity in connection with stock-based compensation arrangements addressed in FAS 123;
- contracts issued by the entity as contingent consideration in a business combination; and
- forward purchase contracts for the reporting entity's shares that require physical settlement.

The last three exceptions above do not apply to the counterparty in those contracts.

13.2.2 What is a derivative?

A derivative is a financial instrument or other contract with the following characteristics: *FAS 133.6*

- its cash flows or fair value must fluctuate and vary based on the changes in one or more *underlying* variables;
- the contract must be based on one or more *notional amounts* or payment provisions or both, even though title to that amount never changes hands. The *underlying* and *notional amount* determine the amount of settlement and even whether or not a settlement is required;
- the contract requires no *initial net investment*, or an insignificant initial net investment; and
- the contract can readily be settled by a net cash payment, or by the transfer of an asset that is readily convertible to cash.

Underlying – An underlying is a variable or index whose market movements cause the fair market value or cash flows of a derivative to fluctuate.   An underlying may be a price or rate of an asset or liability but it is not the asset or liability itself.   *FAS 133.7*

13.2.3   Embedded derivatives

IAS 39.10-11 A derivative may be a component of a hybrid instrument that includes both the derivative and a non-derivative host contract. Such derivatives – embedded derivatives – should be separated from the host contract and accounted for as a derivative if, and only if, all of the following conditions are met:

- the economic characteristics and risks of the embedded derivative are not closely related to the economic characteristics and risks of the host contract;
- a separate instrument with the same terms as the embedded derivative would meet the definition of a derivative; and
- the hybrid (combined) instrument is not measured at fair value with changes in fair value reported in profit or loss.

After separation of the embedded derivative, the host contract should be accounted for under the standard that is applicable to that contract.

IAS 39.10 A derivative that is attached to a financial instrument but has a different counterparty or is contractually transferable independently of that instrument is a separate financial instrument rather than an embedded derivative.

IAS 39.12 If an entity is required to separate an embedded derivative, but cannot separately measure the embedded derivative at either the acquisition date or at a subsequent financial reporting date, the entire combined contract should be accounted for as a financial instrument held for trading.

> **COMMENT**
>
> In April 2005, the IFRIC issued Draft Interpretation D-15 *Reassessment of Embedded Derivatives*. This Draft Interpretation proposes that an entity should assess whether an embedded derivative is required to be separated from the host contract and accounted for as a derivative when the entity first becomes a party to the contract, with subsequent reassessment required when, and only when, there is a change in the terms of the contract.

13.3   ACCOUNTING FOR DERIVATIVES AND HEDGES

13.3.1   General requirements

IAS 39.14,43 An entity should recognise a derivative on its balance sheet at fair value at the time it becomes a party to the contractual provisions of the instrument.

IAS 39.46 After initial recognition, an entity should measure derivative financial instruments at their fair value without any deduction for transaction costs that it may incur on sale or disposal. The only exception is where the derivative is linked to and must be settled by delivery of an unquoted equity instrument and this equity instrument does

Notional amount – While the underlying is the variable in a derivative, the notional amount is the fixed amount or quantity specified in the contract that determines the size of the change caused by the movement in the underlying.

Initial net investment – Derivatives are unique in that the parties do not have to initially invest in or exchange the notional amount.   Though some contracts can settle through physical delivery, e.g. futures and forwards, a derivative really represents an investment in the change in value caused by the underlying, and not an actual investment in the notional amount or quantity of the underlying.

FAS 133.8

13.2.3   Embedded derivatives

Derivatives may be embedded in other instruments, such as a debt instrument where interest payments fluctuate with changes in a recognised quoted share index or where the principal amount is affected by the price of gold.   An embedded derivative should be separated (bifurcated) and accounted for as a derivative instrument under FAS 133 when:

FAS 133.12-16

- the economic characteristics and risks of the embedded derivative are not clearly and closely related to the economic characteristics and risks of the host contract;

- the contract that includes the embedded derivative and the host contract is not re-measured at fair value; and

- the embedded derivative meets the definition of a derivative as set out above.

The bifurcation provisions above do not extend to a derivative embedded in another derivative, such as a cancellable swap.

13.3   ACCOUNTING FOR DERIVATIVES AND HEDGES

13.3.1   General requirements

All derivatives should be recorded on the balance sheet at fair value (see section 14.3F).

FAS 133.17

The accounting for changes in the fair value of a derivative (gains or losses) depends on whether the derivative has been designated and qualifies as part of a hedging relationship and, if so, on the reason for holding it.   The measurement rules for hedged items and hedging instruments are described in section 13.3G.

not have a quoted market price in an active market and its fair value cannot be reliably measured, in which case the derivative will be measured at cost.

The accounting for changes in the fair value of a derivative depend on whether the derivative has been designated and qualifies as part of a hedging relationship and these measurement rules are described in section 13.3.6.

IAS 39.86 IAS 39 recognises the following three types of hedge relationships for which it provides hedge accounting rules:

- fair value hedge – a hedge of the exposure to changes in the fair value of a recognised asset or liability, or an unrecognised firm commitment, or an identified portion of such an asset, liability or firm commitment, that is attributable to a particular risk and could affect profit or loss;

- cash flow hedge – a hedge of the exposure to variability in cash flows that (1) is attributable to a particular risk associated with a recognised asset, liability or highly probable forecast transaction and (2) could affect profit or loss; and

- hedge of a net investment in a foreign operation as defined in IAS 21 *The Effects of Changes in Foreign Exchange Rates.*

IAS 39.87 A hedge of a foreign currency risk of a firm commitment may be accounted for as a fair value hedge or a cash flow hedge.

13.3.2   Hedge criteria – all hedges

IAS 39.88 A hedging relationship qualifies for hedge accounting if, and only if, all of the following conditions are met:

- at the inception of the hedge there is formal designation and documentation of the hedging relationship and the entity's risk management objective and strategy for undertaking the hedge. That documentation should include identification of:
  - the hedging instrument;
  - the hedged item or transaction;
  - the nature of the risk being hedged; and
  - how the entity will assess the hedging instrument's effectiveness;
- the hedge is expected to be highly effective in achieving offsetting changes in fair value or cash flows attributable to the hedged risk, consistently with the originally documented risk management strategy for that particular hedging relationship;
- the effectiveness of the hedge can be reliably measured, i.e. the fair value or cash flows of the hedged item that are attributable to the hedged risk and the fair value of the hedging instrument can be reliably measured; and
- the hedge is assessed on an ongoing basis and determined actually to have been highly effective throughout the financial reporting periods for which the hedge was designated.

IAS 39.9,72 A hedging instrument is a designated derivative or non-derivative financial asset or financial liability whose fair value or cash flows are expected to offset changes in the fair value or cash flows of the item being hedged. However, a non-derivative financial asset or non-derivative financial liability may be designated as a hedging instrument for hedge accounting purposes only for a hedge of a foreign currency risk.

FAS 133 permits 'special accounting' for the following three categories of hedge   *FAS 133.18*
transactions:

- hedges of changes in the fair value of assets, liabilities, or firm commitments (referred to as fair value hedges);

- hedges of variable cash flows of recognised assets or liabilities, or of forecasted transactions (cash flow hedges); and

- hedges of foreign currency exposures of net investments in foreign operations.

Hedge accounting may only be applied when the hedge is effective and hedge criteria have been met.

Either all or a portion of a derivative may be designated as the hedging instrument. The proportion must be expressed as a percentage of the entire derivative so that the profile of risk exposures in the hedging portion is the same as that in the entire derivative.

13.3.2   Hedge criteria – all hedges

Specific hedge criteria exist regarding the different types of hedge identified above,   *FAS 133.18,20*
however, all hedges need to meet the following criteria:

- at inception, there must be formal documentation (designation) of the hedging relationship and the entity's risk management objective and strategy for undertaking the hedge, including identification of the derivative, the related hedged item, the nature of the particular risk being hedged, and how the hedging instrument's effectiveness will be assessed (including any decision to exclude certain components of a specific derivative's change in fair value, such as time value, from the assessment of hedge effectiveness);

- at inception and on an ongoing basis, the hedge must be expected to be highly effective in offsetting exposure due to changes in fair value or cash flows of the hedged item.   The effectiveness in achieving offsetting changes to the risk being hedged must be assessed consistently with the originally documented risk management strategy.   If the derivative provides only one-sided offset against the hedged risk, i.e. an option contract, the increases (or decreases) in the fair value or cash flows of the derivative must be expected to be highly effective in offsetting decreases (or increases) in the fair value or cash flows of the hedged item; and

- for a written option designated as a hedge, the combination of the hedged item and the written option must provide at least as much potential for gains as a result of favourable changes as exposure to losses from unfavourable changes. In other words, a percentage favourable change in the fair value of the combined instruments provides at least as much gain as would the loss incurred from an unfavourable change of the same percentage.   The impact of this requirement is that most written options will not qualify for hedge accounting.

IAS 39.AG94 A written option is likely to have a potential loss that is significantly greater that the potential gain on a hedged item and therefore does not qualify as a hedging instrument unless it is designated as a hedge of a purchased option.

IAS 39.73 Only instruments that involve a party external to the reporting entity can be designated as hedging instruments. Individual entities within a group may enter into hedging transactions with each other and these may qualify for hedge accounting at the individual entity level but they will be eliminated on consolidation.

IAS 39.74 Normally a financial instrument (or proportion thereof) can only be designated as a hedging instrument in its entirety. However, the intrinsic value of an option can be separated out from the total value of an option and be a hedging instrument. Similarly the spot element of a forward contract can be separated out from the interest element and designated as a hedging instrument. These exceptions are allowable on the basis that the elements can generally be reliably measured.

IAS 39.75 A proportion of a hedging instrument may be designated in a hedging relationship, but a hedging relationship may not be designated for only a portion of the time period in which the hedging instrument remains outstanding.

IAS 39.77 Two or more derivatives or non-derivatives, or proportions of them, may be viewed in combination and jointly designated as a hedging instrument.

13.3.3   Hedged item criteria – fair value and cash flow hedges

IAS 39.9,78 A hedged item is an asset, liability, firm commitment or highly probable forecast transaction that exposes the entity to risk of changes in fair value or changes in future cash flows and that, for hedge accounting purposes, is designated as being hedged. The hedged item could also be a group of such items with similar risk characteristics.

The following needs to be taken into account in designating hedged items:

IAS 39.79 • held-to-maturity investments cannot be a hedged item with respect to interest-rate or prepayment risk because designation as held-to-maturity requires an intention to hold until maturity without regard to changes in fair value or cash flows arising from changes in interest rates;

IAS 39.81 • if the hedged item is a financial asset or financial liability, it may be a hedged item with respect to only some of the risks associated with it, if effectiveness can be measured;

IAS 39.82 • if the hedged item is a non-financial asset or non-financial liability, it may be designated a hedged item only with respect to (1) foreign currency risks or (2) in its entirety for all risks, because of the difficulty of isolating any other specific risks other than foreign currency risk; and

IAS 39.83 • if similar assets or similar liabilities are aggregated and hedged as a group, the change in fair value attributable to the hedged risk for each individual item in the group should be expected to be approximately proportional to the overall change in fair value attributable to the hedged risk of the group.

IAS 39.80 Only assets, liabilities, firm commitments or highly probable forecast transactions that involve a party external to the entity can be designated as hedged items. It follows that hedge accounting can be applied to transactions between entities or segments in the same group only in the individual or separate financial statements of those entities or segments and not in the consolidated financial statements of the

13.3.3   Hedged item criteria – fair value and cash flow hedges

In order to qualify for accounting as a fair value or cash flow hedge, the hedged item   *FAS 133.21,28*
needs to meet the following additional criteria:

- if similar assets, liabilities, firm commitments, or transactions are aggregated and hedged as a portfolio, the individual items that make up the portfolio must share the risk exposure designated as being hedged in approximately the same magnitude;

- the hedged item presents an exposure that could affect reported earnings;

- the hedged item cannot be related to an asset or liability that is, or will be, re-measured with the changes in fair value reported currently in earnings (e.g. a debt security classified as trading or its interest cash flows);

- the hedged item cannot be related to a business combination or the acquisition or disposition of subsidiaries, minority interests, or equity method investees, or to an entity's own equity instruments classified in stockholders' equity;

- the risk of changes in market interest rates cannot be hedged for a held-to-maturity debt security or for its cash flows. However, changes in fair value attributable to changes in the obligor's creditworthiness can be hedged;

- for a non-financial asset or liability or its cash flows, the designated risk being hedged must be the risk of changes in fair value or cash flows for the entire hedged asset or liability and not the price risk of a similar asset in a different location or of a major ingredient; and

- if the hedged item is a financial asset or liability, a recognised loan servicing right, or the financial component of a non-financial firm commitment, or the cash flows of such an item, the designated risk being hedged must be:

  (a)   the risk of changes in the overall fair value or cash flows for the hedged asset or liability;

group.   As an exception, IAS 39 allows the foreign currency risk of an intragroup monetary item (e.g. a payable or receivable between two subsidiaries) to qualify as a hedged item in the consolidated financial statements if it results in an exposure to foreign exchange rate gains or losses that are not fully eliminated on consolidation under IAS 21.   Under IAS 21, foreign exchange gains and losses on such items are not fully eliminated on consolidation when they are transacted between two group entities that have different functional currencies.

COMMENT

The IASB in April 2005 issued an amendment to IAS 39 that permits, in consolidated financial statements, the designated hedged item in a foreign currency cash flow hedge of a forecast transaction to be an intragroup transaction provided that:

- the transaction is highly probable and meets all the other hedge accounting criteria (other than the requirement that it involves a party external to the group), and
- the hedged foreign currency transaction is denominated in a currency other than the functional currency of the entity entering into it and affects consolidated profit or loss.

13.3.4   Forecast transaction criteria – cash flow hedges

IAS 39.88
IAS 39.IG F.3.7

A forecast transaction that is the subject of a cash flow hedge must be highly probable and must present an exposure to variations in cash flows that could ultimately affect profit or loss.   The transaction's probability will need to be supported by observable facts and circumstances.   In assessing the likelihood that a transaction will occur, consideration should be given to the following circumstances:

- the frequency of similar past transactions;
- the financial and operational ability of the entity to carry out the transaction;
- substantial commitments of resources to a particular activity;
- the extent of loss or disruption of operations that could result if the transaction does not occur;
- the likelihood that transactions with substantially different characteristics might be used to achieve the same business purpose; and
- the entity's business plan.

The length of time until the forecast transaction is projected to occur will be of relevance in this assessment, as will the reporting entity's past history of successfully or unsuccessfully predicting the likelihood of such forecast transactions.

(b)   the risk of changes in fair value or cash flows attributable to changes in market interest rates;

(c)   the risk of changes in fair value or cash flows attributable to changes in the related foreign currency exchange rates;

(d)   the risk of changes in fair value or cash flows attributable to changes in the obligor's creditworthiness; or

(e)   some combination of the risks enumerated in (b) through (d).

FAS 133 clarifies that a hedging instrument generally can only be a derivative, as defined by the statement.   A non-derivative instrument, e.g. a treasury note, cannot be designated as a hedging instrument except when it results in a foreign currency transaction gain or loss and is designated as hedging the foreign currency exposure of a net investment in a foreign operation or of changes in the fair value of a foreign currency-denominated firm commitment. *FAS 133.20*

13.3.4   Forecast transaction criteria – cash flow hedges

A forecasted transaction may be eligible for designation as a hedged transaction in a cash flow hedge when the following criteria have been met: *FAS 133.29*

- the forecasted transaction can be identified specifically;
- it is probable that the forecasted transaction will occur;
- the counterparty to the forecasted transaction is external to the reporting entity;
- the forecasted transaction does not relate to assets and liabilities that will subsequently be measured at fair value;
- if the variable cash flows of the forecasted transaction relate to a debt security that is classified as held-to-maturity under FAS 115, the risk being hedged is the risk of changes in its cash flows attributable to default or changes in the obligor's creditworthiness;
- the forecasted transaction does not involve a business combination subject to FAS 141;
- if the hedged transaction is the forecasted purchase or sale of a non-financial asset, the designated risk being hedged is: (1) the risk of changes in the functional-currency-equivalent cash flows attributable to changes in the related foreign currency exchange rates; or (2) the risk of changes in the cash flows relating to all changes in the purchase price or sales price of the asset;
- if the hedged transaction is the forecasted purchase or sale of a financial asset or liability or the variable cash inflow or outflow of an existing financial asset or liability, the designated risk being hedged is: (1) the risk of changes in the cash flows of the entire asset or liability; (2) the risk of changes in its cash flows attributable to changes in the designated benchmark interest rate (e.g. LIBOR swap rate); (3) the risk of changes in the functional-currency-equivalent cash flows attributable to changes in the related foreign currency exchange rates; or (4) the risk of changes in its cash flows attributable to default or changes in the obligor's creditworthiness.   An entity may not designate prepayment risk alone as the risk being hedged.

13.3.5   Hedge effectiveness

IAS 39.AG105   A hedge is regarded as highly effective only if both of the following conditions are met:

- at the inception of the hedge and in subsequent periods, the hedge is expected to be highly effective in achieving offsetting changes in fair value or cash flows attributable to the hedged risk during the period for which the hedge is designated; and
- actual results of this hedge effectiveness are within a range of 80-125 percent.

IAS 39.AG106   This effectiveness should be assessed, at a minimum, at the time the entity prepares its interim or annual financial statements.

13.3.6   Accounting for hedges

A   No hedge relationship

If a hedge does not meet the criteria that are required to be met in order to be accounted for as a hedge then the hedged item should be accounted for in accordance with the regular measurement rules of the relevant standard.   The hedging instrument, if it is a derivative, will be measured at fair value with gains and losses through profit or loss.   If the hedging instrument is not a derivative it will retranslated as required by IAS 21 *The Effects of Changes in Foreign Exchange Rates.*

B   Fair value hedges

IAS 39.89   If a fair value hedge meets the hedge criteria described above during the period, it should be accounted for as follows:

- the gain or loss from remeasuring the hedging instrument at fair value (for a derivative hedging instrument) or the foreign currency component of its carrying amount measured in accordance with IAS 21 (for a non-derivative hedging instrument) should be recognised in profit or loss; and
- the gain or loss on the hedged item attributable to the hedged risk adjusts the carrying amount of the hedged item and is recognised in profit or loss.   This applies if the hedged item is an available-for-sale financial asset (and that gain or loss would otherwise be recognised in equity) or if it is otherwise measured at cost.

IAS 39.93-94   This accounting treatment also applies to a fair value hedge of an unrecognised firm commitment, i.e. the change in the fair value of the firm commitment is recognised in the balance sheet with a corresponding gain or loss in profit or loss.   When the asset or liability that results from the realisation of this firm commitment is eventually recognised, its carrying amount is adjusted for this cumulative change in the fair value that is recognised in the balance sheet.

IAS 39.91   An entity should discontinue hedge accounting prospectively when:

- the hedging instrument expires or is sold, terminated, or exercised (for this purpose, the replacement or a rollover of a hedging instrument into another hedging instrument is not considered an expiration or termination if such replacement or rollover is part of the entity's documented hedging strategy);
- the hedge no longer meets the criteria for hedge accounting; or
- the entity revokes the designation.

13.3.5   Hedge effectiveness

The FASB has been purposefully vague in providing guidance as to how much ineffectiveness is permitted before a hedge relationship can no longer be deemed 'highly effective'. FAS 133 refers to prior guidance on correlation, i.e. FAS 80, in which an 80% - 125% effective hedge is considered to be 'highly effective' but anything less effective is considered 'ineffective'. Further, FAS 133 requires a company to define how it will measure the effectiveness of a hedge relationship, at both the inception of the hedge and over the entire life of the relationship.

13.3.6   Accounting for hedges

A   No hedge relationship

Changes in the fair value of derivatives not meeting the criteria to use one of the three hedging categories must be recognised in income.

B   Fair value hedges

Where a designated fair value hedge meets the criteria described above, changes in the fair value of both the derivative and the hedged item attributable to the risk being hedged are recognised in earnings. Thus, to the extent the hedge is perfectly and fully effective, the change in the fair value of the hedged item will be offset in income with no net effect on earnings. Any difference that arises would represent hedge ineffectiveness which would be recognised in earnings. *FAS 133.22*

If a hedged item is otherwise measured at fair value with changes in fair value reported in other comprehensive income, e.g. an available-for-sale security, the adjustment of the hedged item's carrying amount should be recognised in earnings rather than other comprehensive income in order to offset the gain or loss on the hedging instrument. *FAS 133.23*

An entity should discontinue prospectively the hedge accounting for an existing fair value hedge if any of the following occurs: *FAS 133.25*

- any of the hedge criteria are no longer met;
- the derivative expires or is sold, terminated, or exercised; or
- the designation of the fair value hedge is removed.

IAS 39.AG113   The entity discontinues hedge accounting from the last date at which the hedging criteria were met, unless the discontinuance is due to ineffectiveness and this ineffectiveness can be demonstrated to relate to, and only arise after, a particular event.   In this latter case, the entity will discontinue hedge accounting from the date of that identified event.

IAS 39.92   Any adjustment to the carrying amount of a hedged financial instrument for which the effective interest method of accounting is used should be amortised to profit or loss. Amortisation may begin as soon as the adjustment exists and should begin no later than when the hedged item ceases to be adjusted for changes in its fair value attributable to the hedged risk.   The adjustment should be fully amortised by maturity.

C   *Cash flow hedges*

IAS 39.95   If a cash flow hedge meets the hedge criteria described above during the period it should be accounted for as follows:

- the portion of the gain or loss on the hedging instrument that is determined to be an effective hedge should be recognised directly in equity through the statement of changes in equity;
- the ineffective portion should be recognised in profit or loss.

IAS 39.96   More specifically, the accounting should be as follows:

- the separate component of equity associated with the hedged item is adjusted to the lesser of the following (in absolute amounts):
  - the cumulative gain or loss on the hedging instrument from inception of the hedge; and
  - the cumulative change in fair value (present value) of the expected future cash flows on the hedged item from inception of the hedge;
- any remaining gain or loss on the hedging instrument or designated component of it (that is not an effective hedge) is recognised in profit or loss; and
- if the documented risk management strategy for a particular hedging relationship excludes from the assessment of hedge effectiveness a specific component of the gain or loss or related cash flows on the hedging instrument, that excluded component of gain or loss is recognised in accordance with the normal measurement rules for that instrument (effectively in profit or loss for a derivative hedging instrument).

IAS 39.97   If a hedged forecast transaction subsequently results in the recognition of a financial asset or liability, the associated gains or losses that were recognised directly in equity should be recycled into profit or loss in the same period(s) during which the asset acquired or liability assumed affects profit or loss.   However, if it is expected that all or a portion of a loss recognised directly in equity will not be recovered in one or more future periods, the amount that is not expected to be recovered should be immediately recycled into profit or loss.

IAS 39.98-99   If a hedged forecast transaction subsequently results in the recognition of a non-financial asset or liability (or a forecast transaction for a non-financial asset or liability becomes a firm commitment for which fair value hedge accounting is applied) then a choice of accounting policies is available.   In these circumstances, an entity should adopt a consistent policy of either:

C   *Cash flow hedges*

Where a designated cash flow hedge meets the criteria described above, to the extent the hedge is effective, changes in the fair value of the derivative are recognised as a component of other comprehensive income in stockholders' equity until the hedged transaction affects earnings. Any ineffective portion is reported in earnings. The accounting for the hedged transaction is unaffected by the placement of the hedge. *FAS 133.30-31*

Accumulated other comprehensive income associated with the hedged transaction should be adjusted to the lesser of:

- the cumulative gain or loss on the derivative from inception less (1) any ineffective portion, and (2) any gains or losses previously reclassified into earnings; and

- the portion of the cumulative gain or loss on the derivative necessary to offset the cumulative change in expected future cash flows on the hedged transaction from inception, less the derivative's gains or losses previously reclassified into earnings.

The adjustment to other comprehensive income should be taken to earnings, as necessary, together with any remaining gain or loss on the hedging derivative.

Amounts in accumulated other comprehensive income should be reclassified into earnings in the same period or periods during which the hedged forecasted transaction affects earnings. However, a loss in other comprehensive income would be reclassified immediately if an entity expects to recognise a net loss on the combination of the hedging instrument and the hedged transaction in one or more future periods. *FAS 133.31*

An entity should discontinue prospectively the hedge accounting for an existing cash flow hedge if any of the following occurs: *FAS 133.32*

- any of the hedge criteria are no longer met;

- the derivative expires or is sold, terminated, or exercised; or

- the designation of the fair value hedge is removed.

When hedge accounting is discontinued, the net gain or loss will remain in accumulated other comprehensive income, and be reclassified into earnings in the same period or periods during which the hedged forecasted transaction affects earnings.

The net gain or loss would be reclassified into earnings immediately if it is probable that the forecasted transaction will not occur within the specified time period, or within two months thereafter. *FAS 133.33*

- recycling the associated gains and losses that were recognised directly in equity into the income statement in the same period(s) during which the asset acquired or liability assumed affects profit or loss.   However, if it is expected that all or a portion of a loss recognised directly in equity will not be recovered in one or more future periods, the amount that is not expected to be recovered should be immediately recycled into profit or loss; or
- removing the associated gains and losses that were recognised directly in equity and including them in the initial cost or other carrying amount of the asset or liability (referred to as a 'basis adjustment').

IAS 39.100   For all other cash flow hedges (i.e. those that do not result in the recognition of an asset or liability) amounts that had been recognised directly in equity should be recycled into the income statement in the same period(s) during which the hedged forecast transaction affects profit or loss.

IAS 39.101   An entity should discontinue hedge accounting prospectively when:
- the hedging instrument expires or is sold, terminated, or exercised (for this purpose, the replacement or a rollover of a hedging instrument into another hedging instrument is not an expiration or termination if such replacement or rollover is part of the documented hedging strategy).   In this case the cumulative gain or loss that remains recognised directly in equity from the period when the hedge was effective should remain in equity until the forecast transaction occurs.   Thereafter it is required to be dealt with as set out in the paragraphs immediately above;
- the hedge no longer meets the criteria for hedge accounting.   In this case, the cumulative gain or loss that remains in equity is dealt with in same way as in the bullet point above;
- the forecast transaction is no longer expected to occur.   In this case, the cumulative gain or loss on the hedging instrument that remains in equity should be recognised in profit or loss; or
- the designation as a hedge is revoked.   In this case, the cumulative gain or loss that remains in equity is dealt with in the same way as in the first bullet point above.   However, if the transaction is no longer expected to occur, the cumulative gain or loss on the hedging instrument that remains in equity should be recognised in profit or loss.

IAS 39.AG113   The entity discontinues hedge accounting from the last date at which the hedging criteria were met, unless the discontinuance is due to ineffectiveness and this ineffectiveness can be demonstrated to relate to, and only arise after, a particular event.   In this latter case, the entity will discontinue hedge accounting from the date of that identified event.

D   *Foreign currency hedges*

IAS 39.102   Hedges of a net investment in a foreign operation, including a hedge of a monetary item that is accounted for as part of the net investment (see section 5.3.2B), should be accounted for in a similar way to cash flow hedges:
- the portion of the gain or loss on the hedging instrument that is determined to be an effective hedge should be recognised directly in equity through the statement of changes in equity; and
- the ineffective portion should be recognised in profit or loss.

416

D   *Foreign currency hedges*

Consistent with the functional currency concept in FAS 52, an entity may designate   *FAS 133.36*
the following types of foreign currency hedges:

- Fair value hedges of unrecognised firm commitments   *FAS 133.37,39*
  If the firm commitment meets the criteria for a hedged item, a derivative or a non-derivative instrument may be designated as a hedging instrument.   Gains or losses on such hedges should be accounted in income, in accordance with the rules on fair value hedges.

The gain or loss on the hedging instrument relating to the effective portion of the hedge that has been recognised directly in equity should be recognised in profit or loss on disposal of the foreign operation.

Other foreign currency hedges must meet the criteria and be accounted for as either cash flow hedges or fair value hedges as appropriate and as described above.

A non-derivative financial instrument may not be designated as the hedging instrument in a fair value hedge of the foreign currency exposure of a recognised asset or liability:

FAS 133.37A

- Fair value hedges of available-for-sale securities

FAS 133.38

  Derivative instruments may be designated as a hedging instrument in a fair value hedge of available-for-sale securities. Changes in the value of the available-for-sale securities should be recorded in earnings and not in comprehensive income. Gains or losses on the hedging instrument should be accounted for in income, in accordance with the rules on fair value hedges;

- Cash flow hedges

  Cash flows hedge of forecasted foreign currency denominated transactions, either with unaffiliated entities or intragroup, should be accounted for in accordance with the rules on cash flow hedges.

FAS 133.40-41

  A forecasted intragroup transaction qualifies for hedge accounting if all the following additional criteria are met:

  – either the operating unit with the foreign currency exposure, or another member of the consolidating group with the same functional currency (and no intervening subsidiary with a different functional currency), is a party to the hedging instrument;

  – the hedged transaction is denominated in a currency other than the hedging unit's functional currency;

  – if the hedged transaction is a group of individual forecasted transactions, a forecasted foreign currency inflow and a forecasted foreign currency outflow cannot both be included in the same group; and

  – if the hedged item is a recognised foreign currency denominated asset or liability, all the variability in the hedged item's functional currency equivalent cash flows must be eliminated by the effect of the hedge.

  A foreign currency derivative with another member of a consolidated group, e.g. a treasury centre, can be a hedging instrument only if the issuing affiliate either enters into an offsetting derivative contract, or contracts, with an unrelated third party.

- Hedges of net investments in a foreign operation

FAS 133.42

  A derivative instrument or a non-derivative financial instrument that may give rise to a foreign currency transaction gain or loss can be designated as hedging the foreign currency exposure of a net investment in a foreign operation. The gain or loss on a hedging derivative instrument (or the foreign currency transaction gain or loss on the non-derivative hedging instrument) that is designated as, and is effective as, an economic hedge of the net investment in a foreign operation should be reported in the same manner as a translation adjustment to the extent it is effective as a hedge. The hedged net investment should be accounted for in accordance with FAS 52.

Section 14   Financial instruments: Disclosure

14.1   AUTHORITATIVE PRONOUNCEMENTS

* IAS 32

  COMMENT

  In July 2004, the IASB issued exposure draft ED 7 *Financial Instruments: Disclosures.* This exposure draft proposes the development of a new standard that would require disclosures relating to all risks arising from virtually all financial instruments and this new standard would apply to all entities.

  This new standard would require enhanced qualitative and quantitative disclosures from what is already required by IAS 32 and many of the existing disclosures within IAS 32 would be removed and included within this new standard. IAS 32 would be left dealing with only the presentation of financial instruments and IAS 30 *Disclosures in the Financial Statements of Banks and Similar Financial Institutions* would be withdrawn.

  The proposed effective date is for annual periods beginning on or after 1 January 2007, with earlier application encouraged.

14.2   SCOPE

IAS 32.4   The disclosure requirements of IAS 32 apply to all types of financial instruments except for:

* interests in subsidiaries, associates and joint ventures that are accounted for under IAS 27 *Consolidated and Separate Financial Statements*, IAS 28 *Investments in Associates* or IAS 31 *Interests in Joint Ventures* (unless this interest, according to these other standards, is accounted for under IAS 39 or is a derivative on an interest in a subsidiary, associate or joint venture);

* employer's assets under employee benefit plans to which IAS 19 *Employee Benefits* applies;

* contracts for contingent consideration in business combinations, in respect of the acquirer;

* insurance contracts as defined in IFRS 4 *Insurance Contracts (although the standard may apply to derivatives embedded in such contracts);*

* financial instruments that are within the scope of IFRS 4 *Insurance Contracts* because they contain a discretionary participation feature are out of scope of those parts of the Standard relating to the distinction between financial liabilities and equity instruments for the issuer of such instruments; and

* financial instruments, contracts and obligations under share-based payment transactions to which IFRS 2 *Share-based Payment* applies, except for contracts to buy or sell non-financial items in share-based transactions that can be settled net unless they are considered to be 'normal' sales and purchases (see below)

Section 14   Financial instruments: Disclosure

14.1   AUTHORITATIVE PRONOUNCEMENTS

- APB 12
- FAS 6
- FAS 47
- FAS 78

- FAS 107
- FAS 115
- FAS 129
- FAS 133

14.2   SCOPE

The disclosure requirements of FAS 107 *Disclosures about Fair Value of Financial Instruments* apply to all entities that have financial instruments, however, certain financial instruments are excluded from the scope of these requirements primarily on the grounds that they are addressed by other standards, for example: *FAS 107.7-8*

- insurance contracts under FAS 60 *Accounting and Reporting by Insurance Enterprises*, FAS 97, *Accounting and Reporting by Insurance Enterprises for Certain Long-Duration Contracts and for Realized Gains and Losses from the Sale of Investments*; and FAS 113 *Accounting and Reporting for Reinsurance of Short-Duration and Long-Duration Contracts*;

- lease contracts accounted for under FAS 13 *Accounting for Leases*;

- employers' obligations for pension which is covered by FAS 87 *Employer's Accounting for Pensions*;

- post-retirement health and life benefits to which FAS 106 *Employer's Accounting for Postretirement Benefits Other Than Pensions* applies;

- employee stock option and stock purchase plans dealt with under FAS 123R *Accounting for Stock-Based Compensation*;

- investments accounted for under the equity method in APB 18 *The Equity Method of Accounting for Investments in Common Stock*;

- minority interests in consolidated subsidiaries accounted for under ARB 51 *Consolidated Financial Statements*;

and except for requirements relating to treasury shares transacted for purposes of various employee share plans and share based payment arrangements.

IAS 32.8 IAS 32 also applies to contracts to buy or sell non-financial items (such as commodity contracts) that can be settled net in cash unless the contract was originally entered into and continues to be held for the purpose of the receipt or delivery of the non-financial item in accordance with the entity's expected purchase, sale or usage requirements. See section 11.2.1 for further guidance on the ways in which a contract to buy or sell a non-financial item can be settled net in cash or another financial instrument or by exchanging financial instruments.

IAS 32.53 Neither the format of the disclosures, nor their location within the financial statements, is prescribed by IAS 32.

IAS 32.54 The standard emphasises that judgment should be exercised in determining the level of detail to be disclosed, taking into account the relative significance of the particular instruments concerned. A balance should be maintained between providing excessive detail and obscuring important information in aggregated disclosures. Summarised information by reference to particular classes of instrument will be appropriate when dealing with large homogenous groups whilst specific information about an individual instrument may be important when, for example, that instrument represents a material component in an entity's capital structure.

IAS 32.55 Financial instruments should therefore be grouped into classes that are appropriate to the nature of the information disclosed, taking into account matters such as the characteristics of the instruments and the measurement basis applied. In general, classes should distinguish items carried at cost or amortised cost from items carried at fair value and there should be sufficient information to permit a reconciliation to relevant balance sheet line items.

Financial instruments that are not within the scope of IAS 32 constitute a class or classes of financial assets or liabilities separate from those within the scope of the standard. Disclosures about these instruments are also dealt with by other standards.

14.3   DISCLOSURE

A   Terms, conditions and accounting policies

IAS 32.60 For each class of financial asset, financial liability and equity instrument an entity should disclose information about the extent and nature of the financial instruments, including significant terms and conditions that may affect the amount, timing and certainty of future cash flows.

IAS 32.61,66 The following information should be included in the disclosure of the entity's accounting policies:

- the accounting policies and methods adopted, including the criteria for recognition, derecognition, and the basis of measurement (initially and subsequently) applied;

- the basis on which income and expenses arising from financial assets and financial liabilities are recognised and measured; and

- whether 'regular way' purchases and sales of financial assets are accounted for at trade date or settlement date.

- equity investments in consolidated subsidiaries; and,

- equity instruments issued by the entity and included in shareholders' equity.

FAS 115 *Accounting for Certain Investments in Debt and Equity Securities* applies   *FAS 115.3-4*
to all investments in:

- equity securities that have readily determinable fair values except investments in equity securities accounted for under the equity method and investments in consolidated subsidiaries; and

- debt securities, e.g. government bonds, corporate bonds, commercial paper, securitised debt instruments.

The standard does not apply to entities that currently account for all investments in securities at market value or fair value, e.g. investment companies, brokers and dealers in securities.

14.3   DISCLOSURE

A   Investments in marketable equity securities and debt securities

An entity that presents a classified balance sheet should report all held-to-maturity,   *FAS 115.17*
trading, and available-for-sale equity and debt securities as either current or non-current, based on maturities and the entity's intent with regard to those securities, as appropriate under ARB 43.

Presentation of individual amounts for each of the three categories of securities on   *FAS 115.117*
the face of the balance sheet is not required, provided the information is presented in the notes.

Cash flows from purchases, sales, and maturities should be reported gross for each   *FAS 115.18*
category of security and classified in the cash flow statement as follows:

- held-to-maturity and available-for-sale should be classified as cash flows from investing activities; and

- trading should be classified as cash flows from operating activities.

IAS 32.63   If there are potentially significant market, credit, liquidity or cash flow risks created by the issue of financial instruments, disclosure should include detail of:

- principal amounts;

- dates of maturity, execution or expiration;

- any early settlement options or convertibility options;

- amount and timing of future cash payments;

- rate or amount of interest or dividend;

- collateral pledged;

- any required currency payments that are not in the functional currency of the entity; and

- any condition or covenant attached to the instrument that may significantly alter its terms (such as requiring immediate repayment of the liability).

IAS 32.64   If the balance sheet presentation differs to its legal form an explanation is encouraged.

B   Fair values

IAS 32.86   For each class of financial assets and financial liabilities an entity should disclose the fair value of that class of assets and liabilities in a way that permits it to be compared with the corresponding carrying amount in the balance sheet (aside from those relating to investments in unquoted equity instruments or derivatives linked to such equity instruments that are measured at cost under IAS 39 because their fair value cannot be measured reliably).

IAS 32.88   For financial instruments such as short-term trade receivables and payables, no disclosure of fair value is required when the carrying amount is a reasonable approximation of fair value.

IAS 32.90   If investments in unquoted equity instruments or derivatives linked to such equity instruments are measured at cost under IAS 39 because their fair value cannot be measured reliably, that fact should be disclosed together with a description of the financial instruments, their carrying amount, an explanation of why fair value cannot be measured reliably and, if possible, the range of estimates within which fair value is highly likely to lie.   Furthermore, if financial assets whose fair value previously could not be reliably measured are sold, that fact, the carrying amount of such financial assets at the time of sale and the amount of gain or loss recognised should be disclosed.

IAS 32.92   Disclosures relating to methods, assumptions and valuation methodologies should include:

- the methods and significant assumptions applied in determining fair values of financial assets and financial liabilities separately for significant classes of financial assets and financial liabilities;

- whether fair values of financial assets and financial liabilities are determined directly, in full or in part, by reference to published price quotations in an active market or are estimated using a valuation technique;

- whether its financial statements include financial instruments measured at fair values that are determined in full or in part using a valuation technique based

The following information should be disclosed for securities, according to   *FAS 115.19*
classification, analysed by major security type, as of each date for which a balance
sheet is presented:

Held-to-maturity
- the aggregate fair value;
- gross unrealised holding gains and losses;
- gross gains and losses in accumulated other comprehensive income for any
  derivatives that hedged the forecasted acquisition of the securities; and
- net carrying amount.

Available-for-sale
- the aggregate fair value; and
- gross gains and losses in accumulated other comprehensive income.

Companies other than financial institutions can use security types that reflect their   *FAS 115.19*
portfolio holdings. Financial institutions have to include certain specific major
security types, though additional types may be included if appropriate.

Information is required about the contractual maturities of debt securities classified   *FAS 115.20*
as held-to-maturity and separately for securities classified as available-for-sale, as of
the most recent balance sheet date presented. Financial institutions should
disclose the fair value and amortised cost of debt securities based on at least four
maturity groupings: within one year; between one year and five years; between five
years and 10 years; and after 10 years. Other companies have the option of
presenting maturity information in appropriate groupings that reflect the
composition of their investment portfolio.

For each period for which an income statement is presented, an entity should disclose: *FAS 115.21-22*
- the proceeds from sales of available-for-sale securities and the gross realised
  gains and losses on those sales;
- the basis on which cost or amount reclassified out of accumulated other
  comprehensive income was determined in computing realised gain or loss;
- the gross gains and losses included in earnings from transfers of securities
  from the available-for-sale category into the trading category;
- the amount of net unrealised holding gain or loss on available-for-sale
  securities for the period included in accumulated other comprehensive income
  and the amount of gains and losses reclassified out of accumulated other
  comprehensive income for the period;
- the portion of trading gains and losses for the period that relates to trading
  securities still held at the reporting date; and
- for all sales or transfers from the held-to-maturity category; the net carrying
  amount; the net gain or loss in accumulated other comprehensive income for
  any derivative that hedged the forecasted acquisition of the security; the
  realised or unrealised gain or loss at the date of sale or transfer; and the
  circumstances leading to the decision to sell or transfer a security classified as
  held-to-maturity.

on assumptions that are not supported by observable market prices or rates. (and any significant impact from changing any such assumption to a reasonably possible alternative); and

- the total amount of the change in fair value estimated using a valuation technique that was recognised in profit or loss during the period.

IAS 32.93   Disclosure of fair value information includes disclosure of the method used in determining fair value and the significant assumptions made in its application. For example, an entity discloses information about the assumptions relating to prepayment rates, rates of estimated credit losses and interest or discount rates if they are significant.

C   *Risk management policies and hedging activities*

IAS 32.56   An entity should describe its financial risk management objectives and policies, including its policy for hedging each major type of forecast transaction for which hedge accounting is used.

IAS 32.58   An entity should disclose the following separately for designated fair value hedges, cash flow hedges, and hedges of a net investment in a foreign operation:

- a description of the hedge;
- a description of the financial instruments designated as hedging instruments and their fair values at the balance sheet date;
- the nature of the risks being hedged; and
- for cash flow hedges, the periods in which the cash flows are expected to occur, when they are expected to enter into the determination of profit or loss, and a description of any forecast transaction for which hedge accounting had previously been used but which is no longer expected to occur.

IAS 32.59   When a gain or loss on a hedging instrument in a cash flow hedge has been recognised directly in equity, through the statement of changes in equity, an entity should disclose:

- the amount that was so recognised in equity during the current period;
- the amount that was removed from equity and reported in profit or loss for the period; and
- the amount that was removed from equity during the period and included in the initial measurement of the acquisition cost or other carrying amount of a non-financial asset or non-financial liability in a hedged highly probable forecast transaction.

D   *Market risk*

IAS 32.52   Market risk includes three types of risk:

- currency risk – the risk that the value of a financial instrument will change because of changes in foreign exchange rates;
- fair value interest rate risk – the risk that the value of a financial instrument will fluctuate because of changes in market interest rates; and
- price risk – the risk that the value of a financial instrument will fluctuate because of changes in market prices.

B   Other investments

With respect to all other current and non-current marketable securities, i.e. other than equity, other security investments and any other investment, the basis of determining the aggregate amount shown in the balance sheet along with the alternatives of the aggregate cost or aggregate market value at the balance sheet date should be disclosed.

S-X 5-02.2,12

> **COMMENT**
>
> The disclosure requirements of FAS 107 *Disclosures about Fair Value of Financial Instruments* and FAS 133 *Accounting for Derivative Instruments and Hedging Activities* should also be considered as the definition of a 'financial instrument' that is contained in those standards is very wide and includes investments.

C   Current liabilities

The total of current liabilities should be shown on classified balance sheets.

If short-term obligations are excluded from current liabilities because they are expected to be refinanced, a general description should be given of the financing agreement and the terms of any new obligation incurred or equity securities issued (or expected to be incurred/issued) on refinancing.

FAS 6.15

For SEC registrants it is necessary to disclose separately amounts payable to:

S-X 5-02.19-20

- banks for borrowings;
- factors or other financial institutions for borrowings;
- holders of commercial paper;
- trade creditors;
- related parties;
- underwriters, promoters and employees (other than related parties); and
- any other current liability in excess of 5% of total current liabilities.

The amount and terms (including commitment fees and the conditions under which the lines may be withdrawn) of unused lines of credit for short-term financing also should be disclosed, if significant.   The amount of these lines of credit that support a commercial paper borrowing arrangement or similar arrangements should be separately identified.

S-X 5-02.19(b)

It is necessary to disclose current liabilities guaranteed by others, whether oral or written.

FRR 23

Details of all breaches/defaults in debt agreements, sinking fund or redemption provisions at the date of the latest balance sheet should be stated in the notes.   If a default or breach exists but acceleration of the obligation has been waived for a stated period of time beyond the date of the most recent balance sheet being filed, the amount of the obligation and the period of the waiver should be disclosed.

S-X 4-08(c)

D   Long-term debt

For recorded obligations and redeemable stock, disclosure is required, for each of the five years following the date of the latest balance sheet, of:

FAS 47.10
FAS 129.8

- the aggregate amount of payments for unconditional purchase obligations;
- the combined aggregate amount of maturities and sinking fund requirements for all long-term borrowings; and

IAS 32 does not require specific disclosures regarding market risk in general but the entity should follow the general rule of providing disclosures that assist the users to understand the extent of such risks.

E   Liquidity risk

IAS 32.52   Liquidity risk is defined by IAS 32 as the risk that an entity will encounter difficulty in raising funds to meet commitments associated with financial instruments. Liquidity risk may result from an inability to sell a financial asset quickly at close to its fair value.   No specific disclosure requirements exist regarding liquidity risk but the entity should follow the general rule of providing disclosures that assist the users to understand the extent of such risks.

F   Interest rate risk

IAS 32.67   An entity should disclose information, for each class of financial assets and financial liabilities, about its exposure to interest rate risk, including:

- contractual repricing or maturity dates, whichever dates are earlier; and
- effective interest rates.

IAS 32.71   The entity should also disclose which of its financial instruments are exposed to fair value interest rate risk (such as fixed rate assets and liabilities), which are exposed to cash flow interest rate risk (such as floating rate assets and liabilities) and which are not exposed to any interest rate risk.

IAS 32.74   The nature of the entity's business will determine whether disclosure is best presented in narrative form, tabular form or some combination of the two.

G   Credit risk

IAS 32.76   An entity should disclose, for each class of financial assets and other credit exposures, information about its exposure to credit risk, including:

- the amount that best represents its maximum credit risk exposure at the balance sheet date, without taking account of the fair value of any collateral, in the event of other parties failing to perform their obligations under financial instruments; and
- significant concentrations of credit risk.

IAS 32.79-82   If the entity's maximum potential loss from some financial instruments differs significantly to the carrying amount of those instruments additional disclosure should be provided.   Such disclosure may include details of any rights to set off and details of any master netting agreements.   It may also include details of any guarantees that have been provided since such guarantees may result in exposure to credit risk despite there being no financial asset recognised on the balance sheet.

IAS 32.83,85   Concentrations of credit risk are disclosed when they are not apparent from other disclosures and where they result in significant exposure to loss in the event of default by other parties.   This disclosure should include a description of the shared characteristics that identifies each concentration and the amount of the maximum credit risk exposure associated with all financial assets sharing that characteristic.

- the amount of redemption requirements for all issues of capital stock that are redeemable at fixed or determinable prices on fixed or determinable dates, separately by issue or in aggregate.

For long-term debt such as bonds, mortgages etc., the following disclosures should be given for each issue or type of obligation: *S-X 5-02.22*

- the general character of each type of debt including rate of interest;
- the date of maturity or, if maturing serially, a brief indication of the serial maturities;
- if the payment of principal or interest is contingent, an indication of such contingency;
- a brief indication of priority (i.e. subordinated); and
- if convertible, the basis.

The amount and terms (including commitment fees) of unused commitments for long-term financing arrangements should be disclosed if significant.   *S-X 5-02.22(b)*

Disclosure is required of any non-current liabilities guaranteed by others, whether oral or written.   *FRR 23*

Disclosures concerning financial instruments, including debt instruments, are discussed in section 11.

The approximate amounts of assets mortgaged or pledged as collateral and the obligations collateralised should be disclosed.

The rights and privileges of the convertible debt securities outstanding should be disclosed including: *S-X 4-08(b)*

- dividend and liquidation preferences   *FAS 129.4*
- participation rights;
- call prices and dates;
- conversion prices or rates and pertinent dates;
- sinking-fund requirements;
- unusual voting rights; and
- significant terms of contracts to issue additional shares.

Liabilities of a related stock ownership plan that are guaranteed by the company should be reflected in the balance sheet of that company (see section 22.7).   *SOP 93-6*

If a long-term obligation that is or will be callable because of a loan covenant violation is classified as long-term because it is probable the violation will be cured within a specified grace period, the circumstances should be disclosed.   *FAS 78.5*

Any significant changes in the authorised or issued amounts of bonds, mortgages and similar debt since the balance sheet date should be disclosed.   *S-X 4-08(f)*

H   Other disclosures

IAS 32.94   Where certain arrangements in respect of financial assets have been entered into that do not qualify as a transfer of those assets and they continue to be recognised, or are recognised to the extent of the entity's continuing involvement, the following should be disclosed for each class of financial asset:

- the nature of the assets;

- the nature of the risks and rewards of ownership to which the entity remains exposed;

- when the entity continues to recognise all of the asset, the carrying amounts of the asset and of the associated liability; and

- when the entity continues to recognise the asset to the extent of its continuing involvement, the total amount of the asset, the amount of the asset that the entity continues to recognise and the carrying amount of the associated liability.

IAS 32.94   The carrying amount of financial assets pledged as collateral for liabilities and for contingent liabilities should be separately disclosed, along with any material terms and conditions relating to those assets.

IAS 32.94   When collateral has been accepted by an entity that it is permitted to sell or repledge in the absence of default by the owner, the following should be disclosed:

- the fair value of the collateral accepted (both financial and non-financial assets);

- the fair value of any such collateral sold or repledged and whether there is an obligation to return it; and

- any material terms and conditions associated with the use of this collateral.

IAS 32.94   Where a (non-derivative) financial liability has been designated at fair value through profit or loss, i.e. it is not classified as trading, the amount of change in its fair value that is not attributable to changes in a benchmark interest rate, e.g. LIBOR, should be disclosed.   In addition the difference between the carrying amount of such a liability and the amount the entity would be contractually required to pay at maturity to the holder of the obligation should also be disclosed.

IAS 32.94   Disclosure should be made of the carrying amounts of financial assets and financial liabilities that are classified as held for trading and were, upon initial recognition, designated as financial instruments at fair value through profit or loss (i.e. those that are not classified as held for trading).

IAS 32.94   Where a financial asset has been reclassified as one measured at cost or amortised cost rather than at fair value the reason for that reclassification should be disclosed.

IAS 32.94   An entity should disclose the nature and amount of any impairment loss recognised in profit or loss, separately for each significant class of financial asset.

IAS 32.94   With respect to defaults of principal, interest, sinking fund or redemption provisions during the period on loans payable recognised as at the balance sheet date, and any other breaches during the period of loan agreements when those breaches can permit the lender to demand repayment, the following information should be disclosed:

- details of those breaches;

- the amount recognised as at the balance sheet date in respect of the loans payable on which the breaches occurred; and

E   Derivatives and hedge accounting

FAS 107 and FAS 133 contain extensive disclosure requirements.   In addition, the   *S-K Item 303,305*
SEC requires disclosures based on the type of market risk that is being hedged, i.e.   *20-F Item 11*
interest rate, foreign currency and liquidity, in the qualitative and quantitative
disclosures about market risk.

The significant disclosures that are required for all hedging activities are as follows: *FAS 133.44-45*

- the entity's objectives and strategies for holding or issuing derivatives;
- a description of the entity's risk management policy for each type of hedge, including a description of the items or transactions for which risks are hedged;
- the net gain or loss recognised in earnings during the reporting period representing:
  - the amount of the hedges' ineffectiveness;
  - the component of the derivatives' gain or loss, if any, excluded from the assessment of hedge effectiveness; and
  - a description of where the net gain or loss is reported in the income statement or other statement of financial performance.

Although the above requirements apply to all hedging activities, the disclosures
must be segregated between the three types of hedge described below, i.e. fair value,
cash flow, and net investments in foreign operations.

In addition, there are specific disclosure requirements for each type of hedge.

Additional disclosure specific to fair value hedges

- the amount of net gain or loss recognised in earnings at the time the hedge of a firm commitment no longer qualifies as a fair value hedge.

Additional disclosure specific to cash flow hedges

- a description of the transactions or other events that will result in the reclassification into earnings of gains and losses that are reported in accumulated other comprehensive income, and the estimated amount of the existing gains and losses at the reporting date that are expected to be reclassified into earnings within the next 12 months;
- the amount of gains and losses reclassified into earnings as a result of the discontinuance of cash flow hedges, because it is probable that the original forecasted transaction will not occur; and
- the maximum period of time over which the entity is hedging its exposure to the variability in future cash flows for forecasted transactions.   This disclosure is not required for hedges of variable interest rates because disclosure of the maturity of the debt is already required.

Additional disclosure specific to hedges of the net investment in a foreign operation

- the net amount of gains or losses on the hedging instrument included in the cumulative translation adjustment during the period.

Disclosures required by FAS 130 *Reporting Other Comprehensive Income* will   *FAS 133.46-47*
apply to entities using cash flow hedges and hedges of net investments in foreign
operations.   An entity also must display as a separate classification within other

with respect to these amounts, whether the default has been remedied or the terms of the loans payable renegotiated before the date the financial statements were authorised for issue.

comprehensive income the net gain or loss on derivative instruments designated and qualifying as cash flow hedges. Beginning accumulated derivative gains and losses are rolled forward to ending accumulated derivative gains and losses, identifying current period changes, including net amounts reclassified into earnings.

Credit risk

Disclosure should be made of all significant concentrations of credit risk arising from all financial instruments whether from an individual counterparty or groups of counterparties. For each significant concentration, the following disclosure is required:

FAS 107.15A-D

- information about the (shared) activity, region, or economic characteristic that identifies the concentration;
- the maximum amount of loss due to credit risk that, based on the gross fair value of the financial instrument, the entity would incur if parties to the financial instruments that make up the concentration failed completely to perform according to the terms of the contracts and the collateral or other security, if any, for the amount due proved to be of no value to the entity;
- the entity's policy of requiring collateral or other security to support financial instruments subject to credit risk, information about the entity's access to that collateral or other security, and the nature and a brief description of the collateral or other security supporting those financial instruments; and
- the entity's policy of entering into master netting arrangements to mitigate the credit risk of financial instruments, information about the arrangements for which the entity is a party, and a brief description of the terms of those arrangements, including the extent to which they would reduce the entity's maximum amount of loss due to credit risk.

Market risk

An entity is encouraged, but not required, to disclose quantitative information about the market risks of financial instruments that is consistent with the way it manages or adjusts those risks. Appropriate disclosure will differ for different entities but might include disclosing:

FAS 133.531(d)

- more details about current positions and perhaps activity during the period;
- the hypothetical effects on comprehensive income (or net assets), or annual income, of several possible changes in market prices;
- a gap analysis of interest rate repricing or maturity dates;
- the duration of the financial instruments;
- the entity's value at risk from derivatives and from other positions at the end of the reporting period and the average value at risk during the year.

This list is not exhaustive, and an entity is encouraged to develop other ways of reporting quantitative information.

Accounting policies

FAS 133 does not have any specific accounting policy disclosure requirements.   *S-X 4-08(n)*
However, the SEC regulations specify seven specific areas that registrants should
include in their accounting policy disclosures about derivatives.

- a discussion of each method used to account for derivative financial
  instruments and derivative commodity instruments;

- the types of derivative financial instruments and derivative commodity
  instruments accounted for under each method;

- the criteria required to be met for each accounting method used, including a
  discussion of the criteria required to be met for hedge or deferral accounting
  and accrual or settlement accounting, e.g. whether and how risk reduction,
  correlation, designation, and effectiveness tests are applied;

- the accounting method used if the criteria specified above are not met;

- the method used to account for terminations of derivatives designated as
  hedges or derivatives used to affect directly or indirectly the terms, fair values,
  or cash flows of a designated item;

- the method used to account for derivatives when the designated item matures,
  is sold, is extinguished, or is terminated;

- the method used to account for derivatives designated to an anticipated
  transaction, when the anticipated transaction is no longer likely to occur; and

- where and when derivative financial instruments and derivative commodity
  instruments, and their related gains and losses, are reported in the statements
  of financial position, cash flows, and results of operations.

F   Fair values

Fair value of a financial instrument is the amount at which the instrument could be   *FAS 107.5-6*
exchanged in a current transaction between willing parties, other than a forced or   *FAS 107.11,22-29*
liquidation sale.   If a quoted market price is available for an instrument, the fair value
is the product of the number of trading units of the instrument times that market
price (even though the sale of a relatively large holding would yield a different price).
In the case of unquoted instruments, market prices of similar instruments or the
present value of expected future cash flows may be used as measures of fair value.

The following disclosures should be given in financial statements (either in the body   *FAS 107.10*
or in the footnotes) for all financial instruments:

- fair value, together with the related carrying amount in a form that identifies
  the fair value and carrying amounts as assets or liabilities and relates the
  carrying amounts to the reported statement of financial position; and

- method(s) and significant assumptions used to estimate the fair value of
  financial instruments.

FAS 107 does not include specific guidance on what level of aggregation to use in   *FAS 107.10*
making fair value disclosures, other than with examples included in Appendix B to the
standard.   Those examples generally aggregate the disclosures at the same level as is
used in the balance sheet, e.g. cash and cash equivalents, investment securities, loans,
deposits, other borrowings – for a financial institution, and also include separate
disclosures for major categories of off-balance-sheet financial instruments.

In disclosing the fair value of a financial instrument, an entity shall not net that fair value with the fair value of other financial instruments – even if those financial instruments are of the same class or are otherwise considered to be related, for example, by a risk management strategy – except to the extent that the offsetting of carrying amounts in the statement of financial position is permitted under the general principles discussed in section 1.6.3.

FAS 133.531(c)

If it is not 'practicable' to estimate the fair value of a financial instrument or a class of financial instruments, the following should be disclosed:

FAS 107.14

- information pertinent to estimating the fair value of that financial instrument or class of financial instruments, such as carrying amount, effective interest rate, and maturity; and

- the reasons why it is not practicable to estimate fair value.

'Practicable' means that an estimate of fair value can be made without incurring excessive costs. Application of this exception involves judgement and will vary among companies depending on their size, the nature of their business and interpretations as to what constitutes excessive cost. It is a dynamic concept and what is not 'practicable' in one year might be in another.

FAS 107.15

COMMENT

In June 2004 the FASB issued an exposure draft of a Proposed Statement of Financial Accounting Standards *Fair Value Measurements*. The proposed Statement provides guidance for how to measure fair value and would supersede the guidance in FAS 107. The proposed statement would be effective for financial statements issued for fiscal years beginning after June 15, 2005. The FASB expect to issue a final statement in the third quarter of 2005.

G   Risk disclosures

Market risk

There is no specific guidance for interest risk disclosure in financial statements. The SEC requires quantitative and qualitative disclosures about market risk, e.g. interest rate risk or foreign exchange rate risk, under Item 7.A of Form 10-K, or for foreign private issuers, Item 11 of Form 20-F.

Liquidity risk

There is no specific guidance for liquidity risk disclosure in financial statements, other than the SEC requirement to disclose the date of maturity of each type of debt instrument.

S-X 5-02.22(a)

The SEC also requires disclosure of liquidity and capital resources, under Item 7 of Form 10-K or, for foreign private issuers, Item 5.B of Form 20-F, and maturity information under Item 7.A of Form 10-K or, for foreign private issuers, Item 11 of Form 20-F.

Section 15

Inventory and long-term contracts

15.1 AUTHORITATIVE PRONOUNCEMENTS

- IAS 2
- IAS 11

15.2 ACCOUNTING FOR INVENTORY

15.2.1 Definition

IAS 2.6 Inventories are defined as assets which:

- are held for sale in the ordinary course of business;
- are in the process of production for such sale; or
- are in the form of materials or supplies to be consumed in the production of goods or services.

IAS 2.2 The following are excluded from the full scope of IAS 2 *Inventories*:

- work in progress under construction contracts (see section 15.3);
- financial instruments; and
- biological assets related to agricultural activity and agricultural produce at the point of harvest (IAS 41 *Agriculture*).

IAS 2.3,5 The measurement requirements only of IAS 2 do not apply to inventories held by:

- producers of agricultural and forest products, agricultural produce after harvest and minerals and mineral products, to the extent that they are measured at net realisable value in accordance with well-established practices in those industries. When such inventories are measured at net realisable value, any changes in that value are recognised in profit or loss in the period of the change; and
- commodity broker-traders who measure their inventories at fair value less costs to sell. Changes in the fair value less costs to sell of such inventories are recognised in profit or loss in the period of the change. The broker-traders' inventories are those that have been bought with the intention of trading and generating a profit from fluctuations in price or broker-traders' margin.

Section 15

Inventory and long-term contracts

15.1 AUTHORITATIVE PRONOUNCEMENTS

- ARB 43
- ARB 45

- FAS 151
- SOP 81-1

COMMENT

In November 2004 the FASB issued FAS 151 *Inventory Costs an amendment of ARB No. 43, Chapter 4* to converge the wording of portions of ARB 43 related to inventory costs with IAS 2. The statement is effective for inventory costs incurred in fiscal periods beginning after 15 June 2005. Early adoption is permitted for inventory costs incurred in fiscal periods beginning after issuance of the statement.

15.2 ACCOUNTING FOR INVENTORY

15.2.1 Definition

The term inventory refers to those items of tangible assets which: *ARB 43 Ch 4.3*

- are held for sale in the ordinary course of business;
- are in process of production for such sale; or
- are to be currently consumed in the production of goods or services to be available for sale.

15.2.2   Determining the cost of inventory

IAS 2.9   Inventories are measured at the lower of cost and net realisable value.

IAS 2.10-11   Cost of inventories comprises:

- all costs of purchase, which include purchase price, import duties, other non-recoverable taxes, transport and handling costs, and other directly attributable costs. Trade discounts and similar rebates should be deducted from the costs of purchase;

IAS 2.12-14
- costs of conversion, which include direct costs of production and a systematic allocation of fixed and variable production overheads based on the normal capacity of the production facilities. Where more than one product is produced and costs are not separately identifiable, an allocation should be made on a systematic and rational basis. In all cases, the amount of allocated overheads may not exceed the actual overhead costs incurred;

IAS 2.15
- other costs incurred in bringing the inventories to their present location and condition; and

IAS 2.17-18
- certain borrowing costs determined in accordance with IAS 23 *Borrowing Costs*, see section 10.4. However, if an entity purchases inventories on deferred settlement terms where the arrangement effectively contains a financing element, that element is recognised as interest expense over the period of the financing.

IAS 2.19

Where service providers have inventories (usually work in progress), they should measure them at the cost of the directly related labour, other direct costs and attributable overheads. They should not capitalise labour and other costs relating to sales and general administrative personnel nor should they include in the cost of inventories profit margins or non-attributable overheads.

IAS 2.16

Costs which are excluded from the cost of inventories and recognised as an expense when incurred include:

- abnormal production costs;
- storage costs (unless these are necessary in the production process);
- general administrative costs; and
- selling costs.

15.2.3   Costing method

IAS 2.23-24   Where items of inventory are not interchangeable, or relate to specific projects, their costs should be specifically identified and assigned to those items.

IAS 2.25-26   The cost of inventories that do not meet the above criteria should be determined by using the first-in first-out ('FIFO') or weighted average cost formulas. Use of the last-in first-out method ('LIFO') is no longer permitted under the revised version of IAS 2 (for accounting periods beginning on or after 1 January 2005).

The same cost formula should be used for all inventories which have a similar nature and use to the entity. The use of different cost formulas cannot be justified solely on the basis of different geographical locations of the inventories or, for example, the respective tax rules of those locations.

15.2.2   Determining the cost of inventory

The primary basis of accounting for inventory is cost.   Cost has been defined *ARB 43 Ch 4.5* generally as the price paid or consideration given to acquire an asset.   In the context of inventories, cost means the sum of the applicable expenditures and charges directly or indirectly incurred in bringing an article to its existing condition and location.

Inventory cost includes that portion of general and administrative expenses which may be clearly related to production.   Prior to the issuance of FAS 151 there was no explicit reference to production overheads being based on a normal level of activity, ARB 43 states that items such as idle facility expense, excessive spoilage and double freight costs may be so abnormal as to require treatment as current period charges rather than as a portion of the inventory cost.

Under FAS 151, the allocation of fixed production overheads to inventory is based on *FAS 151.2* the normal capacity, or normal range of production levels, of the production facilities, taking into account any loss of capacity resulting from planned maintenance.   During periods of abnormally high production, the amount of fixed overhead allocated to each unit of production is decreased so inventories are not measured above cost. The amount of fixed overhead allocated to each unit of production is not increased during periods of abnormally low production or idle plant.

Unallocated overheads and abnormal costs are recognised as an expense in the period incurred.   Selling expenses are not included in inventory costs.

A change in composition of the elements of cost included in inventory is considered *FIN 1* to be an accounting change.

15.2.3   Costing method

First-in, first-out (FIFO), average cost, and last-in, first-out (LIFO) are all acceptable *ARB 43 Ch 4.6* methods of determining the cost of goods sold.   Companies should choose the method which, under the circumstances, most clearly reflects the periodic income. The AICPA Issues paper on LIFO accounting provides the accounting profession's guidance on what constitutes acceptable LIFO accounting practice.

The LIFO method is popular in the US as the Internal Revenue Service officially recognises LIFO as an acceptable method for the computation of tax provided that it is used consistently for tax and financial reporting purposes.

Interest cost should not be capitalised for inventories that are routinely *FAS 34.10* manufactured or otherwise produced in large quantities on a repetitive basis.

IAS 2.21   Cost measurement techniques, such as the standard cost method or the retail method, may be used for convenience if the results approximate to cost and provided that they are regularly reviewed and revised where necessary.

15.2.4   Lower of cost or net realisable value

IAS 2.6,28 Inventories need to be written down to their net realisable value when their cost is not recoverable. Net realisable value is the estimated selling price in the ordinary course of business less the costs of completion and estimated selling costs.

IAS 2.6-7   IAS 2 distinguishes between net realisable value and fair value. Fair value reflects the amount for which the same item of inventory could be exchanged between knowledgeable, willing parties in an arm's length transaction. Net realisable value is therefore an entity-specific value; fair value is not. As a consequence, net realisable value for inventories may not equal fair value less costs to sell.

IAS 2.29-30 Normally inventories are written down to net realisable value on an item-by-item basis using the most reliable evidence available at the time the estimates are made. However, it may be appropriate to write down a group of similar or related items that cannot practically be evaluated separately. It is not appropriate to write down inventories based on a classification of inventory, for example, finished goods, or all the inventories in a particular industry or geographical segment.

IAS 2.31   Estimates of net realisable value also take into consideration the purpose for which the inventory is held and whether or not this is to satisfy a firm sales contract.

IAS 2.33-34 A new assessment of net realisable value is made in each subsequent period. The carrying amount of inventories sold together with a write-down of inventories to net realisable value and all inventory losses are recognised as an expense in the period in which the related revenue is recognised or the write-down or loss occurs. Any reversal of previously recognised write-downs should be recognised, in the period the reversal occurs, as a reduction in the amount of inventories recognised as an expense. Any reversal of a write-down is limited to the amount of the original write-down.

15.2.5   Disclosure

IAS 2.36-38 An entity should disclose the following information in its financial statements:
*   the accounting policies adopted in measuring inventories, including the cost formula used;
*   the total carrying amount of inventories and the carrying amount in classifications appropriate to the entity (IAS 2 states that commonly used classifications are merchandise, production supplies, materials, work in progress and finished goods);

15.2.4   Lower of cost and market

A departure from the cost basis of accounting is required where the utility of   *ARB 43 Ch 4.8*
inventory is no longer as great as its cost.   The measurement of impairment loss is
generally accomplished by recording inventory at the lower of cost and market.
Market means current replacement cost of the inventory item (by purchase or by
reproduction, as the case may be) except that:

- market should not exceed net realisable value, i.e. estimated selling price in the
  ordinary course of business less reasonably predictable costs of completion
  and disposal; and

- market should not be less than net realisable value reduced by an allowance
  for an approximately normal margin.

The rule of pricing of inventories at the lower of cost and market is intended as a   *ARB 43 Ch 4.10*
guide.   It should be applied realistically in the light of the objectives of accounting
for inventories, i.e. the proper determination of income through the process of
matching appropriate costs against revenues, and with due regard to the form,
content and composition of the inventory.

The most common practice is to apply the lower of cost and market rule separately   *ARB 43 Ch 4.11*
to each item of the inventory.   However, if there is only one end-product category,
the rule of cost and market, whichever is lower, may properly be applied to the total
of the inventory (since the reduction of individual items to market may not always
lead to the most useful result if the utility of the total inventory of the business is
not below its cost).   Similarly, where more than one major product or operational
category exists, application of the rule to the total of the items included in such
major categories may result in the most useful determination of income.

Only in exceptional circumstances (or where it is accepted industry practice) may   *ARB 43 Ch 4.16*
inventories be stated above cost, e.g. precious metals or commodities having a fixed
monetary value with no substantial cost of marketing may be stated at such
monetary value.   The SEC staff's opinion is that all inventories should be stated at
the lower of cost or market unless explicitly provided for by authoritative literature;
they believe such cases to be extremely rare.

The write-down of inventory to the lower of cost and market creates a new cost   *SAB 100*
basis that subsequently cannot be reversed.   *ARB 43 Ch 4.5 fn2*

15.2.5   Disclosure

Disclosure is required separately in the balance sheet or in a note thereto of the   *S-X 5-02.6(a)*
amounts of major classes of inventory such as:

- finished goods;
- costs relating to long-term contracts or programmes (see section 15.3);
- work-in-progress;
- raw materials; and
- supplies.

- the carrying amount of inventories carried at fair value less costs to sell;

- the amount of inventories recognised as an expense in the period, often referred to as cost of sales, consists of costs previously included in the measurement of the inventory which has now been sold plus unallocated production overheads and abnormal amounts of production costs of inventories. The circumstances of the entity may also warrant the inclusion of other costs such as distribution costs;

- the amount of any write-down of inventories recognised as an expense in the period;

- the amount of any reversal of any write-down that is recognised as a reduction in the amount of inventories recognised as an expense in the period;

- the circumstances or events that led to the reversal of a write-down of inventories; and

- the carrying amount of inventories pledged as security for liabilities.

IAS 2.39 If an entity adopts a format for profit and loss which presents an analysis of expenses by nature rather than function, the entity should disclose the costs recognised as an expense for raw materials and consumables, labour costs and other costs together with the amount of the net change in inventories in the period.

15.3 CONSTRUCTION CONTRACTS

15.3.1 Definition

IAS 11.3,5-6 A construction contract is defined as 'a contract specifically negotiated for the construction of an asset or a combination of assets that are closely interrelated or interdependent in terms of their design, technology and function or their ultimate purpose or use.'

IAS 11 includes within its scope service contracts which are directly related to the construction of the asset (e.g. those of project managers or architects) and contracts for the destruction or restoration of assets and the restoration of the environment following the demolition of assets. Accounting for the rendering of services, other than those directly related to a construction contract, is covered in section 19.2B above.

A distinction can be drawn between fixed price contracts and cost plus contracts. Under fixed price contracts, the contractor agrees to a fixed price for the contract or per unit of output, possibly subject to cost escalation clauses. A cost plus contract provides for the contractor to be reimbursed for costs defined under the contract plus a profit margin, which is fixed or a percentage of costs. Some contracts may contain characteristics of both fixed and cost plus contracts in which case the contract must be specifically analysed to determine when to recognise revenue and expenses.

15.3.2 Accounting for construction contracts

A   Combining and segmenting contracts

IAS 11.7 Normally, construction contracts are accounted for on an individual basis, but it may be necessary to combine or segment contracts.

The basis of determining amounts should be disclosed and consistently applied. If inventory amounts are included at cost, a description of the nature of the elements of cost included in inventory should be given. Where goods are stated at above cost, the facts should be fully disclosed.

ARB 43 Ch 4.15
S-X 5-02.6(b)

The method by which amounts are removed from inventory, e.g. LIFO, FIFO, should be described.

The aggregate amount of the general and administrative costs incurred in each period and the actual or estimated amount remaining in inventory at the balance sheet date should be disclosed.

Substantial and unusual losses arising from the application of the lower of cost or market rule must be separately disclosed from 'cost of goods sold' in the income statement. Likewise, accrued net losses on firm purchase commitments for inventory should be identified in the income statement.

ARB 43
Ch 4.14,17

If the LIFO method is used, the excess of replacement or current cost over stated LIFO value should, if material, be disclosed either parenthetically on the balance sheet or in the notes.

S-X 5-02.6(c)

15.3   LONG-TERM CONTRACTS

15.3.1   Definition

There is no specific definition of a long-term contract. References to long-term contracts in disclosure requirements in Regulation S-X include (1) contracts or programmes for which gross profits are recognised on a percentage-of-completion method of accounting, or any variant thereof, and (2) contracts or programmes accounted for on completed contract basis which have associated with them material amounts of inventories or unbilled receivables and which have been or are expected to be performed over a period of more than 12 months. Contracts or programmes of shorter duration may also be included, if deemed appropriate.

S-X 5-02.6(d)

The principal guidance, ARB 45 *Long-Term Construction-Type Contracts* and SOP 81-1 *Accounting for Performance of Construction-Type and Certain Production-Type Contracts* deal with construction and production contracts. Long-term service contracts are specifically excluded from the scope of SOP 81-1, with certain limited exceptions.

Service transaction contracts that fall outside of SOP 81-1 should be accounted for using revenue recognition guidance (see section 19.2.C).

15.3.2   Accounting for construction contracts

A   Combining and segmenting contracts

Contracts may include separately negotiated elements that the contractor agreed to perform whether the others are performed or not. A contractor may segment a

SOP 81-1.39-41

IAS 11.8   Contracts should be segmented when they cover the construction of a number of assets and:

- separate proposals have been submitted for each asset;

- each asset has been subject to separate negotiation and the contractor and customer could have accepted or rejected parts of the contract relating to individual assets; and

- the costs and revenues for each asset can be separately identified.

IAS 11.10   Contracts should also be segmented when they provide for the construction of an additional asset at the option of the customer and:

- the asset differs significantly from the assets under the original contract; or

- the price of the asset was the subject of separate negotiations.

IAS 11.9   Whether they are entered into with one or several customers, contracts should be combined when they were negotiated as a single package, are closely interrelated so that, in effect, they form part of a single project with an overall profit margin and the work is performed concurrently or in a continuous sequence.

B   Revenue recognition

IAS 11.22,30   When the outcome of a contract can be estimated reliably, contract revenue and contract costs of a construction contract should be recognised as revenue and expenses on a cumulative basis by reference to the stage of completion of the contract, i.e. the percentage-of-completion method.

There are a number of possible methods for determining the stage of completion of a contract including the proportion of costs incurred to date to estimated total contract costs, surveys of work performed or completion of a physical proportion of the contract work. By contrast, progress payments and customer advances often do not reflect the actual extent of the work performed.

IAS 11.11-12   Contract revenue comprises the contract price plus, to the extent that they will result in revenue and they can be measured reliably, variations in contract work, claims and incentive payments. Revenue is measured at the fair value of the consideration received or receivable and estimates will need to be revised as events occur and uncertainties are resolved.

IAS 11.16-19   Contract costs are those costs that either relate directly to the specific contract, or are attributable to contract activity in general and can be allocated to the contract, or represent such other costs as are specifically chargeable to the customer under the contract. IAS 11 includes examples of costs which might be included within each category.

IAS 11.20   Costs that cannot be attributed to contract activity or cannot be allocated to a contract are excluded from contract costs. Examples of costs to be excluded are general administration costs and research and development costs for which reimbursement is not specified in the contract, selling costs and the depreciation of idle plant and equipment that is not used on a particular contract.

IAS 11.21   Contract costs include the costs attributable to a contract from the date of securing the contract to final completion. Direct costs incurred in securing a contract may also be included if they are separately identifiable, may be measured reliably and it is

contract if it meets either of two sets of criteria.   First, the contractor must submit two proposals – one on the individual components and the other on the entire project.   The aggregate price of the individual components should be approximately the same as the price for the entire project and the customer can choose either one or more components or the entire project.   If the first set of criteria are not met, a contract may only be segmented if it meets all of the following conditions:

- The terms and scope of the contract or project clearly call for separable phases or elements;

- The separable phases or elements of the project are often bid or negotiated separately;

- The profit margin for each component should vary according to the contractors risk and market conditions;

- Where the profit margin for a segment is greater than that for the entire project, the contractor must have a significant history of providing similar items to other customers;

- The significant history with customers who have contracted for services separately is one that is relatively stable in terms of pricing policy;

- The aggregate segment prices should not be substantially higher than the total project price (the difference attributed to cost savings); and

- The similarity of items in the contract segments and items and prices of such items provided to other customers contracted separately should be documented and verifiable.

For accounting purposes, construction contracts may be combined when they are,   *SOP 81-1.34-37*
in substance, parts of a single project with an overall profit margin as it may not be possible or appropriate to account for these contracts individually.   Only contracts that meet certain specified criteria may be combined and a contractor should consistently apply these criteria.

Both the percentage-of-completion method and the completed-contract method are acceptable methods of accounting for construction contracts.

The percentage-of-completion method is recommended when estimates of costs to   *ARB 45.3,15*
complete and extent of progress toward completion of construction contracts are   *SOP 81-1.23-25*
reasonably dependable.   Where estimating the final outcome is impractical, except to assure that no loss will be incurred, equal amounts of revenue and costs should be recognised until the results can be estimated more precisely.

The completed-contract method, i.e. income recognised only if the contract is   *SOP 81-1.32,52*
completed or substantially so, is preferable when lack of dependable estimates or inherent hazards cause forecasts to be doubtful.

Special rules apply when accounting for cost-plus contracts, i.e. where the   *ARB 43 Ch 11*
contractor is reimbursed for all costs plus a fixed fee amount or percentage.

Under the percentage-of-completion method, contractors measure progress toward   *SOP 81-1.44-51*
completion in many ways and alternative measurement methods can be based on either input or output measures.   Input measures use costs and efforts devoted to a contract, e.g. the cost-to-cost method and the efforts-expended method.   Output measures use the results achieved, e.g. units-of-delivery method and the units-of-

probable that the contract will be obtained. However, if costs incurred in obtaining a contract are recognised as an expense, they must not be reinstated as a contract cost if the contract is secured in a subsequent period.

IAS 11.23   The outcome of a fixed price contract can be estimated reliably when all of the following are satisfied:

- total contract revenue can be measured reliably;
- it is probable that the economic benefits of the contract will flow to the entity;
- both the costs of completion and stage of completion of the contract can be measured reliably; and
- costs attributable to the contract can be clearly identified and measured reliably, allowing a comparison of actual costs incurred and prior estimates.

IAS 11.24   The outcome of a cost plus contract can be estimated reliably when it is probable that the economic benefits of the contract will flow to the entity and the contract costs, whether or not specifically reimbursable, can be clearly identified and measured reliably.

IAS 11.27   Contract costs incurred that relate to future activity on the contract are recognised as an asset provided it is probable that they will be recovered. Such costs are often classified as contract work in progress and are excluded from the determination of the stage of completion.

IAS 11.32-33,35   If the outcome of a contract cannot be estimated reliably, revenue should be recognised only to the extent that it is probable the contract costs incurred will be recoverable and contract costs should be recognised as an expense in the period in which they are incurred. Any expected excess of total contract costs over total contract revenue for the contract should be recognised as an expense immediately. The percentage-of-completion method should be applied when any uncertainties that prevented reliable measurement no longer exist.

IAS 11.36   Foreseeable losses on all construction contracts must be recognised as an expense immediately regardless of whether work has commenced or the stage of completion.

15.3.3   Disclosure

IAS 11.39   An entity should disclose:

- the amount of contract revenue recognised in the period;
- the methods used to determine that revenue; and
- the methods used to determine the stage of completion of contracts in progress.

IAS 11.40-44   For contracts in progress at the balance sheet date an entity should also disclose:

- the aggregate amount of costs incurred and recognised profits (less recognised losses);
- advances received;
- retentions, i.e. progress billings that are only payable when certain conditions are satisfied or defects rectified;
- the gross amount due from customers for contract work, i.e. the net amount of costs incurred plus recognised profits less the sum of recognised losses and

work-performed method. Generally, an output measure is preferable if a reliable measure of output can be established as it provides a direct measure of progress towards completion. However, most contactors use input measures because reliable output measures are not available.

The method used should be applied consistently to all contracts with similar characteristics.

When estimating total revenue, contractors should consider the following major factors; the basic contract price; change orders, options; claims; provisions for penalties; and incentive payments. Under the percentage-of-completion method, the contractor must evaluate these factors throughout the contract's life, and must periodically revise them as necessary, to recognise revenues in the periods they are earned.

SOP 81-1.53-67

Costs must be identified, estimated, accumulated and allocated to contracts with a reasonable degree of accuracy in determining income earned. In general, contract costs should include all direct costs (such as materials, direct labour and subcontracts) and indirect costs where identifiable with or allocable to the contract. General and administrative and selling costs should be expensed as incurred.

SOP 81-1.68-72

Precontract costs incurred for a specific anticipated contract should not be included in contract costs of inventory before receipt of the contract but may be deferred if recoverability is probable. Costs appropriately deferred in anticipation of a contract should be included in contract costs on receipt of the contract. Precontract costs charged to expenses as incurred should not be reinstated on receipt of the contract.

SOP 81-1.73-75

Whenever the current estimate of total contract costs indicates a loss, the estimated loss on the entire contract should be recognised.

ARB 45.6

15.3.3 Disclosure

The method of recognising profits under construction contracts should be disclosed.

ARB 45.15
SOP 81-1.21,45

Where the percentage-of-completion method is used, it is necessary to disclose the methods used in measuring the extent of progress toward completion.

Under the percentage-of-completion method, current assets may include costs and recognised income not yet billed with respect to certain contracts, and liabilities (mainly current) may include billings in excess of costs and recognised income with respect to other contracts.

Where the completed-contract method of accounting is followed, the excess of accumulated costs over related billings should be designated as 'costs of uncompleted contracts in excess of related billings' rather than as inventory or work in process, and classified in current assets if collectable within one year or within an operating cycle if longer. The excess of accumulated billings over related costs should be designated as 'billings on uncompleted contracts in excess of related costs' in current liabilities.

ARB 45.12

progress billings. This should be presented as an asset for all contracts in progress for which costs incurred plus recognised profits (less recognised losses) exceed progress billings; and

- the gross amount due to customers for contract work, i.e. the net amount of costs incurred plus recognised profits less the sum of recognised losses and progress billings. This should be presented as a liability for all contracts in progress for which progress billings exceed costs incurred plus recognised profits (less recognised losses).

IAS 11.45 Any contingent liabilities and contingent assets, which may arise from such items as warranty costs, claims, penalties or possible losses, are disclosed in accordance with IAS 37 *Provisions, Contingent Liabilities and Contingent Assets.*

In respect of amounts due under long-term contracts, the following disclosures should be made in the balance sheet or in a note (for the first and third items, the amounts included which are expected to be collected after one year should be disclosed):   *S-X 5-02.3(c)*

- balances billed but not paid under retention provisions in contracts (if practicable, disclosure should be given of when the amounts not paid under retention provisions are expected to be collected);

- amounts representing the recognised sales value of performance and such amounts that had not been billed and were not billable at the balance sheet date; and

- billed or unbilled amounts representing claims or other similar items subject to uncertainty concerning their determination or ultimate realisation, giving a description of the nature and status of the principal items comprising such amounts.

For inventories related to long-term contracts the following disclosures should be made in a note to the financial statements: *S-X 5-02.6(b)*

- if an estimated average cost per unit method is used, the principal assumptions used to determine amounts removed from inventory (including, when meaningful, the aggregate number of units expected to be delivered under the programme or contract, delivered to date and on order); and

- if general and administrative costs have been charged to inventory, the aggregate amount of general and administrative costs incurred in each period and the actual (or estimated) amount remaining in inventory at each period end.

For long-term contracts or programmes the following information, if applicable, should be disclosed in a note to the financial statements: *S-X 5-02.6(d)*

- the aggregate amount of manufacturing or production costs and any related deferred costs, e.g. initial tooling costs, which exceed the aggregate estimated cost of all in-process and delivered units on the basis of the estimated average cost of all units expected to be produced under long-term contracts and programmes not yet complete, as well as that portion of such amount which would not be absorbed in cost of sales based on existing firm orders at the latest balance sheet date;

- the amount of deferred costs by type of cost, e.g. initial tooling, deferred production costs;

- the aggregate amount representing claims or other similar items subject to uncertainty concerning their determination or ultimate realisation, and to include a description of the nature and status of the principal items; and

- the amount of progress payments netted against inventory at the date of the balance sheet.

Claims in excess of the agreed contract price should be disclosed.   *SOP 81-1*

Section 16 Leasing

16.1 AUTHORITATIVE PRONOUNCEMENTS

- IAS 17
- IAS 40
- IFRIC 4

- SIC-15
- SIC-27

COMMENT

The G4+1 group of standard-setters published two papers on lease accounting – *Accounting for Leases: A New Approach* (1996) and *Leases: Implementation of a New Approach* (2000) – which advocated a fundamental change in lease accounting and recommended that the rights under all leases should be capitalised. Further work on these proposals has been classified as 'Active Research' by the IASB.

IFRIC issued in December 2004, IFRIC 4 *Determining whether an arrangement contains a lease* effective for IFRS reporters for periods beginning on or after 1 January 2006 which is discussed below.

IFRIC has for some time been discussing service concession arrangements and in March 2005 issued three draft interpretations: D12 *Service Concession Arrangements – Determining the Accounting Model*, D13 *Service Concession Arrangements – The Financial Asset Model* and D14 *Service Concession Arrangements – The Intangible Asset Model* that discuss the accounting treatment of such arrangements. A service concession arrangement is a contractual arrangement for the provision of public services. Such contracts are between the 'grantor' and the 'operator'. The grantor (typically a public sector entity) conveys to the operator the right and obligation to provide specified services for the period of the concession. The IFRIC draft Interpretations relate to the accounting by the operator for infrastructure assets that remain under the control of the grantor (rather than the operator).

The first of these three draft interpretations proposes that the operator should not recognise the infrastructure as its property, plant and equipment. Rather, it should recognise the rights it receives in exchange for providing construction or other services (or other consideration) to the grantor as:

- a financial asset: if the grantor has primary responsibility for paying the operator for the concession services; or

- an intangible asset: in all other circumstances, ie if the users have the primary responsibility to pay the operator for the concession services.

The second draft interpretation sets out proposals on how the financial asset model should be applied, and the third sets out proposals on how the intangible asset model should be applied. Disclosure requirements of such service concession arrangements are the subject of SIC-29 *Disclosure – Service Concession Arrangements* that was issued in May 2001.

This section does not address the consolidation of special purpose entity ('SPE') lessors, which is addressed in section 2.6.

16.2 SCOPE

IAS 17.2,4 IAS 17 *Leases* is applied in accounting for all leases (defined as agreements whereby the lessor conveys to the lessee in return for a payment or series of payments the

Section 16   Leasing

16.1   AUTHORITATIVE PRONOUNCEMENTS

- FAS 13
- FAS 28

- FAS 29
- FAS 98

Nine accounting standards, six interpretation statements and several technical bulletins and EITF abstracts have been issued to date on leasing. However, the main requirements are embodied in FAS 13 *Accounting for Leases.*

This section does not address consolidation of special purpose entity lessors (see section 2.7) or guarantees under FIN 45 (see section 18.2.1A).

16.2   SCOPE

A lease is defined as an agreement conveying the right to use property, plant or   *FAS 13.1*
equipment (land or depreciable assets or both) usually for a stated period of time.

right to use an asset for an agreed period of time) other than:

- leases to explore for or use minerals, oil, natural gas and similar non-regenerative resources; and

- licensing agreements for such items as motion picture films, video recordings, plays, manuscripts, patents and copyrights.

IAS 17.2 It is not applied as the basis for measurement for:

- property held by lessees that is accounted for as investment property or investment property provided by lessors under operating leases (IAS 40 *Investment Property*); or

- biological assets held by lessees under finance leases or biological assets provided by lessors under operating leases (see IAS 41 *Agriculture*).

IAS 17.67-69 For existing IFRS reporters, the revised IAS 17 (which introduced significant revisions in respect of clarification of the classification of leases of land and buildings, and the elimination of accounting alternatives for initial direct costs) applies to periods beginning on or after 1 January 2005 with retrospective application encouraged but not required. If the revised Standard is not applied retrospectively, the balance of any pre-existing finance lease is deemed to be properly determined by the lessor, and is accounted for prospectively in accordance with the revised Standard. However, if the entity previously applied IAS 17 (revised 1997), it must apply the revised Standard retrospectively except that if the entity took advantage of the transitional rules in IAS 17 (revised 1997) (which similarly deemed pre-existing finance leases to have been properly determined by the lessor), then the entity must apply IAS 17 retrospectively to all leases entered into since IAS 17 (revised 1997) was first applied.

IAS 17.3 IAS 17 applies to agreements that transfer rights to use assets even if substantial
SIC-29 services by lessors may be called for in connection with operating or maintaining such assets. Service concession arrangements may exhibit those features and it should be noted that SIC-29 *Disclosure–Service Concession Arrangements* contains additional disclosure requirements.

IAS 39.2,AG33 In general, lease rights and obligations recognised in accordance with IAS 17 are not within the scope of IAS 39 *Financial Instruments: Recognition and Measurement* (see section 11.2). However, lease receivables recognised by a lessor are subject to IAS 39's derecognition and impairment provisions, finance lease payables to its derecognition provisions, and embedded derivatives in a lease to its embedded derivatives provisions.

COMMENT

Common lease terms include rental increases in line with a consumer price index, contingent rentals based on sales and contingent rentals based on variable interest rates. The Application Guidance to IAS 39 states that these are closely related to the host contract, and do not need to be separated out, so lessees would continue to expense these contingent payments as incurred (unless, e.g. the lease is leveraged or the index relates to inflation in another economic environment). Care should be taken with evaluating complex lease terms.

IFRIC 4.1,2,5 IFRIC issued in December 2004, IFRIC 4 *Determining whether an arrangement*
IFRIC 4.16-17 *contains a lease*, which is effective for existing IFRS reporters for periods beginning on or after 1 January 2006 (with earlier adoption encouraged). It is applied

A lease, as defined in FAS 13, does not include agreements that are contracts for services that do not transfer the right to use property, plant or equipment from one contracting party to the other. However, agreements that do transfer the right to use property, plant or equipment meet the definition of a lease even though substantial services by the contractor (lessor) may be called for in connection with the operation or maintenance of such assets.

FAS 13 does not apply to lease agreements concerning the rights to explore for or to exploit natural resources such as oil, gas, minerals and timber; nor to licensing agreements for items such as motion picture films, plays, manuscripts, patents and copyrights.

EITF 01-8 *Determining Whether an Arrangement Contains a Lease* provides guidance as to whether an arrangement contains a lease that is within the scope of FAS 13. The consensus should be applied to arrangements agreed to, modified, or acquired in a business combination initiated, after the beginning of an entity's next reporting period beginning after 28 May 2003.

In order to qualify as a lease, an arrangement must:

- involve the use of property, plant or equipment;

- identify the property, plant or equipment (explicitly or implicitly); and

- convey to the purchaser/lessee the 'right to use' the specified property, plant or equipment.

Under EITF 01-8, if property, plant or equipment is not explicitly specified in the contract and it is economically feasible for the seller to perform its obligation independent of the operation of a particular asset, such an arrangement would not contain a lease. Where it is not economically feasible for the seller to perform its obligation through the use of alternative property, plant or equipment, then the asset has been implicitly specified in the arrangement and could be the subject of a lease. The evaluation of whether an arrangement conveys the right to use the asset should be based on the substance of the arrangement.   *EITF 01-8*

The Task Force did not conclude on whether a pro rata portion of the output of an asset can be the subject of a lease but did conclude that physically distinguishable portions of property, plant or equipment can be the subject of a lease.

The assessment of an arrangement under EITF 01-8 should be made at inception and thereafter only (a) if there is a change in the contractual terms, (b) a renewal or an extension is agreed that is not considered a modification of the terms of the original agreement prior to the end of the term of the original agreement, (c) there is a change in the determination as to whether or not performance is dependent on specified property, plant or equipment, or (d) there is a substantial physical change to the specified property, plant or equipment. The assessment should be made based on the facts and circumstances as of the date of the assessment (or reassessment). Changes in estimates would not trigger a reassessment.

FAS 13 requires the separation of a lease that is embedded in a multiple-element arrangement but does not specify how to separate the lease and non-lease payments. EITF 01-8 provides that the arrangement consideration should be allocated between the lease and non-lease deliverables based on relative fair values. Separation is not elective and is required regardless of whether objective evidence of fair value exists.

retrospectively. However, the assessment of whether an arrangement contains a lease may be made at the start of the earliest comparative period presented (and for first-time adopters, at the date of transition) based on the facts and circumstances existing at that date. The Interpretation addresses how to determine whether an arrangement is or contains a lease within the scope of IAS 17, when to make that assessment or reassessment, and how to separate the lease element of the payments. It does not address the classification of any such lease. Arrangements such as outsourcing arrangements (including outsourcing of data-processing functions), telecommunications network capacity contracts and take-or-pay contracts may include lease arrangements involving a right to use an asset, often together with related services or outputs.

IFRIC 4.6-9   Determining whether an arrangement is, or contains, a lease shall be based on the substance of the arrangement and requires an assessment of whether:

- fulfilment of the arrangement is dependent on the use of a specific asset or assets (which may include a portion of a larger asset); and
- the arrangement conveys a right to use the asset.

Although a specific asset may be explicitly identified in an arrangement, it is not the subject of a lease if fulfilment of the arrangement is not dependent on the use of the specified asset, e.g. where the supplier may provide use of alternative assets to fulfil its obligations. However, this first condition is fulfilled, even if no item is explicitly identified, where for example, the supplier owns or leases only one asset with which to fulfil the obligation and it would not be economically feasible or practical for the supplier to fulfil its obligation through the use of alternative assets.

An arrangement conveys a right to use the asset when the purchaser has the right to control the use of the underlying asset, which depends on one of the following conditions being met:

- the purchaser has the ability or right to operate the asset or direct others to operate the asset in a manner it determines while obtaining or controlling more than an insignificant amount of the output (or other utility) of the asset;
- the purchaser has the ability or right to control physical access to the underlying asset while obtaining or controlling more than an insignificant amount of the output (or other utility) of the asset; or
- facts and circumstances indicate that it is remote that one or more parties other than the purchaser will take more than an insignificant amount of the output (or other utility) that will be produced or generated by the asset during the term of the arrangement, and the price the purchaser will pay is neither contractually fixed per unit of output nor equal to the current market price per unit of output as of the time of delivery of the output.

IFRIC 4.10-11   The assessment of whether an arrangement contains a lease should be made at the inception of the arrangement, on the basis of all the facts and circumstances. A reassessment is only made where there is (1) a change in contract terms (except for renewal or extension of the original arrangement), (2) on renewal or extension, unless the term of the renewal or extension had initially been included in the lease term (if there are no changes to the terms of the original agreement, a renewal or extension before the end of the lease term is re-evaluated only in respect of the

renewal or extension period), (3) a change in the determination of whether the arrangement depends on a specified asset, or (4) a substantial change (e.g. physical change) to the specified asset.

A reassessment is made based on the facts and circumstances at the date of reassessment, including the remaining term. Changes in estimates would not trigger reassessment. A change in the determination of whether an arrangement contains a lease is accounted for prospectively from the date the circumstances giving rise to the reassessment changed, except in the case of (2) above, when it is accounted for at the inception of the renewal or extension period.

IFRIC 4.12-15 The payments attributable to the lease element and other elements, where the arrangement contains a lease within the scope of IAS 17, should be separated at the inception of the arrangement (or on reassessment) based on their relative fair values. This may require estimation techniques. IAS 17 is applied to the lease element. If it is impracticable for the purchaser to separate the lease and other elements, in the case of a finance lease, an asset and liability is recognised initially equal to the fair value of the underlying asset that is subject of the lease. An imputed finance charge is recognised using the purchaser's incremental borrowing rate, and payments made reduce the liability. If it is an operating lease, there are changes to the disclosure requirements (see section 16.4.2).

SIC-27.5,7,10-11 SIC-27 *Evaluating the Substance of Transactions Involving the Legal Form of a Lease* requires that an entity applies IAS 17 when the substance of a transaction or arrangement includes the conveyance of the right to use an asset for an agreed period of time. An entity applies the rules in SIC-27 instead of IAS 17 when the substance of the arrangement does not involve a lease. The Interpretation identifies various indicators that individually demonstrate that this may be the case.

The interpretation also discusses the accounting treatment applied in determining, whether in substance, a separate investment account and lease payment obligations represent assets and liabilities of the entity, and the treatment of any fee received by the entity. See section 19.2G for the required disclosures.

16.3   DEFINITIONS

IAS 17.4 A lease is 'an agreement whereby the lessor conveys to the lessee in return for a payment or series of payments the right to use an asset for an agreed period of time.'

A finance lease is a 'lease that transfers substantially all the risks and rewards incidental to ownership of an asset.' Title may or may not eventually be transferred.

An operating lease is 'a lease other than a finance lease.'

From the point of view of the lessee, minimum lease payments are equal to the sum of:

- the payments over the lease term that the lessee is or can be required to make, excluding contingent rent, costs for services and taxes to be paid by and reimbursed to the lessor; and

- any amounts guaranteed by the lessee or a party related to the lessee (maximum amount payable).

16.3   DEFINITIONS

From the standpoint of the lessee the minimum lease payments are equal to the sum of:

FAS 13.5j(i)

- the minimum rental payments over the lease term;
- any guarantee by the lessee of the residual value at the expiration of the lease term; and
- any payment that the lessee can be required to make upon failure to renew or extend the lease at the expiration of the lease term.

If the lease contains a bargain purchase option the minimum lease payments will include the minimum rental payments over the lease term and the payment called for by that bargain purchase.

From the standpoint of the lessor, the minimum lease payments include the amounts as described above plus any guarantee of the residual value or of rental payments beyond the lease term by a third party unrelated to either the lessee or the lessor.

FAS 13.5j(ii)

From the point of view of the lessor, minimum lease payments are equal to the sum of:

- the payments over the lease term that the lessee is or can be required to make, excluding contingent rent, costs for services and taxes to be paid by and reimbursed to the lessor (which is the same as for the lessee); and

- any residual value guaranteed to the lessor by the lessee, a party related to the lessee, or a third party unrelated to the lessor, that is financially capable of discharging the obligations under the guarantee.

If the lease contains a bargain purchase option, i.e. the exercise price of the purchase option is sufficiently lower than the fair value at the exercise date to make exercise reasonably certain, the minimum lease payments will include the minimum rental payments over the lease term to the expected date of exercise of the option and the payment required to exercise the option.

The lease term is the non-cancellable period for which the lessee has contracted to lease the asset, together with any further terms for which the lessee has the option to continue to lease the asset, with or without further payment, providing that at the inception of the lease (the earlier of the date of the lease agreement or of commitment by the parties to the principal provisions of the lease) it is reasonably certain that the lessee will exercise such option. A non-cancellable lease is one that is cancellable only on occurrence of a remote contingency, with the lessor's permission, if the lessee enters into a new lease for the same or equivalent asset with the same lessor, or on payment by the lessee of such additional amount that makes continuation of the lease reasonably certain at lease inception.

Contingent rent is the portion of the lease payments that is based on the future amount of a factor that changes other than with the passage of time – e.g. percentage of sales, amount of usage, price indices, market rates of interest.

The interest rate implicit in the lease is the discount rate that, at inception of the lease, causes the aggregate present value of (1) the minimum lease payments and (2) the unguaranteed residual value, to be equal to the sum of the fair value of the leased asset and any initial direct costs of the lessor.

IAS 17.5,13   Lease classification is made at the inception of the lease. Where the lease agreement includes provisions to adjust lease payments for certain changes in the lessor's costs during the period between lease inception and commencement, the effects of these changes are deemed to take place at inception.

IAS 17.9   Different circumstances of the lessor and lessee may lead to a different lease classification for the same lease.

> **COMMENT**
>
> Detailed definitions of other key terms are provided in IAS 17. Therefore, reference should be made to those definitions in order to determine the appropriate accounting for specific transactions.

16.4   LESSEE ACCOUNTING

IAS 17.4,8   A lessee should account for a lease as a finance lease when that lease transfers substantially all the risks and rewards incidental to ownership to the lessee, even if title is not transferred. All other leases are operating leases.

The lease term is defined as the fixed non-cancellable term of the lease plus all periods, if any: *FAS 13.5f*

- covered by bargain renewal options;
- for which failure to renew the lease imposes a penalty on the lessee in such amount that a renewal appears, at the inception of the lease, to be reasonably assured;
- covered by ordinary renewal options during which a guarantee by the lessee of the lessor's debt directly or indirectly related to the leased property is expected to be in effect or a loan from the lessee to the lessor directly or indirectly related to the leased property is expected to be outstanding;
- covered by ordinary renewal options preceding the date as of which a bargain purchase option is exercisable; or
- representing renewals or extensions of the lease at the lessor's option.

However, in no case should the lease term be assumed to extend beyond the date a bargain purchase option becomes exercisable.

Contingent rentals are increases or decreases in lease payments that result from changes occurring subsequent to the inception of the lease in the factors (other than the passage of time) on which lease payments are based. Lease payments that depend on the future use of the lease property are excluded from minimum lease payments. Lease payments that depend on an existing index or rate (such as the consumer price index) shall be included in minimum lease payments based on the index or rate at the inception of the lease.   *FAS 29.11*

The inception of the lease is the date of the lease agreement or commitment, if earlier.   *FAS 13.5b*

16.4   LESSEE ACCOUNTING

A lessee should capitalise a lease if any one of the following criteria is met (see section 16.6 for special rules for leases involving real estate):   *FAS 13.7*
    FAS 29.10-11

(a)   it transfers ownership to the lessee by the end of the lease term;

461

IAS 17.10,12   The following are indicators (not always conclusive) that a lease should be classified as a finance lease at inception:

- the lease transfers ownership to the lessee by the end of the lease term;
- the lessee has a bargain purchase option;
- the lease term is for the major part of the asset's economic life;

IAS 17.20   • the present value of the minimum lease payments, discounted at the interest rate implicit in the lease, amounts to at least substantially all the fair value of the leased asset;

- the leased assets are of such a specialised nature that only the lessee can use them without major modifications.

IAS 17.11   Additional indications of the existence of a finance lease include conditions that call for the lessee to:

- bear the lessor's losses as a result of the cancellation of the lease;
- absorb the gains or losses from fluctuation in the fair value of the residual value of the asset; or
- extend the lease for a secondary period at a rent substantially below-market rent.

16.4.1   Finance leases

IAS 17.4,20,23-24   At the commencement of the lease term, i.e. the date from which the lessee is entitled to exercise its right to use the leased asset, the lessee shall recognise an asset or a liability under a finance lease at an amount equal to the fair value of the asset being leased or, if lower, the present value of the minimum lease payments (each determined at lease inception) – discounted either at the rate implicit in the lease, or where this is not practicable to determine, the lessee's incremental borrowing rate.   The initial direct costs of the lessee are capitalised as part of the leased asset.   The assets and liabilities under a finance lease may not be presented net in the financial statements.

IAS 17.25   The minimum lease payments are allocated between the finance charge and principal repayments so as to produce a constant periodic interest rate on the remaining liability.   Contingent rents are expensed as incurred.

IAS 17.27,30   The asset recognised under a finance lease must be depreciated, consistent with the depreciation policy that the entity applies to similar assets it owns, over the leased asset's useful life or the lease term if shorter (if it is not reasonably certain that the lessee will obtain ownership of the asset before the lease term ends), and calculated in accordance with IAS 16 *Property, Plant and Equipment* and IAS 38 *Intangible Assets*.   Impairment of the asset is covered by IAS 36 *Impairment of Assets*.

Finance lease payables are subject to the derecognition provisions of IAS 39 (see section 11.3).   This may be relevant, for example in back to back and sub leases.

A   Disclosure

IAS 17.31-32   Lessees shall, in addition to the requirements of IAS 32 *Financial Instruments: Disclosure and Presentation*, make the following disclosures for finance leases:

- the net carrying amount at the balance sheet date for each class of asset;
- a reconciliation between the total of future minimum lease payments at the balance sheet date and their present value;

(b)   there is a bargain purchase option;

(c)   the lease term is for 75% or more of the leased asset's estimated economic life; or

(d)   the present value of the minimum lease payments, discounted at the lessee's incremental borrowing rate (or, if known, the implicit rate in the lease if that is lower) is greater than or equal to 90% of the fair value of the asset to the lessor at the inception of the lease less any investment tax credit retained by the lessor.   Fair value is the price for which the property could be sold in an arm's-length transaction between unrelated parties.

Otherwise, the lease should be classified as an operating lease.   However, where the lessee is involved in the construction of the asset or the lease involves a special purpose lessor, the lessee may effectively have to account for an operating lease as a capital lease.

The last two criteria are not applicable if the inception of the lease is in the final 25% of the asset's economic life, including earlier years of use.

16.4.1   Capital leases

The amount to be capitalised is the present value of the minimum lease payments or the fair value of the leased asset if that is lower.   The asset should be depreciated as for owned assets if it is capitalised under criterion (a) or (b) above or over the lease term for assets capitalised under criterion (c) or (d).   *FAS 13.10-11*

Each minimum lease payment should be split between capital and interest so as to produce a constant periodic rate of interest on the remaining balance of the obligation (i.e. the interest method).   *FAS 13.12*

A   Disclosure

A general description of the lessee's leasing arrangements is required to be disclosed, including: *FAS 13.16(d)*

*   the basis on which contingent rental payments are determined;

*   the existence and terms of renewal or purchase options and escalation clauses; and

*   restrictions imposed by lease agreements, e.g. concerning dividends, additional debt and further leasing.

The SEC Staff also expect disclosure of any obligations with respect to refinancing of the lessor's debt, any significant penalty clauses, and the provisions of any significant guarantees, such as residual value guarantees.   *EITF 90-15*

For each balance sheet presented, the gross amount of assets recorded under capital leases must be disclosed by major classes, according to nature and function, with the related accumulated amortisation thereon (this may be combined with comparable disclosures for owned assets).   *FAS 13.13,16(a)*

The amortisation charge to income on capital leases should be separately disclosed unless included in the depreciation charge, in which case this fact should be stated.   *FAS 13.13*

- the total of future minimum lease payments at the balance sheet date, and their present value, for each of the following periods:
  - not later than one year;
  - later than one year and not later than five years;
  - later than five years;
- contingent rents recognised as an expense in the period;
- the total of future minimum sublease payments expected to be received under non-cancellable subleases at the balance sheet date; and
- a general description of the lessee's material leasing arrangements including, but not limited to, the following:
  - the basis on which contingent rent payable is determined;
  - the existence and terms of renewal or purchase options and escalation clauses; and
  - restrictions imposed by lease arrangements.

The disclosure requirements of IAS 16, IAS 36, IAS 38, IAS 40 and IAS 41 also apply to assets leased under finance leases (see sections 7, 9, 6, 8 respectively).

16.4.2　Operating leases

IAS 17.33　Operating lease payments should be expensed on a straight-line basis over the lease
SIC-15.3,5　term, unless another systematic basis of recognition is representative of the time pattern of the user's benefit. Lease incentives received by the lessee should be recognised over the lease term on the same basis as the operating lease payments, irrespective of their nature or form or the timing of payments.

SIC-15.6　Costs incurred by the lessee, including costs in connection with a pre-existing lease (e.g. termination, relocation or leasehold improvements costs) are accounted for by the lessee in accordance with applicable Standards, even if the costs are effectively reimbursed through an incentive arrangement.

A　Disclosure

IAS 17.35　Lessees should, in addition to the requirements of IAS 32, make the following disclosures for operating leases:

- the total of future minimum lease payments under non-cancellable operating leases for each of the following periods:
  - not later than one year;
  - later than one year and not later than five years;
  - later than five years;
- the total of future minimum sublease payments expected to be received under non-cancellable subleases at the balance sheet date;
- lease and sublease payments recognised as an expense in the period, with separate amounts for minimum lease payments, contingent rents, and sublease payments; and
- a general description of the lessee's significant leasing arrangements including, but not limited to, the following:
  - the basis on which contingent rent payments are determined;

Disclosure is required of the future minimum lease payments under capital lease obligations as of the balance sheet date, in aggregate and for each of the succeeding five years.   *FAS 13.16(a)*

The amounts representing imputed interest should be shown as an adjustment to the aggregate minimum lease payments to reduce them to present value. Additionally, the minimum sublease rentals to be received under non-cancellable subleases of capital leases and total contingent rentals actually incurred for each period should be disclosed.

16.4.2   Operating leases

Operating lease rental expenses should normally be charged to expense over the lease term on a straight-line basis. This also applies to operating lease agreements that include scheduled rent increases 'unless another systematic and rational allocation basis is more representative of the time pattern in which the leased property is physically employed', in which case that basis should be employed. The right to control the use of the leased property is considered as the equivalent of physical use. Hence, recognition of rental expense is not affected by the extent or manner in which the lessee utilises that property.   *FAS 13.15* *FTB 85-3* *FTB 88-1*

Payments made by the lessor to or on behalf of the lessee represent incentives that should be considered reductions of rental expense by the lessee and recognised on a straight-line basis over the lease term.   *FTB 88-1*

A   *Disclosure*

A general description of the lessee's leasing arrangements should be given, e.g. disclosing the existence and terms of renewal of purchase options or escalation clauses.   *FAS 13.16(d)*

The total rental expense for operating leases should be shown with separate amounts for minimum rentals, contingent rentals and sublease rentals.   *FAS 13.16(c)*

For operating leases having initial or remaining non-cancellable lease terms exceeding one year, disclosure is required of future minimum rental payments as of the date of the latest balance sheet presented, in aggregate and for each of the next five years. Additionally, the total of minimum sublease rentals to be received under non-cancellable subleases of operating leases should be disclosed.   *FAS 13.16(b)*

- the existence and terms of renewal or purchase options and escalation clauses; and

- restrictions imposed by lease arrangements.

IFRIC 4.15   If a purchaser in an arrangement that contains a lease in accordance with IFRIC 4 (see section 16.2) concludes that it is impracticable to separate the payments reliably, it shall in the case of an operating lease, treat all payments under the arrangement as lease payments for the purposes of complying with the disclosure requirements of IAS 17, but:

- disclose those payments separately from minimum lease payments of other arrangements that do not include payments for non-lease elements; and

- state that the disclosed payments also include payments for non-lease elements in the arrangement.

16.5   LESSOR ACCOUNTING

16.5.1   Finance leases

IAS 17.4,36,38-39   The lessor records the net investment in assets held under a finance lease as a receivable in the balance sheet.   The net investment is the aggregate of (1) the minimum lease payments receivable and (2) any unguaranteed residual value accruing to the lessor, this total ('gross investment') being discounted by the interest rate implicit in the lease.   Finance income on a lease is recognised on a basis that results in a constant periodic rate of return on the net investment in the finance lease.   Initial direct costs of the lessor (where the lessor is not a manufacturer or dealer) are included in the initial measurement of the receivable.

IAS 17.41   The lessor must regularly review the estimated unguaranteed residual values of the assets held under a finance lease.   If the estimated unguaranteed residual value is reduced, the income allocation over the term of the lease is revised and the reduction related to amounts already accrued is recognised immediately.

Impairment and derecognition of lease receivables is within the scope of IAS 39 (see sections 11.3 and 11.6.3).   This may be relevant, for example in back to back and sub leases.

IAS 17.41A   An asset under a finance lease which is (or is part of a disposal group) classified as held for sale is accounted for in accordance with IFRS 5 *Non-current Assets Held for Sale and Discontinued Operations* (see section 1.9).

IAS 17.4,38,42,45   Manufacturer or dealer lessors recognise a selling profit or loss in accordance with their revenue recognition policy for outright sales.   Where artificially low interest rates are quoted, the selling profit is restricted to that which would apply if a market rate of interest was charged.   Costs incurred in negotiating and arranging a lease are recognised as an expense when the selling profit is recognised and are excluded from the definition of initial direct costs.

IAS 17.44   Sales revenue recognised by the manufacturer or dealer lessor is equal to the lower of (1) the fair value of the asset and (2) the present value of the minimum lease payments, discounted at a market rate of interest.   The cost of sale recognised should be equal to the carrying amount of the leased property less the present value of the unguaranteed residual value.

16.5   LESSOR ACCOUNTING

16.5.1   Capital leases

From the point of view of a lessor, capital leases may be classified as sales-type, direct financing or leveraged leases.

If the lease meets any of the capital lease criteria in section 16.4 and: *FAS 13.6-8,17*

- the collectability of the minimum lease payments is reasonably predictable; and

- no important uncertainties surround the amount of unreimbursable costs yet to be incurred by the lessor under the lease;

the lease should be accounted for as a sales-type or direct financing lease (see below). In either case, the asset should be removed from fixed assets and the lessor should disclose a net investment in the lease (shown as a finance lease receivable).

A   Sales-type leases

Sales-type leases arise when the fair value of the leased property is different from the carrying amount.

The manufacturer's/dealer's profit arising on such leases should be recognised in the income statement. This is calculated as the difference between the present value of the lessor's minimum lease payments and the cost/carrying amount, plus any initial direct costs less the present value of the unguaranteed residual value.

> **COMMENT**
>
> A lease involving real estate which gives rise to a manufacturer's/dealer's profit should be classified as a sales type lease only if it meets criterion (a) in section 16.4.

The lessor records the net investment in the lease as the difference between the   *FAS 13.17* minimum lease payments plus the unguaranteed residual value and the unearned income (the unearned income is the difference between (1) the sum of minimum lease payments and the unguaranteed residual value and (2) the present value using the interest rate implicit in the lease).

The net investment in the lease should be classified as either a current or non-current asset, subject to the same considerations as other assets.

A   Disclosure

IAS 17.47   Lessors shall, in addition to the requirements of IAS 32, make the following disclosures for finance leases:

- a reconciliation between the gross investment in the lease at the balance sheet date, and the present value of minimum lease payments receivable at the balance sheet date;

- the gross investment in the lease and the present value of minimum lease payments receivable at the balance sheet date, for each of the following periods:

  - not later than one year;
  - later than one year and not later than five years;
  - later than five years;

- unearned finance income;

- the unguaranteed residual values accruing to the benefit of the lessor;

- the accumulated allowance for uncollectible minimum lease payments receivable;

- contingent rents recognised as income; and

- a general description of the lessor's material leasing arrangements.

Unearned income should be taken to income at a rate calculated to give a constant rate of return on the net investment in the lease.   No account is taken of the tax flows generated by the lease.

FAS 13.17

B   Direct financing leases

In the case of a direct financing lease, there is no immediate recognition of sales revenue in the income statement.

FAS 13.18

The lessor's net investment in the lease comprises the minimum lease payments plus the unguaranteed residual value less the unearned income plus any unamortised initial direct costs (unearned income is the difference between the sum of the minimum lease payments and the unguaranteed residual value, and the cost/carrying amount of the asset).

Unearned income should be taken to income at a rate calculated to give a constant rate of return on the net investment in the lease, as for sales-type leases.

C   Leveraged leases

A leveraged lease is defined as having all of the following characteristics:

FAS 13.42

- it meets the definition of a direct financing lease;
- it involves at least three parties: a lessee, a long-term creditor and a lessor;
- the long-term creditor provides non-recourse financing (although there may be recourse to the specific property and the unremitted rentals relating to it); and
- once the investment in the lease has been made, the lessor's net investment declines during the early years and rises during the later years of the lease.

FAS 13 prescribes a special accounting treatment for leveraged leases in the lessor's books.   However, where the lease also gives rise to a manufacturer's or dealer's profit it should be accounted for as a sales-type lease (see above).

The method of accounting for leveraged leases is not detailed in this book.   The important differences from the accounting treatment prescribed for a direct financing lease are:

FAS 13.43-46

- the investment in the leveraged lease is recorded net of the non-recourse debt; and
- as the lessor's net investment in the lease is negative in certain years, the net income arising on the lease should be attributed to those years in which the net investment is positive.

D   Disclosure

A general description of the lessor's leasing arrangements should be provided.

FAS 13.23

Total future minimum lease payments with separate deductions for bad debt allowance, unguaranteed residual value and unearned income and, in the case of direct financing leases, initial direct costs should be disclosed.

Disclosure of future minimum lease rentals due for each of the five years after the balance sheet date is required.   Total contingent rentals included in the income statement for each period should also be disclosed.

16.5.2   Operating leases

IAS 17.49,53-54   Lessors must present assets leased under an operating lease in accordance with the nature of the assets. These assets should be depreciated consistent with the depreciation policy the lessor uses for similar assets it owns, and calculated in accordance with IAS 16 and IAS 38. Impairment of the assets is covered by IAS 36.

IAS 17.50,52
SIC-15.3-4   Operating lease income must be recognised in income on a straight-line basis over the lease term, unless another systematic basis of recognition is more representative of the time pattern of the user's benefit. Initial direct costs of the lessor are added to the carrying amount of the asset and recognised as an expense over the lease term on the same basis as lease income. The cost of lease incentives are not added to the carrying amount of the leased asset but are recognised in income on the same basis as the operating lease income.

IAS 17.55   A manufacturer or dealer lessor recognises no selling profit on entering into an operating lease.

A   Disclosure

IAS 17.56   Lessors shall, in addition to the requirements of IAS 32, make the following disclosures for operating leases:
*   the future minimum lease payments under non-cancellable operating leases in the aggregate and for each of the following periods:
    *   not later than one year;
    *   later than one year and not later than five years;
    *   later than five years;
*   total contingent rents recognised as income in the period; and
*   a general description of the lessor's significant leasing arrangements.

IAS 17.57   The disclosure requirements of IAS 16, IAS 36, IAS 38, IAS 40 and IAS 41 also apply to assets provided under operating leases (see sections 7, 9, 6, 8 respectively).

16.6   LEASES INVOLVING LAND AND BUILDINGS

IAS 17.14   Leases involving land and buildings are accounted for as operating or finance leases in the same way as leases of other assets. However, land normally has an indefinite economic life and the lessee normally does not receive substantially all risks and rewards incidental to ownership of the lease of land unless title to the land is expected to pass. Therefore, leases of land are usually operating leases.

For each balance sheet presented, disclosure of the components of the net investment in sales-type and direct financing leases is required, as follows: *FAS 13.23*

- aggregate minimum lease payments to be received;
- the amount of aggregate future lease payments representing (1) executory costs, including any profit thereon, and (2) accumulated allowance for uncollectible minimum lease payments;
- unguaranteed residual values accruing to the lessor's benefit;
- unearned income; and
- initial direct costs (direct financing leases only).

16.5.2   Operating leases

Leases that are not capital leases (sales-type, direct financing or leveraged) are operating leases and the related assets should be classified as fixed assets.   *FAS 13.19*

Income under operating leases should be recognised as it becomes receivable according to the provisions of the lease except where the rentals vary from a straight-line basis, in which case income should generally be recognised on a straight-line basis.   *FAS 13.19(b)*
It should be noted that enterprises may not match the depreciation expense of the assets being leased to lease income by applying annuity methods of depreciation.   *FAS 92.37*

A   Disclosure

For the latest balance sheet presented, the following disclosure is required: *FAS 13.23*

- a general description of the lease arrangement;
- the cost, carrying amount and the accumulated depreciation of assets held for leasing under operating leases by major class of asset; and
- future minimum rentals on non-cancellable leases, in aggregate and for each of the five succeeding years.

Total contingent rentals included in the income statement for each period should also be disclosed.

16.6   LEASES INVOLVING REAL ESTATE

The subject of lessee/lessor accounting is addressed by subdividing leases involving real estate into leases involving:

- land only;
- land and buildings; or
- equipment as well as real estate.

IAS 17.14   A payment made on entering into or acquiring a leasehold accounted for as an operating lease represents prepaid lease payments that are amortised over the lease term, in accordance with the pattern of user's benefit.

IAS 17.15,17   The land and buildings elements of a lease of land and buildings are considered separately for lease classification. Where the land element is immaterial, the elements may be treated as a single leased asset, with an economic life equal to that of the buildings element.

IAS 17.16   Wherever necessary, the minimum lease payments (including any lump-sum upfront payments) are allocated between the land and buildings elements in proportion to the relative fair values of the leasehold interests in the land and buildings elements at the inception of the lease. If the lease payments cannot be allocated reliably between these two elements, the entire lease is classified as a finance lease, unless it is clear that both elements are operating leases, in which case the entire lease is classified as an operating lease.

IAS 17.18-19   Separate measurement of the land and buildings elements is not required when the lessee's interest in both land and buildings is classified as an investment property in accordance with IAS 40 and the fair value model is adopted (see section 8.3). Under IAS 40, a lessee may classify a property interest held under an operating lease as an investment property. In such a case, the property interest is accounted for as if it were a finance lease and the asset is accounted for under the fair value model. The lessee continues to account for the lease as a finance lease even if it subsequently ceases to be classified as investment property, e.g. on transfer to owner-occupation. Where the lessee grants a sublease transferring substantially all the risks and rewards incidental to ownership of the interest to an unrelated third party, the sublease is classified as a finance lease, even if the third party classifies it as an operating lease.

A   Land only

Lessee

If either criterion (a) or (b) in section 16.4 is met, the lease should be accounted for as a capital lease.   Otherwise, it is an operating lease.   *FAS 13.25*   *FAS 98.22(k)*

Lessor

If the lease gives rise to manufacturer's or dealer's profit (or loss) and criterion (a) in section 16.4 is met, the lease should be classified as a sales-type lease and the extent to which manufacturer's or dealer's profit may be recognised is governed by the provisions of FAS 66 *Accounting for Sales of Real Estate* (in the same manner as a seller of the same property – see section 19.3.4).   However, if criterion (a) is not met, the lease is an operating lease.   *FAS 13.25*

If the lease does not give rise to manufacturer's or dealer's profit (or loss) and criterion (a) or (b) in section 16.4 and both criteria in section 16.5.1 are met, the lease should be accounted for as a direct financing or a leveraged lease as appropriate.   However, if the lease does not meet both criteria in section 16.5.1, it should be accounted for as an operating lease.

> **COMMENT**
>
> It should be noted that the conditions of FAS 66 for recognising a sale of real estate are very restrictive.

B   Land and buildings

If the lease meets either criterion (a) or (b) in section 16.4, it should be accounted for as follows: *FAS 13.26*

Lessee

See treatment noted in the case of the leases involving land only (section 16.6A), except that the capitalised value would have to be allocated between the land and buildings in proportion to their fair values at the inception of the lease.   The buildings portion would have to be depreciated in accordance with the lessee's normal depreciation policy.

Lessor

(i)   If the lease meets criterion (a) in section 16.4

If the lease gives rise to manufacturer's or dealer's profit (or loss) and criterion (a) in section 16.4 is met, the lease should be classified as a sales-type lease and the extent to which manufacturer's or dealer's profit may be recognised is governed by the provisions of FAS 66 (in the same manner as a seller of the same property – see section 19.3.4).   However, if criterion (a) is not met, the lease is an operating lease.   *FAS 98.22(l)*

If the lease does not give rise to manufacturer's or dealer's profit (or loss) and meets both criteria in section 16.5.1, the lease should be accounted for as a direct financing or leveraged lease as appropriate.   However, if the lease does not meet both criteria in section 16.5.1, it should be accounted for as an operating lease.

(ii)   If the lease meets criterion (b) in section 16.4

If the lease produces a manufacturer's or dealer's profit (or loss) and criterion (b) in section 16.4 is met, it should be classified as an operating lease.   Leases involving real estate cannot be classified as sales-type leases unless they transfer ownership to the lessee by the end of the lease term (simply to ensure consistency with the requirements of FAS 66).

If the lease does not give rise to manufacturer's or dealer's profit (or loss) and meets both criteria in section 16.5.1, the lease should be accounted for as a direct financing or a leveraged lease as appropriate.   However, if the lease does not meet both criteria in section 16.5.1, it should be accounted for as an operating lease.

(iii)   If the lease does not meet either criterion (a) or (b) in section 16.4

- If the land element of the lease is less than 25% of the total by market value, the lessee and the lessor should consider the land and the building as a single unit and apply criterion (c) or (d) in section 16.5 (and in the case of the lessor, both criteria in section 16.5.1 as well) to determine whether it is a capital/direct financing or leveraged or operating lease.   For the purposes of the 90% test, residual value or first-loss guarantees by the lessee should be included in the minimum lease payments.   If the lease gives rise to a manufacturer's or dealer's profit, the lessor should treat it as an operating lease. *FAS 98.22(m)* *EITF 92-1*

- If the land element is greater than 25%, the land and buildings should be considered separately, the land element being treated as an operating lease and the buildings element being treated as an operating or capital/direct financing or leveraged lease, depending on whether or not it meets at least one of criteria (c) or (d) in section 16.4. *FAS 98.22(n)*

    For those purposes, the minimum lease payments attributable to each element are found by determining the fair value of the land and applying the lessee's incremental borrowing rate to it.   The minimum lease payments applicable to the buildings element is found by deducting those for the land element from the total minimum lease payments.

C   Leases involving equipment as well as real estate

The equipment should be considered, and accounted for, separately; the minimum lease payments applicable to the equipment element of the lease should be estimated by whatever means are appropriate in the circumstances. *FAS 13.27*

Under the consensus reached in EITF 00-11 *Lessor's Evaluation of Whether Leases of Certain Integral Equipment Meet the Ownership Transfer requirements of FASB Statement No.13*, leases of integral equipment, as defined in FIN 43, are considered to be leases of real estate.   EITF 00-13 *Determining Whether Equipment is 'Integral Equipment' Subject to FASB Statements No.66, Accounting for Sales of Real Estate, and No.98 Accounting for Leases* concluded that where the cost to remove plus the decrease in value exceeds 10% of the fair value of the equipment, the equipment is integral equipment. *EITF 00-13*

16.7   SALE AND LEASEBACK

16.7.1   General

IAS 17.59-60,64 In a sale and leaseback transaction, the seller-lessee sells an asset to the buyer-lessor. Where the transaction results in a finance lease, any excess of sales proceeds over the carrying amount is deferred and amortised over the lease term. It is not appropriate to show a profit on disposal on an asset, where the transaction is a means whereby the lessor provides finance to the lessee, with the asset as security. If there is an apparent loss, no adjustment is made to the carrying amount unless there is an impairment under IAS 36.

> **COMMENT**
>
> While the wording is ambiguous, in our view, the leased asset should be recorded at its previous carrying amount, and continue to be accounted for as before. The proceeds are recorded as a liability and accounted for in accordance with IAS 39.

IAS 17.61,63 Where the leaseback is classified as an operating lease the following rules apply:

- sale price equals fair value: the profit or loss on the sale should be recognised immediately;

- sale price below fair value: the profit or loss on the sale should be recognised immediately. However, to the extent the loss is compensated for by future lease payments below market price, the loss should be deferred and amortised in proportion to the lease payments over the period for which the asset is expected to be used;

- sale price above fair value: the difference between the sales price and fair value should be deferred and amortised over the period for which the asset is expected to be used.

However, if the fair value of the asset is lower than its carrying amount, a loss equal to the difference between fair value and carrying amounts is recognised immediately.

IAS 17.65 IAS 17 does not deal explicitly with the use of options in the context of sale and leaseback transactions, and these may affect the overall assessment of the lease. The disclosure requirements for sale and leasebacks, are as for other leases, although attention should be paid to the disclosure of unique or unusual terms.

16.7.2   Sale and leaseback involving land and buildings

There is no specific guidance under International Financial Reporting Standards regarding sale and leaseback transactions involving land and buildings.

16.7 SALE AND LEASEBACK

16.7.1 Sale and leaseback of property other than real estate

Sale-leaseback accounting is a method of accounting for a sale-leaseback transaction in which the seller-lessee records a sale, removes the property and related liabilities from the balance sheet, recognises the profit or loss as required by FAS 28 and classifies the leaseback under FAS 13 as amended by FAS 28.   *FAS 98.70*

Any profit or loss arising on a sale and leaseback transaction other than one involving real estate should be deferred and amortised by the seller-lessee as follows: *FAS 28.3*

- if the leaseback is recorded as a capital lease, in proportion to the amortisation of the leased asset; or

- if the leaseback is an operating lease, in proportion to the gross rental charged to expense over the lease term.

The following are exceptions to the above rule:

- the seller-lessee retains the right to only a minor portion of the remaining use of the property sold, i.e. the present value of a reasonable amount of rental for the leaseback represents 10% or less of the fair value of the asset sold, in which case the sale and leaseback should be accounted for as separate transactions based on their respective terms.

  Potentially, profit on the sale could be recognised in full at the date of sale. However, if the leaseback rentals are not at market value then profit should be deferred or accrued to adjust these to a reasonable level under market conditions;

- the seller-lessee retains more than a minor part but less than substantially all of the use of the property through the leaseback, in which case certain amounts of profit should be recognised immediately insofar as the profit on the sale exceeds the value of the leaseback. 'Substantially all' is measured by reference to the 90% recovery criterion for a capital lease in section 16.4(d);

- the fair value of the asset is less than the carrying amount, in which case a loss should be recognised immediately, up to the extent of that difference.

The EITF considered the accounting treatment of sale and leasebacks where the asset is either subject to an operating lease or subleased or intended to be subleased by the seller-lessee to another party under an operating lease. The Task Force reached a consensus that the seller-lessee-sublessor should record a sale, remove the asset from the balance sheet and classify the leaseback as a lease in accordance with FAS 13 (see section 16.4). Any gain or loss should be recognised or deferred and amortised as discussed above.   *EITF 93-8*

16.7.2 Sale and leaseback involving real estate

A seller-lessee should use sale-leaseback accounting only for those sale-leaseback transactions with payment terms and provisions that: *FAS 98.7*

- provide for a normal leaseback;

- adequately demonstrate the buyer-lessor's initial and continuing investment in the property; and

- transfer all of the other risks and rewards of ownership as demonstrated by the absence of any other continuing involvement by the seller-lessee.

The last two provisions noted above should be assessed by reference to FAS 66 which deals with accounting for sales of real estate (see section 19.3.4). FAS 98 *Accounting for Leases* precludes sale and leaseback accounting where the transaction does not qualify as a sale under FAS 66. Such transactions should be accounted for by the deposit method or as a financing transaction.

A   Normal leaseback

A normal leaseback is one in which the seller-lessee actively uses substantially all of the leased property in its trade or business during the lease term. 'Minor' subleasing is permitted.   *FAS 98.8*

B   Continuing involvement

FAS 66 provides several examples of continuing involvement whereby the risks or rewards of ownership do not transfer to the buyer-lessor. FAS 98 incorporates these restrictions and expands upon them. Three of these examples frequently found in sale-leaseback transactions are provisions in which: *FAS 66.25-43* *FAS 98.11-13*

- the seller-lessee has an obligation or an option to repurchase or the buyer-lessor can compel the seller-lessee to repurchase; or

- the seller-lessee guarantees the buyer-lessor's investment or a return on that investment for a limited or extended period of time; or

- the seller-lessee is allowed to participate in any future profits of the buyer-lessor or the appreciation of the leased property, for example, where the seller-lessee has or has an option to acquire an interest in the buyer-lessor.

Other provisions or conditions that are guarantees and that do not transfer all of the risks of ownership constitute 'continuing involvement' for the purposes of applying the above rules to sale-leaseback transactions. A number of examples of such situations are provided in the standard including the following: *FAS 66.12-13* *FAS 98.12*

- the seller-lessee is required to pay the buyer-lessor at the end of the lease term for a decline in the fair value of the property below the estimated residual value on some basis other than excess wear and tear of the property levied on inspection of the property at the termination of the lease;

- the seller-lessee provides non-recourse financing to the buyer-lessor for any portion of the sales proceeds or provides recourse financing in which the only recourse is to the leased asset;

- the seller-lessee is not relieved of the obligation under any existing debt related to the property;

- the seller-lessee provides collateral on behalf of the buyer-lessor other than the property directly involved in the sale-leaseback transaction;

- the seller-lessee's rental payment is contingent on some predetermined or determinable level of future operations of the buyer-lessor;

16.8 ACCOUNTING FOR SUBLEASES

IAS 17.31,35   International Financial Reporting Standards do not provide separate recognition and measurement rules for subleases (with the exception of a sublease of a leasehold interest accounted for as an investment property – see section 8.2). However, lessees should disclose the following information on subleases:

- the total of future minimum sublease payments expected to be received under non-cancellable subleases at the balance sheet date, separately for property leased under finance leases and operating leases; and

- the seller-lessee enters into a sale-leaseback transaction involving property improvements, e.g. an office building, or integral equipment, i.e. which cannot be removed and used separately without incurring significant cost, without leasing the underlying land to the buyer-lessor;

- the buyer-lessor is obligated to share with the seller-lessee any portion of the appreciation of the property; and

- any other provision or circumstance that allows the seller-lessee to participate in any future profits of the buyer-lessor or the appreciation of the leased property, e.g. the seller-lessee owns or has an option to acquire any interest in the buyer-lessor.

In addition to ensuring that there is no other continuing involvement of the sort described in FAS 66 and FAS 98, terms of the sale-leaseback that are substantially different from those that an independent third party lessor or lessee would accept should also be considered when evaluating the 'continuing involvement' condition noted above. *FAS 98.9*

C   Profit to be recognised

If sale-leaseback accounting is permitted, the profit or loss on the sale portion of the sale-leaseback transaction to be deferred and amortised in accordance with FAS 28 *Accounting for Sales with Leasebacks an amendment of FASB Statement No. 13* i.e. over the leaseback, would be the profit that could otherwise be recognised in accordance with FAS 66. Note that in certain transactions that qualify for sales recognition under FAS 66, the full amount of profit cannot be recognised at the date of sale (see section 19.3.4). *FAS 28.3 fn**

D   Disclosure

In addition to the disclosure requirements of FAS 13 (see section 16.4) and FAS 66, the seller-lessee should disclose the terms of the sale-leaseback transaction, including future commitments, obligations, provisions or circumstances that require or result in the seller-lessee's continuing involvement. *FAS 98.17-18*

Where the transaction is accounted for under the deposit method or as a financing transaction, disclosure is required of:

- the obligation for minimum lease payments as of the date of latest balance sheet presented in aggregate and for each of the five succeeding fiscal years; and

- the total of minimum sublease rentals, if any, to be received in the future under non-cancellable subleases, in aggregate and for each of the five succeeding fiscal years.

16.8   ACCOUNTING FOR SUBLEASES

If an item is subleased, the accounting by the original lessee/sublessor will depend on whether the primary obligation under the original lease remains in force or not. *FAS 13.35-40*

If the primary obligation under the original lease is cancelled under the second agreement and if the original lease was a capital lease, the sublessor removes the asset and obligation from the balance sheet, if applicable, and recognises any profit or loss.

- lease and sublease payments under operating leases recognised as an expense for the period, with separate amounts for minimum lease payments, contingent rents, and sublease payments.

Finance lease payables are subject to the derecognition provisions of IAS 39 (see section 11.3). This may be relevant, for example in back to back and subleases.

16.9   ACCOUNTING FOR LEASE CHANGES

IAS 17.13 Leases are classified at their inception. If the conditions of a lease are changed (other than renewing the lease) in such a way that a different classification would have resulted at inception of the lease, the revised lease agreement is treated as a new lease agreement over its term. Changes in estimates or circumstances, e.g. changes in discount rate or estimated economic life, do not give rise reclassification of existing leases.

If the original capital or operating lease lessee/sublessor is secondarily liable under the sublease, the loss contingency should be treated as described under section 19.3.4.

If the original lease remains in force the sublessor should continue to account for it as before and account for the sublease under the lessor accounting rules in FAS 13 (see section 16.5), except that if the original lease is:

- an operating lease, the sublease should be treated as an operating lease; or
- a capital lease, because it met either criterion (c) or (d) in section 16.4 and not (a) or (b), the sublessor should classify the sublease as a direct financing lease only if it meets criterion (c) in section 16.4 and both criteria in section 16.5.1 – otherwise the sublease is an operating lease.

The only exception to this rule is where the sublease is an integral part of an overall transaction in which the sublessor is just an intermediary, in which case criterion (d) in section 16.4 is also available for classification purposes.

16.9   ACCOUNTING FOR LEASE CHANGES

Specific rules exist on how a lessee and lessor should account for the effects of a renewal, extension, termination or change in the provisions of a lease.   *FAS 13.14*
FAS 13.17(f)

An existing lease is considered a new agreement when it is renewed or extended beyond the original lease term.   The exercise of a renewal option included as part of the original lease term is not a renewal or extension of a lease.   Changes in estimates do not change the classification of a lease.

When both the original lease and the new agreement are classified as capital leases, the recorded asset and obligation balances are adjusted at the date of the revision, by the difference between the outstanding obligation balance and the present value of the future minimum lease payments. The present value of the future minimum lease payments under the revised or new agreement should be computed using the rate of interest used to record the lease initially.   *FAS 13.14*

If a change in the provisions of a capital lease gives rise to a new agreement classified as an operating lease, the transaction should be accounted for under the sale and leaseback requirements of FAS 98 or FAS 28, as applicable.   The original lease continues to be accounted for as a capital lease to the end of its lease term. Thereafter, the new agreement is accounted for as an operating lease. The present value of the future minimum lease payments under the revised or new agreement should be computed using the rate of interest used to record the lease initially.

Termination of a capital lease results in the recognition of a gain or loss for the difference between the remaining asset and obligation balances.

16.10   ONEROUS LEASES

IAS 37.5,66   IAS 17 does not provide specific guidance on accounting for onerous leases.
IAS 37.Appx C.8   However, IAS 37 *Provisions, Contingent Liabilities and Contingent Assets* requires a provision to be recognised for onerous leases equal to the best estimate of unavoidable lease payments.

IFRS 3.Appx B16   Similarly, in the case of a business combination that is an acquisition, IFRS 3 *Business Combinations* requires the acquirer to recognise onerous contracts of the acquiree at the present values of amounts to be disbursed in meeting the obligation, determined at appropriate current interest rates.

16.10   ONEROUS LEASES

Provisions for permanently vacant leasehold properties should be recognised and   *FAS 146.16*
measured at fair value.   The liability for costs to be incurred under a contract for its
remaining term without economic benefit should be recognised at fair value when
the entity permanently ceases using the right conveyed by the contract (the 'cease-
use date approach').   The fair value of the liability at the cease-use date should be
based on the remaining lease rentals, reduced by estimated sublease rentals that
could reasonably be obtained even if the entity does not intend to sublease the
property.   Estimated sublease rentals cannot exceed remaining lease rentals.

The net provision for vacant leasehold properties would be a discounted amount.   *FAS 146.6*
Subsequent changes to the liability should be measured using the credit-adjusted
risk-free rate used for initial measurement.   Changes due to the timing or amount
of estimated cash flows are recognised as an adjustment to the liability and reported
in the same income statement line item(s) as the original provision.   Changes due
to the passage of time are recognised as an increase in the liability and as an
accretion expense but cannot be recorded in interest expense.

Section 17   Taxation

17.1   AUTHORITATIVE PRONOUNCEMENTS

- IAS 12   • SIC-25
- SIC-21

17.2   OBJECTIVES AND BASIC PRINCIPLES

IAS 12.1-2,IN2   IAS 12 *Income Taxes* requires entities to account for taxation using the balance sheet liability method, which focuses on temporary differences in accounting for the expected future tax consequences of events. It applies to income taxes, which include all domestic and foreign taxes based on taxable profits, and taxes payable by a subsidiary, associate or joint venture on distributions to the reporting entity. Taxation recognised in income comprises the current tax and the change in deferred tax assets and liabilities of the entity that is not required to be recognised in equity.

> **COMMENT**
>
> There is a short-term convergence project with the FASB with the aim of eliminating differences between IAS 12 issued by the IASB, and FAS 109 *Accounting for Income Taxes*. The project is wide-ranging and various areas discussed are addressed in the sections below. The IASB intend to publish an exposure draft of amendments to IAS 12 at the same time as the FASB publishes an exposure draft of amendments to FAS 109. However, the IASB do not intend this to be a fundamental rewrite of IAS 12.

17.2.1   Temporary differences and tax base

A   Tax base

IAS 12.5,7   The tax base is 'the amount attributed to the asset or liability for tax purposes.' The tax base of an asset is the amount deductible for tax purposes against any taxable economic benefits that will flow as the entity recovers the carrying amount of the asset.   If those economic benefits are not taxable, the tax base is the carrying amount of the asset.

IAS 12.8   The tax base of a liability is its carrying amount, less any amounts deductible for tax purposes in respect of the liability in future periods.   If settlement of the liability is not deductible, the tax base is the carrying amount.   For revenue received in advance, the tax base is the carrying amount of the deferred income less any revenue not taxable in future periods.

IAS 12.9,68B   Where no asset or liability is recognised on the balance sheet (e.g. research costs, equity-settled share-based payment), the tax base is the difference between the carrying amount of nil and the amounts deductible in future periods.

Section 17   Taxation

17.1   AUTHORITATIVE PRONOUNCEMENTS

- FAS 109

17.2   OBJECTIVES AND BASIC PRINCIPLES

The objectives of FAS 109 *Accounting for Income Taxes* are, first to account for   *FAS 109.6*
taxes in respect of the current year and, secondly, to account for the expected future
tax consequences of events that have been recognised in an enterprise's accounts or
tax returns.   To implement these objectives, in addition to current year amounts,
FAS 109 requires full provision for the tax effects of temporary differences (see   *FAS 109.8,16*
section 17.2.1) using enacted tax rates; the effects of future changes in tax laws or
rates are not anticipated.   The deferred tax charge or credit is the change during the
year in the deferred tax assets and liabilities.

COMMENT

The FASB and IASB are undertaking a joint short-term convergence project to
eliminate differences between IAS 12 *Income Taxes* and FAS 109.   The FASB
expects to issue an exposure draft, which would include all of the proposed
amendments to FAS 109, in the third quarter of 2005.

The FASB has another ongoing project on income taxes which is an interpretation
of FAS 109.   The objective of this project is to clarify the criteria for recognition of
tax benefits, such that an entity's tax benefits recognised in tax returns must be
probable of being sustained before recording the related tax benefit in financial
statements.   Probable as used in this project would be consistent with its use in
FAS 5 *Accounting for Contingencies*.   The FASB expects to issue an exposure
draft in the second quarter of 2005.

17.2.1   Temporary differences

Temporary differences are differences between the tax bases of assets or liabilities   *FAS 109.10-13*
and their carrying amounts that will result in taxable or tax deductible amounts in
future years.   They are created mainly due to timing differences but they can arise
for other reasons, e.g. on an acquisition where the fair values assigned to acquired
assets and liabilities differ from their tax bases (see section 3.4.3J).   Timing
differences are differences between profits or losses as computed for tax purposes
and results as stated in financial statements.   Temporary differences that result in
taxable amounts in future years are known as taxable temporary differences; those
that result in tax deductible differences in future years are referred to as deductible
temporary differences.

IAS 12.10   Where the tax base is not immediately apparent, with some limited exceptions, a deferred tax liability (asset) is recognised whenever recovery or settlement of the carrying amount of an asset (liability) would make future tax payments larger (smaller) than if there were no tax consequences.

IAS 12.52   Where the manner in which an entity recovers (settles) the carrying amount of an asset (liability) may affect the tax base of the asset (liability), the tax base consistent with the expected manner of recovery or settlement is used for measuring deferred tax liabilities and deferred tax assets.

IAS 12.11   In consolidated financial statements, the appropriate tax base is determined using the consolidated tax return in those jurisdictions where such a return is filed, and elsewhere, using the tax return of each entity in the group.

B   Temporary differences

IAS 12.5   Temporary differences are defined as 'differences between the carrying amount of an asset or liability in the balance sheet and its tax base.'

IAS 12.5   Temporary differences may be either:

* taxable temporary differences, which are temporary differences that will result in taxable amounts in determining taxable profit (tax loss) of future periods when the carrying amount of the asset or liability is recovered or settled; or

* deductible temporary differences, which are temporary differences that will result in amounts that are deductible in determining taxable profit (tax loss) of future periods when the carrying amount of the asset or liability is recovered or settled.

COMMENT

There is a short-term convergence project with the FASB with the aim of eliminating differences between IAS 12 issued by the IASB, and FAS 109. At its June 2004 meeting, the IASB discussed the definition of tax base and temporary difference, and tentatively agreed to bring IAS 12 more in line with FAS 109 and also to delete the current requirements to have regard to management intentions in determining the tax base.

17.2.2   Recognition of tax assets and liabilities

IAS 12.5,12-14   Current tax is the amount of income taxes payable (recoverable) in respect of the taxable profit (tax loss) for the period. Current tax for current and prior periods is recognised as a liability to the extent it is unpaid. Payments of taxation for current and prior periods in excess of the amount due are recognised as an asset. Tax losses that can be carried back to recover current tax of prior periods are recognised as an asset in the period the tax loss occurs.

IAS 12.15   A deferred tax liability is recognised by an entity for all taxable temporary differences except to the extent that the deferred tax liability arises from:

* the initial recognition of goodwill; or

* non-deductible goodwill for tax purposes; or

* the initial recognition of an asset or liability in a transaction which (1) is not a business combination and (2) at the time of the transaction, affects neither accounting profit nor taxable profit or loss.

17.2.2   Recognition of tax assets and liabilities

Under FAS 109, it is assumed that reported amounts of assets and liabilities will be   *FAS 109.10*
recovered or settled, and therefore a difference between the tax basis of an asset or
liability and its reported amount will result in taxable or deductible amounts in future
years when the reported amounts of assets are recovered and the reported amounts of
liabilities are settled.   Examples of taxable or deductible amounts include:

- *Revenues or gains that are taxable after they are recognised in financial*   *FAS 109.11*
  income.   An asset (for example, a receivable from an instalment sale) may be
  recognised for revenues or gains that will result in future taxable amounts
  when the asset is recovered.

- *Expenses or losses that are deductible after they are recognised in financial*
  income.   A liability (for example, a product warranty liability) may be
  recognised for expenses or losses that will result in future tax deductible
  amounts when the liability is settled.

There are also special rules for taxable temporary differences associated with investments in subsidiaries, joint ventures, associates and branches described below.

IAS 12.24,34 A deferred tax asset shall be recognised for all deductible temporary differences (and the carryforward of unused tax losses and credits) – to the extent that it is probable that taxable profit will be available against which the deductible temporary difference (or unused tax losses and credits) can be utilised (see below). However, an entity shall not recognise a deferred tax asset that arises from the initial recognition of an asset or liability in a transaction that (1) is not a business combination and that (2) does not affect accounting or taxable profit or loss at the time of the transaction.

There are also special rules for deductible temporary differences associated with investments in subsidiaries, joint ventures, associates and branches described below.

IAS 12.28-30,35 It is probable that taxable profit will be available to utilise a deductible temporary difference (or unused tax losses or unused tax credits) to the extent that:

- there are sufficient taxable temporary differences relating to the same taxation authority and the same taxable entity which are expected to reverse in the same period as the expected reversal of the deductible temporary difference or in periods into which a tax loss arising from the deferred tax asset can be carried back or forward; or

- it is probable that the entity will have sufficient taxable profits relating to the same taxation authority and same taxable entity in the same period as the expected reversal of the deductible temporary difference (or in periods into which a tax loss arising from the deferred tax asset can be carried back or forward), or tax planning opportunities will create taxable profits in appropriate periods. In assessing these future profits, taxable profits arising from deductible temporary differences expected to originate in future periods are ignored, as these will themselves require future taxable profits to be utilised.

When there are unused tax losses and tax credits and insufficient taxable temporary differences as above are present, the detailed guidance in section 17.2.4 is followed.

IAS 12.21-22 Subsequent reductions in a deferred tax liability or asset which was not recognised because it arose from the initial recognition (e.g. because non-tax deductible goodwill is later impaired) are also regarded as resulting from initial recognition and are not recognised. However, a deferred tax liability is recognised if the temporary differences do not result from initial recognition of goodwill (e.g. as the tax deductions are received or impairments are recognised on tax-deductible goodwill).

COMMENT

There is a short-term convergence project with the FASB with the aim of eliminating differences between IAS 12 issued by the IASB, and FAS 109. The exemption from recognition of deferred tax on temporary differences arising on initial recognition of an asset or liability in a transaction which is not a business combination, and at the time of the transaction neither affects accounting nor taxable profit does not appear in FAS 109 and the IASB has tentatively agreed to remove it and replace it with an approach based on a modified version of the 'simultaneous equations' method in US GAAP.

IAS 12.15,66 Temporary differences may arise from the initial recognition of an asset or liability (at
IFRS 3.Appx B16 its fair value) in a business combination. In allocating the cost of the business

- *Revenues or gains that are taxable before they are recognised in financial income.* A liability (for example, subscriptions received in advance) may be recognised for an advance payment for goods or services to be provided in future years. For tax purposes, the advance payment is included in taxable income upon the receipt of cash. Future sacrifices to provide goods or services (or future refunds to those who cancel their orders) will result in future tax deductible amounts when the liability is settled.

- *Expenses or losses that are deductible before they are recognised in financial income.* The cost of an asset (for example, depreciable personal property) may have been deducted for tax purposes faster than it was depreciated for financial reporting. Amounts received upon future recovery of the amount of the asset for financial reporting will exceed the remaining tax basis of the asset, and the excess will be taxable when the asset is recovered.

- *A reduction in the tax basis of depreciable assets because of tax credits.* Amounts received upon future recovery of the amount of the asset for financial reporting will exceed the remaining tax basis of the asset, and the excess will be taxable when the asset is recovered.

- *An increase in the tax basis of assets because of indexing whenever the local currency is the functional currency.* The tax law for a particular tax jurisdiction might require adjustment of the tax basis of a depreciable (or other) asset for the effects of inflation. The inflation-adjusted tax basis of the asset would be used to compute future tax deductions for depreciation or to compute gain or loss on sale of the asset. Amounts received upon future recovery of the local currency historical cost of the asset will be less than the remaining tax basis of the asset, and the difference will be tax deductible when the asset is recovered.

- *Business combinations.* There may be differences between the assigned values and the tax bases of the assets and liabilities recognised in a business combination. Those differences will result in taxable or deductible amounts when the reported amounts of the assets and liabilities are recovered and settled, respectively.

The standard does provide special exceptions to what is otherwise a full provision approach: *FAS 109.9,31-34*

- A tax liability is not required to be recognised for an excess of the amount for financial reporting over the tax basis of an investment in a foreign subsidiary or a foreign corporate joint venture, as defined in APB 18 *The Equity Method of Accounting for Investments in Common Stock*, that is essentially permanent in duration unless it becomes apparent that the temporary differences will reverse in the foreseeable future;

- A deferred tax asset or liability related to goodwill for which amortisation is not deductible for tax purposes or unallocated negative goodwill is prohibited;

- Tax effects of intragroup transfers, such as inventory, are required to be deferred and recognised when the inventory is sold to a third party. It prohibits recognition of a deferred tax asset for the difference between the tax basis of the assets in the buyer's jurisdiction and their cost as reported in the consolidated financial statements.

combination, tax assets (including those from unused tax losses and tax credits) and liabilities are recognised in accordance with IAS 12, but are assessed from the perspective of the combined entity. The resulting deferred tax liability or asset (where it meets the recognition criteria for an asset) affects the amount of goodwill or the amount of any excess of the acquirer's interest in the net fair value of the acquiree's identifiable assets, liabilities and contingent liabilities over the cost of the combination.

IAS 12.23,   In accordance with IAS 32 *Financial Instruments: Disclosure and Presentation*, the
Appx B,   issuer of a compound financial instrument classifies the instrument into equity and
Example 4   liability components. Where the tax base of the liability equals the initial carrying amount of the sum of the liability and equity components, a deferred tax liability is recognised for the temporary difference resulting from the initial recognition of the equity component separately from the liability component (the tax base differs to the recognised liability) and charged to equity. Subsequent changes in the deferred tax liability are recognised in the income statement as deferred tax expense or income.

IAS 12.39,44   An entity shall recognise a deferred tax liability for all taxable temporary differences arising from investments in subsidiaries, branches, associates and joint ventures, except to the extent that both the following conditions are satisfied:

- it is able to control the timing of the reversal of the temporary difference; and
- it is probable that the temporary difference will not reverse in the foreseeable future.

However, a deferred tax asset should be recognised for all deductible temporary differences arising from investments in subsidiaries, branches, associates and joint ventures to the extent that, and only to the extent that it is probable that:

- the temporary difference will reverse in the foreseeable future; and
- taxable profit will be available against which the temporary difference can be utilised.

IAS 12.38   Such temporary differences may arise where the carrying amount – being the parent's or investor's share of net assets of the investment and any goodwill, in consolidated financial statements – differs from the tax base due to, for example, undistributed profits, impairments, or foreign exchange movements.

IAS 12.40,42-43   IAS 12 provides the following further guidance. For a subsidiary or branch, an entity will control the dividend policy and hence the timing of the reversal of the temporary differences. Therefore, where the parent has determined that profits will not be distributed in the foreseeable future, no deferred tax liability is recognised in respect of temporary differences associated with an investment in subsidiary or a branch. However, the entity will not usually control the dividend policy of an associate and the timing of reversal of the temporary differences. Therefore, in the absence of an agreement requiring that the associate's profits are not distributed in the foreseeable future, a deferred tax liability is recognised (where this can not be quantified, but a minimum amount is known, that amount is recognised). Where a joint venture agreement allows a venturer in a joint venture to control profit sharing and it is probable that profits will not be distributed in the foreseeable future, no deferred tax liability is recognised.

- A deferred tax liability or asset is prohibited for differences related to assets and liabilities that, under FAS 52 *Foreign Currency Translation* are remeasured from the local currency into the functional currency using historical exchange rates and that result from (1) changes in exchange rates or (2) indexing for tax purposes.

Certain basis differences may not result in taxable or deductible amounts in future years when the related asset or liability for financial reporting is recovered or settled and, therefore, may not be temporary differences for which a deferred tax liability or asset is recognised.   *FAS 109.14*

Some temporary differences are deferred taxable income or tax deductions and have balances only on the income tax balance sheet and therefore cannot be identified with a particular asset or liability for financial reporting.   For example, when a long-term contract is accounted for by the percentage-of-completion method for financial reporting and by the completed-contract method for tax purposes.   The temporary difference (income on the contract) is deferred income for tax purposes that becomes taxable when the contract is completed.   There is no related, identifiable asset or liability for financial reporting, but there is a temporary difference that results from an event that has been recognised in the financial statements and, the temporary difference will result in taxable or deductible amounts in future years.   *FAS 109.15*

It should be presumed that all undistributed earnings of a subsidiary will be transferred to the parent company.   Accordingly, the undistributed earnings of a subsidiary included in consolidated income should be accounted for as a temporary difference unless the tax law provides a means by which the investment in a domestic subsidiary can be recovered tax free.   However, a deferred tax liability is not recognised for (a) an excess of the amount for financial reporting over the tax basis of an investment in a foreign subsidiary or a foreign corporate joint venture that meets the indefinite reversal criteria (see below), and (b) undistributed earnings of a domestic subsidiary or a domestic corporate joint venture that arose before 15 December 1992 and that meet the indefinite reversal criteria.   *APB 23.10-12*

Indefinite reversal criteria. The presumption that all undistributed earnings of a foreign subsidiary or a foreign corporate joint venture will be transferred to the parent company may be overcome if sufficient evidence shows that the foreign subsidiary or foreign corporate joint venture has invested or will invest the undistributed earnings indefinitely or that the earnings will be remitted in a tax-free liquidation.   If circumstances change and it becomes apparent that undistributed earnings of a foreign subsidiary or a foreign corporate joint venture will be remitted and income taxes have not been recognized by the parent company, or visa versa, the parent company should adjust income tax expense of the current period.

When a foreign entity uses the parent's functional currency as its functional currency, nonmonetary assets such as inventory, land, and depreciable assets are remeasured into the parent's functional currency at historical exchange rates.   After a change in exchange rates, there will be a difference between (a) the amount of foreign currency revenues needed to recover the parent's functional currency cost of those assets and (b) the foreign currency tax basis of those assets.   Although that difference technically meets the definition of a temporary difference, the FASB concluded that the substance of accounting for it as such is to recognize deferred taxes on exchange   *FAS 109.118-119*

COMMENT

There is a short-term convergence project with the FASB with the aim of eliminating differences between IAS 12 issued by the IASB, and FAS 109. The exemptions in relation to investments in subsidiaries, joint ventures, associates and branches are different in both standards. The IASB has tentatively decided that an entity should recognise the income tax consequences of all temporary differences arising in the consolidated financial statements, and to eliminate the concept of 'branches' but following an examination of practical difficulties with this approach, has decided to retain the exceptions in IAS 12 for the recognition of deferred tax liabilities in respect of certain foreign subsidiaries and foreign corporate joint ventures.

IAS 12.41 Temporary differences may arise when the non-monetary assets and liabilities of an entity are measured in its functional currency but its tax base is determined in a different currency (and translated at closing rate). The resulting deferred tax asset (where the asset recognition criteria are met) or liability is charged or credited to profit or loss.

COMMENT

There is a short-term convergence project with the FASB with the aim of eliminating differences between IAS 12 issued by the IASB, and FAS 109. In relation to foreign non-monetary assets and liabilities, the IASB does not propose changing IAS 12, and has suggested the FASB explore the possibility of changing FAS 109 to converge.

IAS 12.68A-68B In some tax jurisdictions, an entity receives a tax deduction that relates to remuneration paid in shares, share options or other equity instruments of the entity. The amount of that tax deduction may differ from the related cumulative remuneration expense, and may arise in a later accounting period. The difference between the tax base of the employee services received to date and the carrying amount of nil, is a deductible temporary difference that results in a deferred tax asset. If the amount the taxation authorities will permit as a deduction in future periods is not known at the end of the period, it should be estimated, based on information available at the end of the period.

IAS 12.68C If the amount of the tax deduction (or estimated future tax deduction) exceeds the amount of the related cumulative remuneration expense, this indicates that the tax deduction relates not only to remuneration expense but also to an equity item. In this situation, the excess of the associated current or deferred tax should be recognised directly in equity.

17.2.3 Measurement of tax assets and liabilities

IAS 12.46 Current tax liabilities (assets) are measured at the amount the entity expects to pay to (recover from) the tax authorities, based on tax laws and tax rates for the relevant periods enacted or substantively enacted by the balance sheet date.

IAS 12.47,51-52 Similarly, deferred tax liabilities (assets) are measured based on tax laws and tax rates that are expected to apply in the period they are settled (realised), which are enacted or substantively enacted by the balance sheet date. In measuring deferred tax liabilities and deferred tax assets, the entity shall reflect the tax consequences (which may impact on the rate and/or the tax base) of the manner in which it intends, at the balance sheet date to settle or recover the carrying amount.

gains and losses that are not recognized under FAS 52. Accordingly, the Board decided to prohibit recognition of deferred taxes for those differences.

FAS 109 requires an company to assess whether the excess of the reported amount of an investment (including undistributed earnings) in a domestic subsidiary for financial reporting purposes over the underlying tax basis is a taxable temporary difference. If the tax law provides a means by which the recorded difference between the parent's book and tax basis of a subsidiary's stock could be recovered in a tax-free transaction (e.g. a tax-free liquidation or a statutory merger) and the company expects that it will use that means, the difference would not be considered a taxable temporary difference. This exception for domestic subsidiaries is not available to corporate joint ventures. *FAS 109.33*

A deferred tax asset for the excess of the tax basis over the book basis of an investment in either a foreign or domestic subsidiary or corporate joint venture is recognised only if it is apparent that the difference will reverse in the foreseeable future. *FAS 109.34*

Income tax regulations specify allowable tax deductions for instruments issued under share-based payment arrangements. Under current US tax law, allowable tax deductions are generally measured at the intrinsic value of an instrument on a specified date. The time value component, if any, of the fair value of an instrument generally is not tax deductible. Consequently, tax deductions generally arise in different amounts and in different periods from the compensation cost. *FAS 123R.58* *APB 25.16*

The cumulative amount of compensation cost that ordinarily would result in a future tax deduction should be treated as a deductible temporary difference based on the compensation cost recognised for financial reporting purposes. The deferred tax benefit (or expense) that results from changes in the temporary difference should be recognised in the income statement. *FAS 123R.59-60*

If a deduction reported on a tax return exceeds the cumulative compensation cost for financial reporting, any resulting excess of realised tax benefit over the related deferred tax asset should be recognised in additional paid-in capital. However, any excess that result other than from changes in the fair value of the entity's shares between the accounting measurement date and the later tax measurement date should be recognised in the income statement. The write-off of a deferred tax asset related to the excess of accounting cumulative compensation expense and the tax return deductible amount, net of any related valuation allowance, should be offset to any remaining additional paid-in capital from excess tax benefits from previous awards with any remaining balance recognised in the income statement. *FAS 123R.61-63* *APB 25.17*

17.2.3　Measurement of tax assets and liabilities

Deferred taxes should be calculated separately under a bottom-up approach for each tax-paying component (an individual entity or a group that submits a consolidated tax return) in each tax jurisdiction using the following procedures: *FAS 109.17*

- identify the types and amounts of existing temporary differences and the nature and amount of each type of tax loss or tax credit carry-forwards;
- calculate the total deferred tax liability for taxable temporary differences;
- calculate the total deferred tax asset for deductible temporary differences, loss carry-forwards and for each type of tax credit carryforward; and

COMMENT

There is a short-term convergence project with the FASB with the aim of eliminating differences between IAS 12 issued by the IASB, and FAS 109. IAS 12 requires measurement of deferred tax using enacted or substantively enacted tax rates, whereas FAS 109 requires enacted legislation to be used. The IASB has tentatively agreed not to change IAS 12 but to clarify the principle that substantively enacted meant the process of enactment was complete such that any future steps in the process will not change the outcome. The IASB agreed at its April 2005 meeting to note in an amended IAS 12 that for US taxing jurisdictions, the point of substantive enactment is when tax laws are enacted. The IASB has also agreed to include similar wording to the FAS 109 on the tax rate to be used when alternative tax systems exist.

SIC-21.5   Deferred tax liabilities (assets) arising from the revaluation of a non-depreciable asset are measured based on the tax consequences that would follow from the sale of the asset.

IAS 12.53   Deferred tax liabilities and deferred tax assets are not discounted.

IAS 12.52A,52B   In some jurisdictions, income taxes may be (1) payable at a higher or lower rate or (2) refundable or payable, if part or all of the net profit or retained earnings is paid out as a dividend to shareholders. In these circumstances, current and deferred tax assets and liabilities are measured at the tax rate applicable to undistributed profits. The income tax consequences of dividends are recognised when a liability to pay the dividend is recognised.

COMMENT

As part of its short-term convergence project on IAS 12 the IASB have decided to use the tax rate applicable to undistributed profits, but where there was an obligation to distribute part of those profits, to measure deferred tax on that portion at the distributed rate.

An entity shall calculate deferred tax liabilities and deferred tax assets using the following procedures:

IAS 12.28-29   • determine temporary differences relating to the same tax authority and the same taxable entity;

   • for each entity and tax jurisdiction compute the deferred tax liabilities and deferred tax assets separately, based on the individual temporary differences and applicable tax rates;

   • determine whether the deferred tax asset meets the recognition criteria (see above and section 17.2.4);

IAS 12.74-76   • determine whether the deferred tax assets and liabilities shall be offset using the criteria detailed in section 17.4.1. Detailed scheduling of the timing of reversal of temporary differences is generally not required under IAS 12. However, under rare circumstances where an entity has a legally enforceable right to set off temporary differences only in certain periods, detailed scheduling may be required.

IAS 12.51   While IAS 12 does not specifically address this subject, application of its principles (i.e. having regard to the manner of recovery or settlement of the tax) would generally require deferred tax on temporary differences arising from intragroup transfers of assets, where the asset is retained in the group, to be measured at the tax rates and laws of the transferee company (an exception might be where tax history of the asset or liability remains with the transferor company).

- determine whether a valuation allowance, i.e. a provision, is necessary to reduce the deferred tax asset to its realisable amount (see section 17.2.4).

The deferred tax expense or benefit for the period is the difference between the deferred tax liability or asset at the beginning and end of the year.

The tax effects of temporary differences and tax loss carryforwards should be calculated using enacted tax rates expected to apply to taxable income in the periods in which the deferred tax liability or asset is expected to be settled or realised. In the case of U.S. federal income taxes, the enactment date is the date the bill becomes law, even if the change in the tax law or rate is retroactive to an earlier date. If alternative tax systems exist in jurisdictions other than the U.S. federal jurisdiction, the applicable tax rate is determined in a manner consistent with the tax law after giving consideration to any interaction between the two systems. FAS 109 does not address specifically how to determine the enactment date in jurisdictions outside the US but the SEC Staff consider that the enactment date is when all steps in the process for legislation to become law have been completed.   *FAS 109.18-19*

Although scheduling the reversal of temporary differences is not specifically required, estimation of the periods of reversal may be necessary:

- to determine the valuation allowance on deferred tax assets (see section 17.2.4);
- to estimate the applicable tax rate when there is a phased-in change in tax rates; or
- to determine the appropriate classification of certain deferred tax assets and liabilities that are not related to an asset or liability that is reported in the balance sheet.

Deferred tax liabilities or assets that are recorded in the balance sheet should be adjusted for the effect of a change in tax law or rates. Any adjustment that is necessary should be included as part of income from continuing operations for the period that includes the enactment date.   *FAS 109.27*

Discounting of deferred tax amounts is prohibited.   *FAS 109.130*

COMMENT

There is a short-term convergence project with the FASB with the aim of eliminating differences between IAS 12 issued by the IASB, and FAS 109. In relation to intragroup transactions, the IASB does not propose changing IAS 12, and has suggested the FASB explore the possibility of changing FAS 109 to converge.

17.2.4   Deferred tax assets

IAS 12.24,34,37 Deferred tax assets are recognised to the extent that it is probable that future taxable
IAS 12.56 profits (see section 17.2.1) will be available against which the deductible temporary differences or carry forward of unused tax losses and unused tax credits can be utilised.   This shall be reassessed at each balance sheet date.   To the extent that it is no longer probable that sufficient taxable profit will be available (or it later becomes probable that it will be available), the carrying amount of a deferred tax asset is reduced (or a previous reduction is reversed).

IAS 12.29,35-36 The criteria for recognising deferred tax assets arising from the carry forward of unused tax losses and tax credits are the same as for other deductible temporary differences, but the existence of unused tax losses is strong evidence that future taxable profits may not be available.   An entity with a history of recent losses shall recognise a deferred tax asset arising from unused tax loses or tax credits only to the extent that it has sufficient taxable temporary differences against which the unused tax losses or credits can be utilised or that there is convincing evidence that sufficient taxable profit will be available before the unused tax or credits expire, taking into account tax planning opportunities.   In determining whether deferred tax assets should be recognised, an entity shall consider whether the unused tax losses result from identifiable causes which are unlikely to recur but may take into account tax planning opportunities that create taxable profit in the appropriate periods.

A   Business combinations

IAS 12.67 An acquirer may consider it probable it will recover its own previously unrecognised deferred tax assets, as a result of a business combination.   The acquirer recognises a deferred tax asset and accounts for it in profit or loss, not as goodwill (or as excess of the acquirer's interest in the net fair value of the acquiree's identifiable assets, liabilities and contingent liabilities over the cost of the combination).

IAS 12.68 If at a later date, a deferred tax asset of the acquiree which did not satisfy the recognition criteria when the business combination was initially accounted for is subsequently recognised, the acquirer shall recognise the resulting deferred tax income in profit or loss.   However, the acquirer shall reduce the carrying amount of goodwill to that which would have been recognised if the deferred tax asset had been recognised at the date of acquisition (i.e. at the tax rates applying at the date of the combination) and must recognise the reduction in the carrying amount of goodwill as an expense.   However, an excess of the acquirer's interest in the net fair value of the acquiree's identifiable assets, liabilities and contingent liabilities shall not be created or increased.

17.2.4 Deferred tax assets

Under FAS 109, deferred tax assets should be recognised in full unless it is 'more *FAS 109.17* likely than not' that some portion or all of the deferred tax assets will not be realised. A provision (or 'valuation allowance') should be made to reduce the tax asset to an amount that is 'more likely than not' to be realised. 'More likely than not' means a level of likelihood that is greater than 50%. In practice, companies that can demonstrate that they are likely to generate sufficient future taxable income will be able to recognise deferred tax assets in full.

Forming a conclusion that a valuation allowance is not needed is difficult if there is *FAS 109.22-24* negative evidence such as:

- cumulative losses in recent years;
- a history of operating loss or tax credit carryforwards expiring unused;
- losses expected in early future years (by a presently profitable entity);
- unsettled circumstances that, if unfavourably resolved, would adversely affect future operations and profit levels on a continuing basis in future years; or
- a carryback, carryforward period that is so brief that it would limit realisation of tax benefits if (1) a significant deductible temporary difference is expected to reverse in a single year or (2) the enterprise operates in a traditionally cyclical business.

Examples of positive evidence that might support a conclusion that a valuation allowance is not needed include the following:

- existing contracts or firm sales backlog that will realise the deferred tax asset based on existing sales prices and cost structures;
- an excess of appreciated asset value over the tax basis of the entity's net assets sufficient to realise the deferred tax asset; or
- a strong earnings history coupled with evidence indicating that any recent loss is an aberration rather than a continuing condition.

An enterprise must use judgment in considering the relative impact of negative and positive evidence.

Management is required to consider tax-planning strategies in determining the amount of the provision to be made. If significant expense or loss would be incurred in implementing a tax planning strategy, the valuation allowance should be increased to allow for the expense or loss.

The effect of a change in the opening balance of a valuation allowance that results from a change in circumstances that causes a change in judgment about the realisability of the related deferred tax asset in future years ordinarily shall be included in income from continuing operations.

COMMENT

While IAS 12 does not specifically address the situation where the acquiree's deferred tax asset recognised on a business combination is subsequently derecognised, application of the general principles would require that this reduction is recognised in profit or loss, rather than as an adjustment to the business combination.

There is a short-term convergence project with the FASB with the aim of eliminating differences between IAS 12 issued by the IASB, and FAS 109. Under IAS 12, deferred tax assets are recognised only where it is probable that the assets will be realised, whereas FAS 109 recognises recognition of all deferred tax assets, and a valuation allowance to the extent it is 'more likely than not' they will not be realised, resulting in different presentation and disclosures. The IASB has tentatively decided not to amend IAS 12, but will clarify that 'probable' means 'more likely than not'. The IASB will discuss any difference between IFRSs and US GAAP in respect of the 'valuation allowance' as part of discussions on uncertain tax positions.

The IASB also tentatively decided that the realisation of a previously unrecognised deferred tax asset of the acquiree would generally be treated as tax income with no adjustment to goodwill, although if realisation occurs within one year of the business combination, there would be a rebuttable presumption that this should be dealt with as an adjustment to the initial accounting for the business combination.

17.3   INTRA-PERIOD TAX ALLOCATION

IAS 12.58,61   Current and deferred tax is included in profit or loss for the period, except to the extent it relates to a business combination or to a transaction or event which is recognised in the same or a different period directly in equity. In the latter case, the related current and deferred tax should be charged or credited directly to equity.

IAS 12.58,62   Items charged to equity include:

- revaluations of property, plant and equipment (IAS 16 *Property, Plant and Equipment* – see section 7);

- adjustments to the opening balance of retained earnings resulting from either a change in accounting policy that is applied retrospectively or a correction of error (IAS 8 *Accounting Policies, Changes in Accounting Estimates and Errors* – see section 1); and

- exchange differences arising on translation of the financial statements of a foreign operation (IAS 21 *The Effects of Changes in Foreign Exchange Rates* – see section 5).

COMMENT

The FASB has an ongoing project on income taxes which is an interpretation of FAS 109. The objective of this project is to clarify the criteria for recognition of tax benefits, such that an entity's tax benefits recognised in tax returns must be probable of being sustained before recording the related tax benefit in financial statements. Probable as used in this project would be consistent with its use in FAS 5 *Accounting for Contingencies*. The FASB expects to issue an exposure draft in the second quarter of 2005.

A   Business combinations

In some business combinations, the acquirer has cumulative losses or other negative evidence, which resulted in a valuation allowance on its deferred tax assets immediately prior to the acquisition, and deferred tax liabilities arise in the business combination that are available to offset the reversal of the acquirer's pre-existing deferred tax assets. As a result of the business combination, the acquiring company considers the pre-existing deferred tax assets are more-likely-than-not to be realised by the combined entity and the valuation allowance should be reduced or eliminated. FAS 109 requires the reduction in the acquirer's valuation allowance be accounted for as part of the business combination, as part of the purchase price allocation, impacting goodwill.   *FAS 109.266*

If a valuation allowance is recognised for the deferred tax asset for an acquired entity's deductible temporary differences or tax loss carryforwards at the acquisition date and that deferred tax asset is subsequently recovered, the amount recovered should be applied: *FAS 109.30*

- first to reduce to zero any goodwill related to the acquisition;
- second to reduce to zero other non-current intangible assets related to the acquisition; and
- third to reduce income tax expense.

17.3   INTRA-PERIOD TAX ALLOCATION

Income tax expense or benefit for the year should be allocated to: *FAS 109.35*

- continuing operations;
- discontinued operations;
- extraordinary items; and
- items charged or credited directly to other comprehensive income or to shareholders' equity, including: *FAS 109.36*
  - adjustments to the opening balance of retained earnings for changes in accounting principles or corrections of errors;
  - gains and losses included in comprehensive income but excluded from net income, e.g. translation adjustments and changes in the carrying amount of certain marketable equity securities and debt securities;
  - an increase or decrease in contributed capital;
  - expenses for employee stock options recognised differently for financial reporting and tax purposes; and

IAS 12.63   Determining the amount of current and deferred tax to be allocated to items credited or charged to equity may be difficult, e.g. when:

- there are graduated rates of income tax and it is impossible to determine the rate at which a specific component of tax profit (tax loss) has been taxed;

- a change in the tax rate or other tax rules affects a deferred tax asset or liability relating to an item that was previously charged or credited to equity; or

- an entity determines that a deferred tax asset should be recognised, or should no longer be recognised in full, and the deferred tax asset relates to an item that was previously charged or credited to equity.

In such cases, the current and deferred tax related to items that are charged or credited to equity is based on a reasonable pro-rata allocation or other method that achieves a more appropriate allocation.

COMMENT

There is a short-term convergence project with the FASB with the aim of eliminating differences between IAS 12 issued by the IASB, and FAS 109. One area under discussion is the allocation of tax charges and credits to equity. Under IAS 12, tax that relates to an item accounted for in equity in current or prior periods is also accounted for in equity, whereas under FAS 109, tax relating to an item accounted for in equity in the current period only is accounted for in equity. At the joint IASB/FASB meeting in April 2005, the IASB agreed to amend IAS 12 to adopt the intraperiod tax allocation requirements of FAS 109.

Various situations where part or the whole of the current or deferred tax is charged or credited to equity are discussed in section 17.2.2 above. Additional guidance on specific situations is given below.

IAS 12.68A-C   In some tax jurisdictions, the tax deduction for share-based remuneration may differ
Appx B,   from the related cumulative remuneration expense and arise in a later period (e.g. tax
Example 5   relief is based on the difference between the share price less the exercise price, at the date of exercise of the option). The difference between the tax base (which at the balance sheet date, will be based on the year end share price, in the example, and pro-rated to the extent employee services have been received in the vesting period) and the carrying amount of the related employee services (often nil) is a deductible temporary difference. If the amount of the estimated tax deduction exceeds the amount of the cumulative remuneration expense, the excess of the associated current or deferred tax is recognised in equity (where not part of a business combination).

IAS 12.52A,52B   In jurisdictions where income taxes are payable at a higher or lower rate, or are
IAS 12.58   refundable or payable if part or all of the net profit or retained earnings is paid out as a dividend to the shareholders of the entity, the income tax consequences of dividends are recognised in profit or loss for the period, except to the extent that the income tax consequences arise from either a transaction or event recognised in the same or different period directly in equity, or from a business combination.

IAS 12.65A   Where an entity is required to pay a portion of its dividends to taxation authorities on behalf of shareholders, that amount ('withholding tax') is charged to equity as part of the dividends. Where, however, the withholding tax relates to intragroup dividends, the general principles of IAS 12 require that the withholding tax is charged to the income statement in the consolidated financial statements (as the dividend is not recognised in equity in the consolidated financial statements).

-   dividends paid on unallocated shares held by an employee share option plan and charged to retained earnings.

The amount allocated to continuing operations should include the following: *FAS 109.35*

-   tax effects of pre-tax income or loss from continuing operations (including the deferred tax effects of temporary differences related to those operations);

-   changes in the valuation allowance for deferred tax assets due to a change in circumstances that result in a change in judgement about future realisation of deferred tax assets;

-   tax effects of changes in tax laws or rates;

-   tax effects of changes in tax status; and

-   the tax effects of tax-deductible dividends paid to shareholders, except for dividends paid on unallocated shares held by an ESOP or any other stock compensation arrangements that are charged to retained earnings.

If there is only one item other than continuing operations (such as a discontinued   *FAS 109.38*
operation, an extraordinary item, or the cumulative effect of a change in accounting policy), the portion of income tax expense or benefit for the year that remains after the allocation to continuing operations is allocated to that one item.

If there are two or more items other than continuing operations, the amount that remains after the allocation to continuing operations is allocated among those other items in proportion to their individual effects on income tax expense or benefit for the year. When there are two or more items other than continuing operations and the sum of the amounts allocated to those other items does not equal the amount of the income tax expense or benefit for the year that remains after the allocation to continuing operations, a further calculation is required to allocate the remaining amount.

As a general rule, the tax benefit of an operating loss carryforward or carry-back   *FAS 109.37*
generally should be classified in the same manner as the source of income or loss in the current year irrespective of:

-   the source of the operating loss carry-forward or taxes paid in a prior year; or

-   the source of expected future income that will result in realisation of the deferred tax asset for an operating loss carry-forward from the current year.

The only exceptions to this rule are the tax effects of deductible temporary differences and loss carry-forwards:

-   acquired in business combinations and for which a tax benefit is initially recognised in subsequent years, i.e. there is a reduction in the 100% valuation allowance, by first reducing goodwill and other non-current intangible assets related to the acquisition to zero; or

-   required to be allocated to shareholders' equity.

SIC-*25.4*   The current and deferred tax consequences of a change in an entity's tax status or that of its shareholders is included in profit or loss for the period. However, if those consequences relate to transactions and events that result in the same or different period in a direct credit or charge to equity, those tax consequences are charged or credited directly to equity.

IAS 12.60   Where the carrying amount of deferred tax assets or liabilities change even though there is no change in the related temporary difference (e.g. due to changes in tax rates or tax laws, reassessment of recoverability of the deferred tax asset, or changes in the expected manner of recovery), the resulting deferred tax is recognised in the income statement, except to the extent it relates to items previously charged or credited to equity.

IAS 12.65   Where an asset is revalued for tax purposes and that revaluation relates to an accounting revaluation of an earlier period, or to one expected to be carried out in the future, the tax effects of both the asset revaluation and adjustment of the tax base are recognised in equity, otherwise in the income statement.

No specific guidance is provided under International Financial Reporting Standards for allocating current and deferred tax to different components of income for the period.

17.4   DISCLOSURE

17.4.1   Balance sheet

IAS 1.68,70   Current tax assets and liabilities, and deferred tax assets and liabilities should be presented as separate line items in the balance sheet. If an entity presents a balance sheet classified into current and non-current assets and liabilities, it shall not report deferred tax assets and liabilities as current assets and liabilities.

> **COMMENT**
>
> There is a short-term convergence project with the FASB with the aim of eliminating differences between IAS 12 issued by the IASB, and FAS 109. IAS 12 requires classification of all deferred tax assets and liabilities as non-current, but FAS 109 requires classification as either current or non-current based on the classification of the related non-tax asset or liability for financial reporting. The IASB has tentatively decided to amend IAS 12 to converge with FAS 109.

IAS 12.74   Deferred tax assets and liabilities shall be offset if and only if:

- the entity has a legally enforceable right to set off current tax assets and current tax liabilities; and
- the deferred tax assets and deferred tax liabilities relate to income taxes levied by the same tax authority on either the same taxable entity, or different taxable entities which intend either to settle current tax on a net basis or to realise current tax assets and settle current tax liabilities simultaneously, in each future period where significant deferred tax liabilities or assets are expected to be settled or recovered.

IAS 12.71   Current tax assets and liabilities shall be offset if and only if the entity has a legally enforceable right to set off and intends either to settle on a net basis or to realise the asset and settle the liability simultaneously.

17.4   DISCLOSURE

17.4.1   Balance sheet

Deferred tax liabilities and assets should be classified as current or non-current *FAS 109.41* based on the classification of the related asset or liability in the balance sheet. A deferred tax liability or asset that is not related to an asset or liability, e.g. deferred tax assets related to tax losses, should be classified according to the expected reversal date of the temporary difference.

For a particular tax-paying component of an enterprise and within a particular tax *FAS 109.42* jurisdiction:

- all current deferred tax liabilities and assets should be offset and presented as a single amount; and
- all non-current deferred tax liabilities and assets should be offset and shown as a single amount.

However, deferred tax liabilities and assets attributable to different tax-paying components of the enterprise or to different tax jurisdictions should not be offset.

17.4.2   Income statement

IAS 12.77   Tax expense or tax income related to profit or loss for the period shall be presented
IAS 1.81   on the face of the income statement as a separate line item.

IAS 12.79-80   An entity shall disclose the major components of tax expense (income) separately in
the financial statements or in the notes.

IAS 12 notes that the components of tax expense (income) may include:

*   current tax expense (income);
*   any adjustments recognised in the period for current tax of prior periods;
*   the amount of deferred tax expense (income) relating to the origination and
    reversal of temporary differences;
*   the amount of deferred tax expense (income) relating to changes in tax rates
    or the imposition of new taxes;
*   the amount of the benefit arising from a previously unrecognised tax loss, tax
    credit or temporary difference of a prior period that is used to reduce current
    tax expense;
*   the amount of the benefit from a previously unrecognised tax loss, tax credit
    or temporary difference of a prior period that is used to reduce deferred tax
    expense;
*   deferred tax expense (income) arising from the write-down, or reversal of a
    previous write-down, of a deferred tax asset; and
*   the amount of tax expense (income) relating to changes in accounting policies
    and errors that are included in profit or loss for the period, because they can
    not be accounted for retrospectively (see section 1).

IFRS 5.33   In respect of discontinued operations, the entity shall disclose separately the tax
IAS 12.81   expense relating to:

*   the gain or loss on discontinuance; and
*   the profit or loss from the ordinary activities of the discontinued operation for
    the period, together with the corresponding amounts for each prior period
    presented.

IAS 12.78   Exchange differences arising on deferred foreign tax liabilities or assets which are
recognised in the income statement may be classified as deferred tax expense
(income) if considered most useful to the users of the financial statements.

17.4.3   Other

IAS 12.81   An entity should disclose the aggregate amount of current and deferred tax related
to items charged or credited to equity.

IAS 12.81,85   A numerical reconciliation should be provided either between:

*   the average effective tax rate and the applicable tax rate; or
*   tax expense (income) and the product of accounting profit multiplied by the
    applicable tax rate(s).

An entity shall disclose the basis on which the applicable tax rate(s) is determined
and explain changes in the applicable tax rate(s) compared to previous periods.

17.4.2   Income statement

The amount of the tax charge allocated to continuing operations, discontinued operations, extraordinary items, the cumulative effect of accounting changes, prior year adjustments and capital transactions should be disclosed for each year for which those items are presented.

FAS 109.45-46

The significant components of income tax expense attributable to continuing operations should be disclosed for each year presented in the financial statements or in the notes.   Those components would include:

- current tax expense or benefit;
- deferred tax expense or benefit;
- government grants (to the extent recognised as a reduction of income tax expense);
- the benefits of operating loss carry-forwards;
- adjustments made to the deferred tax liability or asset in the balance sheet to reflect changes in enacted tax law/rates; and
- adjustments of the opening balance of a valuation allowance because of a change in judgement about the realisability of the related deferred tax asset in future years.

The share of profits of equity accounted investees is disclosed net of tax with no separate disclosure of the tax element required.   In the case of an SEC registrant, where the interest in the investee is deemed 'significant', summarised financial information may be required including the disclosure of net and pre-tax income in the notes or even separate financial statements of the investee.

APB 18.19-20
S-X 4-08(g)
S-X 3-09

In the case of an SEC registrant, disclosure is required of:

S-X 4-08(h)(1)

- the components of income before tax as either domestic or foreign; and
- amounts applicable to US (domestic) income tax, foreign (non-domestic) income tax and other income taxes should also be separately disclosed in each major component.   Amounts applicable to foreign income (loss) and amounts applicable to foreign or other income taxes that are less than 5% of the total of income before taxes or the component of tax expense, respectively, do not have to be separately disclosed.

17.4.3   Other

A   Statement of comprehensive income

An entity may disclose components of other comprehensive income either:

FAS 130.100-105

- net of related tax effects; or
- before related tax effects with one amount shown for the aggregate income tax expense or benefit related to the total of other comprehensive income items.

An entity shall disclose the amounts of income tax expense or benefit allocated to each component of other comprehensive income, including reclassification

FAS 130.24

The applicable tax rate(s) should provide the most meaningful information. While this will often be the domestic tax rate, for an entity operating in several jurisdictions, it may be more meaningful to aggregate separate reconciliations prepared using the domestic rate for the different jurisdictions.

IAS 12.81 The following information is required to be disclosed:

- the amount (and expiry date, if any) of deductible temporary differences, unused tax losses, and unused tax credits for which no deferred tax asset is recognised in the balance sheet;

- the aggregate amount of temporary differences associated with investments in subsidiaries, branches, associates and interests in joint ventures, for which deferred tax liabilities have not been recognised;

- in respect of each type of temporary difference, and in respect of each type of unused tax loss and unused tax credit:
  - the amount of the deferred tax assets and liabilities recognised in the balance sheet for each period presented;
  - the amount of the deferred tax income or expense recognised in the income statement, if this is not apparent from the changes in the amounts recognised in the balance sheet; and

- the amount of income tax consequences of dividends to shareholders of the entity that were proposed or declared before the financial statements were authorised for issue, but are not recognised as a liability in the financial statements.

IAS 12.82 An entity shall disclose the amount of a deferred tax asset and the nature of evidence supporting its recognition when (1) the utilisation of the deferred tax asset depends on future taxable profits in excess of those arising from the reversal of existing taxable temporary differences; and (2) the entity has suffered a loss in either the current or preceding period in the tax jurisdiction to which the deferred tax asset relates.

IAS 12.52A,82A   An entity shall disclose the nature of and also, where practically determinable, the
IAS 12.87A-87C   amounts of the potential income tax consequences that would result from the payment of dividends to its shareholders, where there are special tax consequences of full or partial equity distributions. Additionally, an entity shall disclose whether there are any potential income tax consequences not practicably determinable.

IAS 12.88 Tax-related contingent liabilities and assets shall be disclosed in accordance with IAS 37 *Provisions, Contingent Liabilities and Contingent Assets.* Where changes in tax rates or tax laws are enacted or announced after the balance sheet date, an entity shall disclose any significant effects of these changes on its current and deferred tax assets and liabilities in accordance with IAS 10 *Events after the Balance Sheet Date.*

adjustments, either on the face of the statement in which those components are disclosed or in the notes to the financial statements.

Disclosure of the accumulated balances of each classification of other comprehensive income is covered in section 1.6.6.

B   Other

The types of temporary differences and carryforwards that result in significant portions of a deferred tax liability or asset should be disclosed together with the approximate tax effect of each type of difference (before allocation of any valuation allowance).   Separate disclosure of those tax effects for each major tax jurisdiction is encouraged but not required.

FAS 109.43

A reconciliation of the reported amount of income tax expense attributable to continuing operations to the amount of income tax expense calculated by applying statutory rates to pre-tax income from continuing operations should be presented. A numerical reconciliation may be omitted for non-public companies but the nature of the significant reconciling items should be disclosed.

FAS 109.47

If not otherwise evident, companies should disclose the nature and effect of any other significant matters affecting comparability of information for all periods presented.

A reconciliation need not be provided where no individual reconciling item exceeds 5% of the expected tax charge and the total reconciling difference does not exceed 5% of the expected charge.   Also, reconciling items that are individually less than 5% of the expected charge may be aggregated in the reconciliation.

S-X 4-08(h)(2)

The components of the net deferred tax liability or asset should be disclosed as follows:

FAS 109.43

- the total of all deferred tax liabilities;
- the total of all deferred tax assets; and
- the total valuation allowance recognised for deferred tax assets.

The net change during the year in the total valuation allowance should also be disclosed.

Public companies are required to disclose the tax effect of each type of temporary difference and carryforward that gives rise to a significant portion of deferred tax assets (before any valuation allowance) and liabilities.   Non-public companies may omit disclosures of the tax effects but should disclose the types of temporary differences and carry-forwards that result in significant portions of deferred tax assets (before any valuation allowance) and liabilities.

If a deferred tax liability is not recognised for temporary differences that relate to investments in foreign subsidiaries or foreign corporate joint ventures, the other APB 23 *Accounting for Income Taxes – Special Areas* 'exceptions', a number of additional disclosures are required.

FAS 109.44

The amounts and expiry dates of loss and tax credit carry-forwards for tax purposes must be disclosed.   Also, any portion of the valuation allowance for deferred tax assets for which subsequently recognised tax benefits will be allocated to reduce goodwill or other non-current intangible assets of an acquired entity should be disclosed.

FAS 109.48

Separate disclosure is required of any portion of the valuation allowance for deferred tax assets for which subsequently recognised tax benefits will be allocated to reduce goodwill or other noncurrent intangible assets of an acquired company or directly to contributed capital.

For an accrued tax exposure, it may necessary to disclose (1) the nature and amount of the accrual; and (2) material changes and charges to accruals.

COMMENT

The SEC Staff consider that under FAS 5 a contingent tax liability should be recorded for any difference between the benefit of tax deductions on an income tax return and the tax benefit recognised under the company's accounting policy. The Staff noted that 'confidentiality concerns are not valid reasons for non-compliance with GAAP or the SEC's disclosure rules'.

Where a tax contingency is not accrued because one or both conditions for accrual are not met, or if an exposure to loss exists in excess of the amount accrued, a company should disclose (1) the nature of the contingency; and (2) an estimate of the possible loss or range of loss or statement that an estimate cannot be made. *FAS 5.9-10*

Section 18   Provisions and contingencies

18.1   AUTHORITATIVE PRONOUNCEMENTS

- IAS 37
- IFRIC 1

- IFRIC 3
- IFRIC 5

Appendix C to IAS 37 provides specific examples that illustrate the application of IAS 37 to a variety of practical situations.

COMMENT

As part of its short-term convergence project aimed at reducing the differences between IFRSs and US GAAP and as part of the second phase of the Business Combinations project, the IASB is planning to issue an exposure draft proposing a number of amendments to IAS 37 in the following areas:

- definitions of contingent assets and contingent liabilities;
- recognition and measurement of contingent assets and liabilities when they have associated unconditional rights or obligations and interaction with recognition under IAS 38 *Intangible Assets*;
- definition of a constructive obligation;
- explanation that the outflow of economic resources required to settle an obligation may be the provision of services;
- clarification of the measurement requirements, particularly in respect of 'stand-ready' obligations;
- withdrawal of existing guidance on provisions for restructuring costs and clarification that the existence and announcement of a restructuring plan does not by itself create an obligation. The treatment of costs which are frequently incurred in a restructuring will be specified (and in connection with this, amendments to IAS 19 *Employee Benefits* are proposed in respect of the recognition of termination benefits – see section 25.3);
- onerous contracts; and
- clarification relating to the accounting treatment of rights to reimbursement.

In November 2004 the IFRIC issued draft Interpretation D10 – *Liabilities Arising from Participating in a Specific Market – Waste Electrical and Electronic Equipment* (see section 18.5 below).

18.2   RECOGNITION

IAS 37.1-2   Accounting for provisions and contingencies is dealt with in IAS 37 *Provisions, Contingent Liabilities and Contingent Assets*. The Standard excludes from its scope provisions, contingent liabilities and contingent assets:

- resulting from executory contracts (unless those contracts are onerous); and
- those covered by other Standards.

Section 18   Provisions and
contingencies

18.1   AUTHORITATIVE PRONOUNCEMENTS

- FAS 5
- FAS 47
- FAS 143
- FAS 146

- FIN 14
- FIN 45
- FIN 47

In addition, there are several EITF abstracts, SOPs and SABs dealing with accounting and disclosure of liabilities and contingencies that are referred to below where appropriate.

18.2   RECOGNITION

CON 5 *Recognition and Measurement in Financial Statements of Business Enterprises* and CON 6 *Elements of Financial Statements* (which are not authoritative but serve as a framework) contain general guidance on recognition of liabilities. The recurring principle in the guidance is that provision should only be made where there is an obligation to transfer assets or services at the balance sheet date which has

IAS 37 does not apply to financial instruments (including guarantees) that are within the scope of IAS 39 *Financial Instruments: Recognition and Measurement.*

IAS 37.5 Where another Standard deals with a specific type of provision, contingent liability or contingent asset, an entity applies that Standard rather than IAS 37. For example, IFRS 3 *Business Combinations* addresses the treatment by an acquirer of contingent liabilities assumed in a business combination. Certain types of provisions are also addressed in IAS 11 *Construction Contracts*, IAS 12 *Income Taxes*, IAS 17 *Leases* (although IAS 37 applies to onerous lease contracts), IAS 19 *Employee Benefits* and IFRS 4 *Insurance Contracts* (although IAS 37 applies to the provisions and contingencies of an insurer, other than those arising from rights and obligations under insurance contracts covered by IFRS 4).

18.2.1   Provisions

IAS 37.10,14 A provision is a liability of uncertain timing or amount, which should be recognised only when:

- the entity has a present obligation (legal or constructive) as a result of a past event;
- it is probable that an outflow of resources embodying economic benefits will be required to settle the obligation; and
- a reliable estimate can be made of the obligation.

A   Present obligation

IAS 37.10 A present obligation can be either a legal or a constructive obligation. Legal obligations derive from a contract, legislation or other operation of law. Constructive obligations derive from an entity's actions where:

- by an established pattern of past practice, published policies or a sufficiently specific current statement, the entity has indicated to other parties that it will accept certain responsibilities; and
- as a result, the entity has created a valid expectation on the part of those other parties that it will discharge those responsibilities.

IAS 37.10,17 An obligating event is a past event that creates the legal or constructive obligation that leaves the entity no realistic alternative to settling the obligation.

IAS 37.15-16 If it is not clear whether a present obligation exists, an entity should take into account all available evidence to determine whether it is more likely than not that a present obligation exists at the balance sheet date. Where this is the case, the past event is deemed to give rise to a present obligation and a provision should be recognised. Where it is more likely that no present obligation exists, the entity only has a contingent liability at that stage (see section 18.2.2 below).

IAS 37.20 An obligation always involves another party to whom the obligation is owed, although the identity of that party may be unknown. A management or board decision by itself does not give rise to a constructive obligation unless another party has a valid expectation, arising from a decision communicated before the balance sheet date, that the entity will discharge its responsibilities.

resulted from past transactions or events. The term obligation is not restricted to legally enforceable obligations – it includes equitable and constructive obligations as well. As a general rule, provisions are not made when the effect is to relieve future income statements of charges related to ongoing operations.

As indicated in section 18.1 and 21.2.1, US GAAP does not have a general standard for provisions or contingencies. A number of accounting standards and interpretations deal with specific areas of provision or contingency, including, FAS 5 *Accounting for Contingencies*, FAS 47 *Disclosure of Long-Term Obligations*, FAS 143 *Accounting for Asset retirement Obligations*, FAS 146 *Accounting for Costs Associated with Exit or Disposal Activities*, FIN 14 *Reasonable Estimation of the Amount of a Loss*, and FIN 45: *Guarantor's Accounting and Disclosure Requirements for Guarantees, Including Indirect Guarantees of Indebtedness of Others an interpretation of FASB Statements No. 5, 57, and 107 and rescission of FASB interpretation No. 34.*

18.2.1 Provisions

There is no accounting standard on the general issue of provisions, but detailed rules exist for the recognition and disclosure of liabilities in relation to some specific issues, e.g. costs associated with long-lived asset, or a component of an entity, classified as held for sale in FAS 144 *Accounting for the Impairment or Disposal of Long-Lived Assets* (see section 1), recognition of liabilities as part of a purchase cost allocation in FAS 141 *Business Combinations* (see section 3), costs associated with exit or disposal activities in FAS 146 *Accounting for Costs Associated with Exit or Disposal Activities* (see sections 18.6 and 18.7).

The general principles under CON 6 establish that:

- liabilities are 'probable future sacrifices of economic benefits arising from present obligations of a particular entity to transfer assets or provide services to other entities in the future as a result of past transactions or events';
- a liability has three essential characteristics:
    (i)   it embodies a present duty or responsibility to one or more other entities that entails settlement by probable future transfer or use of assets at a specified or determinable date, on occurrence of a specified event, or on demand;
    (ii) the duty or responsibility obligates a particular entity, leaving it little or no discretion to avoid the future sacrifice; and
    (iii) the transaction or other event obligating the entity has already happened.

These general principles have been extended and modified under various accounting Standards and EITF Abstracts to establish that liabilities should also be accrued in certain specific circumstances where:

- management having appropriate authority to approve the action commits itself to a formal plan of sale, as a direct result of which costs will be incurred; or
- costs will be incurred under an existing contractual obligation, but only if:
    – the costs are not associated with or incurred to generate future revenues or any other future economic benefit to the entity; and
    – the amount of the costs can be reasonably estimated.

IAS 37.18-19,63 Only those obligations arising from past events existing independently of an entity's future actions (i.e. its future conduct of the business) may be recognised as provisions.   No provision may be recognised for costs that need to be incurred to operate in the future, to maintain future economic benefits or for future operating losses, because they do not meet the definition of a liability at the balance sheet date.

IAS 37.21-22 An event that does not give rise to an obligation immediately may do so at a later date because of changes in the law or because an act by the entity gives rise to a constructive obligation.   A proposed new law gives rise to an obligation only when the proposed legislation is virtually certain to be enacted as drafted and, in many cases, such certainty cannot be obtained until the law is actually enacted.

B   *Probable transfer of economic benefits*

IAS 37.23-24 A liability should be recognised when it is more likely than not that an outflow of resources embodying economic benefits will occur to settle that obligation.   The definition of 'probable' as 'more likely than not' as used in IAS 37 does not necessarily apply in other International Financial Reporting Standards.   Where there are a large number of similar obligations the probability of an outflow should be determined for the class of obligation as a whole.

C   *Reliable estimate*

IAS 37.25-26 Except in extremely rare cases, an entity will be able to determine a range of possible outcomes and therefore make an estimate of the obligation that is sufficiently reliable to use in recognising a provision.

In the extremely rare case where no reliable estimate can be made, a liability exists that cannot be recognised.   Consequently, that liability is disclosed as a contingent liability.

A   Guarantees

FIN 45 addresses the disclosures to be made by a guarantor about its obligations under guarantees and the recognition of a liability by a guarantor at the inception of a guarantee.   *FIN 45.2*

At the inception of a guarantee, the guarantor should recognise a liability for the guarantee at fair value, unless the guarantor is required to recognise a liability for the related contingent loss, in which case the liability recognised should be the higher of the two amounts.   The offsetting entry depends on the circumstances in which the guarantee was issued.   The liability initially recognised by the guarantor would typically be reduced (by a credit to earnings) as the guarantor is released from risk under the guarantee.   *FIN 45.9-12*

This Interpretation applies to guarantee contracts that have any of the following characteristics: *FIN 45.3*

- contracts that contingently require the guarantor to make payments based on changes in an underlying related to an asset, a liability, or an equity security of the guaranteed party;

- contracts that contingently require the guarantor to make payments based on another entity's failure to perform under an obligating agreement;

- indemnification agreements that contingently require the indemnifying party to make payments based on changes in an underlying that is related to an asset, a liability, or an equity security of the indemnified party; or

- indirect guarantees of the indebtedness of others even though the payment to the guaranteed party may not be based on changes in an underlying that is related to an asset, a liability, or an equity security of the guaranteed party.

However, this Interpretation does not apply to the following contracts: *FIN 45.6*

- a guarantee or an indemnification that is excluded from the scope of FAS 5 under paragraph 7 of FAS 5 (for example, deferred compensation contracts, stock issued to employees and other employee-related costs);

- a lessee's guarantee of the residual value of the leased property at the expiration of the lease term, if the lessee (guarantor) accounts for the lease as a capital lease under FAS 13 *Accounting for Leases*;

- a contract that is accounted for as contingent rent under FAS 13;

- a contract that provides for payments that constitute a vendor rebate based on either the sales revenues of, or the number of units sold by, the guaranteed party;

- a guarantee (or an indemnification) whose existence prevents the guarantor from being able to either account for a transaction as the sale of an asset that is related to the guarantee's underlying or recognise in earnings the profit from that sale transaction.

The following types of guarantees are not subject to the initial recognition and measurement provisions of this Interpretation but are subject to its disclosure requirements: *FIN 45.7*

- a guarantee that is accounted for as a derivative instrument at fair value under FAS 133 *Accounting for Derivative Instruments and Hedging Activities*;

18.2.2   Contingent liabilities

IAS 37.10,27-28   A contingent liability:

- is a possible obligation that arises from past events and whose existence will be confirmed only by the occurrence or non-occurrence of uncertain future events not wholly within the control of the entity; or

- is a present obligation arising from past events that is not recognised because it is not probable that an outflow of resources embodying economic benefits will be required to settle the obligation or the amount of the obligation cannot be measured with sufficient reliability.

An entity should not recognise a contingent liability in its financial statements. However, certain disclosures are required unless the possibility of an outflow of resources embodying economic benefits is remote (see section 18.9.2 below).

IAS 37.29   If an entity is jointly and severally liable for an obligation, the part it expects to be met by other parties is treated as a contingent liability.

IAS 37.30   Contingent liabilities should be assessed continually to determine whether an outflow of resources embodying economic benefits has become probable. If such an outcome becomes probable for an item previously dealt with as a contingent liability, a provision is recognised in the period in which the change in probability occurs (provided a reliable estimate may be made).

- a guarantee for which the underlying is related to the performance (regarding function, not price) of non-financial assets that are owned by the guaranteed party;

- a guarantee issued in a business combination that represents contingent consideration (as addressed in FAS 141 *Business Combinations*);

- a guarantee for which the guarantor's obligation would be reported as an equity item (rather than a liability);

- a guarantee by an original lessee that has become secondarily liable under a new lease that relieved the original lessee from being the primary obligor under the original lease;

- a guarantee issued either between parents and their subsidiaries or between corporations under common control;

- a parent's guarantee of its subsidiary's debt to a third party; and

- a subsidiary's guarantee of the debt owed to a third party by either its parent or another subsidiary of that parent.

18.2.2   Contingent liabilities

A contingency is defined as an existing condition, situation, or set of circumstances involving uncertainty as to possible gain or loss to an entity that will ultimately be resolved when one or more future events occur or fail to occur. *FAS 5.1*

The estimated loss from a loss contingency should be accrued for if:

- it is probable, based on information available prior to issuance of the financial statements, that a loss has been incurred at the balance sheet date; and *FAS 5.8*

- the amount of loss can be reasonably estimated.

When a loss contingency exists but is not accrued because one or both conditions for accrual are not met, or if an exposure to loss exists in excess of the amount accrued, the following disclosures are required when there is at least a reasonable possibility that a loss or an additional loss may have been incurred: *FAS 5.10*

- The nature of the contingency; and

- An estimate of the possible loss or range of loss, or a statement that an estimate cannot be made.

If the conditions for accrual of a loss contingency are satisfied on the basis of information which becomes available subsequent to the date of the financial statements, but before the financial statements are issued, the charge to income should be recorded in the period that an asset was impaired or a liability was incurred. *FAS 5.11*

The criteria for recognition or disclosure of a loss contingency in such situations is consistent with the criteria for reporting subsequent events in SAS 1 (see section 29).

A loss contingency should be accrued at the balance sheet date when subsequent events provide additional evidence with respect to conditions that existed at the balance sheet date and affect the estimates inherent in the process of preparing financial statements.

A loss contingency should not be accrued at the balance sheet date when subsequent events provide evidence with respect to conditions that did not exist at

18.2.3   Contingent assets

IAS 37.10,31   A contingent asset is a possible asset that arises from past events and whose
IAS 37.33-35   existence will be confirmed only by the occurrence or non-occurrence of one or
more uncertain future events not wholly within the control of the entity.   An entity
should not recognise a contingent asset in its financial statements, as this may result
in the recognition of income that may never be realised.   However, certain
disclosures are required when the inflow of economic benefits is probable (see
section 18.9.2 below).   Contingent assets should be assessed continually and when
the realisation of income is virtually certain, then the related asset is not a contingent
asset and its recognition, together with any related income, is appropriate in the
period in which the change occurs.

18.3   MEASUREMENT

IAS 37.36-37   The amount recognised as a provision should be the best estimate of the
IAS 37.39-41   expenditure required to settle the present obligation at the balance sheet date, as
determined on a pre-tax basis.   The best estimate is the amount that an entity
would rationally pay to settle the obligation or to transfer it to a third party as at the
measurement date.   Where the provision being measured relates to a large
population of items, the expected value of the obligation should be determined by
weighting all possible outcomes by their associated probabilities.   Where a single
obligation is being measured, the individual most likely outcome may be the best
estimate of the liability but the entity should still consider other possible outcomes.
If such outcomes are either mostly higher or mostly lower than the most likely
outcome, the best estimate will be a higher or lower amount.

IAS 37.42-43   Risk and uncertainties should be taken into account in making the best estimate of a
provision, but they do not justify the overstatement of provisions or liabilities.

IAS 37.45,47,60   The amount of a provision should be determined as the present value of the cash
outflows expected to be required to settle the obligation, except where the effect of
the time value of money is immaterial.   The pre-tax discount rate used in
determining the present value of the obligation should reflect the time value of
money and the risks specific to that liability but not the risks that have been adjusted
for in determining the estimates of future cash outflows.   The unwinding of the
discount should be recognised as a borrowing cost.

IAS 37.48,50   An entity should take into account the effects of future events that affect the
amount of a provision where there is sufficient objective evidence that they will
occur.   Similarly, the effect of possible new legislation should be taken into account
where there is sufficient objective evidence that its enactment is virtually certain.

IAS 37.51-52   In determining the amount of a provision, the entity should not take into account
any gains from the expected disposal of assets, even if the disposal of assets is
closely related to the event giving rise to the provision.   Such gains should be
accounted for in accordance with the Standard relevant to the assets concerned.

the balance sheet date but arose subsequent to that date. Some of these events, however, may be of such a nature that disclosure of them is required to keep the financial statements from being misleading.

18.2.3　Contingent gains

Contingent gains are usually not reflected in the financial statements until earned. Disclosure should be given but care should be exercised to avoid misleading implications as to the likelihood of realisation (see section 18.9.1). *FAS 5.17*

18.3　MEASUREMENT

CON 5 and CON 6 also contain general guidance on measurement of liabilities. Specific guidance is available on costs associated with discontinued operations (see section 1), and recognition of liabilities as part of a purchase cost allocation (see section 3).

SAB 92 deals with accounting and disclosures relating to loss contingencies and specifically covers; offsetting probable recovery claims against probable contingent liabilities; apportionment of liabilities between responsible parties; and, the use of estimates, assumptions and discounting for product or environmental liabilities (see section 18.5). *SAB 92 (Topic 5-Y)*

Where it is probable that a liability has been incurred but the reasonable estimate of the cost is a range, an amount should be accrued. If an amount within the range is a better estimate than any other amount within the range then that amount should be accrued. When no amount within the range is a better estimate than any other amount, the minimum amount in the range should be provided. *FIN 14.3*

A provision should be discounted only where the aggregate amount of the liability and the timing of future cash payments are fixed or reliably determinable. Where appropriate, the rate used to discount future cash payments should be the rate that would produce an amount at which the liability could be settled in an arm's-length transaction with a third party or, if this rate is not available, a rate no greater than a risk-free rate. *SAB 92 (Topic 5-Y)*

It is a general rule that assets and liabilities should not be offset except where a right of set-off exists (see section 1.6.3). *APB 10.7*

IAS 37.53-54,56 If some or all of the expenditure required to settle a provision is reimbursable by a third party, but the entity remains ultimately liable for the whole amount in question, the entity should recognise the reimbursement as a separate asset – not exceeding the amount of the provision – when, and only when, its receipt is virtually certain. In the income statement the expense relating to the provision and the reimbursement may be presented on a net basis.

IAS 37.59 At each balance sheet date the entity should review the provisions and adjust them to reflect the current best estimate. Where it is no longer probable that an outflow of resources will be required, the provision should be reversed.

IAS 37.61 A provision should be used only for expenditures for which it was originally recognised.

18.4   MAINTENANCE COSTS

It is not permitted to recognise provisions in connection with major inspections or major overhauls of items of property, plant and equipment. However, when certain conditions are met these expenses may be capitalised (see section 7.2.1C).

18.5   ENVIRONMENTAL COSTS

IAS 37.19,21 Costs for environmental damage should be provided for when there is an obligating event, for example:

- in connection with unlawful environmental damage;
- where existing or new legislation requires rectification of existing environmental damage; or
- when the entity publicly accepts responsibility for rectification of environmental damage.

By contrast, where an entity can avoid the future expenditure by its future actions, such as by changing its future method of operation, it has no present obligation and no provision is made.

18.4　MAINTENANCE COSTS

There is no specific guidance on accounting for and recognition of the cost of planned　*EITF D-88*
major maintenance, inspection or overhaul.　Alternative methods of accounting for
planned major maintenance, inspection or overhaul expenditure include:

- expense as incurred;

- capitalise and amortise over the period to the next planned maintenance,
  inspection or overhaul (any carrying amount remaining from a previous
  maintenance, inspection or overhaul should be written off); and,

- accrue in advance the costs expected to be incurred in the next planned major
  maintenance activity.

COMMENT

AcSEC added a project to its agenda in January 1999 to develop a SOP to address
accounting and disclosure for costs related to property, plant, and equipment to be
capitalized as improvements and expensed as repairs and maintenance and the
accrual of a liability in advance of a planned major maintenance activity.　No
exposure draft has been issued to date.

The SEC staff believes that if a registrant that is currently accruing in advance the
costs expected to be incurred in the next planned major maintenance activity wants
to change from that method to some other method permitted under generally
accepted accounting principles, the SEC staff would not object to a conclusion that
a change from the accrue-in-advance method is preferable.

18.5　ENVIRONMENTAL COSTS

SOP 96-1 *Environmental Remediation Liabilities* interprets FAS 5 *Accounting for*　*SOP 96-1*
Contingencies which requires provision to be made for liabilities if it is probable
that a liability has been incurred and the amount of the loss can be reasonably
estimated.　SOP 96-1 says that the 'probable liability' test is met for environmental
liabilities if, by the time the financial statements are issued:

- litigation, a claim, or an assessment can be asserted, or is probable of being
  asserted; and

- it is probable that the outcome of such litigation, claim, or assessment will be
  unfavourable.

There is a presumption that the probability test will be met if the reporting entity is

IAS 37.22   Where details of a proposed new law have yet to be finalised, an obligation arises only when the legislation is virtually certain to be enacted as drafted.

IFRIC 3.2-3,10   In December 2004 the IFRIC issued Interpretation 3 (IFRIC 3) - *Emission Rights* which applies to accounting periods beginning on or after 1 March 2005 although earlier application is encouraged.   IFRIC 3 applies to participants in an operational cap and trade scheme although some of its requirements may be relevant to other schemes which are designed to encourage reduced emissions levels.

IFRIC 3.5   A cap and trade scheme gives rise to an asset for allowances held, a government grant and a liability for the obligation to deliver allowances equal to emissions made.

IFRIC 3.6-8   Allowances are treated as intangible assets in accordance with IAS 38 and, where issued at less than fair value, should be measured initially at their fair value.   Any difference between the amount paid and fair value is a government grant within the scope of IAS 20.   The grant should initially be recognised as deferred income and subsequently recognised as income on a systematic basis over the period for which the allowances were issued.

As emissions are made, a liability is recognised for the obligation to deliver allowances equal to those emissions.   The liability is a provision within the scope of IAS 37 and will usually be measured as the present market price of the number of allowances required to cover emissions up to the balance sheet date.

COMMENT

In November 2004 the IFRIC issued draft Interpretation D10 – *Liabilities Arising from Participating in a Specific Market – Waste Electrical and Electronic Equipment*.   The EU's Directive on *Waste Electrical and Electronic Equipment* (WE&EE) has given rise to questions about when a liability for the decommissioning of WE&EE should be recognised by manufacturers of certain electrical goods.   Under the Directive, inter alia, the cost of waste management for equipment sold to private households before 13 August 2005 will fall to producers of that type of equipment who are in the market in the period specified in the applicable legislation (the measurement period).   The draft Interpretation states that participation in the market in the measurement period is the obligating event under IAS 37.   A liability does not arise when the products have been manufactured or sold as no obligation is present unless a market share exists in the measurement period.   The liability may or may not arise at the same time as the waste management costs are incurred.

In April 2005 the IFRIC discussed draft Interpretation D10 and decided to make minor amendments to the wording of D10.   Subject to an editorial review of the drafting by IFRIC members and approval by the Board, it is expected that a final interpretation will be issued in the second quarter of 2005.

18.6   DECOMMISSIONING COSTS

IAS 37.19   Decommissioning costs are those that arise, for example, where an oil installation or nuclear power station has to be dismantled at the end of its life.

IAS 37.Appx C   Accounting for decommissioning costs is dealt with in IAS 37 by way of example 3 in Appendix C.   IAS 37 requires an entity to recognise a liability as soon as the decommissioning obligation is created, which is normally when the facility is constructed and the damage that needs to be restored is done.   The total

associated with a contaminated site in respect of which litigation has commenced or a claim or assessment has been asserted (or if such actions are probable).

Measurement of the liability will often be difficult, but at least the minimum amount in the range of possible loss should be accrued. This should be based on both the direct incremental costs of the remediation effort and the payroll cost of those employees who are expected to spend a significant amount of time on it. Where the entity is one of a number of parties against whom the claim is made, it should accrue its share of the costs after taking account of the possible effect of other responsible parties failing to meet their share. The costs accrued should be based on present legislation and technology and presently enacted laws and regulations, and may be discounted only if the aggregate amount of the obligation and the amount and timing of the expenditure are fixed or reliably determinable. The SOP does not indicate an appropriate discount rate to apply, but refers to guidance in SAB 92 which suggests a rate that will produce an amount at which the liability could be settled in an arms-length transaction with a third party. SOP 96-1 further suggests that the rate should be no greater than a risk-free rate.

SAB 92

(Topic 5-Y)

18.6   DECOMMISSIONING COSTS

In June 2001, the FASB issued FAS 143 *Accounting for Asset Retirement Obligations* which is effective for years beginning after 15 June 2002.

FAS 143.24

Under FAS 143 an entity should recognise the fair value of a liability for an asset retirement obligation in the period in which it is incurred if a reasonable estimate of fair value can be made, or as soon as a reasonable estimate of fair value can be made.

FAS 143.3

decommissioning cost is estimated and a liability is recognised based on the percentage of the total decommissioning costs attributable to damage caused by actions to date. The amount recognised is discounted to its present value and added to the corresponding asset's cost. The asset, including the decommissioning cost, is depreciated over its useful life, while the discounted provision is progressively unwound, with the unwinding charge showing as an interest cost in the income statement.

IFRIC 1.3-9   No guidance is provided in IAS 37 on accounting for changes in the decommissioning provision as a result of changes in cost estimates or changes in discount rates. This has been addressed by the IASB with the publication in May 2004 of IFRIC Interpretation 1 (IFRIC 1) – *Changes in Existing Decommissioning, Restoration and Similar Liabilities* which applies to accounting periods beginning on or after 1 September 2004, although earlier adoption is encouraged. Any changes in measurement as a result of implementing IFRIC 1 are changes in accounting policy to be accounted for in accordance with IAS 8.

The basic requirements of IFRIC 1 are summarised below but the specific requirements differentiate between the treatment of the related assets depending on whether they are accounted for under the cost or valuation model under IAS 16 (see sections 7.2.1 and 7.2.2):

- adjustments arising from changes in the estimated cash flows or the current discount rate should be added to or deducted from the cost of the related asset with the adjusted depreciable amount of the asset then depreciated prospectively over the asset's remaining useful life; and

- the periodic unwinding of the discount should be recognised in profit or loss as a finance cost as it occurs (capitalisation, the allowed alternative treatment under IAS 23 *Borrowing Costs*, is not permitted).

IAS 37.Appx D   Example 2 in Appendix D provides an illustration of the disclosures that are
IAS 37.85   required by paragraph 85 of IAS 37 in respect of decommissioning costs.

IFRIC 5.4-5,14   IFRIC Interpretation 5 (IFRIC 5) – *Rights to Interests arising from Decommissioning, Restoration and Environmental Rehabilitation* Funds was issued in December 2004 and applies to accounting periods beginning on or after 1 January 2006, although earlier application is encouraged. IFRIC 5 specifies the accounting by a contributor to decommissioning funds that have the following features:

- the assets are administered separately (either being held by a separate legal entity or as segregated assets within another entity); and

- a contributor's right to access the assets is restricted.

A residual interest in a fund that extends beyond a right to reimbursement may be an equity instrument within the scope of IAS 39 and is not within the scope of IFRIC 5.

IFRIC 5.7-9   The Interpretation requires a contributor to recognise its obligation to pay decommissioning costs as a liability and to recognise separately its interest in the fund unless it has no obligation should the fund fail to pay. A contributor should determine whether it has control, joint control or significant influence over the fund and should account for its interest in accordance with IAS 27, IAS 28, IAS 31 and SIC-12 (see sections 2 and 4 above). If the contributor does not have control, joint control or significant influence over the fund, the right to receive

An asset retirement obligation is a legal obligation associated with the retirement of a tangible long-lived asset that results from the acquisition, construction, or development and (or) the normal operation of a long-lived asset.

FAS 143.2

The fair value of a liability for an asset retirement obligation is the amount at which that liability could be settled in a current transaction between willing parties, i.e. other than in a forced or liquidation transaction. If a quoted market value is not available, the standard suggests that fair value be based on the best available information, including the results of present value techniques inclusive of a profit margin.

FAS 143.7

COMMENT

In June 2004 the FASB issued an exposure draft of a Proposed Statement of Financial Accounting Standards *Fair Value Measurements*. The proposed Statement provides guidance for how to measure fair value. The proposed statement would be effective for financial statements issued for fiscal years beginning after 15 June 2005. The FASB expect to issue a final statement in the second quarter of 2005.

A liability should be recognised, when incurred, for the fair value of an asset retirement obligation that is conditional on a future event (e.g. asbestos in a building which will only be addressed if the building is demolished) if the liability's fair value can be estimated reasonably. An asset retirement obligation would be reasonably estimable if:

FIN 47

- it is evident that the fair value of the obligation is embodied in the acquisition price of the asset;
- an active market exists for the transfer of the obligation; or
- sufficient information exists to apply an expected present value technique.

An expected present value technique would incorporate uncertainty about the timing and method of settlement into the fair value measurement.

An entity would have sufficient information to apply an expected present value technique if either:

- the settlement date and method of settlement have been specified by others (e.g. by law, regulation or contract); or
- the information is available to reasonably estimate (1) the settlement date or range of potential settlement dates, (2) the method of settlement or potential methods of settlement, and (3) the probabilities associated with the potential settlement dates and potential methods of settlement.

Where there is insufficient information available to estimate a range of potential settlement dates for the retirement obligation at the time the liability is incurred, the liability would be initially recognised in the period in which sufficient information is available to make a reasonable estimate of the liability's fair value.

COMMENT

FIN 47 should be effective no later than the end of fiscal years ending after 15 December 2005. Retrospective application for interim financial information is permitted but not required. Early adoption is encouraged.

When an asset retirement obligation is recognised an entity should capitalise an asset retirement cost as an addition to the carrying amount of the related long-lived asset. The capitalised asset retirement cost should be the same amount as the liability and

FAS 143.11

reimbursement from the fund should be recognised in accordance with IAS 37. The reimbursement amount should be the lower of the decommissioning obligation recognised and the contributor's share of the fair value of the net assets of the fund. Changes in the carrying amount of the right to receive reimbursement other than contributions to and payments from the fund should be recognised in profit or loss in the period in which the changes occur.

IFRIC 5.10   When a contributor has an obligation to make potential additional contributions, for example in the event of the bankruptcy of another contributor or as a result of the investment performance of the fund, the obligation is a contingent liability within the scope of IAS 37.   A liability should be recognised only if it is probable that additional contributions will be made.

IFRIC 5.11-13   A contributor should disclose the nature of its interest in a fund and any restriction on access to the assets in the fund.   Other disclosure requirements are in accordance with IAS 37 (see section 18.9 below).

18.7   PROVISIONS IN RESPECT OF VACANT LEASEHOLD PROPERTY AND OTHER ONEROUS CONTRACTS

IAS 37.10,66,68   Contracts are considered onerous when the unavoidable costs of meeting the obligations under the contract (that is, the least net cost of exiting from the contract) exceed the economic benefits expected to be received.   When contracts are onerous, the present obligation under the contract should be recognised and measured as a provision.

IAS 37.69   Before a provision is recognised for an onerous contract, the entity should perform an impairment test on any assets dedicated to that contract in accordance with IAS 36 *Impairment of Assets*.

IAS 37.Appx C   One of the most common examples of an onerous contract in practice relates to leasehold property.   Example 8 in Appendix C to IAS 37 illustrates the application of IAS 37 to an operating lease that becomes onerous.

18.8   ACCOUNTING FOR RESTRUCTURING COSTS

IAS 37.10   IAS 37 defines a restructuring as a programme that is planned and controlled by management, and materially changes either:

- the scope of a business undertaken by an entity; or
- the manner in which that business is conducted.

IAS 37.71   A provision for restructuring costs is recognised only when the general recognition criteria for provisions are met (see section 18.2.1).

should be allocated to expense (depreciated) using a systematic and rational method over its useful life.

Subsequent changes resulting from revisions to the timing or amount of the original estimate of the fair value of the liability should be recognised. Changes in the liability due to the passage of time are recognised as an increase in the carrying amount of the liability and as an operating expense, referred to as accretion expense. Changes due to revisions to the timing or amount of estimated cash flows are reflected in the carrying amount of the liability and the related asset retirement cost capitalised as part of the carrying amount of the related long-lived asset.   Upward revisions in the amount of undiscounted estimated cash flows are discounted using the current credit-adjusted risk-free rate.   Downward revisions in the amount of undiscounted estimated cash flows are discounted using the credit-adjusted risk-free rate that existed when the original liability was recognised, or a weighted-average credit adjusted risk-free rate if the prior period to which the downward revision relates cannot be identified.   The fair value of the liability is not remeasured for changes in the risk-free interest rate used to discount the provision. *FAS 143.13-15*

18.7   PROVISIONS IN RESPECT OF VACANT LEASEHOLD PROPERTY

Provisions for vacant leasehold properties (when permanently vacated) should be recognised and measured at fair value.   The liability for costs to be incurred under a contract for its remaining term without economic benefit should be recognised at fair value when the entity ceases using the right conveyed by the contract (the 'cease-use date' approach).   The fair value of the liability at the cease-use date should be based on the remaining lease rentals, reduced by estimated sublease rentals that could reasonably be obtained even if the entity does not intend to sublease the property. Estimated sublease rentals cannot exceed remaining lease rentals. *FAS 146.16*

The net provision for vacant leasehold properties would be a discounted amount. Subsequent changes to the liability should be measured using the credit-adjusted risk-free rate used for initial measurement.   Changes due to the timing or amount of estimated cash flows are recognised as an adjustment to the liability and reported in the same income statement line item(s) as the original provision.   Changes due to the passage of time are recognised as an increase in the liability and as an accretion expense.   Accretion expense should not be considered interest cost either for potential capitalisation under FAS 34 or for income statement presentation. *FAS 146.6*

18.8   RESTRUCTURING COSTS

The FASB issued Statement 146 *Accounting for the Costs Associated with Exit or Disposal Activities* on the accounting treatment for individual costs often associated with restructurings, distinguishing one-time employee termination benefits, contract termination costs (excluding capital lease contracts) and other associated costs. FAS 146 supersedes EITF Issue 94-3.

IAS 37.72   A constructive obligation to restructure arises only when an entity:

- has a detailed formal plan for the restructuring identifying at least:
    - the business or part of a business concerned;
    - the principal locations affected;
    - the location, function, and approximate number of employees who will be compensated for the termination of their services;
    - the expenditures that will be undertaken; and
    - when the plan will be implemented; and
- has raised a valid expectation in those affected that it will carry out the restructuring by starting to implement that plan or announcing its main features to those affected by it.

IAS 37.74   Furthermore, the implementation of the plan needs to begin as soon as possible and to be completed in a timeframe that makes significant changes to the plan unlikely.

IAS 37.78-79   No constructive obligation arises for the sale of an operation until the entity is committed to the sale, i.e. a purchaser has been identified and there is a binding sale agreement.

IAS 37.80-82   A restructuring provision includes only those direct expenditures that are both necessarily entailed by the restructuring and not associated with ongoing activities of the entity.   A restructuring provision does not include such costs as:

- retraining or relocating continuing staff;
- marketing;
- investment in new systems and distribution networks; or
- identifiable future operating losses up to the date of a restructuring (unless they relate to an onerous contract as defined in IAS 37).

These costs relate to the future conduct of business and are not liabilities for restructuring at the balance sheet date.

IAS 37.9   When a restructuring meets the definition of a discontinued operation, additional disclosures may be required by IFRS 5 *Non-current Assets Held for Sale and Discontinued Operations* (see section 1.9).

A   One-time employee termination benefits

One-time employee termination benefits relate to current employees who are involuntarily terminated under the terms of a benefit arrangement that applies for a specific termination event or for a specified future period.   These do not include termination benefits which are: *FAS 146.2,8*

- part of an ongoing benefit arrangement; or

- payable under the terms of an individual deferred compensation contract.

A liability for one-time benefit costs should be recognised, at its fair value, at the date the plan of termination meets all of the following criteria and has been communicated to employees (the communication date):

- management, having the authority to approve the action, commits to a plan of termination;

- the plan identifies the number of employees to be terminated, their job classifications or functions and their locations, and the expected completion date;

- the plan establishes the terms of the benefit arrangement, including the benefits that employees will receive upon termination, in sufficient detail to enable employees to determine the type and amount of benefits they will receive if they are involuntarily terminated; and

- actions required to complete the plan indicate that it is unlikely that significant changes to the plan will be made or that the plan will be withdrawn.

The timing of recognition and related measurement of the liability depends on whether employees are required to continue working until they are terminated, in order to receive the termination benefits: *FAS 146.9-11*

- If employees are entitled to receive the termination benefits regardless of when they leave, or if employees will not be retained to render service beyond the minimum retention period (i.e. the legal notification period, or 60 days if there is none), a liability shall be recognised at its fair value at the date the termination is communicated to employees.

- If employees are required to continue working until they are terminated to qualify for termination benefits, and will be retained to render service beyond the minimum retention period, a liability should be measured, at its fair value, at the termination date but recognised as employees render service over the future service period, even if the benefit formula used to calculate the termination benefit is based on length of service.

B   Contract termination costs

Costs to terminate an operating lease or other contract are: *FAS 146.14*

- costs to terminate the contract before the end of its term; or

- costs that will continue to be incurred under the contract for its remaining term without economic benefit to the entity.

A liability for costs to terminate a contract before the end of its term shall be recognised and measured at its fair value when the entity terminates the contract in accordance with the contract terms.   *FAS 146.15*

18.9   DISCLOSURE

18.9.1   Provisions

IAS 37.84-85 For each class of provision, an entity should disclose the following:

- a brief description of the nature of the obligation and the expected timing of any resulting outflows of economic benefits;
- an indication of the uncertainties about the amount or timing of those outflows. Where necessary to provide adequate information, an entity should disclose the major assumptions made concerning future events;
- the amount of any expected reimbursement, stating the amount of any asset that has been recognised for that expected reimbursement;
- a reconciliation of the carrying amount of the provision at the beginning and end of the period showing:
    - additional provisions made in the period, including increases to existing provisions;
    - amounts used, i.e. incurred and charged against the provision, during the period;
    - unused amounts reversed during the period; and
    - the increase during the period in the discounted amount arising from the passage of time and the effect of any change in the discount rate.

Comparative information is not required.

IAS 37.91-92 If disclosure of the above information is not practicable, that fact should be disclosed. In the extremely rare circumstances that disclosure of the above information is expected seriously to prejudice the entity in a dispute with other parties, it need not disclose the information but instead should disclose the general nature of the dispute and the reason why, and the fact that, the information has not been disclosed.

A liability for costs that will continue to be incurred under a contract for its *FAS 146.16*
remaining term without economic benefit to the entity shall be recognised and
measured at its fair value when the entity ceases to use the right conveyed by the
contract.   If the contract is an operating lease, the fair value of the liability at the
cease-use date shall be determined based on the remaining lease rentals, reduced by
estimated sublease rentals that could be reasonably obtained for the property, even
if the entity does not intend to enter into a sublease.   Remaining lease rentals
should not be reduced to an amount less than zero.

C   Other costs

Other costs associated with an exit or disposal activity include, but are not limited *FAS 146.17*
to, costs to consolidate or close facilities and relocate employees.

A liability for other costs should be recognised and measured at its fair value in the
period in which the liability is incurred.   The liability shall not be recognised before
it is incurred, even if the costs are incremental to other operating costs and will be
incurred as a direct result of a plan.

18.9   DISCLOSURE

18.9.1   Provisions

Any liability which is not included in one of the other categories of non-current *S-X 5-02.24*
liabilities requiring separate disclosure (i.e. other than a bond, mortgage, other long-
term debt or non-current indebtedness to related parties) and is in excess of 5% of
total liabilities, should be disclosed separately in the balance sheet or in a note
thereto, e.g. deferred tax or provision for liabilities.

In respect of environmental liabilities, the nature, accounting treatment, total *SAB 92*
anticipated amount, and amount accrued to date should be disclosed.   If the *(Topic 5-Y)*
liability relates to assets or businesses previously disposed, that fact should be
disclosed.   Where remediation costs relate to assets held for development or sale,
the treatment of such costs in arriving at an assessment of the assets' recoverability
should be disclosed.

If an environmental liability is measured on a discounted basis, that fact and the *SOP 96-1*
following information should be disclosed: *SAB 92*
(Topic 5-Y)
- the undiscounted amounts any related recovery;

- the discount rate used;

- expected payments for each of the next five years and the aggregate amount
  thereafter; and

- a reconciliation of the expected aggregate undiscounted amounts to amounts
  recognised in the balance sheets.

The following disclosures are required in notes to financial statements that include *FAS 146.20*
the period in which an exit or disposal activity is initiated and any subsequent period
until the activity is completed:
- a description of the exit or disposal activity, including the facts and
  circumstances leading to the expected activity and the expected completion date;

18.9.2   Contingencies

IAS 37.86   Unless the possibility of any outflow in settlement is remote, an entity should disclose for each class of contingent liability at the balance sheet date:

- a brief description of the nature of the contingent liability; and, where practicable;

- for each major type of cost associated with the activity (for example, one-time termination benefits, contract termination costs, and other associated costs):
  (i) the total amount expected to be incurred in connection with the activity, the amount incurred in the period, and the cumulative amount incurred to date;
  (ii) a reconciliation of the beginning and ending liability balances showing separately the changes during the period attributable to costs incurred and charged to expense, costs paid or otherwise settled, and any adjustments to the liability - with an explanation of the reasons therefor;
- the line items in the income statement in which the costs are aggregated;
- for each reportable segment, the total amount of costs to be incurred in connection with the activity, the amount incurred in the period, and the cumulative amount incurred to date, net of any adjustments to the liability - with an explanation of the reasons therefor; and
- if a liability for a cost associated with the activity is not recognised because fair value cannot reasonably be estimated, that fact and the reasons therefor.

Where a liability for costs associated with an exit or disposal activity is recognised, and the activity involves a discontinued operation, the costs should be included in the results of discontinued operations. Where the activity does not involve a discontinued operation, the costs should be included in income from continuing operations.   *FAS 146.18*

The following information should be disclosed for asset retirement obligations: *FAS 143.22*
- a general description of the obligations and associated long-lived assets;
- the fair value of any assets that are legally restricted for settling obligations; and
- a reconciliation of the beginning and ending carrying amount of obligations, showing changes attributable to:
  - liabilities incurred in the current period;
  - liabilities settled in the current period;
  - accretion expense; and
  - revisions in estimated cash flows;

  whenever there is a significant change in one or more of those four components during the reporting period.

If the fair value of an asset retirement obligation cannot be reasonably estimated, that fact and the reasons why should be disclosed.

Liabilities of an employee stock ownership plan should be reflected in the balance sheet of the employer (company) when the liability is either guaranteed by the company or where there is a commitment by the company to make future contributions sufficient to meet the debt service requirements.   *SOP 76-3*
SOP 93-6

18.9.2   Contingencies and guarantees

Disclosure of the nature of the accrual, and in some circumstances the amount accrued, may be necessary for the financial statements not to be misleading.   *FAS 5.9-10*

If a loss contingency exists but is not accrued because one or both conditions for accrual (see section 18.2.2) are not met, or if an exposure to loss exists in excess of

- an estimate of its financial effect;
- an indication of the uncertainties relating to the amount or timing of any outflow; and
- the possibility of any reimbursement.

IAS 37.89   Where an inflow of economic benefits is probable, an entity should disclose a brief description of the nature of the contingent assets at the balance sheet date and, where practicable, an estimate of their financial effect.

IAS 37.91-92   If disclosure of the above information is not practicable, that fact should be disclosed. In the extremely rare circumstances that disclosure of the above information is expected seriously to prejudice the entity in a dispute with other parties, it need not disclose the information but instead should disclose the general nature of the dispute and the reason why, and the fact that, the information has not been disclosed.

the amount accrued, the following disclosures are required when there is at least a reasonable possibility that a loss or an additional loss may have been incurred:

- The nature of the contingency; and
- An estimate of the possible loss or range of loss, or a statement that an estimate cannot be made.

Disclosure of remote contingencies that have the characteristics of guarantees should be made. For example, guarantees of indebtedness of others, guarantees to repurchase receivables that have been sold or assigned, standby letters of credit. *FAS 5.4,12*

If information becomes available before an entity's financial statements are issued indicating that a loss was incurred after the date of the financial statements, disclosure may be necessary to keep the financial statements from being misleading. It also may be desirable to present pro forma information on the face of the balance sheet. *FAS 5.11*

Detailed disclosures regarding judgments and assumptions underlying the recognition and measurement of accrued contingent liabilities should be made. *SAB 92 (Topic 5-Y)*

The amount of unused letters of credit, assets pledged as security for loans and commitments (such as those for plant acquisition or an obligation to reduce debts) should be disclosed but not described as contingencies. *FAS 5.18 S-X 4-08(b)*

Disclosure of contingencies that might result in gains is required, but care should be exercised to avoid misleading implications as to the likelihood of realisation. *FAS 5.17*

A guarantor shall disclose the following information about each guarantee, even if the likelihood of the guarantor's having to make any payments under the guarantee is remote: *FIN 45.13*

- the nature of the guarantee, including the approximate term of the guarantee, how the guarantee arose, and the events or circumstances that would require the guarantor to perform under the guarantee;
- the maximum potential amount of future payments (undiscounted);
- the current carrying amount of the liability, if any;
- the nature of (1) any recourse provisions and (2) any assets held as collateral and, if estimable, the approximate extent to which the proceeds from liquidation of those assets would be expected to cover the maximum potential future payments under the guarantee.

For product warranties that are excluded from the initial recognition and measurement requirements of this Interpretation, the guarantor is required to disclose the following information: *FIN 45.14*

- the accounting policy and methodology used in determining the liability for product warranties; and
- a tabular reconciliation of the changes in the aggregate product warranty liability for the reporting period.

Section 19   Revenue recognition

19.1   AUTHORITATIVE PRONOUNCEMENTS

- IAS 16
- IAS 18
- IAS 20
- IAS 38

- IAS 40
- SIC-27
- SIC-31

COMMENT

The IASB and the FASB are undertaking a joint project on revenue recognition and a Discussion Paper is expected in 2005. The proposed conceptual model for revenue recognition moves away from the risks and rewards approach, the concept of an earnings process and the principle of realisation. Instead, it follows an asset and liability approach to revenue.

IAS 18.1,4,6 IAS 18 should be applied in accounting for revenue arising from the sale of goods, the rendering of services and the use by others of the entity's assets yielding interest, royalty or dividends. It does not, however, deal with revenue arising from lease agreements (see IAS 17 *Leases* – section 16); dividends arising from investments accounted for under the equity method (see IAS 28 *Investments in Associates* – section 4); insurance contracts within the scope of IFRS 4 *Insurance Contracts*; changes in the fair value of financial assets and liabilities or their disposal (see IAS 39 *Financial Instruments: Recognition and Measurement* – section 11); changes in the value of other current assets; initial recognition and from changes in the fair value of biological assets relating to agricultural activity and initial recognition of agricultural produce (see IAS 41 *Agriculture*); or the extraction of mineral ores. Revenue arising from construction contracts (including contracts for rendering of services directly related to construction contracts, e.g. the services of architects and project managers) are dealt with in accordance with IAS 11 *Construction Contracts* (see section 15.3).

Under the GAAP hierarchy in IAS 8 *Accounting Policies, Changes in Accounting Estimates and Errors*, whilst US GAAP cannot override specific requirements of IFRSs or the concepts in the Framework, it may be that companies choose to use US GAAP to formulate appropriate accounting policies, in areas not specifically addressed by IAS 18.

19.2   REVENUE RECOGNITION IN FINANCIAL STATEMENTS

A   Revenue

IAS 18 *Revenue* does not deal with the principles of realisation, which will be determined by national regulation.

IAS 1.34   Not all gains included in income may be included in revenue. An entity undertakes
IAS 16.68 in the course of its ordinary activities, other transactions that do not generate revenue

Section 19   Revenue recognition

19.1   AUTHORITATIVE PRONOUNCEMENTS

- APB 29
- FAS 45
- FAS 48
- FAS 49
- FAS 66

- FAS 91
- FAS 153
- FIN 30
- SAB 104
- SOP 97-2

Generally, most of the guidance either relates solely to a particular industry or deals with the recognition of certain forms of revenue.   In addition:

- the SEC staff has issued SAB 104 *Revenue Recognition* (which updated and revised Topic 13) addressing specific revenue recognition issues faced by registrants.   The SEC has issued several Accounting and Auditing Enforcement Releases ('AAER'), detailing why, in its opinion, issues had not been accounted for properly and citing the preferred accounting treatment;

- there are several EITF consensuses and FASB Technical Bulletins on revenue recognition issues; and

- several SOPs dealing with revenue recognition have been issued by the AICPA.

This section provides a brief summary of the general principles that are applied in practice for the recognition of revenue earned from operations.   Pronouncements dealing with special industry situations or other very specific issues with little general application are outside the scope of this book.

19.2   REVENUE RECOGNITION IN FINANCIAL STATEMENTS

Revenues represent actual or expected cash inflows (or the equivalent) that have occurred or will occur as a result of the entity's ongoing major or central operations.   *CON 6.79*

Revenue recognition involves consideration of two factors: *CON 5.83*
- being realised or realisable; and
- being earned.

IAS 38.113   but are incidental to the main revenue-generating activities, e.g. gains and losses on the disposal of property, plant and equipment.

IAS 18.7   Revenue is the gross inflow of economic benefits received and receivable by the entity, on its own account, during the period, arising in the course of the ordinary activities of an entity, when those inflows result in increases in equity, other than increases relating to contributions from equity participants.

IAS 18.8-10   Revenue should be measured at the fair value of the consideration received or receivable, taking into account any trade discounts and volume rebates allowed. Amounts collected on behalf of third parties, such as sales taxes, are excluded. In an agency relationship, amounts collected on behalf of the entity are not revenue; instead, revenue is the amount of commission.

IAS 18.11,30   Where consideration is deferred, such that this represents a financing transaction, the
IAS 39.9   fair value should be discounted using an imputed rate of interest, based on either the
IAS 39.AG5-AG8   prevailing rate for a similar instrument of an issuer with a similar credit rating, or a rate of interest that discounts the nominal amount of the instrument to the current cash sales price of the goods and services. The interest revenue is recognised on the effective interest method (see section 11.6.1).

IAS 18.18,22,34   In some cases, it may not be probable that the economic benefits associated with the transaction will flow to the entity, until the consideration is received or until an uncertainty is removed. However, when an uncertainty arises about the collectability of amounts included already in revenue, an expense rather than an adjustment to revenue is recorded.

IAS 18.13   The recognition criteria of IAS 18 are usually applied separately to each transaction. However, in certain circumstances, it is necessary to apply the recognition criteria to:

- the separately identifiable components of a single transaction in order to reflect the substance of the transaction; or

- two or more transactions together when they are linked in such a way that the commercial effect cannot be understood without reference to the series of transactions as a whole.

IAS 18 does not establish the criteria for segmenting and combining revenue transactions. IAS 11 addressed this area for construction contracts which may provide appropriate guidance.

B   Sale of goods

IAS 18.14   Revenue from the sale of goods is recognised when all the following conditions have
IAS 18.Appx 1-6   been satisfied:

- the entity has transferred to the buyer the significant risks and rewards of ownership of the goods;

- the entity retains neither continuing managerial involvement to the degree usually associated with ownership nor effective control over the goods sold;

- the amount of revenue can be measured reliably;

- it is probable that the economic benefits associated with the transaction will flow to the entity; and

540

Revenues generally are not recognised until realised or realisable. Revenues are realised when products (goods or services), merchandise or other assets are exchanged for cash or claims to cash and are realisable when related assets received or held are readily convertible to known amounts of cash or claims to cash.

Revenues are not recognised until earned. They are considered to have been earned when an entity has substantially accomplished what it must do to be entitled to the benefits represented by the revenues. There is a presumption that an entity should recognise cash rebates or refund obligations as a reduction of revenue based on a systematic and rational allocation of the cost of honouring rebates or refunds earned and claimed to each of the underlying revenue transactions that result in progress by the customer toward earning the rebate or refund. This presumption is overcome, and the cash consideration should be recognised as a cost incurred, if, and to the extent that (1) the vendor receives an identifiable benefit in exchange for the consideration and (2) the vendor can reasonably estimate the fair value of that benefit.

EITF 00-22

EITF 01-9

All amounts billed to customers for shipping and handling costs, if any, represent revenues earned for the goods provided and should be classified as revenue. Reimbursements received for out-of-pocket expenses incurred should also be classified as revenue in the income statement.

EITF 00-10

EITF 01-14

The SEC Staff believe that for revenue to have been realised or realisable and earned, all of the following criteria must be met:

SAB 104
(Topic 13)

- persuasive evidence of an arrangement exists;
- delivery has occurred or services have been rendered;
- the seller's price to the buyer is fixed or determinable; and
- collectability is reasonably assured.

A   Evidence of an arrangement

When a company's established business practice requires a written sales agreement in order for a sale to be considered final, the absence of a final agreement executed by the properly authorised personnel of both the company and the customer precludes revenue recognition. In addition, if an agreement is subject to subsequent approval, revenue recognition is precluded until the necessary approvals are obtained.

SAB 104
(Topic 13)

If a company does not have a standard or customary business practice of relying on written contracts to document a sales arrangement, it usually would be expected to have other forms of written or electronic evidence to document the transaction. In those situations, that documentation could represent persuasive evidence of an arrangement.

Companies may enter into 'side' agreements to a master contract that effectively amend the master contract. The terms of 'side' agreements should be considered when determining the appropriate accounting for the arrangement. The existence of a subsequently executed 'side' agreement may be an indicator that the original agreement was not final and any revenue recognition was not appropriate.

Revenue recognition is not appropriate in a consignment sale arrangement because the seller retains the risks and rewards of ownership and title does not usually pass to the consignee. In other arrangements title to the delivered products passes to the buyer but the substance of the transaction is that of a consignment, a financing,

- the costs incurred or to be incurred in respect of the transaction can be measured reliably.

IAS 18.16   An entity can retain a significant risk of ownership in a number of ways, for example:

IAS 18.Appx 2,6
- when the entity retains an obligation for unsatisfactory performance not covered by normal warranty provisions;
- when the receipt of the revenue from a particular sale is contingent on the derivation of revenue by the buyer from its sale of the goods;
- when the goods are shipped subject to installation, and the installation is a significant part of the contract which has not yet been completed by the entity. Revenue is normally recognised when the buyer accepts delivery, and installation and inspection are complete. However, it is recognised immediately on buyer's acceptance of delivery when the installation process is simple in nature or performed only for the purposes of final determination of contract prices, e.g. in commodity contracts;
- when the buyer has the right to rescind the purchase for a reason specified in the sales contract and the entity is uncertain about the probability of return. In such cases, revenue is recognised on formal acceptance by the buyer or when the time period for rejection has elapsed; and
- where sales are made to intermediate parties for resale, and the buyer acts in substance as an agent, the sale is treated as a consignment sale under which the buyer undertakes to sell the goods on behalf of the seller. Revenue is recognised when the intermediary, or consignee, sells the goods to a third party.

IAS 18.15, Appx 5   In most but not all cases (e.g. most retail sales), transfer of risks and rewards of ownership coincides with the transfer of legal title or passing of possession to the buyer. For a sale and repurchase agreement, the terms need to be analysed to ascertain whether the risks and rewards of ownership have been transferred or whether it is in substance a financing transaction. There is further discussion of specific situations in the Appendix to IAS 18.

IAS 18 Appx 1   Revenue on bill-and-hold sales is recognised when the buyer takes title if:
- it is probable that delivery will be made;
- the item is on hand, identified and ready for delivery to the buyer at the time the sale is recognised;
- the buyer specifically acknowledges the deferred delivery instructions; and
- the usual payment terms apply.

Revenue is not recognised when there is simply an intention to acquire or manufacture the goods in time for delivery.

IAS 18 Appx 3   Revenue on lay away sales, where goods are delivered only when the buyer makes the final payment in a series of instalments, is recognised when the goods are delivered. However, when experience indicates that most such sales are consummated, revenue may be recognised when a significant deposit is received provided the goods are on hand, identified and ready for delivery to the buyer.

IAS 18.19   Revenue and expenses, e.g. warranty costs, relating to the same transaction should be matched and recognised simultaneously. Where the expenses cannot be measured reliably, any consideration received should be recognised as a liability.

or other arrangement for which revenue recognition is not appropriate. For example, characteristics whereby the buyer has the right to return the product, the buyer does not have economic substance apart from that provided by the seller, or the seller is required to repurchase the product, would preclude revenue recognition even if title to the product has passed to the buyer.

B   Delivery and performance

Revenue recognition is precluded until both title and the risks and rewards of ownership have transferred to the customer.

SAB 104
(Topic 13)

Under local laws in some jurisdictions, including the UK, it is common for a seller to retain a form of title to goods delivered to customers until payment is received so that the seller can recover the goods if the customer defaults on payment. The SEC Staff have confirmed that, presuming all other revenue recognition criteria have been met, revenue recognition on delivery is not precluded where the only rights to title retained by the seller are those enabling recovery of goods in the event of default on payment, e.g. the rights retained under reservation of title clauses (so-called 'Romalpa' clauses in the UK) giving the seller security rights similar to those established in the US Uniform Commercial Code (UCC).

When goods are shipped 'FOB destination', revenue should not be recognised until the customer receives the goods, even if the goods are shipped via common carrier.

If customer acceptance provisions exist, they are presumed to be substantive and revenue recognition is precluded until customer acceptance occurs or the acceptance provisions lapse. Customer acceptance provisions should be viewed from the perspective of the customer. However, this presumption can be overcome where the acceptance provisions are no different from general rights of return or rights under general or specific warranties. Revenue may also be recognised on delivery when the seller reliably demonstrates that a delivered product meets all customer-specific acceptance provisions, even in the absence of formal customer acceptance.

Revenue recognition is precluded unless a vendor has substantially completed all performance obligations. Only clearly inconsequential or perfunctory actions may remain incomplete in order for the vendor's performance obligations to be considered 'substantially complete'. Remaining performance obligations are not inconsequential and perfunctory if they are essential to the functionality of the delivered product. For example, if the seller must install the product, i.e. no one else could do it; this may mean that revenue cannot be recognised until installation is complete. Alternatively, revenue may be recognised on delivery if the delivered equipment is a standard product, the installation activity itself does not alter the equipment's capabilities and other companies are available to perform the installation.

The following sales transactions are impacted by delivery and performance issues:

- bill-and-hold transactions rarely meet the stringent criteria for revenue recognition (a bill-and-hold transaction is where a customer agrees to purchase the goods but the seller retains physical possession until the customer requests shipment to designated locations);
- in licensing and similar arrangements, no revenue should be recognised until the license term begins;

C   *Rendering of services*

IAS 18.20-21
IAS 18.Appx 10-19
When the outcome of a transaction involving the rendering of services can be estimated reliably, revenue is recognised by reference to the stage of completion of the transaction at the balance sheet date. IAS 11 (see section 15.3) requires revenue recognition for construction contracts on a similar basis and its requirements are generally applicable to revenue recognition for a transaction involving rendering of services. The outcome of a transaction can be estimated reliably when all the following conditions are satisfied:

- the amount of revenue can be measured reliably;
- it is probable that the economic benefits associated with the transaction will flow to the entity;
- the stage of completion of the transaction at the balance sheet date can be measured reliably; and
- the costs incurred for the transaction and the costs to complete the transaction can be measured reliably.

IAS 18.25   When services are performed by an indeterminable number of acts over a specified period, revenue is usually recognised on a straight line basis unless there is evidence that some other method better reflects the stage of completion. When a specific act is much more significant than other acts, revenue recognition is postponed until that act is performed.

IAS 18.23   An entity is generally able to make reliable estimates after it has agreed to each party's enforceable rights regarding the service, the consideration and the manner and terms of settlement. It is also usually necessary for the entity to have an effective internal financial budgeting and reporting system.

IAS 18.24   The stage of completion should be determined using a method that measures reliably the services performed. Depending on the nature of the transaction, this may include surveys of work performed, services performed to date as a percentage of total services to be performed, or the proportion that costs incurred to date (reflecting services performed to date) bear to the estimated total costs of performing the services. Progress payments and advances received often do not reflect the services performed.

IAS 18.26-28   When the outcome of the transaction involving the rendering of services cannot be estimated reliably, as may be the case in the early stages of a transaction, revenue should be recognised only to the extent of the expenses recognised that are recoverable, and therefore often no profit is recognised.

SIC-27.8-9   An entity may enter into a transaction or a series of transactions (an arrangement) with an unrelated party or parties that involves the legal form of a lease (see section 16.2). If the arrangement does not in substance include the conveyance of the right to use an asset for an agreed period of time, when IAS 17 applies, then the criteria in IAS 18.20 should be applied to the facts and circumstances of the arrangement in determining when to recognise any fee resulting from that arrangement as revenue. The entity should consider factors such as whether there is continuing involvement in the form of significant future performance obligations necessary to earn the fee, whether there are retained risks, the terms of any guarantee arrangements, and the risk of repayment of the fee. SIC-27 *Evaluating the Substance of Transactions Involving the Legal Form*

- revenue recognition is precluded under 'layaway' sales until merchandise is delivered to the customer; and

- 'street date' restrictions on the right to resale preclude revenue recognition until the restriction expires.

If an arrangement is outside the scope of SOP 81-1 *Accounting for Performance of Construction-Type and Certain Production-Type Contracts* and requires the delivery or performance of multiple 'elements', SAB 104 confirms that the existence of undelivered elements may effect the conclusion as to whether revenue for a delivered element may be recognised, as discussed in EITF 00-21 (see section 19.3.1).

C   Service transactions

There is no guidance that specifically addresses accounting for general service revenues but the revenue recognition principles in CON 5 and SAB 104 refer to the delivery of 'products', which include both goods and services. As such, service revenue is recognised as services are performed, amounts can be objectively determined, and collection is reasonably assured. Performance consists of completing a specified act or acts, or as time passes.

Long-term service arrangements are not within the scope of SOP 81-1 *Accounting for Performance of Construction-Type and Certain Production-Type Contracts*. The SEC Staff has noted that long-term service contracts may be accounted for using the proportionate performance method of revenue recognition, subject to consideration of guidance under SAB 104. The Staff generally would expect an entity to use output measures (similar to those described in SOP 81-1, see section 15.3.2) as the basis for revenue recognition when using the proportionate performance method.

Recognition of revenue relating to service contracts is generally dependent upon the types of acts to be performed in rendering the services:

- For a specified number of similar acts, revenue is recognised equally for each act expected to be performed.

- For a specified number of dissimilar acts, revenue should be allocated to the different acts based on their relative fair values. If insufficient evidence of relative fair value exists, revenue should be recognised on a systematic and rational basis over the service period.

- For an unspecified number of similar acts with a fixed performance period revenue generally is recognised ratably over the performance period.

- For an unspecified number of similar acts for an unspecified period, revenue generally should be recognised ratably over the estimated service period.

A long-term service arrangement that includes multiple deliverables should be evaluated for separation under EITF 00-21 *Accounting for Revenue Arrangements with Multiple Deliverables* (see section 19.3.1).

D   Up-front fees

Up-front fees, even if non-refundable, are earned as the products and/or services are delivered and/or performed over the term of the arrangement or the expected period of performance. Unless the up-front fee is in exchange for products delivered or services performed that represent the culmination of a separate

SAB 104
(Topic 13)

of a Lease discusses specific indicators that individually demonstrate that recognition of the entire fee as income when received, if received at the beginning of the arrangement, is inappropriate.

The fee should be presented in the income statement based on its economic substance and nature.

D   Interest, royalties and dividends

IAS 18.29 Revenue arising from the use by others of entity assets yielding interest, royalties and dividends is recognised when:

- it is probable that the economic benefits associated with the transaction will flow to the entity; and
- the amount of the revenue can be measured reliably.

IAS 18.30,Appx 20   Revenue is recognised on the following bases:

IAS 39.9,AG5-AG8
- interest is recognised using the effective interest method;
- royalties are recognised on an accruals basis in accordance with the substance of the relevant agreement (often on a straight line basis where the licensee has the right to use for a specified period);
- dividends are recognised when the shareholder's right to receive payment is established;

IAS 18.32
- dividends on equity securities which are declared from pre-acquisition profits are deducted from the cost of the securities.   If the allocation between pre- and post-acquisition profits is arbitrary, then dividends are recognised as revenue unless they clearly result in recovery of part of the cost of equity securities; and
- where unpaid interest on an interest-bearing investments is received post-acquisition, only the portion accrued post-acquisition is recognised as revenue.

IAS 18, Appx 20   An assignment of rights for a fixed fee or non-refundable guarantee under a non-cancellable contract which permits the licensee to exploit those rights freely and the licensor has no remaining obligations is a sale.   Examples include a licensing agreement for the use of software when the licensor has no obligations post delivery, and film exhibition rights in markets where the licensor has no control over the distributor and expects to receive no further revenues from box office receipts. Where licence income is contingent on the occurrence of a future event, it is recognised only where it is probable it will be received, normally on occurrence of the event.

E   Upfront fees

These are not specifically addressed by IAS 18 and so the general rules on revenue recognition apply, although the treatment of various specific situations is discussed in the Appendix to IAS 18.

F   Contingent revenue

IAS 37.31-35   The treatment of contingent revenue is addressed by IAS 37 *Provisions, Contingent Liabilities and Contingent Assets*.   If it has become virtually certain that an inflow of economic benefits will arise, the asset and related income are recognised in the financial statements of the period in which the change occurs.

earnings process, revenue should be deferred and recognised systematically over the periods that the fees are earned. Furthermore, in order for up-front fees to be recognised separately from the on-going service or product the criteria for separability discussed in EITF 00-21 must be met (see section 19.3.1).

E   Incremental direct costs

When revenue is recognised over time, incremental direct costs associated with acquiring a revenue-producing contract can be deferred and amortised over the same period as the associated revenue, unless there is no basis for recovery of these costs.

SAB 104
(Topic 13)

Costs in excess of deferred revenues generally should not be deferred unless a contractual arrangement exists guaranteeing a continuing net revenue stream that allows recovery of the costs.

F   Right of return

If the buyer has the right to return the product, revenue should be recognised at time of sale only if all of the following conditions are met:

FAS 48.6

- the seller's price is substantially fixed or determinable at the date of sale;
- the buyer has paid the seller, or is obligated to pay and the obligation is not contingent on resale of the product or would not be changed in the event of theft, physical destruction or damage of the product;
- the seller does not have significant obligations for future performance to directly bring about resale of the product by the buyer;
- the buyer acquiring the products for resale has independent economic substance apart from the seller; and
- the amount of future returns can be reasonably estimated.

Any costs or losses that are expected in connection with any returns should be accrued in accordance with FAS 5 *Accounting for Contingencies*. Reported income should be reduced to reflect estimated returns.

FAS 48.7

If the above conditions are not met at the time of sale, sales revenue and cost of sales should be recognised either when the return privilege has expired or if the conditions subsequently are met, whichever occurs first.

The SEC Staff believe that FAS 48 *Revenue Recognition When a Right of Return Exists* should be applied literally to transactions involving the sale of products. With regard to service transactions with refund provisions, all the factors in FAS 48 must be satisfied in order to conclude that refunds can be reasonably estimated.

For the purpose of estimating the level of future refunds, expected and actual return rates of both products and services should fall within a relatively narrow range to be considered reliable.

When applying FAS 48 by analogy to service transactions, a company introducing services to a new class of customer generally must have at least two years of experience to be able to make reasonable and reliable estimates. Two years of history may not be required for product sales because that would conflict with FAS 48, but the SEC Staff may challenge estimates of product returns when little history of a specific product exists.

G   *Disclosure*

IAS 1.81   Revenue must be included as a line item on the face of the income statement.

> **COMMENT**
>
> As discussed at IFRIC's October 2004 meeting, since finance expense must also be included as a line item on the face of the income statement, it is not appropriate to present this net of finance income, although the gross components of net finance income, could be presented on the face of the income statement with a subtotal for net finance income.

IAS 18.35   An entity shall disclose:

- the accounting policies adopted for the recognition of revenue, including the methods adopted to determine the stage of completion of transactions involving the rendering of services;
- the amount of each significant category of revenue recognised during the period, including revenue arising from:
    - the sale of goods;
    - the rendering of services;
    - interest;
    - royalties;
    - dividends; and
- the amount of revenue arising from exchanges of goods or services included in each significant category of revenue.

SIC-27.10-11   In respect of an arrangement with an unrelated party or parties that involves the legal form of a lease, but does not in substance involve a lease under IAS 17 (see section 19.2C), a description of the arrangement (including the underlying assets and any restrictions on its use; the life and other significant terms of the arrangement; and the transactions that are linked, including any options), the accounting treatment applied to any fee received, the amount recognised as income in the period and the line item in the income statement in which included, shall be disclosed.   These disclosures should be provided for each individual arrangement or in aggregate for each class of arrangement.

It should be noted that FAS 48 does not permit for the deferral of gross margin; instead, it requires that a provision for estimated sales returns should be recorded as a reduction in sales and cost of sales. SAB 104 confirms that FAS 48 does not provide for recognition of sales and cost of sales while deferring gross margin under any circumstances.

G   Contingent revenue

The SEC Staff considered the guidance provided in FAS 29 *Determining Contingent*   *SAB 104* *Rentals,* which indicates that contingent rental income should be recognised in the   *(Topic 13)* period in which the contingency is resolved, may be applied by analogy to other situations for which the realisation of revenue is contingent based on factors other than credit risk. The Staff also state that the use of probability in determining the outcome of future events for the purposes of recording revenue is not acceptable, even if it is probable that a company would achieve a performance target.

H   Disclosure

The SEC Staff consider that a registrant should always disclose its accounting policy for the recognition of revenue as revenue recognition generally involves a high level of judgment. If a company has different policies for different types of revenue transactions, the policy for each material type of transaction should be disclosed. If sales transactions have multiple units of accounting, such as a product and service, the accounting policy disclosure should cover each unit of accounting as well as how units of accounting are determined and valued.

Regulation S-X requires that revenue from the sales of products, services, and other products each be separately disclosed on the face of the income statement. The Staff considers that costs relating to each type of revenue similarly should be reported separately on the face of the income statement.

MD&A requires a discussion of liquidity, capital resources, results of operations and other information necessary to an understanding of a registrant's financial condition, changes in financial condition and results of operations. This discussion would include unusual or infrequent transactions, known trends or uncertainties that have had, or might reasonably be expected to have, a favourable or unfavourable material effect on revenue, operating income or net income and the relationship between revenue and the costs of the revenue. Changes in revenue should not be evaluated solely in terms of volume and price changes, but should also include an analysis of the reasons and factors contributing to the increase or decrease.

Examples of revenue transactions or events that the Staff has suggested should be disclosed and discussed are:

- Shipments of product at the end of a reporting period that significantly reduce customer backlog and that reasonably might be expected to result in lower shipments and revenue in the next period.
- Granting of extended payment terms that will result in a longer collection period for accounts receivable (regardless of whether revenue has been recognised).
- Changing trends in sales that could be expected to have a significant effect on future sales, gross profit margins or sales returns.
- Seasonal trends or variations in sales.

19.3   SPECIFIC RECOGNITION ISSUES

19.3.1   Separately priced extended warranty and product maintenance contracts

IAS 18.13   The general requirements of IAS 18 apply, which require that the recognition criteria are usually applied separately to each transaction, but in certain circumstances, it is necessary to apply the recognition criteria to:

- the separately identifiable components of a single transaction in order to reflect the substance of the transaction; or

- two or more transactions together when they are linked in such a way that the commercial effect cannot be understood without reference to the series of transactions as a whole.

IAS 18, Appx 11   When the selling price of a product includes an identifiable amount for subsequent servicing, that amount is deferred and recognised as revenue over the period during which the service is performed.   The amount deferred is that which will cover the expected costs of the services under the agreement, together with a reasonable profit on those services.

19.3   SPECIFIC RECOGNITION ISSUES

19.3.1   Revenue arrangements with multiple deliverables

A   Basic principles

Revenue arrangements with multiple deliverables should be divided into separate units of accounting if the deliverables meet certain criteria.   The evaluation of all deliverables should be performed at the inception of the arrangement and as each item is delivered.   The delivered item(s) should be considered a separate unit of accounting if all of the following criteria are met:

EITF 00-21

- the delivered item(s) has value to the customer on a standalone basis (either because it is sold separately by any vendor or the customer could resell the delivered item(s) on a standalone basis);
- there is objective and reliable evidence of the fair value of the delivered item(s); and,
- if the arrangement includes a general right of return of the delivered item(s), delivery or performance of the undelivered item(s) is considered probable and substantially in the control of the vendor.

If deliverables can be separated into differing units of accounting, the arrangement consideration should be allocated to the deliverables as follows:

- If there is objective and reliable evidence of the fair value for all units of accounting, and the amount of the total arrangement consideration is fixed or determinable (other than in respect of refunds or performance bonuses), the arrangement consideration should be allocated between the separate units of accounting based on their relative fair values.
- The residual method should be used to allocate consideration where there is objective and reliable evidence of the fair value(s) of the undelivered item(s) but no such evidence for the delivered item(s) and stand-alone value exists for the delivered item.

If any separate unit of accounting is required under GAAP to be recorded at fair value (marked-to-market), the amount allocated to that item should be its fair value. The remainder of the arrangement consideration should be allocated to the other units of accounting based on their relative fair value(s).   This is the only situation where a residual method may be used to determine the amount to be allocated to the undelivered item(s) (i.e. the reverse residual method).

The amount allocated to a delivered item(s) is limited to the amount that is (1) not contingent upon delivery of additional items or meeting other specified performance conditions and (2) not adjusted for the impact of any general right of return pursuant to FAS 48.

The amount recorded as an asset for the excess of revenue recognised over cash or consideration received should not exceed all amounts to which the vendor is legally entitled, including cancellation fees.   The vendor's intention to enforce its contractual rights should be considered in this regard.

The best evidence of fair value is the price of a delivered item when it is regularly sold on a standalone basis and often consists of entity specific or vendor specific objective evidence ('VSOE'). Vendor price lists should not be presumed to be representative of fair value. VSOE is discussed further under software revenue recognition (see section 19.3.2).

A vendor should disclose (1) its accounting policy for revenue recognition of revenue from multiple-deliverable arrangements and (2) the description and nature of such arrangements.

B   *Separately priced extended warranty and product maintenance contracts*

An extended warranty contract is an agreement to provide warranty protection in addition to the scope of the manufacturer's original warranty or to extend the period of coverage provided by the manufacturer's original warranty. A product maintenance contract is an agreement to perform certain agreed-upon services to maintain a product for a specified period of time. A contract is separately priced if the customer has the option to purchase the services provided under the contract for an expressly stated amount separate from the price of the product.
FTB 90-1

Revenue from separately priced contracts should be deferred and recognised in income on a straight-line basis over the contract period, based on the stated price of the contract. If there is sufficient historical evidence that indicates that the costs of performing services under the contract are incurred other than on a straight-line basis, revenue should be recognised over the contract period in proportion to the expected costs of performing services under the contract.

Costs of services performed under the contract should be charged to expense as incurred. Costs that are directly related to the acquisition of a contract generally should be deferred and expensed in proportion to the revenue recognised. A loss should be recognised on extended warranty or product maintenance contracts if the sum of the expected costs of providing services under the contracts and unamortised acquisition costs exceeds related unearned revenue. Contracts should be grouped in a consistent manner to assess whether a loss exists.

C   *Consideration given by a vendor to a customer*

Accounting by a vendor

Cash consideration (including a sales incentive) given by a vendor to a customer is presumed to be a reduction of the selling prices of the vendor's products or services and should be presented as a reduction of revenue in the vendor's income statement. That presumption is overcome and the consideration should be presented as a cost incurred if, and to the extent that, both of the following conditions are met:
EITF 01-9

- The vendor receives, or will receive, an identifiable benefit (goods or services) in exchange for the consideration. The identifiable benefit must be sufficiently separable from the underlying purchase of the vendor's products that the vendor could have transacted with an independent third party to receive that benefit.

- The vendor can reasonably estimate the fair value of the benefit identified. If the consideration paid by the vendor exceeds the estimated fair value of the

benefit received, the excess amount should be presented as a reduction of revenue in the vendor's income statement.

If the consideration consists of a 'free' product or service or equity instruments, the cost of the consideration should be presented as an expense in the vendor's income statement. The SEC Observer indicated that the expense associated with the 'free' products or services delivered at the time of sale of another product or service should be classified as cost of sales.

Application of the criteria above will generally require slotting fees and similar product development or placement fees to be presented as a reduction of revenue.

A rebate or refund redeemable only if the customer completes a specified cumulative level of revenue transactions or remains a customer for a specified time period, should be recognised by the vendor as a reduction of revenue based on a systematic and rational allocation of the cost of honouring the rebates or refunds earned and claimed to each of the underlying revenue transactions that result in progress by the customer toward earning the rebate or refund. Measurement of the total rebate or refund obligation should be based on the estimated number of customers that will ultimately earn and claim rebates or refunds under the offer (that is, breakage should be considered if it can be reasonably estimated). However, if the amount of future rebates or refunds cannot be reasonably estimated, a liability should be recognised for the maximum potential amount of the refund or rebate (that is, no reduction for breakage should be made). However, the following factors may impair a vendor's ability to make a reasonable estimate:

- Relatively long periods in which a particular rebate or refund may be claimed.

- The absence of historical experience with similar types of sales incentive programs with similar products or the inability to apply such experience because of changing circumstances.

- The absence of a large volume of relatively homogeneous transactions.

Accounting by a customer

Cash consideration received by a customer from a vendor generally should be presumed to be a reduction in the price of the vendor's products or services and classified as a reduction of costs of sales. This presumption may be overcome if either of the following conditions are met: *EITF 02-16*

- The vendor receives, or will receive, an identifiable benefit in exchange for the consideration; the conditions stated under EITF 01-9 above are met. In such circumstances, the consideration should be recorded as revenue. Any consideration received in excess of the fair value of the benefit should be recorded as a cost of sales.

- The cash consideration represents a reimbursement of a specific, incremental, identifiable cost incurred by the customer in selling the vendor's product. In such cases, the consideration should be classified as a reduction of that cost.

A rebate or refund of a specified amount of cash consideration that is payable only if the customer completes a specified cumulative level of purchases or remains a customer for a specified period of time should be classified as a reduction of the cost of sales. The allocation of the reduction over the underlying transactions that results in

19.3.2   Software revenue recognition

IAS 18, Appx 19
IAS 18.13

Under International Financial Reporting Standards, there are no specific software revenue recognition rules apart from the example in the Appendix to IAS 18.   Fees from the development of customised software are recognised as revenue by reference to the stage of completion of the development, including completion of services provided for post-delivery service support.   In addition, the general recognition requirements apply, which require that the recognition criteria are usually applied separately to each transaction, but in certain circumstances, it is necessary to apply the recognition criteria to:

- the separately identifiable components of a single transaction in order to reflect the substance of the transaction; or

- two or more transactions together when they are linked in such a way that the commercial effect cannot be understood without reference to the series of transactions as a whole.

progress by the customer toward earning the rebate or refund should be made on a systematic and rational basis provided the amounts are probable and reasonably estimable. If the rebate or refund is not reasonably estimable, it should be recognised as milestones are achieved. The following factors may impair a customer's ability to determine whether a rebate or refund is probable or reasonably estimable:

- the amount relates to purchases that will occur over a relatively long period;
- there is an absence of historical experience with similar products or the inability to apply such experience due to changing circumstances; or
- significant adjustments to expected amounts have been necessary in the past.

19.3.2   Software revenue recognition

A   Basic principles

SOP 97-2 *Software Revenue Recognition (as amended)* provides authoritative guidance on software revenue recognition applying a revenue recognition model based on the relative fair values of the various components of a software arrangement. In order to recognise revenue as each element is delivered, SOP 97-2 requires that stringent requirements for 'vendor-specific objective evidence' must be met for each element's fair value, and no remaining undelivered elements should be essential to the functionality of the delivered elements.

SOP 97-2

> **COMMENT**
> The AICPA staff has issued numerous Technical Practice Aids on accounting and reporting issues related to SOP 97-2.

SOP 97-2 applies to all entities (not just software companies) that earn revenues from licensing, selling, or otherwise marketing computer software. It does not apply to revenue from the sale or licensing of a product containing software that is incidental to the product as a whole.

In an arrangement that includes software that is more than incidental to the other products or services included in the arrangement, the other non-software products or services are also included within the scope of SOP 97-2 if the software is essential to the functionality of those elements.

EITF 03-5

Software arrangements range from those that simply provide a license for a single software product to those that require significant production, modification, or customisation of the software. Arrangements also may include multiple products or services (elements). If the arrangement does not require significant production, modification or customisation of existing software, i.e. contract accounting does not apply, revenue should be recognised when all of the following criteria are met:

SOP 97-2

- persuasive evidence of an arrangement exists;
- delivery has occurred, and no future elements to be delivered are essential to the functionality of the delivered element;
- the vendor's fee is fixed or determinable; and
- collectability is probable, i.e. the fee is not subject to forfeiture, refund or other concessions if the undelivered elements are not delivered.

If an arrangement to deliver software or software systems, either alone or together with other products or services, requires significant production, modification or

19.3.3   Initial fees

A   Franchise fees

IAS 18, Appx 18 Franchise fees may be related to the supply of initial and subsequent services, equipment and other tangible assets, and know-how.   Therefore, franchise fees should be recognised as revenue on a basis that reflects the purpose for which the fees were charged.   The following methods of revenue recognition are appropriate:

- the fair value of supplies of equipment and other tangible assets is recognised as revenue when the items are delivered or title passes;

customisation of software, the entire arrangement should be accounted for as a long-term, construction-type contract (see section 15.3).

Extended payment terms in a software licensing arrangement may indicate that the fee is not fixed or determinable.   Extended payment terms are any payment terms beyond a vendor's normal or customary payment terms.   Further, if payment of a significant portion of the software licensing fee is not due until after expiration of the license or more than twelve months after delivery, the licensing fee should be presumed not to be fixed or determinable.   However, this presumption may be overcome by evidence that the vendor has a standard business practice of using long-term or instalment contracts and a history of successfully collecting under the original payment terms without making concessions.

SOP 97-2 also provides guidance on accounting for specific aspects of software arrangements including discounts, post-customer support and other services, and access keys.

B   Accounting for multiple elements

Software arrangements may provide licenses for multiple software products or for multiple software products and services (multiple elements), e.g. additional software products, upgrades/enhancements, rights to exchange or return software, post-contract customer support, or services, including elements deliverable only on a when-and-if-available basis.   If contract accounting does not apply, revenue recognition should be based on an allocation of the total fee to the individual elements if vendor-specific evidence of fair value exists for each of the elements. If vendor-specific objective evidence exists for all undelivered elements, but not for one or more delivered elements, arrangement consideration may be allocated using the residual method.   If vendor-specific evidence of fair value does not exist for the undelivered elements, revenue from the arrangement should be deferred until sufficient evidence is available, or until all elements have been delivered.

SOP 97-2

C   Determining fair values based on vendor specific objective evidence

Under SOP 97-2, vendor-specific objective evidence is limited to:
- the price charged when the same element is sold separately; or
- if the element has not yet been sold separately, the price for each element established by the software vendor's management having relevant authority. Also, it must be probable that the price will not change before introduction of the element to be sold separately into the marketplace.

SOP 97-2

19.3.3   Initial fees

A   Franchising

Initial franchise fee revenue should be recognised, with an appropriate provision for estimated uncollectible amounts, only when:
- all material services or conditions relating to the franchise sale have been substantially performed or satisfied by the franchisor;
- any obligation to refund cash or forgive receivables has expired; and
- no other conditions or obligations exist.

FAS 45.5

- fees for the provision of continuing services, whether part of the initial or a separate fee, are recognised as revenue as the services are rendered. Sometimes the franchise agreements provide for a separate fee that does not provide a reasonable profit for the supply of continuing services, or the agreement involves the sale of assets to the franchisee at a price lower than that charged to others, or at a price that does not provide a reasonable profit. In such cases, part of the initial fee sufficient to cover (1) the costs of the continuing services, or the estimated costs in excess of the price charged for the assets and (2) a reasonable profit on the sales, should be deferred and recognised as the services are rendered or over the period the goods are likely to be sold to the franchisee. The balance of the initial fee is recognised as revenue when performance of the initial services and other obligations is substantially complete. If the initial fee is collectible over an extended period, and there is significant uncertainty over full collectability, then the fee is recognised as cash instalments are received;

- continuing franchise fees charged for the use of continuing rights granted by the agreement, or for other services provided during the period of the agreement, are recognised as revenue as the services are rendered or the rights used; and

- no revenue is recognised where the franchisor acts as an agent for the franchisee, e.g. the franchisor may order supplies and arrange for their delivery to the franchisee at no profit.

B   Financial service fees

IAS 18, Appx 14   The recognition of revenue for financial service fees depends on the purposes for which the fees are charged and the basis of accounting for any associated financial instrument. The description of fees for financial services may not be indicative of the nature and substance of the services provided. Therefore, it is necessary to distinguish between the following:

- fees that are an integral part of the effective interest rate of a financial instrument are treated as an adjustment to the effective interest rate. These include origination fees received on the creation or acquisition of a financial asset or on issuing a financial liability measured at amortised cost. However, when the financial instrument is measured at fair value with the change in fair value recognised in profit or loss, the fees are recognised as revenue when the instrument is initially recognised. Where commitment fees to originate a loan are received and the loan commitment is outside the scope of IAS 39 (if it is within the scope, it is measured at fair value as a derivative) and it is probable that a specific lending arrangement will be made, the fees are deferred and recognised as an adjustment to the effective interest rate. If the commitment expires without the entity making the loan, the fee income is recognised on expiry;

- fees earned as services are provided are recognised as revenue as the services are provided, e.g. fees charged for servicing a loan, investment management fees. Commitment fees to originate a loan where it is unlikely that a specific lending arrangement will be entered into (and the loan commitment is outside the scope of IAS 39) are recognised on a time proportion basis over the commitment period; and

An appropriate portion of the initial fee should be deferred and amortised over the life of the franchise if it is probable that the continuing fee will not cover the cost (with a reasonable profit allowance thereon) of continuing services to be provided by the franchisor.

FAS 45.7

The relationship between the franchisor and the franchisee may affect recognition of franchise fee revenue. For example, if the franchisor has an option to purchase a franchisee business and there is an understanding that this will be exercised, initial franchise fee revenue should be completely deferred. When the option is exercised, the deferred amount is applied against the franchisor's investment in the business.

FAS 45.10-11

When the initial franchise fee incorporates not only the consideration for the franchise rights and the initial services to be provided by the franchisor but also tangible assets, e.g. equipment or signs, that part of the fee relating to the tangible assets should be separated out, based on the fair value of the tangible assets, and treated as revenue from the sale of assets.

FAS 45.12

B   Financial service fees

The provisions that follow apply to all lending activities and purchases of loans and other debt securities whether or not fees are involved. Hence, for example, loans which may not have fees but do have costs associated with their origination fall within the scope of these provisions.

FAS 91.2-3

Loan origination fees should be deferred and recognised over the life of the loan as an adjustment of yield. Direct loan origination costs generally should be deferred and recognised as a reduction in the yield of the loan.

FAS 91.15

Commitment fees and direct costs incurred to make a commitment to originate (or purchase) a loan should be offset and the net amount generally should be deferred and:

FAS 91.8-9

- if the commitment is exercised, recognised over the life of the loan as an adjustment of yield; or
- if the commitment expires unexercised, recognised in income upon expiration of the commitment.

Credit card fees should be deferred and recognised on a straight-line basis over the period the fee entitles the cardholder to use the card.

FAS 91.10

Loan syndication fees should be recognised when the syndication is complete unless a portion of the syndication loan is retained and the yield on that portion is less than the average yield to the other syndication participants (taking into account the syndication fees paid), in which case a portion of the fee should be deferred so as to produce a yield on the portion of the loan retained that is not less than the average yield on the loans held by the other syndication participants.

FAS 91.11

The net fees or costs that are required to be deferred and amortised as an adjustment of yield over the life of the loan generally should be amortised using the interest method. Variations of the interest method are to be used when the stated interest rate is not constant over the life of the loan.

FAS 91.18

The unamortised balance of loan origination, commitment, and other fees and costs should be disclosed in the balance sheet as part of the related loan balance. The

FAS 91.21-22

- fees earned on the execution of a significant act, e.g. commissions on the allotment of shares to a client, placement fees for arranging a loan between a borrower and an investor, and loan syndication fees – are recognised when the significant act has been completed. In the above examples, this will be on the allotment of shares, the arrangement of the loan and the completion of the syndication (provided the entity arranging the loan retains no part of the loan package for itself or retains a part at the same effective interest rate for comparable risk as other participants).

19.3.4 Disposal of land and buildings

IAS 18, Appx 9
IAS 16.69,72
IAS 38.114,116
IAS 17.58-66
Revenue on the sale of land and buildings is normally recognised when legal title passes to the buyer. However, in some jurisdictions the equitable interest in a property may vest in the buyer before legal title passes, therefore the risks and rewards of ownership have been transferred at that stage, and revenue should be recognised. However, if the seller is obliged to perform any significant acts after the transfer of the equitable and/or legal title, revenue is recognised as the acts are performed.

If real estate is sold with a degree of continuing involvement by the seller such that the risks and rewards of ownership have not been transferred (e.g. sale and repurchase agreements, or where the seller guarantees occupancy or a return on the buyer's investment for a specified period), the nature and extent of the seller's continuing involvement determines how the transaction is accounted for. It may be accounted for as a sale, or as a financing, leasing or some other profit sharing arrangement. If it is accounted for as a sale, the continuing involvement of the seller may delay the recognition of revenue.

A seller must also consider the means of payment and evidence of the buyer's commitment to complete payment. When the aggregate of the payments received provide insufficient evidence of the buyer's commitment to complete payment, revenue is recognised only to the extent cash is received.

It should also be noted that IAS 16 *Property, Plant and Equipment* deals with the measurement of the gains or loss on disposal of an item of property, plant and equipment (see section 7.2.1D) and IAS 38 *Intangible Assets* deals similarly with intangible assets (see section 6.4), in which case IAS 18 applies to the recognition of revenue. IFRS 5 *Non-current Assets Held for Sale and Discontinued Operations* (see section 1.9) includes additional requirements, including measurement rules, for assets held for disposal, which will affect the measurement of the amount of the gain on disposal to be recognised. Sale and leaseback transactions are covered in IAS 17 (see section 16.7).

amounts that are recognised as an adjustment of yield should be reported as part of interest income in the income statement. Amortisation of other fees such as commitment fees included in income when the commitment expires should be reported as service fee income.

19.3.4   Disposal of land and buildings

The recognition of profit on real estate transactions is dealt with in FAS 66 *Accounting for Sales of Real Estate.* FAS 66 provides separate guidance on revenue recognition issues relating to 'retail land sales' and 'real estate sales other than retail land sales'. 'Retail land sales' refer to transactions of the sort entered into by property companies and are not dealt with in this publication. The provisions relating to real estate sales other than retail land sales, e.g. sales of houses, buildings, factories, parcels of land, apply to any type of company and are discussed below.

Real estate time-sharing transactions should be accounted for as non-retail land sales. SOP 04-02 *Accounting for Real Estate Time-Sharing Transactions*, provides additional guidance.

The criteria for recognition of a sale require transfer of the usual risks and rewards of ownership without significant continuing involvement with the property.

Profit from sales of real estate should be recognised in full when the following criteria are met: *FAS 66.3*

- the profit is determinable, i.e. collectability of sales price is reasonably assured or the amount that will not be collectable can be estimated; and
- the earnings process is virtually complete, i.e. seller is not obliged to perform significant activities after the sale to earn the profit.

This method of profit recognition, described as the 'full accrual' method, should not be applied unless the following conditions are met: *FAS 66.5*

- the sale is consummated;
- the buyer's initial and continuing investments are adequate to demonstrate a commitment to pay for the property;
- the seller's receivable is not subject to future subordination; and
- the seller has transferred to the buyer the usual risks and rewards of ownership and does not have a substantial continuing involvement with the property.

When is a sale consummated?

A sale is 'consummated' if the following criteria are met: *FAS 66.6*

- the parties are bound by the terms of a contract;
- all consideration has been exchanged;
- any permanent financing for which the seller is responsible has been arranged; and
- all conditions precedent to closing have been performed.

Adequacy of the buyer's initial and continuing investments

FAS 66 explains what is meant by the buyer's initial and continuing investment and *FAS 66.8-12* provides guidelines for assessing whether they are adequate. These guidelines are based on the lending practices of independent established lending institutions, e.g. the initial investment should represent a significant proportion of the deposit that a buyer would be expected to provide in a leveraged property transaction.

Substantial continuing involvement

Several examples are provided of continuing involvement without transfer of risks *FAS 66.18* and rewards. These include transactions where the seller:

- has an obligation or an option to repurchase the property;
- may be required to repurchase the property because the buyer has a put option; or
- guarantees the return of the buyer's investment.

If a transaction allows the seller to participate in future profit from the property without risk of loss and all the other criteria for recognition of profit under the full accrual method are met, the 'absence of continuing involvement' criterion is presumed to be satisfied.

Other situations where the full accrual method is not appropriate include:

- sale and leasebacks;
- partial sales; and
- sale of property improvements where the buyer leases the underlying land.

Sale and leasebacks

Another common form of continuing involvement is the sale of real estate accompanied by a leaseback to the seller of all or part of the property for all or part of its remaining economic life. Such arrangements should be accounted for under FAS 98 (see section 16.7.2).

Partial sales

A partial sale occurs if the seller retains an equity interest in the property or has an *FAS 66.33* equity interest in the buyer. The difference between the sales value and the proportionate cost of the partial interest sold should be recognised as profit at the date of sale if certain criteria are met.

These are: *FAS 66.34*

- the buyer is independent of the seller;
- collection of the sales price is reasonably assured; and
- the seller is not required to support the operations of the property or its related obligations to an extent greater than its proportionate interest.

If the buyer is not independent of the seller, e.g. where the seller has an equity interest in the buyer, only the part of the profit proportionate to the outside interests in the buyer may be recognised at the date of sale.

19.3.5   Goods on consignment

Inventory held on a consignment basis is common in certain trades.   Essentially, this usually involves the manufacturer retaining title to inventory despatched to dealers.   These arrangements have to be considered in their entirety so that the overall substance can be judged.   The basic question is whether the risks and rewards associated with the inventory have passed in substance, even though legal title has not been transferred.

IAS 18.14 Revenue from the sale of goods should be recognised when all the following conditions have been satisfied:

- the entity has transferred to the buyer the significant risks and rewards of ownership of the goods;

- the entity retains neither continuing managerial involvement to the degree usually associated with ownership nor effective control over the goods sold;

- it is probable that the economic benefits associated with the transaction will flow to the entity;

- the amount of revenue can be measured reliably; and

- the costs incurred or to be incurred in respect of the transaction can be measured reliably.

566

Sale of property improvements where the buyer leases the underlying land

Where the seller sells property improvements, e.g. office building, manufacturing facility, and leases the underlying land to the buyer of the improvements, the transaction should be accounted for as a lease of both the land and improvements if the term of the land lease to the buyer either: *FAS 66.38*

- does not cover substantially all of the economic life of the property improvements; or

- is not for a substantial period, e.g. 20 years.

If the land lease covers substantially all of the economic life of the improvements and extends for at least 20 years, the amount of profit to be recognised on the sale of the improvements at the time of sale should be (a) the present value of rental payments not in excess of the seller's cost of the land plus (b) the sales value of the improvements minus (c) the carrying amount of the improvements and the land. *FAS 66.39*

Alternatives to the full accrual method

If a sale of real estate does not qualify for the 'full accrual method', alternative methods of profit recognition are required. The alternatives are the deposit method, the cost recovery method, the instalment sales method, and the reduced profit method. These methods either postpone or allow piecemeal recognition of profit and their application is discussed in Appendix B to FAS 66. *FAS 66.19-43*

Certain transactions should be accounted for as financing arrangements (or leasing or profit sharing arrangements) rather than a sale. Such transactions include the three examples noted above where the seller has a continuing involvement without transferring substantially all of the risks and rewards of ownership and certain sale-leaseback transactions where the seller has some form of continuing involvement (see section 16.7.2).

19.3.5 Goods on consignment

Many manufacturers and distributors arrange for their products to be sold by retailers or dealers on a consignment basis. Under such an arrangement, the seller (consignor) retains the title to the merchandise, and the dealer (consignee) acts as a selling agent. The dealer earns a commission on the products sold and periodically remits cash from sales, less the commission earned, to the manufacturer or distributor.

The SEC Staff has concluded that products delivered to a consignee under a consignment arrangement are not sales and do not qualify for revenue recognition, or derecognition, until a sale occurs. The Staff consider that revenue recognition is not appropriate as the seller retains the risks and rewards of ownership of the product and title usually does not pass to the consignee. *SAB 104* *(Topic 13)*

In situations where title to delivered products passes to the dealer, but the substance of the transaction is that of a consignment or financing, the consigned inventory should be reported separately from other inventory in the consignor's financial statements under an appropriate caption, such as 'inventory consigned to others'.

IAS 18 Appx 2,6   If one of the first three criteria has not been met, consignment inventory is not considered to have been sold and should remain on the balance sheet of the manufacturer.   If the buyer is acting – in substance – as an agent, the seller should recognise revenue when the goods are sold to a third party.

19.3.6   Sale and repurchase agreements

IAS 18 Appx 5   When the seller is under an obligation or has the right to repurchase the same goods at a later date, the agreement needs to be analysed to ascertain whether the seller has transferred the risks and rewards of ownership to the buyer and is entitled to recognise revenue.   When the seller has retained the risks and rewards of ownership, even though legal title has been transferred, the transaction is a financing arrangement and does not give rise to revenue.   For a sale and repurchase agreement on a financial asset IAS 39 *Financial Instruments: Recognition and Measurement* applies as detailed above.

IAS 32.94   If an entity has transferred a financial asset in such a way that the arrangement does not qualify as a transfer of a financial asset and therefore either continues to recognise all of the asset or continues to recognise the asset to the extent of the entity's continuing involvement it should disclose for each class of financial asset:

- the nature of the assets;
- the nature of the risks and rewards of ownership to which the entity remains exposed;
- when the entity continues to recognise all of the asset, the carrying amounts of the asset and of the associated liability; and
- when the entity continues to recognise the asset to the extent of its continuing involvement, the total amount of the asset, the amount of the asset that the entity continues to recognise and the carrying amount of the associated liability.

Section 16.7 describes the guidance on sale and leaseback transactions.

19.4   NON-MONETARY TRANSACTIONS

19.4.1   General approach

There is no specific International Financial Reporting Standard dealing with non-monetary transactions.   The basic principle in accounting for a non-monetary transaction is that the exchange should be accounted for at the fair value of the assets involved.   However, a further factor that determines the accounting is whether the exchange transaction has or lacks commercial substance.

The following Standards and Interpretations address accounting for non-monetary transactions in particular cases and modify the basic principle:

- IAS 16 *Property, Plant and Equipment* (see section 7.2.1A);
- IAS 18 *Revenue* (see section 19.4.5);
- IAS 20 *Government Grants* (see section 20.3);
- IAS 38 *Intangible Assets* (see section 6.2.3A);
- *IAS 40 Investment Property* (see section 8.2); and

19.3.6   Sale and repurchase agreements

FAS 49 *Accounting for Product Financing Arrangements* deals with arrangements that require an entity (the vendor) to repurchase inventory that it has sold (or to repurchase substantially identical inventory) at predetermined prices. The specified prices are not subject to change except for adjustments to reflect the finance and holding costs incurred by the other party in respect of the arrangement.   *FAS 49.5*

Arrangements falling within the scope of FAS 49 include those where:

- the vendor has given a resale price guarantee to the other party; or

- although not required to repurchase the product, the vendor has an option to do so, the economic effect of which compels it to purchase the product; or

- the other party has the ability to put the product back to the vendor.

Similar arrangements involving products that were originally purchased (rather than produced) or products that have been purchased by another entity on behalf of the vendor company also fall within the scope of the standard.

Product financing arrangements such as those described above should be accounted for as a borrowing. In other words, the products should not be removed from the balance sheet and the proceeds received in respect of them should be recorded as a liability. The finance costs and holding costs of such arrangements should be accounted for in accordance with the entity's accounting policies for such costs, as the other party incurs them. Usually, such costs are expensed.

19.4   NON-MONETARY TRANSACTIONS

19.4.1   General approach

The primary guidance for the accounting for nonmonetary transactions is found in APB 29 *Accounting for Nonmonetary Transactions*. APB 29 generally requires that non-monetary transactions be recorded at fair value, based on the more readily determinable fair value of the asset given up, or the asset received, with certain exceptions as discussed below.

FAS 153 *Exchanges of Productive Assets an amendment of APB Opinion No. 29* eliminates the exception from fair value measurement for non-monetary exchanges of similar productive assets under APB 29 and replaces it with an exception for exchanges that do not have commercial substance. FAS 153 is effective for transactions occurring in fiscal periods beginning after 15 June 2005. The description of nonmonetary transactions below reflects the amendments to APB 29.

FAS 153 nullifies certain issues in EITF 01-2 which codified and reconciled the several EITF abstracts that dealt with non-monetary transactions.

- SIC-13 *Jointly Controlled Entities – Non-Monetary Contributions by Venturers* (see section 4.4.2).

Transfers and exchanges of financial instruments are covered in IAS 39 *Financial Instruments: Recognition and Measurement* (see section 11.3).

19.4.2   Applicability

This is not currently the subject of a specific accounting pronouncement.

19.4.3   Definition of a non-monetary transaction

This is not currently the subject of a specific accounting pronouncement.

19.4.4   Basic principle

This is not currently the subject of a specific accounting pronouncement. The specific requirements of particular Standards are discussed below.

19.4.2 Applicability

The guidance on accounting for non-monetary transactions does not apply to:

APB 29.4

- business combinations accounted for under FAS 141 *Business Combinations*, which include an exchange of a business for a business;
- a transfer of non-monetary assets solely between companies under common control or between a corporate joint venture and its owners;
- non-monetary consideration received in respect of an issue of capital stock;
- stock dividends and splits;
- a transfer of assets to an entity in exchange for an interest in that entity; and
- a transfer of a financial asset within the scope of FAS 140 *Accounting for Transfers and Servicing of Financial Assets and Extinguishments of Liabilities*.

19.4.3 Definition of a non-monetary transaction

An exchange is a reciprocal transfer between entities that results in an entity acquiring assets or services or satisfying liabilities by surrendering other assets or services or incurring other obligations. A transfer of a non-monetary asset is not considered an exchange unless the transferor has no continuing involvement in the transferred asset such that all the risks and rewards of ownership of the asset are transferred. A non-reciprocal transfer of assets or services is a one direction transfer, either to or from an entity or the product's owners.

APB 29.3

Non-monetary transactions are exchanges and non-reciprocal transfers that involve little or no monetary assets or liabilities. If an exchange of non-monetary assets involves a small monetary consideration (referred to as 'boot'), the transaction is considered non-monetary, provided the monetary consideration is less than 25% of the total consideration. In applying this guideline, 'total consideration' is the estimated fair value of the consideration received or the consideration given up, whichever can be estimated more readily.

APB 29.1,4
EITF 01-2

If the monetary consideration exceeds 25% of the fair value of the exchange, the transaction is considered monetary and the exchange should be recorded at fair value, assuming that fair value can be satisfactorily measured.

EITF 01-2 contains specific guidance on accounting for exchanges of 'similar' real estate that are considered to be monetary transactions.

19.4.4 Basic principle

Accounting for an exchange of non-monetary assets should be based on the fair values of the assets involved. Thus, a non-monetary asset received in exchange for another non-monetary asset ordinarily is recorded at its fair value or at the fair value of the asset given up, whichever is more clearly evident, and a gain or loss is recognised if the fair value recorded for the asset received differs from the carrying

APB 29.18-19

19.4.5   Exceptions to the general rule

IAS 16.24-25,68,71
IAS 38.45-47,113
IAS 40.27-29,69

One or more items of property, plant and equipment, investment properties or intangible assets may be acquired in exchange for a non-monetary asset or assets, or a combination of monetary and non-monetary assets. The following discussion refers for simplicity to an exchange of one non-monetary asset for another. The cost of such an item of property, plant and equipment, investment property or intangible asset is measured at fair value unless (1) the exchange transaction lacks commercial substance, or (2) the fair value of neither the asset received nor the asset given up is reliably measurable. The acquired item is measured in this way even if an entity cannot immediately derecognise the asset given up. If the acquired item is not measured at fair value, its cost is measured at the carrying amount of the asset given up. A gain or loss on derecognition is recognised in profit or loss as the difference between the net disposal proceeds, if any, and the carrying amount. A gain on derecognition of property, plant and equipment or an intangible asset is not classified as revenue.

An entity determines whether an exchange transaction has commercial substance by considering the extent to which its future cash flows are expected to change as a result of the transaction. An exchange transaction has commercial substance if:

- the configuration (risk, timing and amount) of the cash flows of the asset received differs from the configuration of the cash flows of the asset transferred; or

- the entity-specific value of the portion of the entity's operations affected by the transaction changes as a result of the exchange; and

- the difference in either of the above two items is significant relative to the fair value of the assets exchanged.

IAS 16.6,25
IAS 38.8,46
IAS 40.28

The entity-specific value is the present value of the post-tax cash flows an entity expects to arise from the continuing use of an asset and from its disposal at the end of its life or expects to incur when settling a liability. The result of these analyses may be clear without an entity having to perform detailed calculations.

The fair value of an asset for which comparable market transactions do not exist is reliably measurable if (1) the variability in the range of reasonable fair value estimates is not significant for that asset or (2) the probabilities of the various estimates within the range can be reasonably assessed and used in estimating fair value. If an entity is able to determine reliably the fair value of either the asset received or the asset given up, then the fair value of the asset given up is used to measure the cost of the asset received unless the fair value of the asset received is more clearly evident.

IAS 18.12

When goods or services are exchanged or swapped for goods or services that are of a similar nature and value, the exchange is not regarded as a transaction which generates revenue. Revenue on exchanges of dissimilar goods or services is measured at the fair value of the goods or services received (or if this can not be measured reliably, the fair value of the goods or services given up), adjusted by the amount of any cash or cash equivalents transferred.

amount of the asset given up. There are certain exceptions to this general rule in order to accommodate problems of measurement and questions about the conditions for recognising revenue.

19.4.5   Exceptions to the general rule

The following are exceptions to the general rule:

APB 29.20-23

- When neither the fair value of the non-monetary asset received nor the fair value of the non-monetary asset given up can be determined within reasonable limits.

- When the transaction is an exchange of a product or property held for sale in the ordinary course of business for a product or property to be sold in the same line of business to facilitate sales to customers other than parties to the exchange.

- Where the transaction lacks commercial substance – a non-monetary transaction has commercial substance if the entity's future cash flows are expected to significantly change as a result of the exchange, i.e. if either:

  - the risk, timing or amount (i.e. configuration) of future cash flows from the assets received and transferred differ significantly; or

  - the entity-specific values of the assets received and transferred differ significantly.

- When the transaction is a pro-rata distribution of non-monetary assets, such as capital stock of subsidiaries, to stockholders in corporate liquidations or plans of reorganisation that involve disposing of all or a significant segment of the business, i.e. spin-offs, split-offs.

In each of the exceptions, the accounting for the transaction is normally based on the carrying amount (after reduction, if necessary, for impairment in value) of the asset given up and there is no gain/loss recognition.

There are circumstances in which some gain or loss is recognised on a non-monetary transaction even though it does not culminate an earnings process. For instance, if the transaction includes monetary consideration, the recipient should recognise a gain to the extent that the amount of the monetary receipt exceeds the proportionate share of the recorded amount of the asset given up. The payer should record the asset received in the exchange at the amount of the monetary consideration paid plus the recorded amount of the non-monetary asset surrendered, i.e. no gain recognition. If a loss is indicated by the terms of the transaction, the entire indicated loss on the exchange should be recognised.

APB 29.22

The EITF has concluded that a non-pro-rata split-off of a business segment should be accounted for at fair value, while a pro rata split-off of a targeted business to the holders of the targeted stock should be accounted for at historical cost. If the targeted stock was created in contemplation of the subsequent split-off, the two should be viewed as one transaction with the split-off being accounted for at fair value.

EITF 01-2

IAS 20.23   Where a government grant takes the form of a transfer of a non-monetary asset, it is
IAS 16.28   usual to account for both grant and the asset at the fair value of the asset.
IAS 38.44   Alternatively, sometimes the asset and grant are recorded at a nominal amount.

19.4.7   Barter credit transactions

This is not currently the subject of a specific accounting pronouncement.

19.4.8   Advertising barter transactions

SIC-31.5   Revenue from a barter transaction involving advertising cannot be measured reliably
by reference to the fair value of advertising services received.   Instead, an entity
should measure revenue at the fair value of the advertising services it provides in a
barter transaction by reference only to non-barter transactions that:

- involve advertising similar to the advertising in the barter transaction;
- occur frequently;
- represent a predominant number of transactions and amount when compared
  to all transactions to provide advertising that is similar to the advertising in the
  barter transaction;
- involve cash and/or another form of consideration (e.g. marketable securities,
  non-monetary assets, and other services) that has a reliably measurable fair
  value; and
- do not involve the same counterparty as in the barter transaction.

Advertising involving similar services does not generate revenue.

19.4.7   Barter credit transactions

In a barter credit transaction an entity exchanges a non-monetary asset for barter credits.   Such transactions may be between principals to the transaction or include a third party, i.e. a barter company.   The barter credits can be used to purchase goods or services, e.g. advertising time, from either the barter company or members of its barter exchange network.   *EITF 93-11*

Barter credit transactions should be accounted for under APB 29.   An impairment of the non-monetary asset exchanged should be recognised prior to recording the exchange, if appropriate, measured as the amount by which the carrying amount of the asset exceeds its fair value.   The fair value should not be based on an estimate of the value of the barter credits to be received, unless an entity can convert the barter credits into cash in the near term, as evidenced by historical practice, or if independent quoted market prices exist for items to be received upon exchange of the barter credits.   The fair value of the non-monetary asset should not exceed its carrying amount, i.e. no gain should be recognised, unless there is persuasive evidence supporting a higher value.

An impairment loss on barter credits should be recognised where:

*   the fair value of any remaining barter credits is less than the carrying amount; or

*   it is probable that not all remaining barter credits will be used.

19.4.8   Advertising barter transactions

An advertising barter arrangement exists when two companies enter into a non-cash transaction to exchange advertising with each other.   The advertisements may be in the form of an image appearing on a website describing the other website, or products and/or services offered on a website or a link to the other website.

The EITF reached a consensus that revenue and expense should be recognised at fair value from an advertising barter transaction only if the fair value of the advertising surrendered in the transaction is determinable based on the entity's own historical practice of receiving cash for similar advertising from buyers unrelated to the counterparty in the barter transaction.   An exchange between the parties to a barter transaction of offsetting monetary consideration does not evidence the fair value of the transaction.   If the fair value of the advertising surrendered in the barter transaction is not determinable within the limits established by the consensus, the barter transaction should be recorded based on the carrying amount of the advertising surrendered, which likely will be zero.   *EITF 99-17*

The population of prior cash transactions that should be analysed to determine fair value should not exceed six months prior to the date of the barter transaction.   In addition, it is inappropriate to consider cash transactions subsequent to the barter transaction to determine fair value.

19.4.9   Involuntary conversions of non-monetary assets to monetary assets

This is not currently the subject of a specific accounting pronouncement.

For advertising surrendered for cash to be considered 'similar' to the advertising being surrendered in the barter transaction:

- the advertising surrendered must have been in the same media and within the same advertising vehicle, e.g. same publication, same website, or same broadcast channel;
- the characteristics of the advertising must be reasonably similar with respect to circulation, market demographics, timing, prominence, and duration; and
- the quantity or volumes of advertising should be equivalent.

19.4.9   Involuntary conversions of non-monetary assets to monetary assets

Involuntary conversions of non-monetary assets to monetary assets are monetary transactions for which a gain or loss should be recognised even though an enterprise reinvests or is obligated to reinvest the monetary assets in replacement non-monetary assets.   In some cases, a non-monetary asset may be destroyed or damaged in one accounting period, and the amount of monetary assets to be received is not determinable until a later period.   The recognition of a gain or loss in those situations is influenced by the requirements in FAS 5 *Accounting for Contingencies* (see section 18.2). *FIN 30*

Section 20   Government grants

20.1   AUTHORITATIVE PRONOUNCEMENTS

- IAS 20
- IAS 41
- SIC-10

COMMENT

In December 1999 the G4+1 group issued a Discussion Paper – *Accounting by Recipients for Non-Reciprocal Transfers, Excluding Contributions by Owners: Their Definition, Recognition and Measurement.* This examined how items such as government grants and charitable donations should be accounted for by those who received them. The paper reviewed the appropriate accounting treatment in the light of the IASB's conceptual framework and concluded that such items should be recognised as assets (or reductions in liabilities) and credited to income when the Framework's definitions and criteria were met, rather than being based on the matching of related revenues and expenses as is done presently by IAS 20 *Accounting for Government Grants and Disclosure of Government Assistance*, an approach that is essentially the same as the one taken by IAS 41 *Agriculture* in respect of government grants of biological assets.

The IASB started discussing IAS 20 in February 2003 as the standard posed specific problems in connection with, what is now, IFRIC 3 *Emission Rights*. The Board considered various options for replacing IAS 20, including withdrawal of the standard and adopting accounting models at present prescribed by pronouncements of other standard-setting bodies. However, ultimately the Board agreed that withdrawing IAS 20 would leave constituents with insufficient guidance and decided to amend IAS 20 by adopting the accounting model for government grants contained in IAS 41.

Given the above developments it seems likely that the IASB will issue an Exposure Draft of the significantly amended IAS 20 in the near future using the same approach as IAS 41.

20.2   NATURE OF GRANTS

IAS 20.2-3
SIC-10.3
Government grants represent assistance by government in the form of transfers of resources to an entity in return for past or future compliance with certain conditions relating to the operating activities of the entity. Government assistance given to an entire category of entities without further conditions also meets the definition of a government grant.

Government grants may be related to specific assets or to income. Excluded from the scope of IAS 20 *Accounting for Government Grants and Disclosure of Government Assistance* are:

- government assistance in the form of tax benefits;
- government participation in the ownership of the entity;

Section 20   Government grants

20.1   AUTHORITATIVE PRONOUNCEMENTS

In 1979, the AcSEC sent a non-authoritative issues paper on accounting for government grants to the FASB for its consideration, but the FASB has not addressed the subject.

20.2   NATURE OF GRANTS

State and local government assistance in the US is usually in the form of investment tax credits, property tax abatements, other tax benefits, or low-interest loans. Accordingly, accounting for and disclosure of government grants, including grant assistance from non-US governments, has not been specifically dealt with.

- assistance to which no value can reasonably be assigned, e.g. where the entity is being favoured by a government's procurement policy or receives a loan at below market interest rates; and
- government grants covered by IAS 41 *Agriculture*.

20.3   ACCOUNTING TREATMENT

IAS 20.7   Government grants should be recognised only when there is reasonable assurance that (1) the entity will comply with the conditions attaching to them and (2) the grants will be received.

IAS 20.12,20   Recognition of government grants in equity is not permitted.   Instead, the grants should be recognised in income on a systematic basis that matches them with the related costs that they are intended to compensate.   Where a grant relates to expenses or losses already incurred, or for the purpose of giving immediate financial support to the entity with no future related costs, the grant should be recognised in income when it becomes receivable.

IAS 41.34-37   Government grants relating to biological assets should only be accounted for under IAS 20 if these biological assets are measured at their cost less any accumulated depreciation and any accumulated impairment losses.   Government grants relating to biological assets measured under the fair value model should be recognised in income only when the grants become receivable and any conditions attached to the grants have been met.

IAS 20.32   A government grant that becomes repayable should be accounted for as revision to an accounting estimate in accordance with IAS 8 *Accounting Policies, Changes in Accounting Estimates and Errors*.   Repayment of a grant related to income should be charged against the related unamortised deferred credit and any excess should be recognised as an expense immediately.   Repayment of a grant related to an asset should be recognised as a reduction of the related unamortised deferred credit or as an increase in the carrying amount of the related asset.   However, in the latter case the cumulative additional depreciation should be charged to income.

IAS 20.9   The accounting for government grants is not affected by the manner in which they are received.   Thus a grant received in cash or as a reduction of a liability to the government are both accounted for in the same manner.

IAS 20.23   A government grant in the form of a transfer of a non-monetary asset, which is intended for use of the entity, is usually recognised at the fair value of that asset. However, the alternative of recognising such assets at a nominal amount is not prohibited.

IAS 20.24-27   Grants that are related to assets should be presented in the balance sheet either:
- by setting up the grant as deferred income; or
- by deducting the grant in arriving at the carrying amount of the asset, in which case the grant is recognised in income as a reduction of depreciation.

IAS 20.29   Grants that are related to items in income are to be presented as a credit in the income statement, either separately or as a reduction of the related expense.

20.3   ACCOUNTING TREATMENT

There are no pronouncements on how to account for government grants. The nature of the grant determines the accounting treatment to be adopted. If the grant is revenue in nature (i.e. it meets the general revenue criteria in CON 5 and CON 6 – see section 19.2), then it is recognised in the income statement in the period when the qualifying expenditure is expensed. If the grant is of a capital nature, e.g. relates to capital expenditure, then it is accounted for either as a deferred credit in the balance sheet or set-off against the cost of the asset. If the grant is for reimbursement of research and development expenses, the grant should be reflected as a reduction in research and development expense on the income statement.

20.4   DISCLOSURE

IAS 20.39   Entities should disclose the following information regarding government grants:

- the accounting policy and presentation adopted in the financial statements;
- a description of the nature and extent of the grants recognised and an indication of other forms of government assistance from which the entity has directly benefited; and
- unfulfilled conditions or contingencies attaching to government assistance that has been recognised.

IAS 20.36   Excluded from the definition of government grants are certain forms of government assistance which cannot reasonably have a value placed upon them (e.g., free technical or marketing advice and the provision of guarantees) and transactions with government which cannot be distinguished from the normal trading transactions of the entity.   The significance of these benefits may be such that the financial statements need to disclose the nature, extent and duration of the assistance to prevent the financial statements from being misleading.

20.4   DISCLOSURE

There are no pronouncements for government assistance but the accounting policy adopted should be disclosed. Other disclosures would depend on the specific circumstances, but might include:

- the amount received or receivable;
- the amount included in income or deferred;
- the basis for recognising any deferred amounts;
- the terms and conditions of receipt; and
- unfulfilled conditions and any contingent liability for repayment.

If benefits are recognised in income as received, the extent to which they are expected to continue in the future might also be disclosed.

Section 21   Segmental reporting

21.1   AUTHORITATIVE PRONOUNCEMENTS

• IAS 14

COMMENT

Segment reporting is currently under review by the IASB as part of its short-term convergence project with the FASB.   In January 2005, the Board decided to adopt the management approach of FAS 131 *Disclosures about Segments of an Enterprise and Related Information.*   Furthermore, in March 2005 the Board decided:

• to retain the scope exclusions for segment reporting currently in IAS 14, but to revisit the issue as part of the project on *Non-publicly Accountable Entities*;

• to follow the approach of FAS 131 and require disclosure of expenditure on all non-current assets with specified exceptions; and

• to add requirements for interim period segment information in IAS 34.

21.2   SCOPE

IAS 14.3,6-7   Entities whose equity or debt securities are publicly traded, and those that are in the process of issuing equity or debt securities in the public securities markets, must report segment information.   If the entity publishes in a single financial report both consolidated financial statements and parent or subsidiary financial statements, segment information only needs to be reported at a consolidated level.   Similarly, if the financial statements of an entity's equity method associate or joint venture are attached to the entity's own financial statements, segment information only needs to be reported on the basis of the entity's own financial statements.   However, no exemption is available to subsidiaries, associates or joint ventures whose securities are publicly traded from presenting segment information in their own separate financial statements.

IAS 14.4-5   Voluntary disclosure is encouraged.   Entities that voluntarily report segment information should comply fully with the requirements of IAS 14 *Segment Reporting.*

21.3   SEGMENT INFORMATION TO BE PRESENTED

IAS 14.Objective   The objective of segment reporting under IFRSs is to provide information about the different types of products and services that an entity produces and the different geographical areas in which it operates.   This information aims to help users of financial statements to understand better the entity's past performance, to assess better the entity's risks and returns and to make more informed judgements about the entity as a whole.

IAS 14.26,33   IAS 14 aims to achieve this objective by defining the principles for reporting financial information by both business and geographical segments, with one being

Section 21   Segmental reporting

21.1   AUTHORITATIVE PRONOUNCEMENTS

- FAS 131

21.2   SCOPE

FAS 131 *Disclosures about Segments of an Enterprise and Related Information*   *FAS 131.9*
applies to all public business enterprises, that is entities:

- with debt or equity securities traded in a public market on a domestic or foreign stock exchange or on the over-the-counter (OTC) market;
- which are required to file financial statements with the SEC; or
- that provide financial statements for the purpose of issuing any class of securities in a public market.

The statement does not apply to entities:

- that do not issue separate financial statements as public entities; or
- whose separate company financial statements also are consolidated or combined in a complete set of financial statements and both the separate company statements and the consolidated or combined statements are included in the same document.

21.3   SEGMENT INFORMATION TO BE PRESENTED

The objective of requiring segmental disclosures is to provide information about the   *FAS 131.3-4*
different types of business activities in which the entity engages and the different economic environments in which it operates. To meet this objective, a company is required to report information about its products and services, the geographical areas in which it operates and its major customers.

Generally, financial information is required to be reported on the basis that it is used   *FAS 131.29-30*
internally for evaluating segment performance and deciding how to allocate resources to segments. This approach may result in differences between the

designated as the primary basis and the other as the secondary basis. Reportable segment information is based on the information used by the board of directors and chief executive officer to evaluate past performance and to make decisions about future allocations of resources.

21.3.1 Segments

A   Business and geographical segments

IAS 14.9,11 A business segment is defined as 'a distinguishable component of an entity that is engaged in providing an individual product or service or a group of related products or services and that is subject to risks and returns that are different from those of other business segments.' Factors relevant to determining whether products and services are related include:

- the nature of the products or services;
- the nature of production processes;
- the type or class of customer for the products or services;
- the methods used to distribute the products or provide the services; and
- if applicable, the nature of the regulatory environment.

Products and services with significantly differing risks and returns are not included within a single business segment and therefore those included in the same business segment are expected to be similar with respect to a majority of the factors above.

IAS 14.9,12 A geographical segment is 'a distinguishable component of an entity that is engaged in providing products or services within a particular economic environment and that is subject to risks and returns that are different from those of components operating in other economic environments'. Geographical segments are identified on the basis of considerations such as:

- the similarity of economic and political conditions;
- relationships between operations in different geographical areas;
- proximity of operations;
- special risks associated with operations in an area;
- exchange control regulations; and
- underlying currency risks.

A geographical segment may be a single country, group of countries or a region within a country, but it does not include operations in economic environments with significantly differing risks and returns.

IAS 14.13-14 Geographical segments can be based either on the location of the entity's operations or on the location of its markets and customers depending on which is judged to be the dominant source of geographical risks.

B   Primary and secondary reporting formats

IAS 14.26 The decision as to whether the primary segment reporting format will be business segments or geographical segments depends on the dominant source and nature of an entity's risks and returns. If differences in products or services have a greater influence on the entity's risks and returns, the primary segment reporting format

measurements used in reporting segment information and those used in the enterprise's general-purpose financial statements.

21.3.1   Segments

FAS 131 requires a 'management approach' to identify reportable business segments, based on the way that management organises segments for making operating decisions and assessing performance.   *FAS 131.4,10-15*

An operating segment is a component of an entity:

- that engages in business activities from which it may earn revenues and incur expenses (including revenues and expenses relating to transactions with other components of the same enterprise);

- whose operating results are regularly reviewed by the entity's chief operating decision maker to make decisions about resources to be allocated to the segment and assess its performance, and

- for which discrete financial information is available.

An operating segment may engage in business activities for which it has yet to earn revenues, for example, start-up operations may be operating segments before earning revenues.

Separate information should be reported for an operating segment meeting any of the following quantitative criteria;   *FAS 131.18*

- reportable revenue (internal and external) is 10% or more of total revenue (internal and external);

- absolute net profit or loss is 10% or more of the greater, in absolute amount, of (1) total profit of all segments that did not report a loss, or (2) total loss of all segments that did report a loss; or

- assets are 10% or more of total assets of all operating segments.

Two or more operation segments may be aggregated into a single operating segment for reporting segmental information if (1) aggregation is consistent with the objective and basic principles of FAS 131 and (2) the segments have similar economic characteristics.   Furthermore, the segments must be similar in each of the following areas: *FAS 131.17*
EITF 04-10

- nature of products or services;

- nature of production process;

- type or class of customer;

- method of distribution of products or services; and

- if applicable, the nature of the regulatory environment.

Operating segments that do not meet the quantitative criteria above may be combined with information about other operating segments that do not meet the quantitative thresholds to produce a reportable segment only if the operating segments have similar economic characteristics and share a majority of the aggregation criteria above.   *FAS 131.19* should be based on business segments with secondary information reported geographically. Where geography has the greater influence on the entity's risks and returns the primary segment reporting format should be based on geographical segments with secondary information reported for groups of related products and services.

IAS 14.27-29 Normally, an entity's primary segment reporting format is determined by how information is reported to the board of directors and chief executive officer. However, business segment information will take precedence over geographical segment information if management receives information based on both segmentations (although IAS 14 does also permit a 'matrix presentation' under which both types of segment are treated as a primary reporting segment). Where management receives segment information based on neither business nor geographical segments, a choice must be made between business segmentation and geographical segmentation as the more appropriate primary segment reporting format.

C   *Identifying reportable segments*

IAS 14.31,33 IAS 14 requires a 'management approach' to be taken in identifying reportable segments, i.e. the segments used for external reporting purposes should be based on those segments for which information is reported internally to the board of directors and the chief operating officer.

IAS 14.32 Internal segments which meet the IAS 14 definition of a business or geographical segment should not be further segmented. Where the segments for internal reporting do not meet the IAS 14 definitions of a business or geographical segment, the entity should look to the next lower level of internal segmentation and determine whether those segments meet the definitions.

IAS 14.34 Two or more internally reported segments that are substantially similar in all of the factors in the appropriate definition of a business or geographical segment may be combined for external reporting when they also exhibit similar long-term financial performance.

IAS 14.35 A business segment or geographical segment is a reportable segment when it derives the majority of its revenue from sales to external customers and:

- its internal and external revenue are 10% or more of total (internal and external) segment revenue; or

- its segment result, whether profit or loss, is 10% or more of the greater, in absolute amount, of (1) the combined results of all profitable segments or (2) the combined results of all segments in loss; or

- its assets are 10% or more of the total assets of all segments.

IAS 14.36-37 If the external revenue of reportable segments is less than 75% of total consolidated or entity revenue, the entity should identify additional reportable segments until at least 75% of total revenue is included in reportable segments – even if the individual segments do not meet the 10% thresholds described above. Internally reported segments may be designated as reportable segments despite their size or may be combined with other similar internal segments into a reportable segment. Segments that are not separately reported or combined for external reporting must be included as an unallocated reconciling item.

588

Additional operating segments, not meeting the quantitative criteria, should be reported until the total external revenue reported by operating segments is at least 75% of total consolidated revenue. Although no precise limit is defined, the standard suggests a practical limit of ten reportable segments. Information about non-reportable business activities and segments should be combined and disclosed in an 'all other' category. Comparative prior-period segmental data should be restated to reflect the newly reportable segments even if those segments were not reportable in those prior periods, unless that information is not available and the cost to develop it would be excessive.

FAS 131.20-24

Additional operating segments may be considered reportable and separately disclosed where management believes that disclosure would be useful to readers of the financial statements.

FAS 135.4(x)

IAS 14.41 An entity's internal reporting system may treat vertically integrated activities as separate selling and buying segments. If the entity does not consider such internal segments to be reportable segments it should combine the selling and buying segments, unless it is unreasonable to do so – in which case the selling segment should be included as an unallocated reconciling item.

21.4   DISCLOSURE

21.4.1   Segment information

A   *Primary segment information*

IAS 14.50-52A The entity should disclose the following information for each reportable segment
IAS 14.55-58,61 based on its primary reporting format:

- segment revenue from external customers;
- segment revenue from transactions with other segments;
- segment result;
- carrying amount of segment assets;
- segment liabilities;
- total cost during the period (on an accruals basis) of acquiring segment assets that are expected to be used in more than one period;
- total for depreciation and amortisation expense included in segment result; and
- the total amount of significant non-cash expenses (other than depreciation and amortisation) included in segment expense for the period.

Segment results relating to continuing and discontinued operations should be shown separately with prior periods being restated so that disclosures are based on the latest period's classification of operations.

IAS 14.64,66 The aggregate amount of the entity's share in the net profit or loss of equity method associates, joint ventures or other investments should be disclosed by segment, if substantially all of an investee's operations are within a single segment. Where this disclosure is made, the aggregate investments in those equity method associates and joint ventures should also be disclosed by segment.

B   *Secondary segment information*

IAS 14.69 If an entity's primary reporting format is based on business segments, it should also report the following geographical information for each reportable segment based on its secondary reporting format:

- segment revenue from external customers, based on customer location, for each geographical segment whose revenue from external sales represents 10% or more of the entity's total revenue from sales to all external customers;
- segment assets, by location of assets, for each geographical segment whose segment assets are 10% or more of the total assets of all geographical segments; and

21.4   DISCLOSURE

21.4.1   Segment information

A   Primary segment information

Segment information is required for each period for which an income statement is presented.   *FAS 131.25*

General information should be disclosed to explain the factors used to identify the entity's reportable operating segments and the types of products and services from which each segment derives its revenues.   *FAS 131.26*

The following information is required for each reportable operating segment identified: *FAS 131.27*

* a measure of profit or loss; and
* total assets.

Where the specified amounts are (1) included in the measure of segment profit or loss reviewed by the chief decision maker, or (2) otherwise regularly provided to the chief decision maker, the following information is required:

* revenue from external customers and revenue from transactions with other segments should be separately identified;
* interest income and expense should be separately identified unless performance is assessed primarily on net interest basis;
* depreciation, depletion and amortisation expense;
* unusual or infrequent items;
* share of the net income of equity method investees;
* income tax expense or benefit;
* extraordinary items; and
* significant non-cash items other than depreciation, depletion and amortisation expense.

The following information should be disclosed for each reportable operating segment identified if the specified amounts are (1) included in the determination of segment assets reviewed by the chief decision maker, or (2) otherwise regularly provided to the chief decision maker: *FAS 131.28*

* the amount of investment in equity method investees; and
* total expenditures for additions to long-lived assets other than financial instruments, long-term customer relationships of a financial institution, mortgage and other servicing rights, deferred policy acquisition costs, and deferred tax assets.

- the total cost incurred during the period to acquire segment assets that are expected to be used during more than one period, by location of assets, for each geographical segment whose assets are 10% or more of the total assets of all geographical segments.

IAS 14.70　If an entity's primary reporting format is based on geographical segments, it should also disclose the following segment information for each business segment whose revenue from sales to external customers is 10% or more of total entity external sales or whose segment assets are 10% or more of total assets of all business segments:

- segment revenue from external customers;
- the total carrying amount of segment assets; and
- the total cost incurred during the period to acquire segment assets that are expected to be used during more than one period.

IAS 14.71　Where an entity's primary reporting format is based on geographical location of assets and this differs from the location of its customers, the entity should also disclose revenue from external customers for each customer-based geographical segment whose revenue from external customers is 10% or more of total entity revenue from sales to all external customers.

IAS 14.72　Where an entity's primary reporting format is based on geographical location of customers and this differs from the location of its assets, the entity should also disclose the following segment information for each asset-based geographical segment whose revenue from sales to external customers or segment assets are 10% or more of total entity sales or assets respectively:

- the total carrying amount of segment assets by location of the assets; and
- the total cost incurred during the period to acquire segment assets that are expected to be used during more than one period by location of the assets.

C　Other disclosures

IAS 14.74　If a business or geographical segment that is reported to the entity's key management is not a reportable segment because the majority of its revenue is derived from sales to other segments, but its sales to external customers are 10% or more of revenue from sales to all external customers, the entity should disclose this fact together with the amounts of revenue from sales to external customers and internal sales to other segments.

IAS 14.81　An entity should indicate the types of products and services included in each reported business segment and the composition of each reported geographical segment, if not disclosed elsewhere in the financial statements or financial report.

　　　　IAS 14 encourages the voluntary disclosure of:

IAS 14.40　●　vertically integrated activities as separate segments, with appropriate descriptions including disclosure of the basis of pricing inter-segment transfers;

IAS 14.49　●　the full primary segment disclosures specified in IAS 14 paragraphs 50 to 67 for each reportable secondary segment;

IAS 14.53　●　measures of segment profitability in addition to the segment result if these can be computed without arbitrary allocations;

If not otherwise disclosed as reportable operating segment information, revenues   *FAS 131.37*
from external customers should be reported for each product and service (or each
group of similar products and services) unless it is impractical to do so.

B   *Secondary segment information*

If not otherwise disclosed as reportable operating segment information, external   *FAS 131.38*
revenues and long-lived assets should be reported for geographical segments,
representing (1) the entity's country of domicile and (2) all foreign countries in total.
However, if amounts attributed to an individual foreign country are material (generally
10% or more of the entity's revenues), those amounts should be reported separately.

In addition, geographical information may be reported for groups of countries.

If providing geographical information is impractical, that fact should be disclosed.

IAS 14.59   •   the nature and amount of any items of segment revenue and segment expense that are of such size, nature, or incidence that their disclosure is relevant to explain the performance of each reportable segment for the period; and

IAS 7.50   •   the amount of the cash flows arising from the operating, investing and
IAS 14.62   financing activities of each reported business and geographical segment (see section 27.9).

21.4.2   Measurement

IAS 14.44,46   Accounting policies applied in preparing the consolidated financial statements should also be applied in preparing segment information. Nevertheless, it is permitted to disclose additional information that is prepared on a different basis when that information is used by the entity's key decision-makers and the alternative basis of measurement is clearly described.

IAS 14.47   Assets that are used by more than one segment should be allocated to segments only if related revenues and expenses are also allocated to those segments.

IAS 14.75   Inter-segment transfers should be measured and reported on the basis that was actually used by the entity to price those transfers. The basis of inter-segment pricing and any changes therein should be disclosed in the financial statements.

IAS 14.16   IAS 14 contains the following detailed definitions of terms that affect the measurement and presentation of segment information:

   •   *segment revenue* is that part of the revenue reported in the income statement that is directly attributable or can be allocated to a segment but, unless the segment's operations are primarily of a financial nature, it excludes interest or dividend income, gains on sales of investments or gains on extinguishments of debt;

   •   *segment expense* is the expense resulting from the operating activities of a segment that is directly attributable or can be allocated to a segment, but excludes the entity's share of losses of equity method investments, income tax expense, general administrative and corporate expenses which relate to the entity as a whole and, unless the segment's operations are primarily of a financial nature, interest, losses on sales of investments or losses on extinguishments of debt;

   •   *segment result* is segment revenue less segment expense, before any minority interest adjustments;

   •   *segment assets* are those operating assets that are directly attributable or can be allocated to the segment. Segment assets exclude income tax assets and are stated after deducting any allowances which are directly offset against the assets in the entity's balance sheet. Where segment result includes interest or dividend income, segment assets include the related receivables, loans, investments or other income-producing assets;

   •   *segment liabilities* are those operating liabilities that are directly attributable or can be allocated to the segment. Segment liabilities exclude income tax liabilities. Where segment result includes interest expense, segment liabilities include the related interest-bearing liabilities.

21.4.2   Measurement

The amounts for segment information reported should be the measure reported to   *FAS 131.29*
the chief operating decision maker for purposes of making decisions about
allocating resources between segments and assessing segment performance.
Adjustments to segment results should only be made if they are included in the
measure of segment profit or loss used by the chief operating decision maker.

If the chief operating decision maker uses more than one measure of a segment's   *FAS 131.30*
results or assets, the reported measures should be those management believes are
most consistent with those used for the corresponding amounts in the entity's
financial statements.

An explanation should be provided for the measurement of segment profit or loss   *FAS 131.31*
and assets for each reportable segment, including as a minimum:

- the basis of accounting for transactions between segments;

- the nature of any differences between the measurements of the reportable
  segments' profits or losses and the entity's consolidated income before
  income taxes, extraordinary items, discontinued operations, and the
  cumulative effect of changes in accounting principles (if not apparent from
  the reconciliations – see section 21.4.3);

- the nature of any differences between the measurements of the reportable
  segments' assets and the entity's consolidated assets (if not apparent from the
  reconciliations – see section 21.4.3);

- the nature of any changes from prior periods in the measurement methods
  used to determine reported segment profit or loss and the effect, if any, of
  those changes on the measure of segment profit or loss; and

- the nature and effect of any asymmetrical allocations to segments, e.g. the
  allocation of depreciation expense to a segment without allocating the related
  depreciable assets to that segment.

Segment revenue includes an entity's share of profits or losses of associates, joint ventures and other investments accounted for using the equity method only if those items are included in consolidated or total entity revenue. Only in cases where segment revenue includes such profits or losses should the related investment be included in segment assets. Segment revenue, expense, assets and liabilities include a joint venturer's share of amounts relating to a jointly controlled entity where proportionate consolidation is used in accordance with IAS 31 *Interests in Joint Ventures.*

IAS 14.20 Segment liabilities exclude borrowings, liabilities under finance leases and other liabilities incurred for financing rather than operating purposes.

IAS 14.24 Segment assets, liabilities, revenue and expense are determined before elimination of intragroup balances and transactions except where such balances and transactions are between group entities within a single segment.

21.4.3   Reconciliations

IAS 14.67 An entity should present a reconciliation between the information disclosed for reportable segments based on its primary reporting format and the entity's financial statements as follows:

- segment revenue should be reconciled to revenue from external customers. Revenue from external customers not included in any segment revenue should be disclosed separately;
- segment result from continuing operations should be reconciled to a comparable measure of entity operating profit or loss as well as to entity profit or loss from continuing operations;
- segment result from discontinued operations should be reconciled to entity profit or loss from discontinued operations; and
- segment assets and liabilities should be reconciled to the entity's assets and liabilities respectively.

21.4.4   Restatement of previously reported information

IAS 14.43-44,76 Changes in the accounting policies for segment reporting that have a material effect on segment information require restatement of the prior period information (unless this is impracticable) and disclosure of:

- a description of the nature of the change;
- the reasons for the change;
- the financial effect of the change, if it is reasonably determinable; and
- a statement that comparative information has been restated or that it was impracticable to do so.

When a segment is identified as a reportable segment for the first time, the prior period segment data should be restated to reflect the newly reportable segment separately, unless it is impracticable to do so.

21.4.3 Reconciliations

Reconciliations should be presented for all of the following: *FAS 131.32*

- the total of the reportable segments' revenues to consolidated revenues;

- the total of the reportable segments' measures of profit or loss to the consolidated income before income taxes, extraordinary items, discontinued operations, and the cumulative effect of changes in accounting principles. However, if an entity allocates items such as income taxes and extraordinary items to segments, the entity may choose to reconcile the total of the segments' measures of profit or loss to consolidated income after those items;

- the total of the reportable segments' assets to the consolidated assets; and

- the total of the reportable segments' amounts for every other significant item of information disclosed to the corresponding consolidated amount.

All significant reconciling items should be separately identified and described.

Operating segment disclosures are required for each period for which an income   *FAS 131.25*
statement is presented, however, reconciliations of balance sheet amounts for reportable segments to consolidated balance sheet amounts are required only for each year for which a balance sheet is presented.

21.4.4 Restatement of previously reported information

If, following a change in the internal organisation, an entity changes the   *FAS 131.34*
composition of its reportable segments, the corresponding information for earlier periods, including interim periods, should be restated unless it is impracticable to do so. An enterprise should disclose whether it has restated the corresponding items of segment information for earlier periods.

Where segment information for earlier periods is not restated to reflect the change   *FAS 131.35*
in reportable segments, the entity should disclose in the year in which the change occurs segment information for the current period under both the old basis and the new basis of segmentation unless it is impracticable to do so.

If a segment identified as a reportable segment in one period no longer meets the size criteria in the next period, management must judge whether the segment is of sufficient continuing importance to warrant separate presentation.

Where an entity changes the identification of reportable segments and does not restate prior period segment information because it is impracticable to do so, it should present segment information based on the old and the new bases of segmentation in the year in which the change takes place.

21.5   INFORMATION ABOUT MAJOR CUSTOMERS

IAS 14.59   There is no specific requirement under IAS 14 to disclose information about major customers.   However, entities are encouraged to disclose the nature and amount of any items of segment revenue and segment expense that are of such size, nature or incidence that their disclosure is relevant to explain the performance of each reportable segment for the period.

21.5   INFORMATION ABOUT MAJOR CUSTOMERS

If revenues from transactions with a single external customer (or a group of *FAS 131.39* customers under common control) amount to 10% or more of an entity's revenues, that fact and the total amount of revenues from each such customer should be disclosed and the segment or segments reporting the revenues should be identified. There is no requirement to disclose the identity of a major customer or the amount of revenues that each segment reports from that customer.

Section 22   Share-based payment

22.1   AUTHORITATIVE PRONOUNCEMENTS

- IFRS 2

COMMENT

In December 2004, the IFRIC issued draft Interpretation D11 – *Changes in Contributions to Employee Share Purchase Plans* to address accounting for changes in employee contributions to an employee share purchase plan (ESPP), particularly the effect of an employee ceasing to make contributions or redirecting contributions into another plan. D11 treats the cessation of contributions by an employee who continues to be employed by an entity as a cancellation to be accounted for in accordance with IFRS 2.28(a). If an employee changes from one ESPP to another, the event should be accounted for as a modification or cancellation in accordance with IFRS 2.28(c).

In April 2005, after considering respondents' comments on D11, the IFRIC reaffirmed its previous conclusion that the event should not be accounted for as a forfeiture. However, it did not reach a conclusion on whether the event should be accounted for as a cancellation or disregarded. Given that IFRIC members were unable to reach a consensus on this issue, the staff advised that they would recommend to the Board that IFRS 2 be amended.

The IFRIC is also considering other IFRS 2-related matters and, in November 2004, it began discussing the following:

- the scope of IFRS 2: In April 2005, the IFRIC decided to issue a draft Interpretation stating that the scope of IFRS 2 is not limited to transactions in which the entity can specifically identify the goods or services received;

- share-based payment transactions in which:

    - the entity grants options to its employees and chooses, or is required, to purchase its own shares when the employees exercise the options; or

    - a subsidiary's employees are granted rights to shares of the parent.

    In April 2005, the IFRIC decided to issue a draft Interpretation that will provide guidance on how to account for such transactions.

22.2   GENERAL APPROACH AND BACKGROUND

Until the publication of IFRS 2 in February 2004, there was no International Accounting Standard which covered the recognition and measurement of share-based payment transactions, including employee equity compensation benefits. However, IFRSs did recognise the importance of disclosure of employee equity compensation benefits and this was dealt with in IAS 19 *Employee Benefits*. Following the publication of IFRS 2, share-based payments are specifically excluded from the scope of IAS 19.

Section 22   Share-based payment

22.1   AUTHORITATIVE PRONOUNCEMENTS

- APB 25
- FAS 123R
- SOP 93-6

- FIN 44
- SAB 107

COMMENT

In March 2005, the SEC issued SAB 107 which provides the staff's views regarding the interaction between FAS 123R and certain SEC rules and regulations. In particular, the SAB provides interpretive guidance regarding the valuation of share-based payment arrangements and the expected volatility and expected term assumptions, the transition from non-public to public entity status, non-GAAP financial measures and the application of the measurement provisions for foreign private issuers.

22.2   GENERAL APPROACH AND BACKGROUND

Typically, non-cash compensatory plans for employees are linked to the company's stock, e.g. a stock option plan or stock appreciation rights granted to employees, giving them a right to receive the appreciation in price of a given number of shares over the plan period. The cost of compensatory plans should be recognised as compensation expense over the periods in which the employee performs related services.

FAS 123 *Accounting for Stock-Based Compensation*, issued in October 1995, defined a fair value based method of accounting for stock-based employee

IFRS 2.1   The objective of IFRS 2 is to specify the financial reporting required when an entity undertakes a share-based payment transaction.   In particular, it requires an entity to reflect in its profit or loss and financial position the effects of such transactions, including expenses associated with the granting of share options to employees.

IFRS 2.7-8   The overall recognition approach required by IFRS 2 is for an entity to recognise goods or services received or acquired in a share-based payment transaction when it obtains the goods or as the services are received.   When the goods or services do not qualify for recognition as assets under the applicable IFRS, they should be recognised as expenses.   The entity should recognise a corresponding increase in equity (equity settled-transaction) or a liability (cash-settled transaction).

22.3   ACCOUNTING FOR SHARE-BASED PAYMENT

A   Scope

IFRS 2.2   IFRS 2 should be applied in accounting for all share-based payment transactions (other than those specifically excluded – see below) including:

- equity-settled share-based payment transactions, in which the entity receives goods or services as consideration for its equity instruments (including shares or share options);

- cash-settled share-based payment transactions, in which the entity acquires goods or services by incurring liabilities that are based on the price (or value) of the shares or other equity instruments of the entity; and

- transactions in which the entity receives or acquires goods or services under an arrangement which gives either the entity or the supplier the choice of whether the entity settles in cash (or other assets) or by issuing equity instruments.

The scope is not restricted to transactions with employees (or others providing similar services) – as defined in Appendix A to IFRS 2 – but applies equally to share-based payment transactions with non-employees.   Also, as noted below, the scope is not restricted to transactions undertaken by a reporting entity itself using its own equity instruments.

IFRS 2.3   The scope of the Standard includes the following, unless the transfer is clearly for a purpose other than payment for goods or services supplied to the entity:

- transfers of an entity's equity instruments by its shareholders to other parties (including employees) in return for goods or services to the entity; and

compensation plans but also allowed an entity to continue to account for those plans using the intrinsic value based method prescribed by APB 25 *Accounting for Stock Issued to Employees*. Although preferred by the FASB, adoption of the FAS 123 fair value basis is not widespread.

In December 2004, the FASB issued FAS 123R *Share-Based Payment*, a revision of FAS 123 that supersedes APB 25 and eliminates the alternative to use the APB 25 intrinsic value based method. The fair value based method in the revised standard is similar in most respects to FAS 123 although there are several key differences. FAS 123R is effective for public companies, other than small business issuers, as of the beginning of the first interim or annual reporting period that begins after 15 June 2005. FAS 123R is effective for public companies, other than small business issuers, no later than the beginning of the first fiscal year beginning after 15 June 2005 (see section 22.7).

FAS 123 also establishes fair value as the basis of measurement for transactions in which an entity acquires goods or services from non-employees in exchange for equity instruments and this guidance is not changed by FAS 123R.

The description of the fair value based method in section 22.3 below reflects the revision of FAS 123.

The accounting for employee stock options granted in a purchase business combination is covered in section 3.4.3A.

22.3 ACCOUNTING FOR SHARE-BASED PAYMENT

A Scope

FAS 123 (revised 2004) requires all entities to apply the prescribed method of accounting for share-based payment transactions which is based on fair value rather than intrinsic value. The statement applies to all arrangements whereby an entity acquires goods or services by issuing, or offering to issue, its shares, share options or other equity instruments (except for equity instruments held by an employee share ownership plan – see section 22.8) or by incurring liabilities to employees or other suppliers in amounts either (1) based, at least in part, on the price of its shares or other equity instruments or (2) that may require settlement in its shares or other equity instruments. *FAS 123R.4*

Accounting for transactions where equity instruments are issued to non-employees in exchange for goods or services is within the scope of FAS 123R but guidance is also provided by EITF 96-18 *Accounting for Equity Instruments That Are Issued to Other Than Employees for Acquiring, or in Conjunction with Selling, Goods or Services.*

The definition of a share-based transaction also extends the scope of FAS 123R to include a transaction in which an entity receives goods or services from an employee or supplier in return for share-based payment from a related party or other holder of economic interests in that entity. *FAS 123R.App E*

Employee share purchase plans satisfying all the following criteria are not compensatory: *FAS 123R.12*

- The plan satisfies at least one of the following conditions:

- transfers of equity instruments of the entity's parent, or of another entity in the same group, to parties that have supplied goods or services to the entity.

IFRS 2.4-6 The following are not share-based payment transactions within the scope of IFRS 2:

- transactions with an employee (or other party) solely in his/her capacity as a holder of equity instruments of the entity (for example, a grant under the terms of a rights issue);
- transactions in which an entity acquires goods as part of the net assets in a business combination to which IFRS 3 *Business Combinations* applies. However, grants of equity instruments to employees of the acquiree in their capacity as employees (for example, in return for continued service) are within the scope of IFRS 2 as are the cancellation, replacement or other modification of share-based payment arrangements because of a business combination or other equity restructuring;
- transactions in which the entity receives or acquires goods or services under a contract within the scope of paragraphs 8-10 of IAS 32 *Financial Instruments: Disclosure and Presentation* or paragraphs 5-7 of IAS 39 *Financial Instruments: Recognition and Measurement*; and
- transactions in which the 'goods' received are financial assets. This exclusion is presumably made on the basis that such assets are within the scope of IAS 32 and IAS 39. However, in the separate financial statements of an investing entity, investments in subsidiaries, associates and corporate joint ventures which are accounted for at cost are not in fact within the scope of IAS 39 and IFRSs have no explicit guidance on the required accounting.

There is no exemption for all-employee share schemes, which are common in certain jurisdictions, unless (as for all other IFRS 2 share-based payment transactions) the effect of applying IFRS 2 is immaterial.

B   Equity-settled share-based payment transactions

Measurement at fair value

IFRS 2.Appx A Fair value is defined as 'the amount for which an asset could be exchanged, a liability settled, or an equity instrument granted could be exchanged, between knowledgeable, willing parties in an arm's length transaction'.

IFRS 2.10 For equity-settled share-based payment transactions, the entity should measure the goods or services received, and the corresponding increase in equity:

- directly, at the fair value of the goods or services received; or
- in cases where the fair value of the goods or services cannot be measured reliably (and only in such cases), indirectly, by reference to the fair value of the equity instruments granted; or

IFRS 2.24 - in the rare cases where neither a direct nor an indirect fair value can be estimated reliably, at the intrinsic value (see separate section below).

The Standard goes on to specify that:

IFRS 2.11-13 - for transactions with employees, and others providing similar services, fair value should be measured indirectly at the date of grant of the award because, typically, it is not possible to estimate reliably the fair value of the employees' services which relate to this particular part of the individuals' remuneration;

(a) the terms of the plan are no more favourable than those available to all holders of the same class of shares; or

(b) any discount from market price does not exceed the per-share amount of share issuance costs that would have been incurred raising capital by public offering (a discount of 5% or less is considered to comply without further justification).

- Substantially all full-time employees that meet limited employment qualifications may participate on an equitable basis.

- The plan incorporates no option features, other than the following:

(a) employees have a short time (not exceeding 30 days) after the purchase price is fixed to enrol in the plan; and

(b) the purchase price is based solely on the market price of the shares at the date of purchase, and employees are allowed to cancel participation before the purchase date and obtain a refund of amounts previously paid.

The accounting for employee share ownership plans is subject to SOP 93-6 *Employer's Accounting for Employee Stock Ownership Plans* (see section 22.8).

B   Equity-settled share-based payment transactions

Measurement at fair value

Share-based payment transactions with employees should be measured based on the grant-date fair value (or in certain situations, a calculated or intrinsic value) of the equity instruments issued or the fair value of the liabilities incurred. The fair value of liabilities incurred should be remeasured at each reporting date until settlement. The amount of the fair value attributed to employee compensation is net of any amount payable by the employee.   *FAS 123R.7,10*

FAS 123R.15

Transactions in which goods or services are the consideration for the issuance of equity instruments to non-employees are accounted for based on the fair value of the equity instruments issued, unless the fair value of the consideration received is more reliably measurable.

Fair value is defined as: 'the amount at which the asset (or liability) could be bought (or incurred) or sold (or settled) in a current transaction between willing parties, that is, other than in a forced or liquidation sale'.   *FAS 123R.App E*

The fair value of an equity share option or similar instrument should be measured based on the market price of a similar option, if available, or estimated using an option-pricing model that takes into account, as of the date of grant, the following: *FAS 123R.22*
FAS 123R
.App A18

- The exercise price of the option.

- for transactions with non-employees there is a rebuttable presumption that the fair value of the goods or services received can be estimated reliably in which case the fair value should be measured at the date the entity receives the goods or the counterparty renders the service; and

- in the rare cases where this presumption is rebutted, the entity should measure the transaction indirectly as at the date the entity receives the goods or the counterparty renders the service.

IFRS 2.IG1-IG7   The Implementation Guidance to IFRS 2 refers to measurement date which, in effect, is grant date for awards to employees (and those providing similar services) and the date on which goods are obtained or services rendered (service date) for transactions with non-employees.

IFRS 2.16-17   For transactions measured indirectly (i.e. by reference to the fair value of the equity instruments granted), the fair value should be measured at the measurement date on the basis of market prices (if available), taking into account the terms and conditions upon which the equity instruments were granted (subject to the treatment of vesting conditions which is considered further below). Where market prices are not available, the fair value should be estimated using a generally accepted valuation technique which incorporates all factors and assumptions that would be considered by knowledgeable and willing market participants.

IFRS 2.18,B1-B41   Appendix B to IFRS 2 contains further detailed guidance on the estimation of fair value including the choice and application of an appropriate valuation model and the minimum inputs into such a model. It notes that the Black-Scholes-Merton option pricing model may not be appropriate for long-lived options which can be exercised before the end of their lives and which are subject to variations in the various inputs to the model, e.g. share price volatility, over the life of the option. However, this model may be appropriate for options with shorter lives and a relatively short exercise period.

Vesting period and vesting conditions

IFRS 2.14-15   A share-based payment arrangement vests when the counterparty has satisfied any
IFRS 2.Appx A   specified vesting conditions so that the award becomes unconditional. The vesting period is the period during which the vesting conditions are to be satisfied. Where services are received by an entity in return for a grant of equity instruments, it

- The expected life or term of the option.
- The current price of the underlying share.
- The expected volatility of the price of the underlying share.
- The expected dividends on the underlying share, as appropriate, over the expected term of the option.
- The risk-free rate(s) of interest over the expected term of the option.

In a closed-form model, e.g. a Black-Scholes model, the expected term is an assumption input to the model. In a lattice model which takes account of the option's contractual term and employees' expected exercise and post-vesting employment termination behaviour, the expected term is an output of the model.

A non-public entity which is unable to reasonably estimate the volatility of its share price should use the historical volatility of an appropriate industry sector index to estimate the fair value of its equity share options. FAS 123R refers to the resulting value as the calculated value. *FAS 123R.23*

In the unlikely event that it is not possible to reasonably estimate fair value at grant date, an equity instrument should be accounted for based on its intrinsic value (see separate section below).

Restrictions or conditions inherent in equity instruments awarded to employees are treated differently depending on whether they continue after the requisite service period and whether they specify a service/performance condition or a market condition. *FAS 123R.17-20*

- A restriction or condition that continues after instruments have vested is considered in estimating the fair value of the instruments at grant date.
- A restriction or condition that affects the forfeitability of instruments prior to vesting is not reflected in the fair value but rather is accounted for by only recognising compensation cost for those awards that vest.
- No compensation cost is recognised for instruments that are forfeited because a service or performance condition is not satisfied. A service condition refers to a condition which depends solely on the employee rendering service to the employer for the requisite period. A performance condition combines a service condition with a condition related to a specified performance target defined solely by reference to the employer's own operations (but which may be defined by reference to the same measure of another entity or group of entities).

The effect of a market condition is reflected in the fair value of the instrument at grant date such that compensation cost is recognised for an award with a market condition provided the requisite service is rendered regardless of whether the market condition is satisfied. A market condition relates to the achievement of (a) a specified price of the issuer's shares or amount of intrinsic value indexed to the issuer's shares or (b) a specified price of the issuer's shares in terms of similar equity securities.

Vesting period and vesting conditions

Compensation cost should be recognised over the requisite service period (often the vesting period), with a corresponding credit to equity (generally, additional paid-in capital). The initial estimate of the service period at grant date should be adjusted, as necessary, based on subsequent information. *FAS 123R.39-40*
FAS 123R.46

should recognise the services as follows:

- if the counterparty does not have to complete a further specified period of service (and therefore the award vests immediately), in full on the grant date, with a corresponding increase in equity;

- if a specified period of service is required before vesting, spread over the vesting period, with a corresponding increase in equity; or

- if vesting depends on both a future period of service and the achievement of a performance condition (see below), the entity should estimate the expected vesting period at grant date, based on the most likely outcome of the performance condition, and recognise the services accordingly.

Where the vesting condition is a market condition (see below), the estimate of the expected vesting period should be consistent with the assumptions used to estimate fair value and should not subsequently be revised. Where the performance condition is not a market condition, the estimate should be revised at each reporting date if subsequent information indicates that the estimated length of the vesting period has changed.

IFRS 2.19-20
IFRS 2.Appx A

A grant of equity instruments may be conditional upon the satisfaction of specified vesting conditions such as:

- market conditions, which are related to the market price of the entity's equity instruments;

- service conditions, which require the other party to complete a specified period of service; and

- performance conditions, which require specified performance targets to be met (either by the entity as a whole or by the other party).

Vesting conditions, other than market conditions, are ignored when estimating the fair value of the equity instruments. Instead, these non market-related vesting conditions are taken into account at each reporting date during the vesting period when, based on the latest information available, the entity should estimate the number of equity instruments likely to vest and adjust the cumulative amount recognised for the transaction accordingly. At the vesting date, the cumulative amount recognised should be based on the number of equity instruments that actually vest and, on a cumulative basis therefore, no amount is recognised if the equity instruments do not vest as a result of failure to satisfy one or more non market-related vesting conditions.

IFRS 2.21

Market conditions are taken into account when estimating the fair value of the equity instruments at the measurement date. Therefore, for a grant of equity instruments with market conditions, an entity should recognise the full fair value to the extent that all other (non market) vesting conditions are satisfied, irrespective of whether the market condition is satisfied.

IFRS 2.22

For options with a reload feature (i.e. an automatic grant of additional share options when the option holder exercises previously granted options using the entity's shares, rather than cash, to satisfy the exercise price), the reload feature should not be taken into account when estimating the fair value at the measurement date but should be accounted for as a new option grant, if and when a reload option is subsequently granted.

The amount of compensation cost recognised should be based on the number of instruments for which the requisite service has been rendered. Initial compensation cost accruals should be based on estimates of the number of options or other equity instruments that are expected to vest, revised, as necessary, based on subsequent information. The effect of a change in the estimated number of shares or options expected to vest is a change in an estimate, and the cumulative effect of the change on current and prior periods is recognised in the period of the change. Compensation cost should be accrued for an award with a performance condition only if it is probable that the condition will be achieved. *FAS 123R.43-44*

Where awards require satisfaction of one or more market, performance or service conditions, compensation cost is recognised only if the requisite service is rendered. The estimate of the fair value of an award at the grant date does not reflect performance or service conditions that affect vesting but is affected by market conditions. Accordingly, previously recognised compensation cost would be reversed for an award with a market condition only if the requisite service is not rendered. *FAS 123R.47-48*

The effect of a reload feature in the terms of an award should not be included in estimating the grant-date fair value of the award but should be accounted for as a separate award when the reload options are granted. A reload feature provides for automatic grants of additional options whenever an employee exercises previously granted options using the entity's shares rather than cash to satisfy the exercise price.

FAS 123R establishes fair value as the basis of measurement where equity instruments are issued to non-employees in exchange for goods or services, being the fair value of the consideration received or the fair value of the equity instrument issued, whichever is more reliably measurable. However, the measurement date, being the date the share price and other inputs on which the fair value of the equity instrument is based, is not prescribed in that standard. *FAS 123R.7-8*

Under EITF 96-18, the measurement date for equity instruments issued to non-employees is generally either the grant date or the vesting date. To achieve a measurement date prior to vesting a performance commitment must exist, under which performance by the counterparty to earn the equity instrument is probable because of a sufficiently large disincentive for non-performance. Usually, this disincentive or penalty should be a specified cash amount; forfeiture of the equity instrument or the potential of being sued for non-performance are not sufficient disincentives. *EITF 96-18*

Where warrants are granted as an inducement for a customer to enter into a long-term sales contract and, for example, the warrants vest as sales are made, it is highly unlikely that a penalty could be large enough to make performance probable. Accordingly, the measurement date would be the vesting dates. Also, if equity instruments issued to a customer will not vest or become exercisable without purchases by the customer, the related cost, which is measured based on the share price over the vesting period, should be reported as a reduction of revenue.

The balance sheet treatment for unvested, forfeitable equity instruments issued to non-employees as consideration for future services is determined by EITF Topic D-90. In Topic D-90 the SEC Staff addressed the situation where, pursuant to *EITF D-90*

After vesting date

IFRS 2.23   Once the equity instruments have vested, the entity should make no further adjustments to total equity and amounts previously recognised should not be reversed, even if the vested equity instruments are later forfeited or options are never actually exercised. Although an entity may not reverse any of the expense through its income statement, it is not precluded from recognising a transfer between separate components of equity.

Measurement at intrinsic value

IFRS 2.24   As referred to above, IFRS 2 acknowledges that there may be rare cases in which the entity is unable to estimate reliably at the measurement date the fair value of equity instruments granted. In these rare cases only, the entity should instead measure the equity instruments at their intrinsic value (the difference between the fair value of the underlying shares and the exercise price (if any) of the award). Under the intrinsic value method:

- the entity measures the intrinsic value of the award at each reporting date between measurement date and settlement (the date on which an award is exercised, forfeited or lapses);
- at each reporting date during the vesting period, the cumulative expense should be determined as the intrinsic value of the award at that date multiplied by the expired portion of the vesting period, with all changes in the cumulative expense recognised in profit or loss; and
- once awards have vested, all changes in their intrinsic value until settlement should be recognised in profit or loss.

As for awards measured at fair value, the cumulative expense during the vesting period should always be based on the best estimate of the number of awards that will ultimately vest. However, unlike awards measured at fair value, there is no distinction between market conditions and other vesting conditions and if a market condition is not met, there will ultimately be no accounting expense under the intrinsic value method. Under the constant remeasurement approach required by the intrinsic value method, the cost of awards will ultimately reflect the number of awards which are actually exercised and consequently, after vesting, any cost previously recognised for awards which, for example, are forfeited or lapse unexercised, will be reversed when the awards are forfeited or lapse.

IFRS 2.25   If an entity applies the intrinsic value method, it is not required to account for modifications, cancellations and settlements in accordance with paragraphs 26-29 (see below), as such modifications to the terms and conditions of an award will already be taken into account in applying the intrinsic value method. However, if an entity settles during the vesting period an award to which it is applying the

610

EITF 96-18, a sufficiently large disincentive for counterparty non-performance exists such that a performance commitment and measurement date have been achieved as of the date of issuance. The Staff concluded that if the issuer receives a right to receive future services in exchange for unvested, forfeitable equity instruments, the fair value (determined in accordance with FAS 123) of such equity instruments should not create an asset at the measurement date.

After vesting date

There is no reversal of previously recognised compensation cost for an instrument which expires unexercised after the requisite service has been rendered.

FAS 123R.45

Measurement at intrinsic value

In the unlikely event that it is not possible to reasonably estimate fair value at grant date, an equity instrument should be accounted for based on its intrinsic value, remeasured at each reporting date through the date of exercise or other settlement. The intrinsic value should continue to be used even if a reasonable estimate of fair value becomes available. Compensation cost should be based on the change (or a portion of the change based on the percentage of the requisite service that has been rendered as of the reporting date) in the intrinsic value of the instrument in each period.

FAS 123R.24-25

intrinsic value method, it should account for the settlement as an acceleration of vesting and recognise any remaining amount as an expense immediately. Any payment made on settlement should be treated as a repurchase of equity instruments, i.e. accounted for as a deduction from equity, except where the payment exceeds the intrinsic value at settlement date in which case the excess should be recognised as an expense in the income statement.

Modification, cancellation and settlement

IFRS 2.26-27 When an entity modifies the terms and conditions of a grant of equity instruments e.g. it changes the exercise price of share options, it must recognise, as a minimum, the cost of the original award as if it had not been modified. This applies unless the award does not vest through failure to satisfy a vesting condition (other than a market condition) which was specified at grant date. The cost of the award will be the original grant date fair value spread over the original vesting period and subject to the original vesting conditions.

In addition to the original cost, the entity must recognise the incremental fair value of any modifications that increase the total fair value of the award or are otherwise beneficial to the employee. The incremental fair value is the difference between the fair value of the modified grant and the fair value of the original grant, both measured on the date of modification. Any additional cost is spread over the period from the date of modification until the vesting date of the modified options which might differ from that of the original award. If, however, a modification is made after the end of the original vesting period and the award is subject to no further vesting conditions, any incremental fair value should be recognised immediately.

IFRS 2.B43-B44 Appendix B to IFRS 2 provides additional guidance on applying the above requirements.

IFRS 2.28-29 If an award is cancelled or settled (i.e. cancelled with compensation) other than by forfeiture due to the non-satisfaction of vesting conditions:

- cancellation or settlement during the vesting period should be accounted for as an acceleration of vesting and any amount that would have been recognised over the remainder of the vesting period should be recognised immediately;

- any compensation paid up to the fair value of the award at cancellation or settlement date (whether before or after vesting) should be accounted for as the repurchase of an equity instrument, i.e. treated as a deduction from equity;

- any compensation paid in excess of the fair value of the award at cancellation or settlement date (whether before or after vesting) should be accounted for as an expense in the income statement; and

- any new equity instruments granted during the vesting period which, on their grant date, are identified by the entity as replacement equity instruments for those cancelled or settled, should be accounted for as a modification of the original grant (in accordance with paragraph 27 and Appendix B – see above) and the incremental fair value should be recognised. The incremental fair value is the difference between the fair value of the replacement equity instruments and the net fair value of the cancelled instruments as at the grant date of the replacement equity instruments. If the new instruments are not identified as replacements, they should be accounted for as a completely new grant.

Modification, cancellation and settlement

A modification of the terms or conditions of an equity award should be treated as an exchange of the original award for a new award with compensation cost recognised for any incremental fair value calculated immediately prior to modification measured based on the share price and other factors at that date.   *FAS 123R.51*

The effects of a modification should be measured as follows:

- Additional compensation cost would be measured as the excess, if any, of the fair value of the modified award over the fair value of the original award immediately before its terms are modified, measured based on the share price and other factors at that date. The effect of the modification on the number of instruments expected to vest also should be considered in determining any additional compensation expense.

- Total recognised compensation cost should at least equal the fair value of the award at the grant date – unless at the modification date performance or service conditions of the original award were not expected to be met.

- A change in compensation cost for an equity award measured at intrinsic value should be measured as the difference between the intrinsic value of the modified award and the original award, if any, immediately before the modification.

The amount of consideration for the repurchase of an award should be charged to equity to the extent that it does not exceed the fair value of the award at the repurchase date. Any excess of purchase consideration over fair value should be recognised as additional compensation cost. Any unrecognised original compensation cost should be recognised at the repurchase date.   *FAS 123R.55*

Cancellation of an award with a concurrent grant (or offer to grant) a replacement award or other consideration should be accounted for as a modification of the cancelled award. A cancellation without a replacement award or other consideration should be accounted for as a repurchase for no consideration and any previously unrecognised compensation cost should be recognised at the cancellation date.   *FAS 123R.56-57*

IFRS 2 does not explicitly address the required treatment for replacement awards granted after the original option has vested.   As the original award will have been fully recognised during the vesting period, it would appear that the replacement award should be treated as if it were a completely new award, i.e. its full fair value should be recognised immediately or, if there are vesting conditions for the replacement award, over the vesting period.

IFRS 2.26   The above provisions on modification, cancellation and settlement also apply to grants of equity instruments to non-employees where those grants are measured by reference to the fair value of the equity instruments granted.   However, in such cases, the date on which the entity obtains the goods or services should be used as the measurement date.

C   Cash-settled share-based payment transactions

IFRS 2.30-32   Cash-settled share-based payment transactions include share appreciation rights, whereby the employee will become entitled to a cash payment which is based on the increase in an entity's share price, and awards where shares are redeemable for cash either mandatorily or at the employee's option.

For cash-settled transactions, an entity should measure the goods or services acquired and the liability incurred at the fair value of the liability.   The ultimate cost will be the cash paid to the counterparty and this will be the fair value at settlement date.   The entity should account for a cash-settled transaction as follows:

- at each reporting date between the measurement date and settlement the fair value of the award is determined;

- during the vesting period, the liability recognised at each reporting date is the fair value of the award at that date multiplied by the expired portion of the vesting period (if the award vests immediately, there is a presumption that services have been received in full and it should be expensed immediately at the grant date);

- from the end of the vesting period until settlement, the liability recognised is the full fair value of the liability at the reporting date; and

- all changes in the liability are recognised in the profit or loss for the period.

IFRS 2.33   The fair value of the liability should be measured by applying an option pricing model, taking into account the terms and conditions of the awards granted and the extent to which services have been rendered to date.

IFRS 2 gives no specific guidance on vesting conditions in the context of cash-settled transactions but it may be concluded that during the vesting period the liability should be based on the best estimate of the number of awards that will vest and the outcome of other performance conditions.   As a cash-settled transaction must ultimately reflect the amount of cash paid, it appears that no distinction should be drawn between market and other conditions and there will therefore be no ultimate cost for an award which has a condition (market or other) which is not satisfied.

D   Share-based payment transactions with cash alternatives

IFRS 2.34   Where either the entity or the counterparty has a choice of whether the entity settles the transaction in cash (or other assets) or by the issue of equity instruments, the entity should account for the transaction, or the components of that transaction, as

C   Cash-settled share-based payment transactions

FAS 150 *Accounting for Certain Financial Instruments with Characteristics of both*   *FAS 123R.29-30*
Liabilities and Equity does not apply to obligations under share-based compensation
arrangements. However, unless FAS 123R requires otherwise, the classification
criteria of FAS 150 should be applied to determine whether to classify as a liability a
freestanding financial instrument granted to an employee in a share-based payment
transaction (see section 12.3).

A puttable (or callable) share is classified as a liability if either (a) the repurchase   *FAS 123R.31*
feature permits the employee to avoid the risks and rewards of share ownership for
a reasonable period from the date the requisite service is rendered and the share is
issued or (b) it is probable the employer would prevent the employee from bearing
those risks and rewards for that period.

Options or similar instruments should be classified as liabilities if (a) the underlying   *FAS 150.32*
shares are classified as liabilities or (b) the entity can be required to settle the option
or similar instrument by transferring cash or other assets.

If an award is indexed to a factor that is not a market, service or performance   *FAS 150.33*
condition it should be classified as a liability and that factor should be reflected in
estimating the fair value of the award at the grant date.

The accounting should reflect the terms of the compensation plan. Generally, the   *FAS 123R.34*
written plan provides the best evidence of the terms but where past practice may
indicate that the substantive terms differ from the written terms, the substantive
terms should be the basis for the accounting.

An award that permits a broker-assisted cashless exercise of options does not result   *FAS 123R.35*
in liability classification for instruments that otherwise would be classified as equity,
provided that:

- the cashless exercise requires a valid exercise of the options; and
- the employee is the legal owner of the shares subject to the option (even
  though the exercise price is not paid before sale of the shares).

Also, the repurchase of shares issued on exercise of options with payment due to
employees withheld to meet the employer's minimum statutory withholding
requirements on exercise (as required by the relevant tax authority) does not result
in liability classification for instruments that otherwise would be classified as equity.

a cash-settled share-based payment transaction if, and to the extent that, the entity has incurred a liability to settle in cash or other assets, or as an equity-settled transaction if, and to the extent that, no such liability has been incurred.

Transactions where the counterparty has a choice of settlement

IFRS 2.35-40 Where the counterparty has the right to choose whether the transaction is settled in cash or by issuing equity instruments, the entity is considered to have granted a compound financial instrument comprising a debt component (the counterparty's right to demand a cash payment) and an equity component (the counterparty's right to demand settlement in equity instruments). The entity should measure and account for such transactions as follows:

- for transactions with parties other than employees in which the fair value of the goods or services received is measured directly, the equity component should be measured as the difference between the full fair value of the goods or services received and the fair value of the debt component, at the date the goods or services are received;

- for other transactions, including those with employees, the entity should measure first the fair value of the debt component and then the fair value of the equity component at the measurement date, taking into account the terms and conditions on which the awards were granted including the fact that the counterparty must forfeit the right to receive cash in order to receive the equity instrument. The fair value of the compound financial instrument is the sum of the fair values of the two components;

- the entity should account separately for the goods or services received or acquired in respect of each component of the compound financial instrument. For the debt component, the requirements relating to cash-settled share-based payment transactions should be applied (see section 22.3C) and for the equity component (if any) the requirements relating to equity-settled share-based payment transactions should be applied (see section 22.3B);

- at the date of settlement, the liability should be remeasured to fair value. If equity instruments are issued rather than cash being paid, the liability should be transferred direct to equity as consideration for the equity instruments issued. If cash is paid rather than equity instruments being issued, the cash payment should be applied to settle the liability in full and any equity component previously recognised should remain within equity (although the entity is not precluded from making a transfer from one element of equity to another).

Transactions where the entity has a choice of settlement

IFRS 2.41-43 Where the entity has the choice of whether to settle in cash or by issuing equity instruments, it should determine whether it has a present obligation to settle in cash. This will be the case if there is no commercial substance to the choice of settlement in equity instruments, the entity has a past practice or a stated policy of settling in cash, or generally settles in cash if requested to do so by the counterparty. The entity should account for the transaction as follows:

- if there is a present obligation to settle in cash, the transaction should be treated as cash-settled (see section 22.3C); or

- in the absence of such an obligation, the transaction should be treated as equity-settled (see section 22.3B).

All awards classified as liabilities should be remeasured at each reporting date until *FAS 150.36-38* settlement and the compensation cost should be based on the change in the value for each period and the proportion of the requisite service rendered at the reporting date.

A public company should measure all awards classified as liabilities at fair value.

The fair value on an equity share option or similar instrument should be measured as for an equity share option under section 22.4A.

A non-public entity must decide whether to measure all liabilities incurred under share-based compensation arrangements at fair value or intrinsic value.

Where the transaction is treated as equity settled, the following approach is adopted when the award is settled:

- if the award is settled in cash, the payment is accounted for as a deduction from equity unless this is the settlement alternative with the higher fair value as at the date of settlement, in which case the entity should also recognise an expense for the excess value, calculated as the difference between the cash paid and the fair value of the equity instruments that would otherwise have been issued; or

- if equity instruments are issued, there is a transfer within equity, if necessary, but no further accounting is required unless this is the settlement alternative with the higher fair value as at the date of settlement, in which case the entity should recognise an additional expense for the excess value, calculated as the difference between the fair value of the equity instruments issued and the amount of cash that would otherwise have been paid.

22.4   INTRINSIC VALUE METHOD

There is no equivalent in IFRSs of the intrinsic value method of APB 25 under US GAAP.

22.4   INTRINSIC VALUE METHOD – APB 25

FAS 123R supersedes APB 25 and eliminates the alternative to use the APB 25 intrinsic value based method effective for public companies, other than small business issuers, as of the beginning of the first interim or annual reporting period that begins after 15 June 2005.

A   Non-compensatory plans

A distinction is made between compensatory and non-compensatory plans for issuing stock to employees.   An employer recognises no compensation expense for stock issued under non-compensatory plans.   A non-compensatory plan should possess at least the following characteristics: *APB 25.7*   *FIN 44*   *EITF 00-23*

- substantially all full-time employees meeting limited employment qualifications may participate;
- stock is offered to eligible employees equally or based on a uniform percentage of salary or wages;
- the time permitted for exercise of an option or purchase right is limited to a reasonable period which is interpreted by the EITF as no greater than 27 months (when the exercise price is based on the fair value of the underlying stock at the grant date) for awards of options granted after 24 January 2002; and
- any discount from the market price is no greater than would be reasonable in an offer of stock to stockholders or others, i.e. the exercise price on the date of grant is no less than 85% of the stock price on that date.

Plans that do not have all the above characteristics are compensatory.

> **COMMENT**
>
> SAYE plans under UK legislation have a minimum contractual term of 36 months and consequently, from 24 January 2002, all new contracts will be compensatory.

B   Fixed compensatory plans

Compensatory plans give rise to compensation expense when the company issues shares or rights to acquire shares to employees at a price lower than the prevailing market price.   Recognition of compensation expense will depend on whether the plan is fixed or variable.

Conventional stock option and stock purchase plans give an employee the right to buy a fixed number of shares of the employer company's stock at a stated price during a specified period, often at a discount from the market price at the date of grant. Fixed plan accounting is only available for stock options granted to employees and board members elected by the shareholders for services provided as a director.

APB 25.1
FIN 44
EITF 00-23

The total compensation cost to be recognised under fixed plans is measured as the difference between the quoted market price of the shares at the measurement date and the amount that the employee is required to pay, i.e. the intrinsic value.

APB 25.10

The measurement date for determining the compensation cost is the first date on which the following are known:

- the number of shares that the employee is entitled to receive; and
- the purchase price the employee is required to pay.

An employee may have to perform services in several periods before an employer issues stock for those services. The employer should accrue compensation expense in each period in which the services are performed. If stock is issued in a plan before some or all of the services are performed, the unearned compensation should be accounted for as expense of the period or periods in which the employee performs the services. The grant or award may specify the period or periods during which the employee performs services, or the period or periods may be inferred from the terms of the plan or from the past pattern of grants or awards.

APB 25.12-14

C   Variable compensatory plans

Variable plans are those plans for which either the number of shares that may be acquired by, or awarded to, an employee or the price to be paid by the employee, or both, are not specified or determinable until after the date of grant or award. Additionally, certain awards that may be settled in cash are accounted for as variable awards. As a general rule, any features of a plan that could result in the exercise price or number of shares changing, either directly or indirectly, are indicators that the plan is variable. Some of the more common provisions that can lead to variable plan accounting include:

FIN 28.2
FIN 44
EITF 00-23
APB 25.11

- an exercise price or number of shares that changes based on time or performance-related criteria;
- cash bonuses paid in connection with the exercise of an option, which are viewed as reductions of the exercise price;
- stock repurchase arrangements such as 'puts,' 'calls' or similar arrangements which effectively turn the award into a cash plan (also, a repurchase of shares within six months of exercise would result in delaying the measurement date);
- shares used to settle withholding taxes exceeding the minimum statutory withholding requirements; and
- nonrecourse employer stock loans which do not meet certain specified criteria or recourse or nonrecourse loans with 'forgiveness' provisions.

Guidance on how to determine the measurement date for certain types of plans is contained in FIN 38 *Determining the Measurement Date for Stock Option, Purchase, and Award Plans Involving Junior Stock* and FIN 44 *Accounting for Certain Transactions Involving Stock Compensation.*

22.5   PAYROLL TAXES ON STOCK COMPENSATION

IFRS 2 does not address specifically the subject of payroll taxes in connection with share-based payment arrangements, but the basic principles of IAS 19 *Employee Benefits* and IAS 37 *Provisions, Contingent Liabilities and Contingent Assets* should be taken into account in addition to IFRS 2.

Compensation cost recognised over the service period should be adjusted in periods up to the measurement date to reflect changes in the market value of the shares based on the proportion of the award that is vested. If the stock appreciation rights or other variable plan awards are granted for past services, the compensation cost should be expensed in the period in which the rights or awards are granted and any adjustments to that compensation cost for changes in the market value of the shares should be recognised immediately.

FIN 28.4

The service period should be presumed to be the vesting period unless it is defined in the plan (or some other agreement) to be a shorter period. Stock appreciation rights and other variable plan awards become vested when the employee's right to receive or retain shares or cash under the rights or awards is not contingent upon the performance of additional services. Frequently, the vesting period is the period from the date of grant to the date the rights or awards become exercisable.

On the exercise of an option, the sum of cash received and the amount of compensation charged to the income statement should be accounted for as consideration received on the issue of stock.

ARB 43 Ch 13B
APB 25.7

The amounts recorded as deferred compensation should be presented in the balance sheet as a deduction from stockholders' equity.

SAB 40

SAYE plans in the UK (and equivalent tax-qualified plans in other jurisdictions) permit the employee to cancel previous contracts (and the related options) and enter into new contracts (and options) whenever the employer offers a new contract. The EITF concluded in EITF 00-23 that an employer's offer to enter into a new SAYE contract at a lower exercise price than existing SAYE options is an offer to re-price stock options and, therefore, causes variable plan accounting for all existing awards subject to the offer. This consensus applies to new contracts offered after 24 January 2002.

EITF 00-23

In addition to the guidance referred to above, there are numerous EITF Abstracts that address stock compensation issues. The guidance contained in those Abstracts has not been included in this book.

D   Related tax effects

A company may obtain an income tax benefit related to stock issued to an employee through a stock option, purchase, or award plan. This may result in a temporary difference because a deduction for income tax purposes may differ from the related compensation expense and the deduction may be allowable in a period that differs from the one in which the company recognises compensation expense in measuring net income. Detailed rules are provided in APB 25 on how to recognise such temporary differences in the financial statements.

APB 25.16-18

22.5   PAYROLL TAXES ON STOCK COMPENSATION

In EITF Topic D-83 the EITF expressed the view that employer payroll taxes on the exercise of stock options should be charged to operating expenses, but did not discuss how or when the tax obligation should be recognised.

EITF D-83

The EITF consensus on issue 00-16 concluded that the event that triggers measurement and payment of the payroll tax is the obligating event and no liability

EITF 00-16

22.6   DISCLOSURE

IFRS 2.44-45   IFRS 2 requires the disclosure of information that enables users of the financial statements to understand the nature and extent of share-based payment arrangements during the period.   As a minimum, the following disclosures are required:

- a description of each type of share-based payment arrangement that existed at any time during the period, including the general terms and conditions of each arrangement, such as vesting requirements, the maximum term of options granted, and the method of settlement (e.g. whether in cash or equity).   An entity may aggregate information on similar types of arrangement, unless separate disclosure is necessary to satisfy the objective above;

- the number and weighted average exercise prices of share options for each of the following groups of options:

  (i)   outstanding at the beginning of the period;

  (ii)   granted during the period;

  (iii)   forfeited during the period;

  (iv)   exercised during the period;

  (v)   expired during the period;

  (vi)   outstanding at the end of the period; and

  (vii) exercisable at the end of the period;

- for share options exercised during the period, the weighted average share price at the date of exercise.   If options were exercised on a regular basis throughout the period, the entity may instead disclose the weighted average share price during the period;

- for share options outstanding at the end of the period, the range of exercise prices and weighted average remaining contractual life.   If the range of exercise prices is wide, the outstanding options should be divided into ranges that are meaningful for assessing the number and timing of additional shares that may be issued and the cash that may be received upon exercise of those options.

IFRS 2.46-47   An entity should also disclose information that enables users of the financial statements to understand how the fair values have been determined.   If the fair value of goods or services has been measured indirectly, by reference to the fair value of the equity instruments granted, the following minimum disclosures are required:

- for share options granted during the period, the weighted average fair value of those options at the measurement date and information on how that fair value was measured, including:

  (i)   the option pricing model used and the inputs to that model;

  (ii)   how expected volatility was determined; and

should be recognised until that event occurs. In the US, for a non-qualified stock option, generally the obligating event is the stock option exercise date.

EITF 00-23 provides detailed guidance on how to treat UK National Insurance contributions in accounting for employee stock options plans.   *EITF 00-23*

22.6 DISCLOSURE

An entity with one or more share-based payment arrangements should provide a description of the share-based payment arrangement(s), including the general terms of awards under the arrangement(s), such as the requisite service period(s) and any other substantive conditions (including those related to vesting), the maximum contractual term of the instruments, and the number of shares authorised for awards. An entity should also disclose the method used for measuring compensation cost from share-based payment arrangements with employees.   *FAS 123R.64-65*   *FAS 123R*   *.App A240*

For the most recent year for which an income statement is provided an entity should disclose:

- the number and weighted-average exercise prices for each of the following groups of share options: (a) those outstanding at the beginning of the year, (b) those outstanding at the end of the year, (c) those exercisable or convertible at the end of the year, and those (d) granted, (e) exercised or converted, (f) forfeited, or (g) expired during the year;
- the number and weighted-average grant-date fair value (or calculated value for a non-public entity that uses a calculated method or intrinsic value) of equity instruments for each of the following groups of equity instruments: (a) those non-vested at the beginning of the year, (b) those non-vested at the end of the year, and those (c) granted, (d) vested, or (e) forfeited during the year.

For each year for which an income statement is provided an entity should disclose:

- the weighted-average grant-date fair value (or calculated value for a non-public entity that uses that method or intrinsic value) of equity instruments granted during the year;
- the total intrinsic value of options exercised, share-based liabilities paid, and the total fair value of shares vested during the year;
- a description of the method used to estimate the fair value (or calculated value) of awards under share-based payment arrangements;
- a description of the significant assumptions used during the year to estimate the fair value (or calculated value) of share-based compensation awards, including (if applicable):
  - (a) expected term of share options and similar instruments, including a discussion of the method used to incorporate the contractual term of the instruments and employees' expected exercise and post-vesting employment termination behaviour into the fair value (or calculated value) of the instrument;
  - (b) expected volatility of the entity's shares and the method used to estimate it. An entity that uses a method that employs different volatilities during the contractual term shall disclose the range of expected

(iii) whether and how any other features of the option grant were incorporated into the measurement of fair value, such as a market condition;

- for other equity instruments granted during the period, the number and weighted average fair value of those equity instruments at the measurement date, and information on how that fair value was measured, including:

  (i) how the fair value was determined if it was not based on an observable market price;

  (ii) whether and how expected dividends were incorporated into the measurement of fair value; and

  (iii) whether and how any other features of the equity instruments granted were incorporated into the measurement of fair value;

- for share-based payment arrangements that were modified during the period:

  (i) an explanation of those modifications;

  (ii) the incremental fair value granted; and

  (iii) where applicable, information on how the incremental fair value was measured (in a manner consistent with the requirements for share options or other equity instruments above).

IFRS 2.48 If the entity has measured directly the fair value of any goods or services received during the period, it should disclose how that fair value was determined e.g. whether it was measured at a market price.

IFRS 2.49 If the entity has rebutted the presumption that the fair value of goods or services may be estimated reliably in transactions with parties other than employees (or similar), the fact should be disclosed together with an explanation of why the presumption was rebutted.

IFRS 2.50-51 An entity should disclose information that enables users of the financial statements to understand the effect of share-based payment transactions on the entity's profit or loss for the period and on its financial position. To give effect to this, the following minimum disclosures are required:

- the total expense recognised for the period arising from share-based payment transactions in which the goods or services received did not qualify for recognition as assets and hence were recognised immediately as an expense. Any amount within the total which relates to equity-settled share-based payment transactions should be disclosed separately;

- for liabilities arising from share-based payment transactions:

  (i) the total carrying amount at the end of the period; and

  (ii) the total intrinsic value at the end of the period of liabilities for which the counterparty's right to cash or other assets had vested by the end of the period.

IFRS 2.44,46
IFRS 2.50,52 If the information required to be disclosed does not meet the disclosure principles of IFRS 2, the entity should disclose any additional information which is necessary to satisfy these principles.

volatilities used and the weighted-average expected volatility. A non-public entity that uses the calculated value method should disclose the reasons why it is not practicable for it to estimate the expected volatility of its share price, the appropriate industry sector index that it has selected, the reasons for selecting that particular index, and how it has calculated historical volatility using that index;

(c)   expected dividends. An entity that uses a method that employs different dividend rates during the contractual term shall disclose the range of expected dividends used and the weighted-average expected dividends;

(d)   risk-free rate(s). An entity that uses a method that employs different risk-free rates shall disclose the range of risk-free rates used; and

(e)   discount for post-vesting restrictions and the method for estimating it;

- total compensation cost for share-based payment arrangements (a) recognised in income as well as the total recognised tax benefit related thereto and (b) the total compensation cost capitalised as part of the cost of an asset; and

- a description of significant modifications, including the terms of the modifications, the number of employees affected, and the total incremental compensation cost resulting from the modifications.

For fully vested share options (or share units) and share options expected to vest at the date of the latest statement of financial position:

- the number, weighted-average exercise price (or conversion ratio), aggregate intrinsic value, and weighted-average remaining contractual term of options (or share units) outstanding; and

- the number, weighted-average exercise price (or conversion ratio), aggregate intrinsic value (except for non-public entities), and weighted-average remaining contractual term of options (or share units) currently exercisable (or convertible).

An entity that grants equity or liability instruments under multiple share-based payment arrangements with employees shall provide the relevant information specified above separately for different types of awards to the extent that the differences in the characteristics of the awards make separate disclosure important to an understanding of the entity's use of share-based compensation.

As of the latest balance sheet date presented, the total compensation cost related to non-vested awards not yet recognised and the weighted-average period over which it is expected to be recognised should be disclosed.

If not separately disclosed elsewhere, an entity should disclose:

- the amount of cash received from exercise of share options and similar instruments granted under share-based payment arrangements and the tax benefit realised from stock options exercised during the annual period; and

- the amount of cash used to settle equity instruments granted under share-based payment arrangements.

The entity's policy, if any, for issuing shares on share option exercise, including the source of those shares (that is, new shares or treasury shares) should be disclosed. If as a result of its policy, an entity expects to repurchase shares in the following

22.7   TRANSITIONAL PROVISIONS

IFRS 1.25B-25C   The following transitional provisions apply to those entities which are already applying IFRS.   For first-time adopters, there are specific provisions set out in IFRS 1.

IFRS 2.53-55,60   For equity-settled share-based payment transactions, IFRS 2 applies in full to awards granted after 7 November 2002 which had not vested at the effective date of IFRS 2 (accounting periods beginning on or after 1 January 2005, although earlier application is encouraged).   If the entity has previously disclosed publicly the fair value of the relevant equity instruments determined at the measurement date, it is encouraged also to apply IFRS 2 to other grants of equity instruments.   Restatement of comparatives and, where applicable, adjustment of opening retained earnings are required.

IFRS 2.56   For all grants of equity instruments to which the Standard has not been applied, the entity is still required to disclose the information specified in paragraphs 44 and 45 (see section 22.6 above).

IFRS 2.26-29,57   If, after IFRS 2 becomes effective, an entity modifies the terms or conditions of a grant of equity instruments to which IFRS 2 has not been applied, the modifications should nevertheless be accounted for in accordance with the requirements of IFRS 2.

IFRS 2.58-59   For liabilities arising from cash-settled share-based payment transactions existing as at the effective date, IFRS 2 should be applied retrospectively with comparatives being restated and the opening balance on retained earnings being adjusted in the earliest period presented for which comparatives have been restated.   Restatement of comparatives is not required if information relates to a period or date earlier than 7 November 2002.   Retrospective application to other liabilities arising from share-based payment transactions is however encouraged.

628

annual period, the entity should disclose an estimate of the amount (or a range, if more appropriate) of shares to be repurchased during that period.

The entity's policy for recognising compensation cost for awards with graded vesting.

In the period that FAS 123R is adopted, an entity should disclose the effect of adoption on income from continuing operations, income before taxes, net income, cash flow from operations, cash flow from financing activities and basic and diluted earnings per share. *FAS 123R.84*

Where the intrinsic value method of APB 25 is applied for any period for which an income statement is presented, all public entities should provide the tabular presentation of the following information:

- Net income and basic and diluted earning per share as reported.
- Share-based employee compensation cost, net of tax, included in net income as reported.
- Share-based employee compensation cost, net of tax, that would have been included in net income if the fair-value-based method had been applied to all awards.
- Pro forma net income as if the fair-value-based method had been applied to all awards.
- Pro forma basic and diluted earnings per share as if the fair-value-based method had been applied to all awards.

22.7   TRANSITIONAL PROVISIONS

The implementation dates for FAS 123R for public companies were deferred by the SEC in April 2005.   FAS 123R is now effective for public companies, other than small business issuers, no later than the beginning of the first fiscal year beginning after 15 June 2005 and for small business issuers no later than the beginning of the first fiscal year beginning after 15 December 2005.   The effective date for non-public entities is the fiscal year beginning after 15 December 2005.

For public and non-public entities that previously used the fair-value based method for either recognition or disclosure, FAS 123R applies to new awards and to awards modified, repurchased or cancelled after the effective date and to the portion of awards outstanding at that date for which the requisite service has not been rendered.   Changes in the previously estimated grant date fair value are precluded. This is referred to as the modified prospective application. *FAS 123R.74-75*

Those entities required to apply the modified prospective application may instead apply a modified retrospective application either (a) to all prior years for which the original FAS 123 was effective, or (b) only to prior interim periods in the year of adoption. *FAS 123R.76-78*

FAS 123R provides specific guidance for the application of the transition methods. *FAS 123R.79-82*

Non-public entities that did not use the fair value based method for either recognition or disclosure should apply FAS 123R prospectively to new awards and to awards modified, repurchased or cancelled after the effective date.   Any portion of awards outstanding at that date should continue to be accounted for under the accounting principles originally applied to those awards. *FAS 123R.83*

22.8   ACCOUNTING FOR EMPLOYEE SHARE OWNERSHIP PLANS (ESOPS)

22.8.1   Measurement

SIC-12   Share-based awards made by an employee benefit trust to an entity's employees are within the scope of IFRS 2, irrespective of whether or not the trust is consolidated by the reporting entity under IAS 27 *Consolidated and Separate Financial Statements*, because the trust is a shareholder of the reporting entity.   However, following the amendment to SIC-12 *Scope of SIC-12 Consolidation - Special Purpose Entities* in 2004 (effective for annual periods beginning on or after 1 January 2005 unless an entity applies IFRS 2 from an earlier date), equity compensation plans held within a special purpose entity, such as an employee benefit trust, are included within the scope of *SIC*-12 and should be consolidated when, in substance, they are controlled by the reporting entity.   Shares in the reporting entity which are held by the trust should be accounted for as treasury shares in accordance with IAS 32 paragraphs 33-34.

22.8   ACCOUNTING FOR EMPLOYEE SHARE OWNERSHIP PLANS (ESOPS)

22.8.1   Measurement

An Employee Stock Ownership Plan (ESOP) is a tax-qualified employee stock benefit   *SOP 93-6*
plan designed to invest primarily in the stock of the sponsoring corporation.   It is
effectively a deferred compensation plan (defined contribution plan) similar to a
profit-sharing plan in that each participant has a separate account.   Periodic employer
contributions and plan earnings are allocated to those separate accounts.

The accounting treatment for ESOPs is complicated and largely depends on the terms
of the plan.   The primary source of guidance on accounting for ESOPs has been
SOP 93-6, *Employers' Accounting for Employee Stock Ownership Plans*.   This
section provides a brief summary of the main guidance in SOP 93-6.   Reference
should be made to the statement when addressing ESOP accounting issues.

There are essentially two basic kinds of ESOPs: leveraged and non-leveraged.   Non-
leveraged ESOPs typically involve periodic contributions of employer stock to the
plan or cash contributions that are used by the plan to purchase employer stock.   A
leveraged ESOP borrows money (the lender usually requires the sponsoring company
to guarantee the debt) to acquire employer stock.   The shares purchased generally
collateralise the ESOP debt.   They are legally released by future debt service
payments and are allocated to individual employees based on a known formula.

A   Leveraged ESOPs

The sponsoring company should report external ESOP debt as a liability.   As the   *SOP 93-6.14-19*
shares transferred from the employer to the ESOP when the ESOP is established   *SOP 93-6.24-27*
are not exchanged for a receipt of assets or services (or a reduction of a liability),
total shareholders' equity should remain unchanged.   The transaction should be
reported only as a change within equity until the shares are 'committed to be
released' for allocation to participants' accounts for services provided.   'Committed
to be released' shares are those that, although not legally released, will be released by
a future scheduled and committed debt service payment and will be allocated to
employees for services rendered in the current accounting period.   Compensation
cost should be recognised in the income statement based on the fair values of shares
'committed to be released' in a period.   The difference between the fair values of
the shares 'committed to be released' in a period and their cost to the ESOP should
be credited to shareholders' equity (generally to additional paid-in capital).

Dividends on allocated ESOP shares must be charged to retained earnings.   *SOP 93-6.21-22*
Dividends on unallocated shares are accounted for as reductions of debt or accrued
interest or compensation cost (if dividends are paid to participants).

22.8.2 Disclosure

The disclosure requirements of IFRS 2 (see section 22.6) apply to share-based payment transactions conducted through an ESOP or similar employee benefit trust. Treasury shares held by an ESOP should be disclosed in accordance with IAS 32.

B　　　*Non-leveraged ESOPs*

The accounting treatment of such plans reflects the fact that they are employee compensation plans. Thus, the compensation cost for the period should generally equal the contribution called for in the period, i.e. fair value of shares contributed or cash. The shares or cash that an employer contributes or commits to contribute to a non-leveraged ESOP for a period is consideration for employee services rendered during that period. As a general rule, dividends on shares held by the ESOP should be charged to retained earnings.

SOP 93-6.40-41

22.8.2　Disclosure

The following disclosures should be made:

SOP 93-6

- a description of the plan should be provided, including:
  - employee groups covered;
  - the basis for determining contributions;
  - for leveraged and pension reversion ESOPs, the basis for releasing shares and how dividends on allocated and unallocated shares are used; and
  - a description of the accounting policies followed for ESOP transactions, including the method of measuring compensation, the classification of dividends on ESOP shares and the treatment of ESOP shares for EPS computations;
- compensation cost recognised during the period;
- the number of allocated, committed-to-be-released, and suspense shares at the balance sheet date;
- the fair value of unearned ESOP shares (accounted for under SOP 93-6) at the balance sheet date;
- the existence and nature of any employer repurchase obligation including the fair value of allocated shares at the balance sheet date that are subject to a repurchase obligation; and
- for all periods presented:
  - actual interest incurred on ESOP debt;
  - the amount contributed to the ESOP; and
  - the amount of dividends on ESOP shares used for debt service by the ESOP.

Section 23   Pension costs

23.1   AUTHORITATIVE PRONOUNCEMENTS

- IAS 19 (amended December 2004)

COMMENT

IAS 19 prescribes the accounting treatment for all employee benefits except those to which IFRS 2 *Share-based Payment* applies (see section 22). The following categories of employee benefits are covered by IAS 19:

- pensions, which are covered in section 23;
- post-employment life assurance and medical care, which are covered in section 24;
- short-term employee benefits, which are dealt with in section 25.2;
- termination benefits, which are discussed in section 25.3; and
- other long-term employee benefits, which are covered in section 25.4.

23.2   GENERAL APPROACH

The general approach of IAS 19 *Employee Benefits* is to require an entity to recognise:

- a liability when an employee has provided service in exchange for employee benefits to be paid in the future; and
- an expense when the entity consumes the economic benefit arising from service provided by an employee in exchange for employee benefits.

23.3   DEFINED CONTRIBUTION PLANS

IAS 19.7,25   Defined contribution plans are post-employment benefit plans that require the entity to pay fixed contributions into a separate entity (a fund). The entity is not under any legal or constructive obligation to pay further contributions to the fund if the fund does not hold sufficient assets to pay all the employee benefits relating to employee service in the current and prior periods. Consequently, the actuarial and investment risks of the plan fall on the employee.

IAS 19.43   Accounting for defined contribution plans is straightforward because the reporting entity's obligation for each period is determined by the amounts to be contributed for that period. Consequently, no actuarial assumptions are required to measure the obligation or the expense and there is no possibility of any actuarial gain or loss to the reporting entity.

IAS 19.44   When an employee has rendered service to an entity during a period, the entity should recognise the contribution payable to a defined contribution plan in exchange for that service:

- as a liability (accrued expense), after deducting any contribution already paid. If the contribution already paid exceeds the contribution due for service

Section 23   Pension costs

23.1   AUTHORITATIVE PRONOUNCEMENTS

- FAS 87
- FAS 88
- FAS 132(R)

23.2   GENERAL APPROACH

The fundamental objective of FAS 87 *Employers' Accounting for Pensions* is to recognise the cost of an employee's pension over that employee's service period.   *FAS 87.6*

A liability (unfunded accrued pension cost) is recognised if net period pension costs charged to income exceed amounts the employer has contributed to the pension plan. An asset (prepaid pension cost) is recognised if net period pension costs charged to income is less than amounts the employer has contributed to the pension plan.   *FAS 87.35*

23.3   DEFINED CONTRIBUTION PLANS

A defined contribution pension plan is one that both; provides pension benefits in return for services rendered; and, has terms that specify how contributions to participants' accounts are to be determined rather than the amount of pension benefits the individual is to receive.   *FAS 87.63*

The pension benefits a participant is entitled to receive under a defined contribution plan depend only on the amounts contributed to the participant's account, forfeitures of amounts initially contributed to other participants' accounts (e.g. due to termination of employment before full vesting) that may be allocated to the participant's account, and the returns earned on investments of those amounts.

An employer's net pension cost for a period is the contribution called for in that period to the extent that the plan's defined contributions to an individual's account are to be made for periods in which that individual renders services.   FAS 87 effectively requires that any contributions made by the employer to a defined contribution plan in excess of amounts allocated to individual accounts by the plan's contribution formula represent prepaid pension cost.   Any prepaid pension cost would be amortised to expense over the shorter of (a) the allocation period called for by the plan's defined contribution formula, or (b) the employees' individual service periods.   *FAS 87.64*

before the balance sheet date, the excess should be recognised as an asset (prepaid expense) to the extent that such prepayment will lead to, for example, a reduction in future payments or a cash refund; and

- as an expense, unless another Standard requires or permits the inclusion of the contribution in the cost of an asset.

IAS 19.45   The contributions to a defined contribution plan should be discounted when they are not wholly due within twelve months after the end of the period in which the service was rendered.

IAS 19.78   The discount rate used should be determined by reference to the market yield on high quality corporate bonds of appropriate currency and term.   In countries where there is no deep market in such bonds, the market yields (at the balance sheet date) on government bonds should be used.

COMMENT

On 8 July 2004, the IFRIC issued draft interpretation D9 *Employee Benefit Plans with a Promised Return on Contributions or Notional Contributions*.   It is common in some jurisdictions for an employer to make contributions to a defined contribution plan and to guarantee a minimum level of return on the assets in which the contributions are invested.   The existence of such a guarantee means that the plan is a defined benefit plan under IAS 19, but this raises questions as to how such a plan should actually be accounted for.   The draft interpretation distinguishes between a benefit of contributions or notional contributions plus a guarantee of a fixed return and benefits that depend on future asset returns.

23.3.1   Disclosure

IAS 19.46   An entity should disclose the expense recognised for defined contribution plans.

IAS 19.47   Where required by IAS 24 *Related Party Disclosures*, an entity should disclose information about contributions to defined contribution plans for key management personnel.

23.4   DEFINED BENEFIT PLANS

IAS 19.7   Defined benefit plans are defined as post-employment benefit plans other than defined contribution plans (see section 23.3 above).

IAS 19.27,49   Under defined benefit plans, an entity's obligation is to provide the agreed benefits to current and former employees.   The most significant difference between defined contribution and defined benefit plans is that, under defined benefit plans, risks of the plan fall on the entity.   This means that if actuarial or investment experience are worse than expected, the entity's obligation may be increased.   Consequently, because the entity is underwriting the actuarial and investment risks associated with the plan, the expense recognised for a defined benefit plan is not necessarily the amount of the contribution due for the period.

IAS 19.48   Accounting for defined benefit plans is complex because actuarial assumptions are required to measure both the obligation and the expense, and there is a possibility of actuarial gains and losses.   Moreover, the obligations are measured on a discounted basis because they may be settled many years after the employees render the related service.

The sponsor of a plan calling for contributions for periods after an employee retires or terminates must accrue the estimated cost during the employee's service period. FAS 87 does not specifically address how this accrual should be determined.

A pension plan having characteristics of both a defined benefit plan and a defined contribution plan requires careful analysis to determine the appropriate accounting. If the substance of the plan is to provide a defined benefit, as may be the case with some 'target benefit' plans, the accounting and disclosure requirements shall be determined in accordance with the provisions of this Statement applicable to a defined benefit plan.

FAS 87.66

23.3.1   Disclosure

The amount of cost recognised for defined contribution plans should be disclosed separately from the amount of cost recognised for defined benefit plans.   The disclosures should include a description of the nature and effect of any significant changes during the period affecting comparability, e.g. a change in contribution rate, a business combination, or a disposal.

FAS 132(R).11

23.4   DEFINED BENEFIT PLANS

A defined benefit pension plan is a pension plan that defines an amount of pension benefit to be provided, usually as a function of one or more factors such as age, years of service, or compensation.   Any pension plan that is not a defined contribution pension plan is a defined benefit pension plan.   Any single-employer plan that, in substance, is a defined benefit pension plan must be accounted for as such.

FAS 87.264

A pension benefit is part of the compensation paid to an employee for services.   In a defined benefit pension plan, the employer undertakes to provide retirement income payments after the employee retires.   The amount of benefit to be paid generally depends on a number of future events incorporated into the plan's benefit formula, including; how long the employee and any dependent survivors live, how many years of service; and, the employee's compensation immediately prior to retirement or termination.   FAS 87 requires the use of assumptions which represent the best estimate of each future event, but also uses the pension plan's benefit formula as a basis for attributing benefits earned and the related costs to specific periods of employee service.

FAS 87.12-14

IAS 19.50   To account for a defined benefit plan, an entity should perform the following steps:

- using actuarial techniques, make a reliable estimate of the amount of benefit that employees have earned in return for their service in the current and prior periods.   This requires an entity to determine how much benefit is attributable to the current and prior periods and to make estimates (actuarial assumptions) about demographic variables (such as employee turnover and mortality) and financial variables (such as future increases in salaries) that will influence the cost of the benefit;

- discount that benefit using the projected unit credit method in order to determine the present value of the defined benefit obligation and the current service cost;

- determine the fair value of any plan assets;

- determine the total amount of actuarial gains and losses and the amount of those actuarial gains and losses that should be recognised;

- where a plan has been introduced or changed, determine the resulting past service cost; and

- where a plan has been curtailed or settled, determine the resulting gain or loss.

Where an entity has more than one defined benefit plan, the entity should apply these steps for each material plan separately.

23.4.1   Actuarial method

IAS 19.64-66   An entity should determine the present value of defined benefit obligations, the related current service cost and, where applicable, past service cost in accordance with the projected unit credit method.   The projected unit credit method sees each period of service as giving rise to an additional unit of benefit entitlement and measures each unit separately to build up the final obligation.   IAS 19 provides an example to illustrate this.   An entity should discount the whole defined benefit obligation, even if part of it falls due within twelve months of the balance sheet date (see section 23.4.2).

IAS 19.67-71   In determining such amounts, the entity should attribute benefits to periods of service under the plan's benefit formula.   If an employee's service in later years will lead to a materially higher level of benefit than in earlier years, the entity should attribute benefits on a straight-line basis from:

- the date when service by the employee first leads to benefits under the plan; until

- the date when further service by the employee will lead to no material amount of further benefits under the plan, other than from further salary increases.

IAS 19 provides additional guidance, including illustrative examples, on the application of the Projected Unit Credit Method.

IAS 19.52-53   An entity should account for both its legal obligation under the formal terms of a defined benefit plan and for any constructive obligation arising from the entity's informal practices.   A constructive obligation exists where an entity's informal practices leave it with no realistic alternative but to pay employee benefits.   In the absence of evidence to the contrary, accounting for post-employment benefits assumes that an entity which is currently promising such benefits will continue to do so over the remaining working lives of employees.

The cost of a benefit can be determined without reference to the extent of funding of the plan. The service cost component is the actuarial present value of benefits attributed to services rendered during the period. The other components of the net periodic pension costs are interest on the projected benefit obligation, actual return on plan assets, amortisation of unrecognised prior service cost and actuarial gain or loss.   *FAS 87.16*

The projected benefit obligation as of a date is the actuarial present value of all benefits attributed to employee service rendered prior to that date. The accumulated benefit obligation differs from the projected benefit obligation in that it includes no assumption about future compensation levels.   *FAS 87.17-18*

Plan assets are assets that have been segregated and restricted (usually in a trust) to provide for pension benefits.   *FAS 87.19*

23.4.1   Actuarial method

The pension cost to be attributed to a period should represent the actuarial present value of the benefits which accrue in respect of the period under the terms of the pension plan. This means that for plan benefit formulas that define benefits similarly for all years of service, the attribution is a benefit/years-of-service approach. For final salary schemes or career-average-salary schemes, the attribution of cost to accounting periods would be the same as using the projected unit credit method. For a flat-benefit plan it is the same as the unit credit method.   *FAS 87.40*

Where there is a substantive commitment to provide pension benefits for employees beyond the written terms of the plan, allowance should be made for such a commitment in the actuarial valuation. Actions of the employer, e.g. communications with the employees, can demonstrate the existence of such a commitment. However, a history of retroactive scheme amendments is not enough, in isolation, to establish a substantive commitment.   *FAS 87.41*
Q&A FAS 87 Q52

IAS 19.69   Employee service gives rise to an obligation under a defined benefit plan even if the benefits are conditional on future employment (i.e. they are not vested). In measuring its defined benefit obligation, an entity considers the probability that some employees may not satisfy any vesting requirements.

23.4.2 Assumptions

IAS 19.72-73,77   Actuarial (demographic and financial) assumptions should be unbiased, mutually compatible and represent the entity's best estimates of the variables that will determine the ultimate cost of providing post-employment benefits. Financial assumptions must be based on market expectations at the balance sheet date for the period over which the obligations are to be settled.

IAS 19.78   The rate used to discount the defined benefit obligations should be determined by reference to the market yields on high quality corporate bonds at the balance sheet date. In countries where there is no deep market in such bonds, the market yields (at the balance sheet date) on government bonds should be used.

IAS 19.83   Post-employment benefit obligations should reflect:

- estimated future salary increases;
- the benefits set out in the formal plan and those resulting from any constructive obligations at the balance sheet date; and
- estimated future changes in the level of any state benefits that affect the benefits payable under a defined benefit plan if (1) those changes were enacted before the balance sheet date or (2) past history or other evidence indicates that those state benefits will change in some predictable manner.

23.4.3 Annual pension cost

IAS 19.61   IAS 19 identifies the following seven components of annual pension cost:

- current service cost;
- interest cost;
- the expected return on any plan assets and on any reimbursement rights;
- actuarial gains and losses as required by the entity's accounting policy;
- past service cost;
- the effect of any curtailments or settlements; and
- the effect of the limit in recognising an asset (see paragraph 58(b)) unless it is recognised outside profit and loss.

The net total of the above should be recognised in profit or loss, except to the extent that another Standard requires or permits their inclusion in the cost of an asset.

IAS 19.56-57   The entity should determine the present value of defined benefit obligations and the fair value of plan assets frequently enough to ensure that the amounts recognised in the financial statements do not differ materially from the amounts that would be determined at the balance sheet date. If the entity uses amounts determined before the balance sheet date, it should update the valuation to take account of any material transactions or changes in circumstances up to the balance sheet date. The involvement of a qualified actuary in the measurement of material post-employment benefit obligations is encouraged but not required.

23.4.2   Assumptions

Each significant assumption necessary to determine annual pension cost, such as   *FAS 87.43-45*
discount rates, return on the plan's assets, or future salary increases, reflects the best
estimate solely with respect to that individual assumption.

23.4.3   Annual pension cost

FAS 87 identifies six components of net periodic pension cost and specifies how   *FAS 87.20*
they are to be measured.   The six components are:

- service cost;
- interest cost;
- actual return on scheme assets, if any;
- amortisation of unrecognised prior service cost, if any;
- gain or loss (including the effects of changes in assumptions) to the extent recognised; and
- amortisation of the unrecognised net obligation or unrecognised net asset existing at the date of initial application of the Statement.

The pension cost for both interim and annual financial statements can be based on   *Q&A FAS 87 Q65*
the last actuarial valuation provided that the obligation obtained after rolling it
forward to the current measurement date is substantially the same as that based on a
new valuation at that date.

A   Service cost

The service cost is the actuarial present value of benefits attributed to services   *FAS 87.21*
rendered by employees during the period.   This cost will be the same irrespective
of whether the plan is unfunded, has minimal funding or is well funded.   The   *FAS 87.198-200*

A Current service cost

IAS 19.64   The current service cost, which should be determined using the projected unit credit method, is the actuarial present value of benefits attributed to services rendered by employees during the period.

B Interest cost

IAS 19.7,82   Interest cost is the increase during a period in the present value of a defined benefit obligation that arises because the benefits are one period closer to settlement. Interest cost is calculated by multiplying the discount rate (see section 23.4.2) at the beginning of the period by the present value of the defined benefit obligation throughout that period, taking into account any material changes in the obligation. The present value of the obligation differs from the liability recognised in the balance sheet because the liability is recognised net of the fair value of any plan assets and because some actuarial gains and losses, and some past service cost, may not be recognised immediately.

C Expected return on plan assets

IAS 19.105-106   The expected return on plan assets is based on market expectations at the beginning of the period for returns over the entire life of the related obligation. The difference between the expected return and actual return on plan assets is an actuarial gain or loss.

D Actuarial gains and losses and past service cost

IAS 19.7,94   Actuarial gains and losses comprise experience adjustments (the effects of differences between the previous actuarial assumptions and what has actually occurred) and the effects of changes in actuarial assumptions. These changes may result from increases or decreases in either the present value of defined benefit obligations or the fair value of any related plan assets and may be attributable to a number of causes, for example:

- unexpectedly high or low rates of employee turnover, early retirement, mortality, increases in salaries or benefits;
- the effect of changes in estimates of future employee turnover, early retirement, mortality, increases in salaries or benefits;
- the effect of changes in the discount rate (see section 23.4.2); and
- differences between the actual return on plan assets and the expected return on plan assets.

IAS 19.92-93   IAS 19 does not require immediate recognition of actuarial gains and losses. Instead an entity need only recognise, subject to IAS 19.58A, a portion of the actuarial gains and losses as income or expense if the net cumulative unrecognised actuarial gains and losses at the end of the previous reporting period exceeded the greater of:

- 10% of the present value of the defined benefit obligation at that date (before deducting plan assets); and
- 10% of the fair value of any plan assets at that date.

assumed discount rate used to calculate the actuarial present value of benefits should reflect the rates at which the pension benefits could effectively be settled. In estimating this rate, it is acceptable to consider rates implicit in annuity contracts that could be used to settle the benefit obligation or returns on long dated gilts. Using such rates would result in a benefit cost which is likely to be greater than the eventual cost of providing the benefits through the plan because a plan could invest in potentially higher yielding assets such as equities.

B   Interest cost

The interest cost component is the increase in the projected benefit obligation (this is the actuarial present value of all benefits attributed to employee service rendered prior to the actuarial valuation date calculated using assumptions about future salary levels) due to the passage of time.

FAS 87.22

C   Actual return on plan assets

For a funded plan, the actual return on plan assets is calculated based on the fair value of the plan assets at the beginning and end of the period, adjusted for contributions and benefit payments.

FAS 87.23

D   Actuarial gains and losses and past service cost

Liabilities resulting from plan amendments or recognition of actuarial gains and losses should be recognised over the future service lives of relevant employees or, in relation to inactive participants, over the remaining life expectancy of those participants.

FAS 87.24-34

The standard specifies in detail the methods of amortising any initial surplus or deficiency, the cost of benefit improvements, i.e. prior service cost, and experience gains and losses.

The gain or loss component of the net periodic pension cost comprises (1) the difference between the actual return on plan assets and the expected return on plan assets, and (2) the amortisation of unrecognised gains and losses from previous periods (the net change in the unrecognised net gain or loss) except that it does not include changes in the projected benefit obligation occurring during the period and deferred for later recognition.

Immediate recognition of prior service cost due to a retroactive plan amendment is permitted only if the employer does not expect to obtain any future economic benefits from that amendment. Immediate recognition of gains and losses is permitted, provided that method is applied consistently each period and to all gains and losses.

Q&A FAS 87 Q19

Q&A FAS 87 Q33

FAS 87 requires that the amortisation of the transition asset or liability and the costs of each past service benefit improvement should be separately tracked. Experience gains and losses, excluding those not yet reflected in market-related values (see section 23.4.6) are dealt with on an aggregate basis and a significance test (the 10%

The above 'corridor test' needs to be applied separately for each defined benefit plan. The excess actuarial gain or loss should be recognised over the expected average remaining working lives of employees participating in the plan. However, an entity may recognise actuarial gains and losses more quickly – as long as the same systematic basis is applied consistently and to both gains and losses – even if they are within the limits of the corridor.

IAS 19.93A-D If actuarial gains and losses are recognised in the period in which they occur, an entity may choose to recognise them outside profit or loss in a 'statement of recognised income and expense' provided that this is done for all of the entity's defined benefit plans and all of its actuarial gains and losses. This statement is a statement of changes in equity and should only comprise those items specified in IAS 1 (see section 1.6.6 above). If an entity recognises actuarial gains and losses in a separate statement of recognised income and expense, it should also include in that statement any adjustments arising from the limit on recognising an asset (see section 23.4.5 below). Amounts which have been recognised directly in a statement of recognised income and expense should be recognised immediately in retained earnings and not subsequently recognised in profit or loss.

IAS 19.7 Past service cost is the increase in the present value of the defined benefit obligation for employee service in prior periods, which occurs in the current period as a result of the introduction of, or changes to, post-employment benefits or other long-term employee benefits. Past service cost may be either positive (where benefits are introduced or improved) or negative (where existing benefits are reduced).

IAS 19.96 In measuring its defined benefit liability, an entity should recognise, subject to IAS 19.58A, past service cost as an expense on a straight-line basis over the average period until the benefits become vested. If benefits vest immediately following the introduction of, or changes to, a defined benefit plan, an entity should recognise past service cost immediately.

E   Settlements and curtailments

IAS 19.112-113 A settlement occurs when an entity enters into a transaction that eliminates all further legal or constructive obligations for part or all of the benefits provided under a defined benefit plan. In some cases, an entity may acquire an insurance policy to fund some or all of the employee benefits relating to employee service in the current and prior periods. The acquisition of such a policy is not a settlement if the entity retains a legal or constructive obligation to pay further amounts if the insurer does not pay the employee benefits specified in the insurance policy.

IAS 19.111 A curtailment occurs when an entity is either demonstrably committed to make a material reduction in the number of employees covered by a plan or amends the terms of a defined benefit plan such that a material element of future service by current employees will no longer qualify for benefits, or will qualify only for reduced benefits. An event is material enough to qualify as a curtailment if the recognition of the curtailment gain or loss would have a material effect on the financial statements. Curtailments are often linked with a restructuring and, in such cases, will be accounted for at the same time as the restructuring.

corridor) is performed at the beginning of the year to assess whether amortisation is necessary.

The minimum amount required to be amortised is the beginning-of-year excess, if *FAS 87.32* any, of (a) the amount subject to amortisation over (b) a 'corridor' equal to 10% of the greater of the projected benefit obligation or the market-related value of plan assets. If amortisation is required, it equals the excess described above divided by the average remaining service period of active employees expected to receive benefits under the plan. However, if all or almost all of a plan's participants are inactive, the average remaining life expectancy of the inactive participants is required to be used instead of average remaining service.

FAS 87 permits any systematic method of amortising unrecognised gains and losses *FAS 87.33* to be used in lieu of the minimum provided that all four of the following conditions are met:

- the minimum method must be used in any period in which the minimum amortisation is greater;
- the alternative method must be applied consistently;
- the alternative method must be applied similarly to both gains and losses; and
- the alternative method used must be disclosed.

Companies with more than one plan do not necessarily have to use the same alternative amortisation method for each one. However, a company should be able to justify why different alternatives are preferable in the circumstances.

Using an alternative amortisation method may be simpler than applying the minimum method but is likely to produce results perceived to be more volatile and unpredictable than under the minimum method.

E   Settlements, curtailments and refunds

There are exceptions to the basic rule on spreading the effects of variations forward.

Settlements

If a settlement occurs thereby relieving the employer of primary responsibility for a *FAS 88.9,11,21* pension obligation, a gain or loss should be recognised in the income statement when the pension obligation is settled, unless the cost of the settlement is not material. The maximum gain or loss subject to recognition is the unrecognised net experience gain or loss plus any remaining unrecognised transitional surplus. If only part of the projected benefit obligation is settled, the employer would recognise in earnings an equivalent pro rata portion of the maximum amount.

Curtailments

A curtailment is an event that significantly reduces the expected years of future service *FAS 88.6* of present employees covered by a pension plan, or eliminates for a significant number of employees the accrual of pension benefits for some or all future services.

IAS 19.109   An entity should recognise gains or losses on the curtailment or settlement of a defined benefit plan when the curtailment or settlement occurs. The gain or loss should comprise:

- any resulting change in the present value of the defined benefit obligation;
- any resulting change in the fair value of the plan assets; and
- any related actuarial gains and losses and past service cost that had not previously been recognised.

IAS 19.110   Before determining the effect of a curtailment or settlement, an entity should remeasure the obligation and any related plan assets using current actuarial assumptions.

IAS 19.115   Where a curtailment relates to only some employees covered by a plan, or only part of an obligation is settled, the gain or loss includes a proportionate share of the previously unrecognised past service cost and actuarial gains and losses.

23.4.4   Discretionary increases to pensions in payment or to deferred pensions

IAS 19.52,98   An entity should account for constructive obligations arising from its informal practices. A constructive obligation exists where an entity's informal practices leave it with no realistic alternative but to pay employee benefits. Discretionary increases to pensions should be recognised in accordance with the guidance on past service cost. However, under- and over-estimates of discretionary pension increases, where an entity has a constructive obligation to grant such increases, should be excluded from past service cost because actuarial assumptions allow for such increases.

23.4.5   Asset valuation method

IAS 19.7   Plan assets comprise assets held by a long-term employee benefit fund and qualifying insurance policies. Assets held by a long-term employee benefit fund are assets (other than non-transferable financial instruments issued by the reporting entity) that:

- are held by an entity (a fund) that is legally separate from the reporting entity and exists solely to pay or fund employee benefits; and
- are available to be used only to pay or fund employee benefits, are not available to the reporting entity's own creditors (even in bankruptcy), and cannot be returned to the reporting entity, unless either:
  - the remaining assets of the fund are sufficient to meet all the related employee benefit obligations of the plan or the reporting entity; or
  - the assets are returned to the reporting entity to reimburse it for employee benefits already paid.

A curtailment may directly cause a decrease in the projected benefit obligation (a gain) or an increase in the projected benefit obligation (a loss). To the extent that such a gain exceeds any unrecognised experience loss (or the entire gain where an unrecognised net gains exists), it is a curtailment gain, or such a loss exceeds any unrecognised experience gain (or the entire loss where an unrecognised net loss exists), it is a curtailment loss.

FAS 88.12-14

Curtailments result in the recognition of a loss for a proportionate amount of unrecognised prior service cost, including any remaining unrecognised transition obligation (but not a transition asset). If the aggregate amount is a net loss, it should be recognised in earnings when it is probable that a curtailment will occur and the effects can be reasonably estimated. If the sum is a net gain, recognition is deferred until the related employees terminate or the plan suspension or amendment is adopted. The recognition of surpluses or deficiencies on account of curtailments is independent of the effect on funding.

Refunds

Any withdrawal (refund) of excess plan assets by an employer should be accounted for as a negative contribution, i.e. a credit to accrued or prepaid pension cost, and would not directly affect the income statement.

Q&A FAS 88 Q5

23.4.4 Discretionary increases to pensions in payment or to deferred pensions

Discretionary pension increases should be allowed for in calculating the pension cost to be attributed to a period if there is a substantive commitment to grant such increases (see section 23.4.2).

FAS 87.41

If no allowance is made for discretionary pension increases, the cost is amortised over the remaining life expectancy of the pensioners concerned if all/almost all of the plan members are inactive. Otherwise, that cost is amortised over the remaining service lives of the active members at the date of the award.

FAS 87.25

A consistently applied less detailed amortisation approach that more rapidly reduces the unrecognised cost is acceptable, e.g. straight-line amortisation over the average remaining service period of relevant employees. The alternative method used should be disclosed.

FAS 87.26

23.4.5 Asset valuation method

For the purposes of deciding whether an additional balance sheet liability should be recognised (see section 23.4.7) the plan assets should be valued at their fair value as of the measurement date.

FAS 87.49

For the purposes of determining the expected return on plan assets and calculating asset gains and losses, the 'market-related value' of plan assets should be used. This is either fair market value or a calculated value that smoothes the effect of short-term market fluctuations over a period of up to five years. To the extent that unrecognised gains and losses based on the fair value of the plan assets are not yet reflected in the market-related value, these may be excluded from the unrecognised gain or loss that is subject to amortisation in the future. Although those excluded gains or losses eventually affect net periodic pension cost in future periods, their impact is delayed through the use of market related value of plan assets.

FAS 87.50
FAS 87.30-31

A qualifying insurance policy is an insurance policy issued by an insurer that is not a related party (as defined in IAS 24 *Related Party Disclosures*) of the reporting entity, if the proceeds of the policy:

- can be used only to pay or fund employee benefits under a defined benefit plan; and

- are not available to the reporting entity's own creditors (even in bankruptcy) and cannot be paid to the reporting entity, unless either:

  - the proceeds represent surplus assets that are not needed for the policy to meet all the related employee benefit obligations; or

  - the proceeds are returned to the reporting entity to reimburse it for employee benefits already paid.

IAS 19.7,102,104 Plan assets should be measured at their fair value which is defined as the amount for which an asset could be exchanged or a liability settled between knowledgeable, willing parties in an arm's length transaction. When no market price is available, the fair value should be estimated. Where plan assets include qualifying insurance policies that exactly match the amount and timing of some or all of the benefits payable under the plan, the fair value of those insurance policies is deemed to be the present value of the related obligations, subject to any reductions required if the amounts receivable under the insurance policies are not recoverable in full.

IAS 19.104A An entity should recognise its right to reimbursement as a separate asset only when it is virtually certain that another party will reimburse some or all of the expenditure required to settle a defined benefit obligation. The entity should measure the asset at fair value. In all other respects the entity should treat that asset in the same way as plan assets. In the income statement, the expense relating to a defined benefit plan may be presented net of the amount recognised for a reimbursement.

23.4.6 Balance sheet amounts

IAS 19.54-55 The defined benefit liability to be recognised in the balance sheet is the net total of:

- the present value of the defined benefit obligation at the balance sheet date (i.e. the gross obligation before deducting the fair value of any plan assets);
- plus actuarial gains less actuarial losses not yet recognised;
- minus any past service cost not yet recognised; and
- minus the fair value at the balance sheet date of any plan assets out of which the obligations are to be settled directly.

IAS 19.58 If the amount determined above is negative, the resulting asset should be measured at the lower of:

- the amount determined above; and
- the total of:

  (i) any cumulative unrecognised net actuarial losses and past service cost; and

  (ii) the present value of any economic benefits available in the form of refunds from the plan or reductions in future contributions to the plan.

IAS 19.58A However, IAS 19 does not permit a gain (loss) to be recognised under the above rule solely as a result of an actuarial loss (gain) or past service cost in the current

23.4.6   Balance sheet amounts

A liability (unfunded accrued pension cost) is recognised if net periodic pension cost *FAS 87.35-37* recognised under FAS 87 exceeds amounts the employer has contributed to the plan.   An asset (prepaid pension cost) is recognised if net periodic cost is less than amounts the employer has contributed to the plan.

If the accumulated benefit obligation (value of accrued benefits without allowance for future salary increases) exceeds the fair value of plan assets, an additional minimum liability may be required to be shown in the balance sheet.   If an additional minimum liability is recognised, an equal amount, but not to exceed the amount of unrecognised prior service cost, should be recognised as an intangible asset.   Any amount not recognised as an intangible asset should be reported in other comprehensive income.

The measurements of plan assets and obligations should be as of the date of the *FAS 87.52* financial statements or, if used consistently, as of a date not more than three months prior to that date.

Amounts should be aggregated for all of an entity's defined benefit plans but *FAS 132(R).6* prepaid benefit costs and accrued benefit liabilities should be shown separately.

period. Instead, an entity should recognise net actuarial losses and past service costs of the current period immediately, to the extent that they exceed any reduction in the net present value of the economic benefits specified under (ii) above. Similarly, an entity should recognise net actuarial gains less past service costs of the current period immediately, to the extent that they exceed any increase in the net present value of the economic benefits specified under (ii) above.

IAS 19.116 An entity may only offset an asset relating to one plan against a liability relating to another plan when it has a legally enforceable right to use a surplus in one plan to settle obligations under the other plan and it intends either to realise the surplus and settle the obligation simultaneously or to settle the obligations on a net basis.

23.4.7 Disclosure

IAS 19.120A-121 An entity should disclose the following information about defined benefit plans:

(a) its accounting policy for recognising actuarial gains and losses;

(b) a general description of the type of plan (including informal practices that give rise to constructive obligations included in the measurement of the defined benefit obligation);

(c) a reconciliation of opening and closing balances of the present value of the defined benefit obligation showing separately, if applicable, the effects during the period attributable to each of the following:

    – current service cost;

    – interest cost;

    – contributions by plan participants;

    – actuarial gains and losses;

    – foreign currency exchange rate changes on plans measured in a currency different from the entity's presentation currency;

    – benefits paid;

    – past service cost;

    – business combinations;

    – curtailments; and

    – settlements;

(d) an analysis of the defined benefit obligation into amounts arising from plans that are wholly unfunded and amounts arising from plans that are wholly or partly funded;

(e) a reconciliation of the opening and closing balances of the fair value of plan assets and of the opening and closing balances of any reimbursement right recognised as an asset (see section 23.4.5) showing separately, if applicable, the effects during the period attributable to each of the following:

    – expected return on plan assets;

    – actuarial gains and losses;

    – foreign currency exchange rate changes on plans measured in a currency other than the entity's presentation currency;

    – contributions by the employer;

    – contributions by plan participants;

    – benefits paid;

23.4.7 Disclosure

COMMENT

In December 2003, the FASB issued Statement 132 (Revised 2003) Employers' Disclosures about Pensions and Other Postretirement Benefits. FAS 132(R) replaces FAS 132 but retains its disclosure requirements and requires additional disclosures about assets, obligations, cash flows and net periodic benefit cost. FAS 132(R) is effective for fiscal years ending after 15 December 2003.

The following disclosures are required to be made, if applicable:

FAS 132(R).5

- a reconciliation of beginning and ending balances of the projected benefit obligation for all balance sheets presented showing separately the effects attributable to:
  - service cost;
  - interest cost;
  - contributions by plan participants;
  - actuarial gains and losses;
  - foreign currency exchange rate changes;
  - benefits paid;
  - plan amendments;
  - business combinations;
  - divestitures;
  - curtailments;
  - settlements; and
  - special termination benefits;
- a reconciliation of beginning and ending balances of the fair value of plan assets for all balance sheets presented showing separately, if applicable, the effects attributable to:
  - actual return on plan assets;
  - foreign currency exchange rate changes;
  - contributions by the employer;
  - contributions by plan participants;
  - benefits paid;
  - business combinations;
  - divestitures; and
  - settlements;

    –   business combinations; and

    –   settlements;

(f) a reconciliation of the present value of the defined benefit obligation in (c) and the fair value of the plan assets in (e) to the assets and liabilities recognised in the balance sheet, showing at least:

    –   the net actuarial gains or losses not recognised in the balance sheet (see section 23.4.3D);

    –   the past service cost not recognised in the balance sheet (see section 23.4.3D);

    –   any amount not recognised as an asset because of the limit in paragraph 58(b) (see section 23.4.6);

    –   the fair value at the balance sheet date of any reimbursement right recognised as an asset (see section 23.4.5 above) together with a brief description of the link between the reimbursement right and the related obligation; and

    –   the other amounts recognised in the balance sheet;

(g) the total expense recognised in profit or loss for each of the following and the line item(s) in which they are included:

    –   current service cost;

    –   interest cost;

    –   expected return on plan assets;

    –   expected return on any reimbursement right recognised as an asset (see section 23.4.5 above);

    –   actuarial gains and losses;

    –   past service cost;

    –   the effect of any curtailment or settlement; and

    –   the effect of the limit in paragraph 58(b);

(h) the total amount recognised in the statement of recognised income and expense for each of the following:

    –   actuarial gains and losses; and

    –   the effect of the limit in paragraph 58(b);

(i) for entities that recognise actuarial gains and losses in the statement of recognised income and expense (see section 23.4.3D), the cumulative amount of actuarial gains and losses recognised in the statement of recognised income and expense;

(j) for each major category of plan assets, which shall include, but is not limited to, equity instruments, debt instruments, property, and all other assets, the percentage or amount that each major category constitutes of the fair value of the total plan assets;

(k) the amounts included in the fair value of plan assets for:

    –   each category of the entity's own financial instruments; and

    –   any property occupied by, or other assets used by, the entity;

(l) a narrative description of the basis used to determine the overall expected rate of return on assets, including the effect of the major categories of plan assets;

- the funded status of the plans, the amounts not recognised in the balance sheet, and the amounts recognised in the balance sheet for all balance sheets presented, including:
  - the amount of any unamortised prior service cost;
  - the amount of any unrecognised net gain or loss (including asset gains and losses not yet reflected in market-related value);
  - the amount of any remaining unamortised, unrecognised net obligation or net asset existing at the initial date of application of this section;
  - the net pension benefit prepaid assets or accrued liabilities; and
  - any intangible asset and the amount of accumulated other comprehensive income recognised (see section 23.4.7);
- the following information about plan assets:
  - the percentage of total plan assets represented by each major category of plan assets;
  - a narrative description of investment policies and strategies;
  - a narrative description of the basis used to determine the overall expected long-term rate of return assumption; and
  - additional disclosure is encouraged concerning assets categories and assets within categories if that information is considered useful in understanding associated risks;
- the accumulated benefit obligation for defined benefit plans;
- the benefits expected to be paid in each of the next five years, and in aggregate for the five years thereafter;
- the contributions expected to be paid to the plan during the next year;
- the amount of net periodic benefit cost recognised for all income statements presented, showing separately:
  - the service cost component;
  - the interest cost component;
  - the expected return on plan assets for the period;
  - the amortisation of the unrecognised transition obligation or transition asset;
  - the amount of recognised gains and losses;
  - the amount of prior service cost recognised; and
  - the amount of gain or loss recognised due to a settlement or curtailment;
- the amount included within other comprehensive income for the period arising from a change in the additional minimum pension liability (see section 23.4.7);
- on a weighted-average basis, the following assumptions used in the accounting for the plans: assumed discount rate; rate of compensation increase; and expected long-term rate of return on plan assets; specifying, in a tabular format, the assumptions used to determine the benefit obligation and net benefit cost;
- the measurements dates used to determine pension measurements for the pension plans that make up at least the majority of plan assets and benefit obligations;

(m)   the actual return on plan assets and the actual return on any reimbursement right recognised as an asset (see section 23.4.5);

(n)   the principal actuarial assumptions used as at the balance sheet date, including, when applicable:

-    the discount rates;

-    the expected rates of return on any plan assets for the periods presented in the financial statements;

-    the expected rates of return for the periods presented in the financial statements on any reimbursement right recognised as an asset (see section 23.4.5);

-    the expected rates of salary increases (and of changes in an index or other variable specified in the formal or constructive terms of a plan as the basis for future benefit increases); and

-    any other material actuarial assumptions used.

The actuarial assumptions should be disclosed in absolute terms (for example, as an absolute percentage) and not just as a margin between different percentages or other variables.

(o)   see section 24.3 below;

(p)   the amounts for the current annual period and previous four annual periods of:

-    the present value of the defined benefit obligation, the fair value of the plan assets and the surplus or deficit in the plan; and

-    the experience adjustments arising on:

  -    the plan liabilities expressed either as an amount or as a percentage of the plan liabilities at the balance sheet date; and

  -    the plan assets expressed either as an amount or as a percentage of the plan assets at the balance sheet date;

(q)   the employer's best estimate, as soon as it can reasonably be determined, of contributions expected to be paid to the plan during the annual period beginning after the balance sheet date.

IAS 19.122   When an entity has more than one defined benefit plan, disclosures may be made in total, separately or in such groupings as are considered to be the most useful. When groupings are used, disclosures should be in the form of weighted averages or relatively narrow ranges.

23.4.8   Implementation

IAS 19.159B-C   The amendments made to IAS 19 in December 2004 should be applied as set out below.

The following amendments apply for annual periods beginning on or after 1 January 2006 (although earlier application, appropriately disclosed, is encouraged):

- amendments relating to multi-employer plans (paragraph 32A – see section 23.6);

- amendments relating to defined benefit plans that share risks between various entities under common control (paragraphs 34-34B – see section 23.6);

- the amounts and types of securities of the employer and related parties included in plan assets, the approximate amount of future annual benefits of plan participants covered by insurance contracts issued by the employer or related parties, and any significant transactions between the employer or related parties and the plan during the period;

- any alternative amortisation method used to amortise prior service amounts or unrecognised net gains and losses (see section 23.4.4);

- any substantive commitment, such as past practice or a history of regular benefit increases, used as the basis for accounting for the benefit obligation;

- the cost of providing special or contractual termination benefits recognised during the period and a description of the nature of the event; and

- an explanation of any significant change in the benefit obligation or plan assets not otherwise apparent in the other disclosures.

Disclosures about pension plans may be aggregated, provided there is additional disclosure of: *FAS 132(R).6*

- the aggregate benefit obligation and aggregate fair value of plan assets for plans with benefit obligations in excess of plan assets; and

- the aggregate pension accumulated benefit obligation and aggregate fair value of plan assets for plans with accumulated benefit obligations in excess of plan assets.

Reduced disclosures are permitted for non-public entities. *FAS 132(R).8*

23.4.8 Implementation

For non-US plans, the statement became effective for periods beginning after 15 December 1988. On implementation, the difference between the projected benefit obligation and the fair value of plan assets as adjusted for previously recorded pension cost accruals or prepayments shown in the balance sheet (this difference is called the transition asset or liability) was generally to be amortised on a straight-line basis over the average remaining service period of the employees. If this period was less than 15 years, the entity could elect to use a 15-year period. If all or almost all of a plan's participants are inactive, the entity should use the inactive participant's average remaining life expectancy period. *FAS 87.76-77*

- amendments relating to the recognition of the components of the defined benefit cost in profit or loss (paragraph 61 – see section 23.4.3); and

- amended disclosure requirements (paragraphs 120-121 – see section 23.4.7).

The option in paragraphs 93A-93D, relating to the recognition of actuarial gains and losses outside profit or loss, may be used for accounting periods ending on or after 16 December 2004.   However, if the option is used for accounting periods beginning before 1 January 2006, the other amendments specified above should also be applied.

IAS 19.160   IAS 8 applies when an entity changes its accounting policies to reflect the changes specified in paragraphs 159B-159C.   Retrospective application is required other than for paragraph 120A(p) which may be applied prospectively from the first annual period in which the entity applies the amendments set out in paragraph 120A.

For first-time adopters of IFRS, there are specific provisions relating to the first-time application of IAS 19 set out in IFRS 1 (see Chapter 2).

> **COMMENT**
>
> The IASB has recorded reservations about certain aspects of IAS 19, including deferred recognition of actuarial gains and losses, and intends to undertake a major project on accounting for post-employment benefits.   Pending this comprehensive reconsideration and also the development of a new format for the income statement (see section 1), the IASB's amendment to IAS 19 in December 2004 allows an entity the option of recognising actuarial gains and losses in a statement of recognised income and expense as an alternative to deferred recognition or immediate recognition in profit or loss (see section 23.4.3D).

23.5   INSURANCE CONTRACTS

IAS 19.39   Where an entity pays insurance premiums to fund a post-employment benefit plan, it should treat such a plan as a defined contribution plan unless the entity has a legal or constructive obligation either to:

- pay the employee benefits directly when they fall due; or

- pay further amounts if the insurer does not pay all future employee benefits relating to employee service in the current and prior periods.

IAS 19.41   If the entity has retained such a legal or constructive obligation it should treat the plan as a defined benefit plan.   In that case, the entity recognises its rights under the qualifying insurance policy as a plan asset and recognises other insurance policies as reimbursement rights (subject to the criteria set out in section 23.4.5).

COMMENT

The SEC staff will accept, for a foreign private issuer adopting FAS 87 for the first time as of the beginning of the first period for which US GAAP data is required to be filed with the SEC, an allocation of the transition asset/liability directly to equity based on the ratio of (1) the years elapsed between 15 December 1988 and the adoption date and (2) the remaining service period of employees expected to receive benefits as estimated at the adoption date.

23.5   INSURANCE CONTRACTS

Under an annuity contract an insurance company unconditionally undertakes a legal obligation to provide specified benefits to specific individuals in return for a fixed consideration.   Some annuity contracts (participating annuity contracts) provide that the employer participates in the experience of the insurance company.   If the substance of a participating contract is such that the employer remains subject to all or most of the risks and rewards associated with the benefit obligation, that contract is not an annuity contract for the purposes of FAS 87.

FAS 87.57

To the extent that benefits currently earned are covered by annuity contracts, the cost of those benefits is the cost of purchasing the contracts.   Benefits covered by annuity contracts should be excluded from the projected benefit obligation and accumulated benefit obligation and annuity contracts should be excluded from plan assets.

FAS 87.58-60

The purchase price of a participating annuity contract is usually higher than the price of an equivalent contract without participation rights.   The difference is the cost of the participation right which should be recognised at the date of purchase as an asset.   In subsequent periods, the participation right should be measured at its fair value if the contract is such that the fair value is reasonably estimable. Otherwise, the participation right should be measured at its amortised cost, and the cost should be amortised over the expected dividend period of the contract.

FAS 87.61

23.6   MULTI-EMPLOYER AND GROUP PLANS

A   Multi-employer plans

IAS 19.7   Multi-employer plans under IAS 19 are defined contribution plans or defined benefit plans, other than state plans, that:

- pool assets contributed by various entities that are not under common control; and

- use those assets to provide benefits to employees of more than one entity, on the basis that contribution and benefit levels are determined without regard to the identity of the entity that employs the employees concerned.

IAS 19.29   An entity should classify a multi-employer plan as a defined contribution plan or a defined benefit plan under the formal terms of the plan but also taking into account any constructive obligations. If a multi-employer plan is classified as a defined contribution plan, it should be accounted for under the guidance applicable to defined contribution plans.

If a multi-employer plan is classified as a defined benefit plan, the entity should account for its proportionate share of the defined benefit obligation, plan assets and costs associated with the plan in the same way as for any other defined benefit plan. The entity should disclose the same information as is required for any other defined benefit plan (see section 23.4.7).

IAS 19.30   If insufficient information is available to use defined benefit accounting for a multi-employer plan that is a defined benefit plan, an entity should:

- account for the plan as if it were a defined contribution plan;

- disclose the fact that the plan is a defined benefit plan and the reason why insufficient information is available to account for it as such; and

- to the extent that a surplus or deficit in the plan may affect future contributions, disclose:
    - any available information about that surplus or deficit;
    - the basis used to determine the surplus or deficit; and
    - any implications for the entity.

IAS 19.32A   There may be a contractual agreement between a multi-employer plan and its participants that determines how a surplus or deficit in the plan will be distributed or funded. Where such an agreement exists and the plan is accounted for as a defined contribution plan, a plan participant should recognise the asset or liability arising from the agreement and the resulting income or expense should be recognised in profit or loss.

IAS 19.32B   In accordance with IAS 37 (see section 18.2.2), a participant in a multi-employer plan should also disclose any contingent liabilities relating to its responsibilities to share the risks for financing the multi-employer plan.

IAS 19.36   An entity should account for state plans in the same way as for a multi-employer plan. State plans are described as plans established by legislation to cover all entities (or all entities in a particular category) and which are operated by national or local government or by another body which is not subject to control or influence by the reporting entity.

23.6   MULTI-EMPLOYER PLANS

A multi-employer plan under FAS 87 is a plan to which, usually pursuant to a *FAS 87.67*
collective-bargaining agreement, more than one unrelated employer contributes.
In a multi-employer plan the assets contributed by one participating employer may
be used to provide benefits to employees of other participating employers, as the
assets in such plans are not segregated or restricted to provide benefits to employees
of that one employer.

A company participating in a multi-employer plan recognises as net pension costs *FAS 87.68*
the required contribution for the period and recognises as a liability any
contributions due and unpaid.

B   *Group plans*

IAS 19.34-34A   Defined benefit plans that share risks between various entities under common control, for example, a parent and its subsidiaries, are not multi-employer plans. An entity which participates in such a plan should obtain information about the plan as a whole, measured in accordance with IAS 19 and using assumptions which apply to the plan as a whole.   If there is a contractual agreement or stated policy for charging the net defined benefit cost of the plan as a whole to individual entities, each entity should recognise the amount it has been charged.   In the absence of such an agreement or policy, the net defined benefit cost should be recognised in the separate or individual financial statements of the entity which is the legal sponsoring employer with other entities recognising in their separate or individual financial statements a cost equal to their contributions payable for the period.

IAS 19.34B   Participation in such a plan is a related party transaction for each individual group entity and IAS 19 requires the following additional disclosures in an entity's separate or individual financial statements:

- the contractual agreement or stated policy for charging the net defined benefit cost or the fact that there is no such policy;

- the policy for determining the contribution to be paid by the entity;

- if the entity accounts for an allocation of the net defined benefit cost, all the information about the plan as a whole should be disclosed (see section 23.4.7); and

- if the entity accounts for the contribution payable for the period, information about the plan as a whole as specified in paragraph 34B.

Section 24

Post-employment benefits other than pensions

24.1 AUTHORITATIVE PRONOUNCEMENTS

- IAS 19 (amended December 2004)

COMMENT

IAS 19 prescribes the accounting treatment for all employee benefits except those to which IFRS 2 *Share-based Payment* applies (see section 22). The following categories of employee benefits are covered by IAS 19:

- pensions, which are covered in section 23;
- post-employment life assurance and medical care, which are covered in section 24;
- short-term employee benefits, which are dealt with in section 25.2;
- termination benefits, which are discussed in section 25.3; and
- other long-term employee benefits, which are covered in section 25.4.

24.2 MEASUREMENT

IAS 19.24   IAS 19 requires application of the same rules to retirement benefits (such as pensions) and to other post-employment benefits (such as post-employment life insurance and post-employment medical care). The description given here of the accounting treatment for post-employment benefits other than pensions differs only in form from that in section 23. The IAS 19 requirements are in substance duplicated in this section in order to facilitate comparison.

The general approach of IAS 19 is to require an entity to recognise:

- a liability when an employee has provided service in exchange for employee benefits to be paid in the future; and
- an expense when the entity consumes the economic benefit arising from service provided by an employee in exchange for employee benefits.

IAS 19 recognises the possibility that post-employment benefits other than pensions may be defined contribution plans. For a description of the applicable accounting requirements in such cases, see section 23.3. In the remainder of this section it is assumed that post-employment benefits other than pensions constitute a defined benefit plan.

Section 24   Post-employment benefits other than pensions

24.1   AUTHORITATIVE PRONOUNCEMENTS

- FAS 106
- FAS 132 (R)
- EITF 93-3

COMMENT

A number of specific accounting standards describe the accounting for different types of employee benefits. This section deals with post-retirement benefits other than pensions. Pension benefits are covered by section 23. Other employee benefits are covered by section 25.

24.2   MEASUREMENT

FAS 106 *Employers' Accounting for Postretirement Benefits Other than Pensions* applies to all employer sponsored post-retirement benefit plans which provide benefits other than pensions (the most common types are health care, dental care and/or life insurance benefits) to current and past employees, their beneficiaries and covered dependents. The standard requires businesses to estimate the total future cost of providing such benefits and recognise that cost as an expense as employees render services, instead of when benefits are paid.   *FAS 106.5-6*

The measurement of obligations and cost under FAS 106 is based on accounting for the substantive plan obligations, assumptions and attribution.

24.2.1   Measurement of cost and obligation

A   *Identifying the substantive plan*

IAS 19.52-53   An entity should account for both its legal obligation under the formal terms of a defined benefit plan and for any constructive obligation arising from the entity's informal practices. A constructive obligation exists where an entity's informal practices leave it with no realistic alternative but to pay employee benefits.   In the absence of evidence to the contrary, accounting for post-employment benefits assumes that an entity which is currently promising such benefits will continue to do so over the remaining working lives of employees.

B   *Assumptions*

IAS 19.72-73,77   Actuarial (demographic and financial) assumptions should be unbiased, mutually compatible and represent the entity's best estimates of the variables that will determine the ultimate cost of providing post-employment benefits.   Financial assumptions must be based on market expectations at the balance sheet date for the period over which the obligations are to be settled.

IAS 19.78   The rate used to discount the post-employment benefit obligations should be determined by reference to the market yields on high quality corporate bonds at the balance sheet date.   In countries where there is no deep market in such bonds, the market yields (at the balance sheet date) on government bonds should be used.

IAS 19.83   Post-employment benefit obligations should reflect:

- estimated future salary increases;
- the benefits set out in the formal plan and those resulting from any constructive obligations at the balance sheet date; and
- estimated future changes in the level of any state benefits that affect the benefits payable under a defined benefit plan if (1) those changes were enacted before the balance sheet date or (2) past history or other evidence indicates that those state benefits will change in some predictable manner.

IAS 19.88-90   The assumptions about medical costs should take account of inflation as well as specific changes in medical costs.   The measurement of post-employment medical benefits requires assumptions about the level and frequency of future claims and the cost of meeting those claims.   Estimates of future medical costs will take into account historic data and will consider the effect of technological advances, changes in health care utilisation or delivery patterns and changes in the health status of plan participants.   Historic data on the level and frequency of claims should be adjusted for changes in the demographic mix of the participants and where there is reliable evidence that historical trends will not continue.

24.2.1   Estimating the benefit obligation

A   Identifying the substantive plan

The basis for estimating the post-retirement benefit obligation should be the   *FAS 106.23*
'substantive plan', or the terms the employee understands and expects will be the
basis for computing his/her post-retirement benefits.   Generally, the substantive
plan will be the extant written plan.   However, there can be situations, e.g. where
there has been past practice of regular increases in certain monetary benefits, which
indicate that the substantive plan includes more than, or is different from, the
written plan document.

B   Assumptions

Estimating the expected post-retirement benefit obligation requires actuarial   *FAS 106.29-42*
techniques and the use of assumptions about future events.   Each assumption used
should individually represent the best estimate of a particular future event.

Principal actuarial assumptions include:

- the probability of payment, e.g. staff turnover, mortality, retirement ages;
- the medical costs for a retiree or dependent at each age during the
  post-retirement period, i.e. the 'per capita claims cost by age';
- future increases in the costs of providing the promised benefits, referred to as
  the 'health care cost trend rate';
- the expected long-term rate of return on plan assets; and
- the appropriate discount rate for determining the present value of expected
  future cash outflows at a given measurement date.

FAS 106 provides guidance on estimating the explicit assumptions that have to be
applied in determining the post-retirement benefit obligation.

The discount rate used to calculate the present value of future benefit payment   *FAS 106.31*
streams should be based on the current rate of return on high-quality, fixed-income
investments whose cash flows match the timing and amount of expected benefit
payments.   This rate will fluctuate year-to-year based on market changes.

The expected long-term rate of return on plan assets should reflect the average rate of   *FAS 106.32*
earnings expected on the existing plan assets and contributions to the plan expected to
be made during the period.   Clearly, this assumption is only appropriate for plans
that are funded (in the US, the majority of plans are unfunded).

For a pay-related plan, assumed compensation levels should reflect the best estimate   *FAS 106.33*
of the actual future compensation levels of the individual employees involved,
including future changes attributed to general price levels, productivity, seniority,
promotion, and other factors.   All assumptions should be consistent to the extent
that each reflects expectations about the same future economic conditions, such as
future rates of inflation.

C　Attribution

IAS 19.64-66　An entity should determine the present value of defined benefit obligations, the related current service cost and, where applicable, past service cost in accordance with the projected unit credit method.　The projected unit credit method sees each period of service as giving rise to an additional unit of benefit entitlement and measures each unit separately to build up the final obligation.　IAS 19 provides an example to illustrate this.　An entity should discount the whole post-employment benefit obligation, even if part of it falls due within twelve months of the balance sheet date (see section 24.2.1B).

IAS 19.67-71　In determining such amounts, the entity should attribute benefits to periods of service under the plan's benefit formula.　If an employee's service in later years will lead to a materially higher level of benefit than in earlier years, the entity should attribute benefits on a straight-line basis from:

- the date when service by the employee first leads to benefits under the plan; until

- the date when further service by the employee will lead to no material amount of further benefits under the plan, other than from further salary increases.

IAS 19 provides additional guidance, including illustrative examples, on the application of the Projected Unit Credit Method.

24.2.2　Net periodic post-retirement benefit cost

IAS 19.61　IAS 19 identifies the following seven components of annual post-employment benefit cost:

- current service cost;
- interest cost;
- the expected return on any plan assets and on any reimbursement rights;
- actuarial gains and losses as required by the entity's accounting policy;
- past service cost;
- the effect of any curtailments or settlements; and
- the effect of the limit in recognising an asset (see paragraph 58(b)) unless it is recognised outside profit and loss.

The net total of the above should be recognised in profit or loss, except to the extent that another Standard requires or permits their inclusion in the cost of an asset.

An employer's share of the expected future post-retirement health care cost for a plan participant is developed by reducing the assumed per capita claims cost at each age at which the plan participant is expected to receive benefits under the plan by: *FAS 106.34-42*

- the effects of coverage by external providers of health care benefits, e.g. Medicare; and

- the effects of the cost-sharing provisions of the plan.

The assumed per capita claims cost should be the best estimate of the expected future cost of the benefits covered by the plan. The standard provides extensive guidance on how the employer should obtain the best estimate of those costs.

C   *Attribution*

An equal amount of the expected post-retirement benefit obligations for an employee generally should be attributed to each year of service in the attribution period. However, if the plan attributes a disproportionate share of the expected post-retirement benefits obligation to employees' early years of service then the costs should be attributed in accordance with the plan's benefit formula. The attribution period normally starts on the date of hire, or at the start of the credited service period at the latest. In all cases, the end of the attribution period should be the full eligibility date.   *FAS 106.43-44*

24.2.2   Net periodic post-retirement benefit cost

The annual expense recognised in the employer's income statement is referred to as the net periodic post-retirement benefit cost. This comprises six components: *FAS 106.46*

- service cost;

- interest cost;

- actual return on plan assets, if any;

- amortisation of unrecognised prior service cost, if any;

- gain or loss (including the effects of changes in assumptions) to the extent recognised; and

- amortisation of the unrecognised net obligation or unrecognised net asset existing at the date of initial application of FAS 106.

A   *Service cost*

The service cost represents the actuarial present value of the portion of the expected post-retirement benefit obligation attributed to employee service during the period.   *FAS 106.47*

IAS 19.56-57   The entity should determine the present value of defined benefit obligations and the fair value of plan assets frequently enough to ensure that the amounts recognised in the financial statements do not differ materially from the amounts that would be determined at the balance sheet date.   If the entity uses amounts determined before the balance sheet date, it should update the results of the valuation to take account of any material transactions or changes in circumstances up to the balance sheet date.   The involvement of a qualified actuary in the measurement of material post-employment benefits is encouraged but not required.

A   Current service cost

IAS 19.64   The current service cost, which should be determined using the projected unit credit method, is the actuarial present value of benefits attributed to services rendered by employees during the period.

B   Interest cost

IAS 19.7,82   Interest cost is the increase during a period in the present value of a defined benefit obligation that arises because the benefits are one period closer to settlement. Interest cost is calculated by multiplying the discount rate (see section 24.2.1B) at the beginning of the period by the present value of the defined benefit obligation throughout that period, taking into account any material changes in the obligation. The present value of the obligation differs from the liability recognised in the balance sheet because the liability is recognised net of the fair value of any plan assets and because some actuarial gains and losses, and some past service cost, may not be recognised immediately.

C   Expected return on plan assets

IAS 19.105-106   The expected return on plan assets is based on market expectations at the beginning of the period for returns over the entire life of the related obligation.   The difference between the expected return and actual return on plan assets is an actuarial gain or loss (see section 24.2.2D below).

D   Actuarial gains and losses

IAS 19.7,94   Actuarial gains and losses comprise experience adjustments (the effects of differences between the previous actuarial assumptions and what has actually occurred) and the effects of changes in actuarial assumptions.   These changes may result from increases or decreases in either the present value of defined benefit obligation or the fair value of any related plan assets and may be attributable to a number of causes, for example:

- unexpectedly high or low rates of employee turnover, early retirement, mortality, increases in salaries, benefits or medical costs;
- the effect of changes in estimates of future employee turnover, early retirement, mortality, increases in salaries, benefits or medical costs;
- the effect of changes in the discount rate (see section 24.2.2A); and
- differences between the actual return on plan assets and the expected return on plan assets.

IAS 19.92-93   IAS 19 does not require immediate recognition of actuarial gains and losses.   Instead an entity need only recognise, subject to IAS 19.58A, a portion of the actuarial gains

B   Interest cost

Interest cost reflects the imputed growth in the accumulated post-retirement benefit obligation because of the passage of time. In many cases, the interest cost for a year will equal the accumulated post-retirement benefit obligation at the beginning of the year multiplied by the assumed discount rate at the beginning of the year.   *FAS 106.48*

C   Actual return on plan assets

For a funded plan, the actual return on plan assets should be determined based on the fair value of plan assets at the beginning and end of the period, adjusted for contributions and benefit payments.   *FAS 106.49*

D   Amortisation of prior service cost

Prior service cost represents the cost of additional benefits resulting from a plan amendment that are attributed to employee service in prior years. Prior service cost should be amortised and recognised as a component of net periodic post-retirement benefit cost by assigning equal amounts to each of the years in the remaining service period (to full eligibility date) of each member of the plan at the date of the amendment. The use of alternative amortisation methods is permitted only if they result in a faster amortisation profile.   *FAS 106.50-54*

In the case of plan amendments that reduce benefits, the reduction in the accumulated post-retirement benefit obligation (or negative prior service cost) should be first offset against any previously unrecognised prior service cost and then any unrecognised transition obligation (see section 24.4). After this offsetting, the remaining negative prior service cost should be recognised in the same manner as positive prior service costs.   *FAS 106.55*

E   Actuarial gains and losses

Gains and losses arise when the actual experience of the plan is different from initial estimate, changes in actuarial assumptions or if the actual return on assets, if any, differs from the expected return. Because gains and losses can fluctuate significantly from year to year, recognition of these amounts may be deferred. However, if the cumulative net amount of previously unrecognised gains or losses exceeds 10% of the accumulated post-retirement benefit obligation, that excess portion must be amortised into income over the average remaining service period to retirement date of active plan participants. Alternative amortisation methods can be used if they result in equal or greater amortisation amounts.   *FAS 106.56-62*

Plan asset gains and losses (the difference between the expected and actual returns on plan assets) not yet reflected in the market-related value of plan assets are not required to be amortised. Although these excluded gains or losses eventually affect the net periodic post-retirement benefit cost in future periods, their impact is delayed through the use of market related value of plan assets. The expected return on plan assets is calculated by multiplying the expected long-term rate of return on plan assets by the market-related value of plan assets.

and losses as income or expense if the net cumulative unrecognised actuarial gains and losses at the end of the previous reporting period exceeded the greater of:

- 10% of the present value of the defined benefit obligation at that date (before deducting plan assets); and
- 10% of the fair value of any plan assets at that date.

The above 'corridor test' needs to be applied separately for each defined benefit plan. The excess actuarial gain or loss should be recognised over the expected average remaining working lives of employees participating in the plan. However, an entity may recognise actuarial gains and losses more quickly – as long as the same systematic basis is applied consistently and to both gains and losses – even if they are within the limits of the corridor.

IAS 19.93A-D   If actuarial gains and losses are recognised in the period in which they occur, an entity may choose to recognise them outside profit or loss in a 'statement of recognised income and expense' provided that this is done for all of the entity's defined benefit plans and all of its actuarial gains and losses. This statement is a statement of changes in equity and should only comprise those items specified in IAS 1 (see section 1.6.6 above). If an entity recognises actuarial gains and losses in a separate statement of recognised income and expense, it should also include in that statement any adjustments arising from the limit on recognising an asset (see section 24.2.4). Amounts which have been recognised directly in a statement of recognised income and expense should be recognised immediately in retained earnings and not subsequently recognised in profit or loss.

E   Past service cost

IAS 19.7   Past service cost is the increase in the present value of the defined benefit obligation for employee service in prior periods, which occurs in the current period as a result of the introduction of, or changes to, post-employment benefits or other long-term employee benefits. Past service cost may be either positive (where benefits are introduced or improved) or negative (where existing benefits are reduced).

IAS 19.96   In measuring its defined benefit liability, an entity should recognise, subject to IAS 19.58A, past service cost as an expense on a straight-line basis over the average period until the benefits become vested. If benefits vest immediately following the introduction of, or changes to, a defined benefit plan, an entity should recognise past service cost immediately.

24.2.3   Valuation of plan assets

IAS 19.7   Plan assets comprise assets held by a long-term employee benefit fund and qualifying insurance policies, both of which are defined in IAS 19 paragraph 7 (see section 23.4.5).

IAS 19.7,102,104   Plan assets should be measured at their fair value which is defined as the amount for which an asset could be exchanged or a liability settled between knowledgeable, willing parties in an arm's length transaction. When no market price is available, the fair value should be estimated. Where plan assets include qualifying insurance policies that exactly match the amount and timing of some or all of the benefits payable under the plan, the fair value of those insurance policies is deemed to be the

24.2.3   Valuation of plan assets

Plan assets should be effectively segregated and restricted so that they cannot be used by the employer for other purposes.   If a trust is established to fund post-retirement benefit obligations it is not necessary to determine that the trust is bankruptcy-proof, i.e. the trust assets are insulated from the claims of the creditors in bankruptcy, for the assets of the trust to qualify as plan assets.   Assets held in a trust which explicitly provides that they are available to the general creditors of the employer in the event of its bankruptcy, however, do not qualify as plan assets. *FAS 106.63-64*
EITF 93-3

For the purposes of disclosure in the notes to the accounts, plan assets should be measured at their fair value as of the measurement date. *FAS 106.65-66*

present value of the related obligations, subject to any reductions required if the amounts receivable under the insurance policies are not recoverable in full.

IAS 19.104A An entity should recognise its right to reimbursement as a separate asset, only when it is virtually certain that another party will reimburse some or all of the expenditure required to settle a defined benefit obligation.   The entity should measure the asset at fair value.   In all other respects the entity should treat that asset in the same way as plan assets.   In the income statement, the expense relating to a defined benefit plan may be presented net of the amount recognised for a reimbursement.

24.2.4   Balance sheet amounts

IAS 19.54-55 The defined benefit liability to be recognised in the balance sheet is the net total of:
*   the present value of the defined benefit obligation at the balance sheet date (i.e. the gross obligation before deducting the fair value of any plan assets);
*   plus actuarial gains less actuarial losses not yet recognised;
*   minus any past service cost not yet recognised; and
*   minus the fair value at the balance sheet date of any plan assets out of which the obligations are to be settled directly.

IAS 19.58 If the amount determined above is negative, the resulting asset should be measured at the lower of:
*   the amount determined above; and
*   the total of:
    (i)   any cumulative unrecognised net actuarial losses and past service cost; and
    (ii)   the present value of any economic benefits available in the form of refunds from the plan or reductions in future contributions to the plan.

IAS 19.58A However, IAS 19 does not permit a gain (loss) to be recognised under the above rule solely as a result of an actuarial loss (gain) or past service cost in the current period.   Instead, an entity should recognise net actuarial losses and past service costs of the current period immediately, to the extent that they exceed any reduction in the net present value of the economic benefits specified under (ii) above. Similarly, an entity should recognise net actuarial gains less past service costs of the current period immediately, to the extent that they exceed any increase in the net present value of the economic benefits specified under (ii) above.

IAS 19.116 An entity may only offset an asset relating to one plan against a liability relating to another plan when it has a legally enforceable right to use a surplus in one plan to settle obligations under the other plan and it intends either to realise the surplus and settle the obligation simultaneously or to settle the obligations on a net basis.

24.2.5   Settlements and curtailments

IAS 19.112-113 A settlement occurs when an entity enters into a transaction that eliminates all further legal or constructive obligations for part or all of the benefits provided under a defined benefit plan.   In some cases, an entity may acquire an insurance policy to fund some or all of the employee benefits relating to employee service in the current and prior periods.   The acquisition of such a policy is not a settlement if the entity retains a legal or constructive obligation to pay further amounts if the

For the purposes of determining the expected return on plan assets and calculating asset gains and losses, the 'market-related value' of plan assets should be used. This is either fair market value or a calculated value that smoothes the effect of short-term market fluctuations over a period of up to five years.   *FAS 106.57*

24.2.4   Balance sheet amounts

The post-retirement benefit obligation amount in the balance sheet comprises the aggregate effect of:

- accruals of net periodic post-retirement benefit cost;
- contributions to the plan or direct benefit payments by the company; and
- where applicable, immediate recognition of the transition obligation (asset) as a cumulative effect of an accounting change.

The measurements of plan assets and obligations should be as of the date of the financial statements or, if used consistently, as of a date not more than three months prior to that date.   *FAS 106.72*

24.2.5   Settlements and curtailments

The effects of plan amendments and gains and losses usually are recognised on a deferred basis. In certain circumstances, e.g. settlements and curtailments, however, recognition of some or all of those previously deferred items may be appropriate.

A   Settlements

If a settlement occurs thereby relieving the employer of primary responsibility for a post-retirement benefit obligation, e.g. through a lump sum payment to plan   *FAS 106.90-93*

insurer does not pay the employee benefits specified in the insurance policy.

IAS 19.111   A curtailment occurs when an entity is either demonstrably committed to make a material reduction in the number of employees covered by a plan or amends the terms of a defined benefit plan such that a material element of future service by current employees will no longer qualify for benefits, or will qualify only for reduced benefits.   An event is material enough to qualify as a curtailment if the recognition of the curtailment gain or loss would have a material effect on the financial statements.   Curtailments are often linked with a restructuring and, in such cases, will be accounted for at the same time as the restructuring.

IAS 19.109   An entity should recognise gains or losses on the curtailment or settlement of a defined benefit plan when the curtailment or settlement occurs.   The gain or loss should comprise:

- any resulting change in the present value of the defined benefit obligation;
- any resulting change in the fair value of the plan assets; and
- any related actuarial gains and losses and past service cost that had not previously been recognised.

IAS 19.110   Before determining the effect of a curtailment or settlement, an entity should remeasure the obligation and any related plan assets using current actuarial assumptions.

IAS 19.115   Where a curtailment relates to only some employees covered by a plan or only part of an obligation is settled, the gain or loss includes a proportionate share of the previously unrecognised past service cost and actuarial gains and losses.

24.3   DISCLOSURE

IAS 19.120A-121   An entity should disclose the following information about defined benefit plans:

(a)   its accounting policy for recognising actuarial gains and losses;

(b)   a general description of the type of plan (including informal practices that give rise to constructive obligations included in the measurement of the defined benefit obligation);

(c)   a reconciliation of opening and closing balances of the present value of the defined benefit obligation showing separately, if applicable, the effects during the period attributable to each of the following:

- current service cost;
- interest cost;
- contributions by plan participants;
- actuarial gains and losses;

members in exchange for their right to receive specified post-retirement benefits or purchasing non-participating insurance contract, the maximum settlement gain or loss is equal to the unrecognised net gain or loss plus any unrecognised transitional asset. The amount of the maximum gain or loss to be recognised is determined based on the percentage reduction of the accumulated post-retirement benefit obligation from the settlement. In other words, if 50% of the accumulated post-retirement benefit obligation is settled, 50% of the maximum settlement gain or loss would be recognised. However, before any benefit obligation settlement gain can be recognised, it first must be offset against any remaining unrecognised net obligation at the date of initial implementation.

B   Curtailments

A curtailment is an event that: *FAS 106.96-99*

- causes a significant reduction in the expected years of future service of present employees covered by the plan; or

- eliminates the accrual of post-retirement benefits for future services for a significant number of employees covered by the plan.

Curtailments include termination of employees' services earlier than expected, e.g. due to closure of a facility; or termination or suspension of a plan so that employees do not earn additional benefits for future service.

The net gain/loss from a curtailment is the sum of two distinct components:

- prior service cost write off, which represents the loss attributable to unrecognised prior service cost (including unrecognised transition obligation) associated with years of service no longer expected to be rendered; and

- curtailment gain or loss, which is the change in the accumulated post-retirement benefit obligation directly caused by the curtailment. If a curtailment gain arises, i.e. decrease in the accumulated post-retirement benefit obligation, the gain must first offset any unrecognised net loss before it can be recognised. In the case of a curtailment loss, the loss must first be offset by any unrecognised net gain (including unrecognised transition asset) before it can be recognised.

24.3   DISCLOSURE

The following disclosures are required to be made, if applicable, similar to those for   *FAS 132(R).5*
pension plans (see section 23.4.8):

- a detailed reconciliation of beginning and ending balances of the accumulated post-retirement benefit obligation;

- a reconciliation of beginning and ending balances of the fair value of plan assets;

- the funded status of the plans, the amounts not recognised in the statement of financial position, and the amounts recognised in the statement of financial position;

- the following information about plan assets:
    - the percentage of total plan assets represented by each major category of plan assets;
    - a narrative description of investment policies and strategies;

- foreign currency exchange rate changes on plans measured in a currency different from the entity's presentation currency;
- benefits paid;
- past service cost;
- business combinations;
- curtailments; and
- settlements;

(d) an analysis of the defined benefit obligation into amounts arising from plans that are wholly unfunded and amounts arising from plans that are wholly or partly funded;

(e) a reconciliation of the opening and closing balances of the fair value of plan assets and of the opening and closing balances of any reimbursement right recognised as an asset (see section 24.2.3) showing separately, if applicable, the effects during the period attributable to each of the following:

- expected return on plan assets;
- actuarial gains and losses;
- foreign currency exchange rate changes on plans measured in a currency other than the entity's presentation currency;
- contributions by the employer;
- contributions by plan participants;
- benefits paid;
- business combinations; and
- settlements;

(f) a reconciliation of the present value of the defined benefit obligation in (c) and the fair value of the plan assets in (e) to the assets and liabilities recognised in the balance sheet, showing at least:

- the net actuarial gains or losses not recognised in the balance sheet (see section 24.2.2D);
- the past service cost not recognised in the balance sheet (see section 24.2.2E);
- any amount not recognised as an asset because of the limit in paragraph 58(b) (see section 24.2.4);
- the fair value at the balance sheet date of any reimbursement right recognised as an asset (see section 24.2.3) together with a brief description of the link between the reimbursement right and the related obligation; and
- the other amounts recognised in the balance sheet;

(g) the total expense recognised in profit or loss for each of the following and the line item(s) in which they are included:

- current service cost;
- interest cost;
- expected return on plan assets;
- expected return on any reimbursement right recognised as an asset (see section 24.2.3);

- a narrative description of the basis used to determine the overall expected long-term rate of return assumption; and

- additional disclosure is encouraged concerning assets categories and assets within categories if that information is considered useful in understanding associated risks;

- the benefits expected to be paid in each of the next five years, and in aggregate for the five years thereafter;

- the contributions expected to be paid to the plan during the next year;

- the amount of net periodic benefit cost recognised;

- on a weighted-average basis, the following assumptions used in the accounting for the plans: assumed discount rate; and, expected long-term rate of return on plan assets; specifying, in a tabular format, the assumptions used to determine the benefit obligation and net benefit cost;

- the measurements dates used to determine pension measurements for the pension plans that make up at least the majority of plan assets and benefit obligations;

- the assumed health care cost trend rate(s) for the next year used to measure the expected cost of benefits covered by the plan and a general description of the direction and pattern of change in the assumed trend rates thereafter, together with the ultimate trend rate and when that rate is expected to be achieved;

- the effect of a one-percentage-point increase and the effect of a one-percentage-point decrease in the assumed health care cost trend rates on:

  - the aggregate of the service and interest cost components of net periodic post-retirement benefit cost; and

  - the accumulated post-retirement benefit obligation;

- the amounts and types of securities of the employer and related parties included in plan assets, the approximate amount of future annual benefits of plan participants covered by insurance contracts issued by the employer or related parties, and any significant transactions between the employer or related parties and the plan during the period;

- any alternative amortisation method used to amortise prior service amounts or unrecognised net gains and losses (see section 24.2.2);

- any substantive commitment, such as past practice or a history of regular benefit increases, used as the basis for accounting for the benefit obligation;

- the cost of providing special or contractual termination benefits recognised during the period and a description of the nature of the event; and

- an explanation of any significant change in the benefit obligation or plan assets not otherwise apparent in the other disclosures.

Disclosures about post-retirement plans may be aggregated, provided there is additional disclosure of the aggregate benefit obligation and aggregate fair value of plan assets for plans with benefit obligations in excess of plan assets. *FAS 132(R).6*

Reduced disclosures are permitted for non-public entities. *FAS 132(R).8*

–   actuarial gains and losses;

–   past service cost;

–   the effect of any curtailment or settlement; and

–   the effect of the limit in paragraph 58(b);

(h)   the total amount recognised in the statement of recognised income and expense for each of the following:

–   actuarial gains and losses; and

–   the effect of the limit in paragraph 58(b);

(i)   for entities that recognise actuarial gains and losses in the statement of recognised income and expense (see section 24.2.2D), the cumulative amount of actuarial gains and losses recognised in the statement of recognised income and expense;

(j)   for each major category of plan assets, which shall include, but is not limited to, equity instruments, debt instruments, property, and all other assets, the percentage or amount that each major category constitutes of the fair value of the total plan assets;

(k)   the amounts included in the fair value of plan assets for:

–   each category of the entity's own financial instruments; and

–   any property occupied by, or other assets used by, the entity;

(l)   a narrative description of the basis used to determine the overall expected rate of return on assets, including the effect of the major categories of plan assets;

(m)   the actual return on plan assets and the actual return on any reimbursement right recognised as an asset (see section 24.2.3);

(n)   the principal actuarial assumptions used as at the balance sheet date, including, when applicable:

–   the discount rates;

–   the expected rates of return on any plan assets for the periods presented in the financial statements;

–   the expected rates of return for the periods presented in the financial statements on any reimbursement right recognised as an asset (see section 24.2.3);

–   the expected rates of salary increases (and of changes in an index or other variable specified in the formal or constructive terms of a plan as the basis for future benefit increases);

–   medical cost trend rates; and

–   any other material actuarial assumptions used.

The actuarial assumptions should be disclosed in absolute terms (for example, as an absolute percentage) and not just as a margin between different percentages or other variables.

(o)   the effect of an increase of one percentage point and the effect of a decrease of one percentage point in the assumed medical cost trend rates on:

–   the aggregate of the current service cost and interest cost components of net periodic post-employment medical costs; and

–   the accumulated post-employment benefit obligation for medical costs.

For the purposes of this disclosure, all other assumptions should be held constant. For plans operating in a high inflation environment, the disclosure should be the effect of a percentage increase or decrease in the assumed medical cost trend rate of a significance similar to one percentage point in a low inflation environment.

(p)   the amounts for the current annual period and previous four annual periods of:

–   the present value of the defined benefit obligation, the fair value of the plan assets and the surplus or deficit in the plan; and

–   the experience adjustments arising on:

      –   the plan liabilities expressed either as an amount or as a percentage of the plan liabilities at the balance sheet date; and

      –   the plan assets expressed either as an amount or as a percentage of the plan assets at the balance sheet date; and

(q)   the employer's best estimate, as soon as it can reasonably be determined, of contributions expected to be paid to the plan during the annual period beginning after the balance sheet date.

IAS 19.122   When an entity has more than one defined benefit plan, disclosures may be made in total, separately or in such groupings as are considered to be the most useful. When groupings are used, disclosures should be in the form of weighted averages or relatively narrow ranges.

24.4   IMPLEMENTATION

IAS 19.159B-C   The amendments made to IAS 19 in December 2004 should be applied as set out below.

The following amendments apply for annual periods beginning on or after 1 January 2006 (although earlier application, appropriately disclosed, is encouraged):

- amendments relating to multi-employer plans (paragraph 32A – see section 24.6);

- amendments relating to defined benefit plans that share risks between various entities under common control (paragraphs 34-34B – see section 24.6);

- amendments relating to the recognition of the components of the defined benefit cost in profit or loss (paragraph 61 – see section 24.2.2); and

- amended disclosure requirements (paragraphs 120-121 – see section 24.3).

The option in paragraphs 93A-93D, relating to the recognition of actuarial gains and losses outside profit or loss, may be used for accounting periods ending on or after 16 December 2004. However, if the option is used for accounting periods beginning before 1 January 2006, the other amendments specified above should also be applied.

IAS 19.160   IAS 8 applies when an entity changes its accounting policies to reflect the changes specified in paragraphs 159B-159C. Retrospective application is required other than for paragraph 120A(p) which may be applied prospectively from the first annual period in which the entity applies the amendments set out in paragraph 120A.

For first-time adopters of IFRS, there are specific provisions relating to the first-time application of IAS 19 set out in IFRS 1 (see Chapter 2).

24.4   IMPLEMENTATION

For public companies and companies with plans with more than 500 members in total, FAS 106 became effective for years beginning after 15 December 1992.   For all other plans (including non-US plans), FAS 106 became effective for years beginning after 15 December 1994.   On implementation, the difference between the accumulated post-retirement benefit obligation and plan assets (if any), minus any post-retirement benefit obligation liabilities recorded in the balance sheet (this amount is referred to as the transition obligation) is generally amortised on a straight-line basis over the average remaining employee service period (see section 24.2.2).   If the remaining service period was less than 20 years, an optional 20-year period could be used.

FAS 106.108-113

24.5   INSURANCE CONTRACTS

IAS 19.39   Where an entity pays insurance premiums to fund a post-employment benefit plan, it should treat such a plan as a defined contribution plan unless the entity has a legal or constructive obligation either to:

- pay the employee benefits directly when they fall due; or
- pay further amounts if the insurer does not pay all future employee benefits relating to employee service in the current and prior periods.

IAS 19.41   If the entity has retained such a legal or constructive obligation it should treat the plan as a defined benefit plan. In that case, the entity recognises its rights under the qualifying insurance policy as a plan asset and recognises other insurance policies as reimbursement rights (subject to the criteria set out in section 24.2.3).

24.6   MULTI-EMPLOYER AND GROUP PLANS

A   *Multi-employer plans*

IAS 19.7   Multi-employer plan under IAS 19 are defined contribution plans or defined benefit plans, other than state plans, that:

- pool assets contributed by various entities that are not under common control; and
- use those assets to provide benefits to employees of more than one entity, on the basis that contribution and benefit levels are determined without regard to the identity of the entity that employs the employees concerned.

IAS 19.29   An entity should classify a multi-employer plan as a defined contribution plan or a defined benefit plan under the formal terms of the plan but also taking into account any constructive obligations. If a multi-employer plan is classified as a defined contribution plan, it should be accounted for under the guidance applicable to defined contribution plans.

If a multi-employer plan is classified as a defined benefit plan, the entity should account for its proportionate share of the defined benefit obligation, plan assets and costs associated with the plan in the same way as for any other defined benefit plan. The entity should disclose the same information as is required for any other defined benefit plan (see section 24.3).

IAS 19.30   If insufficient information is available to use defined benefit accounting for a multi-employer plan that is a defined benefit plan, an entity should:

- account for the plan as if it were a defined contribution plan;

24.5 INSURANCE CONTRACTS

Under an insurance contract an insurance company unconditionally undertakes a legal obligation to provide specified benefits to specific individuals in return for a fixed consideration or premium.   To the extent that benefits currently earned are covered by insurance contracts, the cost of those benefits is the cost of purchasing the contracts.   Benefits covered by insurance contracts should be excluded from the projected benefit obligation and accumulated benefit obligation and insurance contracts should be excluded from plan assets.

FAS 106.67

Some insurance contracts (participating insurance contracts) provide that the employer participates in the experience of the insurance company.   If the substance of a participating contract is such that the employer remains subject to all or most of the risks and rewards associated with the benefit obligation, that contract is not an insurance contract for the purposes of FAS 106.

FAS 106.68

The purchase price of a participating insurance contract is usually higher than the price of an equivalent contract without participation rights.   The difference is the cost of the participation right which should be recognised at the date of purchase as an asset.   In subsequent periods, the participation right should be measured at its fair value if the contract is such that the fair value is reasonably estimable.   Otherwise, the participation right should be measured at its amortised cost, and the cost should be amortised over the expected dividend period of the contract.

FAS 106.69

24.6 MULTI-EMPLOYER PLANS

A multi-employer plan under FAS 106 is a plan to which, usually pursuant to a collective-bargaining agreement, more than one unrelated employer contributes in a multi-employer plan the assets contributed by one participating employer may be used to provide benefits to employees of other participating employers, as the assets in such plans are not segregated or restricted to provide benefits to employees of that one employer.

FAS 106.79-80

A company participating in a multi-employer plan recognises as net post-retirement benefit costs the required contribution for the period and recognises as a liability any contributions due and unpaid.

FAS 106.81

- disclose the fact that the plan is a defined benefit plan and the reason why insufficient information is available to account for it as such; and

- to the extent that a surplus or deficit in the plan may affect future contributions, disclose:

  - any available information about that surplus or deficit;

  - the basis used to determine the surplus or deficit; and

  - any implications for the entity.

IAS 19.32A   There may be a contractual agreement between a multi-employer plan and its participants that determines how a surplus or deficit in the plan will be distributed or funded.   Where such an agreement exists and the plan is accounted for as a defined contribution plan, a plan participant should recognise the asset or liability arising from the agreement and the resulting income or expense should be recognised in profit or loss.

IAS 19.32B   In accordance with IAS 37 (see section 18.2.2), a participant in a multi-employer plan should also disclose any contingent liabilities relating to its responsibilities to share the risks for financing the multi-employer plan.

IAS 19.36   An entity should account for state plans in the same way as for a multi-employer plan.   State plans are described as plans established by legislation to cover all entities (or all entities in a particular category) and which are operated by national or local government or by another body which is not subject to control or influence by the reporting entity.

B   Group plans

IAS 19.34-34A   Defined benefit plans that share risks between various entities under common control, for example, a parent and its subsidiaries, are not multi-employer plans but group plans.   An entity which participates in such a plan should obtain information about the plan as a whole measured in accordance with IAS 19 and using assumptions which apply to the plan as a whole.   If there is a contractual agreement or stated policy for charging the net defined benefit cost of the plan as a whole to individual entities, each entity should recognise the amount it has been charged.   In the absence of such an agreement or policy, the net defined benefit cost should be recognised in the separate or individual financial statements of the entity which is the legal sponsoring employer with other entities recognising in their separate or individual financial statements a cost equal to their contributions payable for the period.

IAS 19.34B   Participation in such a plan is a related party transaction for each individual group entity and IAS 19 requires the following additional disclosures in an entity's separate or individual financial statements:

- the contractual agreement or stated policy for charging the net defined benefit cost or the fact that there is no such policy;

- the policy for determining the contribution to be paid by the entity;

- if the entity accounts for an allocation of the net defined benefit cost, all the information about the plan as a whole should be disclosed (see section 24.3); and

- if the entity accounts for the contribution payable for the period, information about the plan as a whole as specified in paragraph 34B.

Section 25   Other employee benefits

25.1   AUTHORITATIVE PRONOUNCEMENTS

- IAS 19 (amended December 2004)

COMMENT

IAS 19 prescribes the accounting treatment for all employee benefits except those to which IFRS 2 *Share-based Payment* applies (see section 22). The following categories of employee benefits are covered by IAS 19:

- pensions, which are covered in section 23;
- post-employment life assurance and medical care, which are covered in section 24;
- short-term employee benefits, which are dealt with in section 25.2;
- termination benefits, which are discussed in section 25.3; and
- other long-term employee benefits, which are covered in section 25.4.

25.2   SHORT-TERM EMPLOYEE BENEFITS

IAS 19.7-8   Short-term employee benefits are employee benefits (other than termination benefits) which fall due wholly within twelve months after the end of the period of related employee service. They include items such as:

- wages, salaries and social security contributions;
- short-term compensated absences (such as paid annual leave and paid sick leave) where the absences are expected to occur within twelve months after the end of the period in which the employees render the related employee service;
- profit sharing and bonuses payable within twelve months after the end of the period in which the employees render the related service; and
- non-monetary benefits (such as medical care, housing, cars and free or subsidised goods or services) for current employees.

IAS 19.9   Accounting for short-term employee benefits is generally straightforward because no actuarial assumptions are required to measure the obligation or the cost and there is no possibility of any actuarial gain or loss.

A   *Recognition and measurement*

IAS 19.10   When an employee has rendered service to an entity during an accounting period, the entity should recognise the undiscounted amount of short-term employee benefits expected to be paid in exchange for that service:

- as a liability (accrued expense), after deducting any amount already paid. If the amount already paid exceeds the undiscounted amount of the benefits, an entity should recognise that excess as an asset (prepaid expense) to the extent

Section 25   Other employee benefits

25.1 AUTHORITATIVE PRONOUNCEMENTS

- FAS 5
- FAS 43
- FAS 88
- FAS 112

COMMENT

FAS 146 deals with the accounting treatment for individual costs often associated with restructurings, distinguishing one-time employee termination benefits, contract termination costs (excluding capital lease contracts) and other associated costs (see section 18.7). The benefits addressed in FAS 146 are those that would not have otherwise been available to the employees concerned under any of the company's pre-existing plans.

25.2 SHORT-TERM EMPLOYEE BENEFITS

There are no specific rules under US GAAP for accounting for and reporting short-term employee benefits other than compensated absences. Accounting for certain post-employment benefits under US GAAP is discussed in section 25.4.

An employer is required to accrue a liability for employees' rights to receive compensation for future absences when certain conditions are met. For example, a liability shall be accrued for vacation benefits that employees have earned but have not yet taken. However, a liability generally is not required to be accrued for future sick pay benefits, holidays, and similar compensated absences until employees are actually absent. The four conditions are as follows: *FAS 43.6-7*

- the employees' rights to receive the benefits are attributable to services already rendered;
- the employees' rights either *vest* or *accumulate*;
- payment of the benefits is probable; and
- the expected cost of providing the benefits can be reasonably estimated.

FAS 43 defines the following terms:

Vested rights – 'those for which the employer has an obligation to make payment even if an employee terminates; thus, they are not contingent on an employee's future service.' *FAS 43.6(b) fn1*

Accumulate – 'earned but unused rights ... [that] may be carried forward to one or more periods subsequent to that in which they are earned, even though there may be a limit to the amount that can be carried forward.' *FAS 43.6(b) fn2*

that the prepayment will lead to, for example, a reduction in future payments or a cash refund; and

- as an expense, unless another Standard requires or permits the inclusion of the benefits in the cost of an asset.

B   *Compensated absences*

IAS 19.11   An entity should recognise the expected cost of compensated absences in the manner described in section 25.2A as follows:

- in the case of accumulating compensated absences, when the employees render service that increases their entitlement to future compensated absences; and

- in the case of non-accumulating compensated absences, when the absences occur.

IAS 19.13   Accumulating compensated absences may be either vesting (i.e. employees are entitled to a cash payment for unused entitlement on leaving the entity) or non-vesting.   An obligation arises as employees render service that increases their entitlement to future compensated absences.   The obligation exists, and is recognised, even if the compensated absences are non-vesting, but the possibility that employees may leave before they use an accumulated non-vesting entitlement affects the measurement of that obligation.

IAS 19.14   An entity should measure the expected cost of accumulating compensated absences as the additional amount that it expects to pay as a result of the unused entitlement that has accumulated at the balance sheet date.

C   *Profit sharing and bonus plans*

IAS 19.17-18   An entity should recognise the expected cost of profit sharing and bonus payments in the manner described in section 25.2A when, and only when:

- the entity has a present legal or constructive obligation to make such payments as a result of past events; and

- a reliable estimate of the obligation can be made.

A present obligation exists when, and only when, the entity has no realistic alternative but to make the payments.   Where a profit-sharing plan is subject to a loyalty period, a constructive obligation is created during the period in which the relevant profit is earned.   The measurement of any obligation will reflect the possibility that some employees may leave during the loyalty period without receiving a bonus or profit-share payment.

IAS 19.20   An entity can make a reliable estimate of its legal or constructive obligation under a profit sharing or bonus plan when, and only when:

- the formal terms of the plan contain a formula for determining the amount of the benefit;

- the entity determines the amounts to be paid before the financial statements are authorised for issue; or

- past practice gives clear evidence of the amount of the entity's constructive obligation.

D   Disclosure

IAS 19.23   IAS 19 does not require specific disclosures about short-term employee benefits. However, other Standards such as IAS 1 *Presentation of Financial Statements* (section 1) or IAS 24 *Related Party Disclosures* (section 28) may require disclosures.

25.3   TERMINATION BENEFITS

IAS 19.7   Termination benefits are employee benefits that are payable either because the entity has decided to terminate an employee's employment before the normal retirement date or an employee has accepted voluntary redundancy in exchange for those benefits.

A   Recognition

IAS 19.133   An entity should recognise termination benefits as a liability and an expense only when it is demonstrably committed to either:

- terminate the employment of employees before the normal retirement date; or
- provide termination benefits as a result of an offer made to encourage voluntary redundancy.

IAS 19.134   An entity is demonstrably committed when it is without realistic possibility of withdrawal and has a detailed formal plan for the termination, which includes as a minimum:

- the location, function, and approximate number of employees whose services are to be terminated;
- the termination benefits for each job classification or function; and
- the time at which the plan will be implemented (implementation should begin as soon as possible and the period of time to complete implementation should be such that material changes to the plan are not likely).

IAS 19.135-136   Payments which an entity is committed to make to employees when it terminates their employment are termination benefits.   These benefits are typically lump-sum payments but sometimes also include enhancement of retirement or other post-employment benefits and salary until the end of a specified notice period if the employee renders no further beneficial service to the entity.   In some cases, however, benefits are payable regardless of the reason for an employee's departure. The payment of such benefits is certain although the timing may be uncertain. Such payments should be accounted for as post-employment benefits rather than as termination benefits (see section 24).

IAS 19.137-138   Termination benefits should be recognised as an expense immediately.   It may also be necessary for the entity to account for an associated curtailment of retirement or other employee benefits (see section 23.4.3E).

B   Measurement

IAS 19.78   If the termination benefits fall due more than twelve months after the balance sheet
IAS 19.139   date they should be discounted, using a rate determined by reference to the market yields on high quality corporate bonds at the balance sheet date.   In countries where there is no deep market in such bonds, the market yields (at the balance sheet date) on government bonds should be used.

25.3   TERMINATION BENEFITS

Although FAS 112 addresses the accounting for most forms of severance benefits promised to employees, e.g. lump sum payments, future payments, or both, the accounting treatment of 'special' or 'contractual' termination benefits is addressed in FAS 88 *Employers' Accounting for Settlements and Curtailments of Defined Benefit Pension Plans and for Termination Benefits.*

Special termination benefits are those offered by the employer to some or all of its employees for a short period of time for a special purpose, e.g. declining industry may force an employer to reduce the size of its workforce. In those situations, companies may offer a limited-time early retirement offer. A liability generally is recognised for such benefits when: *FAS 88.15*

- the employee accepts the offer; and

- the amount is estimable.

However, if in the example noted above, the company also has the unilateral right and intent to terminate additional employees, if necessary, to achieve its plans, the cost of achieving its intended workforce reduction should be accounted for using the event approach under FAS 112.

Contractual termination benefits provide contractual benefits under the terms of a plan that become payable only if a special event occurs, such as a plant closing. A liability is recognised for such benefits when: *FAS 112.6*

- it is probable that the employees will be entitled to the benefits; and

- the amount is estimable.

Accordingly, redundancy benefits under an ongoing benefit arrangement will often be recognised and measured long before a liability is incurred for one time benefits.

One of the characteristics of an ongoing benefit arrangement is that benefits can be determined or estimated in advance.   Accordingly, the following factors should be considered:

- the frequency and regularity with which an entity has provided termination benefits in the past;

- the similarity of the benefits to be provided under the current plan of termination with termination benefits provided under prior termination plans;

- the existence of statutory minimum benefits for involuntary termination.

If an obligation is not accrued solely because a company cannot reasonably estimate the amounts, the financial statements should disclose that fact.   *FAS 112.7*

IAS 19.140   If the entity has made an offer to encourage voluntary redundancy, the termination benefits should be measured on the basis of the number of employees expected to accept the offer.

C   Disclosure

IAS 19.141   If there is uncertainty about the number of employees who will accept an offer of termination benefits, a contingent liability exists that should be disclosed in accordance with IAS 37 *Provisions, Contingent Liabilities and Contingent Assets.*

> **COMMENT**
>
> The treatment of termination benefits is currently under review by the IASB as part of its short-term convergence project with the FASB.   At its December 2004 meeting, the IASB discussed proposed amendments to the accounting requirements for termination benefits in IAS 19 which will accompany the proposed amendments to the accounting for restructuring costs in IAS 37 (see section 18).   The IASB agreed to propose that:
>
> - benefits for voluntary termination should be recognised when the employees accept the entity's offer of the benefits; and
>
> - benefits for involuntary termination should be recognised when the entity communicates its plan of termination to the affected employees and the plan meets specified criteria.   However, if the benefits are provided in exchange for future services by the employees, the benefits should be recognised over that future service period.
>
> The IASB also reconsidered the measurement of termination benefits and decided to retain the existing measurement requirement of IAS 19.   It also decided:
>
> - to specify that when termination benefits are due more than 12 months after the balance sheet date, an entity should subsequently follow the recognition and measurement requirements in IAS 19 for post-employment benefits; and
>
> - to clarify that when termination benefits are provided through a post-employment benefit plan, the liability and expense recognised initially include only the value of the additional benefits that arises from providing those termination benefits.

25.4   OTHER LONG-TERM EMPLOYEE BENEFITS

A   Applicability

IAS 19.7   Other long-term employee benefits are those benefits (other than post-retirement benefits and termination benefits) which do not fall due wholly within twelve months after the end of the period in which the employees render the related service.

IAS 19.126   Other long-term employee benefits include:

- long-term compensated absences;
- jubilee or other long-service benefits;
- long-term disability benefits;
- profit-sharing and bonuses payable twelve months or more after the end of the period of related service; and
- deferred compensation paid twelve months or more after the end of the period in which it is earned.

25.4 OTHER LONG-TERM EMPLOYEE BENEFITS

There are no specific accounting or reporting rules for other long-term employee benefits. Accounting for compensated absences is discussed under section 25.2 and accounting for certain post-employment and termination benefits is discussed in sections 25.2 and 25.3, respectively.

Post-employment benefits are all types of benefits provided by an employer to former or inactive employees, their beneficiaries, and covered dependants after active employment but before retirement. Examples include salary continuation, supplemental unemployment benefits, severance benefits, disability-related benefits, and continuation of health care benefits and life insurance coverage.   *FAS 112.1,4-5*

Inactive employees are those who are not currently rendering service to the employer and who have not been terminated. They include those who have been laid off and those on disability leave, regardless of whether they are expected to return to active status. Employees working part-time while receiving employer-provided benefits, e.g. disability benefits, generally would be considered active employees.

IAS 19.127   The measurement of other long-term employee benefits is usually subject to less uncertainty than the measurement of post-employment benefits and the introduction of, or changes to, such benefits rarely results in a material amount of past service cost.   As a result, a simplified method of accounting (compared to that required for post-employment benefits) is required which involves immediate recognition of all actuarial gains and losses and past service costs.

B   *Recognition and measurement*

IAS 19.128   The entity should recognise a liability for other long-term employee benefits equal to the net total of the present value of the defined benefit obligation at the balance sheet date and the fair value at the balance sheet date of any plan assets out of which the obligations are to be settled directly.

IAS 19.128-129   For other long-term employee benefits, an entity should recognise the net total of the following amounts as expense or income, except to the extent that another Standard requires or permits their inclusion in the cost of an asset:

- current service cost;
- interest cost;
- the expected return on any plan assets and on any reimbursement right recognised as an asset;
- actuarial gains and losses;
- past service cost; and
- the effect of any curtailments or settlements.

All assets, liabilities, income and expense relating to such benefits should be accounted for in the same way, and subject to the same restrictions on the recognition of assets and income, as those relating to a defined benefit pension plan (see Section 23.4) except that actuarial gains and losses are recognised immediately in profit or loss (i.e. they are not limited to a 'corridor' and may not be recognised outside the income statement) as are all past service costs (i.e. they are not spread over the period to vesting).

IAS 19.130   For benefits where the level of benefit depends on the length of service, such as some long-term disability benefits, an obligation arises when the service is rendered.   If the level of benefit is the same regardless of years of service, the expected cost of those benefits is recognised when an event occurs to trigger the payment of the benefit.

Post-employment benefits do not include benefits provided under pension or other post-retirement benefit plans, individual deferred compensation arrangements, or stock compensation plans.

A   The service period approach

Companies should accrue a liability for employees' rights to receive post-employment benefits if all of the following criteria are met: *FAS 112.6*

- the employees' rights to receive the benefits are attributable to services already rendered;

- the employees' rights either *vest* or *accumulate*;

- payment of the benefits is probable; and

- the expected cost of providing the benefits can be reasonably estimated.

When all of these criteria are met, the cost of providing post-employment benefits should be recognised over the employees' service period, which generally begins when an employee joins the company and ends on the expected date of the event giving rise to an obligation.

This approach is referred to as the 'service period' approach and is based on the requirements of FAS 43 *Accounting for Compensated Absences* (see section 25.3B).

Post-employment benefits typically do not vest. Thus, determining whether such benefits accumulate generally will determine whether a service period approach can be used. In determining whether benefits accumulate, FAS 112 *Employers' Accounting for Postemployment Benefits* provides that if the benefits increase based on the length of service, they are deemed to accumulate whereas if the benefit increase is attributed solely to an increase in salary the benefit does not accumulate.   *FAS 112.18*

FAS 112 does not provide explicit guidance on how to measure the post-employment obligation. When benefits are being recognised under a service period approach, measurement issues similar to those addressed in FAS 87 *Employers' Accounting for Pensions* and FAS 106 *Employers' Accounting for Post-retirement Benefits Other Than Pensions* will arise.

B   Event approach

Post-employment benefits that do not satisfy the criteria for the service period approach should be accounted for when the criteria in FAS 5 *Accounting for Contingencies* are met, i.e. when both of the following conditions are met: *FAS 112.6*
    FAS 5.8

- information available prior to issuance of the financial statements indicates that it is probable that a liability for post-employment benefits has been incurred at the balance sheet date; and

- the cost of the benefits can be reasonably estimated.

This is referred to as an 'event approach' as generally a liability is recorded when an event giving rise to an obligation occurs.

Section 26   Earnings per share

26.1   AUTHORITATIVE PRONOUNCEMENTS

- IAS 33

26.2   APPLICABILITY

IAS 33.2   Entities whose ordinary shares or potential ordinary shares are publicly traded, or are in the process of issuing ordinary shares or potential ordinary shares in the public markets, must disclose earnings per share (EPS) information.

IAS 33.4   If the entity publishes both parent and consolidated financial statements, EPS information only needs to be presented on the basis of the consolidated information.   If an entity chooses also to present EPS information based on its separate financial statements, this information should be confined to presentation in the parent entity income statement and must not be presented as part of the consolidated financial statements.

IAS 33.3   Whether an entity is required to present, or voluntarily presents, EPS information, such information should be calculated and disclosed in accordance with IAS 33 *Earnings Per Share*.

26.3   BASIC EARNINGS PER SHARE

IAS 33.1,11   The Standard's overall objective is to prescribe principles for the determination and presentation of EPS in order to improve performance comparisons between different entities for the same reporting period and between different reporting periods for the same entity.   For basic EPS, the stated objective is to provide a measure of the interests of each ordinary share of a parent entity in the performance of the entity over a reporting period.

26.3.1   Computation

IAS 33.9-10   Basic EPS is calculated by dividing profit or loss for the period attributable to
IAS 33.68,A1   ordinary equity holders of the parent entity (the numerator) by the weighted average number of ordinary shares outstanding during the period (the denominator).   Basic

Section 26   Earnings per share

26.1   AUTHORITATIVE PRONOUNCEMENTS

- FAS 128
- SOP 93-6

COMMENT

In December 2003 the FASB issued an exposure draft for a proposed Statement of Financial Accounting Standards *Earnings per Share an amendment of FASB Statement No. 128.* The proposed standard would prevent entities from overcoming the presumption that contracts that may be settled in cash or shares will be settled in shares and require that shares to be issued on conversion of a mandatorily convertible security be included in the computation of basic EPS. The FASB expects to re-expose the proposal in the second quarter of 2005 and issue a final standard in the third quarter of 2005.

26.2   APPLICABILITY

FAS 128 *Earnings per Share* requires presentation of earnings per share (EPS) by all entities: *FAS 128.6*

- that have issued common stock or potential common stock if those securities trade in a public market (domestic or foreign) or in the over-the-counter market; or
- that have made a filing or are in the process of filing with a regulatory agency in preparation for the sale of those securities in a public market.

The standard does not require presentation of EPS in statements of wholly owned subsidiaries.

Any voluntary presentation of EPS amounts in financial statements should comply with FAS 128.

26.3   BASIC EARNINGS PER SHARE

Basic EPS is intended to measure the financial performance of an entity over the reporting period.   *FAS 128.8*

26.3.1   Computation

Basic EPS is computed by dividing income available to common stockholders by the weighted-average number of common shares outstanding during the period.   *FAS 128.8-9*
  EITF D-42,53,82

EPS should be calculated for both the profit or loss attributable to ordinary equity holders of the parent entity (consolidated profit or loss after adjusting for minority interests) and, if presented, profit or loss from continuing and discontinuing operations attributable to those equity holders.

IAS 33.12 For the calculation of basic EPS, the profit or loss for the period attributable to ordinary equity holders of the parent entity and, where relevant, the profit or loss from continuing operations, should be adjusted for the post-tax amounts of preference dividends, differences arising on the settlement of preference shares, and other similar amounts relating to those preference shares classified as equity.

IAS 33.19-21,23 The weighted average number of ordinary shares outstanding during the period takes into account the portion of the period that any ordinary shares were outstanding by applying a time-weighting factor to the number of shares. Shares are usually included in the weighted average from the date consideration is receivable (generally their date of issue). IAS 33 provides examples of various situations in which ordinary shares might be issued and the relevant timing for the inclusion of those shares in the weighted average calculation.

IAS 33.22 Ordinary shares issued as part of the cost of a business combination are included in the weighted average number of shares from the acquisition date. Reverse acquisitions are not specifically addressed in IAS 33 but appendix B to IFRS 3 *Business Combinations* addresses this matter.

IAS 33.26-28,A2 The weighted average number of ordinary shares outstanding during the period may change because of events, other than the conversion of potential ordinary shares, which change the number of shares without a corresponding change in resources, e.g. a capitalisation or bonus issue (sometimes called a stock dividend), a bonus element in any other issue (such as in a rights issue to existing shareholders), a share split or a reverse share split (consolidation of shares). When such a change occurs and no additional consideration is due, the EPS calculations for all periods presented must be adjusted for the proportionate change in the number of ordinary shares outstanding as if the event had occurred at the beginning of the earliest period presented.

IAS 33.29 In cases where the overall effect of a share consolidation is a share repurchase at fair value, the reduction in the number of shares outstanding is the result of a corresponding reduction in resources e.g. a share consolidation combined with a special dividend. In such cases, the weighted average number of shares outstanding for the period in which the combined transaction takes place is adjusted for the reduction in the number of ordinary shares only from the date the special dividend is recognised and the comparative figures are not adjusted.

IAS 33.64 EPS information for all periods presented should be adjusted retrospectively when a capitalisation or bonus issue, a share split or a reverse share split, as described above, occurs before the financial statements are issued and results in a change in the number of ordinary or potential ordinary shares outstanding. It should also be restated for the effects of errors and adjustments resulting from changes in accounting policies accounted for retrospectively. Where EPS information has been restated this fact should be disclosed.

698

Income available to common stockholders is computed by deducting both dividends declared in the period on preferred stock (whether or not paid) and the dividends accrued for the period on cumulative preferred stock. Additionally, the effects of the redemption or induced conversion of preferred stock also result in adjustments to income available for common stockholders.

In computing the weighted-average number of common shares during the period, shares issued during the period and shares reacquired during the period are weighted for the portion of the period that they are outstanding.

If the number of common shares outstanding changes as a result of a stock dividend, stock split, reverse stock split, or a bonus element (similar to a stock dividend) of a rights issue offered to all existing stockholders, EPS (basic and diluted) should be adjusted for all periods presented to reflect the change in the capital structure. When such a change occurs, the EPS calculations for all periods presented must be adjusted for:

FAS 128.54-56

- the proportionate change in the number of ordinary shares outstanding, when no proceeds are due; or

- the (1) fair value per share immediately before the exercise of rights divided by (2) the theoretical ex-rights fair value per share, when additional proceeds are due.

The theoretical ex-rights fair value per share is the sum of the aggregate fair value of the shares immediately before the exercise of the rights and the additional proceeds, divided by the number of shares outstanding after the exercise of the rights.

If the change in capital structure occurs after the period-end but before financial statements are issued, the EPS calculations should be based on the adjusted number of shares.

Where EPS calculations reflect changes in the capital structure, that fact should be disclosed.

Common shares to be redeemed or repurchased as a result of mandatorily redeemable shares or forward contracts that require physical settlement by repurchase of a fixed number of the issuer's equity shares in exchange for cash should be excluded in calculating basic and diluted earnings per share. Any amounts, including contractual (accumulated) dividends and participation rights in undistributed earnings, attributable to shares to be redeemed or repurchased, that have not been recognised as interest costs, should be deducted in computing income available to common stockholders consistent with the two-class method described in Section 26.3.3.

26.3.2   Own shares held

Example 2 appended to IAS 33 indicates that treasury shares (own shares), which are presented in the accounts as a deduction from equity, should not be included in the weighted average number of shares outstanding.

26.3.3   More than one class of ordinary shares

IAS 33.6,66   IAS 33 recognises that an entity may have more than one class of ordinary shares
IAS 33.A13-14   and states that separate EPS figures should be presented for each class of ordinary shares that has a different right to share in profit for the period.   Earnings should be apportioned over the different classes of shares in accordance with their dividend rights or other rights to participate in profits.

26.3.4   Partially paid shares

IAS 33.A15   In determining the weighted average number of shares outstanding, partially paid shares are treated as a fraction of an ordinary share based on their dividend entitlement during the period relative to a fully paid ordinary share.

26.3.5   Contingently issuable shares

IAS 33.24-25   Contingently issuable shares are treated as outstanding and are only included in the calculation of basic EPS from the date that all conditions for their issue have been met.   Contingently returnable shares (i.e. those subject to recall) are not treated as outstanding and are excluded from the basic EPS calculation until the shares are no longer subject to recall.

26.4   DILUTED EARNINGS PER SHARE

IAS 33.32   The objective of diluted EPS is stated as being consistent with that of basic EPS, that is to provide a measure of the interest of each ordinary share in the performance of the entity, whilst at the same time giving effect to all dilutive potential ordinary shares outstanding during the period.

IAS 33.5   Dilution is defined as 'a reduction in EPS or an increase in loss per share resulting from the assumption that convertible instruments are converted, that options or warrants are exercised, or that ordinary shares are issued upon the satisfaction of specified conditions'.   A potential ordinary share is defined as 'a financial instrument or other contract that may entitle its holder to ordinary shares.

26.3.2   Own shares held

Shares held by consolidated entities are treated as if cancelled and therefore excluded from the calculation of weighted-average shares outstanding. Shares held by an Employee Share Option Plan are also treated as if cancelled, but only until they have been committed to be released or allocated, when they are considered outstanding (using the average number of shares for the period).

SOP 93-6

EITF 97-14

26.3.3   More than one class of common share

Where an entity has more than one class of common shares with different dividend and/or participation rights or other participating securities, the two-class method is used to calculate EPS. The two-class method is an earnings allocation method that calculates earnings per share for each class of common share and participating security according to dividends declared (or accumulated) and participation rights in undistributed earnings.

FAS 128.60-61

EITF 03-6

26.3.4   Partially paid shares

Where an entity has common shares issued partially paid and entitled to dividends in proportion to the amount paid, those shares should be included in the computation of EPS as fractional shares outstanding to the extent that they were entitled to participate in dividends for the period.

FAS 128.64

26.3.5   Contingently issuable shares

Contingently issuable shares are considered outstanding common shares and included in basic EPS only when all necessary conditions have been satisfied. Outstanding common shares that are contingently returnable are treated in the same manner as contingently issuable shares and until the shares are vested or some other contingent criteria are met, the shares should be excluded from basic EPS.

FAS 128.10

> **COMMENT**
>
> The proposed amendments to FAS 128 in the exposure draft would require that shares to be issued on conversion of a mandatorily convertible security be included in the weighted-average number of shares outstanding used in computing basic EPS from the date conversion becomes mandatory using the if-converted method described in section 26.4.2B below.

26.4   DILUTED EARNINGS PER SHARE

Diluted EPS measures the performance of an entity over the reporting period while giving effect to all potential common shares that were dilutive and outstanding during the period.

26.4.1   Computation

IAS 33.30-31   Diluted EPS is calculated by adjusting the profit or loss attributable to ordinary equity holders, and the weighted average number of ordinary shares outstanding, for the effects of all dilutive potential ordinary shares.   As for basic EPS, separate amounts for diluted EPS should be presented for the profit or loss attributable to ordinary equity holders and for the profit or loss on continuing and discontinued operations where these are presented.

IAS 33.33-34   The profit or loss attributable to ordinary equity holders, as used in the calculation of basic EPS, must be adjusted for the after-tax effect of:

- any dividends or other items related to dilutive potential ordinary shares which have been deducted in arriving at the profit attributable to ordinary equity holders;
- interest recognised in the period on the dilutive potential ordinary shares; and
- any other changes in income or expense that would result from the conversion of the dilutive potential ordinary shares.

The expenses associated with the conversion of potential ordinary shares will include transaction costs and any discounts charged in the income statement in accordance with the effective interest method prescribed by IAS 39.

IAS 33.36   The weighted average number of ordinary shares outstanding, as used in the calculation of basic EPS, must be adjusted for the weighted average number of ordinary shares that would be issued on the conversion of all dilutive potential ordinary shares into ordinary shares.   For the purpose of making that adjustment, the conversion into ordinary shares is deemed to have taken place at the beginning of the reporting period or, if later, the date of issue of the potential ordinary shares.

IAS 33.38   Potential ordinary shares are weighted for the period they are outstanding.   Potential ordinary shares that are cancelled or have lapsed during the period are weighted for the period that they were outstanding.   Potential ordinary shares that have been converted during the period are included in the diluted EPS calculation from the beginning of the period to the date of conversion.   From the date of conversion the resulting ordinary shares are included in both basic and diluted EPS figures.

IAS 33.41-42,A3   Potential ordinary shares should be treated as dilutive only when their conversion to ordinary shares would decrease the earnings per share or increase the loss per share from continuing operations (the control number).

IAS 33.44   To maximise the dilution of basic EPS, the most dilutive potential ordinary shares are taken into account first.   Each issue or series of potential ordinary shares is considered in sequence from the most dilutive to the least dilutive, i.e. those with the lowest 'earnings per incremental share' are included first.   The sequence in which potential ordinary shares are considered may affect whether they are dilutive. Options and warrants are generally included first as they do not affect the numerator of the calculation (see section 26.4.2A).

26.4.1   Computation

When computing diluted EPS, the weighted-average number of common shares   *FAS 128.11*
outstanding includes the dilutive potential common shares as if they had been
issued.   Exercise or conversion is assumed as at the beginning of the period or at
the date of grant or issuance, if later.   Dilutive potential common shares which are
issued or which lapse or are cancelled during the period should be included for
diluted EPS only for the period they were outstanding.

For diluted EPS, income is adjusted to add back the following when the effect of
conversion of a security is dilutive:

- any convertible preferred dividends;

- the after-tax amount of interest expense associated with any convertible debt;
  and

- the after-tax effects of any other non-discretionary changes in income or loss
  that would result from conversion of potential common shares.

Diluted EPS is based on the most advantageous conversion rate or exercise price   *FAS 128.12*
from the standpoint of the security holder.   Previously reported diluted EPS data is
not retroactively adjusted for subsequent conversions or subsequent changes in the
market price of the common stock.

Diluted EPS should be adjusted for all periods presented to reflect changes in the   *FAS 128.54-56*
capital structure, just as for basic EPS (see section 26.3.1).

26.4.2   Dilutive potential ordinary shares

IAS 33.7 Examples of potential ordinary shares are:

- financial liabilities or equity instruments, including preference shares, that are convertible into ordinary shares;

- options and warrants; and

- shares that would be issued on satisfaction of contractual conditions, such as the purchase of a business or other assets.

IAS 33.40
IAS 33.A11-A12 A subsidiary, joint venture or associate may issue to parties other than the parent, venturer or investor, potential ordinary shares that are convertible into either ordinary shares of the subsidiary, joint venture or associate, or ordinary shares of the parent, venturer or investor (the reporting entity). If these potential ordinary shares have a dilutive effect on the basic EPS of the reporting entity, they are included in the calculation of diluted EPS.

A   *Options and warrants*

IAS 33.45-46 For the purpose of calculating diluted EPS, an entity shall assume the exercise of dilutive options and warrants. The dilutive effect is calculated as the difference between the number of ordinary shares issued, assuming full conversion, and the number of shares that would have been issued if the assumed proceeds from the dilutive instruments had been exchanged for ordinary shares at the average market price of ordinary shares during the period.

IAS 33.48 Employee share options with fixed or determinable terms and non-vested ordinary shares are treated as options in calculating diluted EPS. Performance-based employee share options are treated as contingently issuable shares.

IAS 33.A16 Partly paid shares that are not entitled to dividends must be treated as the equivalent of warrants or options in the calculation of diluted EPS. The unpaid balance is assumed to represent proceeds used to purchase ordinary shares and the number of shares included in diluted EPS is the difference between the number of shares subscribed and the number of shares assumed to be purchased.

B   *Convertible instruments*

IAS 33.49 The dilutive effect of convertible instruments should be reflected in diluted EPS in accordance with the basis of computation set out in section 26.4.1.

26.4.2   Dilutive potential common stock

A   Options and warrants

The dilutive effect of outstanding call options and warrants (and their equivalents) *FAS 128.17-19* should be reflected in diluted EPS using the treasury stock method.   That method involves three steps:

- exercise of options and warrants should be assumed at the beginning of the period (or on issuance if later);

- the proceeds from exercise should be assumed to be used to purchase common stock at the average market price during the period; and

- the incremental shares (the difference between the number of shares assumed issued and the number of shares assumed purchased) shall be included in the denominator of the diluted EPS computation.

The number of incremental shares included diluted EPS should be computed using *FAS 128.46* the average market price of common stock for the relevant period.   For year-to-date diluted EPS, the number of incremental shares to be included in the denominator should be determined by computing a year-to-date weighted average of the number of incremental shares included in each quarterly diluted EPS computation.

> **COMMENT**
>
> Under the proposed amendments to FAS 128 in the exposure draft (1) the incremental shares included in year-to-date diluted EPS weighted average would be computed using the average market price of shares for the year-to-date period, and (2) when applying the treasury stock method to an instrument classified as a liability but potentially settled in shares, the extinguishment of the liability on issuance of the shares should be included as assumed proceeds in the computation of incremental shares.

B   Convertible securities

The dilutive effect of convertible securities should be reflected in diluted EPS using *FAS 128.26-28* the if-converted method:

- Any convertible preferred stock dividends should be added back to net income.

- For convertible debt; (1) interest charges should be added back to net income; (2) nondiscretionary adjustment based on income should be adjusted to reflect (1); and (3) net income should be adjusted for the tax effects of (1) and (2).

- Convertible preferred stock or convertible debt should be assumed to have been converted at the beginning of the period (or on issuance if later).

However, convertible securities for which conversion is satisfied by delivery of the *EITF 90-19* accreted value in cash and the difference between the conversion value and the accreted value in cash or shares are not subject to the if-converted method.   For those securities there is no adjustment to the numerator in the EPS computation and the number of shares that would be delivered upon conversion should be included in diluted EPS based on the provisions described in Section 26.4.4.

26.4.3   Share-based compensation plans

IAS 33.47A-48   Employee share options with fixed or determinable terms and non-vested ordinary shares are treated as options in the calculation of diluted EPS, even though they may be contingent on vesting.   They are treated as outstanding from the grant date. Performance-based employee share options are treated as contingently issuable shares because their issue is contingent upon the satisfaction of specified conditions in addition to the passage of time.   For share options and other share-based payment arrangements to which IFRS 2 applies, the proceeds figure to be used in calculating the dilution under such schemes should include the fair value of any goods or services to be supplied to the entity in the future under the arrangement.

26.4.4   Contracts that may be settled in shares or cash

IAS 33.58,60   Financial instruments or other contracts that may result in the issue of ordinary shares of the reporting entity to the holder of the financial instrument or other contract, whether at the option of the issuer or the holder, are potential ordinary shares of the entity.   When settlement in ordinary shares or cash is at the entity's option, the entity should presume that the contract will be settled in shares and the resulting potential ordinary shares should be included in diluted EPS if the effect is dilutive.   For contracts that may be settled in shares or cash at the option of the holder, the more dilutive of cash settlement and share settlement should be used in calculating diluted EPS.

26.4.3   Share-based compensation plans

Options and non-vested stock to be issued to an employee under a stock-based   *FAS 128.20*
compensation arrangement that are subject only to service vesting conditions are
considered options for purposes of computing diluted EPS.   Consequently:

- awards should be considered outstanding as of the grant date for purposes of
  computing diluted EPS although their exercise may be contingent upon
  service-based vesting;

- awards are included in the diluted EPS computation even if the employee may
  not receive the stock until some future date; and

- all shares to be issued should be included in computing diluted EPS, if the
  effect is dilutive, using the treasury stock method.

In applying the treasury stock method, as in section 26.4.2, the assumed proceeds   *FAS 128.21*
would be the sum of:

- the amount the employee must pay upon exercise;

- the amount of compensation cost attributed to future services and not yet
  recognised; and

- the amount of tax benefits that would be credited to additional paid-in capital
  assuming exercise of the options.

Options or nonvested stock to be issued to an employee under a stock-based
compensation arrangement that vest based on the achievement of performance or
market conditions (e.g. achieving a specified stock price) are considered contingently
issuable shares.   Therefore, once the conditions described in section 26.4.5 are met,
the treasury stock method described above is applied to these awards.

26.4.4   Contracts that may be settled in shares or cash

If an entity issues a contract that may be settled in common stock or in cash at the   *FAS 128.29*
election of either the entity or the holder, it should be presumed that the contract   *EITF D-72*
will be settled in common stock and the resulting potential common shares included
in diluted EPS if the effect is more dilutive.   The presumption may be overcome if
past experience or a stated policy provides a reasonable basis to conclude that the
contract will be settled in cash.   It may be necessary to adjust the numerator for
any changes in income or loss that would result if the contract had been reported as
an equity instrument for accounting purposes during the period.

> **COMMENT**
>
> The proposed amendments to FAS 128 in the exposure draft would prevent entities
> from overcoming the presumption that contracts that may be settled in cash or
> shares will be settled in shares.

Similarly, where employee stock-based awards may be settled either in stock or cash   *FAS 128.22*
it is presumed that the award will be settled in stock and the resulting potential
common shares included in diluted EPS, if the effect is more dilutive.

26.4.5   Contingently issuable shares

IAS 33.52   Contingently issuable ordinary shares are treated as outstanding shares as at the beginning of the period (or date of the contingent share agreement, if later) if the conditions for issuance have been met. If the conditions have not been met, the number of contingently issuable shares included in diluted EPS should be based on the number of shares that would be issuable if the end of the reporting period were the end of the contingency period and if the result would be dilutive. Restatement of EPS information is not permitted if the conditions are not met when the contingency period expires.

IAS 33.53-57   IAS 33 contains considerable detailed guidance on contingently issuable shares, covering three broad categories: earnings-based contingencies, share price-based contingencies and other contingencies.

26.4.6   Contracts to repurchase own shares

IAS 33.63   Contracts that require an entity to repurchase its own shares, such as written put options and forward purchase contracts, should be reflected in the diluted EPS calculation if the effect is dilutive. If these contracts are 'in the money' during the period, i.e. the exercise or settlement price is above the average market price for the period, the potential dilutive effect should be calculated as follows:

- it should be assumed that, at the beginning of the period, sufficient ordinary shares will be issued (at the average market price for the period) to raise proceeds to satisfy the contract;

- it should be assumed that the proceeds from the issue are used to satisfy the contract (i.e. to buy back ordinary shares); and

- the difference between the number of ordinary shares assumed issued and the number received from satisfying the contract should be included in the calculation of diluted EPS.

26.4.5   Contingently issuable shares

Contingently issuable shares should be considered outstanding and included in the computation of diluted EPS as follows: *FAS 128.30-35*

- if all necessary conditions have been satisfied by the end of the period, those shares should be included as of the beginning of the period in which the conditions were satisfied (or as of the date of the contingent stock agreement, if later);

- if all necessary conditions have not been satisfied by the end of the period, the number of contingently issuable shares included in diluted EPS should be based on the number of shares that would be issuable if the end of the reporting period were the end of the contingency period, assuming the result would be dilutive. These should be included as of the beginning of the period in which the conditions were satisfied (or as of the date of the contingent stock agreement, if later).

The EITF has concluded that contingently convertible instruments should be included in diluted earnings per share computations (if dilutive) regardless of whether the market price conversion trigger has been met. The consensus applies to any instrument where conversion into common stock is possible only if one or more specified contingencies occur and at least one of these contingencies is based on the market price of the issuer's shares (a market price contingency).   *EITF 04-8*

The consensus was effective for reporting periods ending after 15 December 2004.

The Task Force concluded that the consensus should be applied as follows:

- If achievement of the market price contingency alone causes the instrument to become convertible, the dilutive impact should be included in diluted earnings per share from the issuance date.

- If achievement of any non market price contingencies is required for the instrument to become convertible, the dilutive impact should be included in diluted earnings per share from the date that all required non market price contingencies are met (i.e. the market price contingency is ignored, but prior practice continues to be applied to the non market price contingencies).

26.4.6   Contracts to repurchase own shares

Contracts, other than physically settled forward purchase contracts (see section 26.3.1), that require that the reporting entity repurchase its own shares should be reflected in the computation of diluted EPS, if the effect is dilutive, using the reverse treasury stock method. That method involves three steps: *FAS 128.24*

- issuance of sufficient common shares should be assumed at the beginning of the period (at the average market price during the period) to raise enough proceeds to satisfy the contract;

- the proceeds from issuance should be assumed to be used to satisfy the contract, i.e. to buy back the shares; and

- the incremental shares (the difference between the number of shares assumed issued and the number bought-back) should be included in the denominator of the diluted EPS computation.

26.5   ANTI-DILUTION

IAS 33.5,43-44   Anti-dilution is defined as 'an increase in EPS or a reduction in loss per share resulting from the assumption that convertible instruments are converted, that options or warrants are exercised, or that ordinary shares are issued upon the satisfaction of specified conditions'. Potential ordinary shares are anti-dilutive when their conversion to ordinary shares would increase EPS from continuing operations or decrease loss per share from continuing operations. Anti-dilutive potential ordinary shares are ignored in calculating diluted EPS.

26.6   DISCLOSURE

IAS 33.69   The following EPS information should be disclosed, even if the amounts are negative:

IAS 33.66   • basic and diluted EPS based on both the profit or loss attributable to the ordinary equity holders of the parent entity and profit or loss on continuing operations attributable to the ordinary equity holders of the parent entity must, with equal prominence, be presented for all periods on the face of the income statement for each class of ordinary shares that has a different right to participate in the net profit for the period;

IAS 33.68   • if an entity reports a discontinued operation it should present basic and diluted amounts per share for the discontinuing operation either on the face of the income statement or in the notes to the financial statements;

IAS 33.70-71   • the amounts used as the numerators in calculating basic and diluted EPS, and a reconciliation of those amounts to the profit or loss attributable to the parent entity for the period;

• the weighted average number of ordinary shares used as the denominator in calculating basic and diluted EPS, and a reconciliation of these denominators to each other;

• instruments that could potentially dilute basic EPS in the future but were not included in the calculation of diluted EPS because they were anti-dilutive;

• apart from those transactions already taken into account in the EPS calculations, a description of transactions in ordinary shares or potential ordinary shares that occurred after the balance sheet date and which would have changed significantly the number of shares or potential shares outstanding at the period end had the transactions occurred before the end of the reporting period.

26.5   ANTI-DILUTION

To avoid anti-dilution in calculating diluted EPS: *FAS 128.13-16*

- the exercise of options and warrants or conversion of convertible securities is not assumed if the result would be anti-dilutive, such as when a loss from continuing operations is reported or if options are out-of-the-money;

- for maximum dilution, each issue or series of issues should be considered separately and in sequence from the most dilutive to the least dilutive in determining whether potential common shares are dilutive or anti-dilutive; and

- an entity that reports a discontinued operation, an extraordinary item, or the cumulative effect of an accounting change should use income from continuing operations, adjusted for preferred dividends, if any, as the 'control number' in determining whether potential common shares are dilutive or anti-dilutive.

Dilution is a reduction in earnings per share (anti-dilution is an increase in earnings per share or a decrease in loss per share) resulting from the assumption that convertible securities were converted, that options or warrants were exercised, or that other shares were issued upon satisfaction of certain conditions.

26.6   DISCLOSURE

An entity should present on the face of the income statement for all periods   *FAS 128.36*
presented basic per-share amounts, and where applicable, diluted per-share amounts, for both income from continuing operations and net income.

FAS 128 requires that diluted EPS be presented if it is different to basic EPS without regard to materiality. In fact, the FASB noted that the standard materiality clause – 'the provisions of this Statement need not be applied to immaterial items' – does not apply to the difference between two numbers.

If applicable, per share amounts (basic and diluted) for discontinued operations,   *FAS 128.37*
extraordinary items, and the cumulative effect of an accounting change should be presented either on the face of the income statement or in the notes, for all periods presented.

If diluted EPS data is required for any period presented, it must be presented for all   *FAS 128.38*
periods in the presentation. If basic and diluted EPS are the same amounts for all periods presented, dual presentation in one line is permitted.

Where operations of a prior period have been restated, EPS data also should be   *FAS 128.57-58*
restated. The effect of the restatement, expressed in per share terms, should be disclosed in the period of restatement.

For each period for which an income statement is presented, an entity should   *FAS 128.40*
disclose the following:

- reconciliations of the numerators (earnings) and denominators (common shares) for the basic and diluted per-share computations for income from continuing operations;

IAS 33.73   If an entity discloses, in addition to basic and diluted EPS, amounts per share based on a different reported component of the income statement, the basic and diluted amounts based on this component should be disclosed with equal prominence and presented in the notes to the financial statements. The number of shares used in any such additional calculations should be determined in accordance with IAS 33 and an indication should be given of the basis of the profit figure, including whether amounts per share are before or after tax. Where EPS information is based on a component of net profit that is not reported as a separate line item in the income statement, a reconciliation must be provided between that component and a line item in the income statement.

IAS 33.72   Disclosure of certain additional information is encouraged by the Standard.

A   Restatement of prior periods

IAS 33.64   EPS information for all periods presented should be adjusted retrospectively when a change in the number of shares outstanding (in the circumstances described in section 26.3.1 above) occurs before the financial statements are issued. It should also be restated for the effects of errors and adjustments resulting from changes in accounting policies accounted for retrospectively. Where EPS information has been restated this fact should be disclosed.

- if applicable, the effect given to preferred dividends in arriving at income available to common share holders in computing basic EPS; and

- if applicable, securities that could potentially dilute basic EPS in future that were not included in the diluted computation because they would have been anti-dilutive for the periods presented or the conditions for conversion were not met.

A　Restatement of prior periods

If changes in common stock resulting from stock dividends, stock splits or reverse *FAS 128.54* stock splits occur either during or after the close of the period, but before the financial statements are issued, the computation of basic and diluted EPS for all periods presented should be retroactively adjusted to reflect the change in capital structure. The fact that EPS data has been adjusted should be disclosed.

Section 27 Cash flow statements

27.1 AUTHORITATIVE PRONOUNCEMENTS

- IAS 1
- IAS 7

- IFRS 4
- IFRS 5

27.2 APPLICABILITY

IAS 1.8   A cash flow statement is required as part a complete set of financial statements for
IAS 7.1   all entities that prepare their financial statements in accordance with International
Financial Reporting Standards.

27.3 OBJECTIVE

IAS 7.3-5   The purpose of a cash flow statement is to provide information on how the entity
generates and uses cash and cash equivalents.   Used in conjunction with the rest of
the financial statements, this information is useful in assessing the ability of an entity
to generate cash and cash equivalents and examining the relationship between
profitability and net cash flow.

27.4 DEFINITIONS

IAS 7.6-7   Cash comprises not only cash on hand but also demand deposits with banks or
other financial institutions.

Cash equivalents are short-term highly liquid investments that are:

- readily convertible to known amounts of cash;

- subject to an insignificant risk of changes in value.   Normally, only
investments with a maturity on acquisition of less that three months qualify as
cash equivalents; and

- not equity investments unless in substance they meet the above criteria.

IAS 7.8   Bank borrowings are normally part of financing activities.   Nonetheless, bank
overdrafts that are repayable on demand and that form an integral part of an entity's
cash management are included in cash equivalents.

IAS 7.46-47   An entity discloses the policy it adopts in determining the composition of cash and
cash equivalents.   The effect of any change in this policy should be reported in
accordance with IAS 8 *Accounting Policies, Changes in Accounting Estimates and
Errors.*

Section 27   Cash flow statements

27.1   AUTHORITATIVE PRONOUNCEMENTS

- FAS 95
- FAS 102

- FAS 104
- FAS 115

27.2   APPLICABILITY

A statement of cash flows is required as part of a full set of financial statements for all business enterprises other than defined benefit pension plans and certain other employee benefit plans and highly liquid investment companies that meet specified conditions.

FAS 95.3
FAS 102.10

27.3   OBJECTIVE

The primary purpose of a statement of cash flows is to provide relevant information about the cash receipts and cash payments of an enterprise during a period.

FAS 95.4

27.4   DEFINITIONS

Cash includes not only currency on hand but also demand deposits with banks or other financial institutions.

FAS 95.7 fn 1

Cash equivalents are short-term, highly liquid investments that are both:

FAS 95.8

- readily convertible to known amounts of cash; and
- so near their maturity that they present insignificant risk of changes in value because of changes in interest rates.   Generally, only investments with original maturities of less than three months qualify under this definition.

Cash equivalents do not include advances from banks that are repayable within three months, e.g. UK overdrafts.   As a result, movements within advances from banks that are repayable within three months have to be reported in a cash flow statement prepared under FAS 95 *Statement of Cash Flows*.

Under FAS 95, not all investments that qualify as cash equivalents are required to be treated as cash equivalents in the statement of cash flows.   The policy for determining which items are treated as cash equivalents should be disclosed.

FAS 95.10

27.5 FORMAT AND CONTENT OF THE STATEMENT

IAS 7.10 Cash receipts and payments reported in a statement of cash flows should be classified as resulting from:

- operating activities;
- investing activities; and
- financing activities.

IAS 7.12 A single transaction may have to be allocated to cash flows from different activities, e.g. when a loan repayment includes both interest and capital.

A   Operating activities

IAS 7.6,13-15 The principal revenue-producing activities of the entity and other activities that are not investing or financing activities must be classified as operating activities.   Cash flows from operating activities generally result from the transactions and other events that enter into the determination of profit or loss.   Examples include:

- cash receipts from the sale of goods and the rendering of services;
- cash receipts from royalties, fees, commissions and other revenue;
- cash payments to suppliers for goods and services;
- cash payments to and on behalf of employees;
- cash receipts and cash payments of an insurance entity for premiums and claims, annuities and other policy benefits;
- cash payments or refunds of income taxes unless they can be specifically identified with financing and investing activities; and
- cash receipts and payments from contracts held for dealing or trading purposes.

IAS 7.18-19 The cash flows from operating activities must be reported using either:

- the direct method, which requires disclosure of the major classes of gross cash receipts and payments; or
- the indirect method, which takes the net profit or loss as a starting point and makes adjustments for transactions of a non-cash nature, deferrals or accruals of operating cash receipts or payments, and items of income or expense associated with investing or financing activities.

Entities are encouraged to present their cash flows from operating activities using the direct method.

IAS 7.31 Interest and dividends received and paid should be disclosed separately and be classified in a consistent manner as either operating, investing or financing activities.

IAS 7.35 Cash flows from taxes on income are included under operating activities, unless they are directly associated with investing or financing activities.

IFRS 4.37 If an insurance entity presents its operating cash flows using the direct method, cash flows arising from insurance contracts should be disclosed separately.

27.5   FORMAT AND CONTENT OF THE STATEMENT

A statement of cash flows explains the change during the period in cash and cash   *FAS 95.7*
equivalents.   The total amounts of cash and cash equivalents at the beginning and
end of the period shown in the statement of cash flows will be the same amounts as
presented in the balance sheets as of those dates.

Cash receipts and payments reported in a statement of cash flows should be   *FAS 95.14*
classified as resulting from:

- operating activities;
- investing activities; and
- financing activities.

If a cash receipt or payment pertaining to an item has aspects of more than one   *FAS 95.24*
class of cash flows, the appropriate classification should depend on the activity that
is likely to be the predominant source of cash flows for the item.

Net cash provided or used by operating, investing and financing activities and the
net effect of those flows on cash and cash equivalents during the period should be
reported in the statement in a manner that reconciles the total amounts of cash and
cash equivalents at the beginning and end of the period.

A   Operating activities

Operating activities include all transactions and other events that are not defined as   *FAS 95.21-23*
investing or financing activities (including interest charges).   Cash flows from
operating activities are generally the cash effects of transactions and other events
that enter into the determination of net income.   They include receipts from
customers, payments to suppliers and employees, returns on loans, other debt
instruments of other entities, and equity securities, i.e. interest and dividends, and
taxation paid.

The direct method of computation, i.e. reporting gross receipts and payments on   *FAS 95.29*
operating activities along with a reconciliation of net income to net cash flow from
operations in the notes, is encouraged.   However, the indirect method, i.e.
reconciling net income to net cash flow, is also permitted.

B   Investing activities

Investing activities include making and collecting loans and acquiring and disposing   *FAS 95.15-17*
of debt or equity instruments and property, plant and equipment and other
productive assets.

However, cash flows from the following transactions should be classified under   *FAS 102.8-9*
operating activities:

- purchases and sales of securities and other assets specifically acquired for
  resale and carried at market value in a trading account; and
- loans that are acquired specifically for resale that are carried at market value or
  the lower of cost or market.

B   Investing activities

IAS 7.6   Investing activities comprise the acquisition and disposal of long-term assets and other investments not included in cash equivalents.

IAS 7.16   Cash flows arising from investing activities include:

- payments to acquire, and receipts from the sale of, property, plant and equipment, intangibles and other long-term assets (including payments and receipts relating to capitalised development costs and self-constructed property, plant and equipment);

- payments to acquire, and receipts from the sale of, equity or debt instruments of other entities and interests in jointly controlled entities (other than payments and receipts for those instruments considered to be cash equivalents or those held for dealing or trading purposes);

- advances and loans made to, and repaid by, other parties (other than advances and loans made by a financial institution); and

- cash payments for, and receipts from, futures contracts, forward contracts, option contracts and swap contracts except when the contracts are held for dealing or trading purposes, or the cash flows are classified as financing activities.

IAS 7.21,39   Major classes of gross cash receipts and payments from investing activities must be reported separately, except to the extent that certain cash flows can be reported on a net basis (see 30.6 below).   Cash flows resulting from acquisitions and disposals of subsidiaries or business units must be presented separately as investing cash flows.

C   Financing activities

IAS 7.6   Financing activities consist of those activities that affect the size and composition of the contributed equity and borrowings of the entity.

IAS 7.17   Cash flows arising from financing activities include:

- proceeds from issuing shares or other equity instruments;

- payments to owners to acquire or redeem the entity's shares;

- proceeds from issuing, and outflows to repay, debentures, loans, notes, bonds, mortgages and other short or long-term borrowings; and

- payments by a lessee for the reduction of the outstanding liability relating to a finance lease.

IAS 7.21   Major classes of gross cash receipts and payments from financing activities must be reported separately, except to the extent that certain cash flows can be reported on a net basis (see 30.6 below).

27.6   NETTING OFF OF TRANSACTIONS

IAS 7.21   Generally, entities have to report major classes of cash flows on a gross basis.
IAS 7.22   However, presentation on a net basis is permitted for the following:

- cash receipts and payments on behalf of customers that reflect the activities of the customer and not those of the entity; and

- cash receipts and payments for items in which the turnover is quick, the amounts are large, and the maturities are short.

Cash flows from purchases, sales and maturities of investments in equity securities that have readily determinable fair values and all investments in debt securities should be classified as follows: *FAS 115.18*

- if held as available-for-sale securities (see section 11.6C), as cash flows from investing activities and reported gross for each classification;

- if held as trading securities (see section 11.6B), as cash flows from operating activities and may be presented on a net basis.

Cash flows from acquisitions and disposals of businesses are included under investing activities.

C   *Financing activities*

Financing activities include obtaining resources from investors and providing them with a return on (e.g. dividends paid) and a return of their investment; borrowing money and repaying amounts borrowed; and obtaining and paying for other resources obtained from creditors on long-term credit.   *FAS 95.19-20*

27.6   NETTING OFF OF TRANSACTIONS

Generally, cash receipts and payments should all be shown gross. However, certain items may be presented net because their turnover is quick, their amounts are large, and their maturities are short. These items will be cash flows relating to investments (other than cash equivalents), loans receivable, and debt, providing that the original maturity is less than three months.   *FAS 95.11-13,31*

IAS 7.24   In addition, financial institutions may report the following on a net basis:

- cash receipts and payments for the acceptance and repayment of deposits with a fixed maturity date;
- the placement of deposits with, and withdrawal of deposits from, other financial institutions; and
- cash advances and loans made to customers and the repayment of those advances and loans.

27.7   HEDGING TRANSACTIONS

IAS 7.16   Cash flows from a contract that is accounted for as a hedge of an identifiable position should be classified in the same manner as the cash flows of the position being hedged.

27.8   FOREIGN CURRENCY CASH FLOWS

IAS 7.25-27   Cash flows denominated in a foreign currency and cash flows of a foreign subsidiary should be translated into the entity's functional currency using the exchange rate at the date of the cash flow or an appropriate weighted average rate, i.e. that used for income statement purposes.

IAS 7.28   Although unrealised gains and losses on cash and cash equivalents are not cash flows, these exchange differences should be reported in the cash flow statement in order to reconcile the value of cash and cash equivalents at the beginning and end of the period. This reconciling item is shown separately from operating, investing and financing activities.

27.9   OTHER DISCLOSURES

IAS 7.40   An entity should disclose the following additional information in respect of both acquisitions and disposals of subsidiaries or other business units during the period:

- the total purchase or disposal consideration;
- the portion of the purchase or disposal consideration discharged by means of cash and cash equivalents;
- the amount of cash and cash equivalents in the subsidiary or business unit acquired or disposed of; and
- the amount of the assets and liabilities other than cash or cash equivalents in the subsidiary or business unit acquired or disposed of, summarised by each major category.

27.7   HEDGING TRANSACTIONS

Generally, a cash receipt or payment is to be classified according to its nature without regard to whether it stems from an item intended as a hedge of another item. However, cash flows resulting from derivative instruments that are accounted for as fair value hedges or cash flow hedges under FAS 133 *Derivative Instruments and Hedging Activities* may be classified in the same category as the cash flows from the items being hedged provided the accounting policy is disclosed.   If for any reason hedge accounting is subsequently discontinued then any cash flows subsequent to the date of discontinuance shall be classified consistent with the nature of the instrument.

FAS 104.7(b)

FAS 104.5-6

27.8   FOREIGN CURRENCY TRANSACTIONS

Cash flows of foreign currency transactions or foreign operations (e.g. subsidiaries) should be reported using the rate ruling at the date of the transaction, or an appropriate average rate, i.e. that used for income statement purposes.   The effects of exchange rate changes on cash balances held in foreign currencies should be reported as a separate part of the reconciliation of the change in cash and cash equivalents during the period shown in the cash flow statement.

FAS 95.25

27.9   OTHER DISCLOSURES

A reconciliation of net income to cash flow from operating activities should be given in a note.   If the indirect method is used, this reconciliation can be given on the face of the cash flow statement.

FAS 95.29

If the indirect method is used, interest paid (net of that capitalised) and taxes paid should be separately disclosed in a schedule or footnote for each period presented.

FAS 95.30

Disclosure in a separate schedule or footnote is required for investing and financing activities that affect recognised assets or liabilities but do not result in cash receipts or payments.   Examples of these transactions include converting debt to equity or obtaining an asset by entering into a capital lease.

FAS 95.32

Disclosure of the following is also required:

IAS 7.43 • non-cash investing and financing transactions must be disclosed in the financial statements in a way that provides all the relevant information;

IAS 7.45 • the components of cash and cash equivalents and a reconciliation of the amounts in its cash flow statement with the equivalent items reported in the balance sheet;

IAS 7.48 • the amount of significant cash and cash equivalent balances held by the entity that are not available for use by the group, together with a commentary by management; and

IFRS 5.33 • net cash flows attributable to the operating, investing and financing activities of discontinued operations.

IAS 7.50 Disclosure of certain additional cash flow related information is encouraged that may include:

• the amount of undrawn borrowing facilities that may be available for future operating activities and to settle capital commitments, indicating any restrictions on the use of these facilities;

• the aggregate amounts of the cash flows from each of operating, investing and financing activities related to interests in joint ventures reported using proportionate consolidation;

• the aggregate amount of cash flows that represent increases in operating capacity separately from those cash flows that are required to maintain operating capacity; and

• the amount of the cash flows arising from the operating, investing and financing activities of each reported industry and geographical segment.

Entities that use the direct method should, at a minimum, separately report the *FAS 95.27*
following classes of operating cash receipts and payments:

- cash collected from customers, including lessees, licensees and similar;
- interest and dividends received (including dividends from joint ventures and associated undertakings);
- other operating cash receipts, if any;
- cash paid to employees and other suppliers of goods or services, including suppliers of insurance, advertising and similar;
- interest paid;
- taxes paid (including duties, fines or penalties); and
- other operating cash payments, if any.

Section 28

Related party transactions

28.1   AUTHORITATIVE PRONOUNCEMENTS

- IAS 24

28.2   IDENTIFICATION OF RELATED PARTIES

IAS 24.9   A party is related to an entity if:

(a)   directly, or indirectly through one or more intermediaries, the party:

- controls, is controlled by, or is under common control with, the entity (this includes parents, subsidiaries and fellow subsidiaries);

- has an interest in the entity that gives it significant influence over the entity; or

- has joint control over the entity;

(b)   the party is an associate of the entity;

(c)   the party is a joint venture in which the entity is a venturer;

(d)   the party is a member of the key management personnel of the entity or its parent. Key management personnel are those persons having authority and responsibility for planning, directing and controlling the activities of the entity directly or indirectly, including any director;

(e)   the party is a close member of the family of any individual referred to in (a) or (d);

(f)   the party is an entity that is controlled, jointly controlled or significantly influenced by, or for which significant voting power in such entity resides with, directly or indirectly, any individual referred to in (d) or (e); or

(g)   the party is a post-employment benefit plan for the benefit of employees of the entity, or of any entity that is a related party of the entity.

IAS 24.10   In considering each possible related party relationship, attention is directed to the substance of the relationship, and not merely to the legal form.

28.3   TYPES OF TRANSACTIONS REQUIRING DISCLOSURE

IAS 24.9,17   A related party transaction is any transfer of resources, services or obligations between related parties, regardless of whether a price is charged. All related party transactions necessary for an understanding of the potential effect of the relationship on the financial statements must be disclosed.

IAS 24.16   Disclosure is required in respect of key management personnel compensation.

Section 28

Related party transactions

28.1   AUTHORITATIVE PRONOUNCEMENTS

- FAS 57

28.2   IDENTIFICATION OF RELATED PARTIES

If one party controls or can significantly influence the management or operating policies of the other to an extent that one of the transacting parties might be prevented from fully pursuing its own separate interests, those parties are related parties. Another party also is a related party if it can significantly influence the management or operating policies of the transacting parties or if it has an ownership interest in one of the transacting parties and can significantly influence the other to an extent that one or more of the transacting parties might be prevented from fully pursuing its own separate interests. *FAS 57.1,24(f)*

Examples of related party transactions include transactions between:

- a parent company and its subsidiaries;
- subsidiaries of a common parent;
- an entity and trusts for the benefit of employees, such as pension and profit-sharing trusts that are managed by or under the trusteeship of the entity's management;
- an entity and its principal owners (defined as owners of record or known beneficial owners of more than 10% of the voting interests of the entity), management, or members of their immediate families; and
- affiliates (defined as parties that, directly or indirectly through one or more intermediaries, control, are controlled by, or are under common control with, an entity).

28.3   TYPES OF TRANSACTIONS REQUIRING DISCLOSURE

FAS 57 *Related Party Disclosures* requires disclosure of all material transactions with related parties. *FAS 57.2*

No disclosure is required in respect of compensation arrangements, expense allowances and other similar items in the ordinary course of business.

28.4   INFORMATION TO BE DISCLOSED

28.4.1   Material transactions

IAS 24.17   If there have been transactions between related parties the reporting entity must disclose the following information necessary for an understanding of the potential effect of the relationship on the financial statements:

- the nature of the related party relationships; and
- information about the transactions and outstanding balances.

At a minimum disclosures should include:

- the amount of the transactions;
- the amount of outstanding balances and:
  - their terms and conditions, including whether they are secured, and the nature of the consideration to be provided in settlement; and
  - details of any guarantees given or received;
- provisions for doubtful debts related to the amount of outstanding balances; and
- the expense recognised during the period in respect of bad or doubtful debts due from related parties.

IAS 24.18   The above disclosures should be made separately for each of the following:

- the parent;
- entities with joint control or significant influence over the entity;
- subsidiaries;
- associates;
- joint ventures in which the entity is a venturer;
- key management personnel of the entity or its parent; and
- other related parties.

IAS 24.16   An entity should also disclose key management personnel compensation in total and for each of the following categories:

- short-term employee benefits;
- post-employment benefits;
- other long-term benefits;
- termination benefits; and
- share-based payment.

IAS 24.22   Items of a similar nature may be aggregated only where separate disclosure is not necessary for an understanding of the effects of related party transactions on the financial statements of the entity.

IAS 24.21   Disclosure that the related party transactions were on 'arms length' terms should only be made when the claim that the terms were at 'arms length' can be substantiated.

28.4   INFORMATION TO BE DISCLOSED

28.4.1   Material transactions

The disclosures to be made include: *FAS 57.2*

- the nature of the relationship(s) involved.   There is no specific requirement to disclose the name of the related party and the extent of ownership interest in either party unless disclosure of the name is necessary to the understanding of the relationship;

- a description of the transaction (including those to which no amounts or nominal amounts were ascribed) and such other information necessary to gain an understanding of the effects of the transactions on the financial statements;

- the monetary amount of the transaction and the effect of any change in the method of establishing the terms from those used in the preceding period; and

- the amounts due to/from the related party and the terms and manner of settlement if not otherwise apparent.

The SEC's proxy rules (which detail the information required to be given to shareholders by those soliciting shareholder proxies) and the annual report (Form 10-K) rules include specific disclosure requirements for certain relationships and related transactions, some of which may be considered as related party transactions. Such disclosures do not form part of the general-purpose financial statements in the US and the accountant is not usually directly involved in ensuring compliance with those disclosure requirements.

The SEC requires related party transactions which affect the financial statements to be identified and the amounts stated on the face of the balance sheet, income statement, or statement of cash flows.   *S-X 4-08(k)*

Transactions involving related parties should not be presumed to be carried out on an arms-length basis.   Disclosures about related party transactions should not imply that the terms of the transactions were arms-length unless this can be substantiated.   *FAS 57.3*

The SEC requires disclosure of all plan and non-plan compensation awarded to, earned by, or paid to the chief executive officer or person(s) acting in a similar capacity, certain of the registrant's most highly compensated executive officers, and all directors.   The information required to be disclosed and the required presentation are described under SEC Regulation S-K Item 402.   *S-K 402*

A foreign private issuer will be deemed to comply with this disclosure requirement if it provides the information required by Items 6.B. and 6.E.2. of Form 20-F, with more detailed information provided if otherwise made publicly available.

28.4.2   Controlling relationships

IAS 24.12,15   Relationships between parents and subsidiaries should be disclosed irrespective of whether there have been transactions between those related parties. An entity should disclose the name of the entity's parent and, if different, the ultimate controlling party. If neither the entity's parent nor the ultimate controlling party produces financial statements available for public use, the name of the next most senior parent that does so should also be disclosed. This next most senior parent is the first parent in the group above the immediate parent that produces consolidated financial statements available for public use.

28.4.3   Exemptions from disclosure

IAS 24.4   Intragroup related party transactions and outstanding balances are eliminated in the preparation of the consolidated financial statements of a group. However, related party transactions and outstanding balances with other entities in a group are disclosed in the separate financial statements of an entity (including those of a parent).

IAS 24.11   A related party relationship is deemed not to exist merely by virtue of:

- the resulting economic dependence arising from a single customer, supplier, franchisor, distributor or general agent transacting a significant volume of business with the reporting entity;
- two entities sharing a common director or member of key management;
- two venturers sharing joint control over a joint venture; or
- providers of finance, trade unions, public utilities or government departments conducting normal dealings with an entity.

28.4.2   Controlling relationship

If the reporting entity and one or more other enterprises are under common ownership or management control and the existence of that control could result in operating results/financial position of the reporting entity significantly different from those that would have been obtained if the entities were autonomous, the nature of the control relationship should be disclosed even though there are no transactions between the entities.

FAS 57.4

28.4.3   Exemptions from disclosure

Disclosure of transactions that are eliminated on consolidation is not required in consolidated (or combined) financial statements.

FAS 57.2

It is not necessary to duplicate disclosures in an entity's own financial statements, if those separate financial statements are presented in the same financial report as consolidated financial statements which include those separate financial statements.

FAS 57.2 fn 2

Section 29

Events after the balance sheet date

29.1   AUTHORITATIVE PRONOUNCEMENTS

- IAS 1
- IAS 10

IAS 10.1   The objective of IAS 10 is to prescribe:
- when an entity should adjust its financial statements for events after the balance sheet date (known as adjusting events); and
- the disclosures that an entity should give about the date when the financial statements were authorised for issue and about events after the balance sheet date (known as non-adjusting events).

29.2   ADJUSTING EVENTS

IAS 10.3,8   Events occurring after the balance sheet date, but before the financial statements are authorised for issue, may provide evidence of conditions that existed at the balance sheet date.   An entity should adjust its financial statements to reflect such adjusting events after the balance sheet date.

IAS 10.19   When an entity receives information after the balance sheet date regarding conditions that existed at the balance sheet date, it should update disclosures in its financial statements relating to this information.

29.3   NON-ADJUSTING EVENTS

IAS 10.3,10   Events occurring after the balance sheet date, but before the financial statements are authorised for issue, that provide evidence of conditions that did not exist at the balance sheet date but arose subsequent to that date, should not be adjusted for in the financial statements.

IAS 10.21   Nevertheless, where these events are of such a nature that disclosure of them is required to prevent the financial statements from being misleading, the entity should disclose the following information for each significant category of non-adjusting event after the balance sheet date:
- the nature of the event; and
- an estimate of its financial effect or a statement that such an estimate cannot be made.

IAS 10.14   IAS 10 includes one exception to its rule on non-adjusting events.   This arises in the situation where an entity ceases to be a going concern after the balance sheet date. An entity should not prepare its financial statements on a going concern basis if

Section 29 — Events after the balance sheet date

29.1   AUTHORITATIVE PRONOUNCEMENTS

- FAS 5
- SAS 1

29.2   ADJUSTING EVENTS

Events occurring after the balance sheet date but prior to the issuance of the financial statements that provide additional evidence with respect to conditions existing at the balance sheet date and have a material effect on the financial statements should be reflected in the financial statements.

SAS 1

29.3   NON-ADJUSTING EVENTS

Events occurring after the balance sheet date but prior to the issuance of the financial statements which provide evidence with respect to conditions that did not exist at the balance sheet date but arose subsequent to that date should not require adjustments.

SAS 1

Some non-adjusting events may be of such a nature that disclosure of them is required to prevent the financial statements from being misleading.

In some cases the event may be so significant that disclosure can best be made by disclosing pro forma statements giving effect to the event as if it had occurred on the date of the balance sheet. It may be desirable to present pro forma information on the face of the historical statements.

FAS 5.11

In the case of an SEC registrant, a change in capital structure due to a stock dividend, stock split or reverse split occurring after the balance sheet date but before the issuance of the financial statements must be given retroactive effect in the balance sheet and for per share disclosures. Appropriate disclosures should be given for the retroactive treatment, to explain the change made and to state the date the change became effective.

SAB 40
(Topic 4-C)

management determines after the balance sheet date either that it intends to liquidate the entity or to cease trading, or that it has no realistic alternative but to do so.

IAS 10.12-13   If dividends to holders of equity instruments (as defined in IAS 32 *Financial Instruments: Disclosure and Presentation*) are declared after the balance sheet date, an entity should not recognise those dividends as a liability at the balance sheet date.

IAS 1.125   IAS 1 *Presentation of Financial Statements* requires an entity to disclose in the notes to the financial statements the amount of dividends that were proposed or declared before the financial statements were authorised for issue but not recognised as a distribution to equity holders during the period, and the related amount per share.

29.4   DATE OF AUTHORISATION FOR ISSUE

IAS 10.17   The entity should disclose the date when the financial statements were authorised for issue and who gave that authorisation. If the entity's owners or others may amend the financial statements after their issuance, this fact should be disclosed.

29.4   DATE OF AUTHORISATION FOR ISSUE

There is no specific guidance under US GAAP regarding disclosure of the date when the financial statements were authorised for issue.

Section 30   Interim reporting

30.1   AUTHORITATIVE PRONOUNCEMENTS

- IAS 34

COMMENT

Segment reporting is currently under review by the IASB as part of its short-term convergence project with the FASB.   In March 2005, the Board decided to add requirements for interim period segment information in IAS 34 (see section 21.1).

30.2   PREPARATION OF INTERIM FINANCIAL REPORTS

IAS 34.1-2   IAS 34 *Interim Financial Reporting* does not mandate which entities are required to publish interim financial reports, how frequently, how soon after the end of an interim period, or whether these interim financial reports must comply with International Financial Reporting Standards.   These are matters to be decided by National Securities Regulators.

Nevertheless, publicly traded entities are encouraged to prepare interim financial reports at least for the first half of their financial year and to publish them not later than 60 days after the end of the interim period.

IAS 34 applies if an entity is required to or elects to publish an interim financial report in accordance with International Financial Reporting Standards.

30.3   ACCOUNTING

IAS 34.28-32   The same accounting policies are applied in interim financial statements as in the annual financial statements, except for accounting policy changes to be reflected in the next annual financial statements.

The principles for recognising assets, liabilities, income and expense for interim periods are the same as in the annual financial statements.   A cost that does not meet the definition of an asset at the end of an interim period is therefore not

Section 30   Interim reporting

30.1   AUTHORITATIVE PRONOUNCEMENTS

- APB 28 (as amended by FAS 3)   • FAS 130
- FAS 16   • FAS 131
- FAS 128

COMMENT

In December 2003 the FASB issued an exposure draft for a proposed Statement of Financial Accounting Standards *Accounting Changes and Error Corrections a replacement of APB Opinion No. 20 and FASB Statement No. 3*. The proposed Statement would carry forward the guidance in FAS 3 *Reporting Accounting Changes in Interim Financial Statements*.

30.2   PREPARATION OF INTERIM FINANCIAL REPORTS

Under SEC rules, US publicly traded companies must file quarterly reports on Form 10-Q with the SEC for each of the first three quarters (no report is required for the fourth quarter). The financial statements presented in Form 10-Q must be prepared in accordance with Regulation S-X, the principles of accounting measurement in APB 28 and various FASB pronouncements, with two important exceptions (1) the statements may be condensed and (2) certain note disclosures given in annual financial statements may not be required. *S-X 10-01*

Non-US companies need provide only such interim financial information as their various stock exchange listing agreements specify.

Prior to filing, interim financial statements included in quarterly reports on Form 10-Q must be reviewed by an independent public accountant using professional standards and procedures for conducting such reviews. If, in any filing, the company states that an independent public accountant has reviewed interim financial statements, a report of the accountant on the review must be filed with the interim financial statements.

Guidance on conducting a review of interim financial information by the independent accountant is provided in SAS 100 *Interim financial information.*

30.3   ACCOUNTING

Where interim reports are being prepared, each interim period should be viewed primarily as an integral part of an annual period. The interim results should be based on the same accounting principles and practices that are deployed for annual reporting purposes unless there has been a change in accounting policy during the current year. However, certain accounting principles and practices may require modification at interim reporting dates so that the reported results for the interim period may better relate to the results of operations for the annual period. *APB 28.9-10*

deferred, and a liability recognised at an interim reporting date must represent an existing obligation at that date.

Measurement of income and expenses for an interim period is made on a year-to-date basis, recognising that the interim period is part of a larger financial year. The frequency of an entity's reporting therefore does not affect the measurement of the annual results. Income and expenses for an interim period are determined by subtracting (1) year-to-date amount for the previous interim period from (2) year-to-date amounts for the current period. As a result, the current interim period amounts may include the effects of changes in estimates relating to previous interim periods.

IAS 34.23,25,41   Materiality is assessed in relation to the interim period financial data when deciding how to recognise, measure, classify or disclose an item for interim financial reporting purposes, although it is recognised that interim measurements may rely to a greater extent on estimates than measurements used in annual financial data. The overriding goal is to ensure that the interim financial report reliably measures and appropriately discloses all information relevant to understanding the entity's financial position and performance in the interim period. Appendix C to IAS 34 gives more detailed guidance on the use of estimates.

IAS 34 Appx B   Appendix B to IAS 34 provides detailed guidance and examples on applying the recognition and measurement principles of the Standard described below.

A   Accounting policy changes

IAS 34.43   Accounting policy changes that are not subject to the transition rules of a new Standard or Interpretation are accounted for by restating the financial statements of prior interim periods in accordance with IAS 8 *Accounting Policies, Changes in Accounting Estimates and Errors* (see section 1). When it is impracticable to determine the cumulative effect at the beginning of the financial year of applying a new accounting policy to all prior periods, the financial statements of prior interim periods should be adjusted to apply the new policy prospectively from the earliest date practicable, but from a date no later than the beginning of the financial year.

B   Revenue

IAS 34.37   Revenues that are received seasonally, cyclically, or occasionally, within a financial year are not anticipated or deferred as of an interim date, if anticipation or deferral would not be appropriate at the end of the entity's financial year.

C   Costs and expenses

IAS 34.39   Costs that are incurred unevenly during an entity's financial year are anticipated or deferred for interim reporting purposes if and only if it is also appropriate to anticipate or defer that type of cost at the end of the financial year.

A   Accounting changes

A change in accounting policy during the interim period reported on should be highlighted and accounted for in accordance with APB 20 (see section 1.10). In general, companies should adopt changes in accounting principles or policies during the first interim period of a year. If a change is made after the first quarter and accounted for by a cumulative catch-up adjustment, the cumulative effect of the change on retained earnings should be reported as if the change were made in the first quarter. Therefore, in the quarter of change the results should include only that quarter's effect of the change; the effect on each of the previous quarters of that year should be separately disclosed (income and per share), and those quarters should be restated whenever presented.

APB 28.23
FAS 3.9-10

B   Revenue

Revenue should be recognised as earned during an interim period, just as it is for the full year.

APB 28.11

C   Costs and expenses

As many companies do not take physical stock counts each quarter, APB 28 allows interim cost of goods sold to be determined using various estimation techniques, including the use of an estimated gross profit percentage applied to sales for the interim period.

APB 28.14

Costs and expenses not directly associated with revenue may be either charged against revenue in the interim periods as they are incurred or, allocated among interim periods based on an estimate of time expired, benefit received, or activity associated with the periods (e.g. advertising costs may be deferred within a fiscal

APB 28.15

D   Changes in estimates for prior periods

IAS 34.16(d)   An entity that reports interim financial information, measures income and expenses
IAS 34.27,29   on a year-to-date basis for each interim period using information available when
IAS 34.35-36   each set of financial statements is being prepared.   Any changes in estimates of
amounts reported in prior interim periods are included in the current interim period.
Amounts reported in prior interim periods are not retrospectively adjusted, but the
nature and amount of any significant changes in estimates must be disclosed.

E   Income tax provisions

IAS 34.30,   Income tax is recognised in each interim period based on the best estimate of the
Appx B12-B22   weighted average annual income tax rate expected for the full financial year.   This
should, where practicable, be determined separately for each tax jurisdiction and for
each category of income where different tax rates apply, although a weighted
average which gives a reasonable approximation to the use of specific rates may be
used.   Anticipated tax benefits, e.g. for capital expenditure, exports or research and
development costs, which are granted and calculated on an annual basis under most
tax laws and regulations, are generally reflected in computing the estimated annual
effective income tax rate.   However, tax benefits that relate to a one-time event are
recognised in computing income tax expense in that interim period.   Where tax
benefits or credits, while reported on the income tax return, are more similar to a
government grant, they are recognised in the interim period in which they arise.
Where the tax year does not coincide with the financial year, different rates should
be computed for each tax year.   The estimated average annual income tax rate is
re-estimated on a year-to-date basis.

The benefits of a tax loss carryback to recover current tax of a previous period is
recognised as an asset in the period in which the tax loss occurs.   A deferred tax asset
is recognised for the carryforward of unused tax losses and unused tax credits to the
extent that it is probable that future taxable profit will be available, against which these
can be utilised, applying the criteria in IAS 12 *Income Taxes* at the end of each interim
period.   If the criteria are met, the effect of the tax loss carryforward is reflected in
the computation of the estimated average annual effective income tax rate.

Extensive examples of the application of this principle are provided in Appendix B
to IAS 34.

F   Fourth quarter results

IAS 34.26   Estimates of amounts reported in an interim period may change significantly during
the final interim period of the financial year.   Where this is the case and a separate
interim financial report is not published for the final interim period, the nature and
amount of that change in estimate should be disclosed in a note to the annual
financial statements for that financial year.

year if the benefits of an expenditure made clearly extend beyond the interim period in which the expenditure is made).

D   *Changes in estimates in prior periods*

A material nonrecurring adjustment or settlement of litigation or similar claims, income taxes (except for the effects of retroactive tax legislation) or renegotiation proceedings should be accounted for as an adjustment of prior interim periods of the current year if certain criteria are met (including for instance, that the amount of the adjustment or settlement could not be reasonably estimated prior to the current period but becomes reasonably estimable in the current interim period).

FAS 16.13

E   *Income tax provisions*

Companies should make their best estimate of the effective tax rate for the full year and apply this rate when providing for taxes on a current year-to-date basis. FIN 18 provides further guidance on this issue.

APB 28.19
FIN 18

In estimating the annual tax charge, companies should project the deferred tax effects of expected year-end temporary differences. Those with significant deductible temporary differences or operating loss carryforwards should assess (on a quarterly basis) whether a valuation allowance for those deferred tax assets will be required at the year end. A change in a valuation allowance resulting from a change in circumstances which has impacted the realisability of the related deferred tax asset in future years should be recognised as of the date of the change in circumstances and should not be allocated to subsequent interim periods by an adjustment of the estimated annual effective tax rate. If realisation of an operating loss carryforward attributable to losses in prior years is expected because of estimated 'ordinary' income in the current year, the operating loss carryforward should be included in computing the estimated annual effective tax rate.

The estimated effective tax rate should not include tax related to significant, unusual, or extraordinary items that will be separately reported or reported net of related tax either for the interim period or the full year.

APB 28.19

F   *Fourth quarter results*

If a fourth quarter report is not issued, significant year-end adjustments and unusual items recorded in that quarter must be disclosed in the annual report.

APB 28.31
FAS 3

G   Valuations

IAS 34.28,41   The measurement bases for interim reporting are the same as those applied for the
Appx C   previous annual financial statements (unless an accounting policy change is to be
reflected in the next set of annual financial statements).   The measurement
procedures adopted must result in reliable information.   However, this may involve
greater use of estimation methods, and less use of outside experts than at year-ends,
and may simply involve updating the year-end position.   Appendix C to IAS 34
gives guidance in specific areas.

H   Foreign exchange

IAS 34,   An entity measures foreign currency translation gains and losses in the interim
Appx B29-B31   period using the same principles as applied at the financial year end in accordance
with IAS 21 *The Effects of Changes in Foreign Exchange Rates*.   The actual
average rates and closing rates for the interim period are used.

30.4   DISCLOSURE

IAS 34.6-7,9   Interim financial reports shall contain either a complete set of financial statements,
conforming with the requirements of IAS 1 *Presentation of Financial Statements* or
a set of condensed financial statements prepared in accordance with IAS 34.   A
complete set of financial statements included in an interim financial report shall
include all disclosures required by IAS 34 and other Standards and Interpretations.

IAS 34.14   Interim financial reports (condensed or complete) are presented on a consolidated
basis where the most recent annual financial statements were consolidated financial
statements.   Presentation of the parent's separate financial statements, if these were
included in the most recent annual financial report, is neither required nor
prohibited by IAS 34.

IAS 34.8,13   Interim financial reports must include, at a minimum, the following components:
- condensed balance sheet;
- condensed income statement;
- condensed statement showing either (1) all changes in equity or (2) those
  changes in equity other than those arising from capital transactions with
  owners and distributions to owners (using the same format as in the annual
  financial statements);
- condensed cash flow statement; and
- selected explanatory notes.

IAS 34.10,18   The condensed financial statements shall include, at a minimum, each of the headings
and subtotals that were included in the most recent annual financial statements, and
the selected explanatory notes required by IAS 34.   Additional disclosures required
by other standards are not required.   Additional line items and notes are added if
their omission would make the interim financial statements misleading.

IAS 34.11   Basic and diluted earnings per share are presented on the face of the income
statement for an interim period (in condensed or complete financial statements).

G   Valuations

The bases of measurement for interim reporting should be the same as those   *APB 28.15(a)*
applied for the previous year end financial statements, e.g. inventories, investments,
derivative instruments, impairment.   Pension and other post retirement and post   *FAS 87.52-53*
employment cost amounts may be based on valuations and assumptions used at the   *FAS 106.72-73*
previous year end, unless more recent measurements are available.

H   Foreign exchange

Where average rates of exchange are applied for an interim period these should be   *FAS 52.140*
the appropriate average rates for each period.

30.4   DISCLOSURE

The condensed financial statements to be filed on Form 10-Q must include: *S-X 10-01(c)*

- balance sheets as of the end of the most recent quarter and as of the end of
  the preceding year;

- income statements for the most recent quarter, for the period between the
  end of the preceding year and the end of the most recent quarter, and for the
  corresponding periods of the preceding year;

- statements of cash flows for the period between the end of the preceding year
  and the end of the most recent quarter, and for the corresponding period of
  the preceding year;

- sufficient disclosures, either on the face of the financial statements or in
  accompanying footnotes, so as to make the interim information presented not
  misleading.   These disclosures should include significant changes since the
  end of the most recently completed financial year in items such as accounting
  principles, estimations inherent in the preparation of financial statements,
  status of long-term contracts, capitalisation (including significant new
  borrowings or modification of existing financing arrangements and changes in
  the reporting entity resulting from business combinations or disposals).

- per share information (basic and diluted) for each period presented;   *S-X 10-01(b)(2)*

- statements of comprehensive income and disclosure of total comprehensive   *FAS 130.27*
  income for each period presented; and

- limited segmental disclosures for each period presented;   *FAS 131.33*

Article 10-01 of Regulation S-X contains further instructions regarding the
information to be given in quarterly reports, including:

- an analysis of inventory (raw materials, work in progress and finished goods);   *S-X 10-01(a)*

- for development stage companies, condensed cumulative financial statements
  and disclosures as required by FAS 7 *Accounting and Reporting by
  Development Stage Enterprises* to the date of the latest balance sheet
  presented;

IAS 34.20   Interim reports shall include interim financial statements (condensed or complete) for periods as follows:

- balance sheet as of the end of the current interim period and a comparative balance sheet as of the end of the immediately preceding financial year;

- income statements for the current interim period and cumulatively for the current financial year to date, with comparative income statements for the comparable interim periods (current and year-to-date) of the immediately preceding financial year;

- statement showing changes in equity cumulatively for the current financial year to date, with a comparative statement for the comparable year-to-date period of the immediately preceding financial year; and

- cash flow statement cumulatively for the current financial year to date, with a comparative statement for the comparable year-to-date period of the immediately preceding financial year.

IAS 34.21   Where the entity's business is highly seasonal, inclusion of additional financial information for the 12 months ending on the interim reporting date and comparative financial information for the previous 12 months is encouraged.

IAS 34.15-16   The disclosure requirements of IAS 34 recognise that users of interim financial reports have access to the most recent annual financial report of the entity. The entity shall disclose any events and transactions material to an understanding of changes in the financial position and performance of the entity since the last annual report.

IAS 34.16   An entity shall disclose as a minimum, normally on a financial year-to-date basis the following information in the notes to the interim financial statements (unless disclosed elsewhere in the interim financial report:

- the fact that the same accounting policies and methods of computation are followed as in the most recent annual financial statements. Where these have changed, the nature and effect of the changes are disclosed;

- explanatory comments about the seasonality or cyclicality of interim operations;

- the nature and amount of items affecting assets, liabilities, equity, net income, or cash flows that are unusual because of their nature, size, or incidence;

- the nature and amount of changes in estimates of amounts reported in prior interim periods of the current financial year or changes in estimates of amounts reported in prior financial years, if those changes have a material effect in the current interim period;

- issuances, repurchases, and repayments of debt and equity securities;

- dividends paid (aggregate or per share) separately for ordinary shares and other shares;

- segment revenue and segment result based on the entity's primary basis of segment reporting, determined in accordance with IAS 14 *Segment Reporting* (where IAS 14 requires segmental disclosures in the annual financial statements);

- material events subsequent to the end of the interim period that have not been reflected in the financial statements for the interim period;

- summarised income statement information for each subsidiary not *S-X 10-01(b)* consolidated or 50% or less owned entity, or for each group of such entities, for which separate individual or group statements would otherwise be required for annual periods;

- supplemental disclosure of the results for periods prior to the combination for entities in a business combination during the current period accounted for as a pooling of interests;

- pro forma disclosure of results for the current year to the most recent balance sheet presented (and for the corresponding period of the prior year) for a purchase business combination during the current period, as if the entities had combined at the beginning of the period being reported on; and

- the effect on revenues and net income for all periods presented of any disposal of a significant component of an entity during the current period;

Interim financial statements should reflect all adjustments which are, in the opinion of   *S-X 10-01(b)(8)* management, necessary for a fair presentation of the results for the period. A statement to this effect should be included. Where such adjustments are of a normal recurring nature, a statement to that effect should be included; otherwise, details of the nature and amount of other than normal recurring adjustments should be provided.

If a company elects to distribute a quarterly report containing summarised financial   *APB 28.30* information (including fourth quarter reports), the following minimum disclosures should be given:

- sales or gross revenues;
- provision for income taxes;
- net income;
- comprehensive income; and
- basic and diluted earnings per share.

Companies should also report any of the following that are applicable: *APB 28.30*

- business combinations;
- effect of accounting changes;
- disposal of a component of an entity;
- extraordinary, unusual or infrequently occurring items;
- seasonal revenue, costs or expenses;
- contingent items;
- significant changes in estimates or provisions for income taxes; and
- significant changes since the last reporting period in liquid assets, net working capital, long-term liabilities or stockholders' equity.

Where summarised financial information is regularly reported on a quarterly basis,   *APB 28.30* the company should furnish this information for the current quarter and the current year to date or the last 12 months to date, together with comparative information for the preceding year.

IFRS 3.66-73   •   the effect of changes in the composition of the entity during the interim
IAS 34.16(i)   period, including business combinations, acquisition or disposal of subsidiaries
                     and long-term investments, restructurings, and discontinued operations.   For
                     business combinations, the extensive disclosures in IFRS 3 *Business*
                     Combinations, paras. 66 to 73, are required (see section 3.4.7).   Business
                     combinations effected in the interim period that are not individually material
                     (but materiality is based on interim period data) may be aggregated;

               •   changes in contingent liabilities or contingent assets since the last annual
                     balance sheet date.

Various examples of items that would normally be disclosed are given, such as
impairments (and reversals of impairments), writedowns of inventories to net
realisable value (and reversals of such writedowns), restructuring provisions (and
reversals), corrections of prior period errors, litigation settlements, loan defaults and
breaches of loan agreements not remedied on or before balance sheet date, related
party transactions, acquisitions (and commitments for the purchase of) and
disposals of items of property, plant and equipment.

IAS 34.19   Where the interim financial report complies with IAS 34, that fact shall be disclosed.
The interim financial report shall not be described as complying with International
Financial Reporting Standards unless all requirements are complied with.

IFRS 1.45-46   IFRS 1 *First-Time Adoption* requires, in addition, various reconciliations to
previous GAAP where a first–time adopter presents an interim financial report
under IAS 34 for part of the period covered by its first IFRS financial statements.

COMMENT

In June 2004 the FASB issued an exposure draft of a Proposed Statement of Financial Accounting Standards *Fair Value Measurements*. The proposed Statement provides guidance for how to measure fair value but would also require the following additional disclosure in interim financial statements:

(1)   for assets and liabilities that are remeasured at fair value on a recurring (or ongoing) basis during the period, (a) the fair value amounts at the end of the period, in total and as a percentage of total assets and liabilities, (b) how those fair value amounts were determined, and (c) the effect of the remeasurements on earnings for the period (unrealised gains or losses) relating to those assets and liabilities still held at the reporting date; and

(2)   for assets and liabilities that are remeasured at fair value on a nonrecurring (or periodic) basis during the period, (a) the reason for the remeasurements, (b) the fair value amounts, (c) how those fair value amounts were determined, and (d) the effect of the remeasurements on earnings for the period relating to those assets and liabilities still held at the reporting date.

Chapter 4 Principal differences between IFRSs and US GAAP

Introduction

Differences between IFRSs and US GAAP may be categorised broadly into those arising from differences in recognition and measurement requirements and those relating to differences in disclosure requirements. This chapter focuses on the major recognition and measurement differences, as well as the most significant disclosure differences between IFRSs and US GAAP.

The principal differences and similarities between IFRSs and US GAAP are discussed in this Chapter, using the structure and numbering system of Chapter 3.

Section 31 of this Chapter provides a summary of the US regulatory requirements for foreign filers, as set out in Regulation S-X *Form and content of and requirements for financial statements* issued by the SEC.

Section 32 sets out a summary of the principal differences between IFRSs and US GAAP that are due solely to the first time adoption of IFRSs under IFRS 1 *First-time Adoption of International Financial Reporting Standards.*

1   Presentation of financial statements

1.1   Components of financial statements
(Chapter 3 sections 1.2 and 1.5.2)

IFRSs and US GAAP both require a full set of financial statements to include a balance sheet, income statement, statement of changes in equity, cash flow statement, accounting policies and notes. However, there are differences between IFRSs and US GAAP in the layout of each primary financial statement and the classification of individual items within those statements. The SEC requires a full set of financial statements to provide three years' primary financial statements and related note disclosures, except for balance sheets. Balance sheets are required for two years. IFRSs financial statements must cover two years, i.e. the current period and one comparative period.

1.2   Fair presentation
(Chapter 3 section 1.3)

IAS 1 *Presentation of Financial Statements* requires that 'financial statements shall present fairly the financial position, financial performance and cash flows of an entity.' It goes on to state that the application of IFRSs, with additional disclosure when necessary, is presumed to result in financial statements that achieve a fair presentation. Fair presentation also requires an entity to:

- select and apply accounting policies in accordance with IAS 8 *Accounting Policies, Changes in Accounting Estimates and Errors*;

- present information in a manner that provides relevant, reliable, comparable and understandable information; and

- provide additional disclosures when compliance with the specific requirements of IFRSs is insufficient to enable users to understand the impact of particular transactions or events on the entity's financial position and financial performance.

IAS 1 makes it clear that inappropriate accounting policies are not rectified either by disclosure of the accounting policies used or by notes or explanatory material. The Standard caters for those situations where compliance with a Standard or Interpretation would distort fair presentation. Consequently, the Standard provides that in the extremely rare circumstances in which management concludes that compliance with a requirement in a Standard or an Interpretation would be so misleading that it would conflict with the objective of financial statements set out in the IASB's Framework, the entity shall depart from that requirement if the relevant regulatory framework requires, or otherwise does not prohibit, such a departure.

In appropriate circumstances when an entity applies the override, it must disclose the following:

(a) that management has concluded that the financial statements present fairly the entity's financial position, financial performance and cash flows;

(b) that it has complied with applicable Standards and Interpretations, except that it has departed from a particular requirement to achieve a fair presentation;

(c) the title of the Standard or Interpretation from which the entity has departed, the nature of the departure, including the treatment that the Standard or Interpretation would require, the reason why that treatment would be so misleading in the circumstances that it would conflict with the objective of financial statements set out in the IASB's Framework, and the treatment adopted; and

(d) for each period presented, the financial impact of the departure on each item in the financial statements that would have been reported in complying with the requirement.

When an entity has departed from a requirement of a Standard or an Interpretation in a prior period, and that departure affects the amounts recognised in the financial statements for the current period, the Standard requires it to make the disclosures set out in (c) and (d) above.

It is worth noting that the fair presentation override is a requirement (not an option) of IAS 1 to be applied in the extremely rare circumstances in which management concludes that compliance with a requirement in a Standard or an Interpretation would be so misleading that it would conflict with the objective of financial statements set out in the IASB's Framework.

However, at the same time, the IASB has introduced a somewhat contradictory twist to the application of the override. As stated above, the override can be applied only if 'the relevant regulatory framework requires, or otherwise does not prohibit' its use. This means that the Board has built into IAS 1 the possibility of regulatory intervention in its application. IAS 1 provides for the situation where 'the relevant regulatory framework' prohibits departure from a requirement in a particular Standard or Interpretation. In such cases, the Standard requires an entity, to the maximum extent possible, to reduce the perceived misleading aspects of compliance by disclosing:

(a) the title of the Standard or Interpretation in question, the nature of the requirement, and the reason why management has concluded that complying with that requirement is so misleading in the circumstances that it conflicts with the objective of financial statements set out in the Framework; and

(b) for each period presented, the adjustments to each item in the financial statements that management has concluded would be necessary to achieve a fair presentation.

This seems to contradict the clear statement in IAS 1 that 'inappropriate accounting policies are not rectified either by disclosure of the accounting policies used or by notes or explanatory material'. It seems also to create the unwelcome precedent of a standard formally giving regulators the ability to determine how standards should be applied.

The SEC will generally not accept a fair presentation override applied to US GAAP.

1.3 Accounting policies

1.3.1 Selection of accounting policies

(Chapter 3 section 1.4)

Where a Standard or Interpretation under IFRSs specifically applies to a transaction, other event or condition, application of that Standard or Interpretation, together with consideration of any relevant Implementation Guidance, should determine the accounting policy adopted. Where there is no specific requirement under IFRSs, IAS 8 provides principles on the selection of accounting policies that should be selected and applied. In addition, IAS 8 requires management's selection of accounting policies to ensure that the entity's financial statements provide information that is both relevant to the decision-making needs of the users and reliable. In selecting relevant and reliable accounting policies, management should consider the requirements of extant IFRSs dealing with similar issues and the IASB's Framework, and may also consider pronouncements issued by other standard-setters that use a similar conceptual framework. In the absence of specific IFRSs guidance, US GAAP is not the default treatment. Accounting policies should be applied consistently for similar transactions, other events and conditions, unless a Standard or Interpretation specifically requires or permits otherwise.

US GAAP does not contain principles that must be applied in the selection of accounting policies where there is no explicit pronouncement on an issue. However, Statement on Auditing Standards (SAS) No. 69 *The Meaning of Present Fairly in Conformity With Generally Accepted Accounting Principles* sets out a hierarchy of US GAAP and states that, in the absence of a pronouncement or another source of established accounting principles, the auditor may consider other accounting literature, depending on its relevance in the circumstances. Pronouncements by the IASB are included as an example of such accounting literature.

1.4   Comparative information

(Chapter 3 section 1.5.2)

IFRSs requires disclosure of one comparative period for the income statement, balance sheet, cash flow statement, statement of changes in equity and the explanatory notes, whereas under US GAAP, the SEC requires registrants to disclose two comparative periods for all components of financial statements except the balance sheet, for which one comparative year is required.

1.5   Layout of primary financial statements

1.5.1   Layout of the balance sheet

(Chapter 3 sections 1.6.1 and 1.6.2)

The presentation of the balance sheet under IFRSs is detailed in IAS 1 *Presentation of Financial Statements*. IAS 1 does not prescribe a standard layout, but does require a minimum level of disclosure on the face of the balance sheet and a classification under current and non-current except when presentation in order of liquidity is both reliable and more relevant. There is no general requirement under US GAAP to prepare a balance sheet in accordance with a specific layout. However, SEC registrants reporting under US GAAP are required to prepare their balance sheets in conformity with Regulation S-X, which provides a list of items that should appear on the balance sheet. There are no fundamental incompatibilities between the items required by IAS 1 and Regulation S-X. Nevertheless, differences in the layout of IFRSs and US GAAP balance sheets may appear in the following areas:

- entities reporting under US GAAP virtually always present a classified balance sheet that distinguishes between current and non-current items. IAS 1 requires current and non-current items to be presented as separate classifications on the balance sheet except when presentation based on liquidity provides more reliable and more relevant information;

- IFRSs requires presentation of deferred tax as non-current. US GAAP, however, requires classification as current or non-current based on the classification of the related asset or liability in the balance sheet (see section 17.10);

- IAS 28 *Investments in Associates* requires that investments in associates accounted for using the equity method are classified as non-current assets; and

- US GAAP requires more detailed disclosure of individual classes of equity on the face of the balance sheet than does IFRSs, which permits such information to be disclosed instead in the notes to the financial statements.

1.5.2   Reclassification of liabilities

(Chapter 3 section 1.6.2)

A refinancing of a current liability that occurs after the balance sheet date but before the financial statements are issued may qualify for disclosure as non-adjusting in accordance with IAS 10 *Events after the Balance Sheet Date,* and therefore will not result in the reclassification of a liability from current to non-current in the financial statements. US GAAP goes much further as, under FAS 6

Classification of Short-Term Obligations Expected to Be Refinanced, short-term obligations may be reclassified as non-current liabilities if the entity (1) intends to refinance the obligation on a long-term basis, and (2) prior to issuing the financial statements can demonstrate the ability to refinance.

In a similar way, IAS 1 requires that a long-term loan that is payable on demand following a breach of an undertaking is classified as current even if the lender has agreed, after the balance sheet date but before the financial statements are issued, not to demand payment. Under US GAAP, the loan would be classified as non-current if, before the financial statements are issued, the lender has waived the right to demand repayment for more than one year from the balance sheet date.

1.5.3   Offsetting of assets and liabilities

(Chapter 3 section 1.6.3)

Under IFRSs, assets and liabilities and income and expenses should not be offset except where required or permitted by a Standard or Interpretation. Under IAS 32 *Financial Instruments: Disclosure and Presentation* financial assets and liabilities should not be offset against each other unless there is a legally enforceable right of offset and there is an intention to either settle on a net basis or to realise the asset and settle the liability simultaneously. Under US GAAP, it is a general principle that assets and liabilities should not be offset except where a right to offset exists, for example, as part of a master netting agreement, and there is an intention to offset. The SEC staff has expressed its opinion that the right of offset must be a legal right. Detailed rules also exist under US GAAP for the offset of the amounts owed by two parties to each other.

1.5.4   Layout of the income statement

(Chapter 3 section 1.6.4 and 1.6.5)

There is no general requirement under US GAAP for the classification of expenses. However, SEC registrants reporting under US GAAP are required to prepare their income statements in conformity with Regulation S-X, which provides a list of items that should appear on the income statement. IFRSs permit entities to disclose expenses either by their function in the entity or by the nature of the expense. Presentation of this analysis on the face of the income statement is encouraged but not required. However, when an entity presents expenses by function, it must also disclose additional information on the nature of those expenses in the notes.

A number of further differences in the classification of items in the income statement are discussed in sections 1.6 and 1.7 below.

1.5.5   Layout of the statement of changes in equity

(Chapter 3 section 1.6.6)

US GAAP (Regulation S-X) requires the presentation of an analysis of all changes in each caption of stockholders' equity either as a note to the financial statements or as a separate statement. Under IFRSs, entities have the option to present a statement that shows either all changes in each caption of shareholders' equity (a statement of changes in equity) or, alternatively, only changes in equity that did not arise from capital transactions with owners or distributions to owners, the 'statement of recognised income and expense' (SORIE). In the latter case, the entity would be required to disclose additional information on changes in equity in the notes to its financial statements. A SORIE is equivalent to the statement of comprehensive income under US GAAP, see section 1.5.6 below.

1.5.6   Statement of comprehensive income

(Chapter 3 section 1.6.6)

FAS 130 *Reporting Comprehensive Income* requires the presentation of a statement of comprehensive income, showing all movements in equity from non-owner sources, as a primary financial statement. IAS 1 requires an entity to present one of the following:

- a statement comprising all changes in equity; or

- a statement comprising all changes in equity not arising from transaction with shareholders. IAS 19 describes this statement as a statement of recognised income and expense (SORIE).

Entities that avail themselves of the option in IAS 19 (revised) *Employee Benefits* to present actuarial gains and losses in equity rather than the income statement are required to present a SORIE. IFRSs require that the SORIE be presented as a primary statement.

A foreign private issuer may prepare the statement of comprehensive income using either IFRSs or US GAAP. If IFRSs are used, then a reconciliation to US GAAP is encouraged but not required.

Some examples of the alternative approaches to compliance with the SEC's requirements for presentation of a statement of comprehensive income are given in the following extracts.

Extract 1: Nokia Corporation (2003)

36 Differences between International Accounting Standards and U.S. Generally Accepted Accounting Principles [extract]

Presentation of comprehensive income under U.S. GAAP:

	2003 EURm	2002 EURm	2001 EURm
Other comprehensive income:			
Foreign currency translation adjustment	(273)	(465)	(21)
Additional minimum liability, net of tax	3	(3)	-
Net gains (losses) on cash flow hedges, net of tax	(4)	56	96
Net unrealised (losses) gains on securities, net of tax			
Net unrealised holding (losses) gains during the year, net of tax	(71)	(78)	(67)
Transfer to profit and loss account on impairment, net of tax	27	67	74
Less: Reclassification adjustment for gains included in income	(27)	1	(7)
Other comprehensive income	(203)	(422)	(21)
Comprehensive income	3,894	3,181	1,978

Extract 2: Stora Enso OYJ (2003)

NOTE 28 – SUMMARY OF DIFFERENCES BETWEEN INTERNATIONAL FINANCIAL REPORTING STANDARDS AND GENERALLY ACCEPTED ACCOUNTING PRINCIPLES IN THE UNITED STATES [extract]

Consolidated Statement of Comprehensive Income

The Company has adopted SFAS No. 130, Reporting Comprehensive Income, which establishes standards for the reporting and presentation of comprehensive income and its components. The Company has chosen to present comprehensive income using amounts determined in accordance with IFRS.

Components of comprehensive income consist of the following:

	For the year ended December 31,			
	2001	**2002**	**2003**	**2003**
	€	**€**	**€**	**US$**
		(in millions)		
Comprehensive income				
Net income (loss) in accordance with IFRS (restated)	917.9	(240.7)	137.9	173.7
Other comprehensive income				
Foreign currency translation adjustment, net of tax expenses of €9.7 million in 2001 €125.0 million in 2002 and €43.4 million in 2003	19.5	(94.3)	(52.7)	(66.4)
Available-for-sale investments net of tax benefit of €7.4 million in 2001 and €10.2 million in 2002 and expense of €16.5 million in 2003	(21.2)	(24.3)	40.0	50.4
Cash flow hedging, net of tax expense of €1.4 million in 2001 and €81.1 million in 2002 and benefit of €63.6 million in 2003	4.1	199.1	(158.8)	(200.0)
Fair value adjustment related to the adoption of IAS 41, Agriculture as of January 1, 2003, net of tax expense of €240.4 million	–	–	659.4	830.7
Comprehensive income (loss) in accordance with IFRS (restated)	920.3	(160.2)	625.8	788.4

Extract 3: Lihir Gold Limited (2003)

Note 30: Reconciliation to US GAAP [extract]

	2003 US$'000	As Restated 2002 US$'000	2001 US$'000
Comprehensive income			
Net income/(loss) under US GAAP	374	38,625	42,330
Other comprehensive income under IAS GAAP	(137,079)	(123,085)	53,616
Release of valuation allowance under US GAAP	–	(16,426)	16,426
Other comprehensive income under US GAAP	(137,079)	(139,511)	70,042
Comprehensive income/(loss) under US GAAP	**(136,705)**	**(100,886)**	**112,372**

Statement of changes in equity under US GAAP

	2003 US$'000	As Restated 2002 US$'000	2001 US$'000
Accumulated Losses			
Balance at January 1	(478,486)	(377,600)	(489,972)
Comprehensive income / (loss)	(136,705)	(100,886)	112,372
Dividend	(14,185)	–	–
Balance at December 31	**(629,376)**	**(478,486)**	**(377,600)**
Paid up capital			
Balance at 1 January	873,822	873,822	873,822
Shares issued	156,240	–	–
Share issue transaction costs	(4,774)	–	–
Balance at 31 December	**1,025,288**	**873,822**	**873,822**
	395,912	**395,336**	**496,222**

1.6 Unusual or infrequent items

(Chapter 3 section 1.7)

IFRSs and US GAAP both require separate disclosure of material events or transactions that are unusual in nature or occur infrequently.

1.6.1 Extraordinary items

(Chapter 3 section 1.8)

Under IAS 1, entities are not permitted to present any items of income or expense as extraordinary items, either on the face of the income statement or in the notes. US GAAP permits the presentation of extraordinary items but the definition is very restrictive.

1.7 Discontinued operations

(Chapter 3 section 1.9)

The measurement and presentation requirements of IFRS 5 *Non-current Assets Held for Sale and Discontinued Operations* are based on, and therefore similar to, the US rules on reporting discontinued operations under FAS 144 *Accounting for the Impairment or Disposal of Long-Lived Assets*. However, differences are likely to occur in practice as a result of differences in the scope of the two standards and the definitions of discontinued operations.

1.7.1 Definition of discontinued operations

A discontinued operation under IFRS 5 is a component of an entity that either has been disposed of, or is classified as held for sale; and, (1) represents a separate major line of business or geographical area of operations; or (2) is part of a single co-ordinated plan to dispose of a separate major line of business or geographical area of operations; or (3) is a subsidiary acquired exclusively with a view to resale. A component of an entity comprises operations and cash flows that can be clearly distinguished from the rest of the entity, both operationally and for financial reporting purposes.

Under FAS 144, the term discontinued operations refers to the operations of a 'component of an entity' that either: (1) has been sold, abandoned, spun off, or otherwise disposed of; or (2) is classified as 'held for sale'. A 'component of an entity' represents operations and cash flows that can be clearly distinguished from the remainder of the entity, both operationally and for financial reporting purposes. A component of an entity may be an operating segment, a reporting unit, a subsidiary, or an asset group.

Although the definitions of 'held-for-sale' under IFRSs and US GAAP are broadly similar, there may be differences when applying the definitions in practice as the IFRSs definition of a discontinued operation is more restrictive.

1.8   Changes in accounting policies

(Chapter 3 section 1.10)

IAS 8 *Accounting Policies, Changes in Accounting Estimates and Errors* requires changes in accounting policies to be accounted for retrospectively by adjusting the opening balance of retained earnings and restating comparative information.

Generally, US GAAP currently requires changes in accounting policies to be recognised by means of a cumulative catch-up adjustment in the income statement for the current period. Although prior period statements are not restated, the income before extraordinary items and net income computed on a pro forma retroactive basis should be shown on the face of the income statement for all periods presented. In a limited number of circumstances, retroactive restatement of financial statements for all prior periods presented is required by specific accounting pronouncements. A proposed change to US GAAP would require retroactive restatement for changes in accounting principle following adoption of new accounting pronouncements, in the absence of specific transitional guidance, as well as voluntary changes in accounting principles.

1.9   Changes in accounting estimates

(Chapter 3 section 1.11)

IFRSs and US GAAP both prohibit the reporting of changes in accounting estimates by the restatement of prior periods. However, it is important to note that IFRSs requires a change in depreciation method to be treated as a change in accounting estimate, which must be accounted for prospectively. US GAAP, in contrast, currently requires a change in depreciation method to be treated as a change in accounting principle that requires a catch-up adjustment to be made. A proposed change to US GAAP would recognise a change in accounting estimate that is effected by a change in accounting principle, for example, a change in depreciation method, as a change in estimate to be accounted for prospectively.

2   Consolidated financial statements

2.1   Scope

(Chapter 3 section 2.2)

Under IAS 27 *Consolidated and Separate Financial Statements* a parent company should prepare consolidated financial statements in which all subsidiaries are consolidated. However, a parent company need not prepare consolidated financial statements if:

- it is a wholly owned subsidiary itself (or is a partially-owned subsidiary, and its other owners, including those not entitled to vote, have been informed about, and do not object to, the parent company not presenting consolidated financial statements);

- the parent's debt or equity instruments are not traded in a public market;

- the parent did not file, nor is in the process of filing, its financial statements with a securities commission or other regulatory organisation for the purpose of issuing any class of instruments in a public market; and

- the ultimate or any intermediate parent of the parent produces consolidated financial statements available for public use that comply with IFRS.

FAS 94 *Consolidation of all Majority-Owned Subsidiaries* confirms that if an enterprise has one or more subsidiaries, consolidated financial statements rather than parent company financial statements are the appropriate general-purpose financial statements.

2.2   Definition of a subsidiary

(Chapter 3 section 2.3)

The IAS 27 definition of a subsidiary is based on the concept of control. A parent company has control when it has the power to govern the financial and operating policies of an entity so as to obtain benefits from its activities. The existence of potential voting rights that are currently exercisable or convertible is also considered when assessing whether an entity controls another entity. Control is presumed to exist when the parent owns, directly or indirectly through subsidiaries, more than half of the voting power of an entity unless, in exceptional circumstances, it can be demonstrated clearly that such ownership does not constitute control. Control also exists when the parent owns 50% or less of the voting power of an entity, but has certain other legal or contractual powers that result in control. IFRSs also require the consolidation of controlled Special Purpose Entities (SPEs) (see section 2.5 below).

US GAAP requires consolidation of (1) entities in which the parent has a majority voting interest, unless the parent does not in fact control the entity, and (2) variable interest entities where the parent absorbs or receives a majority of the variable interest entity's expected losses and expected residual returns.

The SEC has a broader notion of control than the FASB, more in line with IFRSs, and notes that 'there may be situations where consolidation of an entity, notwithstanding the lack of technical majority ownership, is necessary to present fairly the financial position and results of operations of the registrant'.

2.3   Different reporting dates

(Chapter 3 section 2.3)

Financial statements of a subsidiary with a different reporting date to that of the parent may be consolidated where it is impracticable to prepare additional financial statements for the subsidiary with the same reporting date as the parent, if the difference is no more than three months and is consistent from period to period. However, under IFRSs, it is necessary to make adjustments for the effects of significant transactions or other events between the reporting date of the subsidiary and that of the parent. US GAAP only requires the effect of material intervening events to be disclosed.

2.4   Different accounting policies

(Chapter 3 section 2.3)

IFRSs require consolidated financial statements to be prepared using uniform accounting policies. There is no such specific requirement under US GAAP; however, because the consolidated financial statements represent the financial position and operating results of a single business entity, the accounting policies of consolidated entities would normally be conformed.

2.5   Minority interests

(Chapter 3 section 2.5.5)

2.5.1   Carrying amount of minority interests

The balance sheet measurement of the minority interest in an acquired subsidiary differs between IFRSs and US GAAP.

IFRS 3 *Business Combinations* requires any minority interest arising on acquisition to be stated at the minority's proportion of the fair values of the net assets of the acquired subsidiary. This treatment is not permitted under US GAAP.

The US GAAP treatment would generally result in minority interests being presented in the consolidated balance sheet at an amount equal to the minority's share of the pre-acquisition carrying amount of the subsidiary's net assets. When consolidating the assets and liabilities of an acquired subsidiary that is not wholly owned, the fair value adjustments are limited to the amount attributable to the parent company's ownership percentage. As a result, the assets and liabilities of the subsidiary are included on a 'mixed' basis in the consolidated financial statements.

2.5.2   Presentation of minority interests

Under IFRSs, minority interests classified as equity are presented within equity, but separate from the parent shareholders' equity. In contrast, US GAAP requires minority interests to be presented outside equity, between liabilities and equity.

2.6   Purchase of a non-controlling interest

(Chapter 3 section 2.5.6A)

When a controlling entity acquires additional shares held by a non-controlling entity (minority interest), US GAAP requires that the acquisition be accounted for under the purchase method. There is no specific guidance for transactions between controlling and non-controlling entities under IFRSs, and a number of different approaches are considered to be acceptable.

2.7   Special Purpose Entities (SPEs)

(Chapter 3 section 2.6)

The difficult area of accounting for SPEs has been addressed by the Standing Interpretations Committee (SIC) under IFRSs and by both the FASB and the SEC in the US. SIC-12 *Consolidation – Special Purpose Entities* requires an SPE to be consolidated when the substance of the relationship between an entity and the SPE indicates that the SPE is controlled by that entity. It gives examples of circumstances that may indicate that the SPE is controlled, but the overall approach is to identify the substance of the relationship, based on an analysis of risks and rewards.

The rules in FAS 140 *Accounting for Transfers and Servicing of Financial Assets and Extinguishments of Liabilities* have a more limited scope than SIC-12, since it was issued to provide rules for determining whether a transfer of financial assets constitutes a sale. It should therefore be applied only when the assets held by an SPE are financial assets (see section 11.2) and the SPE is a qualifying SPE (as defined in FAS 140). This type of SPE should not be consolidated if a number of detailed criteria designed to demonstrate that the investor does not control the SPE, are met.

In January 2003, the FASB issued FIN 46, *Consolidation of Variable Interest Entities, an Interpretation of Accounting Research Bulletin (ARB) No. 51.* FIN 46 was revised in December 2003. The FIN 46(R) consolidation model—the variable interests model—determines control (and consolidation) of a variable interest entity. Variable interest entities (VIEs) include many entities referred to as special purpose entities (SPEs), but also may include many other entities not previously thought of as SPEs under US GAAP. VIEs are evaluated for consolidation based on all contractual, ownership, or other interests that expose their holders to the risks and rewards of the entity. These interests are termed variable interests. The holder of a variable interest that receives the majority of the potential variability in expected losses or expected residual returns of the VIE is the VIE's primary beneficiary, and is required to consolidate the VIE.

Even after FIN 46(R) was issued, the US GAAP approach remains different from the IFRSs substance-based approach to identifying the relationship between the reporting entity and its SPE/VIE. It is therefore possible that a VIE under US GAAP may not require consolidation as an SPE under IFRSs, and vice versa.

2.8   Separate parent company financial statements

(Chapter 3 section 2.8)

In separate financial statements presented under IFRSs, investments in subsidiaries, other than those classified as (or included in a disposal group classified as) held for sale, are accounted for either at cost or at fair value in accordance with IAS 39 *Financial Instruments: Recognition and Measurement.* In parent-only financial statements prepared under US GAAP, investments in subsidiaries may be presented either using the cost or equity method.

3   Business combinations

3.1   General approach

(Chapter 3 section 3.2)

The definition of a business combination in FAS 141 *Business Combinations* and the scope of IFRS 3 *Business Combinations* exclude transfers of net assets or exchanges of equity interests between entities under common control. Such transactions are discussed in section 3.4 below.

3.2   The purchase method

(Chapter 3 section 3.4)

All business combinations within the scope of the relevant standards under both US GAAP and IFRSs are accounted for using the purchase method as set out in FAS 141 and IFRS 3, respectively. The basic principles of the purchase method in the two standards are similar, although there are significant differences in detail. The cost of the acquisition is defined as the fair value of the consideration given up plus any directly attributable costs. The assets and liabilities acquired are initially recognised in the acquiring entity's consolidated financial statements based on their fair values (with limited exceptions). The difference between the fair value of the consideration and the fair value of the group's share of assets acquired and liabilities assumed is called goodwill, and (if positive) is capitalised on the balance sheet of the acquiring entity. Although the basic principles of purchase accounting in FAS 141 and IFRS 3 are the same, there are several differences of detail that can cause large measurement and disclosure differences in practice.

3.2.1   Date of acquisition

(Chapter 3 section 3.4.2)

Under IFRS 3, the acquisition date is the date on which the acquirer effectively obtains control of the acquiree. It is possible that this date will be different from the effective date for an acquisition under FAS 141, which is ordinarily the date assets are received and other assets are given, liabilities are assumed or incurred, or equity interests are issued. Under FAS 141, for convenience, and only if certain conditions are met, the parties to an acquisition may designate the end of an accounting period between the date of initiation and consummation of the transaction as the effective acquisition date. This date may be used as the date of acquisition for accounting purposes if a written agreement provides that effective control of the acquired entity is transferred to the acquiring entity on that date without restrictions, except those required to protect the shareholders or other owners of the acquired entity. This alternative is not available under IFRSs.

3.2.2   The cost of the acquired entity

(Chapter 3 section 3.4.3)

A   Date at which the fair value of consideration is measured

Where the purchase consideration includes equity instruments that have been issued by the acquirer, the measurement of the instruments issued is likely to differ under IFRSs and US GAAP. IFRSs and US GAAP use a different measurement date to determine the fair value of the instruments. IFRSs use the date of exchange while US GAAP specifies a reasonable period of time before and after the date the terms of the acquisition are agreed to and announced. Since there may be an extended period of time between the announcement date and closing date, the difference in the measurement date can cause a significant difference in the measurement of the purchase consideration.

B   Contingent consideration

Under US GAAP, contingent consideration is usually recorded only when the contingency is resolved and consideration is issued or becomes issuable. If it is probable that the conditions for payment of contingent consideration would be met, and the amount can be measured reliably, IFRS 3 requires the contingent consideration to be recorded at the date of acquisition. Any subsequent adjustments to contingent consideration will be reflected in the carrying amount of goodwill.

C   Consideration or compensation

EITF 95-8 *Accounting for Contingent Consideration Paid to the Shareholders of an Acquired Enterprise in a Purchase Business Combination*, under US GAAP, provides guidance for the accounting for contingent consideration in a purchase business combination paid to shareholders of an acquired enterprise who could affect the financial results of the acquired enterprise subsequent to the acquisition as employees, officers, directors, consultants, contractors, and the like. The acquirer must analyse the relevant facts and circumstances to determine whether the contingent consideration should be accounted for as an adjustment of the purchase price or as compensation for services. This topic is not specifically mentioned in IFRSs.

3.2.3   Determining the fair value of identifiable assets acquired and liabilities assumed

(Chapter 3 section 3.4.4)

A   General approach

IFRS 3 requires identifiable assets (other than intangible assets) and liabilities (other than contingent liabilities) to be recognised separately on acquisition, if (1) it is probable that there will be an associated inflow of future economic benefits to the acquirer (for an asset) or an outflow of resources in order to settled the obligation (for a liability) and (2) the fair values can be reliably measured. Intangible assets and contingent liabilities are recognised separately where their fair values can be measured reliably, as discussed below.

FAS 141 requires the cost of an acquired entity to be allocated to all identifiable assets acquired and liabilities assumed in a business combination based on their estimated fair values at the date of acquisition.

The principal areas where differences occur are discussed below.

B   *Intangible assets*

IFRSs address the recognition of intangible assets acquired as part of a business combination in IFRS 3 and IAS 38 *Intangible Assets*. Any intangible asset must meet the IAS 38 criteria for recognition: identifiability, control and participation in future economic benefits. An intangible asset acquired as part of a business combination should be recognised separately from goodwill where its fair value can be measured with sufficient reliability. This does not necessarily imply a valuation on an active market. Where there is no active market for a certain type of intangible asset, the acquiring entity takes into account recent arm's length transactions for similar assets or applies valuation techniques for estimating the fair values indirectly. The only circumstances where it may not be possible to measure reliably fair value are when the intangible asset arises from legal or contractual rights and either (1) it is not separable, or (2) it is separable but there is no history or evidence of exchange transactions for the same or similar assets, and otherwise estimating fair value would be dependent on immeasurable variables. If the fair value of the intangible asset cannot be determined reliably, then the asset should not be recognised separately, but instead should be included in the goodwill arising from the acquisition.

FAS 141 requires an intangible asset to be recognised separately from goodwill at its estimated fair value if it arises from contractual or other legal rights, or if it is separable. An intangible asset may be considered separable if it can be sold or otherwise disposed of separately or in combination with a related contract, asset or liability.

The distinction between goodwill and other intangibles has become a crucial one, as both IFRSs and US GAAP do not permit the amortisation of goodwill. However, both systems require the amortisation of other intangible assets if they have finite useful lives (see section 6). Both FAS 141 and IFRS 3 provide long, but not exhaustive, lists of examples of intangible assets that meet the criteria for recognition separately from goodwill, categorised as marketing-related, customer-related, artistic-related, contract-based and technology-based intangible assets.

FAS 141 states clearly that an assembled workforce does not qualify for recognition as a separate intangible asset when it is acquired as part of a business combination. IAS 38 similarly states that an entity usually has insufficient control of the expected useful economic benefits arising from a team of skilled staff for these to meet the definition of a separate intangible asset. An assembled workforce is therefore included within the goodwill recognised in an acquisition under both IFRSs and US GAAP.

For a full discussion of the treatment of goodwill and other intangible assets see section 6 of this chapter.

C   In-process research and development

If amounts allocated to acquired in-process research and development meet the recognition criteria, they should be capitalised under IFRSs and amortised over their useful economic lives. Under US GAAP, a portion of the purchase price paid in a business combination should be assigned to tangible and intangible assets to be used in research and development projects that have no alternative future use and charged to expense at the acquisition date (see Chapter 3 section 3.4.4C).

D   Provisions for reorganisations and future losses

Under IFRS 3, the acquirer should recognise liabilities for terminating or reducing the activities of the acquiree as part of allocating the cost of the combination only when the acquiree has, at the acquisition date, an existing liability for restructuring recognised in accordance with IAS 37 *Provisions, Contingent Liabilities and Contingent Assets* (see Chapter 3 section 3). The acquiree should not recognise liabilities for future losses or other costs expected to be incurred as a result of the combination.

US GAAP allows the acquirer's intentions to be taken into account to an extent when measuring the liabilities acquired with a business, with the result that certain restructuring provisions may also be recognised in the acquired balance sheet under US GAAP.

E   Pre-acquisition contingent liabilities

Under both IFRSs and US GAAP, contingent liabilities are recognised at the acquisition date at fair value even where not previously recognised by the acquiree in accordance with relevant guidance, IAS 37 and FAS 5, respectively.

IFRS 3 specifies that a contingent liability is recognised only if its fair value can be measured reliably. Potentially more contingent liabilities may be recognised on acquisition under US GAAP as FAS 141 requires that a pre-acquisition contingency be recognised at fair value. If fair value cannot be determined then the pre-acquisition contingency should be recognised using the guidance in FAS 5 when it is probable that an asset existed, a liability had been incurred or an asset had been impaired and the amount can be reasonably estimated.

F   Deferred taxation

A deferred tax liability or asset should be recognised for differences between the assigned values and the tax bases of the assets and liabilities recognised in a business combination accounted for under the purchase method. No deferred tax liability is recognised upon initial recognition of goodwill.

Under IAS 12 *Income Taxes*, if a deferred tax asset of the acquiree which was not recognised at the time of the combination is subsequently recognised, the resulting credit is taken to income for the period. This credit is offset by an expense to reduce the carrying amount of goodwill to the amount that would have been recognised had the deferred tax asset been recognised at the time of the combination.

Under US GAAP, the subsequent elimination of a valuation allowance recognised at the acquisition date for deferred tax assets would be applied first to eliminate any goodwill related to the acquisition, second to eliminate any non-current intangible assets related to the acquisition, and third to reduce income tax expense.

G   Minority interests

(Chapter 3 section 2.5.5)

Where an investor acquires less than 100% of a subsidiary, any minority interest arising on consolidation should represent the minority's proportion of the subsidiary's identifiable assets and liabilities. Under IFRSs, the minority's proportion is measured at fair value at the date of the combination. Under US GAAP, minority interests generally represent the minority's share of the carrying amount of the subsidiary's net assets. In practice, this can give rise to a substantial difference between the two systems.

3.3   Accounting for goodwill

(Chapter 3 section 7.4.5)

Goodwill represents the difference between the cost of the business combination and the acquirer's interest in the fair value of the identifiable assets acquired and liabilities assumed.

3.3.1   Positive goodwill

Goodwill under both IFRSs and US GAAP is not amortised but is tested for impairment annually or more frequently if events or changes in circumstances indicate that it might be impaired. However, there are substantial differences in approach to impairment measurement under IFRSs and US GAAP (see section 9.2.2).

3.3.2   Negative goodwill

Under IFRS 3, if the acquirer's interest in the net fair value of the identifiable assets and liabilities exceeds the cost of the business combination, (1) the identification and measurement of the identifiable assets and liabilities and the cost of the business combination should be reassessed, and (2) any excess remaining after the reassessment should be recognised immediately in income.

Under US GAAP, when the acquirer's interest in the fair value of the identifiable assets acquired and liabilities assumed exceeds the cost of the business combination the excess is negative goodwill.

FAS 141 requires negative goodwill to be allocated to reduce proportionately the values assigned to most of the acquired non-financial assets (including in-process research and development assets). Any remaining goodwill, once the value of the acquired non-financial assets has been reduced to zero, is recognised as an extraordinary gain in the period that the acquisition takes place.

3.4   Entities under common control

The definition of a business combination in FAS 141 and the scope of IFRS 3 exclude transfers of net assets or exchanges of equity interests between entities under common control. FAS 141 provides examples of such transactions and accounting guidance (Appendix D), which require that net assets or equity interests transferred are initially recognised at their carrying amounts as recorded by the transferring entity at the transfer date, similar to the pooling-of-interests method of accounting.

In the absence of specific guidance in IFRSs, judgement should be used to develop and apply relevant and reliable accounting policies. In practice, the approaches followed by companies vary, and include both purchase accounting and approaches based on, for example, 'as-if' pooling-of-interest under US GAAP.

3.5 Group reconstructions

A common type of group reconstruction is the creation of a new holding company at the top of an existing group in order to facilitate, for example, the demerger of part of the group's business or its flotation. Under IFRSs, it is not clear whether this type of transaction (1) falls into the category of transactions under common control (see section 3.4 above) or (2) should be treated as a reverse acquisition. In any event it would not be usual practice to apply the purchase method under IFRSs, with remeasurement of the existing group and creation of goodwill, when there has been no real change in ownership of any assets. Comparative figures may be restated to reflect the new structure of the group – for example, if a new holding company has been created on top of an existing group, the financial statements for that group would be prepared as if the new holding company had always been the holding company. US GAAP requires a similar treatment, and specifies that where there has been a change in the reporting entity, all prior periods should be restated.

4 Associates and joint ventures

Both IFRSs and US GAAP require investments over which an entity has significant influence, but not control, to be accounted for using the equity method. The application of the equity method under IAS 28 *Investments in Associates* will in many cases not be different from the accounting treatment required by APB 18 *The Equity Method of Accounting for Investments in Common Stock* under US GAAP. The SEC staff has stated publicly that it believes that there are no differences between IFRSs and US GAAP regarding the application of the equity method.

There is a significant presentational difference between IFRSs and US GAAP in the treatment of joint ventures. Under IFRSs, entities may choose to account for a jointly controlled entity using the equity method or, alternatively, to apply proportionate consolidation. APB 18 applies the same rules to corporate joint ventures as to all other investments of 50% or less of the voting stock in which the equity investor has significant influence, that is, equity method accounting must be applied (see 4.4 below). US GAAP does not permit proportionate consolidation except where it is established industry practice, see section 4.4.

4.1 Definition of associate

(Chapter 3 sections 4.2 and 4.3.1)

IFRSs and US GAAP require the equity method of accounting to be applied to those investments over which the investor has significant influence, i.e. to associates. Under IFRSs and US GAAP there is a rebuttable presumption that the investor has significant influence when it holds 20% or more of the voting stock of the investee.

The definition of an associate in IAS 28 refers to 'an entity, including an unincorporated entity such as a partnership'. Although APB 18 under US GAAP applies to investments in common stock of corporations, there are rules under US GAAP that indicate that the equity method is equally applicable to investments in partnerships and unincorporated joint ventures.

4.2   Significant influence

(Chapter 3 section 4.2)

IAS 28 defines significant influence as 'the power to participate in the financial and operating policy decisions of the investee but not control or joint control over those policies.' APB 18 does not explicitly define significant influence, but the examples given in the standard of situations where significant influence exists are the same as those given in IAS 28.

FASB Interpretation No. 35 (FIN 35) *Criteria for Applying the Equity Method of Accounting for Investments in Common Stock* provides additional criteria on the existence of significant influence under US GAAP. Although there is no equivalent under IFRSs, the criteria in FIN 35 are equally relevant to entities preparing under IFRSs and would therefore not result in a difference between IFRSs and US GAAP in the definition of significant influence. An entity would not therefore be expected to report a reconciling difference with respect to the application of equity method accounting.

4.3   Separate financial statements of the investor

(Chapter 3 sections 2.8 and 4.2)

IFRSs allow the inclusion of stand-alone financial statements of a parent company in the notes to its consolidated financial statements, in contrast to US GAAP. IFRSs also provide principles concerning accounting for associates in the separate financial statements of the investing company. Under IFRSs, investors may account for their investments in jointly controlled entities and associates, other than those classified as held for sale, either at cost or in accordance with IAS 39. The same accounting should be applied for each category of investments. Where separate parent-only financial statements are prepared under US GAAP, investments in subsidiaries may be presented either using the cost or equity method.

4.4   Joint ventures

(Chapter 3 section 4.3.2)

IAS 31 *Interests in Joint Ventures* allows entities to account for investments in jointly controlled entities using either the equity method or proportionate consolidation. US GAAP does not permit proportionate consolidation except for an investment in an unincorporated entity in either the construction industry or an extractive industry where there is a longstanding practice of its use.

The SEC does not require foreign registrants to disclose reconciling differences related to the classification or display of joint ventures when:

- proportionate consolidation is accepted under the issuer's home country GAAP;

- the joint venture would not be consolidated under US GAAP; and

- the joint venture is an operating entity whose significant financial operating policies are jointly controlled by contractual arrangement by all parties having an equity interest in the entity.

Disclosure of the amounts proportionately consolidated is required instead in a footnote.

4.5 Contributions to a jointly-controlled entity

(Chapter 3 section 4.4.2)

Under IFRSs, when a venturer makes a non-monetary contribution to a jointly controlled entity in exchange for an equity interest in that entity the venturer should recognise in profit or loss the portion of the gain or loss corresponding to the equity interests of the other venturers except when:

- the significant risks and rewards of ownership of the contributed non-monetary assets have not been transferred to the jointly controlled entity; or

- the gain or loss on the non-monetary contribution cannot be measured reliably; or

- the contribution transaction lacks commercial substance as described in IAS 16 *Property, Plant and Equipment* (see Chapter 3 section 7.2.1).

If any of these exceptions applies, the gain or loss is regarded as unrealised and is not recognised, unless a venturer also receives monetary or non-monetary assets, in which case an appropriate portion of the gain or loss is recognised.

Under US GAAP, when transactions involve transfers of assets by an enterprise to a newly created entity in exchange for a noncontrolling ownership interest in that entity (1) a gain should be recognised based on the fair values of the assets transferred if the entity accounts for the ownership interest received using the cost method, or (2) a partial gain should be recognised if the entity accounts for the ownership interest received using the equity method. The SEC has noted that an exchange of a consolidated business for an interest in a joint venture would typically not result in gain recognition, absent the receipt of cash or near cash consideration.

4.6 Non-coterminous financial statements

(Chapter 3 section 4.4.3)

Financial statements of a jointly controlled entity or associate may have a different reporting date from that of the investor, where it is impracticable to have financial statements of the jointly controlled entity or associate prepared at the investor's reporting date, if the difference is no more than three months and is consistent from period to period. Under IFRSs, it is necessary to make adjustments for the effects of significant transactions or other events that occur between the reporting dates of the joint venture or associate and that of the investor. US GAAP only requires the effect of material intervening events to be disclosed.

4.7   Impairment

(Chapter 3 section 4.4.4)

Under IFRSs, after application of the equity method, the investor applies the impairment guidance in IAS 39 *Financial Instruments: Recognition and Measurement* to determine whether it is necessary to recognise any impairment loss in relation to its net investment and other interests in a jointly controlled entity or associate. The measurement of any impairment loss is by reference to IAS 36 *Impairment of Assets* for the investor's net investment in a jointly controlled entity or associate, but by reference to IAS 39 for any other interests in the jointly controlled entity or associate. Under US GAAP, the recognition and measurement guidance in APB 18 *The Equity Method of Accounting for Investments in Common Stock* is quite different, and only a loss in value which is other than temporary would be recognised.

4.8   Commencement and cessation of relationship

(Chapter 3 section 4.4.5)

Under IFRSs, a company applies the equity method of accounting at the date of acquisition of a jointly controlled entity or associate. Under US GAAP, APB 18 specifically addresses the situation where an investment qualifies for the use of the equity method as a result of, for example, the acquisition of additional voting stock by the investor. The results of the investor's operations for prior periods, and the retained earnings of the investor, are adjusted retroactively in a manner consistent with the accounting for a step-by-step acquisition of a subsidiary. This results in the recognition of a portion of the associate's results for the prior period, even though the investor did not exert significant influence over the investee during this period. IFRSs do not permit retroactive adjustment of financial statements in accounting for an increase in ownership. Instead, the equity method is applied from the date at which the investment qualifies as a jointly controlled entity or associate: the fair value of the assets acquired is measured at this date, and the group's share of the results of the jointly controlled entity or associate are recognised from this date forward.

When the investor ceases to have significant influence but retains an investment in the associate, application of the equity method should be discontinued under both IFRSs and US GAAP.

4.9   Disclosure

(Chapter 3 section 4.5)

US GAAP requires significantly more detailed disclosures than IFRSs about equity method investments in general, and about significant investees in particular.

Under both IFRSs and US GAAP, the investor's share of the profits or losses of equity method investees should be disclosed separately on the face of the income statement. However, US GAAP additionally requires that extraordinary items and prior period adjustments in those profits or losses are disclosed separately on the face of the income statement. IFRSs do not permit income statement items to be disclosed as extraordinary.

The SEC requires that separate financial statements should be filed for any 50% or less owned entities meeting certain significance criteria.

5   Foreign currency translation

IAS 21 *The Effects of Changes in Foreign Exchange Rates* and *FAS 52 Foreign Currency Translation* do not differ in their fundamental approach to foreign currency translation. However, there are differences between the two standards; most notably the IAS 29 *Financial Reporting in Hyperinflationary Economies* approach to accounting for hyperinflationary economies is very different from the US GAAP approach (see 5.4 below).

5.1   Reporting currency

        (Chapter 3 section 5.2)

Both FAS 52 and IAS 21 require that an entity's assets, liabilities and results of operations should be measured and reported in its functional currency, and provides extensive rules on how to identify it. The concept of an entity's functional currency is broadly the same under both IFRSs and US GAAP.

An entity may wish to present its financial statements in a currency other than its functional currency. Principles governing how to effect the translation into the chosen reporting currency under IFRSs are given in IAS 21 *The Effects of Changes in Foreign Exchange Rates*. Similar rules on translation of foreign currency statements under US GAAP are found in FAS 52.

5.2   Basic requirements – translation to functional and presentation currency

        (Chapter 3 sections 5.2 and 5.3)

FAS 52 and IAS 21 require transactions that are not denominated in the entity's functional currency, i.e. foreign currency transactions, to be translated into the functional currency at the exchange rate in force at the date of the transaction. At each balance sheet date, monetary foreign currency balances are retranslated at the exchange rate at the balance sheet date. Non-monetary balances are not retranslated unless measured at fair value, in which case they are retranslated at the exchange rate at the date the fair value was determined.

If an entity reporting under IFRSs chooses to present its financial statements in a currency other than its functional currency, as permitted by IAS 21, then it must follow a two stage process. The first stage is to translate its assets, liabilities and income statement into its functional currency using the method described above for foreign currency transactions. The second stage is to translate the balance sheet and income statement from the functional currency into the presentation currency. IAS 21 requires assets and liabilities for each balance sheet presented to be translated to the presentation currency at the exchange rate in force at that balance sheet date. Income and expenses are translated at the rates in force at the date of the transaction, or at an approximation to those rates.

An entity reporting under US GAAP may also present its financial statements in a presentation currency different from its functional currency, although this is less common under US GAAP than under IFRSs, because most US entities have a functional currency of, and report in, US dollars. FAS 52 requires the same process as IAS 21, that is, translation first into the functional currency, then into the presentation currency.

When translating the results of a foreign entity into the presentation currency of the group, both IFRSs and US GAAP require the closing rate/net investment method to be used. The balance sheet of the foreign subsidiary is translated into the presentation currency of the group at the rate in force at the closing balance sheet date, and income and expenses are translated either at the rates in force when the transactions take place or, more practicably, using an appropriate weighted average rate for the period.

5.3 Basic requirements – treatment of foreign exchange gains and losses

(Chapter 3 section 5.3)

The general rule under IFRSs and US GAAP is that exchange differences arising on transactions settled during the period, and on the retranslation of monetary items at the balance sheet date, should be included in the result for the year. The following are the important exceptions to this general rule:

- exposures to foreign currency that have been hedged, and whose hedging relationships meet the detailed criteria of IAS 39 *Financial Instruments: Recognition and Measurement* or FAS 133 *Accounting for Derivative Instruments and Hedging Activities*, are accounted for as hedges using the appropriate method set out in those standards (see Chapter 3 section 13.3);

- the exchange differences resulting from the retranslation of the entity's net investment in a foreign operation should be taken directly to equity, and are offset by the exchange movements on any financial instruments hedging that net investment to the extent the hedge is effective (see Chapter 3 Section 13.3);

- FAS 52 permits gains and losses arising on the retranslation of intragroup foreign currency transactions that are of a long-term investment nature to be taken directly to equity. IAS 21 permits exchange differences that arise on monetary items that are regarded as part of an entity's investment in a foreign operation to be taken directly to equity but only where the monetary item is denominated in the functional currency of either the foreign operation or the reporting entity (see Chapter 3 Section 5.3.2).

5.4 Hyperinflation

(Chapter 3 section 5.4.2)

FAS 52 defines a highly inflationary economy as one that has cumulative inflation of 100% or more over a three-year period. IAS 29 gives a number of characteristics that may indicate that an economy is hyperinflationary, including three-year cumulative inflation approaching or exceeding 100%, but also taking into account other qualitative factors such as the attitude of the local population to the stability of the local currency, and prices and wages being linked to price indexes.

IFRSs and US GAAP prescribe fundamentally different methods of reporting the results of an entity whose results are denominated in a hyperinflationary currency.

IAS 29 requires non-monetary balance sheet items and all items in the income statement to be expressed in the measuring unit current at the balance sheet date by applying a general price index. If the entity whose functional currency is the currency of a hyperinflationary economy is also a foreign subsidiary of an entity that prepares consolidated financial statements, then the restated results will be translated from the hyperinflationary currency into the group's presentation currency only after this restatement has taken place.

Under IFRSs, the results and financial position of an entity whose functional currency is the currency of a hyperinflationary economy should be translated into a different presentation currency at the closing rate at the date of the most recent balance sheet. The comparative amounts are those that were presented as current year amounts in the relevant prior year financial statements.

FAS 52 requires an entity operating in a hyperinflationary economy to translate its assets, liabilities and income statement into a stable currency as if the stable currency were the functional currency of the entity. If the entity is also a foreign subsidiary, then the parent company is able to restate the subsidiary's reported results and balance sheet directly into its own functional currency, rather than following the two-stage process required by IFRSs.

Although IFRSs and US GAAP require different treatments of the results of an entity operating in a hyperinflationary economy, the SEC has recognised that it would be unduly onerous for entities to restate their results prepared under IFRSs using the method required by FAS 52 for the purposes of US reporting, since in some cases this would require complete restatement of all lines in the income statement and balance sheet. Therefore the SEC provides an accommodation for foreign entities that file their results using IAS 21 by not requiring those entities to quantify differences in the translation methodology compared to FAS 52. However, it should be emphasised that this accommodation applies to the stand-alone financial statements of foreign entities that reconcile from their home-country GAAP or IFRSs to US GAAP in SEC filings. A US entity with an equity investee or subsidiary in a country considered to be hyperinflationary cannot use the SEC accommodation and would have to translate the financial statements of the investee/subsidiary using the FAS 52 approach.

5.5   *Impairment of a foreign operation*

       (Chapter 3 section 5.5.4)

Under US GAAP, accumulated foreign currency translation differences are considered as part of the carrying amount when evaluating impairment of the net investment in a foreign operation that is held for sale. There is no such specific requirement under IFRSs.

5.6   *Disposal of a foreign operation*

       (Chapter 3 section 5.5.4)

On the disposal of a foreign operation, the cumulative amount of foreign currency translation differences relating to that foreign operation is recognised in profit and loss when the gain or loss on disposal is recognised. For a partial disposal, only the proportionate share of the related cumulative translation differences is included in the gain or loss.

Under IFRSs, a dividend is considered to be part of a disposal when it constitutes a return of the investment. Under US GAAP, the payment of a dividend does not result in the recognition of cumulative translation differences in the income statement.

6   Intangible Assets

6.1   *Initial recognition and measurement*

(Chapter 3 section 6.2)

The initial recognition and measurement of an intangible asset in an entity's balance sheet will depend on whether it has been acquired – either separately or as part of a business combination – or has been generated internally. The relevant governing principles in IFRSs covering all these circumstances can be found in IAS 38 *Intangible Assets.* The US rules for the initial measurement of intangible fixed assets acquired as part of a business combination are found in FAS 141 *Business Combinations.* FAS 142 *Goodwill and Other Intangible Assets* addresses the accounting and reporting for intangible assets acquired individually or with a group of other assets (but not those acquired in a business combination) at acquisition. FAS 142 also addresses the accounting and reporting of intangible assets (including those acquired in a business combination) subsequent to their acquisition. Internally generated intangible assets are covered by a number of other standards, which are listed in Chapter 3 section 6.1.

The recognition of intangible assets acquired as part of a business combination is discussed in detail in section 3.2.3B above. An intangible asset is recognised under US GAAP separately from goodwill if (1) it arises from contractual or other legal rights, or (2) if it is separable from the business acquired. Under IFRSs, if an item meets the definition of an intangible asset it should be recognised separately from goodwill only where its cost, which IAS 38 equates with its fair value, can be measured with sufficient reliability.

Under US GAAP, intangible assets acquired other than in a business combination are not subject to the same FAS 141 recognition criteria. The FASB concluded that where an intangible asset is acquired separately in an arm's length transaction, this provides good evidence of its fair value, and it should be recognised separately at its fair value under FAS 142. The treatment of an intangible asset may therefore be different depending on how it was acquired. IAS 38 also states that if an intangible asset is acquired separately, its cost can usually be measured reliably.

Under IFRSs, the cost of internally developed intangible assets comprises all directly attributable costs necessary to create, produce and prepare the asset to be capable of operating in the manner intended by management. Under US GAAP, costs of internally developing intangible assets that are not specifically identifiable, have indeterminate lives, or are inherent in a continuing business and related to an entity as a whole should be deducted from income when incurred.

6.1.1   Regulatory assets

(Chapter 3 section 6.2.2)

In many countries the provision of utilities (e.g. water, natural gas or electricity) to consumers is regulated by the national government. Regulations differ between countries, but often regulators operate a cost-plus system under which a utility is allowed to make a fixed return on investment. Similarly, a regulator may allow a utility to recoup its investments by increasing the prices over a defined period.

Consequently, the future price that a utility is allowed to charge its customer may be influenced by past costs levels and investment levels. Under FAS 71 *Accounting for the Effects of Certain Types of Regulation*, an entity accounts for the effects of regulation by recognising a 'regulatory' asset (or liability) that reflects the increase (or decrease) in future prices approved by the regulator.

However, 'regulatory assets' do not meet the definition of an intangible asset under IFRSs, because they are not 'a resource controlled by an entity as a result of past events; and from which future economic benefits are expected to flow to the entity'. The right to charge a higher price to customers can only result in economic benefits as a result of future sales to those customers. The economic benefits from sales to customers should be recognised in accordance with IAS 18 *Revenue*, which requires delivery of the goods or services to the customers.

Conversely, an entity may be required by its regulator to reduce prices in a subsequent period. In most circumstances this would not be a provision under IAS 37 *Provisions, Contingent Liabilities and Contingent Assets*; it is not a 'present obligation of the enterprise arising from past events, the settlement of which is expected to result in an outflow from the enterprise of resources embodying economic benefits'; nor is it deferred income under IAS 18 *Revenue* – it simply means that the entity will charge less, and receive less from individual customers in the subsequent periods. A 'regulatory liability' would be recognised only when an entity is required by the regulator to provide a cash refund to a particular group of customers, irrespective of whether or not they remain customers of the entity – in other words, there must be a present obligation, not an undertaking, to charge customers less in future periods.

6.1.2   Emission rights

(Chapter 3 section 6.2.3C)

IFRIC 3 *Emission Rights* requires a participant in an operational 'cap and trade' scheme to account for emission rights (allowances) as an intangible asset under IAS 38. On initial recognition such allowances should be recognised at fair value, even if they were issued for less than fair value. The allowances should subsequently be measured under either the cost model or the revaluation model in IAS 38. The difference between the amount paid and the fair value of the allowances is a government grant that is initially recognised as deferred income in the balance sheet and recognised subsequently in income on a systematic basis over the compliance period for which allowances were issued. US GAAP does not provide specific guidance on accounting for emission rights and practice may therefore vary.

6.2   General research and development

(Chapter 3 section 6.2.4)

The major difference between IFRSs and US GAAP for the treatment of research and development costs is that IAS 38 requires some development costs to be capitalised, whereas FAS 2 *Accounting for Research and Development Costs* requires most development costs to be expensed as incurred. The treatment of certain computer software development costs is addressed separately by FAS 86 *Accounting for the Costs of Computer Software to be Sold, Leased, or Otherwise Marketed* and SOP 98-1 *Accounting for the costs to develop or obtain software for internal use* and is discussed in section 6.4 below.

IAS 38 addresses the treatment of research costs and development costs separately. The costs of research must be expensed as they are incurred. When the technical and economic feasibility of a project can be demonstrated, and further prescribed conditions are satisfied, the costs of the development of the project must be capitalised.

FAS 2 requires general research and development costs that are not covered by separate standards to be expensed as they are incurred. Therefore, there is a potentially large category of development costs that must be expensed when preparing an IFRSs to US GAAP reconciliation.

6.3   Subsequent measurement of intangible assets

(Chapter 3 section 6.2.5)

The allowed alternative treatment in IAS 38 permits intangible assets (other than goodwill) to be carried at a revalued amount. The revaluation must be made by reference to an active market for the specific type of intangible asset; therefore IAS 38 notes that it will be relatively uncommon for the allowed alternative treatment to be applied.

The revaluation of intangible assets is not permitted under US GAAP.

6.4   Computer software development

(Chapter 3 section 6.2.7)

Under IFRSs, computer software costs are covered by the general principles for research and development costs in IAS 38. Therefore once a project reaches the development stage and satisfies the criteria outlined in section 6.2 above, its costs thereafter must be capitalised. Under US GAAP, FAS 86 regards the costs of establishing the technological feasibility of a product as research and development costs. Such costs are expensed as incurred as required by FAS 2. Once the technological feasibility of the product has been established, FAS 86 requires development costs to be capitalised.

FAS 86 is a rule-based standard and specifies several activities which must be evidenced as having been completed before the technological feasibility of a product is established. For example, either a detailed program design must be completed and reviewed, or a product design and a working model of the product must have been completed, before FAS 86 considers the project to be technologically feasible. Costs may be capitalised only once technological feasibility has been established. In contrast, IAS 38 sets out principles that must be applied to the accounting for all types of research and development costs, and does not specifically deal with computer software development costs. It is therefore possible that an entity would be required to commence capitalisation of computer software development costs at different times under IFRSs and US GAAP.

The point at which costs cease to be capitalised may also be different under IFRSs and US GAAP. FAS 86 requires capitalisation to cease when the product is available for general release to customers. IAS 38 defines the cost of an internally generated intangible asset as comprising all directly attributable costs necessary to create, produce, and prepare the asset to be capable of operating in the manner intended by management.

SOP 98-1 provides guidance on accounting for costs of developing software for internal use. Three stages of software development are identified and only costs incurred during the application development stage may be capitalised. Examples of process costs that are incurred during the application development stage are included in SOP 98-1.

6.5   *Amortisation of research and development costs*

(Chapter 3 section 6.2.7)

IAS 38 requires all capitalised development costs, including computer software costs, to be amortised on the same basis as other intangible assets, that is, over their estimated useful lives on a straight-line basis unless another pattern of use can be determined reliably.

FAS 86 requires annual amortisation of computer software costs to be the greater of (a) the ratio of current revenues for a product over current and future revenues for a product; or (b) the straight-line method over the product's estimated economic life. For a product where a high proportion of revenues will be generated in the early years or even months of the product's availability, amortisation matched to the pattern of revenues would be significantly different from amortisation charged on a straight line basis. This may cause a difference between the amortisation charged under US GAAP and that under IFRSs. However, it could be argued that the correct treatment under IFRSs in this case would also be to match amortisation to the pattern of revenue generated by the product.

6.6   *Amortisation of goodwill and intangible assets*

(Chapter 3 section 6.3)

6.6.1   *Amortisation of goodwill*

Goodwill under both IFRSs and US GAAP is not amortised but is tested for impairment annually, or more frequently if events or changes in circumstances indicate that it might be impaired. Differences between the IFRSs and US GAAP approaches to impairment reviews are discussed below in section 9.

6.6.2   *Amortisation of other intangible assets*

Both IAS 38 and FAS 142 require an assessment to be made of the period over which the asset is expected to contribute to the future cash flows of the business, in order to determine the asset's useful life. If, based on an analysis of the relevant factors, there is no foreseeable limit to the period over which the asset is expected to generate net cash inflows to the entity, then its useful life is considered to be indefinite, and it is not amortised but instead reviewed annually for impairment.

7   Property, plant and equipment

7.1   *Scope*

(Chapter 3 section 7.2)

There are some significant differences between IFRSs and US GAAP in their respective approaches to accounting for property, plant and equipment. The most significant of these is the way in which impairment is measured (see section 9 below) and the fact that assets may be revalued under IFRSs whereas under US GAAP all assets must be recorded at depreciated historical cost, net of impairments (if any) see section 7.5 below. However, differences may also arise because of the scope of the relevant standards.

IAS 16 *Property, Plant and Equipment* excludes from its scope property, plant and equipment classified as held for sale in accordance with IFRS 5 *Non-current Assets Held for Sale and Discontinued Operations*; biological assets related to agricultural activity; exploration and evaluation assets; and mineral rights and reserves such as oil, natural gas and similar non-regenerative resources. However, property, plant and equipment used to maintain or develop such biological assets and mineral rights and reserves are within the scope of the standard. Under US GAAP, there is no single comprehensive standard that deals with all aspects of accounting for tangible fixed assets. Instead, there are many standards and interpretations that deal with elements of accounting for specific categories of tangible fixed assets.

7.2   *Definition of costs*

(Chapter 3 section 7.2.1)

IAS 16 provides a definition of the parts (or components) of the cost of property, plant and equipment, whereas under US GAAP there is no single definition. IAS 16 does not permit capitalisation of administrative and general overhead costs, start-up costs and similar pre-production costs (e.g. initial operating losses, relocation costs, advertising and promotion, and training) as a component of property, plant and equipment. SOP 98-5 *Reporting on the Costs of Start-up Activities* under US GAAP also prohibits the capitalisation of start-up costs, either as a separate intangible asset or as part of a component of property, plant and equipment.

The total amount recognised as the cost of an asset may be different under US GAAP compared to IFRSs because of the impact of other accounting standards on the measurement of cost.

7.2.1   Interest costs

(Chapter 3 section 7.2.1)

Interest costs must be included in the capitalised cost of self-constructed assets under US GAAP but there is a choice under IFRSs (see section 10 below). There will therefore be a difference in the base cost of a self-constructed asset if the entity adopts the benchmark treatment under IAS 23 which is to expense all interest costs as they are incurred.

7.2.2   Decommissioning costs

(Chapter 3 section 18.6)

IAS 16 specifies that the costs of dismantling an asset and restoring its site, to the extent that they are recognised as a provision under IAS 37 *Provisions, Contingent Liabilities and Contingent Assets* either when the asset is acquired or as a consequence of using the asset during a period (other than to produce inventories), shall be included as part of the capitalised cost of the asset. The US GAAP treatment, as prescribed by FAS 143 *Accounting for Asset Retirement Obligations*, requires the fair value of any legal obligation associated with the retirement of an asset to be included in the capitalised cost of that asset. In addition to requiring provision to be made for any legal obligations to incur costs, IAS 37 also requires any costs that arise due to a constructive, but not necessarily a legal obligation, to be provided for. An obligation that arose out of a pattern of established practice, rather than a legal obligation, is therefore provided for under IFRSs and included in the cost of the asset, but would not be provided for under US GAAP.

Furthermore, differences between IFRSs and US GAAP may arise when an entity changes cost estimates or discount rates. Under FAS 143, changes in cost estimates should be reflected in the carrying amount of the provision and the carrying amount of the related long-lived asset. However, the liability is not remeasured for changes in the risk-free discount rate as the risk-free interest discount rate used to initially measure the provision is used for all subsequent reductions in the estimated gross future cash flows initially measured. The risk-free discount rate is adjusted, however, to the then-current rate if the estimated gross future cash flows increase. IAS 37 requires the use of a discount rate that reflects the current market assessment of the time value of money at the balance sheet date. No guidance is provided in IAS 37 on accounting for changes in cost estimates or discount rates, but IFRIC 1 requires that adjustments arising from changes in the estimated cash flows or the current discount rate should be added to or deducted from the cost of the related asset.

7.3   Subsequent expenditure

(Chapter 3 section 7.2.1B)

IAS 16 contains principles governing the capitalisation of subsequent expenditure relating to property, plant and equipment. Subsequent expenditure on property, plant and equipment should only be capitalised when it is probable that economic benefits associated with the item will flow to the entity and the cost of the item can be measured reliably. There are no equivalent general principles on subsequent expenditure under US GAAP. As a result, differences in accounting practice may occur. For example, there is no specific US standard on the accounting for the major overhaul of property, plant and equipment. The US allows for the overhaul to be expensed as incurred or, if such expenditure adds significant value or extended life to the property, plant and equipment, costs may be deferred and expensed over the period to the next major overhaul. Costs of regularly recurring major overhauls of an item of property, plant and equipment are recognised as an expense when incurred under IFRSs, except when the reporting entity had already identified a component of the item of property, plant or equipment that represented the major overhaul and had fully depreciated this component. Subject to the usual conditions for subsequent expenditure, the costs of the major overhaul should then be capitalised as a replacement, and any remaining carrying amount of the previous component derecognised.

7.4   *Property, plant and equipment held for sale*

(Chapter 3 section 1.9.2)

Both IFRS 5 *Non-current Assets Held for Sale and Discontinued Operations* and FAS 144 *Accounting for the Impairment or Disposal of Long-Lived Assets* require an asset classified as 'held for sale' to be measured at the lower of its carrying amount and fair value less costs to sell. The asset is not depreciated whilst it is classified as 'held for sale'. The 'held for sale' criteria are also very similar under IFRSs and US GAAP. If these criteria are not met, the asset would continue to be classified as 'held and used' and depreciation must continue to be charged, although it may be necessary to revise the asset's estimated useful economic life and to carry out an impairment review, depending on exactly how the asset is to be disposed of.

7.5   *Revaluation*

(Chapter 3 section 7.2.2)

US GAAP requires tangible fixed assets to be recorded at depreciated historical cost, taking into account possible impairment. IAS 16 requires entities to choose either the cost model or the revaluation model as an accounting policy and to apply the chosen policy to an entire class of property, plant and equipment.

7.6   *Depreciation methods*

(Chapter 3 section 7.2.3)

IAS 16 requires depreciation on a systematic basis to reflect the pattern in which an asset's economic benefits are expected to be consumed. Any method of depreciation (including the straight-line method, the diminishing balance method, and the units of production method) that reflects the expected pattern of consumption of an asset's economic benefits is permitted. Under US GAAP, ARB 43 Chapter 9 specifies that the cost of a productive facility (less salvage value) be spread over its expected life so as to allocate it as equitably as possible to the periods during which benefits are obtained from its use.

7.7   Changes in depreciation method and useful economic life

(Chapter 3 section 7.2.3)

A change in depreciation method is considered to be a change in accounting principle under US GAAP, the cumulative effect of which should be accounted for in the income statement for the period. A change in the estimate of the useful economic life of a tangible fixed asset is considered to be a change in accounting estimate that should be accounted for prospectively. In contrast, under IAS 16 changes in depreciation method, residual value and useful economic life are all considered to be changes in accounting estimates, which should be accounted for prospectively under IAS 8 *Accounting Policies, Changes in Accounting Estimates and Errors.*

7.8   Major inspection or overhaul

(Chapter 3 section 18.4)

The treatment of the costs of a major inspection or overhaul could differ under IFRSs and US GAAP because these are dealt with specifically in IFRSs but not under US GAAP. Under IFRSs, the costs of major inspection or overhaul may be capitalised to the cost of the asset when certain conditions are satisfied, while under US GAAP several alternative accounting methods are available for specific industries (e.g. the airline industry), otherwise such costs are generally required to be expensed as incurred.

8   Investment properties

(Chapter 3 section 8)

There is no specific US standard dealing with accounting for investment properties held directly by a reporting entity that is not a real estate investment entity. This means that under US GAAP some investment property will be accounted for on a cost basis similar to the method used for property, plant and equipment. IFRSs does not recognise a separate accounting regime for real estate investment entities. Instead, IAS 40 *Investment Property* gives entities the option to account for investment property either on a fair value basis or on a historical cost basis in accordance with IAS 16 *Property, Plant and Equipment.* When investment property is accounted for at fair value, the changes in fair value should be recognised directly in income for the period.

9   Impairment

9.1   General principles

(Chapter 3 section 9.2)

It is a well established principle under both IFRSs and US GAAP that an asset must be reviewed for impairment under certain circumstances. Furthermore, if that asset is found to be impaired, it should be written down to its recoverable amount. However, despite this similarity in the overall approach, accounting for impairment can give rise to significant differences in practice.

IAS 36 *Impairment of Assets* is the relevant standard under IFRSs and should be applied to most types of assets, with some exceptions that include inventories, deferred tax assets and financial instruments. Under US GAAP, there are two standards:

- FAS 142 *Goodwill and Other Intangible Assets* deals with accounting for the impairment of goodwill and other non-amortised intangible assets; and

- FAS 144 *Accounting for the Impairment or Disposal of Long-Lived Assets* deals with accounting for impairment of other tangible and intangible fixed assets.

9.2 *When and how to perform an impairment review*

(Chapter 3 sections 9.4 and 9.5)

9.2.1 *Assets other than goodwill that are subject to amortisation*

Both IFRSs and US GAAP require an impairment review to be carried out if events or changes in circumstance indicate that an asset's carrying amount may not be recoverable. The examples of 'indicators of impairment' given in IAS 36 are similar to those in FAS 144 and as the indicators listed in the relevant standards under both IFRSs and US GAAP are not exhaustive, it is unlikely that a GAAP difference would arise in this respect.

If indicators of impairment are present, an impairment review must be carried out for the purposes of both IFRSs and US GAAP. However, an impairment may well be recognised at different times under IFRSs and US GAAP. The IAS 36 methodology for carrying out an impairment review is a two-stage process that requires the reporting entity to consider first whether indicators of impairment are present and, if they are, to compare the asset's carrying amount directly to its recoverable amount – defined as the higher of an asset's fair value less costs to sell and its value in use. Under IFRSs, the value in use calculation involves discounting the expected future cash flows to be generated by the asset to their net present value. FAS 144 requires a three-stage impairment review process: having determined that indicators of impairment are present, a recoverability test must be performed by comparing the estimated sum of undiscounted cash flows attributable to the asset with its carrying amount. Only if the asset fails this recoverability test will the amount of the impairment be calculated by comparing the asset's carrying amount to its fair value. Two examples are given in the extracts below.

Extract 4: Swisscom AG (2003)

42 Differences between International Financial Reporting Standards and U.S. Generally Accepted Accounting Principles [extract]

(e) Write-down of long-lived assets

In 1997 Swisscom recorded an impairment charge of CHF 107 million relating to the write down of certain property, plant and equipment to their realizable value. In determining the realizable amount, Swisscom discounted future cash flows expected to result from the use and eventual disposition of these assets. Under U.S. GAAP, the assets' recoverable amount is determined using undiscounted cash flows. The recoverable amount based on undiscounted cash flow exceeds the carrying value and therefore the impairment charge under IAS was reversed.

As the assets are not written down under U.S. GAAP, additional depreciation expense of CHF 30 million has been recognized in the year ended December 31, 2001. At December 31, 2001 these assets were fully depreciated.

Extract 5: OAO Rostelecom (2003)

35 Differences between International Financial Reporting Standards and Accounting Principles Generally Accepted in the United States [extract]

(a): Reversal of impairment on property, plant and equipment

In 1998, in accordance with IAS 36, "Impairment of Assets", the Group recognized an impairment loss of 8,699 on its property, plant and equipment other than construction in progress. The impairment loss was calculated based on the present value of estimated future cash flows from the continuing use of the assets using a real-terms (inflation adjusted) discount rate of 20%.

IAS 36 requires an assessment of the recoverable amount of an asset whenever there is an indication that the Group's assets may be impaired. Management believed that the Russian economic crisis in 1998 constituted such an indication.

Under US GAAP, SFAS 121, "Accounting for the Impairment of Long-Lived Assets and for Long-Lived Assets to Be Disposed of" (superseded by SFAS No. 144, "Accounting for the Impairment or Disposal of Long-Lived Assets", effective for financial statements issued for fiscal years beginning after December 15, 2001), requires an initial assessment of impairment based on undiscounted cash flows whenever there is an indication that impairment may exist. Due to the fact that the sum of undiscounted expected future cash flows was in excess of the carrying amount of the Group's property, plant and equipment as of December 31, 1998, an impairment loss was not recognized for US GAAP reporting purposes. Management considers that all of the Group's property, plant and equipment, with the exception of construction in progress, represent the lowest level for which there are largely independent and identifiable cash flows.

Since no impairment loss was recognized under US GAAP in 1998, a different asset base is used to compute US GAAP depreciation expense, loss on disposal of property, plant and equipment and the related deferred tax liability commencing 1999.

Based on management's analysis, the sum of undiscounted expected future cash flows was in excess of the carrying amount of the Group's property, plant and equipment as of December 31, 2003, 2002 and 2001, thus, no impairment loss was recognized under US GAAP.

...

These extracts illustrate the fact that this is a highly significant difference between the two systems. In practice, because the US GAAP test is first performed on the basis of undiscounted cash flows, any impairment charge reported under IFRSs will almost certainly be reversed in the US GAAP reconciliation. Moreover, investors will be restricted in their ability to make global comparisons between IFRSs and US GAAP reporting companies, as they will be unable to determine whether or not the companies reporting under US GAAP would have reported asset impairments under IFRSs.

9.2.2   *Non-current assets held for sale*

Under both IFRSs and US GAAP, a non-current asset (or disposal group) held for sale should be measured at the lower of its carrying amount and fair value less costs to sell.

Under US GAAP, accumulated foreign exchange translation differences should be included as part of the carrying amount when evaluating impairment of the net investment in a foreign operation that is held for sale. There is no such requirement under IFRSs.

9.2.3   *Goodwill and intangible assets that are not amortised*

Under FAS 142, goodwill and other intangible assets with an indefinite life are not amortised, but are reviewed annually for impairment. The method of carrying out the impairment review prescribed by FAS 142 is complex and different from that required by IAS 36.

FAS 142 requires all goodwill to be assigned to a reporting unit of the business on acquisition. Each reporting unit that has been assigned goodwill must then be reviewed annually to identify potential impairment. Initially, the fair value of a reporting unit should be compared with its carrying amount. If the carrying amount of a reporting unit, including goodwill, exceeds its fair value then the goodwill should be tested to measure the amount of the impairment loss, if any. This second test compares the implied fair value of the goodwill with the carrying amount of that goodwill.

FAS 142 requires an annual impairment test to be carried out on intangible assets other than goodwill that are not amortised. Additional impairment tests are required when impairment indicators are identified. The impairment test requires the assets' carrying amount to be compared to its fair value, which is defined as the amount at which it could be sold to a willing party. There is no intermediate comparison to associated undiscounted cash flows.

Goodwill is dealt with under IFRS 3 and other intangible assets fall within the scope of IAS 38, but impairment is dealt with under IAS 36 for both. Similar to US GAAP, goodwill and intangible assets with indefinite lives are not amortised but are evaluated for impairment both annually and whenever there are indicators of impairment. Goodwill acquired in a business combination is allocated to each of the cash-generating units on acquisition. The cash-generating units are tested for impairment by comparing the carrying amount including goodwill with its recoverable amount and any impairment loss is recognised. The amount of the impairment will not necessarily be the same under IFRSs and US GAAP.

9.3   *Reversal of impairment charges*

(Chapter 3 section 9.6A)

An entity must assess at each reporting date whether there are indicators that an impairment loss may have reversed and, where this is the case, it should estimate the asset's recoverable amount. IAS 36 requires an impairment charge to be reversed for an asset other than goodwill but only if there has been a change in the estimates used to determine the asset's recoverable amount since the last impairment loss was recognised. US GAAP prohibits the reversal of an impairment loss (except for long lived assets held for sale when there has been subsequent recovery after the impairment). It is less likely that an impairment charge will have been recognised in the first place under FAS 144 because of the initial test for recoverability, which requires comparison with undiscounted cash flows. It is possible for an impairment loss to be recognised in one year under IFRSs but not under US GAAP, and then reversed in the following year under IFRSs because the asset is no longer impaired. This is illustrated by China Petroleum & Chemical Corporation.

Extract 6: China Petroleum & Chemical Corporation (2003)

33 Significant differences between US and US accounting principles [extract]

(e) Impairment of long-lived assets

Under IFRS, impairment charges are recognized when a long-lived asset's carrying amount exceeds the higher of an asset's net selling price and value in use, which incorporates discounting the asset's estimated future cash flows.

Under US GAAP, determination of the recoverability of a long-lived asset is based on an estimate of undiscounted future cash flows resulting from the use of the asset and its eventual disposition. If the sum of the expected future cash flows is less than the carrying amount of the asset, an impairment loss is recognized. Measurement of an impairment loss for a long-lived asset is based on the fair value of the asset.

In addition, under IFRS, a subsequent increase in the recoverable amount of an asset is reversed to the consolidated statements of income to the extent that an impairment loss on the same asset was previously recognized as an expense when the circumstances and events that led to the write-down or write-off cease to exist. The reversal is reduced by the amount that would have been recognized as depreciation had the write-off not occurred. Under US GAAP, an impairment loss establishes a new cost basis for the impaired asset and the new cost basis should not be adjusted subsequently other than for further impairment losses.

The US GAAP adjustment represents the effect of reversing the recovery of previous impairment charges recorded under IFRS.

---

10   Capitalisation of borrowing costs

10.1   *General principles*

(Chapter 3 section 10.2)

Under IAS 23 *Borrowing Costs,* entities have a choice of applying the benchmark treatment, which is to expense all borrowing costs as incurred, or the allowed alternative treatment, which is to capitalise borrowing costs arising on qualifying assets. There is no such choice under US GAAP, since FAS 34 *Capitalization of Interest Cost* makes the capitalisation of interest costs compulsory for certain qualifying assets that require a period of time to get them ready for their intended use.

Many differences between IFRSs and US GAAP have arisen either because the company has adopted the benchmark treatment for IFRSs and expensed borrowing costs which are required to be capitalised by FAS 34, or because of other differences in the accounting for borrowing costs.

Where entities reporting under IFRSs choose not to capitalise qualifying interest costs there will be a GAAP difference, as illustrated by Swisscom.

Extract 7: Swisscom AG (2003)

42 Differences between International Financial Reporting Standards and U.S. Generally Accepted Accounting Principles [extract]

a) Capitalization of interest cost

Swisscom expenses all interest costs as incurred. U.S. GAAP requires interest costs incurred during the construction of property, plant and equipment to be capitalized.

The U.S. GAAP reconciliation includes adjustments arising from the application of the method prescribed by Statement of Financial Accounting Standards (SFAS) No. 34, "Capitalization of Interest Cost".

The effect of capitalization of interest cost, corresponding additional depreciation expense on the increased amount of property, plant and equipment and the disposal of property would be as follows:

CHF in millions	**2001**	**2002**	**2003**
Interest capitalized during year	12	8	8
Depreciation expense	(8)	(9)	(9)
Disposal of property during year	(35)	–	–
Net income statement effect	(31)	(1)	(1)

CHF in millions	**2001**	**2002**	**2003**
Gross amount capitalized	88	96	104
Accumulated depreciation	(38)	(47)	(56)
Net amount capitalized	50	49	48

10.2 Qualifying assets

(Chapter 3 section 10.3)

One important difference between the definitions of a qualifying asset is the requirement under US GAAP to capitalise interest costs related to investments accounted for under the equity method while the investee has activities in progress necessary to commence its planned principal activity. Under IFRSs, such investments would typically not meet the definition of a qualifying asset for which borrowing costs may be capitalised.

Extract 8: China Petroleum & Chemical Corporation (2003)

33 Significant differences between IFRS and US GAAP [extract]

(g) Capitalized interest on investment in associates

Under IFRS, investment accounted for by the equity method is not considered a qualifying asset for which interest is capitalized. Under US GAAP, an investment accounted for by the equity method while the investee has activities in progress necessary to commence its planned principal operations, provided that the investee's activities include the use of funds to acquire qualifying assets for its operations, is a qualifying asset for which interest is capitalized.

10.3 Attributable borrowing costs

(Chapter 3 section 10.4)

IAS 23 permits and FAS 34 requires borrowing costs that are directly attributable to the acquisition, construction, or production of a qualifying asset to be capitalised as part of the cost of that asset. This does not mean that only those interest costs that were incurred on borrowings made specifically for the purchase of the asset may be capitalised. The definition of 'directly attributable' in both standards is those costs that theoretically would have been avoided if the expenditure on the qualifying asset had not been made. IAS 23 goes on to explain that where an entity borrows funds centrally (for example, through a treasury function) and it is not possible to make a direct correlation between borrowings and expenditure on qualifying assets, the amount of borrowing costs to be capitalised will be calculated by applying a weighted average of the borrowing costs to the expenditures on the qualifying asset. Therefore, where the funds that have been used to finance a qualifying asset cannot be specifically identified, both IFRSs and US GAAP permit or require the use of a weighted average based on the entity's total borrowings.

10.4 Foreign exchange differences

(Chapter 3 section 10.4)

IAS 23 specifically states that exchange differences arising from foreign currency borrowings may be capitalised to the extent that they are regarded as an adjustment to interest costs. FAS 52 requires all exchange differences, other than those arising on a hedge of a net investment in a foreign subsidiary or on intragroup transactions, to be included in net income, rather than included in the cost of the asset.

Extract 9: Polska Telefonica Cyfrowa SP ZOO (2003)

29 Differences between IFRS and US GAAP [extract]

a. Removal of foreign exchange differences capitalized for IFRS

In accordance with IAS 23 Borrowing Costs, the Company capitalizes financing costs, including interest and foreign exchange gains or losses and hedging gains and losses, into assets under construction.

For property, plant and equipment under construction, the Company capitalizes interest and foreign exchange gains or losses incurred and directly attributable to the acquisition and

---

construction of the qualifying assets that would have been avoided if the expenditure on the qualifying assets had not been made. The financing costs are capitalized only during the period of construction of the qualifying assets (see Note 14). The Company capitalized financing costs attributable to the acquisition of its GSM 900, GSM 1800 and UMTS licenses, including interest on the related long-term obligation and foreign exchange losses because these licenses are integral parts of the network (see Note 15).

Under Statement of Financial Accounting Standards 52 Foreign Currency Translation, however, foreign exchange differences relating to financing obligations should be included in the income statement of the Company. Consequently, the amounts of foreign exchange differences capitalized in accordance with IAS 23 in the Company's consolidated financial statements are expensed under U.S. GAAP.

10.5   Net investment proceeds

(Chapter 3 section 10.4)

If an entity can associate a specific new borrowing with a qualifying asset, IAS 23 requires the amount of borrowing costs capitalised to be calculated net of any investment income on the temporary investment of those borrowings. US GAAP permits capitalisation up to the gross amount of interest costs incurred but calculated on the average accumulated expenditures for the asset during the period. Consequently, although the methodologies are different, the resulting net amounts of interest capitalised under IFRSs and US GAAP should be materially the same.

11   Financial instruments: recognition and measurement

11.1   Scope

(Chapter 3 section 11.2)

The main standards dealing with financial instruments under IFRSs are IAS 32 *Financial Instruments: Disclosure and Presentation* and IAS 39 *Financial Instruments: Recognition and Measurement*. IAS 32 and IAS 39 apply in principle to all types of financial instruments, but exclude from their scope financial instruments to the extent that they are accounted for under other standards such as, for example, IFRS 4 *Insurance Contracts*, IAS 17 *Leases*, IAS 27 *Consolidated and Separate Financial Statements*, IAS 28 *Investments in Associates* and IAS 31 *Interests in Joint Ventures*.

Guidance on accounting for financial instruments under US GAAP can be found in a range of standards such as FAS 107 *Disclosures about Fair Value of Financial Instruments*, FAS 114 *Accounting by Creditors for Impairment of a Loan (an amendment of FASB Statements No. 5 and 15)*, FAS 115 *Accounting for Certain Investments in Debt and Equity Securities*, FAS 133 *Accounting for Derivative Instruments and Hedging Activities* and FAS 140 *Accounting for Transfers and Servicing of Financial Assets and Extinguishments of Liabilities – a replacement of FASB Statement No. 125*. The US GAAP literature is far more detailed than IFRSs as it has been developed over a longer period and, often, in response to specific financial instruments. Consequently, there are many subtle differences in the scope of standards under IFRSs and US GAAP; the most important of which are described in more detail below.

11.1.1 Normal purchase or sale exemption

(Chapter 3 sections 11.2.1 and 13.2.1)

FAS 133 defines normal purchases and normal sales as contracts that provide for the purchase or sale of something other than a financial instrument or derivative instrument that will be delivered in quantities expected to be used or sold by the reporting entity over a reasonable period in the normal course of business, which is similar to IAS 39. Nevertheless, differences between US GAAP and IFRSs may arise because, for example:

- Under US GAAP, an entity should formally document the designation of a contract that qualifies for the normal purchases and normal sales exception;

- Freestanding option contracts (except power purchase and sales agreements that are capacity contracts) cannot qualify for the normal purchase and sales exemption under US GAAP, while they qualify as normal purchases and sales under IAS 39; and

- Contracts that have a price based on an underlying that is not clearly and closely related to the asset being sold or purchased or that are denominated in a foreign currency that gives rise to an embedded derivative are not considered to be normal purchases and normal sales under US GAAP. Under IAS 39 such contracts may still be considered normal purchases or normal sales even if they contain an embedded derivative.

Further differences may sometimes arise as a result of the detailed guidance contained in FASB's FAS 133 Implementation Issues that interpret the normal purchase and sales exemption under US GAAP.

11.1.2 Loan commitments

Loan commitments meet the definition of a derivative under IAS 39. However, loan commitments that have not been designated as 'at fair value through profit or loss' and that cannot be settled net in cash or another financial instrument are excluded from the scope of IAS 39. Under US GAAP, a commitment to originate a loan is generally not subject to FAS 133. However, a loan commitment that relates to the origination of a mortgage loan that will be held for sale should be accounted for as a derivative instrument by the issuer of the loan commitment. Differences between IFRSs and US GAAP in accounting for loan commitments may therefore be unavoidable in the case of loan commitments that can be settled net and that do not relate to mortgage loans held for sale.

11.2 Definition of financial instruments

(Chapter 3 section 11.2.2)

The term financial instrument is defined somewhat differently under IFRSs and US GAAP. Under IFRSs, the definitions of financial assets and financial liabilities specifically deal with contracts that may be settled in an entity's own equity instruments. Therefore, under IAS 32 instruments such as options and warrants are classified as equity only when they are settled by exchanging a fixed number of own shares for a fixed amount of cash. Consequently IAS 39 does not apply to such instruments. FAS 133 differs in that it does not apply to contracts that are issued or held by an entity that are (1) indexed to the entity's own equity and (2) are classified in stockholders' equity in its statement of financial position.

On the other hand, with the exception of such contracts over an entity's own shares, it is unlikely that any significant differences would arise in practice as a result of the slightly different definition of financial instruments.

11.3 Recognition of assets and liabilities

(Chapter 3 section 11.3.2 and 13.2)

Under IFRSs, an entity recognises a financial asset or a financial liability on its balance sheet when it becomes a party to the contractual provisions of the instrument. However, 'regular way' purchases and sales (i.e. contracts whose terms require delivery of the asset within the time frame established generally by regulation or convention in the marketplace concerned) should be recognised and derecognised using either trade date or settlement date accounting. The method used should be applied consistently for each category of financial assets and financial liabilities.

Although the financial instruments standards under US GAAP do not explicitly address recognition of financial instruments, significant differences are not expected to arise in practice. US GAAP takes a similar approach to 'regular way' purchases and sales as IFRSs, with the exception that financial instruments may only be derecognised when the criteria in FAS 140 have been met. Furthermore, it should be noted that the guidance on 'regular way' transactions under US GAAP applies only to transactions involving securities, rather than the broader notion of financial instruments under IFRSs.

11.4 Derecognition of financial assets

(Chapter 3 section 11.3.3)

Financial assets should be derecognised under US GAAP when the transferor has surrendered control over the transferred assets. FAS 140 focuses on legal considerations (such as legal isolation from the transferor), but does not explicitly consider whether substantially all risks and rewards have been transferred by the transferor.

IAS 39 takes a different approach and generally permits derecognition in the following cases:

(a)   when the rights to cash flows from the financial asset have expired;

(b)   when the entity has transferred substantially all risks and rewards from the financial asset; or

(c)   when the entity (1) has neither transferred substantially all, nor retained substantially all, the risks and rewards from the financial asset and (2) has not retained control of the financial asset.

Derecognition under (b) and (c) may still be possible when the entity (1) has retained its rights to receive the cash flows from the financial asset but (2) at the same has assumed an obligation to pay those cash flows to one or more entities.

Differences between IFRSs and US GAAP are likely to arise in situations where legal control is retained by the transferor while substantially all risks and rewards have been transferred.

If the transaction involves certain types of special purpose entity, then the provisions set out in Chapter 3 section 2.6 must be followed. Differences between IFRSs and US GAAP in this area are discussed in sections 2.5 and 11.7.1 of this chapter.

11.5   Extinguishment of financial liabilities

(Chapter 3 section 11.3.4)

When debt is extinguished and replaced with new debt, it is not always clear whether it is appropriate to recognise a gain or loss on extinguishment of the old debt, or whether finance costs associated with the old debt should continue to be amortised over the term of the new debt. IAS 39 and EITF 96-19 *Debtor's Accounting for a Modification or Exchange of Debt Instruments* provide very similar approaches to this topic and reconciling differences will generally not arise. A gain or loss should be recognised when the new debt is on substantially different terms to the old debt. The terms of the new debt are 'substantially different' from the terms of the old debt when the net present value under the new terms is at least 10% different from the net present value of the remaining cash flows of the original financial liability. EITF 96-19 states specifically that the discount rate to be used to calculate the present value of the cash flows is the effective interest rate, for accounting purposes, of the original debt instrument. Although IAS 39 is silent on the subject, it is generally interpreted as requiring the same approach.

11.6   Troubled debt restructurings

(Chapter 3 section 11.4)

FAS 15 provides guidance on accounting for 'troubled debt restructurings'. That standard requires recognition of a gain by the borrower when the carrying amount of the payable settled exceeds the fair value of the assets transferred, or equity interest granted, to the lender. When the lender agrees to modify the debt agreement, the effect of the modification should generally be accounted for prospectively from the time of the restructuring. The borrower should only recognise a gain when the total future cash payments are less that the carrying amount of the debt.

IFRSs do not specifically address accounting for a troubled debt restructuring; instead, the general rules on accounting for financial assets and financial liabilities apply. If a lender agrees to a substantial modification of the terms of an existing financial liability, this should be accounted for as an extinguishment of the original financial liability – which may result in a gain being recognised immediately – and the recognition of a new financial liability. However, IFRSs do not specifically address accounting for the issuance of equity instruments in the context of a troubled debt restructuring. It is therefore not clear to what extent such transactions give rise to recognition of a gain.

11.7   *Off-balance sheet transactions and accounting for the substance of transactions*

           (Chapter 3 section 11.5)

The treatment of off-balance sheet transactions illustrates the two very different underlying approaches to standard setting under IFRSs and US GAAP. Under IFRSs, it is a fundamental principle that the substance of transactions must be reported rather than their legal form. This is clearly stated in paragraph 35 of the IASB's Framework:

> 'If information is to represent faithfully the transactions and other events that it purports to represent, it is necessary that they are accounted for and presented in accordance with their substance and economic reality and not merely their legal form. The substance of transactions or other events is not always consistent with that which is apparent from their legal or contrived form. For example, an enterprise may dispose of an asset to another party in such a way that the documentation purports to pass legal ownership to that party; nevertheless, agreements may exist that ensure that the enterprise continues to enjoy the future economic benefits embodied in the asset. In such circumstances, the reporting of a sale would not represent faithfully the transaction entered into (if indeed there was a transaction).'

By contrast US GAAP does not contain a principle of substance over form and relies on the application of detailed rules. Indeed, paragraph 160 of the FASB's Concepts Statement No. 2 states:

> 'Substance over form is an idea that also has its proponents, but it is not included because it would be redundant. The quality of reliability and, in particular, of representational faithfulness leaves no room for accounting representations that subordinate substance to form. Substance over form is, in any case, a rather vague idea that defies precise definition.'

This difference of approach could result in different treatment of transactions under two the GAAP systems.

11.7.1   *Securitised assets*

           (Chapter 3 section 11.5.2)

In order to achieve off-balance sheet treatment under IFRSs or US GAAP, a securitisation of financial assets must meet the derecognition criteria of IAS 39 or FAS 140 respectively as discussed in section 11.4 above.

In addition, a securitisation of a group of assets may not be reported as a sale in group financial statements under IFRSs if the other party in the securitisation is a Special Purpose Entity (SPE) that is required to be consolidated under SIC-12 *Consolidation – Special Purpose Entities.* If the other party is an SPE that is in substance controlled by the entity entering into the securitisation, then the SPE must be consolidated by that entity. From the perspective of that entity's consolidated financial statements, the securitisation has not taken place, and any external debt taken on by the SPE is recorded as a liability on the consolidated balance sheet.

Under US GAAP, a securitisation of a group of assets will be reported as a sale in consolidated financial statements only if the other party to the securitisation is a

Qualifying Special Purpose Entity (QSPE) that is not required to be consolidated. FAS 140 sets out the criteria that a special purpose entity must meet in order to qualify as a QSPE. There is no equivalent to the QSPE concept under IFRSs. It is therefore possible that certain QSPEs would require consolidation under IFRSs.

Accounting for SPEs under SIC-12 and FIN 46(R) *Consolidation of Variable Interest Entities, an Interpretation of Accounting Research Bulletin (ARB) No. 51* is addressed in more detail in section 2.5 above and Chapter 3 section 2.6.

11.8   Financial assets

11.8.1   Categories of financial assets
(Chapter 3 section 11.6)

IAS 39 provides for four categories of financial assets:

* at fair value through profit or loss;
* held-to-maturity investments;
* loans and receivables; and
* available-for-sale financial assets.

FAS 115, on the other hand, provides three categories for investments in debt and equity securities:

* trading securities;
* held-to-maturity (debt) securities; and
* available-for-sale securities.

Financial assets within the IFRSs 'loans and receivables' category are outside the scope of FAS 115. Under US GAAP, such financial assets are accounted for at amortised cost similar to the way they are accounted for under IFRSs.

The 'at fair value through profit or loss' category under IAS 39 comprises both items that are designated into this category upon initial recognition and items 'held for trading'. The 'trading securities' category under FAS 115 is narrower because it is not possible to designate items into that category.

Under FAS 115 items are only accounted for as available-for-sale if they do not meet the definition of any of the other categories, while under IAS 39 it is also possible to designate certain financial assets as available-for-sale.

Finally, under IAS 39 it is possible to apply held-to-maturity accounting to any financial asset with fixed or determinable payments and a fixed maturity date. However, under FAS 115 only debt *securities* may be accounted for as held-to-maturity investments (see section 11.8.2B).

11.8.2 Measurement of financial assets

A   Investments in equity securities

(Chapter 3 section 11.2.1)

FAS 115 under US GAAP applies to all investments in equity securities – except investments in consolidated subsidiaries and investments accounted for under the equity method – that have readily determinable fair values. This means that FAS 115 does not apply to non-listed equity investments. Equity securities that are not accounted for under FAS 115 or under the equity method should be accounted for at historical cost under US GAAP. IAS 39 is wider in scope and applies to all investments in equity securities, except investments in consolidated subsidiaries and investments accounted for under the equity method. Under IAS 39, investments in equity securities should always be measured at fair value unless the fair value cannot be reliably measured. This difference can give rise to a measurement difference between IFRSs and US GAAP, as described by UBS:

Extract 10: UBS AG (2004)

Note 41.1 Valuation and Income Recognition Differences between IFRS and US GAAP [extract]

e. Financial investments and private equity

Financial investments available-for-sale
Three exceptions exist between IFRS and US GAAP in accounting for financial investments available-for-sale: 1) Non-marketable equity financial investments (excluding private equity investments discussed below), which are classified as available-for-sale and carried at fair value under IFRS, continue to be carried at cost less "other than temporary" impairments under US GAAP. The opening adjustment and subsequent changes in fair value recorded directly in Shareholders' equity on non-marketable equity financial instruments due to the implementation of IAS 39 have been reversed under US GAAP to reflect the difference between the two standards in measuring such investments. 2) Writedowns on impaired debt instruments can be fully or partially reversed under IFRS if the value of the impaired assets increases. Such reversals of impairment writedowns are not allowed under US GAAP. Reversals under IFRS were not significant in 2004, 2003 or 2002. 3) Private equity investments, as described in the next section.

Private equity investments
UBS accounts for private equity investments as available-for-sale securities in its primary Financial Statements under IFRS, with changes in fair value recognized in Shareholders' equity. Under US GAAP, all of these investments were accounted for at cost less "other than temporary" impairments prior to 1 January 2002.

B   Investments in debt securities

(Chapter 3 section 11.2.1)

FAS 115 under US GAAP applies to all investments in debt securities, e.g. government bonds, corporate bonds, commercial paper, securitised debt instruments. However, the scope of IAS 39 is not restricted to just debt securities, the standard applies to financial assets in general. Therefore, it is possible under IAS 39 to designate, for example, loans and receivables (which are not debt securities) as 'financial assets at fair value through profit or loss' or as 'available-for-sale financial assets' and account for them at fair value with gains and losses arising from changes in fair value initially recognised in income or equity, respectively.

C   *Fair value – bid and ask price*

     (Chapter 3 section 11.6.1)

IAS 39 defines fair value as the amount for which an asset could be exchanged, or a liability settled, between knowledgeable, willing parties in an arm's length transaction. FAS 115 defines fair value in similar terms. Nevertheless, differences may arise because IAS 39 specifically states that the appropriate quoted market price for an asset held or liability to be issued is usually the current bid price and, for an asset to be acquired or liability held, the asking price. When an entity has assets and liabilities with offsetting market risks, it may use mid-market prices as a basis for establishing fair values for the offsetting risk positions and apply the bid or asking price to the net open position as appropriate. US GAAP is silent on the question of whether bid or ask prices should be used.

D   *Effective interest method*

     (Chapter 3 section 11.6.1)

In measuring a financial instrument at amortised cost, both IFRSs and US GAAP require the premium or discount to be amortised based on the effective interest rate on the instrument.

IAS 39 defines the effective interest rate as the rate that exactly discounts estimated future cash payments or receipts through the expected life of the financial instrument or, when appropriate, a shorter period to the net carrying amount of the financial asset or financial liability. When calculating the effective interest rate, an entity should estimate cash flows considering all contractual terms of the financial instrument but should not consider future credit losses. The calculation includes all fees and points paid or received between parties to the contract that are an integral part of the effective interest rate, transaction costs, and all other premiums or discounts.

Under US GAAP, an entity should apply the 'interest' method, the objective of which is to arrive at a periodic interest cost (including amortisation) that will represent a level effective rate on the sum of the face amount of the debt plus or minus the unamortised premium or discount and expense at the beginning of each period. The effective interest rate of a loan is the rate of return implicit in the loan (that is, the contractual interest rate adjusted for any net deferred loan fees or costs, premium, or discount existing at the origination or acquisition of the loan).

In the case of changes in the estimates used in calculating the effective interest rate under IFRSs, an entity should recalculate the carrying amount of the financial instrument by calculating the present value of the remaining cash flows at the original effective interest rate. This adjustment is recognised as income or expense in profit or loss. Under US GAAP, such changes in estimate should be accounted for prospectively.

E   *Available-for-sale financial assets*

        (Chapter 3 section 11.6.1)

There is a difference between IFRSs and US GAAP in the treatment of the movement in the fair value of a foreign currency monetary asset, for example a foreign currency debt instrument, that is designated as an available-for-sale investment. IAS 21 *The Effects of Changes in Foreign Exchange Rates* requires the portion of the change that relates to the underlying movement in exchange rates to be recognised in income, whereas US GAAP requires the entire movement in the fair value of the investment to be recognised in equity, including any part that relates to foreign exchange movements.

11.8.3   *Tainting of held-to-maturity investments*

        (Chapter 3 section 11.6.2)

Under IAS 39, an entity generally may not classify a financial asset as held-to-maturity if it has, during the current financial year or during the two preceding financial years, sold or reclassified more than an insignificant amount of held-to-maturity investments before maturity. FAS 115 contains similar 'tainting' provisions; however, contrary to IAS 39, it does not contain a two-year limitation of the tainting period. However, the SEC staff has concluded, in certain circumstances, that sales of held-to-maturity securities preclude management from credibly asserting the company's ability and intent to hold securities to maturity for at least one year and more likely two years in the future.

11.8.4   *Transfers between categories*

        (Chapter 3 section 11.6.2)

Under IFRSs, an entity should not reclassify a financial instrument into or out of the 'at fair value through profit or loss' category while it is held. An investment will be reclassified as available-for-sale if, as a result of a change in intention or ability, it fails to meet the requirements for classification as held-to-maturity. In addition, if in the current period or two preceding years, the entity has sold or reclassified more than an insignificant amount of held-to-maturity investments before maturity, other than in exceptional circumstances, 'tainting' occurs and any remaining held-to-maturity investments should be reclassified as available-for-sale.

Under US GAAP, transfers between categories should be infrequent and, in the case of transfers from the held-to-maturity category, they should be rare. Given the nature of a trading security, transfers into or from the trading category also should be rare. The SEC Staff consider that sales or transfers of held-to-maturity securities taint the portfolio and the held-to-maturity classification would not be available for new purchases for a period of two years.

11.8.5   Impairment of financial assets

(Chapter 3 section 11.6.3)

A   Determination of impairment

An entity should assess, under IAS 39, at each balance sheet date whether there is objective evidence of impairment of a financial asset – as a result of an event that occurred after the initial recognition of the asset – that has an impact on the estimated future cash flows of the financial asset and can be estimated reliably. Losses expected as a result of future events, no matter how likely, are not recognised.

Under FAS 115, an entity should determine whether a decline in fair value of securities classified as either available-for-sale or held-to-maturity below their amortised cost basis is other than temporary. Under FAS 114, a loan is considered impaired when, based on current information and events, it is probable that a creditor will be unable to collect all amounts due according to the contractual terms of the loan agreement.

Impairment may be recognised at a different point in time under IAS 39 than under FAS 115. IAS 39 requires recognition of an impairment of an investment in an equity instrument when there is objective evidence of a significant or prolonged decline in its fair value below cost. FAS 115 requires recognition when the impairment loss is 'other than temporary'.

IAS 39 requires assessment of impairment at each balance sheet date, whereas FAS 115 requires continuous assessment of impairment. However, it seems unlikely that FAS 115 would require recognition of an impairment that is 'other than temporary' during a reporting period that would have reversed by the end of that reporting period.

B   Collective impairment

An asset that has been assessed individually for impairment under IFRSs and found not to be impaired should be included in a collective assessment of impairment. In performing such a collective assessment of impairment, an entity groups assets by similar credit risk characteristics that are indicative of the debtors' ability to pay all amounts due according to the contractual terms.

Under US GAAP, large groups of smaller-balance homogeneous loans may be evaluated collectively for impairment. However, US GAAP does not provide for a two-stage approach in which balances are first assessed for impairment individually and then assessed for impairment collectively.

C   Reversal of impairment losses

IAS 39 requires reversal of impairment losses on (1) loans and receivables, (2) held-to-maturity investments and (3) available-for-sale debt instruments, when certain criteria are met. Under US GAAP, impairment losses can never be reversed.

11.9   Financial liabilities

11.9.1   Categories of financial liabilities

(Chapter 3 section 11.7)

Under IAS 39, financial liabilities are classified as either:

- at fair value through profit or loss; or

- other financial liabilities.

'Other financial liabilities' are initially measured at fair value less directly attributable transaction costs. Apart from possible differences in the application of the effective interest method (see section 11.8.2B above), this is similar to the measurement of financial liabilities under US GAAP.

The 'at fair value through profit or loss' category does not exist under US GAAP. Use of this category under IAS 39 could therefore give rise to reconciling differences with US GAAP. An entity may be able to avoid such differences to some extent by not designating liabilities as 'at fair value through profit or loss'. However, financial liabilities that meet the definition of 'held for trading' must be accounted for as 'at fair value through profit or loss' under IFRSs.

12   Financial instruments: shareholders' equity

12.1   Shareholders' equity

(Chapter 3 section 12.2)

Equity under IFRSs is defined in the IASB's *Framework* as the residual of an entity's assets minus its liabilities. Stockholders' equity is not defined as a concept in US GAAP. The items usually shown in stockholders' equity, such as common stock, additional paid-in capital, retained earnings and accumulated other comprehensive income, are equivalent to sub-classifications of shareholders' equity permitted by IFRSs.

It should be noted that neither IFRSs nor US GAAP explicitly provide rules on recognition of equity in the balance sheet. Generally, equity instruments are recognised when an entity recognises a corresponding asset or derecognises a corresponding liability. Furthermore, standards such as the ones on share-based payments and financial instruments may also give rise to reclassifications within equity.

The same instrument may be classified differently between debt and equity under IFRSs and US GAAP – see section 12.4 below.

12.2   Distinction between debt and equity

(Chapter 3 section 12.3)

Under IFRSs, an equity instrument is defined as any contract that entitles the holder to a residual interest in the assets of an entity after deducting all of its liabilities. A financial liability is any liability that is:

- a contractual obligation to deliver cash or another financial asset to another entity; or

- a contractual obligation to exchange financial assets or financial liabilities with another entity under conditions that are potentially unfavourable to the entity; or

- a contract that will or may be settled in the entity's own equity instruments and is:

  - a non-derivative for which the entity is or may be obliged to deliver a variable number of the entity's own equity instruments; or

  - a derivative that will or may be settled other than by the exchange of a fixed amount of cash or another financial asset for a fixed number of the entity's own equity instruments. For this purpose, the entity's own equity instruments do not include instruments that are themselves contracts for the future receipt or delivery of the entity's own equity instruments.

Under the FASB's conceptual framework the key distinguishing feature of equity is that it does not carry 'an unconditional right to receive future transfers of assets from the enterprise except in liquidation, and then only after liabilities have been satisfied'. FAS 150 *Accounting for Certain Financial Instruments with Characteristics of both Liabilities and Equity* generally requires liability classification for two broad classes of financial instruments:

- instruments that represent, or are indexed to, an obligation to buy back the issuer's shares, regardless of whether the instrument is settled on a net-cash or gross physical basis; and

- obligations that can be settled in shares but meet one of the following conditions:

  (a)   derive their value predominantly from some other underlying;

  (b)   have a fixed value; or

  (c)   have a value to the counterparty that moves in the opposite direction as the fair value of the issuer's shares.

The substance-based approach to the classification of debt and equity under IFRSs means that many preference shares are classified as liabilities under IFRSs because they include contractual obligations to pay cash distributions or redemptions. The balance sheet classification of a financial instrument as either a liability or equity also determines whether any interest, dividends, gains or losses relating to that instrument are reported in income or equity.

12.3   Split accounting

(Chapter 3 section 12.4)

Where a financial instrument (e.g. convertible debt) comprises a debt and an equity element, IAS 32 *Financial Instruments: Disclosure and Presentation* requires on initial recognition its carrying value to be allocated between the debt and equity components each of which is accounted for separately as debt or equity. This allocation is made by calculating the fair value of the liability component of the instrument and allocating the remainder of the fair value of the instrument as a whole to the equity component. Once this allocation is made, it is not changed.

Where the conversion option is not separable from the debt, US GAAP normally does not permit an allocation of part of the proceeds to the conversion option. However, if the option is 'in the money' at the commitment date, then the intrinsic value of the option is allocated to additional paid in capital. This is different from the IFRSs treatment because the intrinsic value of the conversion feature may not be equal to its fair value, the latter being the value at which it would be recorded under IAS 39 *Financial Instruments: Recognition and Measurement.*

12.4   Convertible debt with a premium put

(Chapter 3 section 12.4.1)

If an entity issues convertible debt with a premium put option, then under IFRSs the entity needs to consider whether the instrument contains an embedded derivative that must be accounted separately for. In addition, split accounting must be applied to the conversion option, as discussed in section 12.3 above. The allocation between debt and equity does not change over the term of the instrument, however the premium put option is measured at fair value at each balance sheet date, unless it is deemed closely related to the host contract and does not require separation.

Under US GAAP, the premium put option combined with the conversion option itself would be analyzed as a unit in determining the effect of Statement 133, and would likely be bifurcated and accounted for separately as a derivative.

12.5   Treasury shares

(Chapter 3 section 12.5.4)

In the US and in many other countries it is possible for an entity to acquire its own shares without the cancellation of those shares. Both IFRSs and US GAAP require such shares – commonly called treasury shares – to be shown as a deduction from equity. Under IAS 32, the acquisition of treasury shares is accounted for as a change in (i.e. deduction from) equity, and subsequent transactions involving these shares, for example their disposal or cancellation, should also be accounted for as a change in equity, with no gain or loss being recognised in the income statement. The US treatment of treasury stock is very similar, with movements being shown either in additional paid in capital or in retained earnings depending on the reason for the purchase of the treasury shares. Under very limited circumstances, if treasury shares are acquired at a price significantly in excess of current market price, a charge to income will be made under US GAAP for the excess of the purchase price over current market price; there is no similar provision in IFRSs (see Chapter 3 section 12.5.4).

13   Financial instruments: derivatives and hedge accounting

13.1   Definitions and scope

13.1.1 Scope

(Chapter 3 section 13.2.1)

There are a large number of minor differences in the scope of application of IAS 39 *Financial Instruments: Recognition and Measurement* and FAS 133 *Accounting for Derivative Instruments and Hedging Activities* that may give rise to reconciling differences:

- neither IAS 39 nor FAS 133 applies to financial instruments that are classified as shareholders' equity (see section 12.2 above), but the standards use a different definition of equity;

- the rules on normal purchases and sales under IFRSs differ slightly from those under US GAAP (see section 11.1.1 above);

- contracts that are not exchange traded and that are based on a climatic, geological or other physical variable are outside the scope of FAS 133. Such contracts are within the scope of IAS 39, unless they meet the definition of an insurance contract under IFRS 4 *Insurance Contracts*;

- options on non-financial assets or liabilities may be considered derivatives under IAS 39, but are specifically scoped out of FAS 133 if they are not readily convertible to cash; and

- IAS 39 and FAS 133 contain different scope exclusions with regards to loan commitments (see section 11.1.2 above).

13.1.2 Definitions

(Chapter 3 section 13.2.2)

A   Notional amount

IAS 39 and FAS 133 define derivative financial instruments differently. Both require a derivative to be a financial instrument the value of which changes in response to an 'underlying', and that requires little or no initial investment. However, where FAS 133 requires that a derivative has one or more notional amounts (i.e. a number of currency units, shares, bushels, pounds, kilograms or other units specified in a derivative instrument) there is no such requirement in IAS 39.

B   Net investment criteria

Both IAS 39 and FAS 133 require that a derivative financial instrument requires either no initial net investment or little initial net investment relative to other types of contracts that have a similar response to changes in market conditions. FAS 149 *Amendment of Statement 133 on Derivative Instruments and Hedging Activities* clarifies that this condition is met under US GAAP if the initial net investment in the contract is less, by more than a nominal amount, than the initial net investment that would be commensurate with the amount that would be exchanged either to acquire the asset related to the underlying or to incur the obligation related to the underlying. The difference in wording between IFRSs and US GAAP suggests that a reconciling item may arise in marginal cases where the net investment in a contract is 'somewhat' lower.

C Net settlement

US GAAP requires that the contract can readily be settled by a net cash payment, or with an asset that is readily convertible to cash. IAS 39 is different in that it requires that the contract is settled at a future date.

One example of where a subtle difference in the definition of a derivative gives rise to a significant measurement difference is described in the following extract from Swisscom's 2003 US GAAP reconciliation.

Extract 11: Swisscom AG (2003)

42 Differences between International Financial Reporting Standards and U.S. Generally Accepted Accounting Principles [extract]

o) Derivative accounting

As described in Note 26, Swisscom subscribed for CHF 100 million of new shares in Swiss for CHF 56 per share effective November 2, 2001. The shares were issued to Swisscom on December 21, on which date the market value of these shares amounted to CHF 79 million. The difference between the commitment price and the market price of CHF 21 million was recorded under financial expense for IFRS purposes. At December 31, 2001, Swisscom recorded a fair value adjustment of CHF 3 million, net of taxes of CHF 1 million, being the difference between the year-end price of CHF 46 and the issue price of CHF 44, through equity. There are restrictions on Swisscom's ability to sell the shares. Accordingly, under U.S. GAAP, the agreement to buy the shares would not be considered a derivative instrument based on the guidance contained in SFAS 133 Implementation Issue No. A14. Therefore, the CHF 21 million difference in commitment price and market price at the date of the issue would be recorded in equity as a fair value adjustment and not taken to the income statement.

Implementation Issue No. A14 referred to by Swisscom provides guidance in interpreting the phrase 'readily convertible to cash' from FAS 133.9(c) and concludes that, in the case of an instrument which entitles the holder to receive equity shares on exercise, that instrument is not readily convertible to cash if there are issuer-imposed restrictions on sale or transfer of those shares within 31 days or less of exercise of the warrant. Due to restrictions on Swisscom's ability to sell the shares, the warrant is not considered readily convertible to cash, therefore it is not a derivative as defined by FAS 133 and must be accounted for using FAS 115 *Accounting for Certain Investments in Debt and Equity Securities* and EITF 96-11 *Accounting for Forward Contracts and Purchased Options to Acquire Securities Covered by FAS 115.* The warrant is treated as a derivative under IAS 39 and the movements in its fair value are recognised in the income statement.

13.2 Embedded derivatives

(Chapter 3 section 13.2.3)

Both IAS 39 and FAS 133 require derivatives that are 'embedded' in other instruments to be accounted for separately as derivatives in their own right if the economic characteristics of the embedded derivative are not closely related to the economic risks and characteristic of the host contract.

Although IAS 39 and FAS 133 give the same basic definition of an embedded derivative, the two standards apply the 'closely related' principle differently in some circumstances and hence may not always agree on whether a given contract contains an embedded derivative. IAS 39 gives several examples of embedded derivatives, and also of contracts that it considers may not contain embedded derivatives. Appendix A to FAS 133 gives further guidance on the application of the clearly and closely related principle. This, and the implementation guidance for both standards, must be taken into account when deciding whether an embedded derivative exists under either framework.

Both IFRSs and US GAAP require an embedded derivative that is deemed not closely related to its host contract to be recognised separately in the balance sheet at its fair value on issuance. Changes in the fair value of the derivative are recognised in the income statement. If the host contract is a debt instrument, it would be recorded on issuance at the amount of net proceeds, which is the balancing figure after subtracting the fair value of the derivative.

Although IFRSs and US GAAP generally identify the same embedded derivatives, there are a number of areas in which significant differences arise in practice:

- contracts that are out of the scope of FAS 133 because they meet the definition of a normal purchase or sale are not assessed for embedded derivatives under US GAAP. IFRSs are different in that they may require separation of embedded derivatives even if the host contract is outside the scope of IAS 39;

- IAS 39 does not require an embedded currency derivative to be separated if a contract is denominated in a currency that is commonly used in contracts to purchase or sell non-financial items in the economic environment in which the transaction takes place (e.g. a relatively stable and liquid currency that is commonly used in local business transactions or external trade);

- options that extend the term of debt instruments are not considered embedded derivatives under US GAAP if they do not *significantly* extend the term of the debt host contract and the interest rate is reset to approximate market rates. IAS 39 may still require separation of an embedded derivative if the debt host contract is extended by a period that is not considered significant under US GAAP; and

- under IAS 39, a call, put, or prepayment option embedded in a host debt contract or host insurance contract is not closely related to the host contract unless the option's exercise price is approximately equal on each exercise date to the amortised cost of the host debt instrument or the carrying amount of the host insurance contract. The rules in FAS 133 are different in that they require a put or call option on debt to be accounted for as an embedded derivative (1) if the debt involves a substantial premium or discount, but only if the put or call option is contingently exercisable or (2) if the payoff amount is determined based on a change in an underlying other than interest rate or credit risk.

Finally, the effective date of the requirement to identify embedded derivatives differs between IFRSs and US GAAP. The transitional rules in IAS 39 require an entity to recognise all embedded derivatives when an entity first applies IAS 39. In contrast, FAS 133 provides an entity the option to apply the requirement to identify embedded derivatives prospectively from 1 January 1998 or 1999 onwards.

13.3   *Accounting for derivatives*

     (Chapter 3 section 13.3)

The basic principle of both IAS 39 and FAS 133 is that derivatives are recorded on the balance sheet at fair value. Gains and losses on derivatives are recognised in the income statement, unless the derivative meets the criteria for a hedging relationship, in which case the gain or loss may be recognised directly in equity or offset in the income statement against an opposite loss or gain on the item it is hedging (see section 13.5 below).

The fair value of a derivative may be estimated in several ways, depending on the type of contract, but the underlying principle for both IFRSs and US GAAP is that a derivative's fair value is the amount for which it could be exchanged or settled between knowledgeable, willing parties in an arm's length transaction. US GAAP is more prescriptive about the methods that may be used to value a derivative.

13.4   *Types of hedging relationship and general criteria*

     (Chapter 3 section 13.3)

Special accounting is permitted by IAS 39 and FAS 133 for the same three categories of hedging relationship: fair value hedges; cash flow hedges; and hedges of net investments in foreign operations.

IAS 39 and FAS 133 provide general criteria which must be met for any type of hedge accounting. The criteria in the two standards are broadly similar:

- both standards require the hedging relationship to be identified and documented in a similar manner at inception;

- the hedge must be expected to be 'highly effective' at inception and on an ongoing basis, this effectiveness to be measured in a manner consistent with the original risk management strategy for that hedging relationship; and

- the hedge must actually be highly effective.

Both standards restrict the use of written options as hedging instruments.

The type of information that must be captured by an entity's systems in order to ensure that a hedging relationship will meet the criteria for hedge accounting is very similar for both IFRSs and US GAAP.

13.4.1   *Fair value hedges*

When applying fair value hedge accounting, the hedging instrument is measured at fair value at each balance sheet date, and changes in its carrying value are recognised in the income statement. The carrying amount of the hedged item is adjusted by the gain or loss on the hedged item that is attributable to the hedged risk, which is also recognised in the income statement. The normal treatment for marketable securities designated as available-for-sale is to measure them at fair value with changes taken directly to equity (see section 11). However, the special accounting rules for a fair value hedge permit these movements to be taken to income and hence offset against the movements of the hedging derivative.

In addition to the general criteria for hedge accounting outlined above, IAS 39 and FAS 133 give further detailed restrictions on the use of fair value hedge accounting (Chapter 3 section 13.3.3). Since the restrictions in each standard are lengthy and detailed it is possible that, for example, a relationship which qualifies for fair value hedge accounting under IFRSs does not qualify under US GAAP, or vice versa.

13.4.2   Cash flow hedges

To account for a cash flow hedge, the portion of the gain or loss on the hedging instrument that is deemed to be an effective hedge is recognised directly in equity (under US GAAP, in other comprehensive income) until the hedged transaction affects earnings.

A   Basis adjustments

Under US GAAP, the cumulative gain or loss in equity relating to the hedging instrument is recycled through the income statement over the same period during which the hedged forecasted transaction affects earnings. The same treatment is permitted under IFRSs. However, as a matter of accounting policy, an entity may opt to account for the gain or loss on hedges of forecast transactions that result in the recognition of a non-financial asset or non-financial liability as a basis adjustment that increases or decreases the carrying amount of that asset or liability. The effect on profit or loss is the same – only the balance sheet differs.

Under both systems any portion of the gain or loss on the hedging instrument that is not an effective hedge is recognised in the income statement immediately as it arises.

B   Forecast transactions

To qualify as a hedged item under IAS 39, a forecast transaction must be highly probable. Under US GAAP, forecast transactions need to be probable to be eligible for designation as a hedged transaction (see Chapter 3 section 13.3.4). The IASB considers 'probable' under US GAAP and 'highly probable' under IFRSs to be consistent; hence this should not give rise to a GAAP difference.

13.4.3   Hedges of net investments in foreign operations

Derivative and non-derivative financial instruments may be designated as hedging the foreign currency exposure of an entity's net investment in a foreign entity under both IFRSs and US GAAP. This type of hedging relationship under IFRSs is subject to the general hedging criteria discussed in section 13.4 above. Under US GAAP, the designation criteria in FAS 133 are less extensive than for fair value hedges and cash flow hedges.

When the hedging criteria for the hedge of a net investment in a foreign entity are met, the gain or loss on the effective part of the hedging instrument is taken directly to equity in the group financial statements, where it will offset, at least partially, the movements on translation of the foreign entity's reserves. The gain or loss on any ineffective part of a hedging instrument should be recognised immediately in the income statement.

FAS 133 requires the operating unit that is exposed to the foreign currency exposure to have the same functional currency as the entity within the group that holds the hedging instrument. This is true for both a hedge of a net investment in a foreign subsidiary and for a foreign currency cash flow hedge. There is no equivalent requirement in IAS 39.

13.5   Designation and effectiveness of hedges
   (Chapter 3 section 13.3)

13.5.1   Highly effective

IAS 39 specifies that it must be possible to measure reliably the effectiveness of the hedging relationship. It requires the entity to expect the changes in the fair value or cash flows of the hedged item to be highly effective in offsetting the changes in the fair value or cash flows of the hedging instrument. When the effectiveness of the hedging relationship is measured, IAS 39 states that the acceptable range of offset is between 80% and 125%. The FASB does not further define the meaning of 'highly effective' in FAS 133, but require an entity to define how it will measure the ineffectiveness of a hedge relationship, both at the inception of the relationship and over its life.

13.5.2   Short-cut method

FAS 133 permits an entity to assume that certain narrowly-defined types of hedging relationships using interest rate swaps, where the critical terms of the swap and the entire hedged asset or liability are the same, will be completely effective, i.e. there will be no ineffectiveness to recognise in the income statement. This assumption can greatly simplify the calculations required to assess the effectiveness of such relationships, and is commonly known as the 'short-cut' method.

There is no equivalent to the 'short-cut' method in IAS 39. However, the IASB pointed out that 'IAS 39 permits the hedging of portions of financial assets and financial liabilities in cases when US GAAP does not'. The Board noted further 'that under IAS 39 an entity may hedge a portion of a financial instrument (e.g. interest rate risk or credit risk), and that if the critical terms of the hedging instrument and the hedged item are the same, the entity would, in many cases, recognise no ineffectiveness.'

13.5.3   Partial term hedges

IAS 39 allows an entity to designate a portion of the cash flows or fair value of a financial instrument as a hedged item, provided that effectiveness can be measured and the other hedge accounting criteria are met. FAS 133 permits identification of a selected portion of an asset or liability as the hedged item; however, in many cases, partial-term hedge transactions will fail to meet the high correlation requirement of FAS 133. Such hedges generally fail because fair value hedging focuses on changes in value – not cash flows – and a partial-term hedge cannot be achieved by simply using a shorter-term derivative.

13.5.4   Macro hedging

Many groups collect exposures to the same types of risk from several divisions and subsidiaries in one place – for example, in the group's treasury function. It is not entirely straightforward to decide whether, in any particular situation, IAS 39 or FAS 133 permits hedge accounting especially when the group's risk is managed on a net basis.

A   Hedging a group of assets and liabilities

IAS 39 and FAS 133 permit a group of assets (or liabilities) to be designated as the hedged item in a hedging relationship, provided that the assets (or liabilities) share the risk exposure for which they are designated as being hedged.

IAS 39 states that the change in fair value attributable to the hedged risk for each individual item in the group should be expected to be approximately proportional to the overall change in fair value attributable to the hedged risk of the group of items. FAS 133 contains similar wording, which it interprets narrowly by adding that 'if the change in fair value of a hedged portfolio attributable to the hedged risk was 10 percent during a reporting period, the change in the fair values attributable to the hedged risk for each item constituting the portfolio should be expected to be within a fairly narrow range, such as 9 percent to 11 percent. In contrast, an expectation that the change in fair value attributable to the hedged risk for individual items in the portfolio would range from 7 percent to 13 percent would be inconsistent with this provision.'

B   Net hedging

IAS 39 states that a net position (for example, fixed rate assets and fixed rate liabilities with the same maturity period) cannot be a hedged item, since to qualify for hedge accounting each hedged item must be matched to a hedging instrument. However, the standard goes on to comment that the effect of hedging a net position may be obtained by designating a portion of the hedging instrument as hedging a portion of the hedged items. It uses the example of a bank that has 100 of assets and 90 of liabilities with risks and terms of a similar nature, that wishes to hedge the net 10 exposure. It can achieve a form of net hedging by designating 10 of the assets as the hedged item. This form of net hedging can be achieved for fair value and cash flows hedges, including a hedge of a firm commitment.

Although FAS 133 does not give as detailed a discussion of this type of net hedging, it does permit a portion of a portfolio of assets or liabilities to be designated as part of a hedging relationship. Consequently, there is, in theory, no reason why an entity should not continue to manage its exposure to a particular type of risk on a net basis and, using the example discussed above, designate a portion of a portfolio of similar assets and liabilities equal to the net exposure as a hedged item. However, differences may arise in respect of hedging of groups of cash flows as described in the extract below.

Extract 12: UBS AG (2004)

Note 41.1 Valuation and Income Recognition Differences between IFRS and US GAAP
[extract]

d. Derivative instruments

Under IAS 39, UBS hedges interest rate risk based on forecast cash inflows and outflows on a Group basis. For this purpose, UBS accumulates information about non-trading financial assets and financial liabilities, which is then used to estimate and aggregate cash flows and to schedule the future periods in which these cash flows are expected to occur. Appropriate derivative instruments are then used to hedge the estimated future cash flows against repricing risk. SFAS 133 does not permit hedge accounting for hedges of future cash flows determined by this methodology. Accordingly, for US GAAP such hedging instruments continue to be carried at fair value with changes in fair value recognized in Net trading income. In addition, amounts deferred under hedging relationships prior to the adoption of IAS 39 on 1 January 2001 that do not qualify as hedges under current requirements under IFRS are amortized to income over the remaining life of the hedging relationship. Such amounts have been reversed for US GAAP as they have never been treated as hedges.

C   Portfolio hedging of interest rate risk

IAS 39 permits designation of a fair value portfolio hedge of interest rate risk only, in which the hedged item is a portion of the portfolio of financial assets or financial liabilities that share the risk being hedged. The key characteristic of this accounting model is that it could reduce the volatility in equity: although derivative hedging instruments would be recorded on the balance sheet at fair value, equivalent changes in the fair value of the hedged assets and liabilities would also be recognised on the balance sheet within assets or liabilities. Similar accounting is not permitted under FAS 133.

13.5.5   Risk components

A   Financial asset or financial liability

IAS 39 allows hedging of a financial asset or financial liability with respect to the risks associated with only a portion of its cash flows or fair value, provided that effectiveness can be measured. FAS 133 specifically defines the following risk components that may be hedged:

- the risk of changes in the overall fair value (or cash flows) of the entire hedged item;

- the risk of changes in its fair value (or cash flows) attributable to changes in interest rate;

- the risk of changes in its fair value (or cash flows) attributable to changes in the related foreign currency exchange rates; and

- the risk of changes in its fair value (or cash flows) attributable to both changes in the obligor's creditworthiness and changes in the spread over the benchmark interest rate with respect to the hedged item's credit sector at inception of the hedge.

Therefore, IAS 39 offers an entity more flexibility in defining the particular risk that is being hedged, which is restricted only by the entity's ability to measure effectiveness of the hedge.

B   Non-financial assets and non-financial liabilities

Non-financial assets and non-financial liabilities can only be designated, under IAS 39 and FAS 133, as a hedged item (1) for foreign currency risks, or (2) in their entirety for all risks. However, it should be noted that there is an exception under FAS 133 that allows a recognised loan servicing right and a non-financial firm commitment with financial components to be designated as a hedged item in a fair value hedge as if they were financial assets or financial liabilities.

13.5.6   Assessment of hedge effectiveness

US GAAP provides more detailed guidance on methodologies to assess hedge effectiveness than IAS 39. Therefore, it is possible that a difference may arise between US GAAP and IFRSs in their assessment of the effectiveness of a given hedge.

13.6   Hedged items and hedging instruments

(Chapter 3 section 13.3)

13.6.1   Non-derivative hedging instruments

Under US GAAP, a non-derivative financial instrument that may give rise to a foreign currency transaction gain or loss under FAS 52 may be designated as hedging only (1) the changes in the fair value of an unrecognised firm commitment attributable to foreign currency exchange risk or (2) the foreign currency exposure on a net investment in a foreign operation. IAS 39 offers more flexibility as it permits designation of a non-derivative financial asset or financial liability as a hedging instrument in a hedge of any foreign currency risk.

13.6.2   Held-to-maturity investments

Under IAS 39, held-to-maturity investments can be a hedged item with respect to currency exchange risk and credit risk, but the interest rate risk and prepayment risk of a held-to-maturity investment cannot be a hedged item.

FAS 133 is different in that it permits an entity to hedge currency exchange risk, credit risk *and* the entire fair value of prepayment options in held-to-maturity investments, while prohibiting hedging of interest rate risks.

13.6.3   Intragroup transactions and monetary items

If a hedged item is denominated in a foreign currency, an entity may designate as the hedged risk in a cash flow hedge under FAS 133 the foreign currency risk on a forecasted intragroup transaction. Under IAS 39, however, the foreign currency risk of an intragroup monetary item (e.g. a payable or receivable resulting from such a forecast) may qualify as a hedged item in the consolidated financial statements only if it results in an exposure to foreign exchange rate gains or losses that are not fully eliminated on consolidation under IAS 21. Furthermore, the foreign currency risk of a highly probable forecast intragroup transaction may qualify as a hedged item in consolidated financial statements provided that the transaction is denominated in a currency other than the functional currency of the entity entering into that transaction and the foreign currency risk will affect consolidated profit or loss.

A further problem with hedge accounting is that many groups use internal derivatives to hedge the exposure of individual divisions to similar types of risk and to collect this risk in the group's treasury function. The definition of a hedged item in IAS 39 requires the hedging instrument to involve a third party, which implies that derivatives entered into between one group entity and another will generally not qualify for hedge accounting in the consolidated accounts. The Guidance on Implementing IAS 39 includes several examples on internal derivatives, and this should be referred to for a fuller understanding of this complex area (see Guidance on Implementing IAS 39 sections F.1.4 to F.1.7, F.2.15 and F.2.16).

FAS 133 does not generally permit hedge accounting for internal derivatives in consolidated financial statements. One exception to this general rule is made for foreign currency derivative contracts that have been entered into with another group company. This type of internal derivative may be designated as a hedging instrument in a foreign currency cash flow hedge of a forecast borrowing, purchase, or sale, or as an unrecognised firm commitment, if a number of detailed conditions are satisfied. Amongst other things, the normal criteria for a foreign currency cash flow hedge must be met from the perspective of the group member using the derivative, and the net exposure being hedged must be laid off by the other group member to a third party. FAS 133 also requires the operating unit that is exposed to the foreign currency exposure to have the same functional currency as the entity within the group that holds the hedging instrument. This is true for both a hedge of a net investment in a foreign subsidiary and for a foreign currency cash flow hedge.

13.6.4 Firm commitments

IAS 39 defines a firm commitment as a binding agreement for the exchange of a specified quantity of resources at a specified price on a specified future date or dates. However, FAS 133 defines a firm commitment somewhat differently as an agreement with an unrelated party, binding on both parties and usually legally enforceable, with the following characteristics:

- The agreement specifies all significant terms, including the quantity to be exchanged, the fixed price, and the timing of the transaction. The fixed price may be expressed as a specified amount of an entity's functional currency or of a foreign currency. It may also be expressed as a specified interest rate or specified effective yield; and

- The agreement includes a disincentive for non-performance that is sufficiently large to make performance probable.

Agreements without a sufficiently large disincentive for non-performance may still meet the definition of a firm commitment under IAS 39. Therefore, it is possible that an agreement qualifies as a hedged item (i.e. firm commitment) in a fair value hedge under IAS 39, while under FAS 133 the same agreement qualifies as a hedged item (i.e. forecasted transaction) in a cash flow hedge.

13.6.5   Business combinations

Under FAS 133, a firm commitment either to enter into a business combination or to acquire or dispose of a subsidiary, a minority interest, or an equity accounted investee cannot be a hedged item. In addition, a forecasted transaction cannot be a hedged item if it involves a business combination subject to the provisions of FAS 141. Under IAS 39, a firm commitment to acquire a business in a business combination cannot be a hedged item, except for foreign exchange risk, because the other risks being hedged cannot specifically be identified and measured.

14   Financial instruments: disclosure

14.1   Scope

There are differences in scope between the IFRSs and US GAAP standards on financial instruments. The disclosures on instruments within the scope of the financial instruments standards are considerably more detailed and onerous than those on financial instruments outside their scope. For example, IFRSs may require more extensive disclosures in respect of non-derivative financial instruments and financial liabilities than US GAAP.

14.2   Disclosure

Both IFRSs and US GAAP require a significant amount of disclosure in respect of financial instruments and risks. Although the purpose of the financial instruments disclosures may not be dissimilar, the actual disclosures required by IFRSs and US GAAP differ considerably. The differences in disclosure requirements – which do not give rise to reconciling items between IFRSs and US GAAP – are too numerous to discuss in this chapter and reference is therefore made to Chapter 3 section 14.

15   Inventory and long-term contracts

15.1   Inventory – scope
(Chapter 3 section 15.2.1)

The definitions of inventory under IFRSs and US GAAP are virtually identical. However, the measurement requirements of IAS 2 *Inventories* do not apply to inventories held by producers of agricultural and forest products, minerals and mineral products, and agricultural produce after harvest, to the extent that they are measured at net realisable value in accordance with well established practices in those industries, or to commodity broker-traders when their inventories are measured at fair value less costs to sell. This means that IFRSs permits the use of industry specific accounting policies for certain types of inventories. Under US GAAP, ARB 43 Chapter 4 *Inventory Pricing*, all inventories should be measured at the lower of cost or market. Only in exceptional circumstances may inventories be stated at above cost, and the SEC staff believe such cases to be extremely rare. Chapter 4 of ARB 43 and the AICPA's Audit and Accounting Guide *Agricultural Products and Agricultural Cooperatives* provide certain exceptions to the general rule to the extent qualifying inventories (e.g. precious metals and harvested crops and livestock) are carried at net realisable value.

15.2 Inventory – costs

(Chapter 3 sections 15.2.2 and 15 2.3)

Although the principles contained in IAS 2 on determining the costs of inventory are similar to US GAAP, there are a number of differences:

- IAS 2 provides more extensive guidance on the nature of costs appropriately included in inventory than does US GAAP;

- US GAAP specifically prohibits capitalisation of interest for inventories that are routinely manufactured, while IFRSs permits capitalisation of directly attributable interest for all assets that necessarily take a substantial period of time to get ready for their intended use or sale; and

- US GAAP permits the use of the FIFO, weighted average and LIFO costing methods. IFRSs permits FIFO and weighted average, but use of the LIFO method is prohibited.

15.3 Inventory – lower of cost and net realisable value

(Chapter 3 section 15.2.4)

When the cost of inventories is no longer recoverable, IFRSs require them to be written down to net realisable value, which is the estimated selling price in the ordinary course of business less the costs of completion and sales costs. US GAAP, however, requires inventories to be written down to their current replacement cost, which should not exceed their net realisable value. Normally this will mean that the written down value under US GAAP (which is determined by reference to the market in which the entity purchases its inventories) is lower than the written down value under IFRSs (which is determined by reference to the market in which the entity sells its inventories).

15.4 Inventory – reversal of impairment

(Chapter 3 section 15.2.4)

IFRSs permit the reversal of a previous impairment of inventory if it is no longer required. This would be reflected in the income statement as a reduction to cost of sales. US GAAP does not permit an impairment to be reversed once it has been recognised.

15.5 Construction contracts – scope

(Chapter 3 sections 15.3.1 and 15.3.2)

IAS 11 *Construction Contracts* defines a construction contract as 'a contract specifically negotiated for the construction of an asset or a combination of assets that are closely interrelated or interdependent in terms of their design, technology and function or their ultimate purpose or use.' All other types of contracts should be accounted for under IAS 18 *Revenue*, which provides principles of revenue recognition in those cases but also refers to IAS 11 for additional guidance.

Accounting for long-term contracts under US GAAP is defined by ARB 45 *Long-Term Construction-Type Contracts* and SOP 81-1 *Accounting for the Performance of Construction-Type and Certain Production-Type Contracts.* ARB 45 implicitly, and SOP 81-1 specifically, exclude service contracts from their scope. Apart from the general revenue recognition principles in CON 5 *Recognition and Measurement in Financial Statements of Business Enterprises* and SAB 104 *Revenue Recognition in Financial Statements*, there is no guidance that specifically addresses accounting for service revenues, hence a difference may arise between IFRSs and US GAAP due to the differing scopes of the standards in this area.

Under IFRSs, long-term contracts should be combined or segmented when certain criteria are met. US GAAP has similar criteria but if these specific criteria are met combining and segmenting contracts is optional.

15.6   Construction contracts – revenue recognition

(Chapter 3 section 15.3.2)

IFRSs and US GAAP both contain standards dealing with the recognition of revenue on construction contracts. Under US GAAP, application of the percentage-of-completion method is preferable when:

* estimates of costs to complete and the stage of completion of construction contracts are reasonably dependable;

* contracts executed by the parties usually include details of enforceable rights regarding goods to be provided, consideration and settlement; and

* both the customer and contractor can be expected to perform their respective obligations under the contract.

If the use of the percentage-of-completion method is not appropriate then US GAAP requires application of the completed-contract method, meaning that income is only recognised when the contract is substantially completed.

Under IFRSs, the percentage-of-completion method should be applied when:

* total contract revenue can be measured reliably;

* it is probable that the economic benefits of the contract will flow to the entity;

* both the costs of completion and stage of completion of the contract can be measured reliably; and

* costs attributable to the contract can be identified clearly and measured reliably, allowing a comparison of actual costs incurred with prior estimates.

If the percentage-of-completion method is not appropriate, IFRSs require revenue to be recognised to match the costs that have been incurred, provided that the costs incurred are recoverable.

There may be borderline cases where the difference in the wording of the criteria for the application of the percentage-of-completion method gives rise to a difference between IFRSs and US GAAP. The use of the completed contract method is prohibited under IFRSs.

If a loss on the contract is foreseen, then both IFRSs and US GAAP would require that loss to be recognised immediately.

16   Leasing

16.1   *General*

All the relevant principles and guidance concerning leases may be found in one standard and three interpretations for IFRSs, but the US rules are contained in several pronouncements: nine accounting standards, six interpretative statements and several technical bulletins and EITF abstracts. IAS 17 *Leases* sets out the general principles for accounting for all but a few specialist categories of leases. FAS 13 *Accounting for Leases* contains detailed rules and thresholds, in contrast to IAS 17's substance-based approach. There are specific US rules on various categories of leases, most notably for real estate transactions.

Although the US guidance is much more specific and rule-based than the IFRSs approach, the overall approaches of IFRSs and US GAAP are in fact very similar. Both focus on classifying leases between finance (or capital) leases and operating leases and both deal separately with lessees and lessors. The most common differences between IFRSs and US GAAP arise in the treatment of sale and leaseback transactions.

16.2   *Accounting by lessees*

(Chapter 3 section 16.4)

Both IAS 17 and FAS 13 require a lease to be classified as either a finance (capital) lease or an operating lease, with the subsequent accounting treatment dependent on the classification. IAS 17 classifies a lease as a finance lease when it transfers substantially all the risks and rewards incidental to ownership to the lessee, and gives examples of circumstances which may indicate that this transfer has taken place. In contrast, FAS 13 gives a straightforward checklist of criteria. If any one of these criteria is met, the lease must be classified as a finance lease. It would be very unusual for a lease to be classified differently under IFRSs and US GAAP, even though the wording of the relevant standards may initially appear to be different, their similarity is illustrated by the following points:

- the transfer of ownership to the lessee by the end of the term of the lease is a criterion or indicator in both standards;

- the existence of a bargain purchase option for the lessee to acquire the asset at a significant discount at the end of the lease is also listed in both standards;

- FAS 13 requires a lease to be classified as a finance lease if the term of the lease is for more than 75% of the leased asset's useful estimated economic life. IAS 17 provides no numerical guidelines but suggests that if the lease term is for the major part of the asset's economic life, then this may indicate that the lease is a finance lease. However in practice, if the lease is for the major part of the economic life of the asset it is likely also to be for more than 75% of the asset's useful estimated economic life; and

- under IAS 17, if the present value of the minimum lease payments is substantially equal to the fair value of the leased asset, then the lease will probably (but not definitely) be classified as a finance lease. Again, FAS 13 is much more specific in its requirements: if the present value of lease payments is greater than or equal to 90% of the present value of the asset, measured in a certain way, then the lease must be classified as a finance lease. Since 'substantially equal' in IAS 17 is in practice often interpreted as 90% or more, it is unlikely that the difference in wording of the two standards would often give rise to a different treatment. Also, IAS 17 requires that the present value of minimum lease payments is discounted using the interest rate implicit in the lease, or if this is impracticable the lessee's incremental borrowing rate, whereas FAS 13 requires the use the lessee's incremental borrowing rate or, if known and if lower, the implicit rate in the lease.

Under both IFRSs and US GAAP, a finance lease is accounted for by recognising the leased asset as a fixed asset in the lessee's balance sheet, measured at the lower of the fair value of the asset and the present value of the minimum lease payments. The lease commitment is recorded as a liability.

The approach to accounting for operating leases is similar under IFRSs and US GAAP. Lease payments, including lease incentives received, are normally charged to income on a straight-line basis over the period of the lease unless another systematic basis is more representative of the time pattern of the benefits of the asset's use.

16.3   Accounting by lessors

(Chapter 3 section 16.5)

A   Finance leases

IFRSs and US GAAP have essentially similar approaches to accounting by lessors for finance leases not involving real estate. If a lease is classified as a finance lease by IAS 17, then the accounting treatment adopted by the lessor reflects the fact that the risks and rewards of ownership have been substantially transferred to the lessee, and a sale is recognised in accordance with normal revenue recognition policies. If there is a difference between the total amount being paid for the asset over the term of the lease (i.e. the present value of the lease payments) and the carrying amount of the asset, this may represent the manufacturer or dealer's profit on the sale, in which case this profit is generally recognised immediately in the income statement to the extent that the fair value of the asset (or, if lower, the present value of the minimum lease payments to the lessor) exceeds the manufacturer's or dealer's cost (being the cost or carrying amount of the leased property less the present value of the unguaranteed residual value). The ongoing finance-type income from the lease payments is recognised over the period of the lease using a constant rate of return. If there is no immediate profit on the sale, then all income is taken to the income statement at a constant rate of return over the lease.

The treatment required by FAS 13 is similar, but not identical. The main difference is that there are two further criteria that must be met in addition to those set out in section 16.2 above in order to treat the lease as a finance lease and recognise an immediate profit on the transaction: (a) the collectability of the lease payments must be reasonably assured; and (b) there must be no important uncertainties surrounding the amount of non-reimbursable costs yet to be incurred by the lessor.

B   *Operating leases*

Both IFRSs and US GAAP require operating lease receipts to be recognised on a straight-line basis over the period of the lease unless another systematic basis is representative of the time pattern of the benefits from the leased asset's use.

C   *Leveraged leases*

FAS 13 defines a further type of finance lease, called a leveraged lease, involving a third party who provides long-term credit. A leveraged lease is accounted for by netting off the investment in the lease and the related non-recourse debt in the lessor's balance sheet. This reflects the fact that the lessor does not bear the risks of the financing because these have been passed onto a third party. Income in the lessor's books is recorded at a constant return on the net investment. IAS 17 does not contain an equivalent classification; therefore the accounting for a leveraged lease under US GAAP will differ from its treatment under IFRSs. This is because IFRSs require both the asset and liability to be shown gross on the balance sheet, and income from the lease will be allocated differently (see Chapter 3 section 16.5.1C).

16.4   *Leases involving real estate*

        (Chapter 3 section 16.6)

Leases involving real estate require special consideration because of the long life – in the case of land, indefinite life – of the assets involved. FAS 13 contains specific rules on accounting for leases involving real estate, and unless the lease transfers ownership to the lessee by the end of the lease term or there is a bargain purchase option, a leasehold interest in land should be accounted for as an operating lease. IAS 17 on the other hand notes that leases involving land and buildings are accounted for using the same principles as for other types of asset, but that the land and buildings elements are considered separately for the purposes of lease classification and the minimum lease payments are allocated between these elements in proportion to their relative fair values at the inception of the lease. As land generally has an indefinite economic life, any lease of land will be deemed to be an operating lease unless title is expected to pass to the lessee. Under IAS 40, a property interest held under an operating lease that otherwise satisfies the definition of an investment property may be classified as an investment property (carried under the fair value model) and accounted for as if it were a finance lease.

16.5   *Sale and leaseback transactions*

        (Chapter 3 section 16.7)

There are significant differences between IFRSs and US GAAP in the accounting for sale and leaseback transactions, particularly when the resultant lease is an operating lease. IAS 17 requires the gain on a sale and leaseback transaction that results in an operating lease to be recognised immediately where the sale price is established at fair value. If the sale price is below fair value any profit or loss is recognised immediately, except where the loss is compensated for by below-market future lease payments, in which case the loss is deferred and amortised in proportion to the lease payments over the period of expected use. If the sale price is above fair value the difference between the sale price and fair value should be deferred and amortised over the period for which the asset is expected to be used. If the sale price is less than the carrying amount at the time of the sale and leaseback the loss should be recognised immediately. Under US GAAP, FAS 28 *Accounting for Sales with Leasebacks* generally requires any gain arising on a sale and operating leaseback to be deferred and only recognised as rental payments are made. China Southern Airlines records a difference in this respect:

Extract 13: China Southern Airlines Company Limited (2003)

33 Significant differences between IFRS and U.S. accounting principles [extract]

(a) Sale and leaseback accounting

Under IFRS, gains on sale and leaseback transactions where the subsequent lease is an operating lease are recognized as income immediately, if the transactions are established at fair value. Differences between the sale price and fair value are deferred and amortised over the period for which the assets are expected to be used. Under U.S. GAAP, such gains are deferred and amortized over the term of the lease.

If a sale and leaseback transaction results in a finance lease, then both IFRSs and US GAAP require any gain or loss on the transaction to be deferred. IAS 17 requires amortisation of the gain or loss over the period of the lease. FAS 28 requires recognition in proportion to the amortisation of the leased asset, which gives a very similar pattern of recognition.

US GAAP gives specific and fairly onerous rules on the treatment of sale and leaseback transactions involving real estate in FAS 98 *Accounting for Leases*. IFRSs do not contain special rules on real estate transactions. This gives rise to a difference in treatment, because US GAAP does not recognise a sale where the sale and leaseback transaction allows for some continuing involvement by the seller in the property. Swisscom reports a difference in this respect:

Extract 14: Swisscom AG (2003)

42 Differences between International Financial Reporting Standards and U.S. Generally Accepted Accounting Principles [extract]

(p) Sale and leaseback transaction

In March 2001 Swisscom entered into two master agreements for the sale of real estate. The first relates to the sale of 30 commercial and office properties for CHF 1,272 million to a consortium led by Credit Suisse Asset Management. The second concerns the sale of 166 commercial and office properties for CHF 1,313 million to PSP Real Estate AG and WTF Holding (Switzerland) Ltd. At the same time Swisscom entered into agreements to lease back part of the sold property space. The gain on the sale of the properties after transaction costs of CHF 105 million and including the reversal of environmental provisions (see Note 28), was CHF 807 million under IFRS.

A number of the leaseback agreements are accounted for as finance leases under IFRS and the gain on the sale of these properties of CHF 239 million is deferred and released to income over the individual lease terms, see Note 28. The accounting is similar under U.S. GAAP. The remaining gain of CHF 568 million represents the gain on the sale of buildings which were either sold outright or which under IFRS qualify as operating leases. Under IFRS, the gain on a

---

leaseback accounted for as an operating lease is recognized immediately. Under U.S. GAAP, the gain is deferred and amortized over the lease term. If the lease back was minor, the gain was immediately recognized. In addition, certain of the agreements did not qualify as sale and leaseback accounting because of continuing involvement. These transactions are accounted for under the finance method and the sales proceeds would be reported as a financing obligation and the properties would remain on the balance sheet and would be depreciated as in the past. The lease payments would be split into an interest part and an amortization of the obligation.

17   Taxation

The broad principle of both IAS 12 *Income Taxes* and FAS 109 *Accounting for Income Taxes* is that a deferred tax liability or asset should be recognised for all temporary differences, with some exceptions. Despite the similar 'full provision' approaches to accounting for taxation under IFRSs and US GAAP, deferred taxation is one of the most common items reported in reconciliations between IFRSs and US GAAP. The reason for this is that a high proportion of other adjustments made to the income statement or balance sheet will have consequential effects on the deferred tax provision. For example, when fixed assets are stated at valuation less depreciation under IFRSs, the revaluation is reversed for US GAAP purposes because US GAAP requires fixed assets to be stated at cost less depreciation. The reversal of an IFRSs revaluation reserve will require the related deferred tax provision to be reversed also.

17.1   General approach

(Chapter 3 section 17.2)

IAS 12 and FAS 109 both require a liability to be recognised in respect of all taxable temporary differences, with a few exceptions as set out in Chapter 3 section 17.2. One important exemption found in both standards is that a deferred tax liability or asset should not be recognised in respect of positive goodwill that is not tax deductible.

Unlike IAS 12, FAS 109 has no exemption from the requirement to provide for deferred tax on initial recognition of an asset or liability in a transaction that is not a business combination and at the time of the transaction affects neither accounting profit nor taxable profit. This could cause a significant difference in the deferred tax provision required by FAS 109 compared to IAS 12.

17.2   Temporary differences arising from investments in subsidiaries, associates and joint ventures

(Chapter 3 section 17.2.2)

FAS 109 does not require a liability to be recognised for the difference between the carrying amount and the tax basis of an investment in a foreign subsidiary or corporate joint venture, unless it becomes apparent that this difference will reverse in the foreseeable future. IAS 12 has a similar exemption for temporary differences in respect of investments where the reporting entity is able to control the timing of the reversal of the temporary difference and it is probable that the temporary difference will not reverse in the foreseeable future.

However, the exemption in IAS 12 applies to investments in subsidiaries, branches, associates and joint ventures where the investor is able to control the timing of the reversal of the temporary difference, whereas the equivalent FAS 109 exemption only applies to investments in foreign subsidiaries and corporate joint ventures (as defined in APB 18 *The Equity Method of Accounting for Investments in Common Stock*). If an entity has the ability to control the timing of the distributions of an investment that is accounted for under the equity method, for example by means of a non-distribution agreement, then the exemption could apply for IFRSs, but not for US GAAP (unless the equity method investment qualifies as a corporate joint venture).

17.3   Deferred tax on elimination of intragroup profits

(Chapter 3 section 17.2.2)

IAS 12 and FAS 109 require different measurements of the deferred tax adjustment that is necessary when intragroup profit is eliminated on consolidation from, for example, inventory. IAS 12 requires the deferred tax provision to be made at the tax rate of the company that is holding the inventory. FAS 109 prohibits recognition of a deferred tax asset for the difference between the buyer's tax basis of the assets and their cost in the consolidated financial statements. The consolidation entries that eliminate intragroup profit also defer the income taxes paid by the seller. The tax benefit or expense deferred is recognised when the asset leaves the consolidated group (e.g. by sale to a third party, depreciation/amortisation or impairment). The FAS 109 deferred tax provision would be made at the tax rate applicable to the selling company. Novartis reports a reconciling item in this respect:

Extract 15: Novartis Limited (2003)

32 Significant Differences Between IFRS and United States Generally Accepted Accounting Principles (US GAAP) [extract]

(h) Deferred taxes

Under IAS 12 (revised) and US GAAP, unrealized profits resulting from intercompany transactions are eliminated from the carrying amount of assets, such as inventory. In accordance with IAS 12 (revised) the Group calculates the tax effect with reference to the local tax rate of the company that holds the inventory (the buyer) at period-end. However, US GAAP requires that the tax effect is calculated with reference to the local tax rate in the seller's or manufacturer's jurisdiction.

17.4   Equity instrument awards to employees

(Chapter 3 section 17.2.2)

Under US GAAP, the cumulative amount of any tax deductible compensation cost should be treated as a deductible temporary difference. Detailed rules are provided in APB 25 *Accounting for Stock Issued to Employees* or FAS 123(R) *Share-Based Payment*, as applicable, on how to recognise such temporary differences in financial statements.

Under IFRSs, the difference between the tax base of the employee services received to date and the carrying amount of nil is a deductible temporary difference that results in a deferred tax asset. If the amount of the tax deduction (or estimated future tax deduction) exceeds the amount of the related cumulative remuneration expense, this indicates that the tax deduction relates not only to remuneration expense but also to an equity item. In this situation, the excess of the associated current or deferred tax should be recognised directly in equity.

17.5 Computation – retranslation of non-monetary assets for tax purposes

(Chapter 3 section 17.2.2)

A difference in treatment arises when non-monetary assets and liabilities of an entity, which are measured in its functional currency, have a tax base that is determined in a different currency. FAS 109 prohibits recognition of a deferred tax liability or asset for differences related to assets that are translated from the local currency into the functional currency using historical exchange rates, when those differences arise either from changes in exchange rates or indexing for tax purposes. In contrast, IAS 12 requires recognition of a deferred tax asset or liability in relation to temporary differences that arise on foreign non-monetary assets that are measured at an historic exchange rate in the reporting entity's functional currency, but whose tax base is in the foreign currency. This difference between IFRSs and US GAAP is illustrated by Grupo TMM.

> *Extract 16: Grupo TMM SA de CV (2003)*
>
> **Note 18 Reconciliation of differences between IFRS and U.S. GAAP** [extract]
>
> **vi. Deferred income tax** [extract]
>
> As mentioned in Note 3, income tax is recorded in accordance with IAS 12 (revised), which among other provisions, requires the recognition of deferred taxes for non-monetary assets indexed for tax purposes. Under U.S. GAAP, the Company follows the procedures established in SFAS No. 109 "Accounting for Income Taxes". This statement does not permit recognition of deferred taxes for differences related to assets and liabilities that are remeasured from local currency into the functional currency using historical exchange rates and that result from changes in exchange rates or indexing for tax purposes.
>
> For U.S. GAAP purposes the deferred tax computation on non-monetary assets and liabilities is based on current historical pesos whereas for IAS purposes amounts in historical US dollars are considered for book purposes and for tax purposes indexation is recognised.

17.6 Computation – applicable tax rate

(Chapter 3 section 17.2.3)

Under IFRSs and US GAAP, deferred tax balances should be calculated based on the enacted tax laws and tax rates that are expected to apply to taxable income in the periods in which they are expected to be settled. IAS 12 requires enacted or 'substantively enacted' tax rates and tax law to be used – the interpretation of 'substantively enacted' will vary from country to country. Although FAS 109 only discusses details of the enactment date of a US federal tax bill, the concept of enacted (versus substantially enacted) is applicable in all jurisdictions and is not influenced by the likelihood of enactment or the perception that the enactment is perfunctory. The SEC Staff has given some further guidance on determining enactment dates of non-US tax law (see Chapter 3 section 17.2.3).

IAS 12 specifically states that when measuring deferred tax liabilities, the entity should take into account the manner in which it intends to settle or recover the carrying amount. For example, if tax allowances on a tangible fixed asset would become taxable (i.e. be clawed-back) in the event that the asset is disposed of, then the claw-back should be taken into account when calculating the deferred tax provision only if the entity intends to dispose of the asset. There is no equivalent requirement in FAS 109, other than in relation to the tax rate to be applied.

17.7   Income or equity?

(Chapter 3 section 17.3)

IAS 12 requires current and deferred tax movements to be included in the income statement for the period, except to the extent that they relate to items that have been recognised directly in equity in the same or a different period. The treatment required by FAS 109 is essentially the same, except that tax effects are charged or credited directly to equity only when they relate to current period amounts recognised directly in equity and some items must always be recognised in income, which can cause a difference between IFRSs and US GAAP.

For example, a difference will arise if the tax law or rate for an item that has been recognised directly in equity subsequently changes. When there is a change in tax rates or tax laws, IAS 12 requires the effect of the change to be shown in the current year income statement, except to the extent that it relates to items whose deferred tax movements were previously recognised directly in equity. FAS 109 on the other hand requires a deferred tax movement caused by a changes in tax rates or tax laws to be recognised in income for the period, irrespective of whether some part of the movement relates to items originally charged to equity.

17.8   Deferred tax assets

(Chapter 3 section 17.2.4)

IAS 12 requires a deferred tax asset to be recognised only to the extent that it is probable that profits will be available to offset the deductible temporary differences. The burden of proof of the availability of taxable profits is high. IAS 12 notes that if an entity has a history of recent losses then this is strong evidence that future taxable profits may not be available, in which case the asset should not be recognised, unless there are sufficient taxable temporary differences or there is convincing other evidence that sufficient taxable profit will be available.

FAS 109 requires deferred tax assets to be recognised in full, but reduced by a valuation allowance to an amount that is more likely than not to be realised. Evidence about future taxable profits and the reversal of existing taxable temporary differences will be taken into account when judging whether a valuation provision is necessary. It is unlikely that a measurement difference between IFRSs and US GAAP would arise in this respect.

17.9 Deferred tax arising from business combinations
(Chapter 3 section 17.2.4A)

Both IAS 12 and FAS 109 require recognition of deferred tax assets or liabilities in respect of temporary differences that arise on acquisition. This is because the tax base of the acquired assets will be different from the value at which they are measured on acquisition (for example, because fixed assets have been revalued to market value). The amount of any deferred tax asset recognised on acquisition is subject to the requirements of both standards (see section 17.8 above).

If as a result of a business combination, an acquirer considers it probable that it will recover its own deferred tax asset that was not recognised before the business combination, IAS 12 would require the acquirer to recognise a deferred tax asset and a credit to income. FAS 109 requires the reduction in the acquirer's valuation allowance be accounted for as part of the business combination, impacting goodwill rather than income.

A different treatment is required by IFRSs and US GAAP also if a deferred tax asset that was not recognised on acquisition is subsequently recognised. FAS 109 requires the tax benefit to be recognised by: first, reducing to zero any goodwill related to the acquisition; secondly, reducing to zero any other non-current intangible assets acquired; and thirdly, reducing income tax expense in the income statement. Under IAS 12, the tax benefit is recognised as a credit to deferred tax in the income statement. In addition, the carrying amount of goodwill is adjusted to what it would have been if the deferred tax asset had been recognised on acquisition. However, this should not result is the creation of negative goodwill. The reduction in the carrying amount of goodwill is recognised as an expense in the appropriate line in the income statement.

17.10 Presentation
(Chapter 3 section 17.4)

Under IFRSs, deferred tax liabilities and assets are presented separately in the balance sheet, but they may not be classified as current liabilities or assets. In contrast, US GAAP requires deferred tax items to be classified as current or non-current based on the classification of the related asset or liability in the balance sheet.

17.11 Reconciliation of expected and reported tax expense
(Chapter 3 section 17.4.3)

IAS 12 requires a reconciliation either between the average effective tax rate and the applicable tax rate; or the tax expense and the accounting profit multiplied by the applicable tax rate, disclosing the basis on which the applicable tax rate is determined. In contrast, FAS 109 requires a reconciliation of the reported tax expense attributable to continuing operations to the income tax expense calculated by applying entity's statutory rate to pre-tax income from continuing operations.

18   Provisions

The accounting for provisions has long been recognised by standard setters as an area which, in the absence of strong accounting standards, may be used to smooth earnings patterns. Provisions for the cost of restructuring a business, or as part of a business combination, have also been focused on by the standard setters.

IAS 37 *Provisions, Contingent Liabilities and Contingent Assets* contains broad principles that must be applied when accounting for provisions and further guidance on accounting for restructuring costs. US GAAP has no equivalent general standards on provisions, but has several standards on specific topics. FAS 143 *Accounting for Asset Retirement Obligations* brings US GAAP closer to IAS 37 in the treatment of the costs of dismantling an asset and FAS 146 *Accounting for the Costs Associated with Exit or Disposal Activities* deals with the accounting treatment for individual costs often associated with restructurings. The FASB has also issued a number of Interpretations and EITF Abstracts. The only US standard that deals with provisions in general is FAS 5 *Accounting for Contingencies*.

18.1   Recognition

(Chapter 3 section 18.2)

Under IFRSs, an entity must recognise a provision when:

*   it has a present obligation – legal or constructive – as a result of a past event;

*   it is probable that an outflow of resources embodying economic benefits will be required to settle the obligation; and

*   a reliable estimate can be made of the obligation.

FASB CON 5 *Recognition and Measurement in Financial Statements of Business Enterprises* and CON 6 *Elements of Financial Statements* (which are not authoritative but serve as a framework) give some guidance on recognition of liabilities that is similar to IAS 37.

18.2   Discounting

(Chapter 3 section 18.3)

IAS 37 requires the time value of money to be taken into account when making a provision. In contrast, US GAAP only permits a provision to be discounted where the amount of the liability and the timing of payments are fixed or reliably determinable, or where the obligation is a fair value obligation (e.g. an asset retirement obligation under FAS 143). Since the very nature of provisions is such that the amount and timing of payments are uncertain, this means that it can be difficult to account for a provision on a discounted basis under US GAAP. This is demonstrated by Swisscom.

Extract 17: Swisscom AG (2003)

42 Differences between International Financial Reporting Standards and U.S. Generally Accepted Accounting Principles [extract]

(l) Telephone poles

Under IAS 37, Swisscom discounted the accrual for dismantlement of telephone poles to its present value. This resulted in a reduction of the liability and an increase in equity in 2000. Under U.S. GAAP, this adjustment is reversed, as the liability is not discounted. For the years ended December 31, 2001 and 2002 the interest expense recorded as an addition to the liability in the amount of CHF 1 million for 2001 and 2002 under IFRS is reversed. Due to a change in law the accrual for dismantlement was reassessed in 2001 and a decrease was recorded. Due to the fact that under U.S. GAAP the liability is not discounted the decrease is higher and additional income is recorded in the amount of CHF 9 million. Effective January 1, 2003, Swisscom adopted SFAS 143 "Accounting for Asset Retirement Obligations" which resulted in a reduction of the liability of CHF 7 million. This adjustment was recorded as a cumulative effect of accounting change in 2003. As a result of this adjustment there is no longer a difference between IFRS and U.S. GAAP for this item.

18.3   Range of outcomes

(Chapter 3 section 18.3)

Where there is a range of possible outcomes, IAS 37 requires a provision for the expected value of the obligation to be made. Where the provision being measured relates to a large population of items, the expected value of the obligation should be determined by weighting all possible outcomes by their associated probabilities. Where a single obligation is being measured, the individual most likely outcome may be the best estimate of the liability but the entity should still consider other possible outcomes. If such outcomes are either mostly higher or mostly lower than the most likely outcome, the best estimate will be a higher or lower amount.

Under US GAAP, where the liability is not measured at fair value and there is a range of possible outcomes, if any outcome within the range is more likely than any other outcome, then that outcome should be accrued. If no amount within the range is a better estimate than any other, then the minimum amount should be accrued. It is therefore possible that a different provision would be required by IFRSs and US GAAP. Where the liability is measured at fair value, all possible outcomes are incorporated into the fair value measurement.

18.4   Major inspection or overhaul

(Chapter 3 section 18.4)

The treatment of the costs of a major inspection or overhaul could differ under IFRSs and US GAAP because these are dealt with specifically in IFRSs but not under US GAAP. Under IFRSs, the costs of major inspection or overhaul may be capitalised to the cost of the asset when certain conditions are satisfied, while under US GAAP several alternative accounting methods are available for specific industries (e.g. the airline industry), otherwise such costs are generally required to be expensed as incurred.

18.5   *Environmental and decommissioning costs*

        (Chapter 3 sections 18.5 and 18.6)

Under IFRSs, the general principles of IAS 37 should be followed for both environmental and decommissioning provisions. This means that a provision is made where there is a legal or constructive obligation to incur costs. If a provision is made for the costs of cleaning up a site after use or returning it to its original condition, for example in the case of an oil-rig that must be dismantled, then the costs provided for are included in the capitalised cost of the fixed asset.

There are specific rules under US GAAP for environmental and decommissioning costs in SOP 96-1 *Environmental Remediation Liabilities* and FAS 143 *Accounting for Asset Retirement Obligations*, respectively.

Under SOP 96-1, the rules require a provision to be recognised when it is probable that a liability has been incurred and the amount can be reasonably estimated. The probability test will be met if litigation can be asserted, or is under way, and it is probable that the outcome of the litigation will be unfavourable. Given the specific nature of the guidance under US GAAP, it is not surprising that differences sometimes occur between IFRSs and US GAAP in this respect

Under FAS 143, an entity should recognise an asset retirement obligation in the period in which it is incurred or as soon as a reasonable estimate of fair value can be made. When an asset retirement obligation is recognised an entity should capitalise an asset retirement cost as an addition to the carrying amount of the related long-lived asset.

Although the US rules on decommissioning are very similar to IFRSs, it remains possible for a measurement difference to occur (1) when the liability does not arise from a legal obligation or (2) when changes in cost estimates or discount rates occur (see section 7.2.2).

18.6   *Accounting for restructuring costs*

        (Chapter 3 section 18.8)

IAS 37 deals specifically with the accounting for restructuring costs. The US guidance is provided by FAS 146.

IAS 37 requires the general recognition criteria for provisions to be satisfied before a provision is recognised for restructuring costs. In addition, management must have a detailed plan for the restructuring, and have created a valid expectation in those affected that the plan will be carried out. In practice, this means that the detailed plan must identify the business or part of the business concerned, location, function and approximate number of employees who will receive termination compensation. A formal public announcement of the restructuring will, if it is made in sufficient detail, create a valid expectation in other parties such as customers, suppliers and employees that the restructuring will take place.

Under FAS 146, even when management has committed itself to a detailed exit plan, it does not follow automatically that the costs of that exit plan may be provided for. Instead, each cost is examined individually to determine when it is incurred. FAS 146 allows the costs of involuntary employee termination to be recognised when management has:

- committed to a detailed plan of termination;

- identified the number, function and location of the employees expected to be terminated; and

- communicated this plan to the employees.

The employee termination costs would be recognised immediately when employees are terminated within the minimum retention period. Otherwise, the costs would be recognised over the future service period.

However, liabilities for other exit costs are simply recognised when they are incurred, which is normally when the goods or services associated with the activity are received. Consequently, other exit costs will probably be recognised later than under IAS 37. This is because IAS 37 places emphasis on the recognition of the costs of the exit plan as a whole, rather than on the recognition of individual liabilities.

18.7   *Disclosure of a contingent liability*

(Chapter 3 section 18.9.2)

Both IFRSs and US GAAP require information about a contingent liability to be disclosed, unless the probability of an outflow of economic benefits is remote. IAS 37 permits reduced disclosure if it would be severely prejudicial to the entity's position in a dispute with other parties over the contingent liability. US GAAP has no similar exemption from disclosure of a contingent liability, including tax contingencies.

19   Revenue recognition

The different approaches of IFRSs and US GAAP to standard-setting are illustrated by the manner in which the respective revenue recognition pronouncements are written.

IAS 18 *Revenue* contains general principles for revenue recognition and illustrative examples of specific transactions. In contrast to this, under US GAAP there are many individual pronouncements that cover particular categories of transaction or particular industries. Additionally, the SEC staff has set out its views on the principles of revenue recognition in SAB 104 *Revenue Recognition in Financial Statements*, providing SEC registrants with further guidance. SAB 104 is based primarily on the Concept Statements in US GAAP.

The US rules are very prescriptive and often apply only to industry-specific cases; in addition, these detailed rules often contain exceptions for particular types of transactions. Under US GAAP, meeting a list of detailed criteria will often decide whether revenue may be recognised or not, rather than applying general principles. Consequently, where differences do arise between IFRSs and US GAAP, they will occur more as a result of rigid application of detailed US GAAP rules than as a result of a fundamentally different approach to whether revenues should be recognised.

In the case of certain industry-specific transactions, it is not unusual for entities preparing their financial statements under IFRSs to apply the detailed US GAAP rules in order to avoid revenue recognition differences arising. However, in so doing, it is important always to ensure that the US GAAP approach adopted is in conformity with IAS 18's general principles.

19.1   General background

(Chapter 3 section 19.2)

The approaches to revenue recognition under both IFRSs and US GAAP follow critical event theory based on the earnings process and the realisation principle. The differences lie in the extremely detailed rules set down in US GAAP.

Revenue is defined in IAS 18 as 'the gross inflow of economic benefits during the period arising in the course of the ordinary activities of an entity when those inflows result in increases in equity, other than increases relating to contributions from equity participants'. The standard provides specific revenue recognition criteria for the sale of goods, the rendering of services, and interest, royalties and dividends. The appendix to IAS 18 provides practical examples of the application of the general principles.

Under US GAAP, revenues represent actual or expected cash inflows (or equivalent) that have occurred or will result from the entity's ongoing major operations and revenue is not recognised until it is both realised or realisable and earned. Revenue is considered to be realised or realisable when products have been exchanged for cash, or related assets that can be easily converted into cash. Revenue is considered to be earned when the entity has substantially accomplished what it must do to be entitled to the benefits represented by the revenue.

19.2   Sale of goods

(Chapter 3 section 19.2)

Both IAS 18 and SAB 104 give several criteria that must all be satisfied before revenue on the sale of goods may be recognised:

- IAS 18 requires the risks and rewards of ownership of the goods to be transferred to the buyer, and requires the seller to retain neither continuing managerial involvement to the degree usually associated with ownership, nor effective control over the goods sold. The equivalent requirement in SAB 104 is that revenue should not be recognised until both title and the risks and rewards of ownership have transferred to the customer. For the simplest sale of goods transactions, this means that revenue should not be recognised before delivery occurs. In most instances, SAB 104 requires delivery to have occurred to validate that sufficient evidence exists that the risks and rewards of ownership have passed. IAS 18 accepts that delivery is not always necessary for revenue to be recognised, because the risks and rewards of ownership may be transferred to the buyer even though the goods have not yet been delivered – for example, it is possible to recognise revenue on bill and hold sales under IFRSs, provided that certain criteria are met. This is rarely permitted by SAB 104 since delivery has not taken place;

- SAB 104 contains a further rule that there must be persuasive evidence of the sale. This means that when a company's standard business practice requires a written sales agreement in order for a sale to be considered final, the absence of a final agreement executed by the properly authorised personnel of both the customer and the company precludes revenue recognition. There is no equivalent specific requirement in IAS 18, although if it was normal practice to obtain a written agreement and no agreement had been obtained in a particular instance, then it might be prudent to inquire whether a sale really has taken place;

- IAS 18 requires that the amount of revenue can be measured reliably. SAB 104 requires that the seller's price to the buyer is fixed or determinable. If the fee a vendor can earn is not fixed or determinable (e.g. due to refund rights provided to the customer or if the vendor has a history of providing concessions after delivery), revenue cannot be recognised; and

- before revenue may be recognised, both IFRSs and US GAAP require that collectability is reasonably assured

19.3   *Multiple-element arrangements*

(Chapter 3 section 19.3.1)

EITF 00-21 *Revenue Arrangements with Multiple Deliverables* and SAB 104 provide rules for transactions that have multiple elements. Multiple deliverables within a revenue arrangement should be divided into separate units of accounting if certain criteria are met at the inception of the arrangement and as each item is delivered. When the separation criteria are met and the amount of the total arrangement consideration is fixed or determinable, the arrangement consideration should be allocated among the separate units of accounting. EITF 00-21 specifies that allocations should be based on (1) the relative fair values of each element or (2) the residual value method when the fair values are known only for all of the undelivered elements. The best evidence of fair value is the price of a delivered item when it is regularly sold on a standalone basis, and is often termed 'vendor specific objective evidence' (VSOE).

IAS 18 includes only general principles and does not provide specific guidance for multiple-element arrangements. However, IAS 18 does deal with combining and segmenting transactions, and in a multiple-element arrangement it may be necessary to apply revenue recognition criteria either to separately identifiable components of a single transaction or to two or more linked transactions. Since 15 June 2003 when US GAAP guidance in EITF 00-21 became effective, certain revenue, previously deferred, may be recognised on delivery. However, even when companies use US GAAP revenue recognition guidance as the basis for IFRSs accounting policies, differences can still arise. For example:

Extract 18: Polska Telefonica Cyfrowa SP ZOO (2003)

3. Principal Accounting Policies [extract]

3.16. Revenue recognition

...

The Company set criteria for revenue recognition of multiple-element transactions and their presentation in the IFRS consolidated financial statements as initiated by SAB 101 and further interpretations, including SAB 104.

...

32. Differences between IFRS and US GAAP [extract]

d. Revenue recognition (SAB 101 / EITF 00-21)

Under IFRS the Company continues the revenue recognition policy applied to prior periods for multi element arrangements.

Under US GAAP, the Company implemented for the arrangements entered into on or after July 1, 2003 principles of EITF 00-21. EITF 00-21 gives detailed interpretation relating to revenue recognition and addresses certain aspects of the accounting of the elements of the multiple-deliverable arrangements as separate units of accounting.

As a result of the implementation of EITF 00-21 the company has identified multiple element arrangements as it pertains to the sale of handsets and the delivery of service. The effect in the income and expenses for the arrangements entered in the period from July 1, 2003 till December 31, 2003 that are deferred and recognized ratably over the average expected life of the customer under IFRS are immediately recognized in income statement account under US GAAP. Total revenues of PLN 58,646 and related costs of PLN 58,646 have thus been recorded for US GAAP.

The arrangements entered into before July 1, 2003 are settled under SAB 101 till termination.

19.4   *Software revenue recognition*

(Chapter 3 section 19.3.2)

SOP 97-2 *Software Revenue Recognition* requires the same four basic criteria as SAB 104 be met before revenue is recognised. For deliverables within the scope of SOP 97-2, EITF 00-21 would not apply. This is because SOP 97-2 requires software vendors preparing financial statements under US GAAP to provide 'vendor specific objective evidence' (VSOE) of the fair value of the different components of a sale in order to recognise each component as it is delivered. However, if VSOE of fair value does not exist for all elements but does exist for all of the undelivered elements, the residual method of allocating the arrangement consideration can be used. If these requirements are not met, then all revenue generally would be deferred until all elements have been delivered or until VSOE of the fair value exists for the undelivered element. VSOE of fair value is usually limited to the price charged when the same element is sold separately by the software vendor. There are no such specific rules in IFRSs, but there is a simple example in the appendix to IAS 18. Although the US rules cannot be imposed on an entity preparing financial statement under IFRSs, many would regard SOP 97-2 to be best practice for software vendors reporting under IFRSs. Consequently, it is unlikely that a difference would arise in this respect.

19.5   Franchise fees

(Chapter 3 section 19.3.3A)

IFRSs and US GAAP require a similar treatment of franchise fee income:

- any portion of the income that relates to the sale of assets should be separated out and treated as revenue from the sale of assets; and

- if the franchise agreement provides prices that do not include a reasonable profit on the provision of goods or services to the franchisee, then a portion of the initial franchise fee should be deferred to cover the continuing cost of these services.

Under US GAAP, FAS 45 *Accounting for Franchise Fee Revenue* contains additional rules on the treatment of franchise fees when the franchisor has an option to purchase the business of the franchisee and it is understood that this option will be exercised. The entire initial franchise fee should be deferred and included in the cost of the franchisor's investment in the business when it is acquired.

19.6   Disposal of land and buildings

(Chapter 3 section 19.3.4)

For revenue to be recognised by the vendor in respect of the sale of land and buildings, both IAS 18 and FAS 66 *Accounting for Sales of Real Estate* require the risks and rewards of ownership of the property to be transferred to the purchaser, without any significant continuing involvement from the vendor. The pattern of payments received from the purchaser must also be considered when determining whether a sale has taken place. However, this is an area where a different treatment may occur under IFRSs and US GAAP .

Because IFRSs are based on principles rather than rules, IAS 18 contains only an example on real estate sales in its appendix. The example discusses, in very general terms, the possible accounting treatments when the vendor retains some form of continuing involvement with the property, or has not received sufficient payment from the purchaser to demonstrate a commitment to complete payment. Rather than giving detailed rules, the standard relies on its principles being applied in order to determine which particular accounting treatment is appropriate. FAS 66, on the other hand, is a detailed standard that applies specifically to real estate sales. It sets out seven different methods of revenue recognition and a series of complex decision trees that must be used to determine which of these seven methods is appropriate. Since the US rules are much more specific than IFRSs, it is possible that a transaction which would be treated as a sale under IFRSs would be treated differently under US GAAP.

19.7   Sale and repurchase agreements

(Chapter 3 section 19.3.6)

Under IFRSs, a sale and repurchase agreement must be analysed to ascertain whether the seller has transferred the risks and rewards of ownership to the buyer. If the seller has retained the risks and rewards of ownership, no revenue is recognised, and the transaction is treated as a financing arrangement. Under US GAAP, FAS 49

Accounting of Product Financing Arrangements only deals specifically with sale and repurchase agreements for inventory, but the required accounting is similar to IFRSs.

19.8   Non-monetary transactions

19.8.1   General background

(Chapter 3 section 19.4)

There is no one standard under IFRSs that deals specifically with non-monetary transactions. The basic principle for measuring the cost of an item of property, plant and equipment, an intangible asset and an investment property which is acquired in a non-monetary exchange is that the cost of the item should be recorded at its fair value unless (1) the exchange transaction lacks commercial substance, or (2) the fair value of neither the asset received nor the asset given up is reliably measurable. The fair value of the asset(s) given up in the exchange is used unless the fair value of the asset(s) received is more clearly evident. If the acquired item is not measured at fair value, its cost is the carrying amount of the asset(s) given up.

When goods or services are exchanged or swapped for goods or services that are of a similar nature and value, revenue is not recorded. Revenue would be recorded if goods or services are exchanged for dissimilar items.

The relevant US rules are found in APB 29 *Accounting for Non-Monetary Transactions* and FAS 153 *Exchanges of Productive Assets an amendment of APB Opinion No. 29.* The rules in APB 29 are similar to IAS 18's principles, and require the accounting entries for sales involving non-monetary transactions to be based on the fair values of the assets involved. The following are exceptions to the general rule:

- When neither the fair value of the non-monetary asset received nor the fair value of the non-monetary asset given up can be determined within reasonable limits.

- When the transaction is an exchange of a product or property held for sale in the ordinary course of business for a product or property to be sold in the same line of business to facilitate sales to customers other than parties to the exchange.

- Where the transaction lacks commercial substance – a non-monetary transaction has commercial substance if the entity's future cash flows are expected to significantly change as a result of the exchange, i.e. if either:

    - the risk, timing or amount (i.e. configuration) of future cash flows from the assets received and transferred differ significantly; or

    - the entity-specific values of the assets received and transferred differ significantly.

- When the transaction is a pro-rata distribution of non-monetary assets, such as capital stock of subsidiaries, to stockholders in corporate liquidations or plans of reorganisation that involve disposing of all or a significant segment of the business, i.e. spin-offs, split-offs.

In each of these exceptions, the accounting for the transaction is normally based on the carrying amount of the asset given up and there is no gain/loss recognition.

If an exchange of essentially non-monetary assets involves some monetary consideration (referred to as 'boot'), and the monetary consideration exceeds 25% of the fair value of the exchange, the transaction is considered by US GAAP to be monetary and should be recorded at fair value, regardless of the types of assets involved, assuming that their fair value can be measured satisfactorily.

Several standards under IFRSs and EITF abstracts under US GAAP address accounting for non-monetary transactions of specific types. The rules on these specific topics, for example, barter credit transactions, exchanges of intangible assets, non-monetary contributions to jointly controlled entities and government grants are set out in Chapter 3 section 4. There are differences between IFRSs and US GAAP in the treatment of advertising barter transactions, as discussed in section 19.8.2 below. Differences in the treatment of other types of non-monetary transactions may occur due to the differing nature of the relevant standards.

19.8.2   Advertising barter transactions

(Chapter 3 section 19.4.8)

Both the SIC and the EITF have taken a similar position on whether revenue should be recognised in respect of the exchange of advertising space, and if so, how it is to be measured.

SIC-31 *Revenue – Barter Transactions Involving Advertising Services* applies to an exchange of dissimilar advertising services. An exchange of similar advertising services does not generate revenue under IAS 18. SIC-31 states that revenue from a barter transaction involving advertising cannot be measured reliably at the fair value of advertising services received. The fair value of the services provided may only be measured by reference to similar non-barter transactions, with a different party, that occur frequently and involve cash or other consideration whose fair value can be reliably measured. SIC-31 also requires that a predominant proportion of the total sales of similar advertising services that are being used to measure the fair value of the barter transaction, as measured by both the number of transactions and value of transactions, should be non-barter transactions. This is a safeguard to ensure that entities do not use a small volume of monetary transactions to justify the value of a much larger volume of non-monetary transactions.

The EITF reached the consensus that revenue should be recognised at fair value from an advertising barter transaction only if the fair value of the advertising surrendered in the transaction is determinable based on the entity's own historical practice of receiving cash for similar advertising. The population of prior cash transactions to be analysed in order to determine the fair value of the advertising given in consideration must be made up of transactions that have taken place with a party separate from the party to the barter transaction, and that are relatively recent (not exceeding six months prior to the barter transaction). The EITF position on advertising barter transactions is therefore similar to that found in SIC-31. However, since both pronouncements contain very detailed provisions on how to measure this type of revenue, it is possible for a difference to arise in a specific instance.

20   Government grants

(Chapter 3 section 20.3)

The relevant standard under IFRSs is IAS 20 *Accounting for Government Grants and Disclosure of Government Assistance.* Government grants should be recognised as income over the periods necessary to match them with the related costs that they are intended to compensate, on a systematic basis. If the grant relates to an asset, then it should be recognised in the balance sheet either as deferred revenue, or by deducting it from the carrying amount of the related asset. There is no prescribed treatment for government grants under US GAAP. However, accounting practices are normally the same as the required IFRSs treatment.

21   Segmental reporting

A broadly similar level of detail is required under IFRSs and US GAAP, therefore the information presented in an entity's IFRSs financial statements will normally suffice in a filing with the SEC. However, certain entities preparing IFRSs to US GAAP reconciliations have presented further disclosures required by US GAAP.

21.1   Definition of segments

(Chapter 3 section 21.3)

US GAAP follows a 'management approach' in requiring the reportable business segments to be based on the way that management organises segments for making operating decisions and assessing performance. Business and geographical segments under IFRSs are defined as a distinguishable component of an entity that is engaged in providing an individual product or service or a group of related products or services (providing products or services within a particular economic environment) and that is subject to risks and returns that are different from those of other business segments (other economic environments). If management does not organise the reporting of the business along the lines of business segments or geographical segments, then the segments that must be reported under US GAAP are different from those required by IFRSs.

21.2   Secondary segment information

(Chapter 3 section 21.4)

IFRSs distinguishe between business and geographical segments of an entity. Entities that use business segments as their primary reporting format must present secondary segment information based on geographical segments. Conversely, entities that use geographical segments as their primary reporting format need to present secondary segment information based on business segments. US GAAP requires disclosure of information by operating segment and by geographical segment, but disclosures for the latter may be less extensive than under IFRSs (see Chapter 3 section 21.3).

21.3   Reported segment result

(Chapter 3 section 21.4.1)

The segment result required to be presented is defined by IAS 14 *Segment Reporting* but US GAAP requires only 'a measure of profit or loss' to be presented for each reportable segment identified.

21.4   Segment accounting policies

(Chapter 3 section 21.4.2)

IFRSs specifically requires that the accounting policies applied in preparing the consolidated financial statements should also be applied in preparing segment information. US GAAP requires the use of internal financial reporting policies in preparing segment information, which may differ from the accounting policies used in the consolidated financial statements and may in some cases not conform to US GAAP. This is an important distinction which must be taken account of when comparing accounts prepared under IFRSs and US GAAP.

22   Employee share option schemes

In the past, the accounting treatment of employee share ownership schemes has been one of the most common reasons for a reconciling item in an IFRSs to US GAAP reconciliation. This was because the lack of any guidance in this area under IFRSs meant that most entities reporting under IFRSs did not recognise any cost in respect of options granted to employees. In contrast, either of the methods of accounting for the cost of employee share option schemes permitted under US GAAP would usually require a cost to be recognised in the income statement, depending on the type of schemes that the entity has put in place.

Since the publication of IFRS 2 *Share-based Payment* and the revision to FAS 123 *Accounting for Stock-Based Compensation*, which eliminated the alternative of using the APB 25 *Accounting for Stock Issued to Employees* intrinsic value based method, IFRSs and US GAAP have similar requirements for accounting for share-based payment. However, despite the objective of convergence, there are still a few areas of difference between IFRSs and US GAAP.

22.1   Share-based payment transactions other than with employees

(Chapter 3 section 22.3)

The scope of IFRS 2 includes all share-based payments arrangements, including those other than with employees. All those arrangements would be accounted for using the modified grant-date method. FAS 123(R) *Share-Based Payment* does not specify a measurement date for share-based payment transactions with non-employees, but leaves unchanged the guidance in EITF 96-18 *Accounting for Equity Instruments That Are Issued to Other Than Employees for Acquiring, or in Conjunction with Selling, Goods or Services* which specifies a measurement date of the earlier of (a) the date at which a commitment for performance by the counterparty to earn the equity instruments is reached; or (b) the date at which the counterparty's performance is complete.

Consequently, under US GAAP, the measurement date for transactions with non-employees could be the vesting date, or some other date between grant date and vesting date. For many awards this will differ from the measurement date prescribed by IFRS 2, being the date the entity receives the goods or the counterparty renders the service, with a resulting difference in the amount of cost recognised.

22.2   Employee share purchase plans

(Chapter 3 section 22.3)

FAS 123(R) includes criteria for determining whether a broad-based employee share purchase plan is compensatory or not. A plan that is not compensatory must meet at least one of the following conditions: (1) the terms must be no more favourable than those available to all holders of the same class of shares and any discount from market price is no greater than 5%; (2) substantially all employees that meet limited employment qualifications may participate; and (3) the plan incorporates no option features. IFRS 2 has no provisions to exempt broad-based employee share purchase plans. It is therefore possible that a share purchase plan for which IFRS 2 requires recognition of compensation expense would not be considered compensatory under FAS 123(R).

22.3   Share options granted by a non-public entity

(Chapter 3 section 22.3B)

Under FAS 123(R), a non-public entity that is unable to reasonably estimate the fair value of its equity share options because it is not practicable to estimate the volatility of its share price should measure its share options at a fair value calculated using the historical volatility of an appropriate industry sector index. IFRS 2 applies the same measurement requirements based on fair value to both public and non-public entities. Both IFRSs and FAS 123(R) permit the use of intrinsic value where it is not possible reasonably to estimate fair value.

22.4   Modifications

(Chapter 3 section 22.3B)

The accounting for a modification of the terms of an award which changes a service or performance condition such that the likelihood of vesting changes from improbable to probable would be different under IFRS 2 and FAS 123(R). Under IFRS 2 the modification would be accounted for as a change only in the number of options expected to vest, and the full grant-date fair value would be recognised over the remainder of the service period. FAS 123(R) would treat such a Type III (improbable to probable) modification in the same way as any other modification, recognising as an expense the fair value of the modified probable award, as the original improbable award would have zero fair value immediately prior to the modification.

22.5   *Payroll taxes*

     (Chapter 3 section 22.5)

IFRS 2 does not address specifically the subject of payroll taxes in connection with share-based payment arrangements. However, by applying the basic principles of IAS 19 *Employee Benefits*, payroll taxes should generally be recognised over the same period as the related share-based payment expense. Under US GAAP, the event that triggers measurement and payment of the payroll tax is the obligating event which is generally the share option exercise date. Payroll taxes generally should be recognised only on exercise of the related share option.

22.5   *Income taxes*

     (Chapter 3 section 17.2.2)

US income tax regulations specify allowable tax deductions for instruments issued under share-based payment arrangements, generally measured at the intrinsic value of an instrument on a specified date. The time value component, if any, of the fair value of an instrument generally is not tax deductible. Consequently, tax deductions generally arise in different amounts and in different periods from the compensation cost. The cumulative amount of tax deductible compensation cost should be treated as a deductible temporary difference. Detailed rules are provided in APB 25 or FAS 123(R), as applicable, on how to recognise such temporary differences in financial statements.

Under IFRSs, the difference between the tax base of the employee services received to date and the carrying amount of nil is a deductible temporary difference that results in a deferred tax asset. If the amount of the tax deduction (or estimated future tax deduction) exceeds the amount of the related cumulative remuneration expense, this indicates that the tax deduction relates not only to remuneration expense but also to an equity item. In this situation, the excess of the associated current or deferred tax should be recognised directly in equity.

23   Pension costs

IFRSs and US GAAP have similar fundamental approaches to accounting for the costs of providing pension schemes to employees. IFRSs and US GAAP both require the net funding position of a defined benefit scheme to be determined by comparing the scheme's assets and obligations. This net funding position is generally a volatile figure, which can be affected by movements in equity valuations and interest rates. IFRSs and US GAAP both apply mechanisms to allow the effect of these movements to be smoothed over time, although there are some differences in the extent to which pension assets and liabilities are recognised in the balance sheet. Also, there is greater opportunity for smoothing under US GAAP than there is under IFRSs. The pension cost in the income statement is a combination of the ongoing cost of benefits earned by current employees, potentially smoothed actuarial movements on the pension scheme assets and liabilities (if an entity does not account for actuarial gains and losses in the SORIE), and other items relating to changes in the benefits and membership of the scheme.

Since the approaches of IFRSs and US GAAP to accounting for pension schemes are similar, and obtaining more than one actuarial valuation adds further costs to an entity's annual reporting cycle, many entities with dual reporting ensure that there are as few differences as possible between the application of FAS 87 *Employers' Accounting for Pensions* and IAS 19 *Employee Benefits* through careful selection of accounting policies and actuarial assumptions. However, differences have arisen because the standards have been applied for the first time in different reporting periods, or because of differences in transitional provisions.

IAS 19 deals with the accounting for all employee benefits other than share-based payments – including pension schemes, other post-retirement benefits and other benefits to which an employee is entitled. The US rules are found in several standards: FAS 87 and FAS 88 *Employers' Accounting for Settlements and Curtailments of Defined Benefit Pension Plans and for Termination Benefits* cover pension schemes. The rules governing other post retirement benefits are contained in FAS 106 *Employers' Accounting for Postretirement Benefits Other than Pensions.* The disclosure requirements of US GAAP may be found in FAS 132(R) *Employers' Disclosure about Pensions and Other Postretirement Benefits.*

Accounting for pension costs is discussed in this section. Accounting for other post-retirement benefits is discussed in section 24 and other employee benefits are covered in section 25 below.

Accounting for defined contribution pension schemes is straightforward under IFRSs and US GAAP, the pension cost being simply the contributions due from the employer in each period.

23.1   Defined benefit pension schemes – general approach

   (Chapter 3 section 23.4)

The amount recognised in an entity's balance sheet in respect of a defined benefit pension scheme is made up of several components, as illustrated by the following summary of disclosures in respect of pension schemes in Swisscom's 2003 20-F. The IFRSs and US GAAP net balance sheet liability is made up of the same basic components, although the method used to calculate certain of them is different under IFRSs and US GAAP, as discussed in the sections that follow.

Extract 19: *Swisscom AG (2003)*

SUMMARISED EXTRACT FROM NOTES TO THE FINANCIAL STATEMENTS

	2003 €m	2003 €m
Total retirement benefits	US GAAP	IAS
Benefit obligation	(6,903)	(6,903)
Fair value of plan assets	4,893	4,893
Funded status	(2,010)	(2,010)
Minimum liability adjustment	(506)	–
Unrecognised actuarial loss	830	788
Unrecognised prior service cost	292	109
Accrued benefit cost	(1,394)	(1,113)

Swisscom reports that the difference between the balance sheet amounts is attributable to how and when the IFRSs and US GAAP pension standards were implemented and the recognition of a minimum liability under US GAAP. The difference in adoption dates results in a change in unrecognised actuarial amounts and the timing of any related amortisation.

23.1.1 Calculation of benefit obligation

  (Chapter 3 sections 23.4.1 and 23.4.3A)

The projected benefit obligation (in FAS 87 terminology) or the defined benefit obligation (in IAS 19 terminology) is the present value at the balance sheet date of the benefits that have accrued to employees through services rendered prior to that date. It is necessary to use actuarial methods to estimate this obligation: IAS 19 specifies that the projected unit credit method must be used to determine the defined benefit obligation, but FAS 87 does not specify the actuarial method that should be used.

The calculation of the defined benefit obligation is extremely sensitive to the assumptions that are input to the actuarial calculation, including the discount rate that is applied to calculate the present value of future payments. IAS 19 specifies that the appropriate discount rate should be determined by reference to market yields on high quality corporate bonds in the same currency and term as the pension scheme's obligations. FAS 87 requires the discount rate used to reflect the rates at which the pension benefits could be effectively settled, and gives both annuity contracts and high-quality fixed-income investments as reference points in determining the interest rate to be used. Since IAS 19 makes no mention of annuity rates, it is in theory possible that different discount rates could be chosen under IFRSs and US GAAP. However, this is unlikely to occur in practice for an entity with dual reporting as the guidance provided by the SEC in EITF Topic D-36 *Selection of Discount Rates Used for Measuring Defined Benefit Pension Obligations and Obligations of Postretirement Benefit Plans Other Than Pensions* suggests applying a discount rate based on an analysis using a hypothetical portfolio of high quality debt instruments with maturities that mirror the pension obligation.

23.1.2 Past service cost

(Chapter 3 section 23.4.3D)

A change in the benefits to which pension scheme members are entitled may cause an increase in the scheme liability as the additional benefits vest to the scheme employees. IAS 19 requires past service costs to be recognised immediately if they are already fully vested, or on a straight line basis over the period until the extra benefits are vested if they do not vest immediately. These costs would be recognised over a different period under US GAAP, since FAS 87 requires prior service costs to be recognised over the expected remaining service life of the scheme employees, even if the benefits are already fully vested.

Extract 20: Syngenta AG (2003)

33 Significant differences between IAS and US GAAP [extract]

d: Pension provisions (including post-retirement benefits) [extract]

Certain defined benefit pension plan amendments resulted in U.S.$nil million (2002: US$2 million; 2001: US$5 million) of past service costs, which were recognized in net income under IAS 19 (revised 2002) but will be amortized over the average future working lives of employees for U.S. GAAP as required by SFAS 87.

23.1.3 Insurance contracts

(Chapter 3 section 23.5)

IAS 19 includes qualifying insurance policies in its definition of plan assets. If plan liabilities are exactly matched by qualifying insurance policies, then IAS 19 deems the fair value of the insurance contracts to be equal to the fair value of the liabilities that they cover. The treatment of fully insured benefits under IFRSs is therefore to include an equal and opposite amount in the calculation of the plan asset and plan obligation. Under FAS 87 the benefits covered by an insurance contract generally are excluded from the calculation of the defined benefit obligation, and the insurance contracts are similarly excluded from plan assets. Although the net balance sheet result under IFRSs and US GAAP would be the same, the grossing up of scheme assets and liabilities under IFRSs could affect the amount of actuarial gains and losses recognised in the income statement (or the SORIE, if applicable). This is because the gross asset and liability figures are used as 'controls' to determine what proportion of actuarial gains and losses should be recognised (see section 23.2.1 below).

23.1.4 Measurement of plan assets

(Chapter 3 section 23.4.5)

IAS 19 requires pension scheme assets to be measured at fair value, which in most cases will be the market value of the assets at the measurement date. FAS 87 requires the use of a 'market-related value' which may either be fair value, or a smoothed version of fair value which recognises market movements over a period of up to five years. In addition, IAS 19 requires the plan assets to be measured at the balance sheet date, whereas FAS 87 permits measurement up to three months before the balance sheet date. It is therefore possible that the valuation of equity investments included in a pension scheme's assets could be different under IFRSs and US GAAP.

23.1.5 Asset cap

(Chapter 3 section 23.4.6)

If the net funding position is positive, i.e. plan assets exceed plan obligations, then IAS 19 imposes certain limits on the recognition of an asset. There is no such limit on the recognition of plan assets in FAS 87; therefore a difference may arise in this respect.

23.1.6 Additional minimum liability

(Chapter 3 section 23.4.6)

FAS 87 stipulates a minimum level of recognition of pension scheme liabilities, by reference to the accumulated benefit obligation, which has no equivalent in IAS 19. The accumulated benefit obligation is the actuarial present value of benefits attributed by the pension benefit formula to employee service rendered prior to the balance sheet date, taking into account current and past but not future compensation benefits. If the accumulated benefit obligation is greater than the value of pension scheme assets, then the minimum liability to be reflected in the balance sheet is the unfunded accumulated pension liability. When an additional minimum liability is required, an equal amount is recognised as an intangible fixed asset up to the amount of any unrecognised prior service cost or transitional liability, and thereafter directly in other comprehensive income. Stora Enso has recognised an additional minimum liability with respect to its domestic and foreign retirement benefit schemes, and discloses the intangible asset and amount recognised directly in equity as follows:

Extract 21: Stora Enso OJY (2003)

28 Summary of differences between International Financial Reporting Standards and Generally Accepted Accounting Principles in the United States [extract]

(a) Employee benefit plans [extract]

The following table sets forth liabilities recognized in the US GAAP balance sheet as of December 31, 2002 and 2003:

	Retirement Benefits as of December 31,			
	2002		2003	
	Domestic	Foreign	Domestic	Foreign
		(€ in millions)		
Accrued benefit liability	(189.2)	(770.5)	(200.4)	(689.3)
Prepaid benefit cost	–	117.4	–	16.3
Intangible asset	–	39.7	–	13.0
Accumulated other comprehensive income	–	104.7	–	91.8
Net amount recognized	(189.2)	(508.7)	(200.4)	(568.2)

For plans where accumulated benefit obligation ("ABO") exceeds the fair value of plan assets under U.S. GAAP, the ABO, projected benefit obligation ("PBO") and fair value of plan assets as of December 31, 2002 and 2003 were as follows:

	Retirement Benefits as of December 31,			
	2002		2003	
	Domestic	Foreign	Domestic	Foreign
		(€ in millions)		
ABO	152.1	908.9	135.9	886.8
PBO	211.2	982.9	194.7	945.2
Fair value of assets	–	323.1	–	329.3

23.2   Annual pension cost

(Chapter 3 section 23.4.3)

The charge for annual pension costs under US GAAP is made up of the following six components:

- current service cost, calculated using the projected unit method;

- interest cost;

- the expected or actual return on plan assets (for an explanation of the difference, see below);

- actuarial gains and losses, to the extent that they are recognised in income;

- past service costs, to the extent they are recognised; and

- the effect of any curtailments or settlements.

In addition, IFRSs have a seventh component: the effect of the limit in recognising a pension asset (i.e. the asset cap – see section 23.1.5).

Since the amounts recognised in the income statement are based in most cases on the amounts recognised in the balance sheet, any of the differences described in section 23.1 above will have a consequential effect on the measurement of the annual pension cost. There are some further reasons for a different annual pension cost under IFRSs and US GAAP, described in sections 23.2.1 and 23.2.2 below.

The precise wording of IAS 19 and FAS 87 might suggest that there is a measurement difference in respect of the return on plan assets. Under IFRSs, the amount credited in respect of return on plan assets is the expected amount as calculated at the beginning of the reporting period, whereas under US GAAP the amount included in this heading is the actual return on assets. However, this amounts to a presentation rather than a measurement difference between IFRSs and US GAAP as, under IFRSs, the actuarial gains and losses recognised in the income statement are adjusted for the difference between the expected and actual return generated by the plan assets during the reporting period.

23.2.1   *Actuarial gains and losses*

(Chapter 3 section 23.4.3D)

The concept of a 'corridor', inside which any actuarial gains and losses need not be recognised, is common to both IFRSs and US GAAP. The corridor smoothes the recognition of potentially volatile actuarial movements in the income statement.

The corridor is applied by comparing the net funding position of the plan with both the defined benefit obligation and the value of plan assets. Any cumulative unrecognised gain or loss that is less than 10% of the greater of these two amounts is not required to be recognised.

Under the corridor approach, the minimum amortisation of actuarial gains or losses, for both IFRSs and US GAAP, is the cumulative amount that falls outside the corridor at the start of the period divided by the expected remaining service life of plan employees. However, both IFRSs and US GAAP do permit recognition of an amount greater than this minimum, provided that a systematic method is used in all periods, and that the same method is applied to recognise previously unrecognised gains and losses.

Under IAS 19, if actuarial gains and losses are recognised in the period in which they occur, an entity may choose to recognise them outside profit or loss in a statement of recognised income and expense; (a SORIE – see section 1.5.5 above) provided that this is done for all of the entity's defined benefit plans and all of its actuarial gains and losses. Amounts that are recognised directly in a statement of recognised income and expense should be taken directly to retained earnings and not subsequently recognised in profit or loss. Recognition of actuarial gains and losses other than through the income statement is not permitted under US GAAP.

23.2.2   *Settlements and curtailments*

(Chapter 3 section 23.4.3E)

Under both IFRSs and US GAAP an entity should recognise gains or losses on a curtailment or settlement when the curtailment or settlement occurs. However, differences can arise in the timing of the recognition of gains or losses on a curtailment. Under IFRSs, a gain or loss is recognised when an entity is demonstrably committed to a curtailment but under US GAAP a curtailment loss should be recognised when it is probable that a curtailment will occur and the effects can be reasonably estimated.

Measurement differences may arise as a result of the calculation of curtailment and settlement gains and losses. Under IFRSs, the gain or loss should include any resulting change in the present value of the defined benefit obligation, any resulting change in the fair value of the plan assets, and any related actuarial gains and losses and past service cost that had not previously been recognised. Under US GAAP, the calculation of curtailment gains and losses and settlement gains and losses is different. A curtailment gain or loss includes the proportionate amount of unrecognised prior service cost, including any remaining unrecognised transition obligation (but not a transition asset) and any gains or losses due to related changes in the projected benefit obligation. The maximum gain or loss subject to recognition on a settlement would comprise the unrecognised net experience gain or loss plus any remaining unrecognised transitional surplus.

23.3   *Multi-employer schemes*

(Chapter 3 section 23.6)

IAS 19 and FAS 87 both address, in different ways, the issue of whether multi-employer schemes should be accounted for as defined contribution or as defined benefit schemes. IAS 19 requires a multi-employer defined benefit scheme to be accounted for as a defined benefit scheme by each individual employer, unless insufficient information is available to the employer to make this possible, in which case the scheme would be accounted for as a defined contribution scheme but with further disclosures.

In contrast, FAS 87 requires an employer participating in a multi-employer scheme to account for the contributions payable by the employer. If an actuarial liability would be created by the employer's withdrawal from the scheme, then FAS 87 requires this to be disclosed as a contingent liability, but not otherwise accounted for.

However, both IAS 19 and FAS 87 draw a distinction between multi-employer plans, where there is a shared actuarial liability, and group administration plans/multiple-employer plans, where the assets of each employer contributing to the plan are aggregated for administration purposes but claims of different employers are segregated. Each employer's share of the plan's assets and liabilities is separately tracked; therefore defined benefit accounting is appropriate under both IFRSs and US GAAP.

24   Post-retirement benefits other than pensions

(Chapter 3 section 24.2.1)

IAS 19 *Employee Benefits* should be applied when accounting for all types of employee benefit plans except share-based payment plans. The standard applies a single set of principles to pension plans and plans for post-retirement benefits other than pensions.

US GAAP deals separately with post-retirement benefits other than pensions in FAS 106 *Employers' Accounting for Postretirement Benefits Other Than Pensions*. The rules in FAS 106 are very similar to those of FAS 87 *Employers' Accounting for Pensions* and FAS 88 *Employers' Accounting for Settlements and Curtailments of Defined Benefit Pension Plans and for Termination Benefits*, which means that many of the differences in treatment of pension benefits described in section 23 apply also to other post-retirement plans.

25   Other employee benefits

(Chapter 3 sections 25.2, 25.3 and 25.4)

Accounting for other employee benefits under IFRSs is covered by IAS 19 *Employee Benefits* and under US GAAP by FAS 112 *Employers' Accounting for Postemployment Benefits (an amendment of FASB Statements No. 4 and 43)* and several other accounting standards.

Compensated absences (i.e. holiday pay) are accrued for under both IFRSs and US GAAP when the right to a compensated absence accumulates during the employee's period of service to the employer.

The accounting treatment of termination benefits is discussed in section 18.6 above, and in Chapter 3 section 25.3.

Under FAS 112, contractual termination benefits which provide benefits under a plan that are payable only if an event occurs, such as a plant closing, are recognised as soon as payment is probable and the amount is estimable. This generally would be earlier than such benefits would be recognised under IFRSs, as it would be before an entity was demonstrably committed to a formal plan for a termination.

26   Earnings per share

There are a number of differences between IFRSs and US GAAP in the reporting of earnings per share. These differences mostly arise because of differences in computational guidance between IAS 33 *Earnings per Share* and FAS 128 *Earnings per Share.*

There is also a difference in the level of disclosure that is required in addition to basic and diluted earnings per share based on net income. IAS 33 only requires disclosure of basic and diluted earnings per share for continuing operations and discontinued operations. By contrast, FAS 128 requires the disclosure of basic and diluted earning per share for continuing operations, discontinued operations, extraordinary items and the cumulative effect of an accounting change.

26.1   Diluted earnings per share

26.1.1   Application of the treasury stock (share) method

(Chapter 3 section 26.4.2A)

The number of incremental shares included in the calculation of diluted EPS should be computed using the average market price of common stock for the relevant period under both IFRSs and US GAAP. However, for year-to-date diluted EPS under US GAAP, the number of incremental shares should be determined by computing a year-to-date weighted average of the number of incremental shares included in each quarterly diluted EPS computation. A proposed amendment to FAS 128 as part of the IFRSs/US GAAP convergence project would eliminate this difference by requiring the incremental shares included in year-to-date diluted EPS weighted average to be computed using the average market price of shares for the year-to-date period.

26.1.2   Stock based compensation plans

(Chapter 3 section 26.4.2A)

Both IAS 33 and FAS 128 provide detailed guidance on the calculation of diluted earnings per share where an entity has stock based compensation plans and both require the use of treasury share/stock methods, which are broadly similar. However, under FAS 128, the number of incremental shares to be included in the denominator for year-to-date diluted EPS should be determined by computing a year-to-date weighted average of the number of incremental shares included in each quarterly diluted EPS computation. Under the proposed amendments to FAS 128 in the exposure draft, the incremental shares included in year-to-date diluted EPS weighted average would be computed using the average market price of shares for the year-to-date period, as required by IAS 33.

26.1.3   Contracts that may be settled in shares or cash

(Chapter 3 section 26.4.4)

Both IFRSs and US GAAP address the treatment of contracts that may be settled in shares or cash, but each takes a slightly different approach.

Under IAS 33, when settlement in ordinary shares or cash is at the entity's option, the entity should presume that the contract will be settled in shares and the resulting potential ordinary shares should be included in diluted EPS if the effect is dilutive. For contracts that may be settled in shares or cash at the option of the holder, the more dilutive of cash settlement and share settlement should be used in calculating diluted EPS.

Under FAS 128, if settlement in common stock or in cash is at the election of either the entity or the holder, it should be presumed that the contract will be settled in common stock and the resulting potential common shares included in diluted EPS if the effect is more dilutive. This presumption may be overcome if past experience or a stated policy provides a reasonable basis to conclude that the contract will be settled in cash. Under the proposed amendments to FAS 128 in the exposure draft, the ability to overcome the share settlement presumption would be eliminated.

26.1.4   Contingently issuable shares

(Chapter 3 section 26.4.5)

The impact of contingently issuable shares on diluted EPS is similar for both IFRSs and US GAAP but there could be differences. If all the conditions for issuance of contingently issuable shares ordinary have been met, under both IFRSs and US GAAP, contingently issuable shares are treated as outstanding shares as at the beginning of the period (or date of the contingent share agreement, if later). If the conditions for issuance have not been met, under IFRSs, the number of contingently issuable shares included in diluted EPS should be based on the number of shares that would be issuable if the end of the reporting period were the end of the contingency period and if the result would be dilutive. Under US GAAP the guidance is similar, except that if the only condition not met is one based on market price, the dilutive impact should be included in diluted EPS from the date of the contingent share agreement, or the date that any non-market price contingencies are met.

27   Cash flow statements

The format of a cash flow statement prepared under IAS 7 *Cash Flow Statements* is essentially the same as a cash flow statement prepared under FAS 95 *Statement of Cash Flows*. Both standards require cash flows to be classified into three broad categories: operating activities; investing activities; and financing activities. Foreign private issuers who are required to file a reconciliation of income and equity from IFRSs to US GAAP with the SEC are not required to prepare a cash flow statement under US GAAP. However, presentational differences can arise due to differences between IFRSs and US GAAP in respect of the definition of cash, and the classification of specific items.

27.1 *Definition of cash and cash equivalents*

(Chapter 3 section 27.4)

Under US GAAP, the definition of cash equivalents does not include advances from banks that are repayable within three months, or amounts outstanding under overdraft facilities. As a result, movements within overdrafts are reported as part of financing cash flows, or as a reconciling item in operating activities. Under IFRSs, overdrafts and other advances from banks that are payable on demand and that form an integral part of the entity's cash management are included in cash equivalents.

27.2 *Allocation of cash flows*

(Chapter 3 section 27.5)

If a cash receipt or payment has aspects of more than one class of cash flows, the appropriate classification under US GAAP depends on the activity that is likely to be the predominant source of cash flows for the item. Instead, IFRSs require, where appropriate, a single transaction to be allocated between cash flows from different activities.

27.3 *Interest and dividends*

(Chapter 3 section 27.5A)

IFRSs permit interest and dividends that are paid or received to be classified as part of operating, investing or financing cash flows. Under US GAAP, interest paid, interest received and dividends received must be classified as operating activities.

27.4 *Income tax*

(Chapter 3 section 27.5A)

US GAAP requires income tax paid to be classified as an operating cash flow. Under IFRSs, income tax paid should be classified as an operating cash flow unless the tax paid can be specifically identified with financing or investing activities.

28   Related party transactions

(Chapter 3 section 28)

Although related parties are defined differently in IAS 24 *Related Party Disclosures* and FAS 57 *Related Party Disclosures*, in practice the differences between IFRSs and US GAAP requirements on reporting related party transactions are limited.

29   Post balance sheet events

(Chapter 3 section 29)

Accounting for post balance sheet events is similar under both IFRSs and US GAAP but differences are possible.

For example, a refinancing of a current liability that occurs after the balance sheet date but before the financial statements are issued may qualify for disclosure as non-adjusting in accordance with IAS 10 *Events after the Balance Sheet Date,* and therefore will not result in the reclassification of a liability from current to non-current in the financial statements. US GAAP goes much further as, under FAS 6 *Classification of Short-Term Obligations Expected to Be Refinanced,* short-term obligations may be reclassified as non-current liabilities if the entity (1) intends to refinance the obligation on a long-term basis, and (2) prior to issuing the financial statements can demonstrate the ability to refinance.

In a similar way, IAS 1 requires that a long-term loan that is payable on demand following a breach of an undertaking is classified as current even if the lender has agreed, after the balance sheet date but before the financial statements are issued, not to demand payment. Under US GAAP, the loan would be classified as non-current if, before the financial statements are issued, the lender has waived the right to demand repayment for more than one year from the balance sheet date.

30   Interim reporting

(Chapter 3 section 30.3)

There is a fundamental difference in approach to interim reporting under the two systems: IFRSs apply the discrete approach (i.e. each interim period is a discrete reporting period; whilst US GAAP applies the integral approach (i.e. each interim period is integral to the full year).

In interim financial statements under IFRSs and US GAAP, the same accounting policies should be applied as are used in preparing annual financial statements. IAS 34 *Interim Financial Reporting* and APB 28 *Interim Financial Reporting* give detailed examples of how to recognise income and costs in interim reporting periods.

30.1   Allocation of costs and expenses

(Chapter 3 section 30.3C)

When deciding whether or not to accrue or defer a cost, IAS 34 requires the same principles to be applied at an interim balance sheet date as at a year-end balance sheet date. APB 28 permits some relaxation of this general principle. For example, if a cost, such as the cost of major repairs, clearly benefits two or more interim periods, then that cost should be allocated to each interim period by creating a prepayment. Such a prepayment would not be permitted at a year-end balance sheet date.

30.2   *Changes in estimates in prior periods*

(Chapter 3 section 30.3D)

Under IAS 34, any changes in estimates of amounts reported in prior interim periods are included in the current interim period. Amounts reported in prior interim periods are not retrospectively adjusted, but the nature and amount of any significant changes in estimates must be disclosed. In certain circumstances, FAS 16 *Prior Period Adjustments* requires an adjustment related to prior interim periods of the current fiscal year to be accounted for as an adjustment of prior interim periods of the current year.

31   US regulatory requirements

All companies wishing to offer securities to the public in the United States are required by the Securities Act of 1933 to register the offered securities with the SEC. Similarly, companies wishing to have securities listed on a US stock exchange such as the New York Stock Exchange, or quoted on NASDAQ, must first register the securities with the SEC under the Securities Exchange Act of 1934.

The registration of existing securities of foreign private issuers under the 1934 Act is generally accomplished by means of a registration statement on Form 20-F. Foreign private issuers also use this form for filing their annual reports. The financial statement requirements are laid down in Items 17 and 18 of Form 20-F, while further detailed regulations concerning the form and content of financial statements are contained within the SEC's Regulation S-X *Form and content of and requirements for financial statements.*

Item 17 requires the financial statements to disclose, inter alia, an information content substantially similar to financial statements that comply with US GAAP and Regulation S-X. The financial statements may be prepared according to US GAAP or according to a comprehensive body of local accounting principles, e.g. IFRSs, if the following are disclosed:

- an indication of the comprehensive body of accounting principles applied;

- a discussion of the material variations from US GAAP and Regulation S-X in the accounting principles, practices and methods used in preparing the financial statements. These material variations have to be quantified in the following format:

  - for each period (including any interim periods) for which an income statement is presented, a reconciliation of net income in tabular format either on the face of the income statement or in a note. A reconciliation of net income of the earliest of the three years presented may be omitted if that information has not previously been included in a filing made under the 1933 Act or 1934 Act.

  - for each balance sheet presented, the amount of each material variation between an amount of a line item appearing in a balance sheet and the amount determined using US GAAP and Regulation S-X. These amounts may be shown in parentheses, in columns, as a reconciliation of the equity section, as a restated balance sheet, or in any similar format that clearly presents the differences in the amounts. In practice, the usual presentation adopted is a reconciliation of shareholders' equity. The reconciliation of shareholders' equity should be in sufficient detail to allow an investor to determine the differences between a balance sheet prepared using, for example, IFRSs and one prepared using US GAAP. In particular:

- reconciling items should be shown gross and not net of taxes;

- adjustments affecting several balance sheet captions should not be shown as one item, e.g. purchase accounting adjustments;

- each adjustment should be made at the subsidiary level to determine the impact on items such as minority interest, taxes and the currency translation adjustment; and

- adjustments for items such as property, plant and equipment or goodwill should be presented gross, with separate disclosure of the amounts of accumulated depreciation and amortisation;

• for each period for which an income statement is presented and required to be reconciled to US GAAP, either a statement of cash flows prepared in accordance with IAS 7 *Cash Flow Statements*, US GAAP, or a quantified description of the material differences between cash flows reported in the primary financial statements and those that would be reported under US GAAP;

• for each period for which an income statement is presented, a statement of comprehensive income prepared using either home country GAAP, e.g. a statement of changes in equity under IFRSs, or US GAAP, is required. These statements may be presented in any format permitted by FAS 130 *Reporting Comprehensive Income*. Reconciliation to US GAAP is encouraged, but not required.

If a company prepares its financial statements under a comprehensive body of accounting principles other than US GAAP, Item 17 permits the inclusion of a cash flow statement in those statements prepared under US GAAP or IAS 7 rather than a statement prepared under the accounting principles used for the rest of the financial statements.

Item 18 requires all of the information required by Item 17 and all other information required by US GAAP and Regulation S-X, unless those requirements specifically do not apply to the registrant as a foreign issuer. Information may be omitted for any period in which net income has not been reconciled to US GAAP.

The distinction between Items 17 and 18 is clarified by SAB 88 *Interpretation of requirements of Item 17 of Form 20-F*. SAB 88 states that the distinction between Items 17 and 18 is premised on a classification of the requirements of US GAAP and Regulation S-X into those that specify the methods of measuring the amounts shown on the face of the financial statements and those prescribing disclosures that explain, modify or supplement the accounting measurements. Disclosures required by US GAAP but not required under the other comprehensive body of accounting principles under which the financial statements are prepared need not be furnished under Item 17. Notwithstanding the absence of a requirement for certain disclosures within the body of the financial statements, some matters may be sufficiently material that their disclosure is required in the Operating and Financial Review and Prospects required by Item 5 of Form 20-F. Instruction 2 to this Item requires discussion of any aspects of the differences between accounting principles used in the preparation of the financial statements and US GAAP, not otherwise discussed in the reconciliation, that the company believes are necessary for an understanding of the financial statements as a whole. Such disclosures might include material undisclosed uncertainties, commitments, credit risk exposures and concentrations, unrecognised obligations and related party transactions.

FAS 130 *Reporting Comprehensive Income* requires the presentation of components of the accumulated balance of other comprehensive income items either on the face of the financial statements or in the notes. In certain countries, some equity components are included in retained earnings and are not separately tracked. Where reconstruction of these amounts may not be practical, the SEC Staff will generally not object if an Item 18 filer concludes, and discloses in its filings, that it is not practical to present the components of the accumulated balance of other comprehensive income items specified by paragraph 26 of FAS 130.

If differences between the accounting principles used in the preparation of the financial statements, and US GAAP, have such a pervasive impact on the financial statements that they render a normal reconciliation as described above confusing to investors, full or condensed financial statements prepared in accordance with US GAAP may be necessary in order for the reader fully to understand the impact of the differences in accounting.

If a foreign private issuer wishes to offer securities to the public in the US to raise funds it will usually have to file a registration statement under the 1933 Act using Form F-1, Form F-2 or Form F-3, depending on its status as the SEC registrant, or on Form F-4 if the securities are to be offered in a business combination or other exchange offer. The registration statement will usually include financial statements that comply with Item 18 of Form 20-F.

32   First-time adoption of IFRSs

There are many areas in which the requirements of IFRSs and US GAAP are similar or even virtually identical. Nevertheless, considerable reconciling differences may still arise as a result of the first-time adoption rules in IFRS 1. An entity preparing an IFRSs to US GAAP reconciliation is required to apply US standards as if it had always applied those standards, i.e. it needs to apply US GAAP fully retrospectively. IFRS 1 on the other hand provides first-time adopters of IFRSs with a number of exemptions and exceptions from full retrospective application. In some cases these rules permit a first-time adopter to base its IFRSs information on measurements under its previous GAAP. Hence, some of the reconciling items in Forms 20-F may reflect differences between a first-time adopter's previous GAAP and US GAAP, rather than differences between IFRSs and US GAAP.

The different types of reconciling items that result from the application of IFRS 1 are discussed below.

32.1   Initial measurement in opening IFRSs balance sheet

Full retrospective application of IFRSs to long-lived assets and liabilities is not only extremely difficult but would often also involve undue cost and effort, for example:

- accounting records for the period of acquisition or the period in which an item arose may not be available anymore. In the case of formerly state-owned businesses, the required accounting records possibly never even existed; or

- the entity may have revalued the items in the past as a matter of accounting policy or because this was required under national law.

Nevertheless, a first-time adopter needs a cost basis for long-lived assets and liabilities in its opening IFRS balance sheet. Therefore, the IASB decided to introduce the following exemptions that allow an entity to use a starting point under IFRSs that is not a 'true' IFRSs compliant amount, but a surrogate that is deemed to be a suitable starting point:

- *Business combinations* – A first-time adopter may elect not to apply IFRS 3 *Business Combinations* retrospectively to business combinations that occurred before its date of transition to IFRSs. This exemption not only affects subsidiaries, but also associates and joint ventures. Consequently, assets and liabilities acquired and goodwill may be stated at amounts that differ considerably from the amounts that would be recognised under US GAAP. These differences in balance sheet valuations will in turn affect future gains and losses on assets and liabilities, depreciation charges and impairment charges;

- *Fair value or revaluation as deemed cost* – Instead of determining the historical cost basis for investment property, intangible assets and property, plant and equipment, a first-time adopter is permitted to use fair value at the date of transition or a revaluation under previous GAAP as a starting point. This will affect both future balance sheets and income statements under IFRSs, and result in reconciling items with US GAAP for as long as the entity owns the assets;

- *Employee benefits* – First-time adopters are allowed to recognise all cumulative actuarial gains and losses at the date of transition to IFRSs, even if they use the corridor approach for later actuarial gains and losses. Therefore, employee benefit costs under IFRSs may differ from those under US GAAP;

- *Cumulative translation differences* – Full retrospective application of IAS 21 would require a first-time adopter to restate all financial statements of its foreign operations to IFRSs from the date of their inception or later acquisition onwards, and then determine the cumulative translation differences arising in relation to each of these foreign operations. As a result of differences in the measurement and recognition of assets and liabilities, the net investment in foreign operations as determined under IFRSs will often differ from that under US GAAP. Therefore, the US GAAP-based cumulative translation adjustment will rarely be appropriate as a starting point under IFRSs. The costs of restating cumulative translation adjustments are likely to exceed the benefits to users of financial statements. Therefore, the IASB decided to permit first-time adopters to reset the cumulative translation difference to zero. This means that upon disposal of the foreign operation, the gain or loss recognised under IFRSs and US GAAP will differ due to the cumulative translation difference up to the date of transition, which is deemed to be zero under IFRSs but must be recognised under US GAAP;

- *Designation of previously recognised financial instruments* – A first-time adopter is allowed to designate a financial instrument at the date of transition to IFRSs (or the beginning of the first IFRS reporting period, if comparatives are not restated) as a 'financial asset or financial liability at fair value through profit or loss' or as available-for-sale. This offers first-time adopters an additional possibility to designate financial instruments under IFRSs differently from US GAAP; and

- *Hedge accounting* – Many entities that currently prepare a Form 20-F apply hedge accounting under their national GAAP, but do not designate hedges for FAS 133 *Accounting for Derivative Instruments and Hedging Activities* purposes. Under the requirements of IFRS 1 many of the transactions accounted for as hedges under national GAAP will continue to receive hedge accounting treatment if hedge documentation is prepared under IFRSs, or are accounted for as discontinued hedges under IFRSs if no hedge documentation is prepared. As such transactions were not considered hedges under US GAAP in the comparative periods, reconciling differences with US GAAP will arise in either case.

32.2   *Prospective application of standards*

IFRS 1 provides the following special rules that allow a first-time adopter not to apply IFRSs to transactions that were entered into before a certain date:

- *Share-based payment transactions* – The transitional rules under IFRS 1 for share-based payments use a different effective date than US GAAP. Therefore, the charge for share-based payments under IFRSs and US GAAP will differ at least until all plans outstanding are within the scope of the respective standards; and

- *Derecognition of financial assets and financial liabilities* – A first-time adopter has the option to apply the derecognition requirements in IAS 39 *Financial Instruments: Recognition and Measurement* (1) prospectively to transactions occurring on or after 1 January 2004 or (2) retrospectively from a date of the entity's choosing. Therefore, if a first-time adopter derecognised non-derivative financial assets or non-derivative financial liabilities under its previous GAAP as a result of a transaction that occurred before 1 January 2004, it should not recognise those assets and liabilities under IFRSs (unless they qualify for recognition as a result of a later transaction or event). The resulting reconciling item in a Form 20-F will reflect a difference between a first-time adopter's previous GAAP and US GAAP, rather than a difference between IFRSs and US GAAP.

32.3   Other first-time adoption exemptions and exceptions

It should be noted that IFRS 1 also provides exemptions and exceptions relating to the following, which may not create additional reconciling differences but could affect the size and nature of existing reconciling differences:

- compound financial instruments;

- assets and liabilities of subsidiaries, associates and joint ventures;

- insurance contracts;

- IFRIC 1 – *Changes in Existing Decommissioning, Restoration and Similar Liabilities*;

- estimates;

- assets classified as held for sale and discontinued operations; and

- exemption from the requirement to restate comparative information for IAS 32 *Financial Instruments: Disclosure and Presentation*, IAS 39 and IFRS 4 *Insurance Contracts*.

The requirements of IFRS 1 are discussed in detail in Chapter 2 of this book.

Appendix A   IFRSs

INTERNATIONAL FINANCIAL REPORTING STANDARDS

INTERNATIONAL ACCOUNTING STANDARDS

INTERNATIONAL ACCOUNTING STANDARDS (continued)

IFRIC INTERPRETATIONS

SIC INTERPRETATIONS

Appendix B   ARBs, APB Opinions and FASB Statements in the US

ACCOUNTING RESEARCH BULLETINS

(issued between 1939-1958)

ACCOUNTING PRINCIPLES BOARD OPINIONS

(issued between 1958-1973)

ACCOUNTING PRINCIPLES BOARD OPINIONS (continued)

No

13   Amending Paragraph 6 of APB Opinion No. 9, Application to Commercial Banks

14   Accounting for Convertible Debt and Debt Issued with Stock Purchase Warrants

18   The Equity Method of Accounting for Investments in Common Stock

20   Accounting Changes

21   Interest on Receivables and Payables

22   Disclosure of Accounting Policies

23   Accounting for Income Taxes—Special Areas

26   Early Extinguishment of Debt

28   Interim Financial Reporting

29   Accounting for Nonmonetary Transactions

30   Reporting the Results of Operations — Reporting the Effects of Disposal of a Segment of a Business, and Extraordinary, Unusual and Infrequently Occurring Events and Transactions

STATEMENTS OF FINANCIAL ACCOUNTING STANDARDS

(issued from 1973)

No

2   Accounting for Research and Development Costs

3   Reporting Accounting Changes in Interim Financial Statements (an amendment of APB Opinion No. 28)

5   Accounting for Contingencies

6   Classification of Short-Term Obligations Expected to Be Refinanced (an amendment of ARB No. 43, Chapter 3A)

7   Accounting and Reporting by Development Stage Enterprises

11   Accounting for Contingencies—Transition Method (an amendment of FASB Statement No. 5)

13   Accounting for Leases

15   Accounting by Debtors and Creditors for Troubled Debt Restructurings

16   Prior Period Adjustments

19   Financial Accounting and Reporting by Oil and Gas Producing Companies

21   Suspension of the Reporting of Earnings per Share and Segment Information by Nonpublic Enterprises (an amendment of APB Opinion No. 15 and FASB Statement No. 14)

22   Changes in the Provisions of Lease Agreements Resulting from Refundings of Tax-Exempt Debt (an amendment of FASB Statement No. 13).

23   Inception of the Lease (an amendment of FASB Statement No. 13)

25   Suspension of Certain Accounting Requirements for Oil and Gas Producing Companies (an amendment of FASB Statement No. 19)

27   Classification of Renewals or Extensions of Existing Sales-Type or Direct Financing Leases (an amendment of FASB Statement No. 13)

STATEMENTS OF FINANCIAL ACCOUNTING STANDARDS (continued)

STATEMENTS OF FINANCIAL ACCOUNTING STANDARDS (continued)

STATEMENTS OF FINANCIAL ACCOUNTING STANDARDS (continued)

STATEMENTS OF FINANCIAL ACCOUNTING STANDARDS (continued)

Index of IFRSs

Framework for the Preparation and Presentation of Financial Statements

IFRIC Interpretations

SIC Interpretations

Index of US literature

**Statement of Financial Accounting
Standards (issued by the FASB)**